ISOBEL DOOLE & ROBIN LOWE
INTERNATIONAL MARKETING STRATEGY
ANALYSIS, DEVELOPMENT AND IMPLEMENTATION

SIXTH EDITION

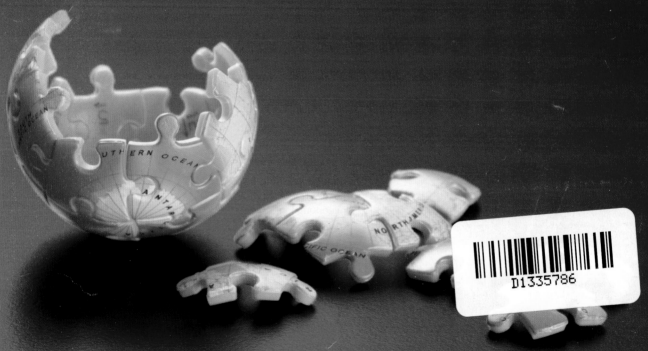

CENGAGE
Learning

Australia • Brazil • Japan • ... • United States

CENGAGE
Learning®

**International Marketing Strategy:
Analysis, Development and
Implementation, Sixth Edition**
Isobel Doole and Robin Lowe

Publishing Director: Linden Harris

Publisher: Brendan George

Development Editor: Annabel Ainscow

Editorial Assistant: Lauren Darby

Project Editor: Alison Cooke

Production Controller: Eyvett Davis

Typesetter: S4Carlisle Publishing Services

Cover design: Adam Renvoize

For product information and technology assistance,
contact **emea.info@cengage.com**.

For permission to use material from this text or product,
and for permission queries,
email **emea.permissions@cengage.com**.

British Library Cataloguing-in-Publication Data
A catalogue record for this book is available from the British
Library.

ISBN: 978-1-4080-4407-0

Cengage Learning EMEA
Cheriton House, North Way, Andover, Hampshire, SP10 5BE
United Kingdom

Cengage Learning products are represented in Canada
by Nelson Education Ltd.

For your lifelong learning solutions, visit **www.cengage.co.uk**

Purchase your next print book, e-book or e-chapter at
www.cengagebrain.com

Printed in China by RR Donnelley
1 2 3 4 5 6 7 8 9 10–14 13 12

*To Andrew and Sylvia
and to our children;*

*Rob, Libby and Will,
Catherine and Jonathan*

BRIEF CONTENTS

CONTENTS

PART I

ANALYSIS   1

PART II

STRATEGY DEVELOPMENT   137

PART III

IMPLEMENTATION   289

9   INTERNATIONAL COMMUNICATIONS   290

10   THE MANAGEMENT OF INTERNATIONAL DISTRIBUTION AND LOGISTICS   324

LIST OF FIGURES, TABLES, ILLUSTRATIONS AND MANAGEMENT CHALLENGES

LIST OF FIGURES

LIST OF TABLES

LIST OF ILLUSTRATIONS

LIST OF MANAGEMENT CHALLENGES

PREFACE

Introduction

Markets and marketing are becoming ever more international in their nature and managers around the world ignore this fact at their peril. To achieve sustainable growth in markets that are becoming increasingly global, or merely to survive in domestic markets that are increasingly attacked by international players, it is essential that organizations understand the complexity and diversity of international marketing and that their managers develop the skills, aptitudes and knowledge necessary to compete effectively around the globe.

This new revised edition of *International Marketing Strategy* continues to meet the needs of the international marketing student and practitioner in an up-to-date and innovative manner. It recognizes the increasing time pressures of both students and managers and so strives to maintain the readability and clarity of the previous editions, as well as providing a straightforward and logical structure that will enable them to apply their learning to the tasks ahead.

The book continues to incorporate new, significant and relevant material with learning innovations that ensure its continued status as the best-selling UK text on international marketing strategy.

Structure of the book

As in previous editions, the book is divided into three main subject areas – analysis, strategy, development and implementation – each of which has four chapters. For each chapter the learning objectives for the reader are stated at the outset and these then lead to the key themes of the chapter, which are explored in the text. Boxed 'Illustrations' throughout the text enable the reader to focus on the key issues and discuss the practical implications of these issues for international marketing strategy development. Boxed 'Management Challenges' in each of the chapters provide examples of the kind of practical dilemmas faced by international marketing managers in their everyday operations. Throughout the book we highlight a number of continuing and emerging themes in the management of international marketing. We provide the opportunity to explore the different mindsets of many types of businesses that depend on international markets for their survival and growth, from small poor farmers, to born global innovative technology businesses, to the global brand giants.

Success in international marketing is achieved through being able to integrate and appreciate the interaction between the various elements of the international marketing strategy development process and this is addressed in two ways. First, at the end of each chapter a case study is included. While the main focus of the chapter 'Case Study' is on integrating a number of the themes of the chapter, the reader should also draw on their learning from the chapters that have gone before to give a complete answer. Second, at the end of each part there is a more comprehensive 'Integrative Learning Activity' for the reader that focuses on international marketing strategy development. At the end of Part 1 this activity is concerned with analysis, at the end of Part 2 with strategy development and at the end of Part 3 with implementation. The format for these learning activities is similar so that the three Integrative Learning Activities, when added together, integrate all the learning from the book and provide a practical and comprehensive exercise in international marketing strategy development for the reader.

New to this edition

All the chapters have been revised and updated to ensure the inclusion of the latest developments in international marketing and in response to the changing focus of international marketing and the new challenges posed by the new patterns of developments in global markets. For this reason we provide many examples of international marketing and innovation in the newly emerging economies of Africa, particularly South Africa, and the Middle East, adding to the examples of development in Asian markets that we also include and build further on the website. We also explain the increasingly global impact of events, such as natural disasters, conflict, the global banking crisis and technological changes on the strategic development and implementation plans of international organizations, large or small.

In Chapter 1 we have included a full section introducing sustainability in an adapted SLEPTS approach to examining the environmental influences on international marketing. Sustainability is about considering the environmental impact of everything we do. This means encouraging a holistic way of thinking in our responses to the global marketing challenges we identify, and assessing the impact of our global marketing strategies – socially, economically and environmentally – in our approach to ensuring sustainability. This is central to the values of responsible international marketing and a theme that we highlight at various stages of strategy development in the chapters of this book.

The global economic crisis sparked a contraction in the volume of global trade and in recent years world trade volume suffered the sharpest decline in more than 70 years. The implications of this changed landscape are discussed in Chapter 2 where we examine the international trading environment and discuss the institutions that aim to influence world trade. Chapters 5 and 6 on international marketing in SMEs and global firms, have been expanded to include a section examining the skills base needed by global managers and the implications of the strategy development issues. Further examples of international companies from emerging markets provide the basis for discussion of the different contexts faced and the alternative growth strategies.

Customers around the world are becoming more comfortable with the use of technology, such as social media and mobile computing, and we highlight this in a number of different business to business and business to consumer situations throughout the chapters of the book, particularly recognizing the different geographic, economic social and cultural contexts that new social media and mobile computing has impacted upon. This is examined particularly in the chapters in Part 3 of the book where we focus on implementation issues. Chapter 12 focuses on this further when we examine how social media and mobile computing, not only support and enable international marketing communications, but also change the process by which the future communication and marketing strategies of organizations in international markets are formulated.

The majority of the case studies, illustrations and management challenges are new or updated. We have endeavoured to ensure the material we use reflects a global perspective and have included practical examples from across the world. However, in this edition we have included a number of our new Case Studies, Illustrations and Management Challenges from North and South Africa and the Middle East in response to the advice and suggestions from reviewers, tutors and students. The authors have focused on responding to the needs of readers who are developing their international marketing skills in Europe, the Americas, Asia and Africa or other parts of the world. Moreover, we believe that organizations operating in these countries face some of the most significant and interesting international marketing challenges today and are developing the most novel solutions. Each Illustration and Management Challenge has questions highlighting specific issues that should be considered in the context of both the industry it focuses on and the area of the world it is spotlighting.

The Integrative Learning Activity (ILA) is an innovative section at the end of each part with the objective of encouraging readers to integrate their learning from the chapters and the parts. All three activities are new to this edition. The ILA at the end of Part 1 highlights the rapid development of the mobile phone services market in Africa and uses this scenario as a backdrop for examining trading infrastructure issues, consumer behaviour issues and examining the development of a latent and exciting market. We focus in ILA 2 on the companies from emerging markets that are challenging the more established players and encourage readers to explore the alternative strategies adopted by these companies to expand their activity. We also encourage readers to consider those companies from emerging markets that have made substantial progress towards becoming global players during the last few years.

In ILA 3 we focus on the opportunities for growth for established consumer brands in emerging markets but also provide the opportunity to consider the contexts that could provide new competition for those global brands.

By obtaining and analyzing data through secondary sources, typically through the Internet, the reader is able to proceed through the steps of the international marketing strategy process, thus acquiring further knowledge and using this opportunity to practice a number of their international marketing skills.

How to study using this book

The aim of the book is for readers to have an accessible and readable resource for use both as a course book and for revision. The text is also recommended reading for students of the CIM qualifications.

It has a clear structure which is easy to use and easy for the reader to follow, thus making it ideal for incorporation into a course delivered in a 12-week teaching semester. Its geocentric view of international marketing, with examples of good practice in competing internationally from around the globe, makes it ideal for use with courses with multicultural students.

International Marketing Strategy has been developed to help the reader learn, understand and practice a number of elements of the international marketing strategy process. The process involves the analysis of a situation, development of a strategy against a background of a number of strategic options and the implementation of the chosen option. It is important to recognize that there is not one 'right' strategy, because success is ultimately determined by many factors and, besides, it will usually take a number of years before the strategy can be seen finally as a success or failure. Therefore, this book provides a framework, within the parts and chapter structure, in which to understand and evaluate the factors that should be taken into account (and which should be dismissed too) in building an international marketing strategy.

Structure of the book

Parts

The three parts focus on the topics of analysis, strategy development and implementation. Each part contains an introduction to the four chapters that have been grouped together.

Readers should realize that these groupings of chapter topics within parts are primarily to provide a clear structure and layout for the book. In practice, however, there is considerable overlap between analysis, strategy development and implementation topics. For example, product strategy and market entry are considered by organizations in some situations to be implementation issues, and technology might be used to support analysis, set the overall international marketing strategy or support implementation.

Part I Analysis Part I focuses on analyzing the international marketing environment. It provides an introduction to how the international marketing environment influences how firms operate. It explores the changing nature of the environment and explains the structures that support and control international trade. Also considered are the social and cultural influences on customer buying behaviour in international markets.

Frameworks and processes that provide the means to systematically identify and evaluate marketing opportunities and carry out market research across the world are explained.

CASE STUDIES AT THE END OF EACH CHAPTER

PART I ANALYSIS

Chapter 1

Tesco in China Here we look at why TESCO view putting the customer at the heart of the business through an empathy with cultural and consumer behaviour in its international markets is fundamental to the success of the world's fourth largest grocery retailer.

Chapter 2

Challenges of the Libyan Market This case study looks at the challenges of marketing to a country which does not as yet have an adequate infrastructure to support market development but where government is investing heavily to enhance its country's infrastructure at all levels and the economy is rapidly expanding.

Chapter 3

Islam, Ramadan and the tent business in the Middle East Lavish tents and marquees have long been a mainstay of the corporate events industry during the holy month of Ramadan in the Middle East. This case looks at two UAE-based companies, Al-Baddad International and Harlequin Marquees & Event Services who had to look at expanding internationally in order to maintain sales in the global downturn.

Chapter 4

How do WGS segment the global mobile phone gambling market? Addressing the issues arising from Cometa Wireless Gaming Systems' attempt to sell mobile phone games to a global market.

Integrative Learning Activity 1: International marketing planning: Analysis

In this ILA we spotlight the rapid development of the mobile phone services market in Africa and use this scenario as a backdrop for examining trading infrastructure issues, consumer behaviour issues and examining the development of a latent and exciting market.

PART II STRATEGY DEVELOPMENT

Part II explains the international marketing strategy options available for small- and medium-sized firms and also the largest organizations that will enable them to compete effectively in global markets. The factors that affect the choice of strategy are considered as well as the challenges that are posed to the managers of these strategies.

A key decision for most organizations is which market entry method to use to exploit the market opportunities from the many options available. This is then followed by the selection and development of the products and service strategy that determine the portfolio that will be offered to customers.

Chapter 5

Global marketing on a tight budget Showing how two small firms in very different situations in Africa build their capability to increase their international market presence through using marketing creativity and innovation, but also explores the challenges faced in making the transition to become a larger business.

Chapter 6

Unilever: redefining product policy for a global future We have included a longer case study to illustrate the range of factors that are influencing the international marketing strategy of a diversified, company that has established global brands in developed markets and a history of building its portfolio of products in emerging markets too.

Chapter 7

When joint ventures go wrong Unforeseen factors cause major problems in promising mergers between companies from developed and developing countries. The case study focuses particularly on Danone's problems in China and looks at where the management made mistakes by not appreciating the different mindsets and cultural differences in managing collaborative working with a Chinese entrepreneur.

Chapter 8

Lego playing with its strengths This case study explores the global toymaker's attempts at diversification in the face of declining sales and profits, and the outcomes of this diversification. It questions Lego's approach to building its brand when challenged by a new generation of consumers, global market changes and the growth of technologically based competitors.

Integrative Learning Activity 2: International marketing planning: Strategy development

Future Global Players examines the different starting points and means used by newcomers from developing economies to build the global competitive capability necessary for them to compete with the more established competitive firms from developed countries.

PART III IMPLEMENTATION

Part III deals with the international communication, distribution and pricing strategies that support the introduction and development of the business in the various worldwide markets. The different local market factors that affect implementation are considered. These factors may allow the associated implementation programmes and processes to be standardized across different markets but, frequently, it is necessary to adapt the strategies to suit local needs.

Finally, technology plays a key enabling role in international marketing strategy implementation. It supports the programme and process delivery and also provides opportunities for creativity that allow innovative firms to gain competitive advantage.

Chapter 9

Greenpeace – global campaigner Greenpeace must balance the need to create awareness, which often requires shock tactics, with the need to raise funds and these two dimensions can sometimes be incompatible. To appeal to its various target audiences it must communicate effectively by adopting and effectively integrating a variety of traditional offline and online media.

Chapter 10

Merry Management Training Presenting the problems arising when a Western management training consultancy and a small Dubai consultancy firm enter into a friendly informal agreement.

Chapter 11

WABCO In this case study a large multinational faces challenges to its positioning and its approach to its global pricing strategy as it tries to compete in a fiercely competitive global market.

Chapter 12

Which way forward for global broadcasting Technology is providing alternatives to traditional broadcasting and, as a result, consumers are changing the way they consume broadcast media. In many emerging markets the broadcasters from developed countries now have to compete with new forms of communication but also much more flexible and responsive local players.

Integrated Learning Activity: International marketing planning: Implementation, control and evaluation

In this ILA we focused on the need for companies from developed countries to secure their position in emerging markets and establish their global brands in new consumer markets by effective implementation of the marketing mix. **Yum brands – eating into new markets** provides an example of this situation. Yum brands has some of the best known fast food brands in its portfolio, but is seeing its business growth and income generation moving from the US to China and other emerging markets. The company must meet not just the needs and wants of consumers but also its local partners, who might also be keen to build their own brands too.

Chapters

After a brief introduction to each chapter the learning objectives for the chapter are set out: these should provide the focus for study. To help to reinforce the learning and encourage the reader to explore the issues more fully the chapters contain a number of additional aids to learning.

Illustrations

The illustrations that have been provided are not present just to reinforce a key issue or learning point that has been discussed within the chapter: the questions that have been added are intended to enable the reader to reflect upon the deeper and broader implications too and thus provide a further opportunity for discussion. Our aim is that the settings for the illustrations be as diverse as possible, geographically, culturally, by business sector, size and type of organization, in order to try to help the reader consider the situations described from alternative perspectives.

Management Challenges

The management challenges included emphasize the point that there are few simple and straightforward management decisions in international marketing. Organizations and managers often face difficult problems that require a decision. The management challenges within a chapter provide the opportunity for the reader to identify those factors that should be taken into account in coming to the decision and, hopefully, consider rather more creative ideas that lead to decisions and solutions that add greater value.

Case studies

The case studies provide the opportunity for the reader to carry out more comprehensive analysis of key chapter topics before deciding what strategic decisions or plans should be made. These short cases provide only limited information and, where possible, readers should obtain more information on the case study subject from appropriate websites in order to complete the tasks. The reader should start with the questions that have been supplied in order to help guide the analysis or discussion. After this, however, the reader should think more broadly around the issues raised and decide whether these are indeed the right questions to ask and answer. International markets change fast and continuously, and new factors that have recently emerged may completely alter the situation.

Integrative learning activities

At the end of each of the three parts of the book we have included an Integrative Learning Activity. Their purpose is to integrate the four chapters that make up each of the parts. More importantly, however, is that as a whole the three activities provide a framework for planning an international marketing strategy and give the opportunity for readers to consider the practical issues involved in developing, planning and implementing an outline international marketing strategy. The objective of these activities is to provide a vehicle through which the reader is able to develop practical skills in research, analysis, evaluation and strategy development. In completing these activities you will need to synthesize the various strands and themes explored throughout the book and apply them to a practical situation.

ID, RL

ABOUT THE AUTHORS

Isobel Doole

Isobel is Professor of International Marketing and Assistant Dean at Sheffield Business School, Sheffield Hallam University. She is an experienced marketing professional and senior academic in international marketing and in the international competitiveness of small firms. With her co-author Robin Lowe she has built an international reputation through the highly successful textbooks *Strategic Marketing Decisions* and *International Marketing Strategy*. She is a senior examiner for the Chartered Institute of Marketing and has acted as an expert advisor on a number of governmental committees.

Robin Lowe

Robin is the Director of Business Advantage at Sheffield Business School, Sheffield Hallam University. Through his research, consultancy and policy development work in international trade, innovation and entrepreneurship, Robin has made a major contribution to government policy and business support. He also has considerable experience of consulting and training with multinationals around the world, including IBM, Microsoft, Astra Zeneca, Renault Nissan, Huawei, and Batelco as well as being an examiner and course director for the Chartered Institute of Marketing. He is the joint author of several best selling texts in international marketing, innovation and entrepreneurship.

ACKNOWLEDGEMENTS

Inevitably, in the task of writing this textbook we have had help, support and valuable contributions from many people. We would especially like to thank our colleagues from Sheffield Hallam University and other universities who have contributed a number of case studies and illustrations. We would also like to thank Andy Cropper at Sheffield Hallam and other case study contributors for their invaluable contributions to the CourseMate digital support resources which accompany this book.

We are indebted to our students from many countries and the managers of many businesses, who have freely given their time to share their expert knowledge of international niche marketing. Also the managers in many larger companies, who have discussed with us the challenges they face in global marketing. Over the years they have all helped to shape and influence our view of international marketing strategy.

The team at Cengage Learning have always encouraged us and we are grateful for their professionalism in turning the manuscript into its finished form.

Every effort has been made to obtain permission from the copyright holders for material reproduced in this book. Any rights not acknowledged here will be acknowledged in subsequent printings if due notice is given to the publisher.

WALK THROUGH TOUR

CHAPTER 1

AN INTRODUCTION TO INTERNATIONAL MARKETING

LEARNING OBJECTIVES

After reading this chapter you should be able to:

- Explain and use the SLEPTS factors to assess international markets
- Discuss the differences between export marketing, international and global marketing
- Understand the criteria required to evaluate a company's international marketing strategy
- Appreciate the key steps in the international marketing planning process

INTRODUCTION

Managers around the globe are recognizing the increasing necessity for their companies and organizations to develop the skills, aptitudes and knowledge to compete effectively in international markets.

The fact that the world economy is open and interdependent, the globalization of consumer tastes and the unabated expansion of mobile internet applications which can be downloaded to smart phones to perform all kind of feats from social networking to online banking all increase the interdependency and interconnections of country economies across the globe. The need for managers to develop the skills to maximize the opportunities such technological developments bring impacts on companies of all shapes, sizes and sectors.

In this chapter, the reader will be introduced to the concepts of international marketing, enabling them to acquire an appreciation of the complexities of marketing on an international basis and how this activity differs from operating purely in domestic home markets. In the following sections we will define international marketing, examine the important trends in the global marketing environment and introduce the reader to the international marketing strategy development and international marketing planning process.

Learning objectives Listed at the start of each chapter, highlighting the key concepts covered in that chapter.

---

58   PART I ANALYSIS

MANAGEMENT CHALLENGE 2.1

South African Exporters target Latin America

The Latin American countries of Brazil, Argentina, Chile and Mexico, are viewed as presenting potential opportunities for trade between South Africa and the Latin American region. Yet in a report published in 2010 South Africa's exports to this region are viewed by the South African DTI to have been disappointing. South Africa's share of exports to Latin America were seen to be less than 1 per cent of the total export value of all the countries they view as their major competitors combined. Australia, Hungary, Malaysia Thailand, Russia and Turkey are all viewed to be better performers. However, a large proportion of the products which these countries export to Latin America are not exported by South Africa. Interestingly none of these countries were seen to have active government policies which encouraged companies to export to Latin America but most of the countries did use similar export promotion instruments as South Africa to support their firms. The South African DTI report suggested, the effectiveness of these instruments depends on the way they are constructed and packaged as part of a comprehensive and global export promotion strategy, and the way that they are targeted at export-ready firms.

In a survey undertaken by the DTI the three most frequently mentioned constraints faced by South African exporters to Latin America are:

- the volatility of the exchange rate;
- the costs of transport; and
- the costs of marketing the product and customs.

Firms that did not export to Latin America perceived making contact with potential buyers and language barriers as the two main impediments to trading with Latin American countries.

Question

1 For an industry of your choice evaluate how the South African DTI can encourage companies within that industry to overcome the constraints of developing exports to Latin America.

References: South Africa Department of Trade and Industry, Increasing Trade with Latin America, Preferences, Challenges and Remedies; policy Position Paper 2010, http://www.dti. gov.za/latin_america.pdt, accessed December 2010.

Management Challenge 2.1 focuses on the efforts of South Africa to encourage its exporters to target Latin America and the perceived constraints they face.

The Asian Pacific Trading Region

Asia Pacific Economic Cooperation

The Asia Pacific Economic Cooperation (APEC) is essentially a forum among 21 member economies who border on the Pacific. Thus, it includes the NAFTA member states, Russia, China and Japan, as well as the founding father Australia, New Zealand, ASEAN nations and Peru and Chile in South America.

Management Challenges International marketing dilemmas and associated questions are located throughout the text and provide a forum for classroom and tutorial discussion.

---

280   PART II STRATEGY DEVELOPMENT

- Achieving marketing synergies, such as channels and promotion, often because of the need to target a new segment.
- Integrating the contributions of marketing and R & D.
- Identifying attractive markets with growth potential.
- Effectively carrying out the NPD process, including pre-development activities, such as idea generation, screening, concept and business case investigation.
- Obtaining support from top management.
- Speed in development.

Key to success in technology sectors is generating a continual flow of new product introductions, but success is by no means guaranteed. Even for technologically leading edge companies not every idea will make it to the market and be a commercial success, so risk-taking and tolerating failure must be accepted by the firm's management. The main focus, however, should be to add value to meet the needs of customers wherever they are in the world.

SUMMARY

- In many business sectors product and service strategies are being affected by the increased globalization of consumer tastes, communications, technological advances and the concentration of business activity. At the same time, however, given the level of competition and choice available, there is an increasing expectation among customers that their individual needs will be met.
- Product managers are balancing the efficiency benefits of standardization in terms of economies of scale and the experience effect with the need and cost of adapting products and services to meet the needs of local customers, regulations and usage conditions.
- The growth of international services is a feature of international marketing and it is being driven by low labour costs and increasing demand in developing countries and the increased possibilities for transferring information through information technology and communications.
- As more products are reaching the mature phase of the life cycle they are becoming commodities, and there is a need to use additional services to differentiate them from competitor offerings. However, services are often difficult to standardize globally because they are affected significantly by the different expectations of service delivery that exist in different cultures.
- The product or service strategy is usually at the centre of international marketing operations. Branding is a key part of product and service management, particularly in international markets, but it is difficult to establish truly global brands that are truly distinctive and have images that appeal to cross-cultural customer segments.
- New product and service development and innovation throughout the marketing process are essential for growth and the renewal of the international portfolio and, particularly for culturally sensitive products and services, it is vital to obtain input from the different stakeholders around the world in order to ensure that they will be successful.

KEYWORDS

Intangibility	Adaptation	International branding
Perishability	International product portfolio	Branding strategies

Summary Featured at the end of every chapter, the summary captures the key issues in each chapter, helping you to assess your understanding and revise key content.

SUMMARY

- For a firm at the start of internationalization, market entry can be regarded as a critical first step which is vital not only for financial reasons, but also because it will set a pattern of future international involvement. It determines not just the opportunities for sales but also a valuable source of market information.
- Market entry methods can be seen as a series of alternatives available to international firms, and a global strategy might utilize a number of different approaches. A firm can make individual decisions based on the factors affecting one specific country or the whole region and choose the most appropriate method for the particular set of circumstances.
- The choice of market entry method should be based on an assessment of the firm's desired involvement in the market and the level of control of its marketing mix in the country, set against the financial and marketing risks.
- For large established companies that already have extensive involvement in international markets, the market entry decision is taken against the background of the competitive nature of the market, the environment, its global strategy and an existing and substantial network of operations.
- The company's competitive strategy is likely to require simultaneous decisions affecting its arrangements in a number of markets in order to improve its competitive position by entering untapped or emerging markets, or expanding its activities in existing markets.
- In order to achieve these objectives within a very short timescale, rather than relying on organic growth the companies have used a variety of market entry strategies, including joint ventures and alliances, often with competitors. This is leading to increasingly complex operations being created in which companies strive to balance the opposing forces of competitiveness and cooperation, and quite frequently such arrangements fail to deliver the expected benefits.

KEYWORDS

Market entry	Trading companies	Wholly-owned subsidiary
Market involvement	Sogo shosha	Contract manufacture
Risk and control	Exporting	Licensing
Indirect exporting	Distributors	Acquisitions
Domestic purchasing	Management contracts	Joint ventures
Export houses	Franchising	Strategic alliance
Piggybacking	Direct marketing	

Keywords Highlighted throughout the book where they first appear, and alerting you to core concepts and techniques. Listed at the end of every chapter and emboldened within the text. Keywords are defined at the end of the book in the Glossary.

Illustrations Illustrative real-life examples are featured throughout the text, showing international companies' marketing strategies, accompanied by a question.

Case studies A longer and in-depth case study is provided at the end of every chapter. They draw upon real-world companies and help to demonstrate theory in practice. Each case is accompanied by questions to test the reader's understanding.

Discussion questions Short discussion questions appear at the end of every chapter. This feature encourages readers to review and/or critically assess their understanding of the main topics covered in the chapter.

Integrative learning activities A series of in-depth learning activities is presented at the end of each part. Each one integrates the four chapters of the associated part.

DIGITAL SUPPORT RESOURCES

Dedicated Instructor Website

To discover the dedicated digital instructor's resources accompanying this textbook please register here for access: http://login.cengage.com

Resources include:

- Instructor's Manual
- ExamView Testbank
- PowerPoint Slides

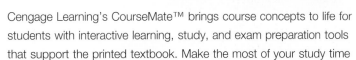

Cengage Learning's CourseMate™ brings course concepts to life for students with interactive learning, study, and exam preparation tools that support the printed textbook. Make the most of your study time by accessing everything you need to succeed in one place. With CourseMate™ you can read your textbook, take notes, review flashcards, and take practice quizzes. CourseMate™ goes beyond the book to deliver what you need!

Interactive Teaching and Learning Tools

CourseMate™ offers a range of interactive learning tools tailored to the sixth edition of *International Marketing Strategy: Analysis, Development and Implementation* including:

- Quizzes
- Case Studies
- Videos
- Games
- Glossary and interactive flashcards
- And much more…

Interactive eBook

In addition to interactive learning tools, CourseMate™ also includes an interactive eBook. You can take notes, highlight, search and interact with embedded media specific to your book.

Engagement Tracker (Lecturer access only)

Lecturers can use the integrated Engagement Tracker in CourseMate™ to assess students' preparation and engagement. The tracking tool can be used to monitor progress of the class as a whole or for individual students.

Accessing CourseMate™

- Students can access CourseMate™ using the unique personal access card included in the front of the book.
- Instructors can access CourseMate™ by registering at http://login.cengage.com or by speaking to their local Cengage Learning representative
- A CourseMate™ demo is available at: www.cengage.com/coursemate

PART I: ANALYSIS

AIMS AND OBJECTIVES

Knowledge and an understanding of the markets in which companies operate are important for all business activities. In international markets, because of geographical distances and the complexities of operating in a number of disparate markets where risk and uncertainty are high, the need for knowledge and understanding becomes of paramount importance. It is this issue that is central to Part 1 of this book. The chapters in this section concentrate on helping the reader generate a greater understanding of the concepts of the international marketing process and the international environment within which companies operate. It aims to extend the range of understanding in order to enable the reader to deal with international marketing situations and to develop the skills to analyze and evaluate non-domestic markets, which in turn will enable their firms to compete effectively in world markets.

In Chapter 1 we focus on the international marketing environment. The book uses the SLEPTS approach to understanding the complexities of the environmental influences on international marketing, thus enabling the reader to acquire an appreciation of the complexities of marketing on an international basis. We examine what is meant by international marketing and introduce the reader to the international market planning process. We also examine the reasons for success and failure in international marketing strategies and the characteristics of best international marketing practice.

In Chapter 2 the focus is on gaining an understanding of the international trading environment. We first examine, at a macro level, the development of international trading structures and the changes in trading patterns, as well as reviewing the major international bodies formed to foster world trade. The evolution of trading regions is analyzed and the implications to international marketing companies assessed.

In Chapter 3 we take a fairly detailed look at the social and cultural influences in international marketing. The components of culture are examined together with the impact of these components on international marketing. We then look at how cultural influences impact on buyer behaviour across the globe both in consumer markets and in business-to-business markets and discuss methods that can be used to analyze cultures both within and across countries.

In Chapter 4 the focus is on the identification and evaluation of marketing opportunities internationally. Segmentation of international markets is discussed, and how to prioritize international opportunities. The marketing research process and the role it plays in the development of international marketing strategies are also examined. The different stages in the marketing research process are discussed, with particular attention being paid to the problems in carrying out international marketing research in foreign markets and coordinating multi-country studies.

CHAPTER 1

AN INTRODUCTION TO INTERNATIONAL MARKETING

LEARNING OBJECTIVES

After reading this chapter you should be able to:

- Explain and use the SLEPTS factors to assess international markets
- Discuss the differences between export marketing, international and global marketing
- Understand the criteria required to evaluate a company's international marketing strategy
- Appreciate the key steps in the international marketing planning process

INTRODUCTION

Managers around the globe are recognizing the increasing necessity for their companies and organizations to develop the skills, aptitudes and knowledge to compete effectively in international markets.

The fact that the world economy is open and interdependent, the globalization of consumer tastes and the unabated expansion of mobile internet applications which can be downloaded to smart phones to perform all kind of feats from social networking to online banking all increase the interdependency and interconnections of country economies across the globe. The need for managers to develop the skills to maximize the opportunities such technological developments bring impacts on companies of all shapes, sizes and sectors.

In this chapter, the reader will be introduced to the concepts of international marketing, enabling them to acquire an appreciation of the complexities of marketing on an international basis and how this activity differs from operating purely in domestic home markets. In the following sections we will define international marketing, examine the important trends in the global marketing environment and introduce the reader to the international marketing strategy development and international marketing planning process.

The strategic importance of international marketing

Last year's world trade in merchandize exceeded US$12 trillion and world trade in commercial services is estimated at around US$4 trillion. While most of us cannot visualize such huge amounts, it does serve to give some indication of the scale of international trade today.

This global marketplace consists of a population of 6.8 billion people which is expected to reach 10 billion by 2050 according to the latest projections prepared by the United Nations.

Global wealth is increasing and this is reflected in higher demand. Increasing affluence and commercial dynamism has seen nations such as China, India, Brazil and countries across Eastern Europe sustain their high growth economies in a period of global economic uncertainty and retrenchment as many of the richer countries seek to resolve the issues of high debt and structural government deficits. Global increasing affluence and demand means that consumers actively seek choice, with the result that globally competition is intensifying as companies compete to win the battle for disposable income.

Population growth and increased affluence together have helped create a 'global youth culture' – teenagers now account for 30 per cent of the population globally. In many countries, more than half the population is pre-adult, creating one of the world's biggest single markets, the youth market. Everywhere adolescents project worldwide cultural icons, Nike, Coke, Apple iPhones and iPads, the Sony Wii and the latest play station. Social networking, twitter, blogs and 'virtual reality' are all now common place creating a one-world youth culture market that potentially can exceed all others as a premier global market segment. Parochial, local and ethnic products may face difficult times.

Older consumers are also increasingly transnational in their consumer identity. They drive globally produced cars, take worldwide holidays, watch programmes from across the globe on television, use globally developed technology and are increasingly plugged into the online digital media technology previously only used by the younger generation. On the supply side, transnational corporations are increasing in size and embracing more global power. The top 500 companies in the world account for 70 per cent of world trade and 80 per cent of international investment. Total sales of multinationals are now in excess of world trade, which gives them a combined gross product of more than some national economies.

To strategically position themselves for global competitiveness, companies are consolidating through mergers, acquisitions and alliances to reach the scale considered necessary to compete in the global arena. At the same time, there is a trend towards global standardization, as companies strive for world standards for efficiency and productivity. Globally last year mergers and acquisitions were worth US$ 3 trillion, with $1 trillion of those being across Europe. Geely, China's biggest privately owned car firm took over Sweden's Volvo cars, The Indian company Tata took over Corus making them the world's largest steel producer, overtaking Mittal (Dutch) who in the same year took over Aecelor of Luxembourg. Rohm and Haas was acquired by Dow Chemical and Apple acquired Quattro Wireless. GSK have a number of global alliances in the pharmaceutical market, creating the world's largest research-based pharmaceutical company. There has also been an increase in the number of joint ventures and international strategic alliances to compete in mature markets. Daimler closed a strategic gap in its global truck operations with a Chinese joint venture with rival Foton to produce trucks for the largest commercial vehicle market in the world. Xerox entered into a joint venture with Fuji to consolidate their global position and the Siemens and Fujitsu joint venture is now the only computer hardware company in Europe following the global consolidation of that sector.

The global marketplace is no longer the summation of a large number of independent country markets but much more multilateral and interdependent, economically, culturally and technically. Information moves anywhere in the world at the speed of light, the ease of transmission being facilitated by the convergence of long distance telecoms, cuts in the cost of electronic processing and the exponential growth in Internet access.

The combination of all these forces has meant that all companies need to develop a marketing orientation which is global in nature and that companies need managers who have the skills to analyze, plan and implement strategies across the world. It is for these reasons that international marketing has become such a critical area of study for managers and an important component of the marketing syllabus of business faculties in universities.

So perhaps now we should turn our attention to examining exactly what we mean by international marketing.

What is international marketing?

Many readers of this textbook will have already followed a programme of study in marketing but, before explaining what we mean by international marketing, let us reflect for a few moments on our understanding of what is meant by marketing itself. The Chartered Institute of Marketing defines marketing as the 'Management process responsible for identifying, anticipating and satisfying customer requirements profitably'. Thus marketing involves:

- focusing on the needs and wants of customers
- identifying the best method of satisfying those needs and wants
- orienting the company towards the process of providing that satisfaction
- meeting organizational objectives.

In this way, it is argued, the company or organization best prepares itself to achieve competitive advantage in the marketplace. It then needs to work to maintain this advantage by manipulating the controllable functions of marketing within the largely uncontrollable marketing environment made up of SLEPTS factors: i.e. Social, Legal, Economic, Political and Technological sustainabily.

How does the process of international marketing differ? Within the international marketing process the key elements of this framework still apply. The conceptual framework is not going to change to any marked degree when a company moves from a domestic to an international market; however, there are two main differences. First, there are different levels at which international marketing can be approached and, second, the uncontrollable elements of the marketing environment are more complex and multidimensional given the multiplicity of markets that constitute the global marketplace. This means managers have to acquire new skills and abilities to add to the tools and techniques they have developed in marketing to domestic markets.

International marketing defined

At its simplest level, international marketing involves the firm in making one or more marketing mix decisions across national boundaries. At its most complex, it involves the firm in establishing manufacturing/processing facilities around the world and coordinating marketing strategies across the globe. At one extreme there are firms that opt for 'international marketing' simply by signing a distribution agreement with a foreign agent who then takes on the responsibility for pricing, promotion, distribution and market development. At the other extreme, there are huge global companies such as Ford with an integrated network of manufacturing plants worldwide and who operate in some 150 country markets. Thus, at its most complex, international marketing becomes a process of managing on a global scale. These different levels of marketing can be expressed in the following terms:

- *Domestic marketing*, which involves the company manipulating a series of controllable variables such as price, advertising, distribution and the product/service attributes in a largely uncontrollable external environment that is made up of different economic structures, competitors, cultural values and legal infrastructure within specific political or geographic country boundaries.

- *International marketing*, which involves operating across a number of foreign country markets in which not only do the uncontrollable variables differ significantly between one market and another, but the controllable factors in the form of cost and price structures, opportunities for advertising and distributive infrastructure are also likely to differ significantly. It is these sorts of differences that lead to the complexities of international marketing.

- *Global marketing management*, which is a larger and more complex international operation. Here a company coordinates, integrates and controls a whole series of marketing programmes into a substantial global effort. Here the primary objective of the company is to achieve a degree of synergy in the overall operation so that by taking advantage of different exchange rates, tax rates, labour rates, skill levels and market opportunities, the organization as a whole will be greater than the sum of its parts.

This type of strategy calls for managers who are capable of operating as international marketing managers in the truest sense, a task which is far broader and more complex than that of operating either in a specific foreign country or in the domestic market. In discussing this, Sarathy *et al.* (2006) comment that: 'the international marketing manager has a dual responsibility; foreign marketing (marketing within foreign countries) and global marketing (co-ordinating marketing in multiple markets in the face of global competition)'.

Thus, how international marketing is defined and interpreted depends on the level of involvement of the company in the international marketplace. International marketing could therefore be:

- Export marketing, in which case the firm markets its goods and/or services across national/political boundaries.

- International marketing, where the marketing activities of an organization include activities, interests or operations in more than one country and where there is some kind of influence or control of marketing activities from outside the country in which the goods or services will actually be sold. Sometimes markets are typically perceived to be independent and a profit centre in their own right, in which case the term multinational or multi-domestic marketing is often used.

- Global marketing, in which the whole organization focuses on the selection and exploitation of global marketing opportunities and marshals resources around the globe with the objective of achieving a global competitive advantage.

The first of these definitions describes relatively straightforward exporting activities, numerous examples of which exist. However, the subsequent definitions are more complex and more formal and indicate not only a revised attitude to marketing but also a very different underlying philosophy. Here the world is seen as a market segmented by social, legal, economic, political and technological (SLEPTS) groupings.

In this textbook we will incorporate the international marketing issues faced by firms, be they involved in export, international or global marketing.

For all these levels the key to successful international marketing is being able to identify and understand the complexities of each of these SLEPTS dimensions of the international environment and how they impact on a firm's marketing strategies across their international markets. As in domestic marketing, the successful marketing company will be the one that is best able to manipulate the controllable tools of the marketing mix within the uncontrollable environment. It follows that the key problem faced by the international marketing manager is that of coming to terms with the details and complexities of the international environment. It is these complexities that we will examine in the following sections.

The international marketing environment

The key difference between domestic marketing and marketing on an international scale is the multidimensionality and complexity of the many foreign country markets a company may operate in. An international manager needs a knowledge and awareness of these complexities and the implications they have for international marketing management.

There are many environmental analysis models which the reader may have come across. For the purposes of this textbook, we will use the SLEPTS approach and examine the various aspects and trends in the international marketing environment through the social/cultural, legal, economic, political and technological and sustainability dimensions, as depicted in Figure 1.1. In this edition we have added a sustainability dimension. Sustainability is about considering the environmental impact of everything we do. This means encouraging a holistic way of thinking in our responses to the global marketing challenges we identify and assessing the impact of our global marketing strategies – socially, economically and environmentally in our approach to ensuring sustainability over the longer term.

FIGURE 1.1 The environmental influences on international marketing

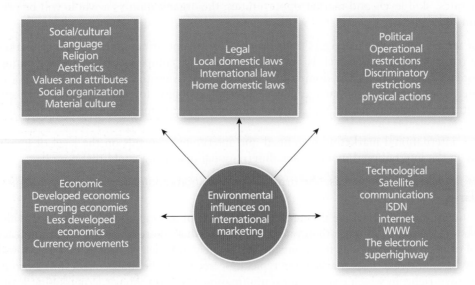

Social/cultural environment

The social and cultural influences on international marketing are immense. Differences in social conditions, religion and material culture all affect consumers' perceptions and patterns of buying behaviour. It is this area that determines the extent to which consumers across the globe are either similar or different and so determines the potential for global branding and standardization.

A failure to understand the social/cultural dimensions of a market are complex to manage, as McDonald's found in India. It had to deal with a market that is 40 per cent vegetarian, had an aversion to either beef or pork among meat-eaters and a hostility to frozen meat and fish, but with the general Indian fondness for spice with everything. To satisfy such tastes, McDonald's discovered it needed to do more than provide the right burgers. Customers buying vegetarian burgers wanted to be sure that these were cooked in a separate area in the kitchen using separate utensils and sauces like McMasala and McImli were developed to satisfy the Indian taste for spice. Interestingly, however, these are now innovations they have introduced into other markets.

Cultural factors

Cultural differences and especially language differences have a significant impact on the way a product may be used in a market, its brand name and the advertising campaign.

Initially, Coca-Cola had enormous problems in China as Coca-Cola sounded like 'Kooke Koula' which translates into 'A thirsty mouthful of candle wax'. They managed to find a new pronunciation 'Kee Kou Keele' which means 'joyful tastes and happiness'.

Other companies who have experienced problems are General Motors whose brand name 'Nova' was unsuccessful in Spain ('no va' in Spanish means 'no go'). Pepsi Cola had to change its campaign 'Come Alive With Pepsi' in Germany as, literally translated, it means 'Come Alive Out of the Grave'. In Japan McDonald's character Ronald McDonald failed because his white face was seen as a death mask. When Apple launched the iMac in France they discovered the brand name mimicked the name of a well established brand of baby laxative – hardly the image they were trying to project.

Operating effectively in different countries requires recognition that there may be considerable differences in the different regions. Consider northern Europe versus Latin Europe, the northwest of the USA versus the south or Bejing and Taipei. At the stage of early internationalization it is not unusual for firms to experience what appear to be cultural gaps with their counterparts in the countries they are expanding into, be it the West going East or the East going West. A campaign by Camay soap which showed a husband washing his wife's back in the bath was a huge success in France but failed in Japan, not because it caused offence, but because Japanese women viewed the prospect of a husband sharing such a time as a huge invasion of privacy.

On the other hand, some commentators argue there are visible signs that social and cultural differences are becoming less of a barrier. The dominance of a number of world brands such as Apple, Sony, Microsoft, Intel, Coca-Cola, McDonald's, Nike, etc., all competing in global markets that transcend national and political boundaries, are testimony to the convergence of consumer needs across the globe. However, it is important not to confuse globalization of brands with the homogenization of cultures. There are a large number of global brands but even these have to manage cultural differences between and within national country boundaries.

There are also a number of cultural paradoxes which exist. For example, in Asia, the Middle East, Africa and Latin America there is evidence both for the westernization of tastes and the assertion of ethnic, religious and cultural differences. Companies like Avon Cosmetics who sell directly through their own distributors are well placed to exploit such paradoxes in emerging markets. There are more than 600 000 Avon ladies now in China and 900 000 in Brazil. In northern Kenya you may well come across a Sambhuru warrior in full traditional dress doing online mobile banking with an app downloaded to his mobile phone. Thus, while there is a vast and, sometimes, turbulent mosaic of cultural differences, there are commentators who believe there is evidence that a global village is potentially taking shape which, as Kenichi Ohmae (2005) says: 'will be a nationless state marked by the convergence of customer needs that transcends political and cultural boundaries'.

The social/cultural environment is an important area for international marketing managers and we will return to this subject in a number of chapters where we examine the various aspects of its strategic implications. Chapter 3 is devoted to a full examination of the social and cultural influences in international marketing. In Chapter 5 we will examine the forces driving the global village and its strategic implication to companies across the world.

Social factors

Growth and movement in populations around the world are important factors heralding social changes. Of the world's population, 80 per cent live in developing countries; by 2025 this is likely to reach 85 per cent. Two out of every five people live in China and India. However, while world population is growing dramatically, the growth patterns are not consistent around the world.

Over the next half century, Africa's population will almost treble and its economy is set to grow substantively (see Illustration 1.1). China's population will rise much more slowly from 1.2 billion to 1.5 billion. With a population of 1.53 billion people, India will have more inhabitants than China in 50 years' time. Europe is the only region where the population is expected to decline; any increase in population in high income countries is entirely due to migration.

There are also visible moves in the population within many countries, leading to the formation of huge urban areas where consumers have a growing similarity of needs across the globe. Nowadays, 50 per cent of the world's population live in urban areas: the world is moving into gigantic conurbations. The population of greater Tokyo is soon to be close to 36 million and Mexico City 22 million. Cities such as Sao Paulo, Shanghai and Jakarta will soon outstrip western cities such as Paris, London and Rome. In the year 2015, no Western European city will be in the top 20 and 19 of the world's 20 mega cities of 10 million plus will be in emerging markets, New York being the only other city. This has powerful implications for international marketing. These cities will be markets in themselves. Urban dwellers require similar products (packaged conveniently and easy to carry). Similarly, they demand services, telephones and transportation of all kinds and modern visual communications. It also means, for the incoming company, that customers are accessible. They are identifiable and firms can communicate with them efficiently via supermarkets, advertising and other marketing communication tools. Table 1.1 shows the ten mega cities in the world forecast for 2015.

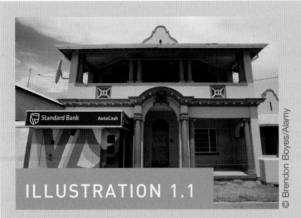

ILLUSTRATION 1.1

Standard Bank Forecasts Exciting Future for African markets

In its report – *African Markets Revealed*, the Standard Bank examined a range of factors that drive markets in 19 African economies across the continent from Egypt to South Africa.

Reviewing the prospects for Africa, Stephen Bailey-Smith, Standard Bank's Head of African Research said:

'Africa would benefit from expected global growth, despite the risks posed by the downturn of the US consumer market, funding problems in European countries and the tightening of monetary policy in China. African markets were facing exciting times.'

'Emerging market growth will attract investment. This will see "frontier markets" such as in Africa becoming economically stronger and reducing the gap existing between them and the broader, more established emerging market economies.'

'The further we get from the nervousness of the 2008 financial crisis, it can be expected that frontier markets such as Africa will outperform relative to developed markets and the more established emerging markets'

Stephen Bailey-Smith, Standard Bank's Head of African Research

Bailey-Smith said that the global financial crisis of 2008 was a significant turning point in the organization of the international economic system. Africa was a major beneficiary of the change.

In its latest World Economic Outlook, the IMF predicted that growth in emerging markets in 2011 would be 6.4 per cent, with growth continuing at an average rate of about 6.4 per cent year-on-year for the next five years. By contrast, the IMF was expecting developed markets to grow only about 2.4 per cent year-on-year for the next five years.

Question

1 What do you see as the major challenges and opportunities for a company wishing to develop the African market?

References: http://www.dailyguideghana.com/ghananews-business/1892-exciting-future-for-african-markets-standard-bank-report.html *accessed 7/3/2011*

Legal environment

Legal systems vary both in content and interpretation. A company is not just bound by the laws of its home country but also by those of its host country and by the growing body of international law. Firms operating in the European Union are facing ever-increasing directives which affect their markets across Europe. This can affect many aspects of a marketing strategy – for instance advertising – in the form of media restrictions and the acceptability of particular creative appeals (see Illustration 1.2). Product acceptability in a country can be affected by minor regulations on such things as packaging and by more major changes in legislation. In the USA, for instance, the MG sports car was withdrawn when the increasing difficulty of complying with safety legislation changes made exporting to that market unprofitable. Kraft Foods sell a product called Lifesavers, which are very similar to the Nestlé Polo brand, in many countries. Using EU law, Nestlé attempted to stop the sale of Lifesavers in the EU purely to protect their market share.

It is important, therefore, for the firm to know the legal environment in each of its markets. These laws constitute the 'rules of the game' for business activity. The legal environment in international

Table 1.1 The world's ten mega cities in 2015

City	Country	Population (millions)
Tokyo	Japan	36
Mumbai	India	22
Mexico City	Mexico	22
Sao Paulo	Brazil	21
New York	USA	20
Delhi	India	19
Shanghai	China	17
Kolkata	India	17
Dhaka	Bangladesh	17
Jakarta	Indonesia	17

Source: www.un.org © United Nations 2000–2011.

marketing is more complicated than in domestic markets since it has three dimensions: (1) local domestic law; (2) international law; (3) domestic laws in the firm's home base.

- *Local domestic laws*. These are all different! The only way to find a route through the legal maze in overseas markets is to use experts on the separate legal systems and laws pertaining in each market targeted.
- *International law*. There are a number of international laws that can affect the organization's activity. Some are international laws covering piracy and hijacking, others are more international conventions and agreements and cover items such as the International Monetary Fund (IMF) and World Trade Organization (WTO) treaties, patents and trademarks legislation and harmonization of legal systems within regional economic groupings, e.g. the European Union.
- *Domestic laws in the home country*. The organization's domestic (homemarket) legal system is important for two reasons. First, there are often export controls which limit the free export of certain goods and services to particular marketplaces, and second, there is the duty of the organization to act and abide by its national laws in all its activities, whether domestic or international.

It will be readily understandable how domestic, international and local legal systems can have a major impact upon the organization's ability to market into particular overseas countries. Laws will affect the marketing mix in terms of products, price, distribution and promotional activities quite dramatically. For many firms, the legal challenges they face in international markets are almost a double-edged sword. Often firms operating internationally face ethical challenges in deciding how to deal with differing cultural perceptions of legal practices.

In many mature markets they face quite specific and, sometimes, burdensome regulations. In Germany, for instance, environmental laws mean a firm is responsible for the retrieval and disposal of the packaging waste it creates and must produce packaging which is recyclable, whereas in many emerging markets there may be limited patent and trademark protection, still evolving judicial systems, non-tariff barriers and instability through an ever-evolving reform programme.

© federico stevanin, shutterstock.com

ILLUSTRATION 1.2

When is a Parma ham not a Parma ham?

The European Court of Justice has decided that it is illegal for the world-famous Parma ham to be sliced and packaged outside the Italian region that gives Parma ham its name. The ruling was a victory for the 200 or so producers of Parma ham who had launched their legal action against Asda, a UK food retailer. The case hinged on the court's interpretation of geographical indications – EU-protected trademarks that recognize the importance of products closely associated with a particular place, whether it is Parma ham, French champagne, Spanish sherry or Stilton cheese from Britain. The Parma producers argued that slicing the ham was an important process that had to be done locally. Asda argued they should be free to slice and pack the ham where they chose in order to cut costs and reduce the price to consumers. The court showed it was more concerned with the protection of the ham producers' rights than market efficiency. However strangely Asda can still use the Parma name when the meat is sliced on a delicatessen counter in front of shoppers?

The question is, how will the world view the decision? Some commentators use such examples to question the commitment of the European Union to freeing trade and becoming more competitive.

Question

1 Do you think the court decision protects local market diversity across European markets, or does it act as a restrictive trade practice?

References: *The Economist,* 21 May 2003 and 'Asda slams "ham-fisted" Parma ruling' BBC News 20 May, 2003

China earned notoriety in the past for allowing infringements of copyright and blatant piracy. However, this is now changing. Some governments are reluctant to develop and enforce laws protecting intellectual property, partly because they believe such actions favour large, rich multinationals. Anheuser Busch (USA) and Budvar (Czech Republic) have been in constant litigation over the right to use the name Budweiser in the European Union and both companies have recently been legally deemed the right to use it.

Piracy in markets with limited trademark and patent protection is another challenge. Bootlegged software exceeds $51 billion in commercial value globally. It is said that pirate products constitutes 87 per cent of all personal computer software in use in India, 92 per cent in Thailand and 98 per cent in China. In China this market is estimated to be worth US$7.6 billion. According to Business Software Alliance for every US$100 worth of legitimate software sold, an additional $75 worth of unlicensed software makes its way into the market somewhere globally.

India is regarded by many firms as an attractive emerging market beset with many legal difficulties, bureaucratic delay and lots of red tape. For example, pairs of shoes cannot be imported which causes huge problems for shoe manufacturers who need to import shoes as production samples. By separating the pairs and importing each shoe to a different port, importers of shoes are using a loophole in the law and trying to overcome this problem. Companies such as Mercedes Benz, Coca-Cola and Kellogg have found the vast potential of India's market somewhat hard to break into. Its demanding consumers can be difficult to read and local rivals can be surprisingly tough. Political squabbles, bureaucratic delays and infrastructure headaches are also major obstacles.

Economic environment

It is important that the international marketer has an understanding of economic developments and how they impinge on the marketing strategy. This understanding is important at a world level in terms of the world trading infrastructure such as world institutions and trade agreements developed to foster international trade, at a regional level in terms of regional trade integration and at a country/market level. Firms need to be aware of the economic policies of countries and the direction in which a particular market is developing economically in order to make an assessment as to whether they can profitably satisfy market demand and compete with firms already in the market.

Among the 194 countries in the world, there are varying economic conditions, levels of economic development and Gross national income per capita (GNIpc). Gross national income in the world is US$70 trillion (purchasing power parity [ppp]). However, it is not shared equitably across the world and the range across the globe is enormous. Norway, with the highest figure has a GNIpc (ppp) of US$60 000 while the lowest, Liberia has a GNIpc (ppp) of US$310. The United Nations classes 75 per cent of the world's population as poor, that is, they have a per capita income of less than US$3470, and only 11 per cent of the population as rich, meaning they have a per capita income of more than US$9000. Perhaps more startling is the UN claim that the richest 50 million people in the world share the same amount of wealth as the poorest 3000 million. Such disparities of incomes set particular challenges for companies operating in international markets in terms of seeking possible market opportunities, assessing the viability of potential markets as well as identifying sources of finance in markets where opportunities are identified but where there is not capacity to pay for goods.

Another key challenge facing companies is the question as to how they can develop an integrated strategy across a number of international markets when there are divergent levels of economic development. Such disparities often make it difficult to have a cohesive strategy, especially in pricing.

The Economist 'Big Mac' Index (Figure 1.2) is a useful tool which illustrates the difficulties global companies have in trying to achieve a consistent pricing strategy across the world. It provides a rough

FIGURE 1.2 An alternative Big Mac index – how many minutes to earn the price of a Big Mac?

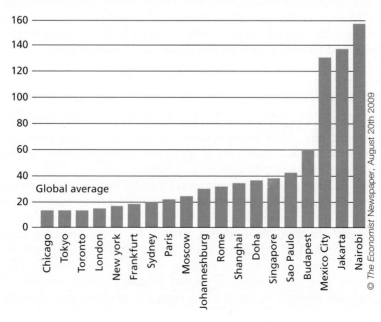

© The Economist Newspaper, August 20th 2009

measure of the purchasing power of a currency. UBS, a bank in the USA, uses the price of the Big Mac burger to measure the purchasing power of local wages around the world. It divides the price of a Big Mac by the average net hourly wage in cities around the world. Fast-food junkies are best off in Chicago, Toronto and Tokyo, where it takes a mere 12 minutes at work to afford a Big Mac. By contrast, employees must toil for over two hours to earn enough for a burger in Mexico City, Jakarta and Nairobi. This causes problems for McDonald's in trying to pursue a standard product image across markets. Priced in US dollars, a Big Mac in Norway would cost US$7.20, whereas in China it would be US$1.95.

In order to examine these challenges further we divided the economies into developed economies and less developed economies.

The developed economies

The developed economies of the North American Free Trade Area (NAFTA), European Union (EU) and Japan account for 80 per cent of world trade. For many firms this constitutes much of what is termed the global market. Even though many companies call themselves global, most of their revenues and profits will be earned from these markets. In the European Union nearly 70 per cent of the international goods traded are traded within the European Union; in NAFTA, 50 per cent of goods exported are to other members of NAFTA. This leads some commentators to argue that most competition, even in today's global marketplace, is more active at a regional level than a global level. It is from these developed economies that the global consumer with similar lifestyles, needs and desires emanates. However, emerging markets are now becoming increasingly economically powerful and moving up the ranks, especially such countries as Brazil, Russia, India and China.

The emerging economies

In countries such as Brazil, Russia, India and China, (the BRIC economies) there is a huge and growing demand for everything from automobiles to cellular phones and all are viewed as key growth markets where there is an evolving pattern of government-directed economic reforms, lowering of restrictions on foreign investment and increasing privatization of state-owned monopolies. All these rapidly developing economies herald significant opportunities for the international marketing firm.

Such markets often have what is termed as a 'dual economy'. Usually there tends to be a wealthy urban professional class alongside a poorer rural population. Income distribution tends to be much more skewed between the 'haves' and the 'have nots' than in developed countries. From negligible numbers a few years ago, China now has a middle class of 100 million which is forecast to grow to 500 million in the next century. Brazil and Indonesia have middle classes of 25 million each.

Less developed countries

This group includes underdeveloped countries and less developing countries. The main features are a low GDP per capita, a limited amount of manufacturing activity and a very poor and fragmented infrastructure. Typical infrastructure weaknesses are in transport, communications, education and healthcare. In addition, the public sector is often slow-moving and bureaucratic.

It is common to find that less developed countries (LDCs) are heavily reliant on one product and often on one trading partner. In many LDCs this product is the main export earner. In Angola, for instance, the sole export is oil and in the Sudan oil accounts for 99 per cent of their exports. In addition, three-quarters of LDCs depend on their main trading partner for more than one-quarter of their export revenue. The risks posed to the LDC by changing patterns of supply and demand are great. Falling commodity prices can result in large decreases in earnings for the whole country. The resultant economic and political adjustments may affect exporters to that country through possible changes in tariff and non-tariff barriers, through changes in the level of company taxation and through restrictions on the

How do you sell to subsistence farmers in Africa?

KickStart International is a non-profit organization that sells irrigation systems to subsistence farmers in Africa. The customers are hard to reach.

They live hours from major cities and many are illiterate. Even though they are a non-profit organization, KickStart needs to build brand loyalty which is difficult in a market where there is a lack of trust in a foreign US company. The other dilemma is given the levels of illiteracy, how do they educate the farmers to use the equipment and how do KickStart get their message across given the small budget they have for such activities?

Question

1 How should KickStart approach this market?

convertibility of currency and the repatriation of profits. In addition, substantial decreases in market sizes within the country are probable.

A wide range of economic circumstances influences the development of the less developed countries in the world. Some countries are small with few natural resources and for these countries it is difficult to start the process of substantial economic growth. Poor health and education standards need money on a large scale, yet the pay-off in terms of a healthier, better-educated population takes time to achieve. At the same time, there are demands for public expenditure on transport systems, communication systems and water control systems. Without real prospects for rapid economic development, private sources of capital are reluctant to invest in such countries. This is particularly the case for long-term infrastructure projects and, as a result, important capital spending projects rely heavily on world aid programmes. Marketing to such countries can be problematic, as in the case of KickStart in Management Challenge 1.1.

Currency risks

While we have examined economic factors within markets, we also need to bear in mind that in international marketing transactions invariably take place between countries, so exchange rates and currency movements are an important aspect of the international economic environment. On top of all the normal vagaries of markets, customer demands, competitive actions and economic infrastructures, foreign exchange parities are likely to change on a regular if unpredictable basis. World currency movements, stimulated by worldwide trading and foreign exchange dealing, are an additional complication in the international environment. Companies that guess wrongly as to which way a currency will move can see their international business deals rendered unprofitable overnight. Businesses that need to swap currencies to pay for imported goods, or because they have received foreign currency for products they have exported, can find themselves squeezed to the point where they watch their profits disappear.

In Europe, the formation of the European Monetary Union (EMU) and the establishment of the Single European Payments Area (SEPA) led to greater stability for firms operating in the market. The formation of the European Monetary Union and the introduction of the single currency across Europe had important implications for company strategies which we will discuss in Chapter 2, when we examine regional trading agreements, and in Chapter 11, when we look at pricing issues in international marketing.

Political environment

The political environment of international marketing includes any national or international political factor that can affect the organization's operations or its decision-making. Politics has come to be recognized as the major factor in many international business decisions, especially in terms of whether to invest and how to develop markets.

Politics is intrinsically linked to a government's attitude to business and the freedom within which it allows firms to operate. Unstable political regimes expose foreign businesses to a variety of risks that they would generally not face in the home market. This often means that the political arena is the most volatile area of international marketing. The tendencies of governments to change regulations can have a profound effect on international strategy, providing both opportunities and threats. The invasions of Afghanistan and Iraq have brought market development opportunities for some but market devastation for others and higher political risk in neighbouring markets for all. The instability in the Middle East and the continued threat of global terrorism have served to heighten firms' awareness of the importance of monitoring political risk factors in the international markets in which they operate. Lesser developed countries and emerging markets pose particularly high political risks, even when they are following reforms to solve the political problems they have. The stringency of such reforms can itself lead to civil disorder and rising opposition to governments. Political risk is defined as a risk due to a sudden or gradual change in a local political environment that is disadvantageous or counter productive to foreign firms and markets.

The types of action that governments may take which constitute potential political risks to firms fall into three main areas:

- *Operational restrictions*. These could be exchange controls, employment policies, insistence on locally shared ownership and particular product requirements.

- *Discriminatory restrictions*. These tend to be imposed on purely foreign firms and, sometimes, only firms from a particular country. The USA has imposed import quotas on Japan in protest at non-tariff barriers which they view as being imposed unfairly on US exporters. They have also imposed bans on imports from Libya and Iran in the past. Such barriers tend to be such things as special taxes and tariffs, compulsory subcontracting or loss of financial freedom.

- *Physical actions*. These actions are direct government interventions such as confiscation without any payment of indemnity, a forced take over by the government, expropriation, nationalization or even damage to property or personnel through riots and war. In 2001 the Nigerian government claimed ownership of Shell's equipment and machinery without any prior warning.

Investment restrictions are a common way governments interfere politically in international markets by restricting levels of investment, location of facilities, choice of local partners and ownership percentage. Recent decisions by certain Latin American countries to compel foreign investors to re-negotiate their investment contracts on sanction of expulsion introduced considerable uncertainty for companies operating in the region. When Microsoft opened its Beijing office, it planned to use its Taiwan operations to supply a Mandarin language version of Windows. The government not only wanted such an operating system to be designed in China but also insisted on defining the coding standards for Chinese characters' fonts, something Microsoft had done independently everywhere else in the world. In a flurry of meetings with officials, Bill Gates argued that the marketplace, not the government, should set standards. But the Chinese electronics industry threatened to ban Windows and President Jiang Zemin personally admonished Gates to spend more time in China and 'learn something from 5000 years of Chinese history'. Gates sacked the original management team and promised to cooperate with Beijing.

The World Trade Organization has led negotiations on a series of worldwide agreements to expand quotas, reduce tariffs and introduce a number of innovative measures to encourage trade among countries. Together with the formation of regional trading agreements in the European Union, North and South America and Asia, these reforms constitute a move to a more politically stable international trading environment. An understanding of these issues is critical to the international marketing manager, which is why in Chapter 2 we examine in some detail the patterns of world trade, the regional trading agreements and the development of world trading institutions intended to foster international trade. In Chapter 4 we will examine in some detail the procedures, tools and techniques which can help the analysis and evaluation of opportunities across such markets.

Courtesy of Cadbury

ILLUSTRATION 1.3

Cadbury's in political faux pas

The Indian division of Cadbury-Schweppes suffered embarrassment around the world and incensed large swathes of Hindu society by running a newspaper advertisement comparing its Temptations chocolate to the war-torn region of Kashmir. The ad carried the tagline:

'I'm good. I'm tempting. I'm too good to share. What am I? Cadbury's Temptations or Kashmir?'.

To make sure nobody missed the point, the ad's creators laid the 'too good to share' catch-line over a map of Kashmir.

The ad caused a national outcry. Arguments over Kashmir have taken India and Pakistan to the brink of nuclear war: using them to sell chocolate was perhaps not the wisest thing to do. Indian politicians were shocked at the very mention of sharing the territory and threatened nationwide protests. To add insult to injury the advertisement was timed to appear on 15 August, India's Independence Day. Cadbury's British roots may have made the ad even harder to swallow. It was British colonial rulers who, at partition in 1947, drew the boundary line between India and Pakistan that the two nations have battled over ever since.

Though Cadbury India has apologized, it does show that in global markets, multinationals can't hide their blunders for long.

Question

1 What are the dangers of a company making such blunders when it operates globally?

References: *The Economist,* 22 August 2002 and BBC News Online 7 October 2002

The political and economic environments are greatly intertwined and, sometimes, difficult to categorize. It is important, however, that a firm operating in international markets assesses the countries in which it operates to gauge the economic and political risk and to ensure they understand the peculiarities and characteristics of the market they wish to develop. Illustration 1.3 examines Cadbury's, who caused huge offence by their misreading of political sentiments in India.

Technological environment

Technology is a major driving force both in international marketing and in the move towards a more global marketplace. The impact of technological advances can be seen in all aspects of the marketing process. The ability to gather data on markets, management control capabilities and the practicalities of carrying out the business function internationally have been revolutionized in recent years with the advances in electronic communications.

Satellite communications, the Internet and the World Wide Web, client–server technologies, ISDN and cable as well as email, faxes and advanced mobile phone applications have all led to dramatic shrinkages in worldwide communications.

Shrinking communications means, increasingly, that in the international marketplace, information is power. At the touch of a button we can access information on the key factors that determine our business. News is a 24 hours a day service. Manufacturers wanting to know the price of coffee beans or the relevant position of competitors in terms of their share price or new product activity have it at their immediate disposal.

As mobile technology renders land cables and telephone lines redundant, developing countries abandoned plans to invest in land-based communication. They have bypassed terrestrial communication systems, enabling them to catch up with and, in some cases overtake, developed countries in the marketplace. In emerging economies consumers are jumping from no telephone to the latest in global communications technology. Wireless application protocol (WAP) technology allows online services to be available to mobile phone users on the move, wherever they happen to be in the world. The use of Global System for Mobile Communications (GSM) technology enables mobile phone operators to determine the location of a customer globally to send them relevant and timely advertising messages.

British Airways operates its worldwide online operations from Mumbai: everything from ticketing to making an 'exceptional request' facility, such as wheelchair assistance needed for a passenger can be managed from the centre in India. The ease of hiring computer-literate graduates by the hundred, who are intelligent, capable, keen and inexpensive to hire, as is local property to rent, has enabled India to build a global advantage in this rapidly developing industry.

The Internet and the world wide web (www)

The Internet and the access gained to the world wide web has revolutionized international marketing practices. Airlines such as easyJet and Ryanair have helped completely change the way we book our airline reservations. EToys, a virtual company based in the US, has no retail outlets but a higher market capitalization than Toys'R'Us. Firms ranging from a few employees to large multinationals have realized the potential of marketing globally online and so have developed the facility to buy and sell their products and services online to the world.

An estimated 2 billion people – some 29 per cent of the global population – now have access to the Internet. However, for many this will be through public-based Internet services in cafes etc. The United Nations estimate that global e-business is now worth more than US$12 trillion, most of which is business-to-business (B2B), not business-to-consumer (B2C) purchases.

The Internet has meant huge opportunities for small- and medium-sized enterprises (SMEs) and rapid internationalization for many. It has enabled them to substantially reduce the costs of reaching international customers, reduce global advertising costs and made it much easier for small niche products to find a critical mass of customers. Because of the low entry costs of operating as an online business it has permitted firms with low capital resources to become global marketers, in some cases overnight. There are, therefore, quite significant implications for SMEs which will be examined further in Chapter 5, where we discuss in some detail the issues in international marketing pertinent to SMEs.

For all companies, the implications of being able to market goods and services online have been far reaching. The Internet has led to an explosion of information to consumers, giving them the potential to source products from the cheapest supplier in the world. This has led to the increasing standardization of prices across borders or, at least, to the narrowing of price differentials as consumers become more aware of prices in different countries and buy a whole range of products via the net. In B2C marketing this has been most dramatically seen in the purchase of such things as, financial services, flights, holidays, music downloads and books. The Internet, by connecting end-users and producers directly, has reduced the importance of traditional intermediaries in international marketing (i.e. agents and distributors) as more companies have built the online capability to deal direct with their customers, particularly in B2B marketing. To survive, such intermediaries have begun offering a whole range of new services, the value added element of their offering no longer being principally in the physical distribution of goods but rather in the collection, collation, interpretation and dissemination of vast amounts of information. The critical resource possessed by this new breed of 'cybermediary' is information rather than inventory. The Internet has also become a powerful tool for supporting networks both internal and external to the firm. Many global firms have developed supplier intranets through which they source products and services from preferred suppliers who have met the criteria to gain access to their supplier intranets. It has become the efficient new medium for conducting worldwide market research and gaining feedback from customers.

Thus the Internet produces a fundamentally different environment for international marketing and requires a radically different strategic approach affecting all aspects of the marketing process. Not all forays into Internet marketing have been successful. Many early dotcom high growth companies became 'dot.bombs' when they failed to sustain their early promise. Levi Strauss stopped its Internet selling operation after finding the cost of servicing returned goods was greater than the revenue generated from new sales.

The dual technological/cultural paradox

On one hand commentators view technological advancement and shrinking communications as the most important driving force in the building of the global village where there are global consumers who have similar needs. On the other hand, to access this global village a person invariably needs a command of the English language and access to the latest technology. In many markets we stumble against the paradox that while in some countries there is a market of well-educated and computer-literate people, in other countries the global electronic highway has completely bypassed them.

Despite all that has been said in previous sections, many developing and emerging markets are characterized by poor, inadequate or deteriorating infrastructures. It is estimated that only 10 per cent of the world's population has direct access to a PC and only 7 per cent have direct access to the Internet. Essential services required for commercial activity, ranging from electric power to water supplies, from highways to air transportation and from phone lines to banking services are often in short supply or unreliable. There are also major disparities in the cost of accessing the Internet. In the USA, accessing the Internet for 20 hours per month would cost 1 per cent of a person's average income; in Mexico it would cost 15 per cent of a person's average income. However, in Bangladesh the same amount of access is equivalent to 278 per cent of the average income and in Madagascar 614 per cent, hardly making access to the Internet feasible for the average person, even if it is technically available.

The huge population shifts discussed earlier have also aggravated the technical infrastructure problems in many of the major cities in emerging markets. This often results in widespread production and distribution bottlenecks, which in turn raises costs. 'Brown outs', for instance, are not uncommon in the Philippines, even in the capital city Manila, where companies and offices regularly lose electric power and either shut down in those periods or revert to generators. Fragmented and circuitous channels of distribution are a result of lack of adequate infrastructure. This makes market entry more complicated and the efficient distribution of a product very difficult. Pepsi Cola in Eastern Europe have a large number of decentralized satellite bottling plants in an attempt to overcome the lack of a distribution infrastructure.

The reader will find that we will examine the impact of the Internet on the relevant marketing practices and processes as we move through the chapters of the book. Chapter 12 of this edition is devoted to examining the implications for the international marketing strategies of companies of such trends in the technology environment.

Sustainability

In considering the environmental challenges to international marketing we also need to take heed of numerous reports that warn of the danger to future prosperity if current over consumption of natural resources is left unchecked. More than three-quarters of the world's people live in countries where national consumption has outstripped biological capacity. Human demands, sometime created by marketers, measure nearly a third more than the Earth can sustain over time. There is increasing evidence of sea levels rising, temperatures warming and uncertain effects on forest and agricultural systems. There is growing evidence of increased variability and volatility in weather patterns which are expected to have a significant and disproportionate impact in the developing world, where the world's poor remain most susceptible to the potential damages and uncertainties inherent in a changing climate.

It is feared by some that as global economic wealth increases, global natural wealth and diversity continue to decline. There is concern that indigenous and national culture and languages can be eroded by the strength of globalized brands. It is also argued by some analysts that globalized markets leave many economically behind. Some countries have been unable to take advantage of globalization of markets and their standards of living are seen to be dropping further behind the richest countries. The gap in income between the 20 per cent richest and poorest countries has grown from 30 to 1 in 1960 to nearly three times that gap. Within many developing markets there are huge gaps between the richest and the poorest.

As responsible global marketers when considering environmental issues we need to ensure in our strategic thinking, we are responding to all the issues we have raised in the previous sections with ethical and socially responsible business practices, that are sustainable in terms of their environmental, societal and economic impact (see Figure 1.3). This involves ensuring in any global marketing action plan we maximize the positive impacts of global marketing while minimizing the negative; whether social or environmental – local, regional or global.

Sustainability interfaces with global marketing through the social and ecological consequences of marketing activities. Sustainability involves ensuring the social, cultural, economic, political and environmental aspects of a global marketing strategy are integrated.

The rise in ethical consumerism and green brands that identify themselves as ethical, has led to a rise in ethic-based decisions across global markets, enabled by increased understanding and information about businesses practices across the globe. Large corporations across the world now see it as a priority that they are seen as socially responsible global citizens who are working ethically and improving the ethical standards of their industry.

Sustainability is about considering the environmental impact of everything we do. This means encouraging a holistic way of thinking in our responses to the global marketing challenges we identify and assessing the impact of our global marketing strategies – socially, economically and environmentally in our approach to ensuring sustainability. This is central to the values of responsible international marketing strategies and a theme that we will return to at various points as we go through the different stages of strategy development in the chapters of this book.

The greatest legacy for the future that we can create, is in the perspectives we take and the skills we use as marketing practitioners. While our global marketing strategies need to be innovative and build global competitiveness we need also to make sure any strategies we develop are grounded in socially and environmentally sustainable business practices. Global marketing strategies should promote sustainable growth, balance prosperity across the world economies and protect our shared global environment. We hope readers of this book in developing international marketing strategies will also make sure we all protect our world environmental capital and manage our global market growth creatively, responsibly and ethically.

FIGURE 1.3 Holistic model of sustainability in global marketing

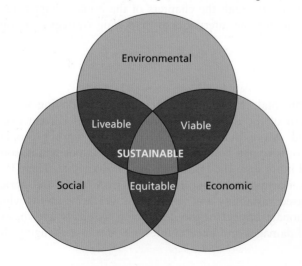

Differences between international and domestic marketing

As we have seen in the previous sections, there are many factors within the international environment which substantially increase the challenge of international marketing. These can be summarized as follows:

1 *Culture*: often diverse and multicultural markets
2 *Markets*: widespread and sometimes fragmented
3 *Data*: difficult to obtain and often expensive
4 *Politics*: regimes vary in stability – political risk becomes an important variable
5 *Governments*: can be a strong influence in regulating importers and foreign business ventures
6 *Economies*: varying levels of development and varying and sometimes unstable currencies
7 *Finance*: many differing finance systems and regulatory bodies
8 *Stakeholders*: commercial, home country and host country
9 *Business*: diverse rules, culturally influenced
10 *Control*: difficult to control and coordinate across markets.

The international competitive landscape

A major difference for managers operating on international markets is the impact all these currents and cross-currents have on the competitive landscape. Wilson and Gilligan (2003) define marketing as 'getting the competitive advantage and keeping it'. The task of achieving this in a competitive environment where firms are subject to local, regional and global competition can be immensely challenging. This is especially so if indigenous local competitors are supported by the government of the country.

Across international markets, advanced countries are seeing significant competition from both emerging markets and less developed countries who are exploiting modern technology and their own low labour costs to compete in markets no longer so protected by tariff walls. The birth of global brand names is no longer the domain of the West (see Illustration 1.4).

The complexity of competition is also heightened by the strategic use of international sourcing of components by multinationals and global firms to achieve competitive advantage.

Given the nature of the challenges and opportunities identified above and the speed of change within the international environment, this means that substantially different pressures are being placed upon management than if they were purely operating in domestic markets. It follows from this that the manager of international marketing needs a detailed knowledge and understanding of how particular environmental variables impact on a firm's international marketing operations.

Perlmutter (1995) identified nine cross-cultural management incompetences which led to failure across a spread of country markets. He defined these core incompetences as: 'the bundle of activities and managerial skills that are mismatched in a great variety of countries where firms do business'.

The first three are interrelated and relate to the failure to be market driven.

1 Inability to find the right market niches.
2 Unwillingness to adapt and update products to local needs.
3 Not having unique products that are viewed as sufficiently higher added value by customers in local markets.
4 A vacillating commitment. It takes time to learn how to function in countries such as Japan.
5 Assigning the wrong people. Picking the wrong people or the wrong top team in an affiliate.
6 Picking the wrong partners. There is a list of difficulties in building alliances; a main limitation is picking partners who do not have the right bundle of capabilities to help reach the local market.

© Ian Dagnall/Alamy

ILLUSTRATION 1.4

From Krating Daeng to Red Bull

Red Bull started life as a truck drivers' pick-me-up in Thailand called Krating Daeng, which translates as 'Red Bull' in English. Based on market share, it is the most popular energy drink in the world. Nowadays in Europe when served with vodka it is seen as a very trendy drink!

Red Bull was initially developed in Thailand, and the rights were then bought by Austrian born Dietrich Mateschitz to market it worldwide excluding Thailand. Thailand continued producing its own brand which has a different formulae and marketing plan to the non-Thailand version.

The internationalization strategy of Red Bull was to open up new markets by securing unusual distribution channels. In the USA a Red Bull sales rep would contact a small distributor to persuade them to sell only Red Bull. If they did not persuade anyone they set up a warehouse and hired younger people to load up the vans and deliver the product. These start-up distributors could focus their entire energies on getting Red Bull fully stocked in stores with prominent shelf placement. They generally broke even within three months and became profitable within six.

In Europe the brand was built through clever repackaging and by developing a niche marketing strategy for the drink as a trendy vodka mixer to the club circuit in Europe. The sales team visited key on-premise accounts: hot clubs and trendy bars to establish distribution. When owners began buying a few cases, they would receive a Red Bull branded cooler and other attractive point of purchase items. Last year, Red Bull's market share stood at 65 per cent, with company worldwide sales being reportedly in the region for US$1 billion.

Question

1 What are the key lessons managers can learn from the building of Red Bull as a worldwide brand?

7 Inability to manage local stakeholders. This includes incompetence in developing a satisfactory partnership relationship with unions and governments.

8 Developing mutual distrust and lack of respect between HQ and the affiliates at different levels of management.

9 Inability to leverage ideas developed in one country to other countries worldwide.

If such mistakes are not to be made in your marketing strategies it is essential to ensure that the company has a robust and rigorous approach to its international marketing planning processes. Approaches to achieving this will be discussed in the following sections.

The international market planning process

In international marketing the very complexity of handling the diverse range of factors that must be considered make planning and control a difficult activity to carry out satisfactorily. For large global companies, the problem becomes one of how to structure the organization so that its increasingly complex and diverse activities around the world can be planned and managed effectively, its goals can be achieved and its stakeholders' expectations satisfied.

In this section we look at the international marketing planning and control process and consider how managers can respond to the challenges posed in the previous sections by ensuring they have robust strategy development and market planning processes.

The planning process

The planning process is the method used by the management of the firm to define in detail how it will achieve its current and future strategic aims and objectives. In doing this, it must evaluate the current and future market opportunities, assess its own current and potential capabilities and attempt to forecast how those changes over which it has no control might help or hinder its efforts to reach its objectives.

The international planning process must allow the company to answer the following three marketing questions.

1 Where is the company now?
2 Where does it want to go?
3 How might it get there?

These questions are fundamental for the majority of businesses whether they are large or small, simple or complex, and they emphasize the firm's need to prepare for the future to ensure its own survival and growth within the increasingly competitive international environment. There is an implication in these questions that the future is likely to be significantly different from the past, so planning is inevitably about forecasting and implementing change which determines the very nature and future direction of the organization.

The starting point of the planning process for any company is to set long-term goals and objectives which reflect its overall aspirations. These goals cannot be set in isolation, however, as the company's history and current levels of success in its different country markets are usually major determinants of its future. Other factors, too, over which the company has little control in international markets, such as the economic and political situation of the countries in which it is operating, the response of the competition and the diverse background, behaviour and expectations of its customers, all have a major impact upon the company's operations and will have a significant effect on determining whether or not it will meet its goals.

Too many firms, particularly smaller ones, fail to prepare contingency plans to cope with the unexpected and, in some cases, even the predictable events in international markets: they are often surprised and unprepared for success too. When unexpected events occur, many companies too easily ignore the plan and develop new strategies as they go along. While it may be possible to survive in a relatively uncomplicated domestic environment by reacting rapidly to new situations as they arise, it is impossible to grow significantly in international markets, as an overly reactive management style is usually wasteful of opportunities and resources.

In international markets, planning and control is essential for both day to day operations and the development of long-term strategies in order to manage the differences of attitudes, standards and values in the extended parts of the organization and avoid the problems of poor coordination and integration of the diverse activities. The plans which are developed must be sufficiently flexible to cope with unfamiliar cultures, rapidly changing political, economic and competitive environments, and the effects of unexpected events which affect global companies in one way or another throughout the world on an almost daily basis.

ILLUSTRATION 1.5

Courtesey of Divine Chocolate

Divine Chocolate Ltd

Kuapa Kokoo is a cooperative of small-scale cocoa farmers in Ghana, who set up Divine Chocolate Ltd (formerly the Day Chocolate Company). The company buys all its cocoa at Fairtrade prices which means the farmers receive a guaranteed minimum price of US$2000 per tonne of cocoa, plus a social premium of US$200 per tonne (these figures reflect an increase made in the last year) which they invest in farm and community development projects. Divine Chocolate has two brands, Divine and Dubble, which carry the Fairtrade Mark licensed by the international Fairtrade Labelling Organization (FLO).

The mission of Divine Chocolate is to improve the livelihoods of West African cocoa farmers by bringing their brand of Fairtrade chocolate to the mainstream world markets. Their milk chocolate recipe was developed with UK tastes in mind, and both Divine and Dubble were created to a quality standard and designed to compete with major brands. Prices also matched those of equivalent products already available on the market.

In July 2006 the Body Shop donated its shares in Divine Chocolate Ltd to Kuapa Kokoo, growing the cooperatives' stake from 33 per cent to 45 per cent of the company. With this very special farmer–ownership model for the business and two successful Fairtrade brands, Divine has a strong appeal to today's more conscientious consumer. In 2010 Kuapa Kokoo permitted Divine to buy the first consignment of Sierra Leone's only Fairtrade certified cocoa extending the opportunity further into the African continent.

Armed with a delicious product and a compelling story, and the clout of supporting charities such as Comic Relief (UK) and Christian Aid, Divine Chocolate has succeeded in getting both Divine and Dubble listed in all the top UK supermarkets, as well as many independents. They also supply chocolate for own label products in the Co-op in the UK and Starbucks across the UK and Europe. The company now has a sister company in the USA and has growth in the USA and other European markets in their sights. However, given their limited resources, can they build on their UK success and take their message to new countries and new cultures with very different consumer behaviour patterns and varying attitudes to the importance of Fairtrade?

Question

1 How can the Divine Chocolate Company develop a marketing plan to help them develop into new international markets?

Source: Jeanette Baker, Sheffield Hallam University.

References: www.divinechocolate.com and www.dubble.co.uk

As a company moves into international markets, having previously been marketing solely to domestic markets, the processes of planning and control remain largely the same, but the complexity of the process increases dramatically. In a domestic situation misunderstandings between different departmental managers can be relatively quickly sorted out with a face to face discussion, but in the international situation this is much harder and often impractical. More impersonal communications, along with longer lead times, different cultures and the use of different languages, results in seemingly inconsistent and often negative attitudes in international managers.

Major evolutionary stages of planning

As most companies move gradually into international markets they go through the major evolutionary stages of planning: the unplanned stage, the budgeting stage, the annual business planning and the strategic planning stage (see Illustration 1.5).

The unplanned stage: In its early stages of international marketing, the company is likely to be preoccupied with finding new export customers and money to finance its activities. Frequently business is very unpredictable and is consequently unplanned, so that a short-term 'crisis management' culture emerges.

The budgeting stage: As the business develops, a system for annual budgeting of sales, costs and cash flow is devised, often because of pressure from external stakeholders such as banks. Being largely financial in nature, budgets often take little account of marketing research, product development or the longer term potential of international markets.

Annual business planning: Companies begin to adopt a more formalized annual approach to planning by including the whole of the business in the planning review process. One of three approaches to the process of international market planning generally emerge at this stage:

1 *Top-down planning*: this is by far the simplest approach, with senior managers setting goals and developing quite detailed plans for middle and senior staff to implement. To be successful, this clearly requires the senior managers to be closely in touch with all their international markets and for the business to be relatively uncomplicated in the range of products or services offered. It has the advantage of ensuring that there is little opportunity for misinterpretation by local managers, but the disadvantage of giving little opportunity for local initiative. Most of the strategic decisions at McDonald's and Coca-Cola are taken in the US, and by Sony in Japan.

2 *Bottom-up planning*: in this approach the different parts of the company around the globe prepare their own goals and plans and submit them to headquarters for approval. While this encourages local initiative and innovation, it can be difficult to manage as the sum of the individual parts that make different demands on resources, financial returns and marketing profiles rarely add up to a feasible international development plan.

3 *Goals down, plans up*: in an attempt to benefit from the positive elements of the first two approaches, this third approach is based upon senior management assessing the firm's opportunities and needs, setting corporate global objectives and developing broad international strategies. Financial goals are then set for each part of the company, which has the responsibility for developing individual strategies and plans to achieve these targets. For this approach to work effectively the senior management generally allows considerable flexibility in the way that the goals are achieved by the component parts of the firm around the globe. This approach is adopted particularly by companies that have a very diverse portfolio of businesses and products.

The strategic planning stage: So far, the stages discussed have been concerned with relatively short-term planning (one to two years), but for many aspects of international marketing such as new market entry, growth strategies and brand management, much longer-term planning is essential. By developing strategies for a five year timescale, it is possible to avoid short-term, highly reactive and frequently contradictory and wasteful activity. The annual marketing plan then becomes a more detailed version of the five year strategic plan which can be rolled forward year on year.

The obvious benefits of strategic planning are that all staff can be better motivated and encouraged to work more effectively by sharing a vision of the future. There are, however, potential dangers too. Long-term strategic plans often fail to cope with the consequences of unexpected events, either environmental or political. There is often confusion between managers over what are strategic issues and what are operational tactics. What a manager in a foreign subsidiary might consider to be a strategic issue, such as achieving a substantial market share increase in the country, might be regarded as an operational matter by a senior manager at the headquarters, which does not consider success in that particular country a priority for the company.

The international marketing planning process

There are a number of elements in the international marketing plan, as detailed in Figure 1.4.

Stakeholder Expectations The complexities of the international marketing environment mean another major difference for companies competing on international markets is that the company has many more organizations and people who have a stake in how they conduct their business and so consequently many more stakeholders whose differing expectations they have to manage. The ability of a company to pursue its chosen marketing strategy is determined to a large degree by the aims and expectations of the stakeholders, who directly or indirectly provide the resources and support needed to implement the strategies and plans. It is important to clearly identify the different stakeholder groups, understand their expectations and evaluate their power, because it is the stakeholders who provide the broad guidelines within which the firm operates. Figure 1.4 identifies the typical stakeholders of a multinational enterprise. Body Shop, the environmentally conscious UK toiletries retailer, is always likely to have problems balancing the widely differing pricing and profit expectations and environmental concerns of its franchisees, customers and shareholders.

While the senior management of the firm aim usually to develop and adopt strategies which do not directly oppose these stakeholder expectations, they do, of course, frequently widen or alter the firm's activities due to changes in the market and competition. Moreover, a wide range of stakeholders influence what multinational enterprises (MNEs) do by giving greater attention to the political, commercial and ethical behaviour of the organizations as well as taking more interest in the actual operation of the business and the performance and safety of the products. As a result of this, companies need to explain their strategies and plans to shareholders through more detailed annual reports, to staff through a variety of briefing methods and to pressure groups and the community in general through various public relations activities, particularly when their activities have an impact on the local environment or economy. In international marketing it is particularly important that the firm addresses the concern of its host country stakeholders, who may be physically and culturally very distant from the headquarters.

Particular attention should be paid to the different expectations of the stakeholders and their power to influence the firm's strategic direction. Given the different expectations of the firm's stakeholders it is inevitable that conflicts will occur. For example, shareholders usually want a high return on their investment and may expect the firm to find countries with low production costs, but the workers in these countries want an adequate wage on which to live. It is often the firm's ability to manage these potential conflicts that leads to success or failure in international marketing (See Figure 1.5).

International pressure groups are another important stakeholder MNEs have to manage. Global communications and the ability of the Internet to draw together geographically dispersed people with shared interests have led to the growing power of globally based pressure groups. Such has been the success of a number of these, it is now the case that pressure-groups are seen by many global operators as one of the key stakeholders to be considered in international strategy decision-making. The role of pressure groups in global markets tends to raise awareness of issues of concern. Among those that have received wide press coverage affecting international marketing strategies are:

- the Greenpeace efforts to raise awareness to threats on the environment;
- the anti-globalization lobby demonstrating against the perceived dark global forces they see manifested in the World Trade Organization;
- the anti-child labour movement.

Gap, the clothes manufacturer and retailer, responded to a revelation that companies who had a licence to produce their products were using child labour by applying the employment guidelines and dismissing

FIGURE 1.4 Aspects of international marketing planning

Stakeholder expections
- Shareholders, customer, host government, employees in each country, pressure groups

Situation analysis
- Evaluation of the environment and individual markets

Resources and capabilities
- Individual small business unit strengths and weaknesses analysis
- Capability to deal with threats and opportunities

Corporate aims and objectives
- Financial, market, area, brand and mix objectives

Marketing strategies
- Growth strategies
- Standardization and adaptation

Implementation of the plan
- Individual SBU and marketing mix plans
- Regional, global or multidomestic integration

Control and feedback
- Setting relevant standards, measuring performance, correcting deviations

the 'child'. This only exacerbated the anger of the pressure groups. Levi, another target of the anti-child labour movement, finding themselves exposed to the same bad publicity, dismissed the child but agreed to fund the child's education up to the point when they would be eligible to seek employment. This pacified the pressure group in the short term, but one is left wondering what Levi would do if they subsequently discovered that there were another few thousand under-age employees across other factories they use, or if there was a sudden influx of employees that were recruited and then declared themselves under age in order to seek educational support.

One of the main roles of international public relations is to try to manage the expectations and aspirations of pressure groups and all the stakeholders of a company. In international marketing one of the key responsibilities is to establish good practice to respond to publicity generated by pressure groups on issues where they have been seen not to meet stakeholder expectations.

As the international business environment becomes more competitive, dynamic and complex, there is a greater need for individual managers to be aware not simply of their immediate situation, but also of the possible impact of changes taking place in surrounding areas too.

Situation analysis

Situation analysis is the process by which the company develops a clear understanding of each individual market and then evaluates its significance for the company and for other markets in which the business operates. As the international business environment becomes more competitive, dynamic and complex, there is a greater need for individual managers to be aware not simply of their immediate situation, but also of the possible impact of changes taking place in surrounding areas too. Individual national markets can be both surprisingly similar and surprisingly dissimilar in nature, and it is important to understand these linkages and the implications of the changes which take place. Chapters 2 and 3 give the reader a detailed insights into the factors to consider in carrying out a situational analysis of the international marketing environment.

FIGURE 1.5 Some typical stakeholders of multinational enterprises

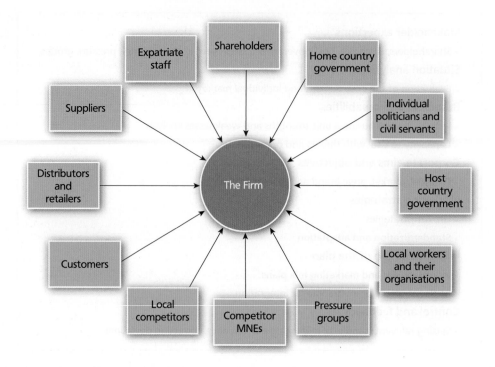

The processes and procedures for segmenting international markets and carrying out the necessary research to build the situational analysis are examined in some depth in Chapter 4.

A detailed analysis of each of these factors as they affect both the local and international market environments is necessary in order to forecast future changes. The most frequently adopted approach by firms is to extrapolate past trends. However, with so many factors to consider and the increasing frequency with which unexpected events seem to occur, it may be extremely difficult and misleading to build up one all-embracing vision of the future. Firms are responding to this uncertainty by developing a series of alternative scenarios as the basis of the planning process. An effective and robust strategy needs to contain contingency plans to deal with a variety of situations in which the company might find itself.

Resources and capabilities

In stressing the need to analyze and respond to external forces over which even global companies have little control, there can be a temptation among some managers to believe that the current capabilities of the organization are inadequate when facing the future. A more thorough analysis of the firm's situation is needed and the SWOT framework (analyzing the firm's strengths, weaknesses, opportunities and threats) is appropriate for this purpose. It is important, therefore, to audit not just the most obvious company weaknesses, but also the strengths of the company, which are often taken for granted but which are really its source of competitive advantage. This is particularly important in international markets as, for example, customer and brand loyalty may be much stronger in certain markets than others, and products which may be at the end of their life in the domestic market may be ideal for less sophisticated markets. SWOT analysis should, therefore, be carried out separately on each area of the business by function, product or market and focus upon what action should be taken to exploit the opportunities and minimize the threats that are identified in the analysis. This will lead to a clearer evaluation of the resources that are available or which must be acquired to ensure the necessary actions are carried out.

Knowledge management

The increasing globalization of business, particularly because it is being driven by information technology, has led many firms to re-examine what contributes to their global competitive advantage. They have recognized the fact that it is the pool of personal knowledge, skills and competencies of the firms' staff that provides its development potential and they have redefined themselves as 'knowledge-based' organizations. Moreover, these firms have acknowledged that they must retain, nurture and apply the knowledge and skills across their business if they wish to be effective in global markets. The growth potential can only be exploited if the firm becomes a learning organization in which the good practice learned by individual members of staff can be 'leveraged', transferred and built upon throughout its global activity.

Corporate objectives

Having identified stakeholder expectations, carried out a detailed situation analysis and made an evaluation of the capabilities of the company, the overall goals to be pursued can be set. It is important to stress that there is a need for realism in this, as too frequently corporate plans are determined more by the desire for short-term credibility with shareholders than with the likelihood that they will be achieved. The objectives must be based on realistic performance expectations rather than on a best case scenario. Consideration must also be given to developing alternative scenarios so that realistic objectives can be set and accompanied by contingency plans in case the chosen scenario does not materialize.

The process adopted for determining long-term and short-term objectives is important and varies significantly depending on the size of the business, the nature of the market and the abilities and motivation of managers in different markets. At an operational level, the national managers need to have an achievable and detailed plan for each country, which will take account of the local situation, explain what is expected and how performance will be measured. For most companies the most obvious international strategic development opportunities are either in increasing geographical coverage and/or building global product strength. This is discussed in much further detail in Chapter 5 from the viewpoint of the SME and in Chapter 6 from the viewpoint of globally based organizations. Management Challenge 1.2 helps you consider this question from the viewpoint of fast food firms trying to grow their global business.

Marketing strategies

Having set the objectives for the company, both at corporate and the subsidiary level, the company will develop detailed programmes of the marketing strategies and activities which will achieve the objectives. Decisions will need to be made as to how the company will segment and target its international markets? How will it position itself in different international markets? How will it add value to its efforts through its product portfolio, communications, distribution and pricing strategies? It is this that is at the heart of the following chapters of this book as we take the reader through the detailed considerations in developing an international marketing strategy. A central consideration in marketing strategy development for international markets is the dilemma facing all international managers as to how far they can standardize marketing strategies in different country markets. This essential question will be examined as we go through different aspects of international marketing strategy development and implementation.

Implementation of the marketing plan

Having agreed the overall marketing strategy, plans for implementation are required at a central and local subsidiary level. Firms usually allocate resources to individual subsidiaries on a top-down basis, but this needs to be modified to include the special allocations made to enable foreign subsidiaries to resource specific market opportunities or difficulties encountered in particular markets. Agreement is reached through a process of discussion between the operating department and management levels. Detailed budgets and timescales can then be set for all areas of marketing including those outside

The fast food challenge

Fast food restaurants have faced varying fortunes across the globe. In the USA sales have been falling but in some markets, such as Japan, France and Britain, total spending on fast food increased. McDonald's with its global reach has remained stable but many, such as Burger King, have seen sales fall.

China is the place where most fast-food chains, like so many industries, see big expansion. If so, then Yum!, which has the greatest presence in China of any Western fast-food company, is ideally placed. Already around 30 per cent of the company's profits come from China, and in the next five years this is expected to grow to 40 per cent. India also looks like a succulent opportunity. Others plan to serve up more business in Russia and elsewhere in Europe.

Question

1 If Fast Food firms want to keep growing their international portfolios what are the key environmental challenges they face

---

agencies (such as marketing researchers, designers and advertising agencies) in order to ensure that their contributions are delivered on time and within the budget. Some allowance must be made for those activities which might be more difficult to estimate in terms of cost or time, such as research and development of new products.

We have, so far, emphasized the need for careful, detailed and thorough preparation of the plan, but it is essential that the plan is action oriented and contains programmes designed to give clear direction for the implementation, continuous evaluation and control of all the firm's marketing activity. The plan must, therefore, be: *strategic*, by fulfilling the corporate and marketing objectives and coordinating the individual strategic business unit (SBU) plans; *tactical*, by focusing upon individual SBU marketing activities in each country; and *implementable*, by detailing the individual activities of each department within the SBU.

The control process

The final stage of the planning process is setting up an effective system for obtaining feedback and controlling the business. Feedback and control systems should be regarded as an integrated part of the whole planning process, and they are essential in ensuring that the marketing plans are not only being implemented but are still appropriate for the changing international environment.

There are three essential elements of the control process:

1 *Setting standards*: the standards that are set need to be relevant to the corporate goals such as growth and profits reported by financial measures, return on capital employed and on sales, and non-financial indicators, e.g. market share. Intermediate goals and individual targets can be set by breaking the plan down into measurable parts which when successfully completed will lead to the overall objectives being achieved. The standards must be understandable, achievable and relevant to each local country situation.

2 *Measuring performance against standards*: to obtain measurements and ensure rapid feedback of information, firms use a variety of techniques, including reports, meetings and special measurements of specific parts of the marketing programme, such as cost–benefit analysis on customers, product lines and territories or marketing audits for a thorough examination of every aspect of marketing in a particular country. They also use benchmarking, which allows comparisons of various aspects of the business, such as efficiency of distribution, customer response times, service levels and complaints, with other companies that are not necessarily from the same business sector.

FIGURE 1.6 Essential elements of the international marketing plan

Does the plan contain:

International analysis

- assumptions about the world economy and the environment trends in the principal markets?
- details of historical performance (sales, cost, profitability)?
- forecast of future performance based on (a) an extrapolation of the past (b) alternative scenarios?
- identified opportunities and threats?

Company capability assessment

- analysis of the company strengths, weaknesses and future capabilities in comparison with local and international competition?

International mission statement with:

- long-term aims and objectives and the strategies to achieve them?
- one year marketing objectives and individual strategies (for example, budgets, brand objectives and development of personnel)?

Operational plans

- detailed country by country forecasts and targets?
- detailed country by country plans for all marketing activities and coordination with other functions (for example, manufacturing)?
- an explanation of how country plans will be integrated regionally or globally if appropriate?

Contingencies and controls

- a summary of the critical factors for success?
- an assessment of the likely competitor response?
- a contingency component for when things do not go to plan?
- a control process for feedback, evaluation and taking corrective action?

3 *Correcting deviations from the plan*: perhaps the most difficult decisions that must be made are to determine when performance has deviated sufficiently from the plan to require corrective action to be taken either by changing the plan or the management team charged with the responsibility of carrying out the plan.

A checklist of the essential elements of the international marketing plan is summarized in Figure 1.6.

Reasons for success

Hamel and Prahalad (1996) suggest the firms operating globally that succeed are those that perceive the changes in the international environment and are able to develop strategies which enable them to respond accordingly. The firms that will do well will base their success largely on the early identification of the changes in the boundaries of markets and industries in their analysis of their international marketing environment. Management foresight and organizational learning are, therefore, the basis of a sustainable competitive advantage in global markets.

The increasing globalization of business, particularly because it is being driven by information technology, has led many firms to re-examine what contributes to their global competitive advantage. They have recognized the fact that it is the pool of personal knowledge, skills and competencies of the firm's staff that provides its development potential and they have redefined themselves as 'knowledge-based' organizations. Moreover, these firms have acknowledged that they must retain, nurture and apply the knowledge and skills across their business if they wish to be effective in global markets. The growth potential of international markets can only be exploited if the firm becomes a learning organization in which the good practice learned by individual members of staff in one market can be leveraged and built upon throughout its global activity.

NEVER BE WITHOUT A FRIEND

ILLUSTRATION 1.6

Courtesy of Fisherman's Friend

Fisherman's Friend

Fisherman's Friend lozenges were initially developed for sailors and Fleetwood fishermen who were work-ing in the severe weather conditions of the North Atlantic fishing grounds. For an entire century the company made around 14lb of lozenges a month which were only sold in the local area. Their first overseas shipment was to Belgium in 1974. However, since then they have expanded into a worldwide operation. Norway was an early attractive opportunity that was investigated and it is now the market with the highest sales per head of population. Surprisingly, the lozenge was a success in many hot countries too. Italy was the largest export market at one point before being overtaken by Germany. Although the lozenge needs no adaptation – a cough needs no translation – promotion of Fisherman's Friend differs greatly from country to country. The traditional concept has been the centre of advertising in the UK, but overseas promotional themes are quite different. An Italian TV commercial showed a girl who breathed so deeply after eating a lozenge that the buttons pop off her blouse to reveal her cleavage; in Denmark a man breathes fire; in the Philippines butterflies flutter against pastel shades accompanied by gentle music. Fisherman's Friend is now available in over 100 countries worldwide and in many it is seen as a strong sweet, not as medicated confectionery. Exports now account for over 95 per cent of the company's total production.

Question

1 What are the reasons for the success of Fisherman's Friend?

However, firms are increasingly vulnerable to losing these valuable personal assets, because of the greater mobility of staff, prevalence of industrial espionage and the security risks and abuse associated with the Internet. Moreover, with the increase in communications it is becoming more difficult to store, access and apply the valuable knowledge that exists among the huge volume of relatively worthless data that the company deals with. Consequently, effective knowledge management is now critical for success. This means having online database systems that facilitate effective data collection, a cloud computing capability, storage in data warehouses and data mining (the identification of opportunities from patterns that emerge from detailed analysis of the data held).

Successful global operators use the knowledge gained to assess their strengths and weaknesses in light of their organizational learning and ensure they have the company capability and resources to respond to their learning in order to sustain their competitive advantage. This is particularly important in international markets as, for example, customer and brand loyalty may be much stronger in certain markets than others, and products that may be at the end of their life in the domestic market may be ideal for less sophisticated markets. In the dynamic international markets, therefore, if a firm is to succeed it must develop the ability to think, analyze and develop strategic and innovative responses on an international, if not global scale, perhaps such as Mrs Lofthouse did for the Fisherman's Friend in Illustration 1.6.

Characteristics of best practice in international marketing

It is apparent, therefore, that firms and organizations planning to compete effectively in world markets need a clear and well-focused international marketing strategy that is based on a thorough understanding of the markets which the company is targeting or operating in. International markets are dynamic entities that require constant monitoring and evaluation. As we have discussed, as markets change so must marketing techniques. Innovation is an important competitive variable, not only in terms of the product or service but throughout the marketing process. Countertrading, financial innovations, networking and value-based marketing are all important concepts in the implementation of a successful international strategy.

The challenge, then, of international marketing is to ensure that any international strategy has the discipline of thorough research and an understanding and accurate evaluation of what is required to achieve the competitive advantage. Doole (2000) identified three major components to the strategies of firms successfully competing in international markets:

- A clear international competitive focus achieved through a thorough knowledge of the international markets, a strong competitive positioning and a strategic perspective which was truly international.

- An effective relationship strategy achieved through strong customer relations, a commitment to quality products and service and a dedication to customer service throughout international markets.

- Well-managed organizations with a culture of learning. Firms were innovative and willing to learn, showed high levels of energy and commitment to international markets and had effective monitoring and control procedures for all their international markets.

SUMMARY

- In this chapter we have discussed the growing strategic importance of international marketing and examined the issues associated with successfully competing in international markets. The chapter examines the main differences between domestic and international marketing, the different levels at which international marketing can be approached and the more complex and multidimensional uncontrollable elements of the international marketing environment.

- We have examined the major aspects of the SLEPTS factors in the international marketing environment. The environments in which international companies must operate is typically characterized by uncertainty and change – factors which, taken together, increase the element of risk for international marketing managers.

- It has been suggested that marketing managers need to have a properly planned approach to any international activity because, without this, the costs and likelihood of failure are likely to increase. We examined the international marketing planning and control process and considered how managers can respond to the challenges posed in the international marketing environment by ensuring they have robust strategy development and market planning processes.

- The reasons for success and failure on international markets were examined and it was suggested the firms operating globally that succeed are those that perceive the changes in the international environment and are able to develop strategies which enable them to respond accordingly. Management foresight and organizational learning are, therefore, the basis of a sustainable competitive advantage in global markets.

■ The reader has been introduced to many of the concepts that are important to the international marketing management process and will have gained an understanding of the issues to be addressed. All the various aspects of the international marketing strategy process introduced in this chapter will be examined in more detail in the following chapters. In Chapter 2 the international trading environment and the trends and developments in trading patterns will be examined.

KEYWORDS

World trade	Cultural paradoxes	North American Free Trade Area
International trade	European Union	
Global youth culture	Piracy	World Trade Organization
Export marketing	Gross national income	Emerging economies
International marketing	Purchasing power parity	Multinational enterprise
Global marketing	Less developed economies	Globalization

CASE STUDY

© Lou Linwei/Alamy

Tesco in China

Putting the customer at the heart of the business through an empathy with cultural and consumer behaviour in its markets is fundamental to the success of the world's fourth largest grocery retailer. And while a study carried out for the Sunday Times newspaper by research group CACI 12 revealed that Tesco has almost total control of the food market in 108 of Britain's postal areas, international business accounts for almost £20 billion of Tesco's £62.5 billion sales (*Sunday Times 30/5/2010*).

Retaining its place as the UK's number 1 retailer is a hard battle based on a simple formula – listening to customers, responding to their changing needs and expectations, and providing a range that meets the needs of a diverse customer base that closely represents the demographics of the UK population. The

global expansion strategy of Tesco has followed the same principles as can be illustrated in its expansion into the Chinese market.

Understanding the local culture, shopping habits and needs of local customers feature high on the agenda of the growth strategy into China. China is viewed by Tesco as their most important and fastest growing overseas operation. It is anticipated that Tesco will invest £500m in China this year, more than in any other foreign market as it battles to establish itself against the competition from Wal-Mart and Carrefour. Wal-Mart's share of Chinese hypermarket sales is about 45bn yuan, Carrefour's 33bn yuan, while currently Tesco accounts for 11bn yuan, according to data from Euromonitor. The battle for the global market share is now being played out in China. However, the company still has a long way to go before it ranks as a top retailer in China.

Tesco entered Chinese market in 2004 by founding a 50:50 partnership with Ting Hsin International Group, which operated 25 Hymall stores. In 2006, they increased their stake from 50 per cent to 90 per cent. They are now growing their business in three regions in the East of the country, including Shanghai; the North, including Beijing; and the South, including Guangzhou. They now have 58 hypermarkets in China.

Ken Towle, Tesco China President, is very ambitious In the next five years, he plans to open more new retail space in China (40m sq ft) than Tesco has built up in the UK in the nine decades since it was founded. If everything goes according to plan, after more than £4 billion of investment together with its partners, Tesco China will also have a property empire of 80 self-built shopping centres, many of them boasting skyscrapers full of apartments, cinemas and gyms. More than 50 000 shoppers turned out for the opening of the Qingdao centre, which is described as feeling a lot more 'local' that the standard foreign hypermarket, with much noise and bustle and the sale of live turtles and fresh stingray adding to the atmosphere.

However, despite the importance of such centres, central to the promotional and marketing campaigns in China is price. Ken Towle, was quoted in the *Daily Mail* as saying: 'You have to be extremely careful in China – a few jiao (pence) off the price of eggs can mean the difference between brisk trading and a riot'.

Understanding the mindset of the Chinese consumer and embracing their culture is the key to Tesco's success in China. The blueprint for growth is based on a combination of getting the price right and promoting local Chinese brands under the umbrella of a Tesco hypermarket. Success lies in creating a traditional shopping experience with wet markets, encouraging the purchase of daily essentials with fresh foods displayed traditionally, and product placement of price sensitive staples in the Chinese diet at the front of the stores.

Tesco is strengthening its understanding of local culture through working with local committees. It has made a point of employing local staff throughout its stores and embracing traditional practices by encouraging locals to gather for early morning Tai Chi outside its stores. It plays music to support these activities and offers hot drinks to those exercising in the winter months.

Another important strand to their Chinese strategy is a strong distribution and logistics operation. They have a distribution centre and a Fresh Food Distribution Centre in Shanghai. TESCO consider these centres as essential to their strategy of ensuring customers are provided with a consistent quality throughout their stores in China. They have strict quality control processes with advanced equipment and well-trained staff. Through their centralized distribution strategy they have been able to reduce deliveries to stores from 100 every day to just 2 or 3.

China is also important to Tesco as a prime location to source good value and high quality products to sell in stores all over the world. About US$1.1 billion worth of products from China is sold in Tesco stores across the world.

By 2016 Tesco plans to spend £2 billion opening 80 shopping malls in China – a massive expansion programme that will give it 40m sq ft of shopping space, this compares to a current 33m sq ft in the UK.

Questions

1 Evaluate the reasons behind the success of Tesco in China.

2 What are lessons TESCO offers to managers trying to develop strategies for international markets?

References: *Daily Mail City Focus*: Tessa Thorniley 11th January 2010 Tesco plans full of Eastern promise: http://www.cn.tesco.com/en/aboutus/aboutus_inchina_is.htm accessed September 2010 and Julia Finch Tesco increases market share www.Guardian.co.uk accessed 10.11/10

Source: Kate Morse Sheffield Hallam University

DISCUSSION QUESTIONS

1 What are the major environmental influences which impact on international marketing? Show how they can affect international marketing strategies.

2 Using examples, examine the reasons why marketing strategies fail in international markets.

3 Identify three major global pressure groups. Examine how they have influenced the international marketing strategies of particular firms.

4 What skills and abilities are necessary requirements for an effective international marketing manager? Justify your choices.

5 How can marketing managers accommodate the multiplicity of international markets into a cohesive international marketing strategy and plan?

REFERENCES

1. Dicken, P. (2010) *Global shift-mapping the changing contours of the world economy*, 6th edn. Sage.
2. Doole, I. (2000) 'How SMEs Learn to Compete Effectively on International Markets', Ph.D.
3. El-Kahal, S. (2006) *Introduction to international business*. McGraw-Hill.
4. Haliburton, C. (1997) 'Reconciling global marketing and one to one marketing – A global individualism response', in Doole, I. and Lowe, R. (eds), *International marketing strategy – contemporary readings*, ITP.
5. Hamel, G. and Prahalad, C.K. (1996) *Competing for the future*. Harvard Business School Press.
6. Hofstede,G, Hofstede, G.J. and Minkov, M., (2010) *Cultures and Organizations: Software for the Mind,: Intercultural Cooperation and Its Importance for Survival*, McGraw Hill 3rd edn. Kotabe, M. and Helsen, K. (2008) *Global marketing management*, 4th edn. J. Wiley and Sons.
7. Ohmae, K. (2005) *The next global stage: the challenges and opportunities in our borderless world*. Pearson Education.
8. Perlmutter, M.V. (1995) 'Becoming globally civilised, managing across culture', Mastering Management Part 6, *Financial Times*, 1 December.
9. Porter, M.C. (1990) *The competitive advantage of nations*. Macmillan.
10. Quelch, J. and Deshpande. R. (2004) *The global market: developing a strategy to manage across borders*. Wiley and Sons.
11. Rugimbana, R. and Nwankwo, S. (2003) *Cross cultural marketing*, Cengage.
12. Sarathy, R., Terpstra, V. and Russow, L.C. (2006) *International marketing*, 9th edn. Dryden Press.
13. Wilson, R. and Gilligan, C. (2003) *Strategic marketing management: planning implementation and control*, 3rd edn, Butterworth-Heinemann.

CHAPTER 2

THE WORLD TRADING ENVIRONMENT

LEARNING OBJECTIVES

After reading this chapter the reader should be able to:

- Discuss the effects and implications of the factors impacting on world trade

- Explain the key trends in the major regional trading blocs around the globe

- Understand the role of the major world institutions that foster the development of multilateral free trade across the world

INTRODUCTION

International marketing takes place within the framework of the world trading environment. If the reader is to have the skills necessary to develop international marketing strategies, some understanding of the parameters of the world trading environment in which they operate is needed.

In this chapter we examine the development of world trade in recent years and the international trading environment in the context following the global financial crisis in 2008–09. We will analyze the growth and changing patterns of world trade and discuss the institutions that aim to influence world trade.

We will also look at the changing regional trading blocs and the implications these have on trading structures around the globe.

World trading patterns

The world economy consists of over 194 nations with a population of 6.8 billion and a gross domestic product (GDP) output totalling US$61 trillion at purchasing power parity (ppp). Last year global GDP grew by less than 2 per cent following the downturn resulting from the global financial crisis. World trade in merchandize totals US$12 trillion and trade in services is currently estimated by the World Trade Organization (WTO) to be about US$4 trillion.

Together, Asia, North America and the European Union account for 86 per cent of world trade and the world gross GDP. Figure 2.1 highlights the major trade flows between the three points of what has become known as Ohmae's triad (2005) after the Japanese writer who first coined the phrase.

However, such figures mask the potential of future market opportunities. Of the world's population, 85 per cent live in emerging markets and at market exchange rates their current share of the world economy accounts for only 30 per cent. Measured in ppp terms it is now over 50 per cent. It is anticipated that by 2050 the combined GNP of emerging economies will eclipse that of the developed countries. The International Monetary Fund (IMF) estimate that in the next five years emerging economies as a whole will grow between 7–10 per cent per annum compared to a rate of less than 2 per cent by developed countries.

Brazil, Russia, India and China are four of the biggest emerging economies (now known as BRICs after being grouped together under the acronym by Goldman Sachs).

Economies such as China (8.3 per cent GDP growth) and India (8.1 per cent), are obvious stars and there is much debate as to which one will achieve future dominance; China, Brazil and Russia actually produce more than India at present in real terms. However, according to the CIA fact-book (2010), measured on a purchasing power parity (ppp) basis, all four economies would rank in the world's top ten of economies.

The centre of gravity and dynamism in Asia in the past decade has been China. China is developing the potential to dwarf most countries as it continues its rapid development and speedy economic growth. Commentators are interested to see whether it is China or India that will dominate the global trading structures of the 21st century.

However, as the BRIC countries develop, interest turns to identifying the next set of countries likely to develop. The Next Eleven (or N-11) are 11 countries – Bangladesh, Egypt, Indonesia, Iran, Mexico, Nigeria, Pakistan, the Philippines, South Korea, Turkey and Vietnam – identified by Goldman Sachs investment bank as having a high potential of becoming the world's largest economies in the 21st century along with the BRICs. The bank chose these states due to their promising outlooks for investment and future growth. This of course is a much longer term prediction, time itself will tell how accurate that prediction turns out to be.

In global trade, emerging economies are now major players; their share of world exports has jumped from 20 per cent in 1970 to nearly 50 per cent. Rising exports give countries more money to spend on imports. Over the next decade it is expected that one billion new consumers will enter the global marketplace as incomes in emerging countries across Asia and Africa rise further and households start to have more disposable income to spend on non-essential goods.

The global downturn has helped reduce global imbalances in trade. The top three exporters account for 27 per cent of total exports which is down from being over a third the previous year. China is perhaps having the biggest impact and is now the single largest exporter in the world overtaking Germany and the USA (see table 2.1). This is a huge development. China did not even warrant a place in this top ten table in the 2001 edition of this textbook, by the 2003 edition it had moved up to sixth place and third position in the 2008 edition giving some indication of the trajectory of the growth of its economy. In this edition South Korea has entered the top ten table for the first time.

While China is now the world's biggest exporter of merchandize exports, followed closely by Germany, it is the USA that is the biggest exporter of commercial services. The USA accounts for 15 per cent of world exports in commercial services which puts it far in front of any other competitors. The UK, the next largest supplier of services, has only 7.5 per cent of world exports followed by Germany with 6.4 per cent. France and Japan have approximately a 4 per cent share each.

FIGURE 2.1 Global trade flows

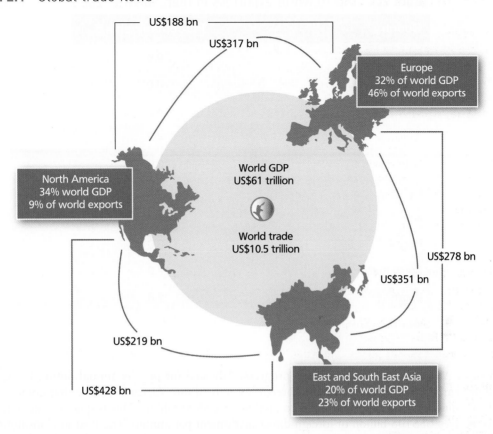

Source: Adapted from P. Dickens (2007) *Global shift – mapping the changing contours of the world economy*, 5th edn, Sage. Reproduced by permission of SAGE Publications, London, Los Angeles, New Delhi and Singapore.

The UK's share of global merchandize exports has declined appreciably over the past 30 years. Compared with a 7.5 per cent share in the 1980s, the UK currently accounts for only 2.8 per cent of global merchandize exports. The pattern of change over the period is very similar to that of US exports who have also moved down the rankings having been taken over by both Germany and China.

Future prospects

The global economic crisis sparked a 12.2 per cent contraction in the volume of global trade in 2009 and world trade volume suffered the sharpest decline in more than 70 years. However the WTO forecasts that world trade is set to rebound by growing at 9.5 per cent in the next year, and will then continue to grow year on year in the next decade.

In the same period the world GDP fell by 2.2 per cent. The global economic crisis originated in the financial sector in the USA. At the core appear to have been unsound lending practices by financial institutions, notably in the private mortgage lending sector, and unsatisfactory risk management practices. The contagion seems to spread worldwide, causing an unprecedented credit squeeze as inter-bank lending came to a virtual hold. In consequence, businesses in many countries have faced liquidity squeezes and consumers have cut back their expenses. Worldwide GDP growth has slowed from 5.0 per cent in 2007 to 1.4 per cent (–3.8 per cent in advanced economies and +1.5 per cent in emerging and developing economies).

Table 2.2 examines the annual percentage change in GDP and consumer prices (inflation). China and India continue to have the leading growth rates in terms of GDP among the larger economies. However, a number of African nations all have growth rates in excess of 10 per cent per annum. In the past decade

Table 2.1 Top 10 world exporters in merchandize, 2009

Country	Percentage share
China	9.6
Germany	9.0
United States	8.5
Japan	4.7
Netherlands	3.9
France	3.8
Italy	3.2
Belgium	3.0
South Korea	2.9
Britain	2.8

Source: www.wto.org, © WTO

the continent of Africa has made remarkable progress. Adjusted for ppp its annual output has grown by an average of nearly 5 per cent per annum. Foreign investment into Africa is double that going into India and has grown nine fold since the year 2000 to just under US$90 billion. This is quickly catching up with China who receives US$108 billion of foreign direct investment per annum. The Boston Consulting Group estimate that Africa's top 500 companies have grown at an average of 8.3 per cent in the last decade.

In Table 2.3, China, Japan, Russia and Germany all exhibit an exceptionally strong and healthy balance of payment surpluses. The US, however, is still forecast to have a huge trade deficit (US$568.7 billion), as does the UK and India. In Chapter 1 we discussed the difficulties of marketing to countries with high inflation rates. According to Table 2.2 firms are likely to have difficulties in such markets as Venezuela, Libya and Angola where inflation is in excess of 23 per cent. However even countries that offer potentially attractive market opportunities such as India, Egypt, Rwanda and Argentina could be problematic given they all currently have inflation rates of over 10 per cent. The African nations identified are of particular interest given the potential opportunity they present for market development and growth.

Table 2.2 Percentage change on previous year in real GDP/GNP and consumer prices

Country	Growth rate (%)	Inflation rate (%)
Angola	13.2	23.9
Argentina	4.0	10.9
Australia	3.3	2.9
Brazil	4.5	5.4
China	8.3	3.0
Euro zone	1.3	1.5

Table 2.2 Continued

Country	Growth rate (%)	Inflation rate (%)
Egypt	5.4	11.8
France	1.4	1.6
Germany	1.6	1.1
India	8.1	11.4
Japan	1.6	−0.9
Libya	3.8	25.4
Malaysia	4.0	1.7
Netherlands	1.5	1.2
Nigeria	6.0	11.0
Poland	3.4	2.5
Russia	4.0	6.4
Rwanda	11.2	17.4
Saudi Arabia	3.7	3.5
Sweden	2.7	1.3
South Africa	3.7	5.2
South Korea	4.0	3.0
Thailand	4.1	3.5
Turkey	3.9	8.7
UK	1.9	3.0
USA	2.8	1.7
Venezuela	−2.5	33.2

References: *World Development Indicators* (2010) and *The Economist* (2010) and www.imf.org (2009).

The reasons countries trade

International trade is a vital part of world economic activity but it is not a new phenomenon. While the growth of international trade has accelerated in the past 40 years, it goes back far beyond then and has been developing throughout the ages since the time when barter was used.

The great growth period for trade was in the 18th and 19th centuries when many of today's important trading links were forged and developed.

A major source of many of the conflicts in the 19th century was the desire by nations to win the right to trade in foreign markets. One of the reasons why Great Britain went to war with Napoleon was to open the French markets to our newly industrialized nation. The colony of Hong Kong and the associated New Territories returned to China in 1997 were acquired by the UK in the early 19th century for trading purposes.

Table 2.3 Trade balances in merchandize trade

Country	US$ billion
Argentina	14.4
Australia	−4.2
Brazil	17.8
China	156.6
Euro zone	32.3
Egypt	32.3
Germany	210.4
India	−110.2
Japan	79.5
Malaysia	36.6
Netherlands	53.3
Russia	152.6
Saudi Arabia	104.4
Spain	69.5
Taiwan	15
Turkey	−52.6
UK	−134.7
USA	−568.7
Venezuela	30

Source: World Bank (2007) World development indicators.

The reasons nations trade are many and varied: the two key explanations of why nations trade, however, are based on the theory of comparative advantage and the international product life cycle.

The theory of comparative advantage

The rationale for world trade is based largely upon Ricardo's theory of comparative advantage. At its simplest level, the theory suggests that trade between countries takes place because one country is able to produce a product at a lower price than is possible elsewhere. An illustration of this is provided by the way in which Japanese companies such as Sony and Hitachi came to dominate the European television market. Their strategy was based upon higher product quality, better design and, more importantly for our purposes here, the lower prices that were made possible by far greater economies of scale and better manufacturing technology than was currently being achieved by the European producers.

It is this notion of relative cost that underpins world trade; in other words, countries concentrating upon producing products in which they have a comparative advantage over their foreign competitor countries.

How comp

A comparative

- Sustained
- Lower la
  emerging
  the USA
  Philippin
  for them
  compour
  Illustrati
  as global
- Proximit
  case with
- Subsidies
  farmers,
  their inte
  compete
- Building
  Japanese
  targeted

Some countrie
products and
advantage thr

- Factor c
  infrastru
- Demand
- Related
  industrie

- Firm strategy, structure and rivalry: the conditions in the nation governing how companies are created, organized and managed and the nature of domestic rivalry.

The international product life cycle

The theory of comparative advantage is often used as the classic explanation of world trade. Other observers, however, believe that world trade and investment patterns are based upon the product life cycle concept. Writing from an American perspective, Vernon and Wells (1968) suggested that on an international level, products move through four distinct phases:

1. US firms manufacture for the home market and begin exporting.
2. Foreign production starts.
3. Foreign products become increasingly competitive in world markets.
4. Imports to the USA begin providing significant competition.

This cycle begins with the product being developed and manufactured, for example, in the USA for high-income markets, subsequently being introduced into other markets in the form of exports. The second phase begins to emerge as the technology is developed further and becomes more easily transferable. Companies in other countries then begin manufacturing and, because of lower transportation and labour costs, are able to undercut the American manufacturers in certain markets.

© Bartosz Hadyniak, iStockphoto.com

ILLUSTRATION 2.1

China and India: The technology challenge

China is now the third-biggest buyer of hi-tech goods and services in the world; behind America and Japan. China and India make an interesting contrast in their technological development. They have roughly the ... China spends 2.5 times as ... ogy as India. China is the world's ... phone market with some 800 million ...sers, and has the second-largest market ... India has some 545 million cell phones, en- ... to serve about 45 per cent of the population, ... only about 366 million people or 31 per cent of the population had access to improved sanitation. China had around 384 million Internet users compared with 51 million in India,. The two countries are adopting technology at different paces and in different ways.

A further difference is that China's manufacturing strength means hi-tech gear is available locally at low cost, whereas India must import it. India has focused more on software and services, which can be delivered via networks without bureaucratic interference, unlike China which has focused on competing in physical goods. However, India is seen as playing an invaluable role in the global innovation chain. Motorola, Hewlett-Packard, Cisco Systems, Google and other tech giants now rely on their Indian teams to devise software platforms and the tech hubs in such places as Bangalore. These companies are spawning companies producing their own chip designs, software and pharmaceuticals at an exhilarating pace of innovation.

Question

1 Compare and contrast the opportunities and challenges of competing in the market for a high tech product in India and China.

References: http://www.economywatch.com/ 2010 and http://in.reuters.com/.

The third phase is characterized by foreign companies competing against US exports which, in turn, leads to a further decline in the market for US exports. Typically, it is at this stage that US companies either begin to withdraw from selected markets or, in an attempt to compete more effectively, begin investing in manufacturing capacity overseas to regain sales.

The fourth and final stage begins when foreign companies, having established a strong presence in their home and export markets, start the process of exporting to the US and begin competing against the products produced domestically.

It is these four stages, Vernon suggests, that illustrate graphically how American automobile firms have found themselves being squeezed out of their domestic markets having enjoyed a monopoly in the US car market originally.

Although the product life cycle provides an interesting insight into the evolution of multinational operations, it should to be recognized that it provides only a partial explanation of world trade as products do not inevitably follow this pattern. First, competition today is international rather than domestic for all goods and services. Consequently, there is a reduced time lag between product research, development and production, leading to the simultaneous appearance of a standardized product in major world markets.

Second, it is not production in the highly labour-intensive industries that is moving to the low labour-cost countries but the capital-intensive industries such as electronics, creating the anomalous situation of basing production for high-value, high-technology goods in the countries least able to afford them. Nor does the model go very far in explaining the rapid development of companies networking production and marketing facilities across many countries. Thus, global business integration and sharing of R&D, technological and business resources is seen as a more relevant explanation of today's world trade.

Barriers to world trade

Marketing barriers

While countries have many reasons for wishing to trade with each other, it is also true to say that all too frequently an importing nation will take steps to inhibit the inward flow of goods and services.

One of the reasons international trade is different from domestic trade is that it is carried on between different political units, each one a sovereign nation exercising control over its own trade. Although all nations control their foreign trade, they vary in terms of the degree of control. Each nation or trading bloc invariably establishes trade laws that favour their indigenous companies and discriminate against foreign ones.

Thus, at the same time as trade has been developing worldwide, so has the body of regulations and barriers to trade. The WTO lists the technical barriers to trade that countries use in their attempts to protect their economy from imports. The main protagonists are seen as the USA, Italy, France and Germany.

However, the major barriers to trade are becoming increasingly covert, i.e. non-tariff barriers which are often closely associated with the cultural heritage of a country and very difficult to overcome. The complex distribution patterns in Japan are one such example. Thus, while Japan is seen not to have many overt barriers, many businesses experience great difficulties when trying to enter the Japanese market. In Russia recently 167 500 Motorola handsets were seized at a Moscow airport. They were alleged to have been smuggled, to be counterfeit, to violate a Russian patent and to be a danger to public health. As a result some 50 000, it was claimed, were destroyed by the Interior Ministry, but surprisingly, a large number of Motorola phones appeared on the Russian black market. Whatever the rights and wrongs of the intentions, trade distortion practices can provide nightmare scenarios for the international marketer. It is thus important to be aware of the practices of the countries being targeted and the types of barriers companies face. Trade distortion practices can be grouped into two basic categories: tariff and non-tariff barriers, as illustrated in Figure 2.2.

FIGURE 2.2 Market entry barriers

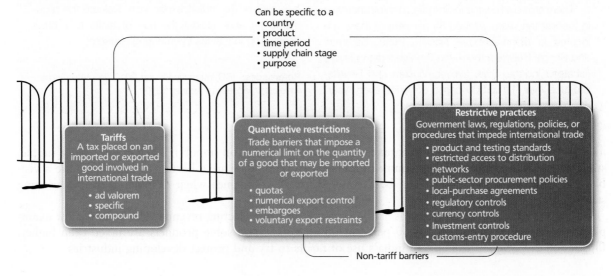

© Bill Grove, iStockphoto.com

ILLUSTRATION 2.2

To protect or not protect?

25 million Indians drink red wine which is just 2 per cent of India's population. They consume approximately 18 million litres of wine a year. Market watchers predict that soon 10 per cent of Indians will be drinking wine. Given that nearly 75 per cent of India's population is under 25 years old wine is seen to be a potential growth market.

There are now 65 wineries in India, a tenfold increase in the last ten years. Around 85 per cent of these are located in Maharashtra – Nashik, Pune, Baramati and Sangli. Between them, the top five Indian players (Château Indage, Sula, Grover, Vinsura and Reveilo) produce over 1 700 000 cases of wines every year.

Pernod Ricard, Mallya's United Spirits and the multi award-winning new brand Château d'Ori) produce a further 480 000.

The 80 registered wine importing firms in India currently bring in over 120 foreign wine labels to the country and statistics show that the French control 45 per cent of the imported wine market share. Their dominance is being challenged by new world wines from Australia and Italy, which together control almost 30 per cent of the market.

The EU and the USA wants to export wine to India However high tariffs of 150 per cent and legislative barriers mean there are huge obstacles to foreign wine producers. The WTO rules allow countries to have tariffs, but require that they satisfy a 'national treatment' rule. This means that, once foreign products have entered the country and paid the duty, they must be taxed and regulated just like domestic goods. Thus was the point of a dispute between the EU, USA and India which went to the WTO dispute panel. The panel initially found in favour of India. However, this decision was overturned on appeal.

Goa, Maharashtra and Tamil Nadu, which represent important potential import wine markets, imposed additional discriminatory domestic taxes on foreign wines, while exempting domestic wines to try to encourage the growth of the industry. The Indian producers argued this was necessary and justified as a protective measure that gave domestic firms room to grow. Abolishing the taxes would mean their small producers facing unfair competition from global giants.

Question

1 In light of the Indian experience evaluate the arguments for and against the use of tariffs to protect developing industries in emerging markets.

References: JBC International Jan 2010 and http://indian-wine.com/, accessed August 2010.

Tariff barriers Tariffs are direct taxes and charges imposed on imports. They are generally simple, straightforward and easy for the country to administer. While they are a barrier to trade, they are a visible and known quantity and so can be accounted for by companies when developing their marketing strategies.

Tariffs are used by poorer nations as the easiest means of collecting revenue. The Bahamas for example has a minimum import tax of 30 per cent on all goods, and some products are taxed even higher. Illustration 2.2 gives an example of India's use of tariffs to try and protect developing industries.

Tariffs are also imposed to simply protect the home producer, as in the US and Australia. Both of these countries have high tariff walls for certain industries they wish to protect – for example, agricultural products. The trend towards the lowering of tariff barriers across the globe in recent years (the average tariff is now 5 per cent whereas in 1945 it was 45 per cent), together with the opening up of new markets to foreign investment, notably Asia and South America, has greatly complicated the decision for many companies as to where to place manufacturing facilities.

These trends have made global production much more possible, but it has also reduced the need for many overseas plants. Markets that previously demanded local production facilities because tariff levels made importing prohibitive can now be supplied from non-domestic sources.

A good example of these dynamics can be seen in Australia in the automotive sector. Tariffs on imported cars have fallen from 57.5 per cent to 5 per cent. Japanese manufacturers, therefore, found they no longer needed to have plants in Australia to serve the market.

Tariffs can take many forms, as can be seen in Figure 2.2. The most common, however, are:

- *Specific*: charges are imposed on particular products either by weight or volume and usually stated in the local currency.

- *Ad valorem*: a straight percentage of the import price.

- *Discriminatory*: in this case the tariff is charged against goods coming from a particular country, either where there is a trade imbalance or for political purposes.

Non-tariff barriers

In the past 40 years, the world has seen a gradual reduction in tariff barriers in most developed nations. However, in parallel to this, non-tariff barriers have substantially increased. Non-tariff barriers are much more elusive and can be more easily disguised. The effect can, however, be more devastating because they are an unknown quantity and are much less predictable.

Non-tariff barriers take many different forms:

- Increased government participation in trade is one that is gaining more dominance and which is used by nations to gain competitive advantage, as in the case of the US wheat subsidy previously discussed.

- Customs entry procedures can also impede trade. These take many forms: administrative hold-ups, safety regulations, subsidies and differing technical standards are just a few. In Angola enforcing a contract involves 47 procedures and takes over 1000 days. A World Bank study of non-tariff barriers showed that out of the 35 least business-friendly countries in the world, 27 were in Sub-Saharan Africa.

The need for customs modernization and harmonization has become a priority for companies who find their operations severely hampered by administrative delays at borders and which stand to be disadvantaged even more as economic globalization gathers pace.

Clearly the extent of customs delays and red tape varies enormously from country to country but everywhere there is a need for governments to take account of business needs for simple, transparent, coordinated and harmonized customs procedures.

- Quantitative restrictions such as quotas are another barrier. These are limits on the amount of goods that may enter a country. An import quota can be more restrictive than a tariff as there is less flexibility in responding to it. The Japanese car industry faced quotas both in Europe and the US and so developed manufacturing capacity in these markets as a means of overcoming the barriers. The US also imposes quotas on imports from China. However, China, according to the US, has been transhipping products through other ports such as Hong Kong in order to circumvent the quotas.

- Financial controls were last seen in the UK in the mid-1970s but have been used recently in Mexico and South America where high inflation and lack of hard currency required stringent monetary controls. This is probably the most complete tool for the regulation of foreign trade as it gives the government a monopoly of all dealings in foreign exchange. A domestic company earning foreign exchange from exporting must sell it to the national bank and, if goods from abroad need to be bought, a company has to apply for foreign exchange. Thus foreign currency is scarce. The International Monetary Fund has placed stringent controls on several countries, in particular, Indonesia, Brazil and Argentina. The latter countries especially have huge external debts which are viewed as unsustainable.

Countries practising exchange controls tend to favour the import of capital goods rather than consumer goods. The other major implication to companies operating in foreign markets is the restrictions on repatriating profits in foreign currency, requiring either countertrade dealings or the use of distorted transfer prices to get profits home (see Chapter 11 on pricing issues).

Non-tariff barriers become much more prevalent in times of recession. In the US and Europe we have witnessed the mobilization of quite strong political lobby groups, as indigenous industries which have come under threat, lobby their governments to take measures to protect them from international competition.

The last major era of protectionism was in the 1930s. During that decade, under the impact of the most disastrous trade depression in recorded history, countries around the world adopted high tariffs and abandoned their policies of free trade. Even today a number of governments impose different types of restrictions on imports to protect their home industries as Illustration 2.2 shows. In 1944 there was a reaction against the high tariff policy of the 1930s and significant efforts were made to move the world back to free trade. In the next section we will look at the global institutions that have been developed since that time to foster world trade and provide a trade climate in which such barriers can be reduced.

In the 1930s world trade was at low ebb, protectionism was rife and economies were strangling themselves. Several initiatives were born, primarily out of the 1944 Bretton Woods conference, to create an infrastructure that fostered trading relations. These initiatives fell into three areas:

- *Need for international capital*: the International Bank for Reconstruction and Development (IBRD).
- *International liquidity*: International Monetary Fund.
- *Liberalization of international trade and tariffs*: General Agreement of Tariffs and Trade, which became the World Trade Organization.

International Bank for Reconstruction and Development (IBRD)

The World Bank, officially called the International Bank for Reconstruction and Development, was founded together with the International Monetary Fund (IMF) in 1944. The World Bank began operating in June 1946 and membership of the Bank is open to all members of the IMF. Currently, there are 187 member countries. The Bank is owned and controlled by its member governments. Each member country subscribes to shares for an amount relative to its economic strength. The largest shareholder in the World Bank at the moment is the United States.

The World Bank is a vital source of financial and technical assistance to developing countries around the world. They help governments in developing countries reduce poverty by providing them with money and technical expertise they need for a wide range of projects – such as education, health, infrastructure, communications, government reforms and for many other purposes. Most recent Bank lending to developing countries by the IBRD and its sister organization the International Development Agency (IDA) totalled just under $47 billion. The IDA is the part of the World Bank that helps the world's poorest countries. Established in 1960, IDA aims to reduce poverty by providing interest-free credits and grants for programmes that boost economic growth, reduce inequalities and improve people's living conditions. The IDA complements the International Bank for Reconstruction and Development (IBRD) – which serves middle-income countries with capital investment and advisory service.

The scope of the Bank's operations has increased phenomenally during the past two decades. It now provides more than five times as much financial help to developing countries than it did 20 years ago. The Bank provides support for a wide variety of projects related to agriculture, education, industry, electricity, rural development, tourism, transportation, population planning, urban development, water supply and telecommunications. The Bank lends money only for productive purposes and gives serious consideration to the prospects of repayment before granting the loan.

While the countries who are members subscribe to the share capital of the World Bank, it relies mainly on private investors for its financial resources through borrowing in various capital markets. In this way, private investors become involved in the development efforts of developing countries. Since the IBRD obtains most of its funds on commercial terms, it charges its borrowers a commercial rate of interest. Loans are usually repayable over a 20-year period.

This has led to what has been euphemistically termed the 'debt crisis'. Many of the poor developing countries, recipients of large capital loans, are finding it impossible to meet the burden of debt facing them. Some of this debt is unpayable when the interest on the debt is greater than what the country produces. However, in some cases this is what is known as 'Odious debt', debt incurred by undemocratic countries and misspent. It is estimated that developing countries owed US$1.2 trillion to the world's richest nations. The World Bank Group provides debt relief to the poorest countries through the HIPC Initiative and the Multilateral Debt Relief Initiative (MDRI). The Initiative calls for the voluntary provision of debt relief by all creditors, whether multilateral, bilateral or commercial, and aims to provide a fresh start to countries with a foreign debt that places too great a burden on export earnings or fiscal revenues.

However, since the global banking crisis the level of debt has become a heavy burden to a number of major exporting countries as well as developing countries as Table 2.4 indicates.

In the 1950s it became obvious that many of the poorer countries needed loans on much easier terms than the World Bank could provide. The International Development Association (IDA) was established in

Table 2.4 The heavy burden of debt

	Debt as a % of GDP
Zimbabwe	304.30
Japan	192.10
Lebanon	160.10
Italy	115.20
Greece	108.10
Sudan	104.50
Iceland	100.60
USA	90.80
Nicaragua	87.00
Egypt	79.80
United Kingdom	68.50
India	60.20

Source: CIA Fact book 2010

1960 to help meet this need. It was made an affiliate of the World Bank and was to be administered in accordance with the Bank's established methods. The IDA makes soft loans of about US$7 billion annually. Almost all are granted for a period of 15 years without interest, except for a small charge to cover administrative overheads. Repayment of loans does not start until after a ten-year period of grace. Both the IDA and the IBRD lay down stringent requirements that have to be met before any loans are granted. In many cases this has meant that in order to be granted the investment the countries have had to make quite hard political decisions in order to achieve the balanced budget required. In some cases this has led to severe hardship and social disorder, for which the institutions have been severely criticized.

International Monetary Fund (IMF)

The objective of the IMF was to regain the stability in international exchange rates that had existed under the gold standard. Although the system of pegged rates failed to keep up with the growth in international trade, the functions of the IMF have continued to develop.

The main function is to provide short-term international liquidity to countries with balance of payments deficit problems enabling them to continue to trade internationally. The IMF, with its 187 members, provides a forum for international monetary cooperation enabling the making of reciprocal agreements among countries and the monitoring of the balance of payments positions of countries. Thus, it serves to lessen the risk of nations taking arbitrary actions against each other, as happened before it came into being, and it can also sound a warning bell for nations with potential liquidity problems.

The IMF's seal of approval is, for emerging markets, essential to attract foreign investment and finance. It is also a precondition of financial assistance from the Fund. Georgia, Ukraine, Hungary, Iceland, Latvia, Pakistan, Turkey and Sri Lanka have all been recent recipients of IMF funding. Earlier this decade Brazil and Argentina were recipients of the Fund's largest-ever loans. The IMF experienced a sharp decline in its lending business in recent years until the present global financial crisis led to a resurgence in lending. Its role has also started to change as it took on the global role of examining policies that underpin prosperity and poverty and tries to guide nations to the former. The Group of 20 (G20) empowered the IMF by making it the key lending institution for crisis-affected countries in need of balance of payments support. As a result, the IMF's lending portfolio has increased over the past year and the cumulative amount of its loans now stands at $47.9 billion.

The World Trade Organization

The predecessor of the World Trade Organization was the General Agreement on Tariffs and Trade (GATT). Established in January 1948, it was a treaty not an organization, with the signatories being contracting parties. Prior to the Doha Round which commenced in 2001 there had been a series of eight trade liberalization 'rounds'. These entailed tens of thousands of tariff concessions on industrial goods and covered trade flows worth hundreds of billions of dollars. In all, 23 countries participated in the 1948 opening round when 45000 tariff concessions were agreed covering US$10 billion worth of trade. Under the first eight GATT rounds, the average tariff on manufactured products in the industrial world fell from around 45 per cent in 1947 to under 5 per cent. This has been an important engine of world economic growth which, in turn, has stimulated further increases in world trade. Signatories to these treaties account for well over 90 per cent of world trade.

The last round of negotiations to be completed was the Uruguay Round with 107 participants. It was widely seen as the most complex and ambitious round ever attempted. This was due to the sheer volume of its coverage – 15 sectors and US$1 trillion worth of trade. An important part of the treaty was the formation of the World Trade Organization, which commenced in 1995 and replaced GATT. The WTO currently has 153 members and another 31 countries who have observer status.

The WTO preaches a gospel of multilateral trade and most-favoured-nation status which obliges each signatory to the treaties to grant the same treatment to all other members on a non-discriminatory basis. It has evolved regulations which it has tried to enforce through its adjudicatory disputes panels and complaints procedures. Since its start in 1995, over 400 disputes have been through the dispute settlement mechanism of the WTO. The USA, the EU, China and India have been its biggest users. Last year major WTO members including the EU and the USA launched 77 complaints against China with a value of about US$10 billion, 40 per cent of these were from India. Most of the cases against China are related to its cost advantage of cheap labour costs. India recently announced a six-month ban on imports of toys from China in a move that has been seen by observers to be aimed at protecting Indian manufacturers from cheaper Chinese imports. The most notable disputes between the USA and China have been over copyright, piracy and the use of brand names. Between the USA and the European Union it has often been over quotas and the enforcement of regulations. The USA considers the EU's refusal to approve genetically modified (GM) foods illegal under the WTO trade rules and launched a formal complaint against them. Barring US producers from exporting GM crops to the EU is estimated to cost US producers several hundred million dollars a year. Interestingly, however, the WTO has recently allowed the EU to impose up to US$4 billion of tariffs against America as recompense for a US foreign tax sales break which the WTO has deemed an illegal subsidy. However, India has also been at odds with the USA and Europe over their developing wine industry as Illustration 2.2 illustrates.

The main aim of the WTO is to promote a free market international trade system. It promotes trade by:

- working to reduce tariffs
- prohibiting import/export bans and quotas
- eliminating discrimination against foreign products and services
- eliminating other impediments to trade, commonly known as non-tariff barriers.

The latest round of negotiations is called the Doha Round, In this round members of the WTO are attempting to liberalize trading rules in a number of areas, including agricultural subsidies, textiles and clothing, services, technical barriers to trade, trade-related investments and rules of origin.

Over three-quarters of the WTO members are developing countries. The Doha Round has been dubbed the Development Round as it specifically aims to ease trading restrictions for these countries. It is estimated that developing countries face trade barriers four times those applied by rich countries to each other. These barriers reduce export earnings by US$100 billion per annum. Two of the main problem areas for negotiators are the international trading of textiles and agriculture, which accounts for 70 per cent of developing countries' exports. Average tariffs for textiles are 15–20 per cent compared to an average of 3 per cent for industrialized goods. In the European Union and the USA agricultural subsidies amount to US$1 billion per day, six times the annual amount spent on aid by these two regions.

The Doha Round of talks started in 2001 with the aim of fully implementing all parts of the Doha Declaration by 2013. Progress towards this objective has been seriously stalled several times and many think the objectives of the round will not be achieved. The main problem being the USA's unease due to the developing countries refusal to open up markets to the extent demanded. Of equal concern to the developing countries is the refusal by the USA to reduce the trade-distorting subsidies which developing countries view as leading to the unlawful dumping of produce from the USA onto global markets. Of equal concern is the EU's refusal to reduce the agricultural tariffs which block developing countries from EU markets.

It is believed by some that during the 50 years of global economic expansion under the auspices of GATT, despite the long-term commitments to multilateral trade and all the work to develop a fee multilateral trading system across the world, what we have in reality are a series of giant trading blocs. We will explore some of the more important ones in the next section.

The development of world trading groups

The formation of the European Monetary Union in 1999 was, perhaps, the most significant trading bloc to be formed. When the Single European Market was formed in 1993, the United States effectively became the second largest market in the world. Given the rise of the economies of China and India, the question that interests many observers of the global competitive battles now being fought is who will dominate the global markets of the future? There is a fear that the world economy may divide into three enormous trading blocs dominated by the world's major trading regions, the EU, NAFTA and China/East Asia, rather than a world of multilateral free trade, particularly if the implementation of the DOHA Declaration does not fully succeed. Some commentators argue that national economies are becoming vulnerable to the needs of the trading blocs within which trade is free, currencies are convertible, access to banking is open and contracts are enforceable by law. While this scenario may be a long way from the present position, we are already seeing the growing strength of trading blocs such as the North American Free Trade Association (NAFTA), Association of South East Asian Nations (ASEAN) and the formation of the European Monetary Union.

In this section we will examine in detail the regional trading blocs that are emerging, but first let us examine different forms of trade agreements.

Forms of market agreement

There are nine levels of market association ranging from limited trade cooperation to full-blown political union (see Table 2.5). At the lower level of association, agreements can be purely for economic cooperation in some form, perhaps a decision to consult on or coordinate trade policies. At the next level of cooperation, there will be the development of trade agreements between countries on either a bilateral or multilateral basis. Often these are for a particular sector – for example the multi-fibre agreement on textiles. Sometimes such agreements, especially trade preference ones, will act as a forerunner to closer ties. As far as formal trade groupings are concerned, there are five major forms: free trade areas, customs unions, common markets, economic unions and political unions.

Free trade area

The free trade area type of agreement requires different countries to remove all tariffs among the agreement's members. Let us assume that there are three nations – A, B and C – that agree to a free trade area agreement and abolish all tariffs among themselves to permit free trade. Beyond the free trade area A, B and C may impose tariffs as they choose. The EEA (European Economic Area) formed between the EU and EFTA (European Free Trade Area) and the LAFTA (Latin American Free Trade Area) illustrate the free trade area type of agreement, as does NAFTA, the agreement between the USA, Canada and Mexico, and the Asian Free Trade Area (AFTA).

Customs union

In addition to requiring abolition of internal tariffs among the members, a customs union further requires the members to establish common external tariffs. To continue with the example (countries A, B and C), under a customs union agreement B would not be permitted to have a special relationship with country X – A, B and C would have a common tariff policy towards X. Prior to 1993, the EC was, in reality, a customs union. Both the Economic Community of Central African States (ECCAS) and the Economic Community of West African States (ECOWAS) have the objective of being a customs union. Mercosur is now a customs union. Their cooperative effort started as a free trade area and now they have developed into a customs union.

Common market

In a common market type of agreement, not only do members abolish internal tariffs among themselves and levy common external tariffs, they also permit free flow of all factors of production among themselves. Under such an agreement, countries A, B and C would not only remove all tariffs and quotas among themselves and impose common tariffs against other countries such as country X, but would also allow capital and labour to move freely within their boundaries as if they were one country. This means that, for example, a resident of country A is free to accept a position in country C without a work permit.

The European Union is essentially a common market, with full freedom of movement of all factors of production. Similarly the Andean nations in South America have formed ANCOM, the Central American

Table 2.5 Main types of trade associations

Type	Description	Degree of policy harmonization among members	Common external tariff	Free movement of capital and people	Example
Economic cooperation	Broad agreement for consultations on and possible coordination of economic trade policies	None/very low	No	No	Canada–EC framework agreement, APEC
Bilateral or multilateral trade treaty	Trade regulation and often, but not necessarily, liberalization in one or more specified sector(s)	Low	No	No	The Peru, Chile Accord
Sectoral free trade agreement	Removal of internal tariffs in a specified sector may include non-tariff barrier reduction	Medium (within Specified sector(s)	No	No	The multi-fibre agreement
Trade preference agreement	Preferred trade terms (often including tariff reduction) in all or most sectors, possibly leading to free trade area	Low/medium	No	No	South African Development Cone (SADC)
Free trade area (or agreement)	Removal of internal tariffs and some reduction of non-tariff barriers in all or most sectors	Medium	No	No	ASEAN, NAFTA
Customs union	Free trade area but with a common external tariff, harmonization of trade policy toward third countries	Medium/high	Yes	Possibly	**ECOWAS & EECSA ECOWAS** COMESA, ANCOM, CACM Mercosur
Common market	Customs union, but with provisions for the free movement of capital and people, removal of all trade barriers, elaborate supranational institutions, significant harmonization of internal market structure and external policies				European single market
Economic union	Common market, but with integration of monetary policies, possibly common currency, significant weakening of national powers of member states	Very high	Yes	Yes	European Monetary Union **CEMAC**
Political	Full or partial federalism, including sharing of powers between supranational institutions and national governments	Highest	Yes	Yes	Would resemble federal states (e.g. US, Canada, Germany)

nations have grouped themselves as CACM, the Caribbean community have formed CARICOM and Southern Africa have formed the Common Market for Eastern and Southern Africa (COMESA).

Economic union

Under an economic union agreement, common market characteristics are combined with the harmonization of economic policy and member countries are expected to pursue common fiscal and monetary policies. Ordinarily this means a synchronization of money supply, interest rates, regulation of capital market and taxes. The Economic and Monetary Community of Central African States (CEMAC), has the objective of being an economic Union. In effect, an economic union calls for a supranational authority to design an economic policy for an entire group of nations. This is the objective of the European Monetary Union.

Political union

This is the ultimate market agreement among nations. It includes the characteristics of economic union and requires, additionally, political harmony among the members. Essentially, it means nations merging to form a new political entity: Germany and the USA are perhaps the closest examples historically. Yugoslavia, which was created after the First World War, was a political union, as was the Soviet Union, although neither of these still exist.

Figure 2.3 shows the major trading regions to have developed significantly in the past decade, together with their member countries. In the following sections we will examine these major trading groups and the developments they have undergone.

FIGURE 2.3 Regional trading areas of the world

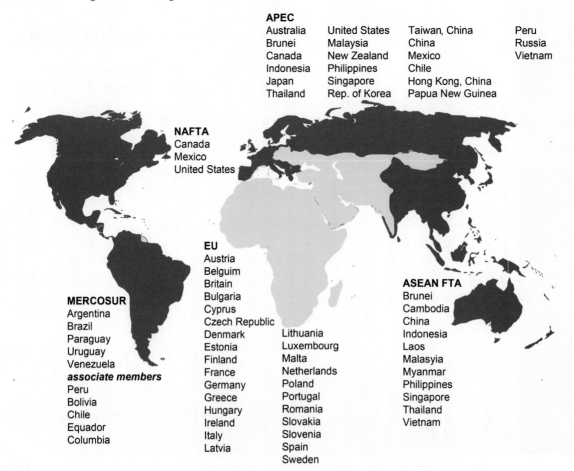

The European Union

Since 1987 and the signing of the Single European Act, Europe has undergone momentous changes, the key among these being:

- the creation of the EU and its single market
- formation of the European Monetary Union (EMU)
- the expansion of the European Union (EU) to include members of the European Economic Area (EEA) and central, eastern and southern Europe.

The Single European Market

The formation of the European Union meant that the EU became the largest trading bloc in the world with an estimated population of over 500 million people (2011), making it a powerful competitive force in the global markets. This, of course, was the key objective of the moves towards unification and the formation of the single market across the union. In the early 1980s it was recognized that if European companies were to compete successfully in the increasingly interdependent and global economy, a free and unbridled large internal market was necessary. This would enable companies to develop the critical mass needed to compete globally. The highly fragmented and restricted European market was seen as a major barrier to the ability to compete in global markets.

The EU was formed as a result of the signing of the Single European Act in 1986 which created, within Europe, 'an area without internal priorities in which the free movement of goods, personal services and capital is ensured in accordance with the provision of the Treaty of Rome'.

The key changes were:

- *Removal of tariff barriers*: a single customs check at all intra-EU borders enabling goods and services to move freely across Europe.
- *Removal of technical barriers*: a major impediment to trade was the differing and complex standards required in each country. Harmonization of these standards has paved the way for product standardization throughout Europe.
- *Public procurement*: public procurement amounts to 15 per cent of EU GNP, only 2 per cent of which went to foreign suppliers. By opening up the market to all European suppliers and by ensuring its enforcement, it is estimated that 17.5 billion Euros are saved per annum.
- *Free movement of labour and workers' rights*: nationals of member states now have the right to work in other member states.
- *Opening up of professions*: through mutual recognition of qualifications, professionals in certain categories have their qualifications recognized by other member states.
- *Financial services*: the opening up of banking, insurance and investment services through the introduction of a single banking licence and the harmonization of banking conditions.
- *Transport, haulage and coastal cabotage*: road haulage permits and quotas have been abolished. A more competitive air transport industry is also being pursued, as is unlimited cabotage for transport through the EU. Trucks are now allowed to pick up goods in any EU country and drop them off where required without the bureaucracy of permits and border documentation.
- *Company law*: several European developments in the area of company law are taking place in the fields of takeover bids, health and safety, cross-border merger, etc. The road to greater control from Brussels is now becoming especially apparent in this area.
- *Fiscal barriers*: there are many EU variations of fiscal policies, e.g. VAT. The UK has a standard rate of 20 per cent but VAT rates vary across the EU from 15 per cent in Cyprus to 25 per cent in Denmark. Moves are being made to reduce these disparities.
- *The environment*: the European Environment Agency was established to try to provide an integrated and Europe-wide policy for environmental protection.

Most analysts agree that the formation of the EU has greatly enhanced market opportunities for European companies. Since its formation it is estimated to have created about 2.5 million jobs and generated prosperity equivalent to 1 trillion Euros. As a result of its formation, there is a potential home market of 500 million consumers for companies within its walls. Intra-regional trading among EU members accounts for 75 per cent of all trade. With such interdependency, it is little wonder that so much effort has been put into completing the unification. However, 15 or so years on, while most goods are now crossing Europe's national borders with little or no hindrance, the liberalization of trade in services has not made the same progress. Europe's service providers are hindered by all sorts of petty bureaucratic rules, often justified on health, safety or consumer protection grounds, which discourage them from entering new European markets. In some cases, the European Commission has itself hampered progress by granting certain industries exemptions from the normal rules of fair competition, although these exemptions are starting to be undone.

European Monetary Union

The idea of a single European currency had been around since the early 1960s. As trade between member countries increased, various attempts were made to stabilize exchange rates. Previous systems such as the Exchange Rate Mechanism (ERM) attempted to create monetary stability through a system of fixed and floating exchange rates. This proved, however, to be incapable of coping with capital flows, which resulted in problems for sterling and the lira in September 1992, with the remaining currencies also facing problems the following year. Pressure for further integration in the Community resulted in the move to monetary union and a single European currency. This created the Economic and Monetary Union (EMU), sometimes called the Euro zone as countries within the zone all use the Euro as a domestic currency. Britain and countries such as Sweden and some recent members to the EU are not members of the Euro zone. Firms from these countries however, trading in the European Union, are affected by the Euro and economic activity in the Euro zone. Companies not in the Euro zone have to convert their customer invoices and accounts, credit notes and prices into Euros. Company computer systems for customer and/ or supplier accounts have had to be adapted to deal with Euros as many companies who operate across Europe follow a strategy of pricing all products in Euros for instance Marks and Spencer price in sterling and the Euro in the UK.

Strategic implications

The EMU was not just a monetary event, but one that has had a serious impact on the real economy. Prices and wages became transparent; consumers now shop around for the best deals; middlemen try to exploit any prevailing regional price differences and margins everywhere are now coming under pressure.

The competitive environment is viewed by many as being tougher under the EMU. The development of the EMU in Europe affected companies both inside and outside the Euro zone, but companies operating inside the Euro zone have had to adjust more quickly than companies operating outside it.

Global European companies such as Hewlett Packard, BMW, Daimler-Benz and Siemens for example, use Euro zone pricing policies. Pharmaceutical companies introduce new drugs across the EU at a single pan-European price. The banks have been significant losers in terms of the business of buying and selling European currencies. The formation of the Single European Payments Area (SEPA), discussed in Chapter 11 has further impacted on the margins previously achieved by European banks. The biggest difference, however, has not been between industries but between efficient, flexible companies and those that have stuck to their old national ways and found it difficult to compete in the new open and competitive landscape.

Companies that have concentrated on their national markets have been particularly vulnerable to takeover or extinction at the hands of their more far-sighted European competitors. Those businesses already used to competing internationally have had a strong advantage. As sources of supply widen, specializations based on national talents have developed further. French and German companies, for example, run call centres from Dublin, where multilingual Irish operators (or continental expatriates) provide advice or take orders over the telephone more cheaply and flexibly than would be possible in the companies' home countries. Another effect of the single currency has been to open the European market for those small- and medium-sized companies who have previously concentrated on their domestic customers. It has been estimated that currency fluctuations and the costs of dealing with them previously deterred a third of small- and medium-sized German companies from venturing abroad. Many who did export concentrated exclusively on countries where currencies were informally linked to the Deutschmark, such as Austria and the Netherlands.

Widening European membership

Enlargement of the European Union has happened at several stages of its development over the past 50 years, and there have been four previous enlargements.

In 1993 the European Council adopted the Copenhagen Criteria for admission to the EU. These require that member countries attain the following:

- Stable institutions guaranteeing democracy and the rule of law.
- A functioning market economy, as well as the capacity to cope with the competitive pressure and market forces within the EU.
- The ability to fulfil membership obligations, including adherence to the aims of political, economic and monetary union.

To date 12 countries from southern, central and Eastern Europe have joined the EU. Turkey, Croatia, Macedonia and Romania are in the application stages of accession.

The 12 new member states of Central and Eastern Europe have enjoyed a higher average percentage growth rate than their Western European counterparts since joining the EU. The reasons for this include government commitments to stable monetary policy, export-oriented trade policies, low flat-tax rates and the utilization of relatively cheap labour. It is reasonable to expect such a differential to continue in the medium-term and as such the member states of Central and Eastern Europe may be where the exciting market opportunities are in Europe. Illustration 2.3 discusses one such example.

However, given that the EU is now a tariff free trade area, the inclusion of central Europe makes the disparities between the wealth of members more pronounced. Denmark is one of the wealthiest countries of the 27 EU members with a GDP *per capita* of US$62 000. This compares to a GDP *per capita* in Portugal of US$22 000 and Poland of US$13 000 and Bulgaria of US$6500. The EU average is US$32 600. Clearly this poses challenges for marketers trying to establish a consistent marketing position across the European Union.

The free trade area of the Americas

The North American Free Trade Area (NAFTA) consisting of the US, Canada and Mexico, is regarded as the world's richest single market, with a combined population of 444 million people and has a combined economy of over US$17 trillion. Together the NAFTA members account for 34 per cent of the world GDP.

The main provisions of the NAFTA agreement aimed to:

- Eliminate tariffs on manufactured goods.
- Eliminate tariffs on 57 per cent of the agricultural produce from Mexico.
- Harmonize and streamline customs procedures and bureaucracy.
- Liberalize telecommunications, transport, textiles, banking and finance.
- Establish a NAFTA trade commission to settle trade disputes.

The attractive feature of NAFTA is that by virtue of the fact that Mexico is at a different stage of economic development from the US and Canada, the gains through specialization have been relatively large, allowing the US to specialize in more complex products that are intensive in their use of knowledge, technology and capital equipment.

© MICHAEL DUNLEA/Alamy

ILLUSTRATION 2.3

Škoda has the last laugh

The Czech word Škoda means pity or shame so on seeing a passing Škoda car, Czechs used to say 'there goes a shame' – and nobody would argue much. Today Škoda Autos (of the Czech Republic), once a butt of jokes, has now completely overhauled its image. Now 98 per cent of its drivers say they would recommend Škoda to a friend. Škoda uses this to guide its future strategic development and marketing. Škoda UK used this to develop their marketing strategy based on the confident slogan, *'the manufacturer of happy drivers'* of its brand image. With the help of its German partner Volkswagen who have the controlling share in Škoda, its profitability has consistently grown. The company employs about 4 per cent of the Czech workforce, or 150 000 people, directly or indirectly. In addition to the Czech Republic, Škoda cars are now made in Ukraine, India, Bosnia and Herzegovina, Kazakhstan, China and Russia. Cars are assembled in country from parts and components exported from the Czech Republic and they have worldwide sales of over 700 000.

Productivity in its plants is higher than Western levels and labour costs are much lower than at other VW plants in Europe. Analysts reckon that Škoda is the most successful company from a former Communist region. They produce 700 000 cars and are central Europe's largest car manufacturer. Last year sales were CZK220 billion. The growth has been driven by exports. Ten years ago around 30 per cent of Škodas were sold abroad, now over 80 per cent are exported. Its major sales success has been in China, where Škoda has doubled its sales in one year. Its controlled expansion into Western Europe has continued apace, especially into Germany, the firm's biggest Western market. The best selling Škoda model worldwide is the Octavia which sells 158 024 cars a year.

Volkswagen's presence in central Europe has had three advantages. First, it increased Volkswagen's leadership in Europe through the conquest of local central European markets. Second, it increased competitiveness through local manufacturing and purchases. Third, it has allowed them the possibility of using Škoda to develop its worldwide presence.

Question

1 Evaluate the reasons for Škoda's success.

References: www.Škoda-auto.com, http://www.thetimes100. co.uk/downloads/Škoda/ and http://www.autoexpress.co.uk/ news/autoexpressnews.

The available evidence suggests that this is precisely what has happened. US exports to Mexico of electronic goods, transport equipment and services have increased substantially. Meanwhile, most of the anecdotal evidence about US workers harmed by NAFTA comes from light manufacturing industries and agriculture.

However, it must be said that the scale of change induced by NAFTA is probably quite small relative to other factors impinging on the US economy over the last decade, such as technological change and their foreign policy initiatives.

For many, the creation of NAFTA was a US response to the formation of the single market in Europe. However, for others it has signalled the era of the drive by the US to create a free trade area across the Americas. The **Free Trade Area of the Americas** (FTAA) is a proposed agreement to eliminate or reduce trade barriers among all nations in the American continents (except Cuba) and involves negotiations with the Central American Common Market, the Andean Community and Mercosur. Spearheaded by the United States, the FTAA was intended to unite Latin America and North America in one broad trade accord. However, there is opposition and a number of Latin American and the Caribbean nations have formed The Bolivarian Alliance for the Peoples of Our America (ALBA) in opposition to the FTAA. The ALBA aims to achieve regional economic integration of its members. They use a virtual trading currency called the SUCRE and eventually aim for this to become a hard currency.

Mercosur, has also played a key role in the failure of the FTAA (Free Trade Agreement of the Americas). The Mercosur members and the then-autonomous Venezuela rejected the FTAA agreement in 2005 over concerns it would lead to increased inequality in the region. Proponents of the FTAA have not been able to make any significant progress since. Discussions have also faltered over similar issues to those in the Doha round of World Trade Organization talks. The USA and Canada are endeavouring to expand trade in services and increase intellectual property rights, while the central and South American nations are seeking to end the trade distorting agricultural subsidies in the USA.

Mercosur

Mercosur is the trading bloc linking Argentina, Brazil, Paraguay, Uruguay and Venezuela. The associate members of Bolivia, Chile, Columbia, Ecuador and Peru have a free trade agreement with Mercosur. This South American southern cone is the fourth largest trading bloc in the world and consists of 300 million people with a combined GNP of over US$2.4 trillion. Geographically Mercosur is four times the size of the European Union.

The creation of Mercosur has played an integral part of the formula across South America to conquer inflation, expand the size of its markets and attract substantial foreign direct investment, and this has, on the whole, been successful.

As a result Mercosur itself has developed and formed its own supra Mercosur institutions which include the policy-making Common Market Council and the Common Market Group. These implement policies and monitor compliance with the council's decisions. A Mercosur parliament has advisory powers only with its 90 members being drawn from member countries' national parliaments.

However, while the Customs Union has laudable and shared aims it has been driven by disputes among its members. As Brazil's car industry has become increasingly competitive, Argentina responded by imposing tariffs on Brazilian steel imports. Argentina and the union's smallest country, Uruguay, clashed over plans to build two large pulp mills along the border – the biggest foreign investments Uruguay had ever attracted. The bloc's smaller members, Paraguay and Uruguay, complain of restricted access to markets in Argentina and Brazil and have sought to set up bilateral trade deals outside Mercosur, which the rules are supposed to forbid.

The other fear is that Mercosur is becoming politicized and moving away from its freetrade origins. Talks to secure a trade accord with the EU have stalled, with farm subsidies and tariffs on industrial goods being among the stumbling blocks. Mercosur's blockage of the FTAA and its general disinterest in trade with the United States has discouraged warm relations between the two.

As trade barriers have fallen, especially in intra-regional trade, many multinationals have tried to bring the Mercosur countries into their worldwide strategy. For example, as part of its drive to dominate the global ice-cream industry Unilever bought Kibon, Brazil's largest ice-cream maker. However, besides the challenges described above, these companies have found there are three strategic issues they have had to face when trying to build a presence in the Mercosur markets:

- *Infrastructural weaknesses*: although the region has achieved remarkable growth in internal trade in the past few years, its infrastructure has to be substantially improved to facilitate a more competitive flow of materials, machinery and goods. This will allow corporations to develop fully integrated regional strategies. As things stand, the inefficient infrastructure hampers companies' efforts to achieve the economies of scale needed for regional competitiveness.

- *The need to develop industrial 'clusters'*: a nation's successful industries are usually linked through clusters of vertical and horizontal relationships. The vehicle assembly industry based in São Paulo, which has been successful for decades, illustrates how clustering of related businesses (glass, rubber, pistons and steel) is a driving force behind an industry's competitiveness. Such clusters should increase the opportunities for small- and medium-sized companies – not just the big corporations – to profit from the process of regional economic integration.

- *The business mindset*: a major obstacle to development is the business culture among traditional entrepreneurs. A mindset based on paternalism, centralization of authority and casual opportunism can pose problems for carrying out business in such countries.

MANAGEMENT CHALLENGE 2.1

South African Exporters target Latin America

The Latin American countries of Brazil, Argentina, Chile and Mexico, are viewed as presenting potential opportunities for trade between South Africa and the Latin American region. Yet in a report published in 2010 South Africa's exports to this region are viewed by the South African DTI to have been disappointing. South Africa's share of exports to Latin America were seen to be less than 1 per cent of the total export value of all the countries they view as their major competitors combined. Australia, Hungary, Malaysia Thailand, Russia and Turkey are all viewed to be better performers. However, a large proportion of the products which these countries export to Latin America are not exported by South Africa. Interestingly none of these countries were seen to have active government policies which encouraged companies to export to Latin America but most of the countries did use similar export promotion instruments as South Africa to support their firms. The South African DTI report suggested, the effectiveness of these instruments depends on the way they are constructed and packaged as part of a comprehensive and global export promotion strategy; and the way that they are targeted at export-ready firms.

In a survey undertaken by the DTI the three most frequently mentioned constraints faced by South African exporters to Latin America are:

- the volatility of the exchange rate;
- the costs of transport; and
- the costs of marketing the product and customs.

Firms that did not export to Latin America *perceived* making contact with potential buyers and language barriers as the two main impediments to trading with Latin American countries.

Question

1 For an industry of your choice evaluate how the South African DTI can encourage companies within that industry to overcome the constraints of developing exports to Latin America.

References: South Africa Department of Trade and Industry, Increasing Trade with Latin America, Preferences, Challenges and Remedies; policy Position Paper 2010, http://www.dti.gov.za/latin_america.pdf, accessed December 2010.

Management Challenge 2.1 focuses on the efforts of South Africa to encourage its exporters to target Latin America and the perceived constraints they face.

The Asian Pacific Trading Region

Asia Pacific Economic Cooperation

The Asia Pacific Economic Cooperation (APEC) is essentially a forum among 21 member economies who border on the Pacific. Thus, it includes the NAFTA member states, Russia, China and Japan, as well as the founding father Australia, New Zealand, ASEAN nations and Peru and Chile in South America. APEC members account for approximately 40.5 per cent of the world's population, approximately 54.2 per cent of world GDP and about 43.7 per cent of world trade.

The APEC forum has worked to reduce tariffs and other trade barriers across the Asia-Pacific region, with the aim of creating efficient domestic economies and increasing exports. Key to achieving APEC's vision are what are referred to as the 'Bogor Goals' of free and open trade and investment in the Asia–Pacific region. It has three key objectives:

- to develop and strengthen the multilateral trading system across APEC;
- to increase the interdependence and prosperity of member economies; and
- to promote sustainable economic growth in the region.

Courtesy of Banyan Tree Resorts

ILLUSTRATION 2.4

The Asian global brands

Asia has not traditionally been known to produce many global brands. Aside from a handful of brands originating from Japan, such as Sony, Toyota and Honda; and from South Korea, Samsung and LG there are probably less than ten truly global Asian brands. However, now that is all changing, Asian brands such as Haier and China's biggest computer manufacturing firms, Lenovo, I-Flex and Banyan Tree have successfully leveraged excellent service, one of Asia's traditional strengths, to offer customers an unparalleled brand experience and established global brands.

Samsung is an South Korean electrical goods manufacturer and the global leader in memory chips and flat screens for computers and televisions. Samsung has built its global brand from scratch but their strategy was to focus more on brand values than the brand itself. There are four components to the Samsung brand values:

- technology value;
- product value;
- marketing value; and
- reputation value.

In the service sector Singapore Airlines (SIA) and its iconic Singapore Girl has consistently been one of the most premier Asian global brands and has always had the reputation of a trendsetter and industry challenger which they credit to a dedicated, professional brand strategy throughout a diversified, global organization. However, the new globally developing brands are now taking a hold globally. Both Haier and Lenovo companies used the 2008 Olympics as a springboard to create a global recall and brand recognition for their products.

I-flex is viewed as an important emerging India global brand. According to Rajesh Hukku, chairman of I-flex solutions of India, the process of building a global brand has three stages:

> 'Get people around the world to become customers of the brand; show them that the quality and reliability is better than competition; and create the success story over and over by building solid company leadership that understands the brand and how to communicate it.'

Banyan Tree Holdings Limited is a leading manager and developer of premium resorts and are best known for their signature Banyan Tree and Angsana resorts, spas and galleries. Banyan Tree have successfully built a global brand in the luxury resort market. The company began in Thailand but now have a presence in 23 countries and a strong brand identity across the globe.

Question

1 Evaluate the environmental factors that are fuelling the growth of these emerging market super brands.

References: http://www.banyantree.com/ http://knowledge .insead.edu/ and http://www.reuters.com/.

Some members of the group would like an Asia-Pacific trading bloc to emerge because they fear being excluded from traditional US markets.

Combining FTAA, East Asian and Australasian countries into one Asia–Pacific bloc would mean that nearly 70 per cent of their trade would be intra-regional. However, there is marked resistance among Asian members of APEC to an enhanced role of the group. The US is giving a high priority to the APEC grouping and intends to forge closer trade and investment ties across the Pacific.

The Asia Pacific region has the fastest growth in the world. Asia is the principal export region for US products. Transpacific trade is 50 per cent greater than its transatlantic trade and more than 40 per cent of US trade is now in the Asian region. To foster this growth, the United States supports a more active APEC. It is from this region too that a number of the new global brands are emerging, as discussed in Illustration 2.4.

MANAGEMENT CHALLENGE 2.2

Rwanda: Darling or Devil?

Rwanda has received considerable international attention due to its 1994 genocide, in which an estimated 800 000 people were killed. Since then the country has made a recovery and is now considered as a model for developing countries. In 2009 a CNN report cited Rwanda as Africa's biggest success story, having achieved stability, economic growth and international integration. Although still small (US $5 billion) Rwanda's GDP has doubled in the last five years and is growing at 6 per cent per annum. According to Transparency International, a Berlin based anti-corruption monitoring agency, Rwanda is the least corrupt nation in East Africa. It has made significant progress in overcoming the obstacles to carrying out business and investing in the region. The government objective is to establish Rwanda as a trading hub between the Congo and East Africa and it recently joined the East African Community which includes Burundi, Kenya, Tanzania and Uganda. As a result, Rwanda has scrapped immigration procedures for East Africans. However, it is still a very poor country, it has a GNP *per capita* of US$900, continues to receive substantial aid money and obtains IMF-World Bank Heavily Indebted Poor Country (HIPC) initiative debt relief. About 90 per cent of the population in Rwanda are engaged in (mainly subsistence) agriculture and some mineral and agro-processing. In 2008, minerals overtook coffee and tea as Rwanda's primary foreign exchange earner. The government has embraced an expansionary fiscal policy to reduce poverty by improving education, infrastructure, and foreign and domestic investment. They are also pursuing market-oriented reforms, although energy shortages, instability in neighbouring states, and lack of adequate transportation linkages to other countries continue to handicap growth.

Question

1 What opportunities and challenges does Rwanda pose to companies trying to develop a presence in east Africa?

References: *The Economist,* 7 August 2010, www.cia.gov, and www.ft.com/companies/africa.

The members of the Association of South East Asian Nations (ASEAN) – Thailand, Indonesia, Singapore, Brunei, Malaysia and the Philippines, Vietnam, Myanmar, Cambodia and Laos – plan to complete the formation of the ASEAN free trade zone (AFTA) by 2015 and form an Asian Economic Region by 2020.

ASEAN is already well on the way to creating a largely tariff-free market of 580 million people, nearly one-tenth of the global population. The goal is to increase 'the region's competitive advantage as a production base geared for the world market'. The primary mechanism for achieving this is the Common Effective Preferential Tariff (CEPT) scheme, which established a schedule for phased tariff reductions to a rate between 0–5 per cent. Total trade of the ASEAN members is now US$1 trillion and they have a combined GDP of US$1.5 trillion.

However, some observers are sceptical about the potential development of AFTA. Geographical distances and cultural and political disparities have meant that previous attempts at closer economic integration have failed. These nations are keenly competitive and some members have not kept to agreements to lower trading restrictions. ASEAN has also failed to support action against its rogue state of Myanmar, thus making many doubt the political will of the group. Where EU and NAFTA integration has been based on treaties, in Asia so far it has been based on market forces, the chief of these being the region's fast rate of growth. Asia accounts for about a third of world production. Increasingly growth is also coming from intra-Asian trade, which recent estimates have put as high as 45 per cent.

ASEAN-China Free Trade Area (ACFTA)

A significant development in the progress of ASEAN has been the formation of the China-ASEAN Free Trade Area in 2010. The new free trade area brought together the ASEAN countries and China to create a trading bloc with a combined population of 1.9 billion, a combined gross domestic product (GDP) of up to US$6 trillion and total trade volume of US$4.5 trillion.

Barriers to developing a cohesive trading region While an Asian trading bloc may never have the cohesion of either Europe or America as the fastest-growing economic region in the world, any move towards integration will be watched closely by international competitors. There are particular barriers to developing a liberalized Asian trading bloc. First, there is a huge diversity among the nation states, not just culturally but in historical, religious and economic terms. Japan currently has a GDP *per capita* of US$39 400, Myanmar US$462. Politically, the countries embrace very different systems. Vietnam and Laos have communist dictatorships, Myanmar and Thailand have military juntas and Brunei is an absolute monarchy. In a number of countries the institutions are either non-existent or too weak to ensure the economic fairness necessary to sustain the progress to regulation of markets and trust in the rule of law which is crucial to any commercial relationship. Furthermore, the geographical area is huge and there are no natural groupings of nation states. Management Challenge 2.2 focuses on the opportunities and challenges that Rwanda poses to companies trying to develop a presence in east Africa.

SUMMARY

- In this chapter we have discussed the major developments in international trade. The world economy consists of over 194 nations with a population of 6.8 billion and an output (GDP) totalling US$61 trillion (ppp). World trade in merchandize totals US$12 trillion and trade in services is currently estimated by the WTO to be about US$4 trillion.

- In the last 50 years multilateral trade has flourished and a number of institutions have been developed to foster international trade. The World Bank, the IMF and the WTO all play important roles in ensuring a multilateral and fair international trading environment. It is important for the reader to have an understanding of how they may impact on the international marketing strategy of a company.

- The major trading regions around the globe are at different stages and their continuing development has been discussed. The creation of the EU and the formation of the Economic and Monetary Union (EMU) have changed the competitive landscape across the globe radically. Other areas are now formally developing as trading regions with free trade areas emerging in Asia, the Pacific and the Americas. Some commentators believe this is moving world trade to a more regionally focused trading pattern.

- In recent years there have been substantive changes in the global competitive structures as emerging markets strengthen their economic foundations and regional trading areas become more cohesive. The BRIC economies, Brazil, Russia, India and China are viewed as the star performers in emerging economies.

- The centre of gravity and dynamism of the Asia Pacific economy in the past decade has been China. China is developing the potential to dwarf most countries as it continues its rapid development and speedy economic growth. Commentators are interested to see whether it is China or India that will dominate the global trading structures of the 21st century.

KEYWORDS

Next Eleven (or N-11)

trade deficit

international product life cycle

comparative advantage

tariff

non-tariff barriers

hard currency

International Monetary Fund

World Bank

International Development Association (IDA)

balance of payments

Doha Round

trading blocs

Single European Market

Association of South East Asian Nations (ASEAN)

Asian Free Trade Area

Mercosur

Exchange Rate Mechanism

Economic and Monetary Union

Free Trade Area of the Americas

© Kurt Drubbel, iStockphoto.com

CASE STUDY

Challenges of the Libyan Market

Libya is situated in North Africa between Egypt and Algeria, with the Mediterranean to the north and Chad and Niger on its southern borders.

A former Roman colony, Libya is a mostly desert country, apart from the coastal strip and the mountains in the south, its landscape is desert or semi-desert. Libya is famous for its old Roman cities, its Green Mountain and its beautiful desert and its stunning 1900km costal line. In the past Libya saw invasions by Vandals, Byzantines, Arabs, Turks and more recently Italians before gaining independence in 1951. Oil was discovered in 1959 and made the state wealthy. Ten years later, King Idris was overthrown in a coup led by the 27-year-old Muammar Gaddafi, and Libya embarked on a radically new chapter in its history. In 2011 this all changed again when political crisis engulfed the country and plunged it into armed conflict which resulted international intervention.

Libya's strategic position in North Africa and its abundant oil and gas resources makes it an important trading partner for European countries. Libya is the fourth largest country in Africa by area, and the seventeenth largest in the world. The capital, Tripoli, is home to 1.7 million of Libya's 5.7 million people. The three traditional parts of the country are Tripolitania, Fezzan and Cyrenaica. Libya has the fourth highest GDP (PPP) *per capita* in Africa, behind the Seychelles, Equatorial Guinea and Gabon. This is largely due to its large petroleum reserves and low population. Libyans will tell you that Libya is the centre of the world in terms of its geographical location.

Libya, once shunned by much of the international community over the 1988 bombing of a PanAm plane above the Scottish town of Lockerbie, underwent a dramatic rehabilitation after taking formal responsibility for the bombing in 2003. The UN lifted sanctions, and Libya's subsequent renunciation of weapons of mass destruction further improved relations with the West. However, the armed conflict and political economic crisis in 2011 deeply impacted on the economic, political and social landscape of Libya, posing a serious threat to companies trading in the region as well as its oil and gas industrial infrastructure.

International investment in Libyan markets between 2003 and 2011 had grown steadily and in 2010 was around US$14 billion. Multinationals and international investors saw great opportunities in Libya as the economy started to develop. In this period, the country attracted the growing interest of a number of international companies across different market sectors. The Libyan economy depends primarily upon revenues from the oil sector and in this period enjoyed a low level of both absolute and relative poverty which made it potentially a interesting market, seen by many as being on the cusp of rapid development.

Even before 2011 Libya did not have an adequate infrastructure to support industrial development. The communication infrastructure had significantly improved due to huge investment and was viewed as being well connected through its telecommunication and mobile communication, however the events of 2011 seriously impacted on this. The lack of a viable transport infrastructure has always been seen as a major logistics barrier by a number of companies. For example, in Tripoli traffic jams are a huge problem and waste lots of time and money. There is a lack of a public transport system, so the car is the only means of travel. This weakness again has been made more severe since 2011. Education is compulsory in Libya and while there is a good level of basic education there is now a severe shortage of skilled labour and so companies find it problematic to recruit.

Stringent regulations, political unease and opaque Libyan commercial laws were always a challenge to companies looking to develop the Libyan market but the events of 2011 meant such difficulties diminished in significance in view of the even more serious threats to the survival of many companies who had invested in the country in the preceding years.

Libya is the gateway to Africa so its location is an important attraction. Libya has huge untapped resources. However, in Libya politics and business are inescapably intertwined and the success of a company developing this market will depend on how it manages its operations in a highly volatile politically and economically unstable environment.

Questions

1 What do you see as the major risks to a company wishing to develop a business in a market with such high levels of economic and political uncertainty?

2 For a sector of your choice, what advice would you give to a company wishing to enter and develop the Libyan market?

References: http://news.bbc.co.uk/1/hi/world/africa/country_profiles/819291.stm, accessed 11/3/2011.

DISCUSSION QUESTIONS

1 Identify barriers to the free movement of goods and services. Explain how barriers influence the development of international trade.

2 What do you consider to be the macro forces impacting on the development of world trade? Show by examples how they are changing the nature of international business.

3 To what extent do you agree with the view that the open global market no longer exists but simply consists of closed trading regions within which trade now moves freely?

4 How has the emergence of China as a major global competitor impacted on global marketing?

5 Recent mega mergers in the pharmaceutical and media industry are becoming increasingly evident. What is the rationale behind such mergers and how will it lead to global competitive advantage?

REFERENCES

1. Agtmael, A. (2007) *The emerging markets century*, Simon and Schuster.
2. Dicken, P. (2007) *Global shift – mapping the changing contours of the world economy*, 5th edn. Sage.
3. Griffin, R.W. and Pustay, M.W. (2009) *International business*, 6th edn. Pearson/Prentice Hall.
4. Porter, M.C. (1990) *The competitive advantage of nations*. Macmillan.
5. Vernon, R. and Wells, L.T. (1968) 'International trade and international investment in the product life cycle', *Quarterly Journal of Economics*, May.
6. World Bank, The 'China 2020: development challenges in the new century', available at http://www.econ.worldbank.org.

USEFUL WEBSITES

http://www.economist.co.uk

http://news.ft.com/

http://www.imf.org

http://www.wto.org

http://www.oecd.org

https://www.cia.gov/library/publications/the-world

http://www.google.com/publicdata/directory

http://www.un.org

http://www.worldbank.org

CHAPTER 3

SOCIAL AND CULTURAL CONSIDERATIONS IN INTERNATIONAL MARKETING

LEARNING OBJECTIVES

After reading this chapter you should be able to:

- Discuss and evaluate social and cultural factors impacting on an international marketing strategy

- Understand the cross-cultural complexities of buying behaviour in different international markets

- Assess the impact of social and cultural factors on the international marketing process

- Carry out a cross-cultural analysis of specified international markets

INTRODUCTION

Markets in countries around the world are subject to many influences, as we saw in Chapter 1. While it is possible to identify those influences common to many country markets, the real difficulty lies in understanding their specific nature and importance.

The development of successful international marketing strategies is based on a sound understanding of the similarities and differences that exist in the countries and cultures around the world. The sheer complexity of the market considerations that impinge on the analysis, strategic development and implementation of international marketing planning is a major challenge.

In this chapter we will examine the social and cultural issues in international marketing and the implications they have for strategy development.

Social and cultural factors

Social and cultural factors influence all aspects of consumer and buyer behaviour, and the variation between these factors in different parts of the world can be a central consideration in developing and implementing international marketing strategies. Social and cultural forces are often linked together. While meaningful distinctions between social and cultural factors can be made, in many ways the two interact and the distinction between the various factors is not clear-cut. Differences in language can alter the intended meaning of a promotional campaign and differences in the way a culture organizes itself socially may affect the way a product is positioned in the market and the benefits a consumer may seek from that product. A sewing machine in one culture may be seen as a useful hobby: in another it may be necessary to the survival of a family.

Kotler *et al.* (2009) included such things as reference groups, family, roles and status within social factors. While this is a useful distinction from the broader forces of culture, social class and social factors are clearly influenced by cultural factors. Take the example of the family, which is an important medium of transmitting cultural values. Children learn about their society and imbibe its culture through many means, but the family influence is strong, particularly during the early formative years of a child's life. Furthermore, the way in which family life is arranged varies considerably from one culture to another. In some cultures the family is a large extended group encompassing several generations and including aunts and uncles, while in other cultures the family is limited more precisely to the immediate family of procreation, and even then the unit might not be permanent and the father and mother of the children might not remain together for the entirety of the child-rearing process. Thus, social and cultural influences intertwine and have a great impact on the personal and psychological processes in the consumer and buyer behaviour processes and, as such, play an integral part in the understanding of the consumer in international markets. Toys'R'Us found quite distinct differences in the type of toys demanded in their various international markets. Whereas the US children preferred TV, and movie-endorsed products, Japanese children demanded electronic toys, South East Asian children wanted educational toys and the more conservative cultures of the European markets expected a choice of traditional toys.

It is not feasible to examine all the social or cultural influences on consumer and buyer behaviour in one chapter, neither is it possible to describe all the differences between cultures across the world. In the first section we will highlight the more important sociocultural influences which are relevant to buyer behaviour in international markets. In the following section we will focus on developing an understanding of the components of culture, its impact on consumer behaviour and the implications for international marketing strategies. We will then discuss the methodologies which can be used to carry out cross-cultural analyzes to enable comparisons to be made across cultures. Finally we will examine business-to-business marketing and the impact of culture in these types of markets.

What is culture?

Perhaps the most comprehensive definition of culture is that of Matsumoto (2010) who said culture 'is a unique meaning and information system, shared by a group and transmitted across generations that allow the group to meet the basic needs survival by co-ordinating social behaviour to achieve a viable existence and to transmit successful social behaviours'. (p5) Or perhaps, more appropriately: 'The way we do things around here'. In relation to international marketing, culture can be defined as: 'The sum total of learned beliefs, values and customs that serve to direct consumer behaviour in a particular country market'.

Thus, culture is made up of three essential components:

Beliefs: A large number of mental and verbal processes which reflect our knowledge and assessment of products and services.

Values: The indicators consumers use to serve as guides for what is appropriate behaviour. They tend to be relatively enduring and stable over time and widely accepted by members of a particular market.

Customs: Overt modes of behaviour that constitute culturally approved or acceptable ways of behaving in specific situations. Customs are evident at major events in one's life, e.g. birth, marriage, death and at key events in the year, e.g. Christmas, Easter, Ramadan, etc.

Such components as values, beliefs and customs are often ingrained in a society and many of us only fully realize what is special about our own culture – its beliefs, values and customs – when we come into contact with other cultures. This is what happens to firms when they expand internationally and build up a market presence in foreign markets: often the problems they face are a result of their mistaken assumption that foreign markets will be similar to their home market and that they can operate overseas as they do at home. Frequently in international markets the toughest competition a firm may face is not another supplier but the different customs or beliefs as a result of cultural differences. This means that for a company to succeed in that market they often have to change ingrained attitudes about the way they do business. The beliefs and values of a culture satisfy a need within that society for order, direction and guidance. Thus, culture sets the standards shared by significant portions of that society, which in turn sets the rules for operating in that market.

Hofstede *et al.* (2010) identify a number of layers within a national culture.

Layers of culture

- A national level according to one's country which determines our basic cultural assumptions.
- A regional/ethnic/religious/linguistic affiliation level determining basic cultural beliefs.
- A gender level according to whether a person was born as a girl or as a boy.
- A generation level which separates grandparents, parents and children.
- A social class level associated with educational opportunities, a person's occupation or profession.

All of these determine attitudes and values and everyday behavioural standards in individuals and organizations.

Given such complexities, market analysts have often used the 'country' as a surrogate for 'culture'. Moreover, culture is not something granted only to citizens of a country or something we are born with, it is something we learn as we grow in our environment. Similar environments provide similar experiences and opportunities and hence tend to shape similar behaviours.

Sarathy *et al.* (2006) identify eight components of culture which form a convenient framework for examining a culture from a marketing perspective (see Figure 3.1).

The components of culture

Education The level of formal primary and secondary education in a foreign market will have a direct impact upon the sophistication of the target customers. A simple example will be the degree of literacy.

FIGURE 3.1 A cultural framework

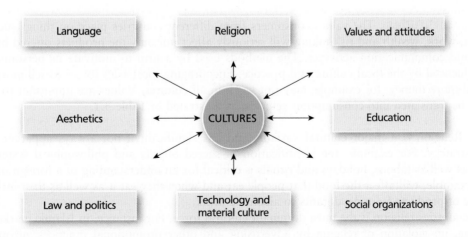

Source: Data adapted from Sarathy, R., Terpstra, V. and Russow, L.C. (2006) *International marketing*, 9th edn. Dryden Press.

The labelling of products, especially those with possibly hazardous side-effects, needs to be taken seriously for a market that has a very low literacy rate. The UK company ICI markets pesticides throughout the world: in developed countries its main form of communication is advertising and printed matter. In developing countries they rely heavily on training and verbally based educational programmes to get their message across.

Social organization This relates to the way in which a society organizes itself. How the culture considers kinship, social institutions, interest groups and status systems. The role of women and caste systems are easily identifiable examples – if the firm has a history of successfully marketing to 'the housewife/homemaker', life is more difficult in a culture where women have no social status at all. House ownership is another example. In Switzerland the majority of people rent rather than own their houses and expect to rent property with domestic appliances already installed, which means the banks, not individual families, are the largest purchasers of washing machines.

Technology and material culture This aspect relates not to materialism but to the local market's ability to handle and deal with modern technology. Some cultures find the idea of leaving freezers plugged in overnight, or servicing cars and trucks that have not yet broken down difficult to understand. In instances such as these the organization is often faced with the choice of either educating the population (expensive and time-consuming) or de-engineering the product or service (difficult if you have invested heavily in product development).

Law and politics The legal and political environments in a foreign market are usually regarded as consequences of the cultural traditions of that market. Legal and political systems are often a simple codification of the norms of behaviour deemed acceptable by the local culture. This aspect was dealt with in some detail in Chapter 1. **Cultural sensitivity** to political issues in international markets is of the utmost importance. Thus, an advertizement for the Orange mobile phone network in Ireland with the strapline 'The future's bright, the future's orange', clearly did not have any awareness of political sensitivities in Northern Ireland.

Aesthetics This covers the local culture's perception of things such as beauty, good taste and design, and dictates what is acceptable or appealing to the local eye. A firm needs to ensure that use of colour, music, architecture or brand names in their product and communications strategies is sympathetic and acceptable to the local culture. For the unwary, there are many, many traps in this area. Pepsodent tried to sell its toothpaste in the far reaches of East Asia by emphasizing that it 'whitens your teeth'. Unfortunately they did not realize there was a practice among local natives in some areas of chewing betel nuts to blacken their teeth to make them attractive. Colour can mean completely different things in different cultures and brand colours sometimes do not travel well because of this, as we can see in Illustration 3.1.

Values and attitudes The values consumers from different countries place on things such as time, achievement, work, wealth and risk-taking will seriously affect not only the products offered but also the packaging and communication activities. The methods used by a firm to motivate its personnel are also strongly influenced by the local culture and practice. Encouraging local sales forces to sell more by offering cars and more money, for example, may not work in all cultures. Values are important to marketers as they can be translated into consumption vehicles, as illustrated in Table 3.1.

Religion Religion is a major cultural variable and has significant if not always apparent effects on marketing strategy. For example, the identification of sacred objects and philosophical systems, beliefs and norms as well as taboos, holidays and rituals is critical for an understanding of a foreign market. Religion, for example, will affect the food that people eat and when they eat it as well as their attitudes to a whole range of products from deodorants to alcoholic drink.

  In some countries religion is the most dominant cultural force. For instance, in Islamic markets such as Saudi Arabia, no violation of religion by advertising and other promotional practices, no matter how

Courtesy of Cadbury

ILLUSTRATION 3.1

Cadbury's: Lady Purple or Aunty Violet?

Like ourselves, colours may or may not be aesthetically pleasing but they all have a personality. When we look at a colour a whole spectrum of thoughts, feelings and emotions are evoked in our minds. Some of these associations are instinctive in us all, others we learn from the environment in which we live. From the passionate excitement of red to the playful happiness of yellow, colours are constantly eliciting subconscious responses in us.

For international marketers this notion is particularly pertinent. In our efforts to cue the customer into positioning our brand in a certain way, the colours used in the design, packaging and advertising of a product can send very powerful messages about the personality of our brand. However, as the meaning of colour is often derived from the cultural environment, the messages and thus the personality may fluctuate greatly across countries and cultures.

In a recent study, the Cadbury's brand was perceived very differently by UK and Taiwanese participants. While in the UK Cadbury's was seen to be luxurious, stylish, expensive, classy and silkily feminine, the Taiwanese had an image of an old, warm, friendly, but essentially poor brand, low in quality and lacking in class.

In the same study, participants from the two countries were asked to discuss their perceptions of the colour purple – a colour that Cadbury's is currently attempting to register as a trademark.

Once again, the British made associations with luxury, style, sophistication, youth and femininity. The Taiwanese, on the other hand, talked of a warm, old, quiet colour, serious, a little sad but dignified. In both cultures, all the feelings, emotions and characteristics associated with the colour purple had been transferred to give very different meaning to the Cadbury's brand.

When taking colour abroad, therefore, marketers may do well to heed some of mother's most motherly advice, 'Looks aren't everything. It's the personality that counts!'

Question

1 How can marketers ensure they understand such cultural sensitivities when entering new markets?

Source: Anthony Grimes, Manchester Business School, University of Manchester

insignificant, will go unnoticed or unpunished either by the government or the consumer. This can cause problems for advertisers. Shaving advertizements cannot be shown if the male actor shows too much of his chest. Likewise, in certain Gulf States, an advertizement where someone uses their left hand to handle food could upset local sensibilies. Major violations of religion are sometimes punished in more liberal and so-called secular markets within the Islamic world. Rules surrounding religious laws require heightened insight and empathy by international companies. Comparative ads are banned as, according to the laws of Islam, pegging one product against another diminishes the sense of unity and social community. Companies operating in these markets need to understand the difference between three key terms: *Haraam, Halal* and *Makruh*.

Haraam are subjects or things that are absolutely unlawful and strongly prohibited in Islam, such as alcohol and cheating. These taboo subjects are banned in advertising and other promotional activities in countries such as Saudi Arabia, Kuwait and Iran. *Halal* is the opposite to *Haraam* and is a term designating any object or an action which is permissible to use or engage in, according to Islamic law. The term is commonly used to designate food seen as permissible according to Islamic law. *Makruh* are subjects which are seen as distasteful: they are discouraged in Islam but are not banned. Smoking is not forbidden in Islam but it is highly discouraged.

Table 3.1 Cultural values and their relevance to consumer behaviour

Value	General features	Relevance to consumer behaviour
Achievement and success	Hard work is good; success flows from hard work	Acts as a justification for acquisition of goods ('You deserve it')
Efficiency and practicality	Admiration of things that solve problems (e.g. save time and effort)	Stimulates purchase of products that function well and save time
Progress	People can improve themselves; tomorrow should be better than today	Stimulates desire for new products that fulfil unsatisfied needs; ready acceptance of products that claim to be 'new' or 'improved'
Material comfort	'The good life'	Fosters acceptance of convenience and luxury products that make life more comfortable and enjoyable
Individualism	Being oneself (e.g. self-reliance, self-interest, self-esteem)	Stimulates acceptance of customized or unique products that enable a person to 'express his or her own personality'
External conformity	Uniformity of observable behaviour, desire for acceptance	Stimulates interest in products that are used or owned by others in the same peer group
Youthfulness	A state of mind that stresses being young at heart and a youthful appearance	Stimulates acceptance of products that provide the illusion of maintaining or fostering youthfulness

Source: Schiffman, L.G. and Kanuk, L.L., Consumer Behaviour 9/e © 2008, p. 416, Pearson Education Inc., Upper Saddle River, N.J., reproduced with permission.

Language   Language can be divided into two major elements: the spoken language of vocal sounds in patterns that have meaning and **silent language,** which is the communication through body language, silences and social distance. This is less obvious but is a powerful communication tool. To many commentators language interlinks all the components of culture and is the key to understanding and gaining empathy with a different culture. In the following section we will examine the different components of language.

Language and culture

Spoken language   **Spoken language** is an important means of communication. In various forms, e.g. plays and poetry, the written word is regarded as part of the culture of a group of people. In the spoken form the actual words spoken and the ways in which the words are pronounced provide clues to the receiver about the type of person who is speaking.

   Chinese is spoken as the mother tongue (or first language) by three times more people than the next largest language, English. However, Chinese is overtaken by English when official language population numbers are taken into account. However, the official language is not always spoken by the whole population of a country. For example, French is an official language in Canada but many Canadians have little or no fluency in French. English is often but by no means always the common language between business people of different nationalities.

   Speaking or writing in another language can be a risky activity (see Illustration 3.2). In advertising, particular attention needs to be paid when translating from one language to another. The creative use of copy to gain attention and to influence comprehension of the target audience can result in a clever use of words. However, inadequate translation often results in clumsy errors. In Germany a General Motors'

ILLUSTRATION 3.2

Written language: but what does it mean?

- In France the Toyota MR2, pronounced emm-er-deux, is written phonetically as merde.

- The car maker AMC were confident Matador meant bullfighter, but when they launched the Matador in South America they found to their cost that it actually meant 'killer'.

- Japanese hotel notice to hotel guests: 'You are invited to take advantage of the chambermaid'.

- Acapulco hotel notice regarding drinking water: 'The manager has personally passed all the water served here'.

- Visitors to a zoo in Budapest were asked 'Not to feed the animals. If you have any suitable food, give it to the guard on duty'.

- A Bangkok dry cleaner to potential customers: 'Drop your trousers here for best results'.

- A Roman laundry innocently suggested: 'Ladies leave your clothes here and spend the afternoon having a good time'.

- A Hong Kong dentist claims to extract teeth 'By the latest Methodists'.

- A Copenhagen airline office promises to 'Take your bags and send them in all directions'.

Question

1 What unusual translations have you come across when reading international advertizements?

References: BBC News online and the *Sunday Times*.

advertizement mentioned a 'body by Fischer' which became 'corpse by Fischer'. This is clearly a straightforward translation error, directly resulting from the mistranslating of the word 'body'. The Hertz company's strapline, 'Let Hertz put you in the driving seat', became 'Let Hertz make you a chauffeur'. Instead of communicating liberation and action as intended, this translation provided an entirely different meaning, implying a change of occupation and status. In India an advertizement for the milky drink Horlicks was translated into Tamil as '20 men asleep under the tree'.

Language in web marketing The choice of language to use for a company website is also problematic for companies operating across many borders. Should it be multilingual, thus incurring greater costs in ensuring its sustainability, or should it be in one language? Surprisingly, while English is a widely spoken language throughout the world, it is only the first language of 6 per cent of the world's population, yet 96 per cent of all e-business sites are written in English.

Managers have previously assumed that English is the international language of the Internet. While this was so in the early days, according to Forrester Research, web contact time is doubled on sites localized for language and culture. Japanese businessmen, for example, are three times more likely to conduct an online transaction when addressed in Japanese. The US consultancy Global Reach estimates that for every US$2 million a US site generates from domestic sales, another US$1 million is lost when non-Americans do not easily understand the website.

Obviously a preferred solution for many companies is to build the web capability to offer a multilingual website, localized to the language and cultural sensitivities of the market. A global brand then needs to centralize the message, translate it and colloquialize it. A second reason for localization is to ensure a company is compliant with local regulations. In France, for instance, consumers enjoy a one-week grace period after they receive an online purchase. In Germany, comparative advertising is banned on the web and in China, clients' companies may they find their websites are monitored by the Chinese government.

The same issue of course is faced by advertisers on social networking sites. Illustration 3.3 looks at how Adidas has responded to this challenge on its Facebook site.

ILLUSTRATION 3.3

© Julie Woodhouses / Alamy

Global brand localizes Facebook content

Adidas Originals' Facebook page currently has more than 1.9m global fans. However, they wanted to make their pages more useful to their fans and more appealing for Adidas advertising. The solution Adidas and Facebook came up with was more localization of the campaigns and e-commerce links. As a result they have introduced a new tab to its fan page that tailors advertising content according to the location of the Facebook user.

There are now a number of localized versions for countries including the US, UK, France, Italy, Japan and South Africa. Facebook are currently developing localized versions for cities and a regional Latin America version.

Tara Moss, Adidas global head of digital marketing, said:

'Facebook is a global platform and, as Adidas is a brand that celebrates originality, it was important for us to be relevant in our engagement with all of our consumers worldwide. Innovation is in our DNA and is what consumers expect from Adidas. Innovation coupled with the connection that social media is how we'll continue to get closer to our consumers and build meaningful relationships with them online and beyond.'

Question

1 How important do you think it is for global brands such as Adidas to localize their communications given the global nature of its brand platform?

References: www.guardian.co.uk, Monday June 1 2009 and McEleny, C., 'Adidas Originals ramps up localised content on Facebook fan page', *News Media Age*, Tue, 2 Jun 2009 and **www.hedgehogs.net/**

Silent language   Silent language is a powerful means of communication and the importance of **non-verbal communication** is greater in some countries than others. In these cultures people are more sensitive to a variety of different message systems. Silent Language examines the many influences we face each day, influences that are silent in that they are not verbal but that are quite loud in terms of the effects they have on our development, our relationships and so on. Hall (1997) suggested that many of these influences are cultural, attitudes and behaviours we inherit from our cultural heritage and learning. As different cultures speak different verbal languages so does our culture give rise to differences in the silent languages used to communicate. Such silent language influences important in international marketing are, attitudes to time, which influences the importance of being on time, attitudes to space, which impacts on the conversational distance between people. In Asian cultures the significance of trusted friends as a social insurance is very important. Therefore, the communication coming from a person recognized as a friend is much more trusted than someone who has not yet achieved that status.

Silent languages are particularly important in sales negotiations and other forms of business meetings. They will, in addition, influence internal communications in companies employing people from different countries and cultures.

Difficulties can arise even between cultures which are geographically close to each other but have different perceptions of language. The word *konzept* in German means a detailed plan, in French the word concept means an opportunity to discuss. Executives could meet with hugely varying expectations if a conceptual discussion was on the agenda.

Cultural learning The process of **enculturation**, i.e. learning about their own culture by members of a society, can be through three types of mechanism: formally, through the family and the social institutions to which people belong; technically, through the educational processes, be it through schools or religious institutions; and informally, through peer groups, advertising and various other marketing-related vehicles.

This enculturation process influences consumer behaviour by providing the learning we use to shape the toolkit of labels, skills and styles from which people construct strategies of action, e.g. persistent ways of going through the buying process.

The process of acculturation is the process international companies need to go through to obtain an understanding of another culture's beliefs, values and attitudes in order to gain an empathy with that market. As we have seen, culture is pervasive and complex and it is not always easy for someone outside a given culture to gain an empathy with that market.

Having examined the main components of culture and the various important dimensions, we will now look at how culture impacts on consumer behaviour.

Culture and consumer behaviour

There are several important ways in which the various components of culture influence a consumer's perception, **attitude** and understanding of a given product or communication and so affect the way a consumer behaves in the buying process. Jeannet and Hennessey (2006) identify three major processes through which culture influences consumer behaviour as depicted in Figure 3.2.

Culture is seen as being embedded in elements of society such as religion, language, history and education (cultural forces). These elements send direct and indirect messages to consumers regarding the selection of goods and services (cultural message). The culture we live in determines the answers to such questions as: Do we drink coffee or juice at breakfast? Do we shop daily or on a weekly basis? and so affects the consumer decision process.

The body of theory on which our understanding of **consumer behaviour** is based predominantly hails from the USA. Usunier and Lee (2009) argue that the means by which international marketing managers understand consumer behaviour is flawed because the theoretical principles on which we base our understanding do not necessarily hold true across different cultures. There are some important assumptions which international marketers need to question when applying Western theoretical principles in order to understand consumer behaviour across international markets:

1 That Maslow's hierarchy of needs is consistent across cultures.
2 That the buying process in all countries is an individualistic activity.
3 That social institutions and local conventions are similar across cultures.
4 That the consumer buying process is consistent across cultures.

FIGURE 3.2 Cultural Influences on buyer behaviour

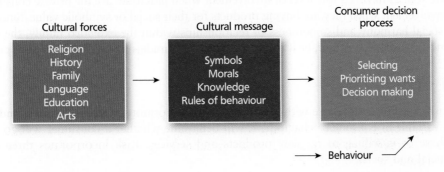

Source: Adapted from Jeannet and Hennessey (2006)

That Maslow's hierarchy of needs is consistent across cultures

Culture influences the hierarchy of needs (Maslow 1970) on two levels. First, the axiom that one need must be satisfied before the next appears is not true for every culture, and second, similar kinds of needs may be satisfied by different products and consumption types.

For example, in some less developed countries, a consumer may go without food in order to buy a refrigerator and, therefore, satisfy the dominant need of social status before physical satisfaction. A study identified that self-esteem needs were most important to Chinese consumers, and physiological needs the least important. Physiological needs include food, water, shelter, etc., self-esteem needs include prestige and success.

In building a presence in the Chinese market, companies would need to target consumers with high self-esteem needs by linking a product such as credit cards to success in business or beer to success in sporting activities.

Likewise, similar kinds of needs may be satisfied in very different ways. For example, to a Hindu the need for self-realization does not necessarily imply material consumption, as in Western cultures, but in fact abandoning all worldly possessions.

That the buying process in all countries is an individualistic activity

Many Western buying behaviour models are primarily based on individual purchases with reference to family decision-making in the context of husband and wife decisions. They assume buying decisions are focused on an individual's decision-making process. In Asian or Arabian cultures a family may be a complex structure and an individual would need to take into account all members of the family in making major purchase decisions, so the decision-making is of a much more collectivist nature.

That social institutions and local conventions are similar across cultures

Institutions such as the state, the religious institutions, trade unions and the education system also influence consumer behaviour.

The UK company ROMPA, which serves the market for people with learning disabilities, found enormous cultural differences across their European market due to the varying influences the national institutions had on how charities and social institutions should be organized. In Germany the market was highly organized and strongly supported financially by the state. In Spain the state lottery was the prime benefactor of major national charities, whereas in Italy the church was the major benefactor, with very little involvement by the state.

That the consumer buying process is consistent across cultures

There are many inconsistencies in the buying processes across cultures around the globe. Three aspects which are particularly pertinent to our discussion are the differences in the level of consumer involvement, the perception of risk in a purchase and the cognitive processes of consumers.

Consumer involvement

The Chinese are seen as having a low level of involvement when purchases are for private consumption but a high level of involvement when they are buying products for their social or symbolic value. Since the Chinese greatly value social harmony and smoothness of relationships within the extended family, the social significance of products is highly important, be it to express status, gratitude, approval or even disapproval.

Perceived risk

The level of risk consumers associate with a purchase varies enormously across cultures, and as such it is an important variable in consumer behaviour. It will determine whether a consumer will go for the comfortable purchase or is willing to try new products and services. Risk incorporates three components: physical, financial and social.

Whereas in some countries, *physical risk* may be important (e.g. the fear of AIDS), others may be more sensitive to *social risk* and the loss of social status if a wrong buying decision is made (i.e. the Chinese fear of losing face). *Financial risk* closely relates to the level of economic development in a country. It is likely to be less in the more affluent economies where if a wrong purchase decision is made the financial hardship suffered may not be so profound.

The level of brand loyalty found in a market is also closely related to the **perception of risk**. There are huge variations in attitudes to brand loyalty across different cultures. In the US the standard buyer behaviour is that of disloyalty. A consumer will shift from one brand to another because it is standard behaviour to test several competitive products and so foster price competition. Thus, in the US it is relatively easy for a new entrant to persuade Americans to try their product, but much harder to get them to keep buying it.

In other cultures, consumers are more fundamentally loyal, less brand-conscious and not so used to cross-product comparisons. In Australia and South East Asia buyers have a greater need for brand security, are less confident with regard to trying unknown products and so are less willing to take risks.

Cognitive style

Western consumer behaviour models assume a logical buying process with rational steps, including the formation of awareness, the searching for information, reviewing the information, evaluating alternatives and finally making a choice. Sometimes by attacking traditional cognitive styles advertisers have had surprising success.

Many authors argue that internationally there are many different models of the buying process. Asian consumers tend to have a quite different cognitive style to Western consumers. The Chinese as well as the Japanese have a more synthetic, concrete and contextual orientation in their thought patterns, as opposed to the Americans who tend to have a more analytical and abstract decision-making process. Thus, culture not only impacts on how we behave as consumers but on the whole decision-making process. Marketing managers need to be aware of how cultural sensitivities can impact on how they communicate in different cultures as in the case of Saudi Arabia in Management Challenge 3.1.

Analyzing cultures and the implications for consumer behaviour

As we have seen in previous sections, there are many social and cultural influences which determine our values, beliefs and customs and combine to form a **cultural identity** which in turn influences the process of decision-making when buying products. All these aspects need to be examined to understand the consumer in any international market.

Blackwell *et al.* (2006) suggest the following steps should be undertaken when analyzing consumer behaviour in international markets. They propose that if a company is to fully empathize with a culture they must pose a series of questions about buyer behaviour, culture and the suitability of various marketing communications approaches for that culture. These steps consist of:

- *Determine relevant motivations in the culture.* What needs are fulfilled with this product in the minds of members of the culture? How are these needs presently fulfilled? Do members of this culture readily recognize these needs?

- *Determine characteristic behaviour patterns.* What patterns are characteristic of purchasing behaviour? What forms of division of labour exist within the family structure? How frequently are products of this type purchased? Do any of these characteristic behaviours conflict with behaviour expected for this product? How strongly ingrained are the behaviour patterns that conflict with those needed for distribution of this product?

- *Determine what broad cultural values are relevant to this product.* Are there strong values about work, morality, religion, family relations and so on that relate to this product? Does this product denote attributes that are in conflict with these cultural values? Can conflicts with values be avoided

MANAGEMENT CHALLENGE 3.1

Doing Business in Saudi Arabia

Saudi Arabia is considered a very high context culture. This means that the message people are trying to convey often relies heavily on other communicative cues such as body language and eye-contact rather than direct words. In Saudi Arabian culture particular emphasis is placed on tone of voice, the use of silence, facial cues and body language. It is vital to be aware of these non-verbal aspects of communication in any business setting in order to avoid misunderstandings. For instance, silence is often used for contemplation and you should not feel obliged to speak during these periods. It is also wrong to assume that the person who asks the most questions holds the most responsibility. In Saudi Arabia this person is considered to be the least respected or least important. The decision-maker is more often than not a silent observer. Communications occur at a slower pace in Saudi Arabia and patience is often necessary. In Saudi Arabia the spoken word has much more weight than written agreements. An agreement is only final when both parties have parted. Until then it is open to negotiation, even if the contract has been signed.

Question

1 What do you think are the do's and don'ts of carrying out sales negotiations in Saudi Arabia?

References: The CIA World Factbook.

by changing the product? Are there positive values in this culture with which the product might be identified?

■ *Determine characteristic forms of decision-making.* Do members of the culture display a studied approach to decisions concerning innovations, or an impulsive approach? What is the form of the decision process? Upon which information sources do members of the culture rely? Do members of the culture tend to be rigid or flexible in the acceptance of new ideas? What criteria do they use in evaluating alternatives?

■ *Evaluate promotion methods appropriate to the culture.* What role does advertising occupy in the culture? What themes, words or illustrations are taboo? What language problems exist in present markets that cannot be translated into this culture? What types of sales staff are accepted by members of the culture? Are such sales staff available?

■ *Determine appropriate institutions for this product in the minds of consumers.* What types of retailers and intermediary institutions are available? What services do these institutions offer that are expected by the consumer? What alternatives are available for obtaining services needed for the product but not offered by existing institutions? How are various types of retailers regarded by consumers? Will changes in the distribution structure be readily accepted?

Self-reference criterion

As we have discussed, it is of crucial importance when examining foreign markets that the culture of the country is seen in the context of that country. It is better to regard the culture as different from, rather than better or worse than, the home culture. In this way, differences and similarities can be explored and the reasons for differences can be sought and explained. The differences approach avoids the evaluative and often superior approach based on one's own self-reference criterion.

'Self-reference criterion' (SRC) characterizes our unconscious reference to our own cultural values when examining other cultures. Usunier and Lee (2009) suggests a four-step approach to eliminate SRC.

1 Define the problem or goal in terms of home country cultural traits, habits and norms.

2 Define the problems or goals in terms of the foreign culture, traits, habits and norms.

3 Isolate the SRC influence in the problem and examine it carefully to see how it complicates the problem.

4 Redefine the problem without the SRC influence and solve for the foreign market situation.

The process of enculturation to gain empathy with a foreign country market is not an easy one. It requires:

■ *Cultural empathy*: the ability to place yourself in the position of the buyer from another culture. In this way a strong attempt is made to understand the thinking approaches, the decision-making process and the interactions between this and the cultural and other forces influencing the buyer.

■ *Neutrality*: the ability to identify the differences that exist without making value judgements about 'better' or 'worse' cultures. Inevitably, self-reference will exist. If the focus is placed on differences rather than superiority, the chances of achieving accurate cross-cultural analysis are increased.

To ensure they achieve this, companies follow a number of policies. They may recruit foreign staff at their head office, collaborate with local firms when entering a new market or they may put managers through acculturation programmes. Guinness understood the importance of avoiding SRC in developing their knowledge base of the new international markets in which they were operating, so they ensured they had a management team in each market which was truly multinational, as well as including managers with a local knowledge.

Cross-cultural analysis

So far our discussions have been concerned primarily with understanding what is meant by culture, examining its components and surveying its influence on consumer behaviour and how that differs across cultures.

However, strategists and students of international marketing need to move beyond this and endeavour to develop ways to compare and contrast consumers, market segments and buyers across cultures. In today's global environment where culture is becoming increasingly de-territorialized and each culture is penetrated by the influences of other cultures, this is becoming increasingly complex as a research task. Cultural influences are much more diffuse and opaque than previously. This means that cultural analysis does not necessarily equate to country analysis and any research design must account for such complexities.

International marketers must decide the relevant cultural segments/grouping for analysis and then need appropriate frameworks or conceptual schemata to enable comparisons to be made and contrasts and similarities to be drawn across cultural groupings.

For the most part, **cross-cultural** classification approaches tend to be either mere lists or incredibly theoretical complex structures. There is a recognized lack of a universal, broadly generalizable framework within which to visualize cross cultural analysis. The contextual approach and the work of Hofstede *et al.* (2010) is used by many researchers as the basis for methodologies of cross-cultural analysis. A further framework has been developed through the GLOBE programme which focuses on cross cultural leadership attributes. In the following sections we will examine how these concepts can be used by firms in attempting to analyze consumer behaviour across cultures and will then highlight some further frameworks which readers may find useful.

The high/low context approach

The main thesis of the contextual approach to analyzing culture is that one culture will be different from another if it understands and communicates in different ways. Languages are therefore seen as the most important component of culture.

The language differences between some cultures will be large and therefore there will be marked differences in their cultures. Language and value differences between the German and Japanese cultures, for instance, are considerable. There are also differences between the Spanish and Italian cultures but they are much less; both have languages based on Latin, they use the same written form of communication and have similar although not identical values and norms.

In different cultures the use of communication techniques varies. In some languages communication is based on the words that are said or written (spoken language). In others, the more ambiguous elements such as surroundings or social status of the message-giver are important variables in the transmission of understanding (silent language). Hall used these findings to classify cultures into what he referred to as 'low context cultures' and 'high context cultures'.

- *Low context cultures* rely on spoken and written language for meaning. These are cultures where people tend to have many connections but of short duration or for some specific reason. In these societies, cultural behaviour and beliefs may need to be spelled out explicitly so that those coming into the cultural environment know how to behave. Senders of messages in low context cultures encode their messages expecting that the receivers will accurately decode the words used to gain a good understanding of the intended message. Germany, Switzerland, UK and the USA are viewed as low context cultures. These cultures have a high explicit content in their communications.

- *High context cultures* are those cultures where people have close connections over a long period of time. Many aspects of cultural behaviour are not made explicit because most members know what to do and what to think from years of interaction with each other. High context cultures use and interpret more of the elements surrounding the message to develop their understanding of the message. In high context cultures the social importance, knowledge of the person and the social setting add extra information and will be perceived by the message receivers. Saudi Arabia, Japan, Asia and South America are seen as high context cultures. These cultures have subtle and complex ways of communicating with people according to their age, sex and the relative and actual social positions of the people conversing.

The greater the contextual difference between those trying to communicate, the greater the difficulty firms will have in achieving accurate communications. Table 3.2 outlines the communication differences between low and high context cultures.

Hofstede's cultural dimensions

Hofstede (2010) was primarily interested in uncovering differences in work-related values across countries. He identified five dimensions of culture: individualism, power distance, uncertainty avoidance, masculinity and Confucianism. These dimensions, he argued, largely account for cross-cultural differences in people's belief systems and behaviour patterns around the globe.

Individualism

Individualism (IDV) describes the relationship between an individual and his or her fellow individuals in society. It manifests itself in the way people live together, for example in nuclear families, extended families or tribes, and has a great variety of value implications. At one end of the spectrum are societies with very loose ties between individuals. Such societies allow a large degree of freedom and everybody is expected to look after his or her own self-interest and possibly that of the immediate family. Societies of this type exemplify high individualism (high IDV) and display loose integration. At the other end are societies with very strong ties between individuals. Everybody is expected to look after the interests of their in-group and to hold only those opinions and beliefs sanctioned by the in-group which, in turn, protects the individual. These 'collective' (low IDV) societies show tight integration. Hofstede identified highly individualistic countries as the USA, Great Britain and the Netherlands. Collectivist countries were Colombia, Pakistan and Taiwan. The mid-range contains countries such as Japan, India, Austria and Spain.

Table 3.2 Communication Styles in Low and High Context Cultures

Factor	High-context culture	Low-context culture
Overtness of messages	Many covert and implicit messages, with use of metaphor and reading between the lines.	Many overt and explicit messages that are simple and clear.
Locus of control and attribution for failure	Inner locus of control and personal acceptance for failure.	Outer locus of control and blame of others for failure.
Use of non-verbal communication	Much nonverbal communication.	More focus on verbal communication than body language.
Expression of reaction	Reserved, inward reactions.	Visible, external, outward reaction.
Cohesion and separation of groups	Strong distinction between ingroup and outgroup. Strong sense of family.	Flexible and open grouping patterns, changing as needed.
People bonds	Strong people bonds with affiliation to family and community.	Fragile bonds between people with little sense of loyalty.
Level of commitment to relationships	High commitment to long-term relationships. Relationship more important than task.	Low commitment to relationship. Task more important than relationships.
Flexibility of time	Time is open and flexible. Process is more important than product.	Time is highly organized. Product is more important than process.

Source: Straker, D., (2008) *Changing Minds: in Detail*, Syque Press

Power distance

Power distance (PDI) involves the way societies deal with human inequality. People possess unequal physical and intellectual capacities which some societies allow to grow into inequalities in power and wealth. However, some other societies de-emphasize such inequalities. All societies are unequal but some are more unequal than others The Philippines, India and France score relatively high in power distance (see Illustration 3.4). Austria, Israel, Denmark and Sweden show relatively low PDI scores, while the United States ranks slightly below midpoint.

Combining power distance and individualism reveals some interesting relationships (see Figure 3.3). Collectivist countries seem to show large power distance but individualist countries do not necessarily display small power distance. For example, the Latin European countries combine large power distance with high individualism. Other wealthy Western countries combine smaller power distance with high individualism. It is interesting to observe that in Hofstede's sample, almost all developing countries tend to rate high on both collectivism (low individualism) and power distance. Of the countries Hofstede studied, only Costa Rica combined small power distance with high collectivism (low individualism).

Uncertainty avoidance

Uncertainty Avoidance (UA) reflects how a society deals with uncertainty about the future, a fundamental fact of human existence. At one extreme, weak UA cultures socialize members to accept and handle uncertainty. People in such cultures tend to accept each day as it comes, take risks rather easily, do not work too hard and tolerate opinions and behaviour different from their own. Denmark, Sweden and Hong Kong all rated low in UA. The other extreme – strong UA societies – fosters the need to try to beat the future, resulting in greater nervousness, aggressiveness and emotional stress. Belgium, Japan and France ranked relatively high in uncertainty avoidance while the United States scored somewhat below midpoint.

ILLUSTRATION 3.4

© Arterra Picture Library / Alamy

France: image vs reality?

France scored relatively high in power distance dimension in Hofstede's analysis, and certainly some regard it as a culture that is inherently conservative and resistant to change. It is argued due to the evident characteristics of large power distance it should be a blocked society with too many top-down bureaucratic

rules which breed distrust among people and a resistance to change among individuals. Consequently individuals perceive innovation and risk-taking with suspicion and so will be hostile to an open global market which encourages diffusion of cross-cultural ideas and new products and services. Globscan, a polling group, found that 71 per cent of Americans agreed that the free market economy was the best system available, as did 66 per cent of the British and 65 per cent of Germans. Only 36 per cent of French respondents agreed.

Yet France boasts some of the most successful companies operating on global markets. Carrefour's empire spreads the globe and virtually in every sector there are world class French firms, cars (Renault), tyres (Michelin), cosmetics (L'Oréal), luxury goods (LVMH) and food (Danone).

Question

1 How do you account for the contradiction in the image of France as a bureaucratic culture resistant to change and the reality of the performance of French companies on global markets?

FIGURE 3.3 Power distance/individualism dimensions across culture

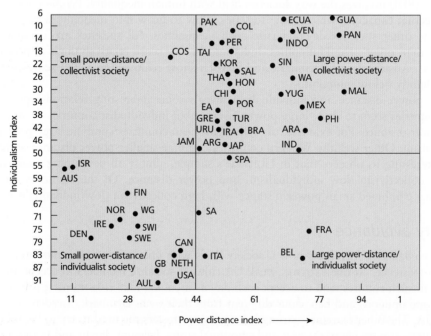

Masculinity

Masculinity (MAS) deals with the degree to which societies subscribe to the typical stereotypes associated with males and females. Masculine values stress making money and the pursuit of visible achievements: such societies admire individual brilliance and idolize the successful achiever, the superman. These traditional masculine social values permeate the thinking of the entire society, women as well as men. Hofstede's research indicated that within his sample, Japan, Austria, Venezuela and Italy ranked highest in masculinity.

In more feminine societies, both men and women exhibit values associated with traditionally feminine roles such as endurance and an emphasis on people rather than money. Societal sympathy lies with the underdog, the anti-hero rather than the individually brilliant. Sweden, Norway, the Netherlands and Denmark rank as some of the most feminine societies studied by Hofstede. The United States scored fairly high on the masculinity dimension, placing it near the top one-third.

An assertive salesperson would be better accepted in a highly masculine culture such as Austria than in Denmark's more feminine culture. The level of masculinity also explains part of the perception that business people have of each other. In feminine countries where relationships are more highly valued, the supplier–client relationship is seen much more as a partnership than in more masculine cultures. Thus, the affective aspects of the business relationship are seen as of vital importance, particularly in negotiations as we will see in the section on cross-cultural negotiating later in this chapter.

Confucian dynamism

The Confucian dynamism dimension assesses cultures on the degree they are universalistic or particularistic. Universalistic cultures believe that what is true and good can be determined and defined and can be applied everywhere. Particularistic cultures evolve where 'unique circumstances and relationships are more important considerations in determining what is right and good rather than abstract rules'(Hofstede 2010). Confucian philosophy traditionally pervades Chinese culture. Its major characteristics include a strong bias towards obedience, the importance of rank and hierarchies and the need for smooth social relations. Within Confucian ethics, four basic relations were, between ruler and those ruled, father and son, husband and wife and friend and friend. Everyone is expected to know where they stand in the hierarchy of human relations and one's place carries with it fixed standards of how one behaves towards others.

Culture/communication typologies

A number of writers have developed frameworks that can be utilized for cross-cultural analysis which have built on the above work. In this section we will discuss the communication typologies and the relationship between the cultural dimensions identified by Hofstede and the adoption of new products.

Communication typologies

Four verbal communication typologies were suggested by Gudykunst *et al.* (2005) which can be used as a basis for cross-cultural analysis. These are as follows:

1 *Direct vs indirect* refers to the degree of explicitness of the verbal message of a culture. The Chinese use the indirect style, often hiding their real feelings and being more concerned with group harmony and the feelings of others. The use of the indirect style refers to the high context culture and Hofstede's collective dimension.

2 *Elaborative vs succinct* reflects the quantity of talk that people feel comfortable with in a particular culture. The succinct style is where quantity of talk is relatively low. This reflects high uncertainty avoidance and a high context culture. Elaborative styles may be used more in low context cultures where the spoken language is of greater importance, as in the US.

3 *Personal vs contextual* contextual style focuses on the role of the speaker and the role of relationships. The role and hierarchical relationship of the parties in conversation will be reflected in

ILLUSTRATION 3.5

The use of humour in international advertising

Every culture enjoys some form of humour, but humour has difficulty crossing cultural boundaries because what is funny in one culture is often not so in another. In cultures where the desire to avoid uncertainty is high, as in Germany, humour with its inherent ambiguity is likely to be restrained in advertising. In an analysis of beer advertising across Europe, researchers found humour dominated British commercials, whereas it was used more sparingly in German or Dutch commercials.

In Europe typical examples of humorous advertising include commercials that tell a funny story, use of irony or making fun of typical situations. In Thailand, however, advertising that has made its mark in terms of creativity and popularity is primarily characterized by humour, sometimes black, sometimes slapstick and always identifiably Thai. This is probably indicative of a trait across Asia which surprised Unilever when they found they had greatly under-utilized the use of humour when addressing women consumers. Their study showed that 83 per cent of women in Asia preferred the portrayal of humour over the traditional Western heavy-handed use of emotions in advertising.

In B2B cross-cultural advertising status is an important consideration. In some countries people may loosen up as they get promoted and be more receptive to humour, but in more hierarchical cultures, such as France, the reverse is more likely to be the case. Seniority is largely determined by intellectual achievement and academic credentials. Consequently, French executives are keen to avoid being branded lightweight. So while clever and sophisticated humour is acceptable, the risk of appearing foolish, with the accompanying loss of credibility and intellectual standing, tends to inhibit other forms of humour. The self-mocking humour for which British advertising is renowned is likely to be completely misunderstood.

In international advertising it may be as well to remember the old Chinese proverb: 'You get sick by what you put in your mouth, but you can be hurt by what comes out of your mouth'.

Question

1 Evaluate the implications of using humour in cross-cultural advertising.

---

the form of address and words that are used. This type of communication reflects high power distance, collectivism and high context cultures such as Japan.

4 *Instrumental vs affective* defines the orientation of the speaker. In the affective verbal style the speaker is process orientated. There is concern that neither the speaker nor the receiver will be put in an uncomfortable position. The speaker also listens to and closely observes the receiver in order to interpret how the message is being taken. This is a reflection of a high context collective culture, such as South East Asia.

Such typologies may influence the receptiveness of consumers across cultures to humour in advertising. We explore this in Illustration 3.5.

Hofstede's cultural dimensions vs rate of product adoption　Singh (2006) suggests that particular dimensions of culture are critical in determining whether consumers of certain cultures are likely to easily adopt new products or services or not. Essentially he measured the propensity of a culture to innovate and found that cultures characterized by a small power distance, weak uncertainly avoidance and masculinity are more likely to be innovative and accept new product ideas than cultures where there was a large power distance, strong uncertainty avoidance and more feminine traits exhibited. Equally he suggested that cultural dimensions were also linked to the preferred type of communication. Individualistic cultures are more likely to be swayed by more impersonal channels, whereas collectivist cultures are more likely to be swayed by interpersonal communications. Heineken tapped into the need for social acceptance to avoid uncertainty in collectivist cultures in their innovative campaign in Asia. They built a perception of popularity by asking staff in bars selling Heineken to leave bottles on tables by not pouring full beers into glasses and not collecting the empties. Suddenly little green bottles were seen everywhere and it didn't take long for customers to start asking for that particular brand.

Globe programme   The GLOBE (Global Leadership and Organizational Behaviour Effectiveness) programme is an extensive research project, which has built on previous studies on cultural divergences and patterns. It is working to integrate previous research to develop one single platform to carry out cross cultural analysis on leadership attributes. Across 62 countries, the GLOBE programme investigates how cultural values are related to organizational practices, conceptions of leadership, the economic competitiveness of societies and the human condition of its members. The programme identifies the following nine cultural dimensions:

- uncertainty avoidance;
- power distance;
- collectivism (two forms of it);
- gender egalitarianism;
- assertiveness;
- future orientation;
- performance orientation; and
- humane orientation.

Social and cultural influences in business-to-business marketing

Much of the discussion relating to the influences of social cultural factors on international marketing assumes a market for predominantly fast-moving consumer goods where decisions are made on either a family or individual basis. Yet a considerable proportion of exports relates to industrial goods and services where companies are primarily concerned with company-to-company or business-to-business marketing and dealing, therefore, with primarily organizational or even government buyers. The question we now need to address is how relevant the social/cultural factors we have been discussing are to these types of markets.

In business-to-business marketing there are essentially two types of buyers: organizations and governments. In this section we will highlight some of the social/cultural influences on these types of buyers which are particularly relevant to international marketing. Following this we will discuss the impact of culture on cross-cultural negotiating styles and the practice of gift-giving in international business relationships.

Organizational buyers

Business buying decisions are influenced by decisions about technology, the objectives and tasks of the company, the organizational structure of the buying company and the motivations of people in the company. The technology decision is an interesting area. Some companies rely on their own internal capability to produce solutions to problems they need to solve in the areas of technology and how to manufacture the product. However, Japanese companies have encouraged their suppliers to help them by providing technological improvements. This approach is now influencing business practices across the world. The US adversarial approach of developing a precise buying specification and then challenging supplying firms to win the contract by providing the best deal is now less common.

Culture at the organizational level can play a significant part in the way in which the various roles are enacted. When it comes to international encounters, humour for instance can be a double-edged sword. The dangers of a joke backfiring are increased when the parties concerned do not share a common culture. Different cultures have different beliefs and assumptions which determine when humour is considered appropriate, what can be joked about and even who can be joked with. Attitudes to uncertainty, status and the sanctity of business influence the extent to which humour is allowed to intrude on proceedings.

There are a number of different corporate cultural characteristics in European countries which influence buyer behaviour. The French have a hierarchical system of management with a strong tendency to centralism, consequently it is often difficult for sales people to reach the top manager as that individual may well be buffered behind half a dozen assistants. Spanish and Italian decision-making tends to be highly autocratic and based on the model of the family; decision-making is shared, with systems that tend to be informal. The German position is influenced by earned respect for formal qualifications and technical competence. Leadership depends upon respect rather than subservience.

Government buyer behaviour

In many countries the government is the biggest buyer, far larger than any individual consumer or business buyer. Governments buy a wide range of goods and services: roads, education, military, health and welfare. The way in which governments buy is influenced by the extent to which public accountability in the expenditure of public money is thought important.

It has been estimated that 20 per cent of the gross domestic product of the European Union is controlled through the value of purchases and contracts awarded by the public sector. In the US approximately 30 per cent of the gross national product is accounted for by the purchases of US governmental units. For some companies their international business comprises government buyers in different countries. It is important, therefore, to understand the government buying processes.

Usual forms of buying procedure are the open tender and selective tender. In open bid contracts, tenders are invited against a tight specification, and contracts are usually awarded to the lowest-price bid. Selective tender contracts are offered to companies who have already demonstrated their ability in the area appropriate to the tender. Only those companies on the selective tender list will be invited to tender. As with open tender, the lowest price is often used to adjudicate the bids.

In the European Union specific rules have been drawn up in an attempt to remove the barriers between potential suppliers of government contracts from different countries of the EU. Suppliers from all EU member states should have an equal opportunity to bid for public authority contracts and public works contracts must be advertized throughout the EU.

The business-to-business buying process

In the B2B buying processes the various types of buying are classified into three different classes of buying: straight re-buy, modified re-buy and new task.

A straight re-buy represents the bulk of the business buying. The buy signal is often triggered through information systems when stock levels reach a predetermined replenishment point. The modified re-buy indicates a certain level of information search and re-evaluation of products/services and supplies before the purchase is made. The new task represents an area of considerable uncertainty in which the company needs to make decisions about what it wants, about performance standards and about supplier capabilities. The new task, particularly if the purchase is of major importance to the company, will involve senior management and might take a long time to complete.

The way in which a company manages each of the buy classes will be influenced by cultural factors. Companies with a strong ethnocentric orientation may limit their search for suppliers to suppliers from their own country. For more internationally oriented companies, the country of origin effect will distort information collection and appraisal. The influence of established relationships in cultures in which personal contacts and relationships are important will act as a barrier to companies which operate in a more formal way.

Relationship marketing is very important in business-to-business marketing, where companies may gain competitive advantage not necessarily from the product but through the added value they have built because of their relationship. This is especially important in markets such as China. The Chinese rely heavily on personal relationships in business dealings. It is important for foreign companies to understand the dynamics of these relationships (known as *guanxi*). There is a saying in Chinese, 'If you do not have a relationship you do not exist'.

Personal selling and negotiation between the buyer and seller as they go through the interaction process in order to build a business relationship which is mutually beneficial is an important part of international marketing. It is in this process of negotiation and relationship building that cultural factors have their greatest impact.

The role of culture in negotiation styles

Culture can be a major determinant in the success or failure of business negotiations. In Saudi Arabia business may look informal and slow paced, but in negotiations a businessman would be grossly insulted if they were expected to negotiate with a representative rather than the top person. Indian negotiators bargain much longer and tend to be much more competitive and persistent in trying to maximize their gains.

However, some commentators suggest that while a lack of understanding of the cultural differences in negotiation styles may be a major cause of negotiation failure, awareness of cultural differences may not be a major factor in negotiation success, unless that awareness is accompanied by a deeper understanding of how culture impacts on the whole negotiation process. A negotiation process can be broken down into four stages:

1 Non-task discussion

2 Task-related exchange of information

3 Persuasion

4 Concession and agreement.

The first stage, *non-task discussion*, describes the process of establishing rapport between members of the negotiation teams. Japanese negotiators would spend considerable time and money entertaining foreign negotiating teams in order to establish a rapport, whereas US executives saw the delays as frustrating and the money spent as wasteful. GEC Alsthom sales executives found karaoke sessions very useful when negotiating with the North Koreans for a contract for high-speed trains between Seoul and Pusan. The firm understood from the outset that the first stage of negotiations needed to include a broad range of activities, such as singing, to help establish a rapport on which the relationship could be built.

The *task-related exchange of information stage* describes the exchange of information that defines the participants' needs and expectations. Well over 90 per cent of all large Japanese companies and most of the smaller ones use a decision-making process called *ringi*. The system is based on the principle that decisions are made only when a consensus is reached by the negotiating team. Proposals are circulated among the negotiating team for each to affix their own personal seal of approval. Without the group's approval, which takes a long time to acquire, no proposal will be accepted. What may appear to US negotiators as stalling tactics is often simply the different process by which the Japanese reach a decision.

The *persuasion stage* for US executives is the one that consumes time, whereas for Japanese negotiators who have previously taken the time to understand each other's expectations, it is seen as unnecessary. Japanese negotiators may, as a result, remain silent. This is not because they do not agree with the proposal but because they are either waiting for more information or, for them, agreement has been reached and therefore negotiations are complete.

This often leads to misunderstanding at the *concession and agreement stage*. An extension of the Japanese preference for establishing strong personal relationships is their dislike for the formal Western-style contract. A loosely worded statement expressing mutual cooperation and trust developed between negotiating parties is much preferred. The advantage of these agreements is that they allow a great deal of flexibility in the solution of unforeseen problems, whereas Western negotiators may feel the need to bargain to the end and do not see their job as complete until they have actually obtained a signature. Table 3.3 gives an interesting summary of differences in buyer–seller negotiating styles in selected countries.

Usunier and Lee (2009) suggests a number of ways to minimize cultural impact in negotiations in order to build effective trans-cultural relationships:

- *Adaptation*. In international business meetings, people who do not appear to feel the need to adapt may be considered indolent: 'Those who adapt are aware of differences, whereas those to whom others adapt remain unaware' (Usunier and Lee (2009)).

- *Interpreters*. Be aware that interpreters influence meaning. They may translate better from one language into another than in the opposite direction. The loyalty of interpreters needs to be considered. Are they more in favour of one party than the other? Should you use your own interpreter? Should you use several interpreters to reduce stress errors and bias?

- *Cultural blocks*. Not everything will translate – it is not possible to translate meaning exactly for all elements in an interpretation. Culture-specific elements will block some attempts at translation.

- *The stereotype*. Avoid negative stereotyping which is likely to increase negotiation conflicts and difficulties.

- *Intercultural preparation*. Good prior preparation in intercultural understanding is a necessary investment to improve international business effectiveness.

Ethical issues in cross-cultural marketing

Cultural sensitivity is often at the heart of the ethical dilemmas that managers face when operating in international markets. There are few, if any, moral absolutes and few actions for which no one can provide reasonable justification. Almost every action can be justified on the basis that it is acceptable in one particular culture. In thinking about ethics managers need to be aware that simply defining what is ethical by the standards, values and actions from their own culture may be insufficient in satisfying all the stakeholders of a multinational enterprise. What is often seen as an acceptable business practice in one culture can be seen as ethically questionable in another. The SRC effect discussed earlier is particularly relevant to the discussion of how cultural sensitivities impact on what is an ethical business practice. Managers from different cultures will always be able to challenge, for instance, the US, African, or Japanese perspective of what is ethical.

The **ethical challenges** facing international marketing managers are many. In recent years such issues as environmental abuse, the use of child labour, poor working conditions and the low levels of pay in Third World factories have received particular attention. Western consumers choosing brands look for reassurance that the product has been produced in what they see as a socially responsible manner Some clothing brands such as, Primark, Nike and Gap have suffered adverse publicity when it has been made known that child labour has been used to produce their products. However, valiant attempts by some brands to ensure ethical standards in their international operations has in some cases led to criticism elsewhere (See Illustration 3.6).

Consumers globally are becoming better informed through better education and faster and more effective communications. Increasingly, therefore, they are able to question the actions of multinational enterprises, as we saw in the discussion of the role of pressure groups in Chapter 1. For their part, while the largest multinationals are extending their influence within the global markets, they are becoming more vulnerable to criticism. Over the past few years quality and service have improved considerably, but now firms are increasingly expected to ensure that their behaviour is ethical and in the interests of the global community which makes up their market.

However, international marketing executives operating across cultures will find themselves facing moral and ethical dilemmas on a daily basis on a wide range of issues when faced with the ethical dilemmas operating in countries where bribery and corruption are endemic.

Table 3.3 Differences in buyer–seller relationships styles

International market	Climate	Importance of relationships	Process	Decision-making
United States	Sometimes viewed as an aggressive or confrontational climate	Of less importance. Focus is on achieving desired results	Ordered process where each point is discussed in sequence	Can be either an individual or group decision process
Canada	Positive, polite climate. Hard sell will not work here	Of less importance. Focus is on achieving desired results	Ordered process where each point is discussed in sequence	Can be either an individual or group decision process
Latin America	Positive and hospitable climate	Personal, one-on-one relationships very important	Relationship building through socialization will precede negotiations	Decisions are usually made by a high-level individual
United Kingdom	Traditional, polite climate. Hard sell will not work here	Of less importance. Focus is on achieving desired results	Ordered process where each point is discussed in sequence	Can be either an individual or group decision process
Germany/ Austria	Rigid, sober climate	Low. Germans remain aloof until negotiations conclude	Systematic process with emphasis on contractual detail	Even the most routine decisions are made by top-level officials
France/ Belgium	Formal, bureaucratic Climate. Hard sell will not work here	Formal, arm's-length relationships with attention to etiquette	French teams use argument to generate discussion	Usually a group process headed by a senior negotiator
Japan	Formal polite climate with many idiosyncratic nuances	Great importance. Long-term relationships are what matter most	First all general items are agreed on, then details are discussed	A total group process with all levels involved in the final decision
China	Bureaucratic climate with an abundance of 'red tape'	Very important. Traditional, cultural courtesies are expected	Discussions are long and repetitive. Agreements must be in writing	Usually a group process headed by a senior negotiator
Russia	Bureaucratic climate with an abundance of 'red tape'	Low. Russians will remain reserved until negotiations conclude	Cumbersome process due to bureaucratic constraints	Usually a group process headed by a senior negotiator

Source: Data adapted from Lewin, J.E. and Johnston, W.L. (1997). 'Managing the International Salesforce'. *Journal of Business and Industrial Marketing*. 12 (3/4).

© Paul Prescott / Alamy

ILLUSTRATION 3.6

Ensuring ethical standards in international operations

A number of global brands have tried hard to ensure they avoid the sort of damaging scandals that have hit the reputation of Nike and Gap by introducing codes of practice with regard to the use of child labour. However, some have found even when trying to operate to high ethical standards there can be unintended consequences. Reebok inaugurated the Reebok Human Rights Production Standards, covering nine areas including 'No Child Labour'. They regularly monitor all suppliers to ensure that child labour is not used in stitching footballs so that their footballs can bear the label 'Guaranteed: Manufactured Without Child Labour'. They also built a centralized stitching factory to ensure better control, but then were criticized because a consequence of moving from home-working to a centralized workplace meant that the number of women in the workforce fell dramatically.

Levi Strauss used to manufacture its own products close to the places where they were sold. It has increasingly sub-contracted the work in low wage locations in Africa and Asia. They developed 'Global Sourcing and Operating Guidelines', stipulating that workers must be at least 15 years of age to work for them or their suppliers. When they found that suppliers were using child labour in Bangladesh, Levi Strauss reportedly negotiated corrective action with their suppliers which involved removing the children from the factories, placing them in education and paying their wages until they reached an age at which they could return to work. The company also supports good causes, including AIDS charities, and (in South Africa) a home for children who have suffered serious physical or sexual abuse.

However market pressures took their toll on Levi Strauss. Sales of its main products, jeans and Dockers casual-wear, has consistently declined since the mid-1990s. The company cut 18 000 jobs in high-wage locations, and has closed 30 factories in North America, and seven in Europe over the last five years. There is now the fear that cutting costs to the bone could damage the integrity of the brand if it is seen to be exploiting the workforce at home while supporting expensive good causes overseas.

Questions

1 Is it possible for a global brand to have a geocentric ethics strategy which meets the needs of all its operations around the globe?

2 How should global companies resolve the ethical dilemmas identified above?

References: BBC World Service.com.Inside Global Giants: 'Levi's – Balancing ethics with profit', and http://www.unicef.org.uk/publications/all.

Bribery and corruption

An integral part of conducting business internationally is the practice of gift-giving. However, in many Western countries such practice is seen as bribery/corruption and is tightly regulated and controlled. Business gift-giving – or bribery, depending on your point of view – if improperly executed, could stop sensitive negotiations and ruin new and potential business relationships. German and Swiss executives tend to feel uncomfortable accepting gifts, which they view as bribes, as they will not want to be seen as being under obligation to the other party. However, business gift-giving in many cultures is an important part of persuasion. In cultures where a business gift is expected but not given, it is an insult to the host.

MANAGEMENT CHALLENGE 3.2

The Moral Challenge of bribery in Nigeria

Nigeria is the economic powerhouse of West Africa and has one of the fastest growing economies in the world. Much of this growth is driven by the gas and oil sectors – Nigeria is the world's eighth largest exporter of oil. Yet 92 per cent of the population lives on less than $2 per day and doing business in Nigeria is notoriously difficult. Chief among the many challenges is the pervasiveness of bribery and corruption in the country. Transparency International ranks Nigeria as one of the world's most corrupt countries. Despite strong government initiatives to tackle the problem, the Economic and Financial Crimes Commission say that bribe payment to government officials by businesses in the country is on the increase. The police, Power Holding Company of Nigeria (PHCN), and the Nigeria Customs Service lead the corruption chart.

The problem for international companies operating in the markets is that bribes are often paid without a precise goal, which means that companies are required to pay bribes often without any clear benefit being given to them or any clear reason being given as to why they have to pay the bribe. This makes carrying out business in Nigeria complex, fraught with difficulties and, expensive. It also presents moral dilemmas to export managers trying to send goods to the Nigerian market as the Nigerian Customs Service may well demand a bribe prior to allowing goods to enter the country. Failure to pay a bribe could result in the goods being returned, simply being lost or being left to stand on the dockside for many months. This presents a moral challenge to managers whose home country has signed up to the OECD Anti-Bribery Convention and are committed to the banning of the payment of any bribe by its citizens in whatever country they are operating.

Question

1 As an export manager, how would you manage the moral dilemma outlined above?

References: http://www.transparency.org/news_room/ and BBC News.co.uk.

Cultures that view bribery as an acceptable business practice tend to fall into the high context category. In such a culture the communication style is more implicit, non-verbal and more reliant on hidden cues in the context of personal relationships. In Japan, for example, a highly developed and affluent society, gift-giving practices are widespread in the business culture. Refusing to participate in gift-giving in such cultures can cause bad feeling and misunderstandings between business clients. In high context cultures, financial inducements are often seen as important steps in bringing a person into the inner circle of a business relationship or to strengthen the relationship between a buyer and a seller.

By contrast, people in low context cultures rely on explicit contracts, communication is more formal and explicit and negotiations based on a more legalistic orientation. Laws applying to bribery tend to be very well laid out. In some cultures, all business gifts will be viewed as illegal bribes; on the other hand, other cultures view gifts, pay-offs and even bribes merely as a cost of business. Bribery and corruption are part of the commercial traditions of many parts of Asia, Africa and the Middle East. Transparency International, a global counter-corruption watchdog, ranks Somalia as the most corrupt country, followed closely behind by Afghanistan and Myanmar. The problem, as outlined in Management Challenge 3.2 is that to many countries bribery and corruption are simply a means of getting business done. To many international marketing managers operating in those markets, how to respond to the demand for a bribe could be a problematic ethical dilemma. It can sometimes be very difficult to empathize with the cultural values of another country if they challenge your own personal morals. Management Challenge 3.2 looks at the case of Nigeria.

Piracy

Piracy has been a particular problem to the global music and software industry.

Different cultures have varying perspectives on piracy. The US courts take a very stringent view and prosecute offenders that are caught. In China and India views on intellectual property rights are much more difficult to define. The International Intellectual Property Alliance claims that despite now being members of the WTO piracy is still a big problem in China.

In China, Havoscope estimate at least US$26 billion-worth of goods sold each year inside the country are counterfeit. However according to Fox News the Chinese authorities are now cracking down on product piracy, in just three months in 2011 they arrested 3001 people, confiscated huge amounts of pirated products and closed some 300 websites selling counterfeit and fake goods.

Worldwide sales of counterfeit goods are estimated by Havoscope to be in the region of US$532.93 Billion Over 5.5 billion cigarettes, or 20 per cent of all cigarettes sold in South Africa, are either smuggled or counterfeit cigarettes. Procter and Gamble estimates that 10–15 per cent of its revenues are lost each year to counterfeit products. The Ukraine now exports counterfeit optical discs, Russia markets counterfeit software, Paraguay markets imitation cigarettes. Counterfeit pharmaceuticals are routinely marketed to countries unable to afford the expensive products of the authentic drug companies; often these are substandard, or have fake labels. It is estimated by the World Health Organization that between 5 and 7 per cent of drugs sold are counterfeits, with potentially fatal consequences.

American industries lose US$200–250 billion a year to counterfeiting. The fact that many global manufacturers have moved their production to low-cost bases around the world is seen by some to have opened the floodgates to counterfeiting. The global brands have been able to take advantage of low labour costs but gave insufficient attention to securing intellectual property rights in such countries. In today's markets, where so much of the added value of a product is in its brand identity, counterfeiters have been able to exploit consumers' expectations of quality and service with counterfeit products. Brands such as Louis Vuitton, Nike, Microsoft, Gucci and Prada are among the most counterfeited of global brands.

Much of the problem stems from cultural attitudes to the rights of anyone to own intellectual property. The Chinese have argued that if all ideas were copyrighted they should be able to patent the compass, ice-cream, noodles and many other products they have given to the world. Recently Starbucks won a high profile case against a Chinese company using the Chinese version of its name, the court ruling that the company had the sole right to its name in both English and Chinese. The French cognac company Hennessey also won a piracy case in China against two companies copying its brand and selling it as French cognac brandy even though it was produced and bottled in China. In Europe, the European Commission has proposed new rules to harmonize member states' legislation on IPR enforcement. This has been particularly important because the EU embraced new members from Eastern Europe, where counterfeiting is a serious problem in some countries.

Although nations and organizations often provide ethical guidelines on bribery, counterfeiting, etc., ultimately international managers have to make decisions based on their own personal views of what is and is not ethical. Managers need to form a view when operating across different cultures as to what constitutes ethical decision-making within an organization. Managers need to reflect on what constitutes ethical behaviour, how decisions will be viewed by stakeholders and the perceived and real impact upon the organization of making a decision that breaches ethical standards. Central is the importance the company places on the need for an ethically responsible approach to their operations in the global markets.

Companies are increasingly of the view that organizational behaviour considered to be unethical can decrease a firm's wealth, while behaviour considered by stakeholders to be ethical can enhance a company's competitive advantage on global markets. Attempting to take an ethically responsible decision, though, could mean the loss of perhaps an efficient and cheap source of supply or in some cases the loss of a potential deal. Any decision would need very careful consideration.

The consequence of an ethically responsible approach would involve increased resources and attention being applied to a number of areas, such as:

- The increased need for accurate and timely information.
- Increased attention to press, public reaction and global pressure groups.
- Closer relationships with stakeholders and members of the supply chain to ensure all interests are taken into consideration.
- Being prepared, when serious risks are identified, to take positive and constructive action.

SUMMARY

- The influence of social and cultural factors in international marketing is complex and often extremely difficult for a firm operating in foreign markets to analyze and understand. In today's global environment, where culture is becoming increasingly de-territorialized and each culture is penetrated by the influences of other cultures, the issue of examining and understanding cultural sensitivities is becoming increasingly complex.

- If the firm is operating across a number of markets, finding consistent methods of analyzing their cross-cultural markets poses particular challenges. The cultural dimensions of Hofstede, the contextual classification of cultures and the GLOBE programme dimensions are three frameworks that can be used.

- This chapter has focused on developing an understanding of the components of culture and how these components impact on consumer beliefs, values, attitudes and purchasing behaviour.

- Culture also affects the way that business is carried out in different markets. Culture underpins the legal structure of a country and ethical attitudes to decision-making and the acceptability of bribes, etc. Managers need to form a view when operating across different cultures as to what constitutes ethical decision-making within an organization and what constitutes ethical behaviour.

- Culture has a significant impact, therefore, on the international marketing strategies of firms, both in consumer and business-to-business markets. In this chapter the reader should have acquired an awareness of the possible methods that can be used to categorize differences across cultures to enable a cross-cultural analysis to be carried out. In Chapter 4 we go on to look at the methods of analyzing and researching international markets.

KEYWORDS

Social and cultural factors	Non-verbal communication	Cross-cultural
Beliefs	Enculturation	Low context cultures
Values	Attitude	High context cultures
Customs	Consumer behaviour	Individualism
Cultural sensitivity	Perception of risk	Ethical challenges
Silent language	Cultural identity	Piracy
Spoken language	Self-reference criterion	

CASE STUDY

© Juanmonino, iStockphoto.com

Islam, Ramadan and the tent business in the Middle East

Ramadan represents one of the five pillars of Islam, which all Muslims are expected to follow, the other four are 'Faith' or *Shahadah*; 'Prayer' or *Salah*, 'Charitable Giving' or *Zakah* and the 'Pilgrimage to Makkah' or *Hajj*. The month of Ramadan is a time for spiritual reflection and prayer. Ramadan is usually observed in the ninth month of the Islamic lunar calendar and is one of the most important months for Muslims as it is believed this is the month that the Quran was first revealed to the Prophet Mohammed. During this month all healthy Muslims fast from sunrise to sunset when they must refrain from all food, drink, gum chewing, any kind of tobacco use and any kind of sexual contact.

Muslims believe their good actions bring greater reward during these 30 days because the month has been blessed by Allah. 'Fasting' reminds Muslims of the suffering of the poor who often don't get to eat well. During the 'holy month' of Ramadan most Muslims will tend to wake up just before sunrise to have a

meal or *Suhoor*. They will then not be able to eat or drink again until sunset when it is traditional to open the fast with a date and then eat and this meal is known as *Iftar*. People open their fasts with a 'date' as it is believed that the Prophet Mohammed broke his fast with such a fruit.

Ramadan has both spiritual and physical significance. Certain individuals and/or groups hold *Iftar* parties (where they prepare lots of food and then invite people round to eat). Ramadan often lasts anything between 29 to 30 days, depending on the sighting of the new moon, which marks the celebration of *Eid El Fitr*. Prior to this final day of celebration, tents and/or marquees are traditionally put up by the privileged to cater for the less privileged in the spirit of *charitable giving* during this sombre and sober month.

Lavish tents and marquees have long been a mainstay of the corporate events industry during the holy month of Ramadan in the Middle East. However, recently due to the financial crisis the marquee business has suffered as big corporations cut spending and marquee companies began to 'feel the pinch'.

Depending on the quality and size of the structure, a complete tent costs a minimum of between Dh200 000 and Dh250 000 (£33 334 and £42 000) for the month of Ramadan alone. Even large businesses such as the likes of Tamani Hotel, Dubai Marina and the Hilton Hotel, Dubai Jumeirah, have moved their *iftars* and *suhoors* indoors after having previously had tents outdoors for the Ramadan period.

Two UAE-based companies, Al-Baddad International and Harlequin Marquees and Event Services both compete in this market so had to start looking further afield in order to maintain sales in the downturn.

Al-Baddad International (henceforth Al-Baddad), a subsidiary of Al-Baddad Global, was established in the UAE capital, Abu Dhabi in 1971 (the same year the country attained independence from Great Britain) by the late Hajj Hassan Al-Baddad. The company is a leading provider of innovative mobile halls and prefabricated buildings in the Middle East and North Africa (MENA) region. The company provides outdoor solutions, exhibitions, conferences, weddings, special events, private occasions, festivals, camps, warehouses and temporary accommodations.

Since its founding, *Al-Baddad* has continually built a business across the Middle East and North African (MENA) region with Egypt and Libya being the latest markets it has entered (see Table 1). The company claims leadership in mobile halls and tents in the

Table 1 Al-Baddad Branches worldwide

Year of entry	City/Country	Year of entry	City/Country
1971	Abu Dhabi (UAE)	2001	Riyadh (Saudi Arabia)
1989	Al-Ain (UAE)	2002	Jeddah (Saudi Arabia)
1989	Sharjah (UAE)	2005	Ras Al-Khaimah (UAE)
1992	Dubai (UAE)	2005	Kuwait
1996	Qatar	2009	Damman (Saudi Arabia)
1996	California (USA)	2010	Egypt
1997	Jordan	2010	Libya

Source: http://www.albaddadintl.com/aboutus.htm

region – manufacturing large quantities of tents and pre-fabricated buildings all year round through a company known as 'Al-Baddad Capital'.

Al-Baddad's marketing strategy is to 'explore, create, and always adopt new techniques and innovations to keep its solutions ahead of the curve', as it strives to guarantee its place among the top suppliers in its industry both regionally and internationally. As one of the major tents companies in the region, it now is facing the challenge of a downturn in business due to a decline in corporate sponsorship and so needs to think through how it might expand into new markets.

Commenting on how they were now faring, Bilal Hamdan, the company's marketing manager remarked that '… this year we were more creative'. This creativity underlined the company's marketing strategy including offering hotels price discounts in exchange for their branding to be displayed at the venues. They also looked at other cultural events and other opportunities across the MENA region having observed that some hotels had decided to use the structures they had set up for the recently concluded FIFA World Cup as Ramadan tents.

The second company Harlequin Marquees & Event Services (*Harlequin* henceforth), established in 1998, is a company that claims to be at the *forefront of Gulf Hospitality*, catering for all the usual events – from product launches to gala dinners and various other festivals. *Harlequin* also boasts Arabesque themed solutions in its opulent Ramadan *Majlis* (an Arabic term meaning 'a place of sitting' used to describe various types of special gatherings) tents.

Founder, Carmen Clews, a former employee of Britain's Royal Air Force air traffic control team, partnered with Charlie Wright to guide the full-service event design and rental company into a 45-employee operation that claims to have some of the world's biggest blue-chip companies as its clients. Indeed the creative enterprise of designing '*modern Arabia*' event environments, complete with frosted arabesque-pattern tent windows and white LED-lit 'star' fabrics, satisfies Harlequin's hunger for unique challenges. The company enjoys a dual advantage. First is the favourable climate – hot weather conditions and the second is the strategic location of the country. Indeed Dubai's location – almost midway between Europe and Asia – makes it both a hub for international commerce and a notable attraction for workers from around the world.

While this presents itself as an opportunity for *Harlequin* who consider themselves '… *fortunate to have a fantastic team who all communicate, listen and talk very well together*', it also poses a cultural challenge with ethnically diverse clientele (Arabic, Asian and/or Western). As part of its marketing strategy, the company considers itself a patient player, '*we have to be extra careful, taking nothing for granted and never assuming anything*'. But while acknowledging the virtue of such patience, Clews was quick to point out that a bit of impulsiveness – '*acting immediately on ideas that feel right*', had got her and Harlequin where they are today.

Like the previous case, *Harlequin* has seen a downturn. According to Camilla Quinn, the client services manager of *Harlequin*, 'we're finding that the main reason hotels have pulled out this year has been because they've not been able to get the sponsorship'. Another member of the company's management team stated, 'We had four clients who were all quite far down the line with putting structures up, but they were all based on receiving corporate sponsorship. With all four of them it fell through at the last minute and they all completely pulled their Ramadan tents.'

Discussion Questions

1 Compare and contrast the social and cultural dimensions of the different market segments *Al-Baddad* and *Harlequin Marquees* are targeting in the MENA region.

2 Compare and contrast the international marketing-mix strategies used by *Al-Baddad* and *Harlequin Marquees* in response to these markets.

Source: Nnamdi O. Madichie, PhD

References: Bundhun, R. (2010) 'Now is the summer of our discount tent', Abu Dhabi: *The National Newspaper*, Business Section, 2 September.

Daniyah Hafiz (2008) 'What is Ramadan?' BBC Lancashire, UK (5 September 2008). Online at: http://www.bbc.co.uk/lancashire/content/articles/2006/10/09/ramadan_feature.shtml [Accessed 3 September 2010]

Huda (about.com) Ramadan Information. Online at: http://islam.about.com/od/ramadan/tp/ramadan-hub.htm; Official website of *Harlequin Marquees & Event Services, online* at http://www.harlequinmarquees.com/

DISCUSSION QUESTIONS

1   Discuss the view that culture lies at the heart of all problems connected with international marketing.

2   What is culture? Is it important for international marketers to take account of it or is globalization going to make it a thing of the past?

3   Given the cultural sensitivities to ethical dilemmas, can there ever be a global harmonization of ethical business practices in international marketing?

4   How do social and cultural influences impact on international business negotiations? Using examples, advise a company preparing for cross-cultural negotiations.

5   It has been suggested that firms from developed countries should market to developing countries by establishing partnerships in a neighbouring developing country. Explain the reasons behind such a proposition and the implications for a firm developing a globalization strategy.

REFERENCES

1.   Blackwell, R.D., Miniard, P.W. and Engel, J.L. (2006) *Consumer behaviour*, 9th edn. The Dryden Press.

2.   Broways, M.J. and Price, R. (2008) *Understanding cross Cultural Management*, Prentice Hall.

3.   Gudykunst, W.B. (2005) *Cross-cultural and intercultural communication*, Sage Publications.

4.   Hall, S. (1997) *Representation: Cultural Representations and Signifying Practices (Culture, Media and Identities series)*, Sage Publications.

5.   Hawkins, D.I., Mothersbaugh, D.L. and Best, R.J. (2009) *Consumer behaviour*, 11th edn. Irwin.

6.   Hofstede, G. (2003) *Culture's consequences: comparing values, behaviours, institutions and organisations across nations*, 2nd edn. Sage.

7.   Hofstede, G., Hofstede, G.J. and Minkov, M. (2010) *Cultures and Organizations: Software for the Mind: Intercultural Cooperation and Its Importance for Survival*, 3rd edn. McGraw Hill.

8.   Jeannet, J.-P. and Hennessey, H.O. (2006) *Global marketing strategies*, 2nd edn. Houghton Mifflin.

9.   Kotler, P., Keller, K.L., Brady, M, Goodman, M. and Hasen, T. (2009) *Marketing management*, Pearson.

10. Lewin, J.E. and Johnston, W.L. (1997) 'Managing the international salesforce', *Journal of Business and Industrial Marketing*, 12 (3/4).

11. Maslow, A.H. (1970) *Motivation and personality*, 2nd edn. Harper and Row.

12. Matsumoto, D. and Van de Vijver, F.J.R. (2010) *Cross Cultural Research Methods in Psychology (Culture & Psychology)*, Cambridge.

13. Sarathy, R., Terpstra, V. and Russow, L.C. (2006) *International marketing*, 9th edn. Dryden Press.

14. Schiffman, L.G., Kanuk, U. and Hansen, H (2008) *Consumer behaviour*, 6th edn. Prentice Hall.

15. Singh, S. (2006) 'Cultural differences in and influences on consumers propensity to adopt innovations', *International Marketing Review*. 23(2) 173–91.

16. Straker, D. (2008) *Changing Minds: in Detail*, Syque Press.

17. Usunier, J.C. and Lee, J.A. (2005) *Marketing across cultures*, 4th edn. FT Prentice Hall.

18. Usunier, J.C. and Lee, J.A. (2009) *Marketing Across Cultures*, 5th Edn. FT Prentice Hall.

CHAPTER 4

INTERNATIONAL MARKETING RESEARCH AND OPPORTUNITY ANALYSIS

LEARNING OBJECTIVES

After reading this chapter you should be able to:

- Appreciate the key roles of marketing research in international marketing

- Understand the concepts and techniques to identify and evaluate opportunities internationally

- Build a market profile analysis of a foreign country market

- Discuss the difficulties and issues that arise in developing multi-country primary research studies

INTRODUCTION

Discussions in previous chapters have illustrated the highly risky and complex environment in which the international marketing manager operates. If a company is to survive in the international marketplace, it is important that it searches for methods to reduce the risk of making a wrong decision as far as possible.

This is why **marketing research** is so fundamentally important to the international marketing process, for while it cannot help a manager reduce risk to the point of zero, it can ensure that the starting point for decision-making is knowledge, rather than guesswork. Lack of knowledge of foreign markets is one of the first major barriers an international marketing manager will encounter. An effective marketing research strategy is the first step in overcoming that barrier.

The purpose of this chapter is to examine the place of marketing research in international strategy and the contribution it makes to the decision-making process. We will, therefore, be examining such concepts as the role of marketing research and opportunity analysis in international markets and the building of an international marketing information system. We will also examine some of the aspects of primary marketing research in international markets and discuss the practicalities and problems in implementing multi-country studies.

The role of marketing research and opportunity analysis

Marketing research can be defined as the systematic gathering, recording, analysis and interpretation of data on problems relating to the marketing of goods and services.

The role of research is primarily to act as an aid to the decision-maker. It is a tool that can help to reduce the risk in decision-making caused by the environmental uncertainties and lack of knowledge in international markets. It ensures that the manager bases a decision on the solid foundation of knowledge and focuses strategic thinking on the needs of the marketplace, rather than the product. Such a role is, of course, necessary in all types of marketing.

In international marketing, because of the increased uncertainties and complexities in world markets, the capacity to ensure a systematic planned process in the research and the use of secondary information, prior to field research, is of paramount importance if quality information is to be obtained. The research process (Malhotra *et al.* 2006) consists of six key stages. These steps are the logical process for any research study to go through in its implementation and will be relevant for all research studies:

1 *Defining the problem*. It is important to decide what information is needed and set the objectives of the research, ensuring it is both commercially worthwhile and that the objective is feasible and achievable.

2 *Developing the approach to be taken*. The planning phase will concern itself with timescales, resources to carry out the work, the expertise required to meet the objectives and the decision as to whether a qualitative or quantitative approach is to be taken.

3 *Designing the research*. In designing the research strategy consideration will be given to the different action steps that need to be taken. Ensuring full use of secondary data sources will be important, as will the use of a pilot study to ensure the development of an effective and meaningful questionnaire.

4 *Carrying out the field work*. Decisions as to how the questionnaires will be administered (telephone, mail, personal interviews or focus groups) will be made as well as decisions as to who will do the work and what resources are required.

5 *Analyzing the data*. The data analysis stage will need to take full account of the objectives of the research and the client's needs. Many researchers will argue that the methodology to be used should be decided in the first stages of the research planning as it will impact on the questionnaire design and how the interviews are administered.

6 *Preparing the report and presentation*. The report and presentation are the researcher's outputs and vital in establishing the credibility of the research methods used and the validity of the findings of the research.

The role of international marketing research

The ability for research to deliver fast and yet sensitively analyzed results across a range of different countries in today's global markets is crucial for competitive success. In the past decade, we have seen the speed of business increase substantively with the global diffusion of computers, digital technologies and instant global telecommunication. Instant communication has become the standard across global markets, which means that marketing research has a critical role in feeding into decision-makers' time-sensitive insights and changes in market behaviours around the globe. As such, the Internet has transformed the way we find information on our customers and track our markets worldwide. Web bases information suppliers are able to offer more selective, dynamic and up to date information to a larger number of user enabling marketers to save on the expensive research costs of collecting data from different countries. Companies worldwide are able to get information that was previously impossible or too expensive to come by if they have access to the web. This is now available 24 hours a day, often at a reasonable cost and sometimes free of charge. This is hugely beneficial to smaller companies for whom accessing up to date information used to be a huge barrier to competing internationally. Now SMEs have the power of information giving them access to new markets worldwide.

The development of better decision tools and decision support systems and of globally based research supplier networks have in turn led to an increase in the usage of continent-wide and worldwide on-line surveys which transcend national boundaries. The development of specialist global niche marketing research strategies and a rapid increase in the rate and spread of product innovation, with which research must keep pace, have all meant that the old days of slow-moving local or national marketing research studies are long gone. In just a short time span the Internet has transformed all areas of marketing research simply because it allows the researcher to make instant connections to multiple sources of competitive and customer information. This enables the researcher to mine for customer information, competitor information and permits marketers to monitor customer activity across the globe with great ease. The use of Social network sites to carry out global marketing research is also expanding rapidly. According to eMarketer's most recent forecast, $4.3 billion is now spent on social networks globally. This increased capability has created an information explosion. The availability of online databases and web enabled information sources have transformed the nature of international marketing research and the role it plays in the marketing process. Global web networks enable companies across the globe to build the ultimate in customization strategies or 'one-to-one' marketing plans. It is estimated that over three quarters of revenue for marketing research agencies is derived from online research. Equally the role of the marketing researcher has become much more closely aligned with the decision-making processes of organizations.

Research into international market issues can incorporate three major roles:

- *cross-cultural research*: the conducting of a research project across nation or culture groups;
- *foreign research*: research conducted in a country other than the country of the commissioning company;
- *multi-country research*: research conducted in all or important countries where a company is represented (Sarathy *et al.* (2006)).

This does not in any way convey the enormity of the task involved in developing an international market intelligence system which would be sufficient to provide the information necessary to make sound international marketing decisions. Such an information system would not only have to identify and analyze potential markets, but also have the capacity to generate an understanding of the many environmental variables discussed in the previous three chapters. Many levels of environmental factors will affect international marketing decisions, from macro-level economic factors to political–legal factors, as well as the micro market structures and cultural factors affecting the consumer. It is a truism of international marketing that in competing internationally uncertainty is generally greater and the difficulties in getting information are also greater. It is frequently said that it is the lack of market knowledge which is the greatest obstacle to companies succeeding on international markets, and it is access to such knowledge that makes it possible for the internationally experienced company to extend their activities to new markets.

As such, the role of the international market researcher is to provide an assessment of market demand globally, an evaluation of potential markets and of the risks and costs involved in market entries, as well as detailed information on which to base effective marketing strategies.

To achieve this, the researcher has three primary functions to carry out:

1 Scanning international markets to identify and analyze the opportunities.
2 Building marketing information systems to monitor environmental trends.
3 Carrying out primary marketing research studies for input into the development of marketing strategies and to test the feasibility of the possible marketing mix options, both in foreign country markets and across a range of international markets.

In the next three sections we will examine each of these in some detail.

Opportunity identification and analysis

Scanning international markets

There are 194 countries in the world (including Taiwan and the Vatican City). Even a large multinational corporation would find it difficult to resource market development in all these countries. Thus, the first task for the researcher is to scan markets to identify which countries have the potential for growth. International markets are scanned primarily at this stage to identify countries that warrant further research and analysis: thus the researcher will look for countries that meet three qualifying criteria:

1 *Accessibility*. If a company is barred from entering the market, it would be an ineffective use of resources to take research further. The scanning unit would assess such things as tariffs, non-tariff barriers, government regulation and import regulations to assess the accessibility of the market. Japan is still seen as a highly profitable market, but it is viewed by some as inaccessible due to the perception of the difficulties involved in overcoming trade barriers.

2 *Profitability*. At this level the researcher would assess factors that at a macro level could render the market unprofitable – for example, the availability of currency, the existence of exchange regulations, government subsidies to local competition, price controls and substitute products. Many countries in Africa are fully accessible, but companies question the ability of trade partners in some of these countries to pay. The extra risk of non-payment reduces the profit return calculations of those markets.

3 *Market size*. An assessment is made of the potential market size to evaluate whether future investment is likely to bear fruit.

The specific indicators a company will look for tend to be very product-and market-specific. Thus a hand tool manufacturer in the north of England specializing in tools for woodworking craftsmen looked for evidence of a hobby market (accessibility), high levels of disposable income (profitability) and large numbers of educated, middle-aged men with leisure time (market size). In Management Challenge 4.1 the reader is asked to consider how H&M, a Swedish clothing retailer should specify each indicator. At the scanning stage the researcher is attempting to identify countries where marketing opportunities exist. Having identified those opportunities, the researcher will need to make an assessment of their viability for further investigation. In principle, there are three types of market opportunities:

1 Existing markets. Here customers' needs are already serviced by existing suppliers; therefore, market entry would be difficult unless the company has a superior product or an entirely new concept to offer the market.

2 Latent markets. In this type of market there are recognized potential customers but no company has yet offered a product to fulfil the latent need. As there is no direct competition, market entry would be easier than in existing markets as long as the company could convey the benefits of its product to the market. Coca-Cola and Pepsi Cola dominate the global market. Qibla Cola, however, has tapped into a latent market by targeting consumers who do not want to buy a Western global brand. They launched their cola not on its product benefits but as an alternative for consumers around the globe who oppose western policies in the Middle East and who wish to support ethical causes, as well as that Qibla gives 10 per cent of all profits made to good causes. Management Challenge 4.2 asks you to think through why the Saudi Arabian market is a latent market for a technology company.

3 Incipient markets. Incipient markets are ones that do not exist at present but conditions and trends can be identified that indicate the future emergence of needs that, under present circumstances, would be unfulfilled. It may be, of course, that existing companies in the market are positioning themselves to take advantage of emerging markets but at present there is no direct competition.

The nature of competitive products can be analyzed in a broadly similar way, with three distinct product types: competitive products, improved products and breakthrough products. A competitive

H&M identify potential markets

H&M is a Sweden based company. The firm designs, produces and retails clothing items and accessories (including cosmetic products). Its range of product includes clothing for men, women and children. The company aims to reflect international trends through different concepts and ranges of clothes that cover different 'style' with above all classics, basics and, a line depending on international trends.

They currently operate approximately 2000 retail outlets in 37 countries. Its major markets are in Germany, Sweden and the UK. The company also allows its customers to buy on the Internet through their online shop although this is not available in all the countries in which it operates.

H&M has a keen understanding of its target market – which is the low price, high fashion end of the clothing sector – and is closely attuned to what mainstream consumers want. It enjoys a strong following among women, particularly those in younger age groups, who make up the majority of its customers. By selling a broad range of fashionable collections which are renewed frequently, by offering attractive prices, and by maintaining a strong presence in prime shopping locations, H&M has ensured its stores enjoy a steady flow of customers.

Question

1 In scanning global markets what indicators with regard to: accessibility, profitability and market size should H&M monitor, to identify countries with potential development opportunities?

product is one that has no significant advantages over those already on offer. An improved product is one that, while not unique, represents an improvement upon those currently available. A breakthrough product, by way of contrast, represents an innovation and as such, is likely to have a significant competitive advantage.

The level and nature of competition that a firm will encounter can, therefore, be analyzed by relating the three types of market demand to the three types of competitive products. This is illustrated in Figure 4.1 and can be used as a basis for determining first, whether market entry is likely to succeed, and second, whether the company possesses any degree of competitive advantage. This, in turn, provides an insight into the nature of the marketing task needed. In saying this, however, it needs to be emphasized that this sort of insight provides an initial framework for analysis and nothing more. What is then needed is a far more detailed assessment of the degree of competitive advantage that the company possesses.

Obviously the greatest opportunities, together with the greatest risk and potential for profit, are in the identification of incipient markets. The problem is that because markets do not yet exist there is no market data. Researchers, therefore, use analytical techniques to make sure they identify and recognize conditions in incipient markets, thus enabling their companies to develop strategies by which to be first into the market.

In the research techniques used, the basic principle is to compare, contrast or correlate various factors in the market under study with some external variant to identify similarities within the market or with other markets, thus assessing whether the right conditions exist for a market to emerge.

Some of the key techniques used are now discussed.

Demand pattern analysis

In this technique, it is assumed that countries at different levels of economic development have differing patterns of demand and consumption. By comparing the pattern of demand in the country under study with the pattern of demand in an established market when the product was first introduced, a broad estimate of an incipient market can be achieved.

FIGURE 4.1 Nature of competition and level of market development

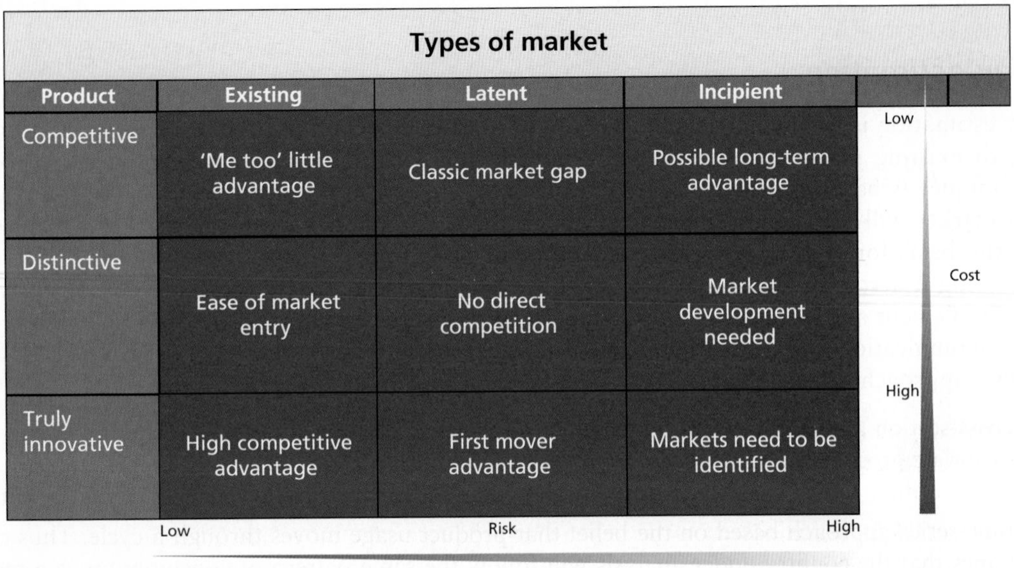
Types of market
Product
Existing
Latent
Incipient
Competitive
'Me too' little advantage
Classic market gap
Possible long-term advantage
Distinctive
Ease of market entry
No direct competition
Market development needed
Truly innovative
High competitive advantage
First mover advantage
Markets need to be identified
Low
Cost
High
Low
Risk
High

MANAGEMENT CHALLENGE 4.2

Optcan assess Saudi Arabia

A Canadian company, Optcan, is in the business of Free Space Optics (FSOs), an emerging technology that transports data via laser technology. They are considering entering the Saudi Arabian market and so wish to carry out a feasibility study to help them decide whether they should set up a presence in the market. However, there is no actual market data as there is no company, as yet, operating directly in the market. The company hope that once they are established in Saudi Arabia to expand into countries such as UAE, Kuwait, Oman and Qatar. However, in these countries too the shortage of data is often a problem for researchers trying to evaluate market potential.

Questions

1 How should Optcan evaluate whether Saudi Arabia is potentially viable and how should they assess the level of potential risks involved?

2 How should they approach researching the countries they wish to expand into?

Multiple factor indices

This assumes that the demand for a product correlates to demand for other products. By measuring demand for the correlated product, estimates of potential demand can be made. For example, a manufacturer of frozen foods may make an assessment by measuring the number of houses with freezers. Not all market potential indexes are developed from a single comparison; some are combinations of several factors, occasionally as many as 20. Many of these indexes are developed by particular companies or industries to measure market potentials for their products in a given country where the market is seen as incipient. Multiple market indexes are designed to measure the relative potentials of different markets for a particular product. Such indexes have the advantage of taking into account several factors that influence the sales of the given product and so help the company identify potential markets.

Analogy estimation

Analogy estimation is used where there is a lack of market data in a particular country. Analogies are made with existing markets comparing and contrasting certain ratios to test for market potential. This techniques is based on the theory of diffusion of innovation. It assumes that the innovation in the new market will diffuse and develop in much the same manner as in the market which is being used as the basis for comparison. This technique arouses mixed levels of enthusiasm, since experiences of using it across international markets have been variable. In addition, it is an expensive technique to implement and doubts have been expressed about the accuracy of its forecasts in a world of instant communication and global launches of new products. Those who have used it typically adopt one of two approaches:

- A cross-section approach, where the product market size for one country is related to some appropriate gross economic indicator in order to establish a ratio. This ratio is then applied to the specific country under analysis to estimate the potential for the product market in that country.
- A time-series approach based on the belief that product usage moves through a cycle. Thus one assumes that the country under analysis will follow the same pattern of consumption as a more advanced economy, albeit with a predetermined time lag.

Macrosurvey technique

This method is essentially anthropological in approach and can help companies to establish themselves early in emerging countries with obvious long-term marketing benefits. The technique is based on the notion that as a community grows and develops, more specialized institutions come into being. Thus, one can construct a scale of successively more differentiated institutions against which any particular country can be evaluated to assess its level of development and hence its market potential.

These techniques highlight the importance of comparative research and regular market screening if incipient demand is to be identified at an early stage. However, the value of several of the techniques does rest upon the assumption that all countries and their consumption patterns will develop along broadly common lines. If firms are to make effective use of many of these techniques, the assumption of common economic development patterns must stand. Increasingly, however, evidence is emerging to suggest that global commonality does not exist to this degree and there are strong arguments for companies grouping country markets for the purposes of this sort of comparative analysis.

Risk evaluation

As previously stated, incipient markets offer the greatest opportunity for profit potential, but with profit comes risk.

The risk factor in opportunity analysis cannot be over-estimated. Sometimes political risk itself can be the most important determining factor to the success or failure of an international marketing campaign. In the markets where opportunities have been identified, researchers need to make an assessment first as to the type of risk apparent in that market (political, commercial, industrial or financial), and second as to the degree of that risk. Matrices such as the one identified in Figure 4.2 can be useful in carrying out such assessments.

Over recent years marketers have developed various indices to help assess the risk factor in the evaluation of potential market opportunities. Nowadays a number of such indices are readily available on line. The Knaepen package, an OECD sponsored classification, and the Business Environment Risk Index (BERI), are perhaps two of the most well known ones.

FIGURE 4.2 The four-risk matrix

Country						
Risk level Risk type	A Low	B Moderate	C Some	D Risky	E Very risky	F Dangerous
Political Commercial						
Industrial Financial						

The Knaepen Package

The Knaepen Package, is a system for assessing country credit risk and classifying countries into eight country risk categories (0–7). It measures the country credit risk, i.e. the likelihood that a country will service its external debt. The classification of countries has two basic components:

1 the Country Risk Assessment Model (CRAM), which produces a quantitative assessment of country credit risk; and

2 a qualitative assessment which considers, political risk, commercial and other risk factors not taken into account in the CRAM model.

The final classification, is a consensus decision of Country Risk Experts who meet several times a year. These meetings are organized so as to guarantee that every country is reviewed whenever a fundamental change is observed and at least once a year. The list of country risk classifications is published after each meeting.

Business Enhancement Risk Index (BERI)

The BERI provides country risk forecasts for 50 countries throughout the world and is updated three times a year. This index assesses 15 environment factors, including political stability, balance of payments volatility, inflation, labour productivity, local management skills, bureaucratic delays, etc. Each factor is rated on a scale of 0–4 ranging from unacceptable conditions (0) to superior conditions (4). The key factors are individually weighted to take account of their importance. For example, political stability is weighted by a factor of 2.5. The final score is out of 100 and scores of over 80 indicate a favourable environment for investors and an advanced economy. Scores of less than 40 indicate very high risk for companies committing capital.

The main value of subscribing to such indices is to give companies an appreciation of the risk involved in opportunities identified. There are a number of organizations around the globe who publish country risk ratings – Standard and Poor, the OECD, *The Economist* and Moodys – so information on risk evaluation is readily available to the Internet researcher.

Major global corporations such as IBM, Microsoft and ICI have specialist political risk analysts, monitoring environmental trends to alert senior managers to changes and developments which may affect their markets.

International marketing segmentation

At the scanning stage, the manager researching international markets is identifiying and then analyzing opportunities to evaluate which markets to prioritize for further research and development. Some framework is then needed to evaluate those opportunities and try to reduce the plethora of countries to a more manageable number. To do this, managers need to divide markets into groups so they can decide which markets to prioritize or even to target.

Market segmentation is the strategy by which a firm partitions a market into submarkets or segments likely to manifest similar responses to marketing inputs. The aim is to identify the markets on which a company can concentrate its resources and efforts so that they can achieve maximum penetration of that market, rather than going for a market-spreading strategy where they aim to achieve a presence, however small, in as many markets as possible.

The Pareto law usually applies to international marketing strategies with its full vigour. The most broad-based and well-established international firms find that 20 per cent of the countries they serve generate at least 80 per cent of the results. Obviously these countries must receive greater managerial attention and allocation of resources. The two main bases for segmenting international markets are by geographical criteria (i.e. countries) and transnational criteria (i.e. individual decision-makers).

Geographical criteria

The traditional practice is to use a country-based classification system as a basis for categorizing international markets. The business portfolio matrix (Figure 4.3) is indicative of the approach taken by many companies. In this, markets are classified in three categories.

FIGURE 4.3 Business portfolio matrix

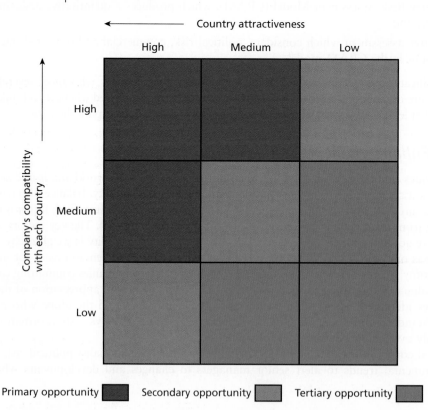

Source: Adapted from: Harrell, G.D. and Keifer, R.D. (1993) 'Multinational Market Portfolio in Global Strategy Development', *International Marketing Review* 10 (1), Emerald Insight.

The business portfolio matrix

Primary opportunity These markets indicate the best opportunities for long-term strategic development. Companies may want to establish a permanent presence and so embark on a thorough research programme.

Secondary opportunity These are the markets where opportunities are identified but political or economic risk is perceived as being too high to make long-term irrevocable commitments. These markets would be handled in a more pragmatic way due to the potential risks identified. A comprehensive marketing information system would be needed.

Tertiary opportunity These are the catch-what-you-can markets. They will be perceived as high risk and so the allocation of resources will be minimal. Objectives in such countries would be short term and opportunistic, companies would give no real commitment. No significant research would be carried out.

Figure 4.3 illustrates the business portfolio matrix. The horizontal axis evaluates the attractiveness of each country on objective and measurable criteria (e.g. size, stability and wealth). The vertical axis evaluates the firm's compatibility with each country on a more subjective and judgemental basis. Primary markets would score high on both axes.

This is a particularly useful device for companies operating in a portfolio of markets to prioritize market opportunity. Ford Tractor carried out such an analysis of key markets. In assessing market attractiveness they explored four basic elements:

1 market size;
2 market growth rate;
3 government regulations; and
4 economic and political stability.

Competitive strength and compatibility were defined in the international context and such factors as market share, market representation, contribution margin and market support were examined. Using this analysis they identified Kenya, Pakistan and Venezuela as primary markets.

Equally, a company may use the BERI index, Hofstede's cultural dimensions or the Knaepen package as a basis for classifying countries. Whatever measurement base is used, once the primary markets have been identified, companies then normally use standard methods to segment the markets within countries using such variables as demographic/economic factors, lifestyles, consumer motivations, geography, buyer behaviour, psychographics, etc.

Thus the primary segmentation base is geographic (by country) and the secondary bases are within countries. The problem here is that depending on the information base, it may be difficult to fully formulate secondary segmentation bases. Furthermore, such an approach can run the risk of leading to a differentiated marketing approach which may leave the company with a very fragmented international strategy.

Infrastructure/marketing institution matrix

Sheth and Arma (2005) suggest international markets be categorized by the country's infrastructure and marketing institutional development. A country's infrastructure development refers to roads, telecommunication, legislative bodies, open and free justice systems, etc. Infrastructure development is usually associated with economic development. The availability of media efficiency of the distribution channels are used as indicators for marketing institutional development as it is associated with competitive marketing offerings, i.e. competitive, efficient and effective marketing institutions, are available to marketers in country with highly developed marketing institutions, which generally includes efficient and effective distribution channels.

Using these dimensions countries can be classified as *Developed infrastructure and developed marketing institutions*, e.g. the US, UK and Scandinavia. *Developed infrastructure but restricted marketing development*, e.g. Japan and Germany. Examples of marketing development restrictions are countries that have time restrictions on when the store can be open (e.g. Germany) or restrictions on the size of stores (e.g. Japan). *Low levels of infrastructure development but have developed marketing institutions* such as retailers and media, e.g. India and Mexico. The last category is both low *infrastructure development and low marketing institutional development*. Typically these are countries that have not developed efficient and effective distribution systems due to geography (e.g. Indonesia) or legal restrictions (e.g. Vietnam).

A major drawback with the country-based approach is that countries do not buy products, consumers do. Global markets, therefore, need to be understood in terms of groups of buyers who share the need and desire for a product and the ability to pay for it, not just those who share a national border (as is the case in Illustration 4.1). If companies are to establish brand positions across a number of international markets, an increasingly common strategic goal, then they need to use a segmentation strategy that enables them to build a consistent brand position across those markets. If a company is to try to achieve a consistent and controlled marketing strategy across all its international markets, it needs a transnational approach to its segmentation strategy. If the basis for global market segmentation is one that cuts across national boundaries, then marketing strategies can be developed that will work for similar segments around the globe.

Transnational segmentation

Buyers in any particular segment seek similar benefits from and exhibit similar behaviour in buying a product. According to Hassan and Stephen (2005), although these consumers may live in different areas of the world and come from very different backgrounds and value systems, they have commonalities in association with a given global brand. To achieve a transnational approach to segmentation therefore, a country as a unit of analysis is too large to be of operational use. An alternative approach is to examine the individual decision-maker (Hassan and Stephen 2005). Key bases for segmentation would include such variables as value systems, demographic, psychographic and behavioural criteria.

Demographic variables have obvious potential as cross-national segmentation criteria. The most commonly used variables include sex, age, income level, social class and educational achievement. Frequently use is made of a battery of demographic variables when delineating transnational market segments.

Psychographic segmentation involves using lifestyle factors in the segmentation process. Appropriate criteria are usually of an inferred nature and concern consumer interests and perceptions of 'a way of living' in regard to work and leisure habits. Critical dimensions of lifestyle thus include activities, interests and opinions. Objective criteria, normally of a demographic nature, may also be helpful when defining lifestyle segments. Research International, when researching the transnational segments of young adults globally, divided them into four broad categories. 'Enthusiastic materialists' are optimistic and aspirational and to be found in developing countries and emerging markets like India and Latin America. 'Swimmers against the tide', on the other hand, demonstrate a degree of underlying pessimism, tend to live for the moment and are likely to be found in southern Europe. In northern Europe, the US and Australasia consumers are the 'new realists', looking for a balance between work and leisure with some underlying pessimism in outlook and, finally, the 'complacent materialists' are defined as passively optimistic and located in Japan.

Behavioural variables also have a lot of potential as a basis for global market segmentation. In particular, attention to patterns of consumption and loyalty in respect of product category and brand can be useful, along with a focus on the context for usage. Variables such as the benefit sought or the buying motivations may be used. Behaviourally defined segments may be identified in terms of a specific aspect of behaviour which is not broad enough to be defined as a lifestyle. Goodyear have effectively used behavioural characteristics to develop a global segmentation strategy (see Illustration 4.2).

Mosaic Global

One of the trends enabling segmentation using individualistic characteristics to become a feasible strategy for many companies is the development of geodemographic databases. One such database is the Mosaic Global from Experian. Mosaic Global is a single, consistent classification providing insight and

ILLUSTRATION 4.1

Corporates go ethnographic

While retailers mine data from microchipped loyalty cards to segment markets and target special offers, this kind of number-crunching misses the bigger picture of how products are chosen and how they could be improved. A heightened level of understanding and insight can generate the breakthroughs companies need and seek to create a competitive advantage on global markets. To make sure their products succeed across national boundaries global brands are turning to ethnographic market research. As the costs of launching new products rises exponentially companies have to minimize the risk of failure, and ethnographical research, a technique developed by anthropologists can help them develop deep insights into their global market segments and develop innovative marketing platforms. Ethnographic research is the systematic study of how people go about their daily living. In the business world it means actually observing how customers use products and services and make buying decisions

Today, corporations such as IBM, Microsoft, Pitney Bowes, Procter & Gamble and Intel have in-house ethnographers.

Like many high-tech companies, Intel makes long-term bets on how markets will develop. They ask such questions as:

- Will television and PC technology converge?
- Will today's consumers retain their TV habits and web search activities as they age, or are they comfortable shifting to new media?
- Will smartphones take over most of the functions of personal computers?

However, people often can't articulate what they're looking for in products or services. By understanding how people live, researchers discover otherwise elusive trends that inform the company's future strategies. With smartphones, for example, they can contrast the technology perspectives of teenagers, who have used cell phones since they were in elementary school, with those of older generations, who came to them only after becoming proficient with PCs. The job of the ethnographic researcher is to help Intel understand their consumers and translate that into understanding how future markets will develop. Ethnography has proved so valuable at Intel that the company now employs two dozen anthropologists and other trained ethnographers, probably the biggest such corporate staff in the world.

Question

1 What do you see as the major advantages and disadvantages of the use of ethnographic research by Intel?

References: Jackson, S. (2009) http://www.examiner.com/business-commentary; Anderson, K. (2009) *Ethnographic Research: A Key to Strategy*, Harvard Business Review.

understanding on the demographics, lifestyles and behaviour of 880 million people from the world's most prosperous economies including North America, Europe and Asia Pacific.

It is based on the idea that the world's cities share common patterns of residential segregation. Each have their enclaves of Metropolitan Strugglers, suburbs of Career and Family and communities of Sophisticated Singles, and each of these can be characterized into neighbourhoods that display strong similarities in terms of their demographics, lifestyles and behaviour, regardless of where they are found. The result is a classification that identifies ten distinct neighbourhood types each with a set of distinctive demographic and lifestyle characteristics that can be found in every country covered by the classification.

The Ten Mosaic Global types are:

- Sophisticated Singles
- Bourgeois Prosperity

- Career and Family
- Comfortable Retirement
- Routine Service Workers
- Hard Working Blue Collar
- Metropolitan Strugglers
- Low Income Elders
- Post Industrial Survivors
- Rural Inheritance.

ILLUSTRATION 4.2

© Kelvin Webb / Alamy

Goodyear global segmentation research

Goodyear is one of the world's largest tyre companies, with operations in most regions of the world. Together with its subsidiaries and joint ventures, Goodyear develops, markets and sells tyres for most applications. It has 57 plants in 23 countries. Goodyear is the world's 3rd largest tyre maker and aims to be a market-focused tyre company providing superior products and services to end-users and to their channel partners.

Goodyear were one of the first companies in this sector to develop a transnational segmentation strategy that could be applied globally to their world markets. The requirement was that the strategy would provide a practical base for a global marketing strategy and prove to be consistent and durable.

After considerable research they identified three decision orientations which could constitute primary attitude segments when buying tyres: brand, outlet and price.

From consumer research they then developed six consumer segments:

1 The *Prestige Buyer* makes the brand decision first and the outlet decision second. This segment is male-dominated, very 'upscale', brand and retailer loyal, does very little information-gathering prior to making a purchase and is predisposed to major brands.

2 The *Comfortable Conservative* looks for the outlet first and the brand second. This segment has the same characteristics of the first group but includes more women who are dependent on the retailer for expert advice. These shoppers tend to develop a lasting relationship with a retailer.

3 The *Value Shopper* considers brand first and price second. This segment is seen as Mr Average. Its members are predisposed to major brands, have a very low retailer loyalty and search for information extensively to educate themselves prior to making the purchase.

4 The *Pretender* wants a major brand but the price ultimately determines the choice. The first decision is price, the second is brand. This group has two sub segments – the aspiring young and emulating old – but all these shoppers exhibit very little loyalty to retailers or brands and do a lot of information searching.

5 The *Trusting Patron* chooses the outlet first and the price second. This group is somewhat 'downscale', heavily female and extremely retailer loyal. The brand is totally unimportant and little searching for information is undertaken.

6 The *Bargain Hunter* shops for price first, outlet second but price is really the only consideration. This group primarily consists of young, 'downscale' people who have low retailer and brand loyalty and who delay the tyre purchase as long as possible.

Question

1 Do you think these segments are valid across all global markets?

The distribution of these typologies can be mapped by country and across the 29 countries in which it operates. Given the addresses of a company's customers, the system gives the researcher the ability to identify the type of people using certain products and services and to identify at a local level where the similar geodemographic types are, thus acting as an aid to the segmentation of markets and the identification of primary and secondary markets. Mosaic Global will also be of use in identifying the sample in a research survey and for building lists in a direct marketing exercise.

Despite the attractiveness of using individualistic characteristics, it is apparent there is strong potential for significant differences in the patterns of consumer behaviour within global segments derived using this method. Also, international similarities in lifestyle and behaviour do tend to be specific, and relevant primarily to specialist products and niche markets.

Hierarchical country – consumer segmentation

To overcome some of the above problems, a compromise approach would be to implement a procedure for global segmentation which integrated features of both processes.

Hassan and Stephen (2005) propose a hierarchical approach to global market segmentation that takes into account country factors but also incorporates individual behaviourist characteristics into a segmentation strategy that helps companies develop cross-national segments to allow for a global positioning strategy.

On this basis the marketing strategy would build on the premise that world markets consist of both similarities and differences and that the most effective strategies reflect a full recognition of similarities and differences *across* rather than *within* markets. Thus, companies competing internationally should segment markets on the basis of consumers, not countries. Segmentation by purely geographical factors leads to national stereotyping. It ignores the differences between customers within a nation and ignores similarities across boundaries. Colgate and Palmolive reached such a conclusion when carrying out an analytical review of their own segmentation strategies, and now use the hierarchical approach.

Any global segmentation strategy needs to be carried out in stages:

1 Identify those countries that have the infrastructure to support the product and are accessible to the company.

2 Screen those countries to arrive at a shorter list of countries with the characteristics that make the market attractive, e.g. a frozen dessert manufacturer may say that for a market to be attractive they need to beat at least five million refrigerators per market.

3 Develop mini-segments within these countries based on factors such as:

   ■ information search behaviour;
   ■ product characteristics required.

   The outcome of this process would be a series of mini-segments within qualified countries.

4 The development of transnational segments begins by looking for similarities across segments. Factor analysis of the behavioural patterns of these segments would enable managers to understand the characteristics of the demand of each segment as regards marketing mix issues. Each mini-segment would, therefore, be rated on several strategic factors in terms of potential response.

5 Cluster analysis is then used to identify meaningful cross-national segments, each of which, it is thought, would evoke a similar response to any marketing mix strategy.

It is argued that this approach would enable marketers to design strategies for cross-national segments and so take a more consumer-orientated approach to international marketing. In prioritizing markets, companies would use consumers as their primary base. Some writers argue that companies still need a secondary segmentation stage to identify the key countries where these transnational segments can be found.

The market profile analysis

Analyzing foreign country markets

Having completed the scanning stage, the researcher will have reduced the number of potential countries to a feasible list requiring further research. The researcher needs then to systematically evaluate the markets identified and to build an analytical picture of the foreign country markets. This is primarily the role of the market profile analysis.

In building a market profile, the objective of the company is first, to develop a cost-effective information flow between the environment in which the company operates and the head office decision-makers and, second, to use a consistent approach to facilitate cross country comparisons.

Using the 12C environmental analysis model in Table 4.1, this can help the researcher achieve these two objectives. The information input into the 12C analysis will help the researcher to draw up a market profile analysis, as shown in Figure 4.4.

The objective of a market profile analysis is to enable the company to use the environmental information to identify opportunities and problems in the potential marketing strategies. For example, the fact that television advertising is prohibited in a country will have major implications for a promotional strategy.

It is this type of detailed assessment that helps companies determine the degree of competitive advantage they may possess and the most appropriate method of market entry. Using consistent frameworks also enables the researcher to make cross-country comparisons much more easily.

Sources of information

In building a MIS, companies would utilize a variety of information services and sources. The starting point for most international researchers in the UK is UK Trade and Investment. This government department helps businesses export and grow overseas, and provides a variety of support services to such organizations. The majority of Western nations have similar government-sponsored organizations helping exporters to develop information on international markets.

Some reports have been critical of the deficiencies in the provision of market intelligence by government departments and of firms' abilities to use this information. The main criticisms are:

- information is non-specific to particular industries;
- firms experience problems with the bureaucratic nature of some government services;
- data is often in a form which is unsuitable for the company's needs, or too general to be of use;
- services have been available only in the capital city;
- inadequate publicity about the information and services available.

Other institutions that offer advice and information to companies researching international markets include:

- business libraries
- university libraries
- international chambers of commerce
- UK Trade and Investment: national and regional international marketing intelligence centres
- local business links
- embassies
- banks
- trade associations
- export councils
- overseas distributors
- overseas sales subsidiaries
- foreign brokerage houses
- foreign trade organizations.

Table 4.1 The 12C framework for analyzing international markets

Country
- general country information
- basic SLEPT data
- impact of environmental dimensions

Concentration
- structure of the market segments
- geographical spread

Culture/consumer behaviour
- characteristics of the country
- diversity of cultural groupings
- nature of decision-making
- major influences of purchasing behaviour

Choices
- analysis of supply
- international and external competition
- characteristics of competitors
- import analysis
- competitive strengths and weaknesses

Consumption
- demand and end use analysis of economic sectors that use the product
- market share by demand sector
- growth patterns of sectors
- evaluation of the threat of substitute products

Contractual obligations
- business practices
- insurance
- legal obligations

Commitment
- access to market
- trade incentives and barriers
- custom tariffs

Channels
- purchasing behaviour
- capabilities of intermediaries
- coverage of distribution costs
- physical distribution
- infrastructure
- size and grade of products purchased

Communication
- promotion
- media infrastructure and availability
- which marketing approaches are effective
- cost of promotion
- common selling practices
- media information

Capacity to pay
- pricing
- extrapolation of pricing to examine trends
- culture of pricing
- conditions of payment
- insurance terms

Currency
- stability
- restrictions
- exchange controls

Caveats
- factors to beware of

FIGURE 4.4 Market profile analysis

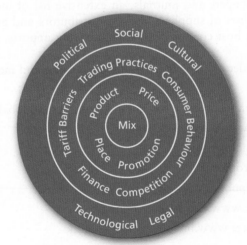

Online databases

As previously stated in an earlier section of this chapter, one of the main developments in the availability of secondary information for international markets is the plethora of web based information sites, online databases, company customer response management (CRM) databases and online research services.

Online databases are systems which hold computerized information which can be accessed through the Internet, making a wide range of information available from an online database to a manager in a matter of seconds. Information can be transmitted from anywhere in the world instantaneously, bringing obvious benefits.

There are numerous advantages in using online databases. They are regularly updated – two or three times per day – and are therefore much more current than traditional printed sources. Retrieving information online is much more cost-effective than manual searching and is considerably faster. Online databases can be accessed 24 hours a day, seven days a week. You also retrieve – and consequently pay for – only the information you want.

Online data sources can also be a solution for carrying out cross-cultural marketing research when primary data collection is prohibitive due to its cost. Marketing information globally is now becoming much more consolidated as global organizations develop databases that are excellent for cross-country comparisons and for accessing global market information. Table 4.2 gives examples of some of the globally based online databases that managers wishing to carry out comparative studies or globally based marketing research may find useful.

Organizations in developing countries are increasingly using online computerized databases for their market research work as they become better equipped with telecommunication facilities. The type and volume of trade information available through online databases has expanded dramatically over recent years, with new databases of interest to business and trade organizations continuously being introduced to the market.

The use of the Internet for marketing intelligence, therefore, is one of the most important ways in which connectivity can improve a firm's ability to develop international markets. Buying or commissioning market research reports can be a prohibitively expensive business. For a fraction of the cost, and in some cases free of charge, much of the same information can be gathered electronically. Given the time and expense associated with the collection of primary data, the use of web based online databases are now central to building marketing information on international markets. However, researchers do need to be wary using such databases and ensure they fully evaluate the credibility and worthiness of the data they obtain from such sources to ensure the accuracy and validity. The volume of relevant international marketing information available on the Internet is too extensive to describe in detail in this chapter, but includes numerous online newspapers and journals, an extensive list of individual country and industry market research reports, trade lists of suppliers, agents, distributors and government contacts in a large number of countries, details on host country legislation covering imports, agency agreements, joint ventures, etc.

Some of the best sites for undertaking general country screening and international marketing research include:

- Brand data: www.brandchannel.com; www.gbrands.com; www.globalstrategies.com
- *BusinessWeek*: www.businessweek.com
- *The Economist*: www.economist.com
- European Union: http://europa.eu/
- Google: www.google.com/publicdata
- UK Trade and Investment: www.uktradeinvest.gov.uk
- UK Chambers of Commerce: www.britishchambers.org.uk
- United Nations: www.un.org
- World Bank: www.worldbank.org
- World Fact Book: www.cia.gov/cia/publications/factbook
- World Trade Organization: www.wto.org

Table 4.2 Online databases

Company Information	
Duns Marketing Database:	166.5 million business records globally
European Kompass:	26 million companies in 19 countries
DataStream:	Financial data on companies worldwide
Extel:	Worldwide company and market information
Predicast:	Overview of market and technology Company data
Trade Data	
Google public data:	Large global publicly available datasets
WTO gateway:	World Trade Organization data sets
Reuters:	Global market data
UN Comtrade:	Global Merchandize Trade Statistics
Global Trade Information Services:	International merchandize trade data
Croners:	Comprehensive guide to exporting goods to over 170 countries
Eurostat:	Detailed statistics on the EU countries
IMF/World Bank/UN:	World trade statistics
Market Information	
MINTEL	Global market and consumer data
Business Monitor International:	Analysis, ratings, rankings and forecasts covering 175 countries and 22 industry sectors
CIA World fact book	Profiles of countries and territories around the world
Euro Monitor:	International market intelligence
Profound/MAID:	Full text market research reports

These are just a few examples of the large number of websites which provide access to sources of international trade and marketing data as well as other useful services.

Problems in using secondary data

In carrying out marketing research internationally, problems arise by virtue of the very nature of the number and complexities of the markets being investigated. While the use of secondary data is essential in international marketing research, the reader needs to be aware of its limitations and some of the problems that occur in using secondary data.

Perhaps the most frequently discussed issue is the availability and accessibility of quality secondary information in international markets. The collection of secondary data concerning the economy and the business infrastructure in some countries varies in quality and consistency, and evaluation of secondary data is critical for international marketing research. Different countries, even for internationally based statistics, may report different values for a given statistic, such as GDP, because of differences in the way the unit is defined. Measurement units may not be equivalent across countries and the accuracy of secondary data may also vary from country to country. Business and income statistics are affected by the taxation structures and the extent of tax evasion. Population censuses may vary in frequency and year in which the data is collected.

One of the reasons for the distortion of data in some countries is the political considerations of governments. The International Labour Organization found the actual unemployment rate in Russia was 10 per cent rather than the officially reported 2 per cent. The Indian government estimates that India's middle class numbers 250 million but, according to a recent survey of consumer patterns conducted by the National Council of Applied Economic Research in Delhi, the Indian middle-class probably totals 100 million at best and there is much stratification among them. This problem might be solved by obtaining authentic data from international organizations such as the OECD, EU, World Bank, etc.

The inconsistencies which can be found in the classification of various types of data in various countries are also a problem when carrying out any comparative analysis across markets. Sarathy *et al.* (2006) say that the most important problem associated with the secondary data, especially in developing countries, is its scarcity. A further problem which can be quite misleading is the timeliness of the collected secondary data: it might have been collected several years earlier and never updated and is therefore outdated and of little value for future planning. Thus it can be a problem when accessing on-line databases where the year the data actually refers to may be a few years before the actual publication date. This may result in the researcher being misled into thinking they are viewing current data.

Many countries attempt to attract foreign investment by overstating certain factors that make the economic picture look better. On the other hand, some countries understate certain factors, making the economic situation appear worse in order to attract foreign aid.

The Asia-Pacific market is an important market and so obtaining reliable information in this region is of crucial importance for many companies. In a recent survey by INSEAD of one thousand managers of European companies operating in the Asia-Pacific region, it was found that only in Japan and Singapore were companies able to easily access data that was viewed as being of a reliable quality. In China, Taiwan and Vietnam data was not trusted by researchers. Even though Japanese data was relatively accessible, there were still difficulties due to the fact that the information was over-abundant and so it was difficult to select and interpret the relevant data or to give it any practical application.

None of the limitations discussed above should devalue the importance of secondary data in international marketing research. For many smaller companies lacking the resources to carry out primary research in markets which are geographically distant, it may be the only information to which there is relative ease of access (see Illustration 4.3).

Primary research in international markets

We have discussed scanning international markets to identify potential market opportunities and the building of market information systems from which the market profile analysis is formulated. So far we have only discussed obtaining information from secondary sources. It is unlikely that a researcher will be able to obtain the information for input into a marketing information system from secondary sources alone. Having exhausted these sources the researcher will need to embark on the collection of primary data to obtain the information required.

In the following sections we will discuss the issues facing the researcher which should be considered when endeavouring to carry out primary research studies. To do this we use the seven-step framework (Malhotra *et al.* 2006) depicted in Figure 4.5.

Courtesey of Ogilvy & Mather

ILLUSTRATION 4.3

Segmenting the Islamic Global Market

At a recent Global Islamic Branding and Marketing Forum, Miles Young the chairman of the global advertising agency Ogilvy, challenged business and marketing leaders to stop segmenting global markets simply by country but look for global vertical segments that cut through country boundaries.

He argued that the world is re-balancing, and that the business of marketing and branding is only just beginning to acknowledge this. The theme of his talk was the Muslim consumer who he estimates conservatively as being a third of one billion across the globe. The market is bigger in value and numbers than India

or China, and yet, he claims, receives a tiny fraction of the attention.

'The GDP of the five large Middle Eastern countries is the same size as India, but on a population which is one-third of it. Most global enterprises, whether from the West or the East, have a BRIC strategy, and many are starting to look at N-11 in the same way. 53% of the population of the N-11 are Muslim. Finally, Muslim countries are some of the youngest in the world. There are more than 750 million Muslims under the age of 25, representing 43% of the global Muslim population, and 11% of the world's population.'

He went on to outline two challenges which Western marketers face when contemplating this opportunity.

'The first is that global enterprises still operate within matrix structures in which the primary axis is geographic. However, the Islamic world is a powerful vertical segment which unifies attitudes and behaviours, but not always by geography.

'The second is the tendency of the marketing and advertising industry to see it as just another interesting segment. In this mindset, it becomes equated with 'greys', or the 'Pink Dollar'; or Latinos in the US. Of course, all these are very valid targets for segmentation strategies, but the Islamic opportunity surely differs qualitatively. An American Muslim is a Muslim first and an American second. An American grey is an American first, and grey is a qualifier. In other words, much of the conventional marketing canon does not really cope intellectually with the Islamic opportunity.'

Question

1 What are the characteristics of a global market segment. How would you research the Islamic global segment?

References: Speech by Miles Young, CEO of Ogilvy at the Inaugural Oxford Global Islamic Branding and Marketing Forum.

Problem definition and establishing objectives

The precise definition of the marketing research problem is more difficult and more important in international marketing research than in domestic marketing research. Unfamiliarity with the cultures and environmental factors of the countries where the research is being conducted can greatly increase the difficulty of obtaining accurate findings. Often there are no clear geographical boundaries to the market you are trying to investigate which can make the design of the research problematic (see Management Challenge 4.3).

MANAGEMENT CHALLENGE 4.3

How to research the Canadian market

The account manager of a small food manufacturer in Groningen, in the Netherlands, was keen to expand the business in Canada. The company had 50 employees and manufactured a traditional Dutch ready-meal dish. The account manager was convinced from her knowledge of the marketplace that there were huge opportunities in Canada. Canada and the Netherlands had a strong relationship with a larger number of Dutch expatriates residing in Canada; English and French were the key 'second languages' for the account manager and her fellow employees. She had also read in a European Food Association newsletter that a UK manufacturer of a UK traditional dish, 'bangers and mash', had entered the Canadian market and used it as a springboard into the US. As a small company the board of directors were reluctant to invest in overseas markets without the possibility of substantial return; the home market had declined and resources to invest were precious. Having persuaded the board to consider exporting, another member of the board felt that testing a market with closer proximity to the Netherlands such as Germany would be cheaper and easier.

The account manager had four weeks to provide a business case for Canada.

Question

1 Without visiting the marketplace and no budget to purchase market information, how could the account manager identify sufficient evidence in such a short period of time to substantiate her proposal to invest in Canada?

Reference: Alexandra Anderson, Sheffield Hallam University

On a practical level, the differences in climate and infrastructure create problems. A survey on floor-cleaning products across Europe would have to take account of the fact that Scandinavians have wooden floors, there are lots of tiled and stone floors in the Mediterranean, and in the UK many houses have carpets.

Many international marketing efforts fail not because research was not conducted but because the issue of comparability was not adequately addressed in defining the marketing research problem. This is why, as we saw in Chapter 3, it is so important to isolate the impact of self-reference criteria (SRC) and the unconscious reference to our own cultural values when defining the problem we are attempting to research in international markets.

Developing an innovative approach

It is important in international marketing research to maintain flexibility in the approach you may have in the initial stages of the research. In the first stage of primary research, companies often use informal means to gather preliminary information and extensive use is made of the network of contacts available to the company both at home and abroad. It is unlikely that a full understanding of the foreign market will be obtained without visiting that market to gain information first hand. The first steps in doing this would be by networking and obtaining information through relatively informal means such as networking consortia or multi-client studies. The company in Management Challenge 4.3 was looking for such an innovative approach.

Networking

The use of contact networks to build information is vitally important because of the sometimes prohibitive cost of carrying out detailed market research studies overseas. Before any detailed studies are undertaken, trade contacts need to be fully explored.

FIGURE 4.5 The international marketing research process

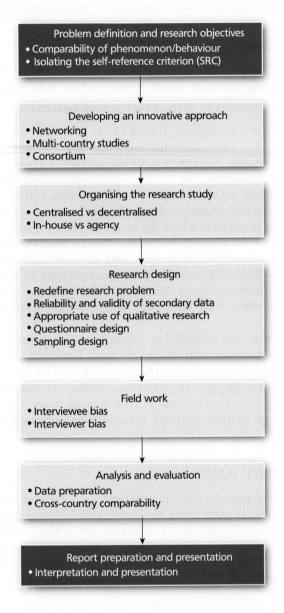

Source: Data adapted from Malhotra, N.K. and Birks, D. (2006) *Marketing Research and Applied Approach*, 3rd edn. FT Prentice Hall

In order to find solutions to the many international marketing research problems, improvisation in international research is essential.

Most companies will make extensive use of their existing networks to build the market profiles and develop information bases. These could be agents, distributors, licensees, joint venture partners or other companies operating in the country under investigation.

Consortia

Marketing research consortia enable the comparison of data across different cultures and aid international marketing research efforts. Consortia are used by companies as a way of overcoming the difficulties involved in gathering data and establishing contacts in foreign markets. Essentially a group of companies will come together to research a particular market area in which they have a common interest. The advantages are:

- the consortium is more visible in the foreign market;
- it is more likely to enjoy the support of the home export promotion organization;
- it achieves economies through the joint use of export facilities both at home and in foreign markets;
- it increases the resources available to support the research operation.

However, if a company is to join a consortium, then it has to be prepared to have its autonomy reduced; this fact alone is the major reason most consortia fail. There also has to be a strong reason to join together for the relationship to develop. Nevertheless, by the pooling of resources, consortia are very useful in giving companies the resources needed to acquire knowledge on markets. Often agencies will offer Omnibus studies which have much the same benefits (see Illustration 4.4).

Due to the problems and considerations we have discussed above, it may be that detailed research studies will only be carried out in markets where the market viability is seen to be positive and when detailed consumer/market information is required to develop marketing strategy. The cost of primary field research can be high and so it will only be carried out after all other sources have been investigated.

A survey carried out by INSEAD of European companies operating in the Asia-Pacific region showed that companies perceived the most significant sources of information as being personal contacts of the companies themselves, whether these were customers, other business relationships or their own market surveys.

A second tier of usefulness was then identified as consisting of other direct sources such as government contacts and contacts with competitors or trade associations. Finally, there was a third tier comprising publicly available information such as newspapers and magazines. This information may be widely read but relatively little weight seems to be given to its strategic value. The importance of directly collected information seems to confirm the view that business in Asia depends more heavily on the creation of a network of relationships than on analysis of hard data collected through surveys or other published information.

The collection of primary data

The cost and effort of collecting primary data in new markets is far higher than that of collecting such data in the domestic market. This is particularly the case in developing countries where no marketing research infrastructure or experience is available. Primary research in these circumstances would entail substantial investment costs in developing basic information relating, for example, to sampling frames or trained qualified interviewers. This, of course, reinforces the importance of secondary data for research purposes and the need for a systematic planning process when embarking on a primary research project.

Organizing the research study

There are two major organizational questions which the international marketing manager will need to address:

- Should the research be carried out by foreign local subsidiaries or should all marketing research be centralized at headquarters?
- Should the fieldwork be carried out in-house or by an agency?

Centralization vs decentralization

If a centralized approach is adopted, then decisions have to be made regarding the specific responsibilities of the operating unit and what managerial arrangements should exist between the unit and headquarters

ILLUSTRATION 4.4

© Fernando Blanco Calzada, shutterstock.com

Omnibus surveys

Omnibus studies have the advantage of enabling the client to participate in large surveys with focused questions at much less expense than would be the case otherwise. A significant growth in this type of field research has been seen in the past few years, particularly as more companies have become operational on international markets. An omnibus is a syndicated survey where several clients can buy as few or as many questions as they wish for a fixed cost per question. The traditional analogy is that it is like buying seats on a bus. Many companies now offer omnibus surveys globally.

Orient Express, an online market research company, uses online, face-to-face, telephone and mixed methodology research to offer insights of consumers in countries worldwide. For companies researching worldwide markets this offers cost-effective and fast access to the opinions of consumers across the world.

The company regularly researches the opinions of 1000 nationally representative adults in over 80 countries. The omnibus respondents are chosen by their demographic details including age, gender and social class or income. The omnibus survey is used by companies to gather customer feedback in a variety of areas including international buying habits, attitudes, opinions and global trends.

Clients can specify the type of people they wish to be surveyed from Orient Research's online panels, including the UK, Germany, France, Italy, Spain, the Netherlands, Austria, Sweden, North America, Canada, China, Japan, Korea and many other countries.

Question

1 Identify a number of examples where omnibus studies could be used as a primary marketing research tool in international markets.

---

staff. Further to this, decisions have to be taken as to what relationship is to exist between the local research staff who are ultimately responsible to headquarters and the local line management.

If a decentralized approach is chosen, then arrangements have to be made for research findings to be transferred from one operating unit to another. There is also the question of who has the overall responsibility for administering and overseeing the market research budget to ensure that resources are not wasted by a possible duplication of research effort.

Such issues are complex and are also related to overall organizational issues, which are examined in some depth in Chapter 5. In this chapter we will concentrate our discussion on the decision as to whether the company should carry out international research itself, or involve independent research agencies.

In-house or agency

Whether a company chooses to do all the research in-house or to use an agency will largely be determined by factors such as company resources, market expertise and product complexity.

If a company operates in a specialist B2B market with highly technological and complex products and has significant experience in the market, it may have no choice but to carry out research itself as it may be difficult to find an agency with the necessary competence.

However, if the company is operating in the consumer markets then a different scenario applies. Consumer research may require an established field force and the size of the markets may mean that a research company with field work resources is needed. A priority could well be to obtain an independent objective assessment of a foreign country; this could require specialist interviewing skills which a company alone might not be able to resource and thus would require the services of an agency. If the company is carrying out a multi-country study and needs a consistent research approach across all markets, then an international agency with resources across markets may be much more able to handle the research programme. Often, however, research in foreign markets may require a local firm to do the field work, gather data and provide some analysis and interpretation. The selection and use of a foreign firm may be extremely important to the success of the whole project.

In choosing an agency, a company has six basic options:

- a local agency in the market under investigation;
- a domestic agency with overseas offices;
- a domestic agency with overseas associate companies;
- a domestic agency which subcontracts field work to an agency in the market under investigation;
- a domestic agency with competent foreign staff;
- a global agency with offices around the world.

Which solution is best for the researcher will depend on a number of factors: the ease of briefing the agency, supervizing and coordinating the project, the probability of language problems arising, the requirements of specialist market knowledge, the standard of competence required and the budget available.

Thus, no single option is universally the best to select. It is primarily dependent on the budget available, the requirements of the research, the expertise within the company and, of course, the market under investigation. In a research study in Saudi Arabia the UK agency wished to maintain control and coordination of the project. However, Western interviewers would have had little success in eliciting meaningful information from Saudi businessmen. Therefore, it was decided to employ a Cypriot field work agency to translate the questionnaire into Arabic and carry out the interviews etc. This led to certain control and communication problems, but it was the only realistic methodology to obtain the required information.

It may often be the case that in a multi-country study a combination of agencies are used. A typical multi-country study will go through the following steps:

1 The project is discussed at length with the client.
2 The field work agencies in each country are selected.
3 The questionnaire is designed centrally.
4 The questionnaire is translated locally and the translation is checked centrally.
5 The questionnaire is piloted locally.
6 The questionnaire is finalized centrally.
7 The interviewers are briefed locally by an executive of the central company.
8 The field work is carried out locally.
9 The coding and editing plan is provided for the local agencies.
10 The edited and coded questionnaires are returned to head office.
11 A coding and editing check is carried out centrally.
12 Computing and analysis are carried out centrally.

Research design

In formulating a research design, considerable effort is needed to ensure that the methods used will ensure comparability of data. In order to handle problems such as cultural bias in research design and interpretation of data etc., perspectives of researchers from different countries and cultures could be incorporated in the process so that the bias is minimal. However, this method will only work if there are no major problems of communication between researchers from different environments. If this is not the case, there is a possibility that some other kind of unknown bias might be introduced into the research process which could be even more harmful. A study of the cultural and social values and the method of conducting research in the host country could play an important role in facilitating the process of international marketing research.

One of the first factors to consider in developing a research design is the reliability and validity of the secondary data used. As we have previously discussed, the accuracy of secondary data varies enormously across countries. This means that the database being used to develop primary research may be inaccurate or highly biased, or lack the capability to make multi-country comparisons.

Further to this, the research design needs to incorporate methods which will be feasible in the foreign country markets, as well as allowing the international researcher to obtain meaningful and relevant findings.

For example, in India there is a highly variable literacy rate across the country and across genders. According to www.india.gov, the literacy rate in the country is 65 per cent, 75 per cent for males and 54 per cent for females. However, in some rural areas it is much lower. In Bihar there is a literacy rate of 47 per cent, in Jammu and Kashmir it is 55 per cent. There are hundreds of languages and there can be very real fears that the interviewer, in some rural areas, is a government inspector in disguise. In such a scenario, a researcher would have problems throughout the research process in establishing the basic sample, designing the questionnaire and applying analytical techniques. However, India also has a rapidly growing affluent and educated middle class that in absolute terms is larger in size than the total population of any Western European country.

Social and cultural factors are one of the most important issues which affect the process of international marketing research. In collecting primary data, the researcher needs to consider the issues facing them in evaluating the possible methods under consideration.

In this context, qualitative research, survey methods, questionnaire design and sampling considerations are particularly important.

Qualitative research

Because the researcher is often unfamiliar with the foreign market to be examined, qualitative research is crucial in international marketing research. In the initial stages, qualitative research can provide insights into the problem and help in developing an approach by generating relevant research questions and hypotheses, models and characteristics which influence the research design. Thus, qualitative research may reveal the differences between foreign and domestic markets. It may also help to reduce the psychological distance between the researcher and the respondent. In some cases, the researcher must rely on qualitative research because secondary data may not be available. Some problems associated with qualitative techniques in developing countries are such things as accessibility (different concept of time), sampling (extended demographic factors such as religion and tribal membership), shorter span of attention and less familiarity with abstract thinking.

Focus groups can be used in many settings, particularly in newly emerging markets where there is scant data and companies are trying to establish the cultural sensitivities in the market to their products and services. In some cultures, such as in the Middle or Far East, people are hesitant to discuss their feelings in a group setting. In these cases, in-depth interviews can be used.

The use of projective techniques is sometimes appropriate. Association techniques (word association), completion techniques (sentence completion, story completion) and expressive techniques (role playing, third-person technique) involve the use of verbal cues and so are all good cross-cultural research techniques.

Survey methods

There are several issues to consider in evaluating the various interviewing methods available.

Online surveys. As the Internet achieves greater penetration even in less developed markets, online surveys are now becoming predominant globally. Speed of execution, the obtaining of timely responses, ease of interview and speed of analysis are all major benefits to international marketing researchers. Globally access to the Internet is still scarce in some countries and in others subject to government controls. This could mean potential bias in both the sampling and in the answers given by respondents.

© Dmitriy Shironosov, shutterstock.com

ILLUSTRATION 4.5

The use of social networks to understand global consumer opinion

Unilever, who use a range of qualitative research techniques, such as focus groups, psychological testing and in-depth interviewing to understand their customers have now added social networking to their primary research portfolio of tools.

Unilever has created bespoke social networks across its brands to involve consumers in its product development process. The FMCG giant, whose brands include Lynx, Magnum and Pot Noodle, now integrates social media into its product development research aimed at gaining insights into customer preferences. They first used social networks to research and test their men's fragrance Lynx Twist in the UK and in the USA and now use them for a range of products. They have even used a social media campaign to help research, market test and then launch a new product in the shape of Marmite XO. Marmite XO is an 'extra mature, extra strong' version of the manufacturer's yeast spread, which is known for its 'Love it or Hate it' brand positioning.

Unilever's move highlights a trend among global brands to create invite-only online communities to gain greater understanding of consumer opinions. The chairman of Unilever sees the use of social networks for research on its markets worldwide as a major step forward in helping them access the opinions of millions of their users across the globe. However, there are limitations and he warns of a 'lost generation' of research and brand managers who do not understand the web and social networks. Traditional marketing agencies he says are struggling to adapt to the digital world and the array of new online marketing research tools which are now presented to them.

Question

1 Identify the main advantages and disadvantages of using social networks to understand consumers in global markets.

As more of us share personal information online through sites like Facebook, MySpace and Linkedin, companies are using these networking sites as a means of contacting customers. This gives them the opportunity to analyze consumption patterns, examine behavioural targeting, cost effective online product testing and as a means of building direct contact with the consumer to access a plethora of information. Illustration 4.5 gives one such example.

Telephone interviewing. With the setting up of global call centres, Internet telephony and the collapse in the price of international telephone calls, multi-country studies are now often conducted from a single global location and are now much cheaper and easier to control. Most telephone data collection is conducted through CATI (Computer aided telephone interviews) which are cost-effective as well as reliable. CATI/telephone surveys are the most effective method of collecting data from global customers as it can be organized from one location and administered globally. In the US, Canada and Europe, the telephone has achieved almost total penetration of households. In most developing nations, such as across Africa however, mobile phones are more prevalent than land lines and it could be that only a few households have telephones. Even in countries like Saudi Arabia, where telephone ownership is extensive, telephone directories can be incomplete and out of date.

Therefore, telephone interviews are most useful when employed with relatively upscale consumers who are accustomed to business transactions by phone, be it mobile or land line, or consumers who can be reached by phone and can express themselves easily.

Mail interviewing. Because of the rise of the online survey the use of mail interviews internationally has declined dramatically. However, in countries where literacy is high and the postal system is well developed and where there are still problems in terms of access to the Internet mail surveys still continue to be used. In Africa, Asia and South America, however, the use of mail surveys and mail panels is low because of illiteracy and the large proportion of population living in rural areas.

No questionnaire administration method is superior in all situations. Table 4.3 presents a comparative evaluation of the major modes of collecting primary data in the context of international marketing research.

Questionnaire design

The questionnaire or research instrument should be adapted to the specific cultural environment and should not be biased in terms of any one culture. This requires careful attention to each step of the questionnaire design process. It is important to take into account any differences in underlying consumer behaviour, decision-making processes, psychographics, lifestyles and demographic variables.

The use of unstructured or open-ended questions may be desirable if the researcher lacks knowledge of the possible responses in other cultures. Unstructured questions also reduce cultural bias because they do not impose any response alternatives. However, unstructured questions are more affected by differences in educational levels than structured questions. They should be used with caution in countries with high illiteracy rates.

The questions may have to be translated for administration in different cultures. A set of guidelines has been proposed by Brislin (2001) for writing questionnaires in English so that they can be easily translated. These include:

- use short and simple sentences;
- repeat nouns rather than using pronouns;
- avoid metaphors;
- avoid adverbs and prepositions related to place and time;
- avoid possessive forms;
- use specific rather than general terms;
- avoid vague words;
- avoid sentences with two different verbs if the verbs suggest different actions.

The problems of language and translation were discussed in Chapter 3 and equally apply in marketing research. A translation of a questionnaire might be grammatically correct but this does not necessarily mean that it is conveying the appropriate message. For example: value for money is not a common phrase in Spain; the equivalent phrase is 'price for product'. In the Middle East 'payment' is a transactional word; it refers to repaying a debt and so would be inappropriate in the context of purchasing a product.

Another problem is that countries sometimes have more than one official language: a decision has then to be made as to what the most appropriate language is. In Malaysia and Singapore, for instance, consumer surveys regularly employ three languages (English, Malay and Chinese). An interviewer may need a command of several languages or dialects to undertake field work. In Pakistan, the official language is Urdu, but most of the official work in government departments is done in English. However, most local nationals who understand English also usually understand Urdu. There is also a particular segment of social class in the country which prefers English to Urdu in their daily routines. Should the researcher use English or Urdu?

Table 4.3 A comparative evaluation of survey methods for use in international marketing research

Criteria	Online	Telephone	Personal	Mail
High sample control	1	1	1	2
Difficulty in locating respondents at home	1	1	2	1
Inaccessibility of homes	1	1	2	1
Unavailability of a large pool of trained interviewers	1	1	2	1
Large population in rural areas	1	2	1	2
Unavailability of current telephone directory	1	2	1	2
Unavailability of mailing lists	1	1	1	2
Low penetration of telephones	2	2	1	1
Lack of an efficient postal system	1	1	1	2
Low level of literacy	1	2	1	2
Face-to-face communication culture	2	2	1	2

Note: 1 denotes an advantage: 2 denotes a disadvantage.
Source: Data adapted from Malhotra, N.K. and Birks, D. (2006) *Marketing Research an Applied Approach*, 3rd edn. FT Prentice Hall.

The literal translation of a questionnaire can pose problems. A different language is not just a matter of different spellings but of different linguistic concepts. This is why translation agencies recommend back translation into the original language. This identifies and corrects many of the problems faced in simple translation. The technique of 'decentring' in translation, where the material is translated and re-translated each time by a different translator, also minimizes mistakes being made.

Sample frame

The problems of obtaining valid sampling frames tend to be more complicated in researching international markets. It might be difficult or even impossible to obtain a reliable sampling frame. Due to problems associated with the validity and reliability of secondary data in some countries, experience and judgement need to play an important part in constructing the sample where there is no reliable database. It may mean that accepted techniques of marketing research in developed countries cannot always be directly transferred, even to other developed countries where data might have to be collected through less formalized methods. This applies especially in countries lacking a marketing infrastructure where, unless sufficient care is taken in selecting the sampling frame, the sample chosen will invariably be distorted.

Field work

Interviewee bias The major problems in field work are errors caused through bias in the interviewing stage of the process which can mean that reliable multi-country studies where results can be compared and contrasted across different countries are sometimes difficult to achieve.

Different cultures will produce a varied response to interviews or questionnaires. For example, purchase intentions for new products frequently peak in Italy because Italians have a propensity to over-claim their likelihood to buy, whereas German results are much closer to reality. If Germans say they will buy a product they probably will.

Another problem is that in some countries it is not possible for the female members of a household to respond personally to a survey. In such countries, mail or on-line surveys for researching the female market might obtain a much better rate of response.

In some countries the rate of response of a particular segment of society might be quite low due to tax evasion problems, with respondents unwilling to provide any information which gives an idea of their economic status (Sarathy *et al.* 2006). Even within the same country, different social classes of customers could have differing responses to marketing research techniques. In some cultures the respondent may cause bias by attempting to please the interviewer and give the answers they think they want to hear. This happened to BSN in Japan. The French conglomerate carried out a study in Japan to find out people's attitudes to yogurt. The results indicated that the Japanese were becoming much more Westernized in their food and eating habits and that there was a potential market for yogurts. BSN launched their products, set up distribution and invested heavily in promotion. However, the sales were disappointing. Follow-up research showed that the questions used in the original research were too simplistic to elicit accurate responses. The Japanese were far too polite to reply NO to a question. Therefore the responses to yes/no questions were highly misleading. Likewise, they did not wish to offend Westerners by criticizing the usage of a spoon as an eating implement.

Interviewer bias   Interviewer biases are often due to communication problems between the interviewer and respondents. Several biases have been identified in multicultural research, including rudeness bias, 'I can answer any question' bias, courtesy bias, sucker bias, hidden premises bias, reticence–loquaciousness bias, social desirability bias, status difference bias, racial difference bias and individual group opinion bias (Malhotra and Peterson *et al.*, 2006).

Extensive training and close supervision of the interviewers and other field staff may be required to minimize these biases.

The selection, training, supervision and evaluation of field workers are critical in multi-country research. Local field work agencies are unavailable in many countries. It may be necessary, therefore, to recruit and train local field workers or import trained foreign workers. The use of local field workers is desirable as they are familiar with the local language and culture. They can thus create an appropriate climate for the interview and be sensitive to the concerns of the respondents.

Data analysis   A number of issues need to be considered at the data analysis stage. First, in preparing data for analysis in multi-country or cross-cultural studies, how do you deal with 'outliers'? These are countries where the data is quite obviously different from the bulk of the data. It may not be a problem at all but, likewise, it could be due to some cultural bias, a problem in the sampling or a problem of translation in the questionnaire.

Second, is the issue of how to ensure comparability of data across cultures. Some researchers prefer to standardize data to ensure comparability. In contrast, others prefer statistics based on non-standardized data on the basis that this allows a truer comparative analysis.

Report preparation and presentation

In any research study there is the chance of cultural bias in the research findings. International research often involves researchers from one cultural environment conducting research in another cultural environment or communicating with researchers from another cultural environment. In international research situations, effective communication between the respondents and the researcher is essential to avoid problems of misinterpretation of the data. The phenomenon of cultural self-reference criteria is cited as a possible cause of the misinterpretation of data and can lead to a systematic bias in the findings. The reader is referred to the discussion in Chapter 3 and the discussion on the steps that can be taken to remedy self-reference criteria.

Some agencies follow the practice of always ensuring foreign market studies are written in the local language and include interpretation as well as analysis. The nuance can then be discussed with the translator.

Face-to-face debriefings with agencies and researchers are also a good way to synthesize the results from multi-country surveys and form coherent conclusions through open discussions with representatives who have participated in the research across a range of countries.

Continuous research   In this chapter, in order to discuss the relevant issues in a logical manner, we have used the six-step research design framework. It is perhaps important to stress, however, that international market research, while expensive, is by no means a 'one-off' activity. In today's dynamic environment where changes occur almost on a daily basis in some rapidly growing markets (e.g. India and China), it is important that research be on a continuous basis to ensure a company keeps ahead of its competition.

SUMMARY

- In this chapter we have examined the three main roles of the international marketing researcher: scanning international markets, building up market profiles and carrying out primary research across global markets. The rise of the Internet has impacted critically on the role of international market research and led to the development of better decision tools and the development of globally based research supplier networks and global databases.

- International research is, in many cases, a complex, expensive and time-consuming task and evidence suggests that for these reasons many international firms fail to research markets to the extent that is really necessary. The consequences of this are significant in terms of both missed opportunities and the failure to meet existing and developing market demand.

- The issues relevant to the identifying and analyzing of opportunities across the globe were discussed and the problems involved in categorizing and segmenting international markets identified. Several models used in the segmentation process of international markets were presented.

- Within this chapter, we illustrated the strategic importance of opportunity analysis and the contribution that market research can make to the decision-making process.

- In examining the international marketing research process the six-step research design framework was used. It was suggested that many international marketing efforts fail not because research was not conducted, but because the issue of comparability was not adequately addressed in defining the marketing research problem. The importance of self-reference criteria (SRC) was discussed and at each of the six stages the relevant issues for the international marketer highlighted.

KEYWORDS

marketing research	Market segmentation	websites
research process	Pareto law	secondary data
cross-cultural research	differentiated marketing	primary data
marketing information	transnational	Omnibus studies
Existing markets	segmentation	multi-country study
Latent markets	global segments	qualitative research
Incipient markets	market profile analysis	
comparative research	Online databases	

Stock.xchng

CASE STUDY

How do WGS segment the global mobile phone gambling market?

WGS developed a whole new business by transferring the 'feel of the casino/slot machine' to the mobile phone. Mobile phones provided an ideal platform to deliver casino style games.

Market research showed there were few companies delivering fruit machine-style games on mobile phones. Closer inspection of their games revealed the games were basic and designed from the perspective of a games designer rather than a fruit machine designer. Estelle research also estimated that the mobile gambling market was set to rise rapidly to $50 billion by 2020. The market for mobile gambling games therefore had huge growth potential. WGS was able to deliver superior quality games compared with its competitors, bringing the feel of playing on the Las Vegas slots to the mobile phone. Games could be played any time, anywhere; on the way to work on the bus/train, waiting in

the bus queue, etc. Competitors, however, had a few years' foothold in the market, acquired key partners and had begun to establish a mobile casino brand.

The mobile gambling market was split into a number of sectors providing different style games. The lottery and bingo style games, more traditional fruit machine/casino games including roulette and blackjack, skills-based games such as quiz games, points for prizes games and non-gambling games such as just for fun slot machines where players paid just for the download to their phone. It also included more functional gambling services such as placing bets for horse racing, football and other sporting activities. WGS focused on delivering games which encompassed its core expertise, i.e. the fruit machine/casino style gambling games. Its initial portfolio of games included a range of slot machine style games such as 'Adders and Ladders', 'Cop the Cash', casino style games such as roulette, blackjack and poker as well as bingo, virtual horse racing and a World Cup shoot out.

Global market potential looked promising. WGS were confident in their ability to design high-quality games based on superior software design. The platform on which the mobile casino operated, Arcadia™, was patent protected and WGS had a team of highly qualified software designers led by a technical director with experience in the fruit machine industry. WGS sold their mobile casino package to industry intermediaries around the globe who could reach the 'mobile gambler'. Therefore, as a business to business operation, WGS needed to consider how to segment the global markets to identify companies with the largest penetration of potential mobile phone gamblers. This meant understanding:

a the profile of the mobile phone gambling game player around the world; and

b which companies could best reach those players globally.

WGS sold their mobile casino games via a website where players downloaded games directly to their mobile phones. This meant they had to identify which companies would want to operate their own mobile casino. In principle anybody could set up their own mobile casino, however, given that WGS's revenue streams would be based on a percentage of gambling revenues, their target customers needed to have access to a large database of potential mobile gambling games players. Which companies had access to such a large database of potential players? how should they best be identified and reached? Would online casinos look for a mobile arm to their operations, or would entrepreneurs with sufficient revenues want to manage their own mobile casino? The latter would need a heavily supported promotional campaign to build a large enough database to capture a percentage of mobile phone gamblers.

Given the 'virtual' nature of the product and its user, i.e. the online mobile casino and the mobile gambler, WGS had a difficult decision to make in trying to segment the global market. In its simplest terms the mobile phone gambler could be anyone in the world with a mobile phone with the capacity to download games, but segmenting the world market on that basis would be costly and ineffective. In terms of the mobile gambling game player, was their profile the same as the fruit machine player, i.e. the 18 to 35 male? Was it the same as the mobile phone games player? Research showed an increase in the number of women playing mobile gambling games. Did they play the same games as men? Did they fall in the same income, age brackets or life-stage segments? It was more likely that the mobile phone gambler was a niche customer located in different countries across the world.

Geography was only an issue in terms of gambling legislation. Players could be global but legislation was not. Culture and legal issues played a big role in the gambling sector. Many gambling-style companies were basing operations offshore, or had to acquire expensive gambling licences. Legislation was continually changing. The US outlawed gambling over a telephone wire, although 'games of chance' were not. In the UK the law states that the place where a bet is taken in the UK must have a license, e.g. if it is taken in a bookmakers then that bookmakers must have a licence to take bets, if that bookmaker is overseas, in the case of Internet gambling, then it is 'out of the jurisdiction' of the British government. In order to advertise gambling in the UK, a company must be in a jurisdiction that is on the British government's 'white list'. France and Germany were reported to be in breach of European law for outlawing online gambling while allowing state-run online Lottos. Spain allowed Internet gambling from European destinations. Italy's attempted ban recently backfired and online gambling has been allowed. Legislation and the lack of conformity across regions meant WGS would have to segment the global market carefully.

WGS knew it had the right combination of expertise in games and software design and experience in the fruit machine sector. It only needed to find the best way to reach the mobile gambling game player around the globe and identify the best route to the market ensuring it did not breach gambling legislation.

Questions

1 Critically evaluate the arguments for and against the use of country by country versus global market segment descriptors as bases for the segmentation of the global mobile phone gambling market.

2 How can WGS develop a global segmentation strategy that could be used as the basis for a global marketing plan?

3 Advise WGS on how they should research the global opportunities to better understand the market for mobile gambling.

Source: Alex Anderson, Sheffield Hallam University

DISCUSSION QUESTIONS

1 What are the problems in carrying out multi-country studies? As an international market researcher, how would you avoid these dangers?

2 Many companies are looking to emerging markets in their internationalization programmes. What are the problems in researching these markets? How, if at all, may they be overcome?

3 Identify the principal methods that companies might use in assessing and reviewing opportunities across international markets. Suggest the alternative means by which firms can prioritize and segment international markets.

4 As firms become more global so does their requirement to gather global information. Outline the key categories of a global information system and explain their relevance.

5 Citing specific examples, show how the spread of the Internet has impacted on international market research. What are the problems and limitations of using web-based research?

REFERENCES

1. Brislin, R.W. (2001) *Understanding cultures' influence on behaviour*, 2nd edn. Harcourt.
2. Czinkota, M.E. and Ronkainen, I.A. (2009) *Principles of International marketing*, 9th edn. S.W. College USA.
3. Douglas, S.P. (2005) *International Marketing Research*, 3rd edn. John Wiley and Sons.
4. Gorton, K. and Doole, I. (1989) *Low cost marketing research*, John Wiley.
5. Hamill, J. and Stevenson, J. (2002) 'Internet forum', *International Marketing Review*, 19 (5) 545.
6. Harrell, G.D. and Keifer, R.D. (1993) 'Multinational market portfolio in global strategy development', *International Marketing Review*, 10 (1).
7. Hassan, S.S. and Stephen, H.C.T. (2005) 'Linking global market segmentation decisions with strategic positioning options', *Journal of Consumer Marketing*, 22 (2) 81–9.
8. Malhotra, N.K. and Birks, D. (2006) *Marketing Research an Applied Approach*, 3rd edn. FT Prentice Hall.
9. Malhotra, N.K., Peterson, M. and Uslay, C. (2006) 'Helping marketing research earn a seat at the table for decision-making. An assessment and prescription for the future', *European Business Review*, 18 (4) 294–306.
10. Sarathy, R., Terpstra, V. and Russow, L.C. (2006) *International marketing*, 9th edn. Dryden Press.
11. Sheth, J. and Ama, A. (2005) 'International e-marketing: opportunities and issues', *International Marketing Review*, 22 (6) 611–22.

INTEGRATIVE LEARNING ACTIVITIES

An Introduction

Successful international marketing is about taking a planned approach to analysis, strategy development and implementation. The chapters of this book focus upon providing the underpinning knowledge to support the process of planning an international marketing strategy. The purpose of the three integrated learning activities at the end of each of the three parts of the book is to integrate the four chapters that make up each of the parts. More importantly, however, is that as a whole, the three activities provide a framework for planning an international marketing strategy and give the opportunity for readers to consider the practical issues involved in developing, planning and implementing an outline international marketing strategy.

Learning Objectives

On completing the three integrated learning activities you should be able to:

- Analyze the international marketing environment of a given company situation critically

- Apply relevant concepts and models to each of the development stages of an international marketing strategy

- Make clear links between analysis and the chosen response. The issues identified in the analysis should lead directly to the development and implementation of a strategy

- Develop a realistic and cohesive international marketing strategy

The aims of the integrated learning activities (ILAs) therefore are much wider in scope than the short case studies found at the end of each chapter. The objective is to provide a vehicle through which the reader is able to develop practical skills in research, analysis, evaluation and strategy development. In completing these activities you will need to synthesize the various strands and themes explored throughout the book and apply them to a practical situation. To complete each of the activities the reader must move well beyond the boundaries of the textbook, researching new material and exploring the interplay of the concepts discussed in the text and possible solutions to the practical problems identified in each activity.

Each ILA depicts very different scenarios.

Part 1: We spotlight the rapid development of the mobile phone services market in Africa and use this scenario as a backdrop for examining trading infrastructure issues, consumer behaviour and cultural issues and examining the development of a latent and exciting market.

Part 2: We identify a number of companies from emerging markets that are developing as global brands competing against entrenched Western global players. How do such companies compete effectively against existing global competitors, and how can they ensure they build a sustainable competitive advantage?

Part 3: Yum brands has a portfolio of some of the best known fast food brands. Due to changes in the market environment, customer expectations and competition, it must use creative approaches in implementing its international marketing strategies to maintain its growth.

In each of the activities a series of questions is posed, together with suggestions on how to get started, a framework depicting the key factors to consider in completing the task, and suggested websites you may find useful.

Additional observations are also made that will assist you in addressing the key issues and how you could develop the activity further.

In all the activities we have provided only outline information on the scenarios. A key skill in international marketing is *finding* information about international markets, analyzing it, deciding what is most important and preparing a structured, logical rationale for the decisions that must ultimately be made. In each activity, therefore, you will need to seek information outside of the case to complete the task. Much of the information you can use is available online. You should not have to approach staff in the organizations depicted for further information to complete the task.

INTEGRATIVE LEARNING ACTIVITY

INTERNATIONAL MARKETING PLANNING: ANALYSIS

Introduction

In this activity we explore the development of the mobile phone services' market in Africa and the attendant challenges and opportunities faced in its development by companies trying to develop a marketing strategy across the region to enable them to become globally competitive. We explore the international marketing opportunities and challenges companies face in this market face.

The mobile phone services' market in Africa, especially Southern Africa, can be defined as a latent market with huge growth potential. However, there are huge challenges in terms of lack of infrastructure and the ability of many in the market to pay, which mean it is a highly challenging market. Anyone entering the market needs to develop a thorough understanding of the complexities of the African marketing environment in which they are competing and decide how to segment the market, which segment to target and how to develop a positioning strategy to achieve competitive leverage. Increasing global competition in this market necessitates greater innovation, not just in products and services, but in all aspects of the operation. To understand such issues we need to build the skills to research, analyze and evaluate how such factors impact international strategy development. We hope the reader will develop these skills in this activity.

Learning Objectives

On completing this activity you should be able to:

- Identify and analyze international market opportunities and challenges
- Use appropriate conceptual frameworks to develop a market profile analysis
- Identify sources of information, methods of information collection and methods of information analysis suitable for international marketing operations
- Understand the complexities of researching international markets and be able to identify possible solutions

The scenario: Market information

In a world where more people have access to mobile phones than to flushing toilets, telecommunications operators in search of growth are naturally drawn to countries where phone usage is still low. Yet fixating on so-called penetration rates – the number of mobile subscribers as a percentage of the population – can be a mistake. The Egyptian operator Orascom, for example, entered what, on that measure, was the ultimate growth market, North Korea. Two years later, the mobile penetration rate there was still barely above 0 per cent.

Operators have had better luck in Africa. Penetration across the continent has increased over the past decade from 2 per cent to 45 per cent. Africa is in the grip of a mobile phone revolution. In the past ten years, subscribers in sub-Saharan Africa have risen from 72 000 (excluding South Africa) to 25.5 million. While many rural villagers huddle around paraffin lamps as darkness falls, neon lights come to life as they illuminate the mobile phone masts proliferating across the African landscape.

According to Mobile Africa the number of mobile phone subscriptions far exceeds fixed-line subscriptions. The International Telecommunication Union reckon that more Africans have begun using phones in the past decade than in the whole of the previous century! Use of mobile phones has been increasing at an annual rate of 65 per cent, more than twice the global average.

Ten years ago Africa was dubbed 'the hopeless continent'. Since then its progress has been remarkably hopeful. McKinsey (June 2010) pointed out that, thanks to rising living standards, some 200 million Africans will enter the market for consumer goods in the next five years. The consultancy also notes that the continent's working-age population will double from 500 million today to 1.1 billion in 2040.

Africa's annual output is growing by approximately 5 per cent (adjusted for purchasing-power parity), twice as fast as in the previous ten years and faster than the global average. Foreign direct investment to the region increased from $10 billion to $88 billion – more than India ($42 billion) and, even more remarkably, catching up with China ($108 billion). The Boston Consulting Group notes that the revenues of Africa's 500 largest companies (excluding banks) have grown at an average of 8.3 per cent a year over the past decade.

Consumer-goods companies ranging from Western giants such as Procter & Gamble to emerging-market car companies such as China's Great Wall and India's Tata Motors are pouring into Africa. Foreign firms are starting to use Africa as a base for manufacturing as well, as labour costs in India and China rise.

The mobile phone market has been an integral part of this growth.

In Africa, average penetration of mobile phones stands at nearly half the population, and in North Africa it is almost two-thirds. Gabon, the Seychelles and South Africa now boast almost 100 per cent penetration. Only five African countries – Burundi, Djibouti, Eritrea, Ethiopia and Somalia – still have a penetration of less than 10 per 100 inhabitants.

Uganda, the first African country to have more mobiles than fixed telephones, is cited as an example of cultural and economic transformation. Penetration has risen from 0.2 per cent ten years ago to 23 per cent now, with operators making huge investments in infrastructure, particularly in rural areas. Given their low incomes, only about a quarter of Ugandans have a mobile subscription, but street vendors offer mobile access on a per-call basis. They also invite those without access to electricity to charge their phones using car batteries.

Popular mobile services include money transfers, allowing people without bank accounts to send money by text message. Many farmers use mobiles to trade and check market prices.

Company Information

Companies are now investing heavily in this market. France Telecom says it is willing to spend €7 billion over the next five years to expand its footprint there. Bharti Airtel paid $10 billion for a group of African mobile companies and it has recently acquired Zain Africa.

Bharti, India's largest cell phone company, is aiming to more than double within three years in the number of mobile phone users in Africa. In Africa it intends to pursue the low-cost outsourced business model of operations that has served it so well at home.

The Indian operator segments Africa by language and has divided its operations in Africa into three separate divisions to meet their needs. These divisions include Bharti Anglophone (comprising the English speaking nations – Ghana, Kenya, Malawi, Sierra Leone, Tanzania, Uganda, Zambia), Bharti Francophone (comprising the French speaking nations – Burkina Faso, DRC, Chad, Congo B, Madagascar, Niger, Gabon), while Nigeria, the continent's largest market will be a separate unit.

There are also a number of strong more local brands. Essar Telecom offers services under the 'Yu' brand in Kenya, while Warid has mobile networks in Uganda and Congo. Both Essar Telecom and Warid are in the process of extending operations to more geographies in Africa.

Internet technologies

Mobile Internet technologies play a very important role in making Internet services available to many in Africa. Africans are using them for more than calling their friends and family, many are using them to do their banking. About half a million South Africans now use their mobile phones as a bank. For these new banking customers both the mobile phone and the whole system of banking are new to them.

Besides sending money to relatives and paying for goods, they check balances, buy mobile airtime and settle utility bills. Traditional banks offer mobile banking as an added service to existing customers, most of whom are quite well off. Wizzit, and to some extent First National Bank (FNB) and MTN Banking, are chasing another market: the 16 million South Africans, over half of the adult population, with no bank account. Significantly, 30 per cent of these people do have mobile phones. Previously ignored as the bottom of the pyramid and of little commercial importance to the large corporations, such customers are now being courted. Wizzit hired and trained over 2000 unemployed people, known as Wizzkids, to drum up business. It worked: eight out of ten Wizzit customers previously had no bank account and had never used an ATM.

People using advanced technology to manage their finances had until now depended on the archaic system of barter. They have leapfrogged telephony technology and jumped from dealing only in cash or barter to the world of cellular finance. A simplified kind of account called *Mzansi* has been launched to reach the non-banking customers, and portable banks and ATMs have been rolled out in townships and in the countryside.

In most of Africa, only a fraction of people have bank accounts – but there is huge demand for cheap and convenient ways to send money and buy prepaid services such as airtime. In Kenya, a pilot scheme called M-Pesa is being used to disburse and pay micro-loans by phone. Meanwhile Celpay is offering platforms for banks and phone companies in Zambia and Congo. In countries like Somalia, with chaotic conditions, cash transfers by phone will be a bonus.

By clicking a few keys on a mobile phone, money can be zapped from one part of Kenya to another in seconds. For urban migrants sending money home to their villages, and for people used to queuing at banks for hours to pay bills or school fees, the M-PESA money-transfer service, operated by Safaricom, Kenya's largest mobile operator, is a godsend. It is used by 9.5 million people, or 23 per cent of the population, and transfers the equivalent of 11 per cent of Kenya's GDP each year. The most ambitious is Africa's biggest operator, MTN, which is rolling out mobile-money schemes in several African countries. Its scheme in Uganda has signed up 890 000 users since its launch and is expected to soon reach 2 million.

Interestingly it has inspired more than 60 similar schemes across the world many in the developed world. Operators in other countries have been doing their best to imitate Safaricom.

Market challenges

There are many difficulties on the way. Not all potential consumers are ready to make the leap. Many think banking too expensive and complicated, and helping new customers become financially literate takes time. The technology remains a problem in some cases, with downloads requiring dozens of text messages. Several rival platforms are still in the fight, but so far those that emphasize simplicity and ease-of-use over state-of-the-art technology and security have made the greatest strides. A lot also hangs on putting the right laws and regulations in place. They need to be tight enough to protect vulnerable users and discourage money laundering, but open enough to allow innovative mobile banking to grow.

However the main barrier to further expansion remains the cumbersome regulatory frameworks. Countries with similar economic circumstances but with a liberalized market generally show higher penetration rates. Taxes can also act as a barrier, particularly import

duties on handsets or special mobile communications surcharges. The mobile industry has been seen as a cash cow by governments in some countries who have used its popularity for generating tax revenues but haven't invested in the infrastructure for its growth. To expand coverage into rural and remote areas, government support will be required.

Rural areas in some countries are also often economically unattractive for operators to invest in. This is usually not due to a lack of demand but rather to lack of basic infrastructure. The roads in Africa can be notorious, the infrastructure under-developed and the continent has more than its fair share of conflicts and crises.

The cost of making calls and sending texts in Africa is also relatively high and many of its countries are poor. In South Africa, running a mobile phone costs the average user 3 per cent of a monthly income, according to International Telecommunication Union data. Yet in countries such as Kenya, Tanzania, Rwanda and Niger, it costs between 25 per cent and 60 per cent. Big chunks of some markets remain unreachable because of this.

A 'digital divide' also persists in terms of Internet access. Australia, a country with 21 million inhabitants, has more broadband subscribers than the whole of Africa. There is also a huge gap in terms of broadband speed. Governments need to address this situation and bring the continent more meaningfully online if the industry is to expand.

References

http://www.reuters.com

http://news.bbc.co.uk

http://timesofindia.indiatimes.com

http//www.economist.com

http://www.guardian.co.uk

The task

1 Analyze and evaluate the major environmental influences that will impact on the growth of the mobile phone services market.

2 Building on the results of your analysis from Question 1, and with reference to a company of your choice, draw up a market profile analysis for the area.

3 Propose and justify an effective segmentation strategy of the African market that will form the basis on which a company of your choice can build a regional marketing strategy. This should form the basis on

which the company you have chosen can enter and develop the market.

4   For the company referred to in Question 2, show how the company should develop some of the segments identified. In doing so, you will need to fully appraise them of the challenges and problems they will face and how they should respond to these challenges.

Useful websites

www.southafrica.net

allafrica.com

www.gamos.org

news.bbc.co.uk

www.globaldashboard.org

www.wto.org

www.ita.doc.gov/tradestats

www.worldbank.com

www.foreign-trade.com

Getting started

In international markets it is exceedingly difficult to obtain a comprehensive understanding of the relevant market environment. Africa is particularly difficult due to the scarcity of reliable data. In tackling the task it is useful to categorize the elements of the environment into social and cultural, legal, economic, political and technological forces (SLEPT).

In the increasingly global marketplace, companies are trying to identify methodologies for segmenting and evaluating international markets that transcend national and cultural boundaries. You are asked to develop a segmentation strategy. It is important here to remember that simply segmenting the market on a geographical basis

will be too simplistic and not form a basis on which the company can build a regional strategy. You will need a hierarchical approach where your segmentation strategy has several steps and can incorporate the multidimensional aspects of a global niche segment.

It is important in building a market profile analysis to develop a systematic method for building a market information on the markets you have prioritized. The 12C framework is a useful tool when developing profiles of international markets. Finally, you need to think through the implications of your research and consider the issues the analysis has highlighted and consider the implications for developing a strategy. Of particular importance, consider these issues in the light of possible resources/cultural/management constraints that the company you choose may face.

In summary, therefore, the framework shown in Table I provides a guide to the key factors that needs to be considered in tackling the task identified.

The way forward

After reading Part 2 of the textbook you may wish to return to plan the next stage of your strategy. The most important issue is deciding how quickly the firm should develop internationally and how – country by country, concentrating on a particular segment or seeking a regional presence distribution. You should define a strategy that builds upon the firm's competitive advantage, identifying a positioning strategy that meets the needs of the target segment you have chosen. Then you should identify the criteria that will determine the choice of market entry.

After reading Part 3 you will be in a position to define the implementation plan and make decisions on the marketing mix elements, relationship building and supply chain management. You can identify how management and technology systems might support the international expansion. Finally, you will be able to identify the monitoring and control systems that will be used.

Table I   Key factors to consider

The element of the plan	Some concepts, models and issues to be addressed
Environment	• The global SLEPT factors, including political and economic issues and socio/cultural factors affecting the opportunities for the firm
	• The changing global trends in competition and customer expectations that impact on business
	• The international challenges to be met

The element of the plan	Some concepts, models and issues to be addressed
Home and possible international markets	• The level of market development and competitive structures • Prioritization of markets using country attractiveness and latent assessment of markets • Commercial, home, host country stakeholder expectations and ethical issues
Company capability	• SWOT, competitive advantage • Products: international product life cycle, knowledge and capability
Segmentation	• Basis of segmentation/criteria for global segmentation/global niche possibilities • Hierarchy of segmentation
Market Information	• Market profile analysis and the information systems, data collection and management to support it • Market and environmental risk and potential commercial opportunity using the 12C framework
Strategic options	• Potential strategic alternatives for the company • The challenges faced and potential responses to the issues identified in the analysis • The resource constraints

PART II: STRATEGY DEVELOPMENT

AIMS AND OBJECTIVES

Having identified and analyzed the opportunities that exist within international markets in the first section of the book, we now turn our attention to the ways in which firms can use international marketing to develop their international business in order to exploit these opportunities profitably. The focus in Part 2 is on developing an international marketing strategy that is appropriate for the firm, given the environment and market context in which it is working, the firm's capability and the ambition of its management. Throughout the section we emphasize the importance of the mindset of the management of the firm in planning their international marketing and take decisive action to deal with the challenges posed by the business and market context, analyzed in section 1.

The first chapter in Part 2, Chapter 5, concentrates on the international marketing strategies of small- and medium-sized enterprises. The discussion ranges from firms taking their first steps in international markets, or marketing to international customers from their home base, to those dynamic small firms that have the ambition and capability to grow quickly to become the major global players of the future.

When we think of globalization it is the very largest firms in the world that come to mind. Chapter 6 is concerned with the global strategies of the firms that operate within a global context and build brands that are instantly recognizable. Their global strategies aim to appeal to customers worldwide and ensure that as many customers as possible choose their products and services.

For any firm moving into a new international market the key step is to decide which market entry method should be chosen in order to achieve the best outcome from the investment that is made.

In Chapter 7 we discuss the factors that firms must consider in selecting an appropriate market entry method.

In Chapter 8 we consider the product and service management strategy and focus upon the need to have a constantly evolving portfolio of products and services that meet the current and future needs of global customers.

CHAPTER 5

© R_R, Shutterstock

INTERNATIONAL NICHE MARKETING STRATEGIES FOR SMALL- AND MEDIUM-SIZED ENTERPRISES

LEARNING OBJECTIVES

After reading this chapter you should be able to:

- Appreciate the nature and types of international marketing undertaken in the SME sector

- Compare the different strategic approaches and mindsets of SMEs in international marketing

- Understand the factors affecting SME international strategic management

- Identify the characteristics of the different stages of international development of SMEs

- Be able to evaluate the factors for success and failure in SME international marketing

INTRODUCTION

Small and medium-sized enterprises (SMEs) have always been significant creators of wealth and employment in domestic economies, but are a less powerful force outside their home territory, usually because of their limited resources. Indeed many SMEs, despite what may be obvious business capability, never move into international markets at all. However, for reasons which will be explored in this chapter, SMEs have growth potential both in fast-growing business sectors that involve applying new technology and in market niches, where innovation in mature industry sectors can lead to new opportunities. In less developed markets entrepreneurs can play a vital role in countering poverty by creating new businesses to employ local people. The impact of these SMEs in regenerating the economy can increase considerably if they can gain access to international markets.

In this chapter we discuss the factors which influence the patterns of international development of small- and medium-sized firms, including the strategic options available to them and the particular problems they face in implementing their strategy. We also emphasize the different mindsets of SMEs needed to exploit their business situation.

The traditional model of SME internationalization is exporting, in which goods are manufactured in one country and transferred to buyers in other countries, but many SMEs are involved in a broader range of international marketing activity and it is for this reason we observe many international niche marketing companies. Small service providers generate revenue from customers in foreign markets either by providing services from the home country which customers can access wherever they are situated (for example, information and advice supplied via the Internet) or by providing services in the firm's home country, and requiring the customers to visit (for example, tourism, training and education residential courses).

Increasingly, large firms are finding that operating on a global scale often makes them inflexible and unresponsive to fast-changing markets, with the result that smaller, more entrepreneurial firms with an innovative idea, can compete globally in their chosen niche market from the start (born globals). To be successful all these international market approaches require an understanding of the factors affecting international marketing and what capabilities are needed to grow the business internationally.

The SME sector and its role within the global economy

A number of definitions of the small- and medium-sized firm sector exist, but the most commonly used terms relate to the number of employees in the company. The European Union, for example, defines SMEs as those firms employing less than 250 staff. This characterization, however, effectively includes 99 per cent of all firms in Europe and accounts for roughly 50 per cent of employment and, because it includes sole operators as well as quite sophisticated businesses, is not particularly useful for segmenting the smaller firms sector.

In this chapter, therefore, the review of smaller firm international strategies is not restricted to firms with a specific number of employees, but instead focuses on those issues that apply to businesses in general which have the mindset to think and act like small- and medium-sized enterprises. The reason for adopting this stance is that a garment-making firm with 250 employees has a very restricted capacity to internationalize, whereas a 250-employee financial services or computer software company could be a significant international player. Many quite large companies take business decisions within a small group of major shareholders or senior managers in much the same way that the family owners of small firms take decisions. Many of the fastest-growing international firms grow rapidly through the 250 employee ceiling without making significant changes to their international strategic approach or management style. Our discussion, therefore, relates to issues affecting firms which could not be described as large multinational enterprises (MNEs) with the global power to dominate their sector, but we do consider some of the implications for firms growing from being SMEs to global players.

SMEs can be vulnerable to changes in the competitive environment and there are high failure rates. Because of globalization, the liberalization of trade policies and removal of protectionism and most trade barriers, virtually all firms are part of the global market, simply because their suppliers, customers and competitors are likely to be global players. In practice, however, many SMEs do remain focused on the domestic market, which may soon become over-supplied and this may be one reason why many firms fail to grow. Only a small percentage of SMEs, perhaps less than 5 per cent, grow significantly and an even smaller percentage have the ambition to become international traders.

Despite this the SME sector is increasingly recognized as a creator of wealth and employment because over the last 20 years many large firms have periodically downsized by reducing their workforce, rationalizing their operations and outsourcing their activities, often to smaller firms. Public sector organizations have also increased their outsourcing and in many countries this has left the small- and medium-sized firms sector as the only significant growing source of wealth and employment.

The role of SME internationalization in economic regeneration

Encouraging entrepreneurship is seen by many experts as the route to future prosperity for emerging markets. It can be argued that growing the private business sector helps put money in people's pockets, increases domestic demand, generates tax revenues and reduces dependency on international aid. Indeed there is considerable debate about the proportion of international aid that should be used for alleviating hunger, addressing basic health care and education and improving a country's infrastructure, as opposed to supporting and promoting business creation and development.

In practice, however, it can be argued that it is those SMEs that trade internationally which are most important. SMEs that market their products and services in the domestic economy often grow at the expense of other domestic SMEs because of the relatively limited home market. However, export markets offer seemingly unlimited scope for SMEs to grow and have the effect of importing jobs and foreign currency, so creating wealth in the domestic economy. Of particular significance in less developed countries, as we shall see in Chapter 7, is the first 'level' of international market entry strategies. This includes domestic purchasing in which the international customer purchases products from the emerging market SME in its home country. Examples would include a supermarket sourcing fruit or coffee shop chains sourcing coffee beans from African farmers. In Chapter 7 we discuss this in more detail and Illustration 5.1 provides an example of domestic purchasing from the Maasai in Kenya.

ILLUSTRATION 5.1

© Britta Kasholm-Tengve, iStockphoto.com

Maasai – leaders in high fashion

Sitting under a spreading acacia tree in Nairobi, a group of Maasai women thread beads into intricate patterns to create breast plates, earrings and bracelets that convey their social and marital status. But this is no longer purely the traditional work that left the women with very small amounts of money for long days at work making products for the local market in Kenya and for tourists. The women are part of a co-operative that continues the tradition but at the same time increases their earnings. Their beads are heading for a new market, for European designers who are innovating in the use of the beads to create new designs for the next season's high fashion.

What has changed their work and prosperity is Safari bead run by Zimbabwe-born Lisa Barratt, who acts as an intermediary winning profitable orders abroad. The new designs are distributed to the rural communities where the products are made. Ms Barratt collects the finished products, checks for consistent quality and drops off the next assignment. Because the aim is for the women to receive a fair wage, the products have to be charged at higher prices than High Street shops would be prepared to pay, so the products need to be sold into the couture end of fashion, where individual designs and original patterning will be used in dresses selling for thousands of dollars.

The women had only been taught the traditional designs by their mothers and aunts but the new designs ordered by the fashion designers will inevitably influence the way the Maasai bead motifs develop in the future and the Maasai men can look forward to being the height of fashion too!

Question

1 What do you consider to been the risks faced by the Maasai women and how could they be reduced?

Reference: S Smith beads hit the catwalk, BBCOnline, accessed on 24 September 2010.

The challenges for SMEs from less developed countries

Small organizations from emerging markets are often severely disadvantaged in international marketing. For example, small farmers from poor countries are frequently exploited by aggressive multinational retailers who ruthlessly use the global competition among small organizations. The poor negotiating position of the farmers and the perceived demand from consumers for low prices forces down the prices paid to farmers to one which is so low that it results in workers living below the poverty line. Although the multinational retailers sign up to ethical social corporate responsibility principles, many fail to behave ethically in their everyday transactions and there are many stories of unacceptable behaviour.

Fairtrade and the protection of the interests of farmers Nicholls and Opal (2005) discuss the Fairtrade organization (www.fairtrade.org) which was developed to promote ethical consumption. It is an independent consumer label which appears on products as an independent guarantee that disadvantaged producers in the developing world are getting a better deal.

For a product to display the Fairtrade mark it must meet international Fairtrade standards. These standards are set by the international certification body Fairtrade Labelling Organizations International (FLO), which inspects and certifies them. They receive a minimum price that covers the cost of sustainable production and an extra premium that is invested in social or economic development projects. Fairtrade principles include:

- direct purchasing from producers;
- transparent and long-term trading partnerships;
- cooperation not competition;
- agreed minimum prices to cover the costs of production, usually set higher than market minimums;
- focus on development and technical assistance via the payment to suppliers of an agreed social premium (often 10 per cent or more of the cost price of goods);
- provision of market information; and
- sustainable and environmentally responsible production.

By 2007 Fairtrade claimed to have certified 422 producer groups in 49 countries, who were selling to hundreds of Fairtrade registered importers, licensees and retailers in 19 countries. Fairtrade turnover had reached in excess of £1 billion.

There are arguments for and against the Fairtrade principles. The major argument against Fairtrade is that it acts as a kind of subsidy and creates artificially high prices which can then encourage the creation of surpluses. In practice, the key step is connecting the farmers better with their distant markets, helping them to develop their market knowledge, build their export or processing capability, or to diversify to meet newly identified demand. Fairtrade provides examples including coffee growers developing citrus or macadamia nuts, banana farmers moving into other premium tropical produce, or investment in alternative income-generation projects such as ecotourism, as well as support for community health and education programmes.

Infrastructure weaknesses The challenges for international marketers from emerging markets are huge. Many of the emerging countries have difficult geography and terrain with remote areas and an inhospitable climate. Many have a poorly developed infrastructure and suffer unreliable and often poor quality supplies of utilities, such as energy, water and power. Fixed line telecommunications and transport are slow and unreliable. Usually there is an overly bureaucratic and inefficient financial and business support infrastructure. The informal economy is huge in less developed countries (LDCs) and, in addition, bribery and corruption are rife at all levels. War and terrorism can have a devastating long-term effect on trade.

However, organizations from emerging markets can and do succeed in building their businesses despite these challenges if they can connect with their market and thus build the knowledge and capabilities to compete. For example, simply knowing what the actual international market price is for their products, rather than relying for price information on a buyer or a third party, is crucial and can have a huge

© Diana Lundin iStockphoto.com

ILLUSTRATION 5.2

Chocolate bringing a better future for villagers in Sierra Leone

Sierra Leone has been ravaged by civil war and poverty for decades and it is in places like this that Fairtrade can have its greatest impact but also its greatest challenges.

Wata Nabien, like many people here, has had her cocoa plantation for most of the 40 years of her life and her three year old daughter has never tasted the results of her labour. She works alone except when the neighbours help with the harvesting, chasing monkeys and birds away from the ripening fruit, trying to avoid hidden snakes … or men.

The country is at the bottom of the UN list of wealth and development. One in six women die in childbirth and one in four children will not reach the age of five. Wata has never been to school. Wata's father, who planted the cocoa trees, and her brother died in the civil war. Rape and murder were common, children were forced to become soldiers and amputation was the usual punishment for opposition.

The cocoa buyers ruthlessly exploited the situation. The buyers would visit the villages during the dry season, 'the hunger season' and lend the families rice. When the crop was ready in January the buyers would reclaim the debt – but it would be at grotesquely unfair rates, one sack of cocoa beans for one sack of rice, but the villagers were unaware of the real value of their crop and the market price – and they had to feed their children.

In the midst of war the farmers planned for the future when they would manage their own exports and an alliance was formed with Africa's most successful co-operative Kuapa Kokoo (Good Cocoa Farmers' Company). Kuapa with 47 000 farmer members owns nearly half of Britain's Divine chocolate company and is the main source of Fairtrade chocolate, now supplying Cadbury (for Dairy Milk) and (Mars for KitKat). The farmers had to be retrained to relearn their business and grow better cocoa to attract higher prices. Because they cannot get hold of chemicals the crop, of course, is organic. The Sierra Leone farmers have been successful and generated surpluses which have been used to build storage sheds and an office for the co-operative. Life is still not easy though. As the cocoa buyers see the balance of power shifting they are still trying to put the co-operative out of business. But at least now everyone owns a pair of shoes.

Question

1 Why should global companies support their extended supply chain and what are the benefits?

Reference: A Renton, Chocolate gives Sierra Leone's villagers new hope, *The Observer*, 19 September 2010.

impact on the viability of a small organization. By enabling a real time connection with international market information that bypasses incomplete, unreliable and out-of-date infrastructure, mobile computing could bring about the next 'industrial revolution'. It is also important for these SMEs to understand the value contributions of the supply chain, identifying changing customer demands and expectations, market trends, understanding what quality standards are required and knowing how to meet them and appreciating the power of branding to raise the perception of the products.

In countries that have a small, unsophisticated domestic market these issues may not be so significant, but in international markets the goods and services must compete with those from other countries, even though they may be cheaper or unique. This poses the problem of the customers' perceptions of the quality of their goods and service. What is acceptable in a local emerging market may not be acceptable to consumers in a developed country. Illustration 5.2 shows how even in a country ravaged by war Fairtrade principles can made a significant improvement. While the obvious route to the international market is by becoming a contract manufacturer or grower, the Internet offers further potential. To address the imbalance in power between the supplier and major international customers, improved networking of small growers and manufacturers can help.

Government support

We have explained the potential contribution of entrepreneurs and SMEs to the regeneration of national economies in terms of jobs and wealth creation through internationalization and the challenges they face. It is hardly surprising, therefore, that governments in developed and developing countries encourage SMEs to internationalize by running export promotion programmes providing support and advice.

Governments often provide support in the form of resources and advice but at significantly different levels, ranging from help with documentation, comprehensive country market information, export credit guarantees, trade missions and, in some cases, target country representative offices. OECD (2009) emphasize the need for policy-makers to be more concerned with determining what assistance might be useful in helping firms to become more marketing oriented and focused on satisfying customer needs by improving quality, service and specifications to meet international standards and becoming more effective in conducting business overseas. While help with language training is usually available, it is cultural training in both the social and business culture that is often more important. In South Africa, Proudly South African (www.proudlysouthafrican.co.za) is an initiative of the National Economic Development and Labour Council (Nedlac) and is supported by organized business, organized labour, government and the community to encourage firms to achieve the high standards necessary to compete against international competition and in foreign markets. Governments also preferentially may support exporting from particular regions of the country or support particular sectors that have exhibited the greatest growth potential. For example, the South African Department of Trade and Industry supports a number of sectors including agro-processing, chemicals, electronics and textiles.

The OECD suggest the role of private sector organizations, such as Chambers of Commerce, could be enhanced citing a number of examples, as well as public sector agencies, such as local authorities, local business support agencies, banks and accountants, which also provide SMEs with a range of services to support their international marketing activity. The support activities should focus particularly on addressing the barriers to internationalization by, for example, redressing managerial capacity barriers and also providing a wide range of actions to support the motivating factors.

Management Challenge 5.1 is concerned with the role of marketing in stimulating business in some of the poorest countries, but also prompts the broader question about how to get the best value from public money provided by governments to small firms.

We know that SMEs play different roles in the global economy, they have different ambitions and exploit different types of opportunity. It is this diversity that leads to SMEs adopting different approaches to international development.

The nature of SME international marketing strategies

In exploiting these opportunities to generate revenue from international markets SMEs have a number of alternative strategies which provide a useful method of categorization of SME internationalization.

- *Exporting* is primarily concerned with selling abroad domestically developed and produced goods and services.
- *International niche marketing* is concerned with marketing a differentiated product or service overseas, usually to a single customer segment, using the full range of market entry and marketing mix options available.
- *Domestically delivered or developed niche services* can be marketed or delivered internationally to potential visitors.
- *Direct marketing including electronic commerce* allows firms to market products and services globally from a domestic location.

MANAGEMENT CHALLENGE 5.1

International marking helping social enterprises

For the most part in this book we discuss international marketing as it applies to private sector organizations and occasionally we refer to the larger global charities, such as Oxfam and Save the Children.

In practice the for-profit and not-for-profit sectors converge in the area of social entrepreneurship. There has been unprecedented interest from public, private and charitable organizations and companies in addressing the problems of Africa, for example through UN initiatives, interventions by companies and campaigns, such as Make Poverty History.

The Skoll World Forum on Social Entrepreneurship founded by Jeff Skoll, the first president of eBay, suggests that such initiatives do not work and that the people in the country can succeed in business provided a longer-term view of investment is taken.

The principles of international marketing are fundamental to and can be applied to all aspects of the work of campaigning, interventions and generating success for small firms in the poorest parts of the world.

Question

1 How can marketing help people in the poorest parts of the world?

Reference: www.skollfoundation.org/.

■ *Participation in the international supply chain* of an MNE can lead to SMEs piggybacking on the MNE's international development. This may involve either domestic production or establishing a facility close to where the MNE's new locations are established in other countries.

Exporting

The emergence of global competition and the opening up of international markets has stimulated many firms to embark on the internationalization process: for many of them, exporting is the first significant stage. Exporting has been the most popular approach adopted by firms to enter and penetrate foreign markets as it requires less commitment of resources, has little effect on the firm's existing operations and involves low investment and financial risks. Leonidou *et al.* (2007) identify the factors stimulating smaller firms to export. However, exporting, when defined as the marketing of goods and/or services across national and political boundaries, is not solely the preserve of small- and medium-sized businesses, nor is it a temporary stage in the process of internationalization for many firms. Many companies, both large and small, do not progress beyond the stage of relatively limited involvement in international markets.

Motivation

In OECD (2009) there are references to a large volume of literature covering exporting, including export stimuli, barriers to exporting and promotion programmes. Despite the wide variation in the contexts in which the research was carried out some broad conclusions can be reached.

The research primarily focuses on proactive stimuli but it is also important to recognize that motivations to export can also be reactive too. Two examples of reactive strategies are:

1 If a product has reached maturity or is in decline in the home market, the company may find new foreign markets where the product has not reached the same life cycle stage and which, therefore, offers potential for further growth.

2 Companies may seek new markets abroad to utilize their production facilities to their full capacity.

In these circumstances companies may well embark on marginal pricing and sell at lower prices on the export markets, seeking only a contribution to their overall cost for their home base market.

The following are reactive stimuli:

- adverse domestic market conditions;
- an opportunity to reduce inventories;
- the availability of production capacity;
- favourable currency movements;
- the opportunity to increase the number of country markets and reduce the market-related risk;
- unsolicited orders from overseas customers.

To reduce risk, OECD (2009) identify proactive stimuli for exporting as growth motives, including profits, an increased market size, a stronger market position and market diversification. If a company sees only limited growth opportunities in the home market for a proven product it may well see market diversification as a means of expansion. This could lead to the identification of new market segments within a domestic market, but it may well lead to geographic expansion in foreign markets. Thus, companies try to spread risks and reduce their dependence on any one market. Equally the firm may identify market gaps.

The proactive company with Knowledge assets, including the management's previous international experience and capability, innovation capability, unique products or services, resources and a well-managed marketing information system will identify foreign market opportunities. This could, of course, be by undertaking formal structured research. Proactive companies, however, highlight the importance of networks, supply chain links and social ties, through immigrant communities in global markets.

The following are proactive stimuli:

- attractive profit and growth opportunities;
- the ability to easily modify products for export markets;
- public policy programmes for export promotion;
- foreign country regulations;
- the possession of unique products;
- economies resulting from additional orders.

And certain managerial elements including:

- the presence of an export-minded manager;
- the opportunity to better utilize management talent and skills;
- management beliefs about the value of exporting.

Barriers to internationalization

Many companies with export potential never become involved in international marketing, and a series of export studies have found that it is often a great deal easier to encourage existing exporters to increase their involvement in international markets than to encourage those who are not exporting to begin the process. The reasons given by companies for not exporting are numerous. The biggest barrier to entry into export markets for these companies is the fear that their products are not marketable overseas: consequently they become preoccupied with the domestic market. Other SMEs believe that because of the particular nature of their business sector, their domestic market continues to offer the best potential for market growth or market share growth and is not so vulnerable to international competition, so a domestically focused strategy makes the best use of their resources.

The OECD (2009) have summarized a large number of recent research studies into the SME internationalization barriers. The following are the areas which are identified:

- Shortage of working capital to finance exports.
- Inadequate knowledge of overseas markets and lack of information to find and analyze markets.

ILLUSTRATION 5.3

German SME, Zetec, winning through the recession

Coming out of the recession, the German economy accelerated at a pace not experienced since the reunification 20 years previously. The turnaround was completely unexpected with the automobile industry contributing £76 billion, reversing all its export losses of 2009. Sales of German cars to China tripled and 11 500 workers at VW gave up their summer holidays to help meet demand and get themselves out of their personal financial problems.

The turnaround in large firms was mirrored in small firms. Ingo Hell the chairman of Zetec, a metal components maker with 30 staff near Stuttgart, believed in May 2009 that his company had two months to survive, as orders had halved and credit had dried up. However, within months the company had won back all its orders and with the export boom it had embarked on a project to double the size of its factory. The key to being able to exploit the rapid turn-around was that the German government provided enhanced benefits for short time working, which avoided large scale redundancies and loss of the skills that are vital to successful manufacturing, so when the demand picked up again Zetec was well placed to exploit the opportunity.

Question

1 What steps can small firms take to reduce their risks during recessions?

Reference: M Woodhead, For Germany, the darkest days are over, *Sunday Times*, 3 October 2010.

- Inability to contact overseas customers, including finding the right partner, the right representation and suitable distribution channels.
- Lack of managerial time, skills and knowledge, including differences in managers' perceptions and psychological barriers to internationalization.

There is significant risk too because SMEs have little influence over environmental change and recession often leads to many business casualties. SMEs can over extend themselves financially by growing internationally too quickly. If there is a downturn in demand they may not be able to generate sufficient cash and profits to service their debt and often end up being taken over or going bankrupt.

Illustration 5.3 shows how a firm came close to this but because of good government policy and flexibility in their own approach they survived and thrived by quickly adapting to the new situation.

Non exporters tend to highlight issues such as the perceived bureaucracy associated with international markets and trade barriers, whereas experienced exporters tend to believe that these problems should be addressed through managerial proactivity, for example, by training staff and seeking expert assistance. A number of studies suggest other factors that might be specific in some contexts. For example, a study of 120 firms in Nigeria by Okpara *et al.* (2010) added other barriers to the above including factors such as poor infrastructure, and corruption and bureaucratic bottlenecks.

Niche marketing Having identified the motivations and barriers to exporting it is tempting to conclude that many exporters are characterized by being product-oriented – selling abroad the products and services that are successful in the domestic market. Moreover, exporters often seem to throw away their successful domestic marketing strategies in international markets, preferring instead to delegate their marketing to agents and distributors. In doing this they seem to overlook the alternative market entry and marketing mix strategies that are available to them, opting instead for a strategy of least involvement. In many cases this approach may meet the exporting firm's immediate objectives, especially if, for example, they are simply seeking to offload excess production capacity, but it does not provide them with a sound basis for substantially increasing their international market presence.

Table 5.1 The difference between exporting and international niche marketing

Marketing Strategy	Exporting Selling production capacity	International Marketing Meeting customer needs
Financial Objective	To amortize overheads	To add value
Segmentation	Usually by country and consumer characteristics	By identifying common international customer benefit
Pricing	Cost based	Market or customer based
Management focus	Efficiency in operations	Meeting market requirements
Distribution	Using existing agents or distributor	Managing the supply chain
Market information	Relying on agent or distributor feedback	Analyzing the market situation and customer needs
Customer relationship	Working through intermediaries	Building multiple level relationships

Source: http://www.unctad.org © UNCTAD, © United Nations 2000–2011.

By contrast, international niche marketing occurs where firms become a strong force in a narrow specialized market of one or two segments across a number of country markets. Parrish, Cassill and Oxenham (2006) explain how niche marketing can be used in a mature sector – for example, global textiles – to increase competitiveness, despite the presence of strong rivals.

Brown and McDonald (1994) explain that the segments must be too small or specialized to attract large competitors: true niche marketing does not include small brands or companies that are minor players in a mass market offering undifferentiated products. For the international niche to be successful the product or service must be distinctive (highly differentiated), be recognized by consumers and other participants in the international supply chain and have clear positioning.

To sustain and develop the niche the firm must:

- have good information about the segment needs;
- have a clear understanding of the important segmentation criteria;
- understand the value of the product niche to the targeted segment(s);
- provide high levels of service;
- carry out small scale innovations;
- seek cost efficiency in the supply chain;
- maintain a separate focus, perhaps, by being content to remain relatively small;
- concentrate on profit rather than market share; and
- evaluate and apply appropriate market entry and marketing mix strategies to build market share in each country in which they wish to become involved.

There are, therefore, significant differences between the traditional view of exporting and international niche marketing and these are summarized in Table 5.1.

Niche marketing of domestically delivered services

In the travel industry domestic firms such as hotels, tour operators and leisure attractions generate foreign earnings for the country by attracting visitors. International destination marketing of cities, regions and countries, such as Prague, the wildlife reserves of Botswana and Vietnam is increasingly important for economic success in certain areas. It is usually undertaken by relatively small organizations such as tourist boards that represent a huge network of dependent providers of accommodation, catering, leisure activities and experiences. Their role is becoming increasingly important as the economies of the destinations become ever more dependent on tourism and competition between destinations and the number of potential visitors increase.

With increased international travel and improved access to worldwide communications a much wider range of services is being offered to visiting customers. Examples include the provision of education, specialized training, medical treatment, sports, cultural and leisure events and specialist retailing, such as luxury goods. For example, around 400 000 foreign students study at 165 higher education institutions in the UK and many more study at colleges and private language schools. The British Council supports the international marketing efforts of what are largely independent institutions.

Clearly these activities lead to wealth and jobs being generated in the local economy in much the same way as with exporting and niche marketing. The international marketing strategy processes and programmes are similar too, in that the products and services must meet the requirements of, and be promoted to, international customers. Consequently, issues of standardization and adaptation of the marketing mix elements are equally important. The additional challenge is that the benefits obtained from the service provided must be unique and superior and thus outweigh the benefits to the consumer of their locally available services, as well as the cost of travel that the customers will incur in the purchasing and consumption process.

In addition to the services designed to be offered to individuals in both consumer and business-to-business markets, a whole range of additional services which fall into this category of being domestically delivered are concerned with developing solutions for opportunities or problems identified abroad. These might include technology developments, such as research into new drugs, trial and testing facilities, software development and product and packaging design services.

There are many examples of research and development companies, such as Imagination Technologies and ARM in computer microchip design that licence their new technologies to customers around the world.

Importing and reciprocal trading

Importing is clearly the opposite process to international marketing and as such might be seen by governments as 'exporting' jobs and potential wealth. However, the purpose of considering importing here is to highlight the nature of international trade as it is today. Rarely do supply chains for products and services involve solely domestic production and delivery. There has been a substantial increase in outsourcing, not only by large firms but by SMEs too.

Exporting and importing have become inextricably linked so that the challenge is one of adding value to imported components and services, no matter where they are sourced, so that they can then be re-exported in order to meet the international customers' needs effectively and profitably.

Importing activity can also considerably enhance a company's potential to network, leading ultimately, perhaps, to reciprocal trading in which, as a result, the supplier might take other products or services in return from the customer.

Foreign Direct Investment It might be concluded from this that raising the level of value-adding supply chain activity in a particular country is the ultimate aim of governments. Most governments take this further by encouraging Foreign Direct Investment (FDI) by multinationals in the belief that as well as aiding the economy through increasing employment and tax revenues, the MNEs' operations will benefit the indigenous SME supply sector by:

- providing additional B2B sales opportunities for the SME suppliers to provide components, subcontracted fabrication work and non-core services as part of the MNE's supply chain; and
- setting and establishing higher international quality standards among the suppliers, which will then enable them to compete better in international markets.

The danger with FDI is that MNEs will only maintain their operations in a particular country while it is financially advantageous. When the MNE finds a lower labour cost country location for its operations it will move on. Many countries have found that low-cost assembly-type manufacturing or call centre operations can be easily relocated with the associated loss of jobs and tax revenues. While the government can take action to encourage continuing high levels of FDI through financial incentives, ensuring a well-educated and flexible workforce, an efficient, responsive and flexible SME supply chain will also be a significant factor in MNE location decisions.

Direct marketing and electronic commerce

Cross border direct marketing and, in particular, electronic commerce continues to grow as customers become more confident in buying goods from abroad. Direct marketing offers the benefits of cutting out other distribution channel members such as importers, agents, distributors, wholesalers and retailers, by using a variety of communications media, including post, telephone, television and the Internet. For SMEs' suppliers these allow borders to be crossed relatively easily with limited investment and risk, and without the SMEs having to face many of the barriers already highlighted in this chapter. Illustration 5.4 shows how a website, www. etsy.com provides a platform for small craft work businesses to gain access to global customers.

Direct marketing also has a number of disadvantages. Despite the range of media available, communicating can still be problematic as personalization of the communication is essential for direct marketing success. In cross-border direct marketing there is always the danger of cultural insensitivity and language mistakes in the communications. Many of the following comments apply to both traditional direct marketing using physical media and electronic commerce, but we have focused on online trading as it is this method that has had the most impact on SME internationalization.

If customers speak different languages then it may be necessary for online retailers to have multilingual websites. This can add cost in setting up and servicing the website. The continued growth of online retailers may depend on selling to international customers who do not speak the home country language. Moreover, because of the need to manage large numbers of customers it is necessary to use databases which must be up to date, accurate and be capable of dealing with foreign languages. Even an incorrectly spelt name can be insulting to the recipient.

The Internet provides smaller firms with a shop window and also the means of obtaining payment, organizing and tracking shipment and delivery. For some products and services it can provide the means by which market information can be accumulated and new ideas collected, developed and modified by customers and other stakeholders.

Electronic commerce has led firms to redefine their business and it can also be a business in its own right. For example, many electronic commerce services take the form of information transfer and this can become the basis of the product or service itself, for example, specialist advice on personal finance, travel and hobbies.

As well as being a route to market in its own right in the form of direct commerce, the Internet as an interactive marketing information provider has an increasingly important role in each of the above international niche marketing strategies.

The Internet offers the benefits to SMEs of real time communications across distances and the levelling of the corporate playing field, leading to more rapid internationalization as well as achieving competitive advantage by:

- creating new opportunities;
- erecting barriers to entry;
- making cost savings from online communications;
- providing online support for inter-firm collaboration, especially in research and development, as an information search and retrieval tool;
- the establishment of company websites for marketing and sales promotion; and
- the transmission of any type of data including manuscripts, financial information and CAD/CAM (computer-aided design/computer-aided manufacture) files.

There are some disadvantages, especially the relative ease with which it is possible to become flooded with electronic messages (spam) and orders. While this may be manageable for certain products and

ILLUSTRATION 5.4

© zhang bo, iStockphoto.com

Crafting a money spinner

Around the world there are obsessive crafters hand spinning wool, silk painting, leatherworking or wood carving and every item is personal and means something. Nearly six million hand crafted items are for sale on Etsy (www.etsy.com) and, whereas few of the 400 000 worldwide sellers would make enough money to set up a traditional shop, setting up shop on Etsy is free. The site was set up by a 25-year-old American furniture maker, Rob Kalin, who was frustrated by the lack of places to sell his crafts. Each item costs 20 cents to list (it is an American site) and 3.5 per cent of the selling price is charged by Etsy, compared to 10 per cent by eBay. By 2010 39 million potential customers visited the site and monthly sales were around $22 million.

Because the sellers are doing the work for love rather than money, prices are often bargains. The ever-changing featured items are chosen as favourites by other sellers. The site is also a community and meet-ups are organized for members in cities around the world.

Question

1 What are the advantages for crafters of a niche sales platform like Etsy compared to a mass market platform like eBay or Taobao?

References: J Salter Money spinner, *The Daily Telegraph Magazine.*

---

services where production volumes can easily be increased or decreased, sales feasts and famines can cause havoc where production capacity is less flexible.

As advanced search engines become more sophisticated it is essential (and expensive) to make sure that the firm's offer is listed on the first page of search results for key words. The implications of this are that instead of marketing being essentially passive in electronic commerce, the marketing input required in designing websites needs to become increasingly sophisticated in promoting the products, providing interactive product design, development and safe payment arrangements. Technical and customer service support and initial customer segmentation and targeting are increasingly important to the delivery of an effective, focused business. Thus, while many SMEs see the Internet as a low-cost distribution channel, the greater competition and more sophisticated versions of electronic commerce make it more difficult for SMEs to compete. SMEs frequently face the dilemma of how to cope with powerful competitors. For example, dealing with niche markets used to be problematic for MNEs because of the difficulty of managing millions of small transactions, so SMEs could operate with more freedom in their chosen niche, but now information and communications technology allows MNEs to more cost effectively manage relatively small volumes and values, making them more competitive in niche markets.

The advent of e-business and the Internet appears, therefore, to offer the benefits to SMEs of being able to ignore borders and make more direct interaction possible between international SMEs and their customers. However, Servais, Madsen and Rasmussen (2007) explain that even 'born global' SMEs use the Internet only to a limited extent to sell their products and as a tool to support existing relationships. Considerable opportunities exist therefore for more creative direct marketing by SMEs.

The nature of international development

The internationalization process differs enormously depending on whether the company first serves the domestic market and later develops into foreign markets (adaptive exporter), or is expressly established from its inception to enter foreign markets (born global). Adaptive and born global exporters differ in a variety of ways, including their respective market assessment processes, reasons for international market involvement, managerial attitudes and the propensity to take risks. Successful born globals are seen to overcome their distinctive challenges with flexible managerial attitudes and practices.

Many exporting firms, especially in high-technology or industrial markets, internationalize through their network of relationships. Firms in any market establish and develop relationships through interactions with other individuals and firms, leading the parties to build mutual trust, respect and knowledge. Kulmeier and Knight (2010) explain that it is the quality of the relationships in four dimensions:

- communication;
- co-operation;
- trust; and
- commitment,

that are critical. Internationalization of the firm, therefore, becomes a consequence of the interaction between the firms in the network they have formed. The network of business relationships comprises a number of different stakeholders – customers, customers' customers, competitors, supplementary suppliers, suppliers, distributors, agents and consultants – as well as regulatory and other public agencies. In any specific country, different networks can be distinguished. Any or all of these relationships may become the conduit for the internationalization of a company. In these cases the internationalization process of a company is more aptly visualized as a series of multilateral cycles rather than a linear process (see Figure 5.1).

Thus the internationalization process manifests itself by the development of business relationships in other countries:

- through the establishment of relationships in country networks that are new to the firm, i.e. international extension;
- through the development of relationships in those networks, i.e. penetration;
- through connecting networks in different countries, i.e. international integration.

Relationship and network building are especially important in the fast changing, global environment, but particularly in high technology industries. Studies of the internationalization process of small hi-tech firms indicate that some of these companies follow the traditional internationalization patterns, while others behave differently. They go directly to more distant markets and rapidly set up their own subsidiaries. One reason seems to be that the entrepreneurs behind those companies have networks of colleagues

FIGURE 5.1 The multilateral aspects of the internationalization process

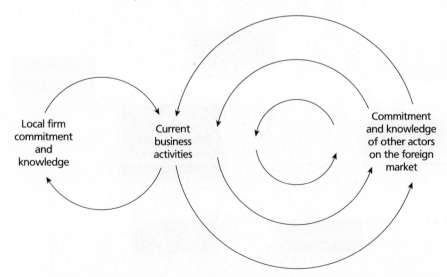

Source: © Johannson J. and Vahlne J.E. (1992) 'The Mechanism of Internationalization,' *International Marketing Review*, Emerald Insight.

dealing with the new technology. Internationalization, in these cases, is an exploitation of the advantage created by networking and may benefit from external facilitation.

Crick and Spence (2005) found that internationalization strategy formation for high performing SMEs is not always systematic and capable of being described by one single theory. Some firms take a much more opportunistic approach towards their internationalizing strategy and it is necessary to take a more holistic view of the organization and its context to explain its decisions.

Balabanis and Katsikea (2003) explain the further dimensions and add that there is some evidence to suggest that an entrepreneurial approach, which involves risk-taking, being proactive and innovative in developing strategies, is useful in international marketing development.

Geographic development of SMEs

For SMEs, country market selection and development of market share within each country are particularly important for growth. Given their limited resources and narrow margin for failure it is vital that their method of country market development is effective. The various patterns of SME international development are shown in Figure 5.2.

The conventional approach is for new companies to test the viability of their products in the domestic market before spreading internationally, but we have already indicated that a number of firms become international players almost immediately after they have been formed, either because they are born global

FIGURE 5.2 Geographic development of SMEs

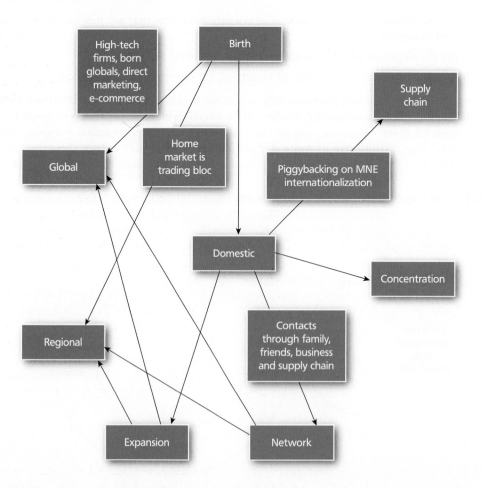

Source: Data adapted from *McKinsey 7S framework*, Thomas J. Peters and Robert H. Waterman (1982) *In Search of Excellence*, Warner.

or they operate within a common regional market. The different patterns of international spreading are now discussed.

Market expansion and concentration

The conventional view of country selection is that from a sound domestic base SMEs develop either by choosing between expanding into many markets, gaining a superficial presence and accepting a low overall market share, or concentrating their marketing activities in a small number of markets in which they can build a significant market share. The research in this area is inconclusive about the precise reasons why firms adopt one strategy or another.

Katsikeas and Leonidou (1996) found that market concentrators tend, in general, to be smaller firms, because of their greater interest in export profitability and lesser concern with export sales objectives. Typically they make regular visits overseas and this appears to play a key role in their strategy for penetrating the market. Concentrators experience more problems associated with product adaptation to the needs of their customers but pricing and their marketing organization needs present less of a problem.

Market expanders tend to be larger firms who are more concerned with export sales objectives, do more export marketing research and have greater overall market share expectations. They place less emphasis on profitability, personal visits are less important and they perceive fewer product adaptation-related problems. E-commerce businesses are typical market expanders.

Where the domestic market is redefined

The lowering or removal of barriers between countries and the move, for example, in the EU to the harmonization of standards, the removal of tariff barriers, reduction of non-tariff barriers and the introduction of a common currency within a regional trading bloc mean that SMEs are more likely to be active in more than one country market because the regional market is considered to be their domestic market. This is particularly the case, for example, in mainland Europe where there are no additional costs in travelling to a neighbouring country and, often, a common language may be used.

Where the SME international development is the result of networking

Many SMEs adopt what appears to be a rather unsystematic approach to country market selection. Their patterns of development tend to be the result of a network approach where the selection of the market is not merely made on the relative attractiveness of the markets and their match with the company capability, but rather on the reduction of the risk of entering unknown markets by working with individuals or companies they know. International development through using existing networks of contacts is more typical of Asian firms than SMEs from Western countries.

Internationalizing through networking using a small business management model still provides entrepreneurs with the means of achieving security, often because it allows fast adaptation in a rapidly changing world. Through a global network many small units can come up with a variety of solutions at an acceptable level of risk. Hardman, Messinger and Bergson (2005) have taken this further and suggest that to compete effectively with the largest competitors, with their scale advantages, small organizations will have to achieve virtual scale by working in alliances to achieve the necessary leverage. The Internet can facilitate this and the success of social networking is leading to greater online business networking.

Family networks

Nueno (2000) explains that the Chinese can be very effective entrepreneurs. While 1 per cent of the population of the Philippines is ethnic Chinese they control 40 per cent of the economy, half the economies

ILLUSTRATION 5.5

Family networking

Success in Asia still runs on power, prestige, influence, favours given and received, family fortune and connections. Without these even the simplest deal can come unstuck for no obvious reasons. For example, the Chinese, Japanese, Koreans and Indians have their own special connections and their business styles come down to trust and credibility – who vouches for whom.

There are six big economic groups in Asia that are growing fast as a result of networking. These are:

- Japanese *keiretsu* company connections;
- Koreans with *chaebol* conglomerates;
- mainland Chinese with party and military links;
- ethnic or overseas Chinese with their stored wealth, extended family, dialect and guild connections;
- the emerging *pribumi* and *bumiputera* (indigenous) business leaders of Indonesia and Malaysia with their political connections;
- the Indians with their family dynasties.

It is networking on a grand scale that provides the basis of the international operations as there are an estimated 57 million Chinese and 18 million Indians

that are living abroad. A Singaporean Chinese trader may have family connections in Taiwan, Hong Kong, Guandong, Fujian or Vietnam that can provide legal, banking and support services when moving across borders.

A small group of families also control the Indian economy and are successfully developing their global businesses. However, it is internal family disagreements that are their major concern. For example, the giant conglomerate, Reliance Industries was built as a rags to riches story over decades by Dhirubhai Ambani. After he died his sons, Anil and Mukesh fell out over the direction of the company. By 2005 they could no longer work together and their mother brokered a demerger into two groups. But the feud continued with Mukesh blocking Anil's telecom group's efforts to merge with South Africa's MTN. A dispute followed regarding gas prices and ended in court. Anil won and Mukesh appealed the ruling, but the oil ministry stepped in when it realized how damaging it was for the government when two wealthy men were seen to be fighting over the resources that should belong to the country.

The traditional power of the mainland Chinese dynasties was disrupted during the communist era and new dynasties will be created.

In the West many of the old, great family business dynasties have declined in importance and given way to the new entrepreneurs who have exploited new technologies, such as Rupert Mudoch of News International, which includes Sky. Perhaps such organizations are creating new family dynasties.

Question

1 To what extent do you expect the old family groups to be the future successes and to what extent do you expect the new groups that have created their wealth through new technologies succeed them?

of Indonesia and Thailand are controlled by 4 per cent and 10 per cent ethnic Chinese respectively and in Malaysia two-thirds of the economy is controlled by ethnic Chinese.

They operate effectively within a family network and, because the Chinese are spread throughout the world, they can lay the foundations for stronger links among businesses across borders as a network of entrepreneurial relationships. As we indicated earlier, in practice most SMEs operate within a network of personal contacts, but this is much more formalized in some cultures, such as the Chinese, because it is based on *guanxi* and the obligation to return favours. The Confucian tradition of hard work, thrift and respect for one's social network provides continuity, and the small network-based enterprises bound by strong cultural links is well suited to fast-changing markets. Illustration 5.5 explains the impact of family groups on international trade and gives an example of the effect of family feuds.

Networking and relationship marketing are now emphasized as key components of most SME internationalization strategies.

Where the SME is born global

Some SMEs market their products and services globally from birth or soon after because the customer segment or competition is global (especially in high technology, breakthrough products) or because the distribution method is global, for example, direct marketing and telecommunications-based international marketing (e.g. Internet). A survey for the Global Entrepreneurship Monitor (2009) identifies the percentage of early stage entrepreneurs that have an international orientation, and the extent to which customers are from other countries, whether it is export sales, selling to international customers online or as a consequence of international travel. Typically countries with a greater size, for example, India, Iran, Brazil, Russia, China and Australia have lower international orientation. Few US entrepreneurs, for example, have high international orientation of over 25 per cent of their customers, whereas three quarters have a small percentage of international customers. Interestingly Eastern European countries tend to have high international orientation.

A number of studies of born global firms have been made in different country contexts. Mort and Weerawardena (2006) explain that the new concept of international entrepreneurship has followed research into born global firms and highlighted the importance of relationships and networking in enabling the identification and exploitation of market opportunities and facilitating the development of knowledge-intensive products. Harris and Wheeler (2005) focus on the role of the entrepreneur's interpersonal relationships in the internationalization process and explain that strong, deep relationships are developed in wide social/personal and business situations that do not just provide information and access to networks but, more importantly, can be influential in directing strategy and can lead to the transformation of the firm.

Crick (2009) examines the differences between born global firms and international new ventures (INVs) and concludes that they do exhibit different characteristics as the born global management views the world as its marketplace from the outset whereas INVs' management see foreign markets as adjuncts to the domestic market and hence typically focus on regional markets. The majority of born globals are formed by active entrepreneurs and tend to emerge as a result of a significant breakthrough in some process or technology. They may apply cutting-edge technology to developing a unique product idea or to a new way of doing business. The products and services that born globals sell directly involve substantial value added and the majority of such products may be intended for industrial use. They do not compete on price.

Several trends have given rise to the emergence of born global firms:

- The increasing role of niche markets, especially in the developed world. As markets mature, products increasingly become commodities, and SMEs respond by identifying sub segments of customers that require a more specialized or customized product or service.

- To compete with large, powerful MNEs smaller firms must specialize. However, while the demand from a domestic niche market may be very small, the global demand can sustain an SME that is prepared to supply the niche on a worldwide basis.

- Recent advances in process technology mean low-scale batch production can be economical and new technologies mean that SMEs can compete with large firms to produce sophisticated products.

- Communications technologies allow SMEs to manage across borders and information is more readily accessible to everyone. It is now much less expensive to go international than it was just 20 years ago.

- Quicker response time, flexibility and adaptability to foreign tastes and specific customer requirements give these firms an immediate competitive edge.

- SMEs can gain access to funding and support, benefit from joint research programmes and technology transfer and employ cross-border educated managers more easily than ever before.

- Increasingly, international business is facilitated through partnership with foreign businesses – distributors, trading companies, subcontractors and alliances – allowing new specialist firms to participate in global networks more easily than before.

Supply chain internationalization

The pattern of internationalization of firms that are part of the supply chain of an MNE is usually determined by the international strategy adopted by the MNE. In a continual effort to achieve focus and operational efficiency, firms continually think about what are their core competence and answer the question 'what business are we in?'. The response to this question leads MNEs to identify those components and services that were part of the overall product offer but which they regarded as being peripheral to their business. As a result of this many decide to outsource more of their supplies, either from MNE specialist component makers and service providers, or from SMEs that have exploited these new opportunities to grow.

The reasons for MNEs to outsource can be summarized as follows:

- It reduces the capital requirements of the business (the supplier rather than the MNE invests in new processes and facilities).

- It overcomes the difficulty of developing quickly and maintaining in-house knowledge in many different specialist knowledge areas.

- It improves flexibility, as some firms are better equipped and can carryout small production runs, special designs and development tasks more quickly.

- The MNE can take risks in more peripheral activities where their expertise is weak, stopping the firm from falling behind in the effectiveness of its non-core operations.

- The economies of scale of suppliers may make components much cheaper through outsourcing rather than from in-house supplies.

- The expertise of business support service providers, for example in transport and delivery systems, cannot be matched.

- Downsizing without outsourcing can lead to management resources becoming too stretched and unfocused.

The disadvantages of outsourcing are:

- *Loss of know-how* – Western businesses in many sectors have outsourced manufacturing to Asian firms who have subsequently opened up as competitors.

- *The costs of managing the outsourced supplies* – Managing outsourced components and services does require time and technical expertise and, particularly in the case of IT, there have been some difficulties of integrating the service with the firm's primary strategic objectives.

Both large and smaller firms have been the beneficiaries of this increased outsourcing but for smaller firms there are particular challenges. These include:

- The need to become closely linked with one or two major customers, upon which the SME is almost entirely dependent for survival and success.

- Internationalization is driven by the demands of the MNE. Failure to follow their product or market development demands may result in the loss of all the business as the MNE will seek alternative suppliers.

- They are under continual pressure to make operational efficiencies and design improvements in order to offer even better value for money.

- Concentration on developing the relationship with the MNE may lead to the firm becoming relatively weaker in external marketing, putting the firm at a disadvantage if it needs to find new customers when difficulties occur.

The advantages for SMEs are:

- The opportunities to learn from working with the MNE. This is likely to improve the smaller firms' strategic and operational management systems, communications and purchasing efficiency.

MANAGEMENT CHALLENGE 5.2

Rising costs, lower prices: no longer cleaning up

Over the last few years small manufacturing firms in developed countries have found it difficult to compete with factories in low labour cost countries, such as China, and many have outsourced manufacturing there. At the same time the large number of emerging middle class consumers in emerging countries are used to basic products at very low prices, which makes it difficult for small western businesses to compete. Nine years ago Nick Grey invented and patented a cordless electric floor cleaner. His company Gtech has revenues of £7 million and a workforce of 27. Sales through major retailers amount to 75 per cent of his revenues. He could get much larger volumes in international markets but would need to charge much lower prices. The problem is that manufacturing costs are rising rapidly. He outsources this production to China but the attitude of his Chinese manufacturing partner of nine years has changed dramatically. Whereas previously they were supportive now Grey considers them cold and unresponsive, refusing to discuss cost increases and

regularly losing their temper when he tries to discuss price. They will even change prices halfway through an order.

The reason is that now retailers are buying cheap products in larger volumes directly from the factory as 'own label' products. Shipping costs have trebled in a year driven up by increasing demand for space on containers and higher fuel prices. Gtech's gross margin has plummeted from 50 per cent to 20 per cent in three years as the company tries to maintain retailer price points, such as £29 and £39. Faced with the higher costs abroad companies would like to bring manufacturing back home but many of the supporting industries, such as injection moulders are no longer there, so it is not really possible. Whatever manufacturing solution the company goes for Gtech know that they must move the brand up market and focus on building demand for higher priced products by educating customers at home and in international markets of the value of design and quality. The company needs to innovate as Grey intends to discontinue cheaper products that average less than 4.5 out of 5 on customer ratings on Amazon.

Question

1 What advice would you give to Nick Grey?

References: Hurley, J., 'Gtech is looking to solve the Chinese puzzle', *Daily Telegraph*, 12 October 2010.

- They get greater business security through reliable and predictable ordering while the customer is successful.
- The opportunity to focus on production and technical issues rather than being diverted by the need to analyze changes to the market, customer and competition to the same degree.

Developing relationships

The key to success in working within the supply chain of an MNE is developing an effective relationship which can build upon the advantages and minimize the disadvantages of cooperative working between firms which may have some business objectives in common, but also may have a number of differences. As more SMEs become involved in international supply chains, the ways in which relationships between smaller suppliers and the MNE differ between Western and Asian styles of management become particularly significant.

The Western way of arranging sourcing is a much more competition-based approach and has the advantage of a much sharper focus on cost reduction, profit and individual creativity. The Asian approach is much more cooperative-based and includes ensuring that more than one strong supplier is available, expertise is shared and built upon, and the competitive focus is always on the much larger market opportunity. However, the Management Challenge 5.2 faced by Gtech is an example of the problems that outsourcing can cause.

Over the past few years the number of cooperative arrangements between Western and Asian styles within one supply chain has increased and, as a result, arrangements which could be described as a combination of the two have been developed in which longer-term contracts have been agreed in order to maximize the cooperation between the MNE and supplier, but without the insistence on sharing information with the losing contractor, which was often a feature of the Asian approach.

International strategic marketing management in SMEs

Having considered the various categories of SME internationalization and the nature of SME international development, we now turn to the factors which influence the international marketing management of SMEs. The McKinsey 7S framework, shown in Figure 5.3, is useful for discussing the elements.

The McKinsey 7S framework

The first three elements – strategy, structure and systems – are considered to be the hardware of successful management and as such can be implemented across international markets without the need for significant adaptation. The other four – management style, staff, skills and shared values – are the software, and are affected by cultural differences. Often it is the management of these aspects of the business that highlights good management in the best firms and relatively unimpressive management in poorer performing firms. It is quite obvious too that it is these elements of the framework which can vary considerably from country to country and provide the most significant challenges for SMEs developing from their home base into an organization with involvement in a number of different countries.

The characteristics of these four software elements are:

1 *Style*: In organizations such as McDonald's, it is the consistency across the world of the management and their operational style that is one of the distinguishing features of the companies. For SMEs the management and operational style often reflects the personality, standards and values of the owner, and is often maintained as the firm matures, as is the case with Richard Branson of Virgin and Steve Jobs of Apple.

2 *Skills*: The sorts of skills that are needed to carry out the strategy vary considerably between countries and also over time as the firm grows rapidly and new strategies and systems are introduced. Because the levels and quality of education of staff may vary considerably too, an effective human resource development strategy can be important to identify and build the necessary skills.

FIGURE 5.3　McKinsey 7S framework

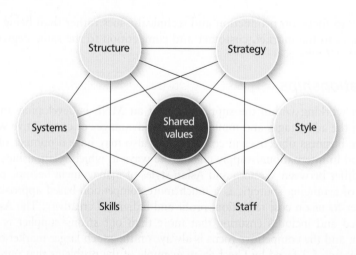

Source: Data adapted from McKinsey 7 S framework, Thomas J. Peters and Robert H. Waterman (1982) In Search of Excellence, Warner

3 *Staff*: The people that are recruited around the world need to be capable, well trained, and given the jobs that will best allow them to make use of their talents. Recognition of the contributions of the staff, the criteria for advancement, acceptance of appraisal and disciplinary processes vary considerably between countries.

4 *Shared values*: Despite the fact that staff come from different cultural backgrounds there is a need for employees to understand what the organization stands for, where it is going and to share the same organizational values.

The first part of the next section on international strategic management focuses broadly upon the 'hardware' and the second part on the 'software' of the McKinsey 7S framework.

The generic marketing strategies for SME internationalization

While there are an infinite number of individual implementation strategies that an SME might adopt, the generic marketing strategies provide a useful starting point.

Segmentation, targeting and positioning The principal approach to marketing strategy development follows three stages, normally referred to as segmentation, targeting and positioning (STP marketing):

1 Identification of the various segments that exist within the sector, using the various segmentation methods which we discussed in Chapter 4. It is important for the SME to define cross-border segments with clearly identifiable requirements that it is able to serve.

2 The firm must then target the segments which appear to be most attractive in terms of their size, growth potential, the ease with which they can be reached and their likely purchasing power.

3 In seeking to defend and develop its business the firm needs to position its products or services in a way that will distinguish them from those of its local and international competitors and build up barriers which will prevent those competitors taking its business.

Competitive strategies In order to create the competitive advantage necessary to achieve growth, Porter (1990) suggests that firms should adopt one of the following three generic competitive strategies. However, each poses particular challenges for SMEs in international markets:

1 *Cost leadership* requires the firm to establish a lower cost base than its local or international competitors. This strategy has typically been adopted by companies that are located in countries with lower labour costs that are component or service providers. Because of their limited financial resources, however, SMEs that adopt a low-cost strategy spend little on marketing activity and are vulnerable to either local firms or larger multi-nationals temporarily cutting prices to force the firm out of the market. Alternatively changes in currency exchange rates or other instability in the economic climate can result in newer, lower priced competitors emerging.

2 *Focus*, in which the firm concentrates on one or more narrow segments and thus builds up a specialist knowledge of each segment. Such segments in the international marketplace are transnational in nature and companies work to dominate one particular segment across a number of country markets. Typically this strategy necessitates the SME providing high levels of customer and technical service support, which can be resource intensive. Moreover, unless the SME has created a highly specialized niche, it may be difficult to defend against local and international competition.

3 *Differentiation* is achieved through emphasizing particular benefits in the product, service or marketing mix, which customers think are important and a significant improvement over competitive offers. Differentiation typically requires systematic incremental innovation to continually add customer value. While SMEs are capable of the flexibility, adaptability and responsiveness to customer needs necessary with this strategy, the cost of maintaining high levels of differentiation over competitors in a number of international markets can be demanding of management time and financial resources.

FIGURE 5.4 Ansoff growth matrix

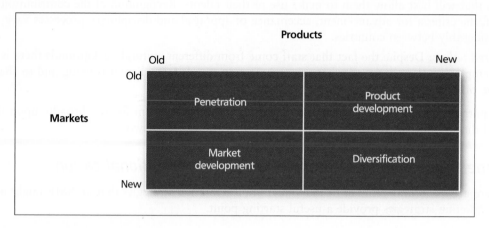

Many SMEs base their international strategy on the generic strategy which has given them competitive advantage in domestic markets and then attempt to apply this same successful strategy in international markets. US and Chinese firms benefit from having a huge domestic market. By contrast, SMEs from emerging markets and from countries with smaller domestic markets often have to export merely to find enough customers to enable them to survive.

Growth strategies   Typically SMEs have limited resources and so need to make difficult decisions about how to use these resources to grow the business. Ansoff (1957) identified four growth strategies – product penetration, market development, product development and diversification – and these are shown in Figure 5.4. Following a product penetration strategy is appropriate if a company has an existing portfolio of products and a presence in its target markets, which offer considerable potential expansion of sales. The resources available to the company under these circumstances can be best used in concentrating on doing more of what is already being done well.

Diversification, on the other hand, is a strategy used in international markets in situations where demand for the company's existing products is falling rapidly (for example, in recent years in the defence industry), where resources are available but would not generate an acceptable return if used on existing activities. Also, in the case of firms run by entrepreneurs, the owner can often becomes bored with the firm's current activities and seeks out new challenges, by developing a new product for a new market.

For most companies the most obvious strategic development opportunities are in increasing geographical coverage (market development) – which is discussed in Chapter 7 – and product development – which is discussed in Chapter 8 – perhaps by further differentiating a current product or applying their current technology to a new application. However, these options compete for resources and firms have to choose which approach will generate a greater return on investment.

The factors which affect the choice of an SME's international marketing strategy

Figure 5.5 indicates a number of the factors which influence the choice and development of an SME's international strategy. Particular issues include environmental trends, the market and industry structure, the customer requirements from different countries, the nature and intensity of local and international competition and the degree to which the SME can defend its niche. In SMEs, however, specific company factors are particularly important in the decision. These include the resources available, the products and services that have been developed and the firm's attitudes to international development and management of risk. These will result in the firm adopting a specific approach to individual country selection as the strategy develops.

FIGURE 5.5 Factors affecting SME internationalization

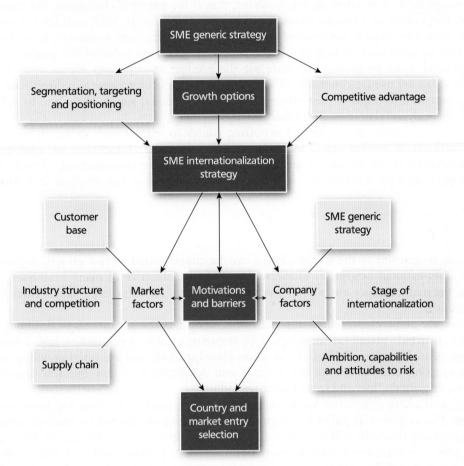

Market factors

The most significant factor inherent in SMEs is their relatively small size and lack of power in most international markets in which they wish to be active. This puts them at a disadvantage to local competitors and MNEs, as they often lack the management resources to spend researching new markets, the contacts necessary to quickly develop effective distribution of their products and sufficient financial resources to enable them to compete with the promotional spend of their competitors and thus be strong enough to withstand a 'price war'.

At the same time smaller size means that SMEs can offer customers the benefits of a more personal service from the firm's owners or senior managers, faster decision-making and, usually, a greater willingness to listen. Of course, the SME must work out how to profit from international market developments by building on these potential strengths.

The SMEs' challenge is to communicate some unique selling propositions to their customers and create other competitive advantage dimensions, thus building barriers to entry around the niche that they have identified in order to stop attacks by competitors. There are a number of ways that this can be done. First, underpinning any product/service offer must be a significant improvement in customer added value – there is little point in SMEs trying to market 'me-too' products internationally.

Second, if the product is a technical or design breakthrough it should be protected wherever possible by patent or copyright. It is worth saying, however, that if the patent is challenged, the costs of fighting a court case, particularly in a foreign country, can be prohibitive for an SME with limited resources.

Third, the firm must exploit any creative way of shortcutting the route to market, for example by convincing experts or influential participants in the supply chain of the value of the product offer so they might recommend it, or by gaining exposure for the product at important events or in highly visible places. Some SMEs are using e-commerce to achieve some of these objectives: as a direct route to their international customers, to improve their efficiency in an international supply chain and to achieve greater effectiveness through collaboration with other SMEs.

Fourth, instead of using the traditional exporting routes to market such as agents and distributors, alternative methods of market entry, for example using licensing, franchising or joint ventures, can increase the diffusion of the product or service into the market more cost-effectively. Finally, more SMEs are now cooperating with other firms – a customer, competitor or a firm engaged in a complementary activity.

Company factors

Only a minute proportion of the world's SMEs can be characterized as fast growth organizations and become the multi-national enterprises of the future. The sole objective of many businesses, such as the corner shop, the market trader and the car mechanic is to look for sufficient business from the domestic market to survive.

The smaller size and entrepreneurial approach of SMEs offers the advantages of flexibility and adaptability to new demands placed on them, speed of response to new opportunities and, usually, very focused management. However, SMEs lack adequate planning skills and are often unwilling or unable to devote sufficient time and finances to the research and development of new business opportunities and this can result in wasted effort and some expensive failures.

Frequently SMEs have insufficient knowledge of the culture, market structure and business practices of new markets. The response of SMEs to international marketing is affected by their perceptions of this risk. At one extreme the SME will be deterred from becoming involved at all. At the other extreme the risk-taking SME will experiment with international marketing, perhaps with very little preparation, believing that the firm will be able to respond quickly enough to deal with any difficulties that emerge. More cautious SMEs will attempt to assess and manage the risks involved by evaluating the market opportunity and planning their use of management operations and financial resources to enable a cost-effective internationalization approach to be developed.

Underlying the diversity in the range of a firm's attitudes to risk are the owners' ambition for the firm and how this fits with the firm's capabilities. To be successful the firm needs a vision of its international future which can be delivered using capabilities and resources that already exist, but also include those that can be acquired over a realistic timescale. It is often the case that successful SMEs are those that are able to clearly recognize the threats and opportunities in each marketplace, correct their weaknesses and build upon their strengths. SMEs that are unsuccessful in internationalizing are those that do not understand how their market is changing and what new resources and skills are needed, or are unwilling or unable to acquire them.

It is worth saying that many SMEs are so dominated by their owner that they become almost the personification of the owner, whose opinions, knowledge and attitudes determine the strategies adopted and decisions made. Usually decision-making is well thought-through with the owner being aware, understanding and managing the risks of working in an unfamiliar market, but sometimes owners lacking international expertise make decisions that can be irrational and even foolhardy.

Country selection

High levels of existing competition in developed countries make market entry challenging for SMEs. At the same time the new high growth emerging markets offer opportunities for SMEs to develop their

ILLUSTRATION 5.6

Young entrepreneurs shaping the future on three continents

Whereas in the past emerging country businesses have been controlled by senior and well respected figures, today it is young entrepreneurs that are leading the way and they have a global outlook. Globals is a fast growing Indian IT business that was founded in 2000 and now has offices in 11 countries. The chairman and chief executive is Suhas Gopinath, aged just 24. Demography forecasts that the emerging countries will have a young population while the developed countries are ageing. Therefore, their entrepreneurs are likely to be much younger too. In 2020 the median age in India will be 29, compared with 38 in America, 45 in Western Europe and 49 in Japan. This seems to be leading to a group of entrepreneurs that are creating born global companies.

The seven founders of Infosys, one of the companies identified in ILA 2 were in their twenties when they launched the company in 1981. It now has 63 offices and development centres in India, China, Australia,

the Czech Republic, Poland, the UK, Canada and Japan. Infosys and its subsidiaries have over 120 000 employees.

Herman Kojo Chinery-Hesse is a software engineer by profession and 19 years ago he co-founded SOFT-tribe Limited, which is now the leading software and business management systems house in West Africa. Fifteen years ago Herman decided to abandon his comfortable life in the United Kingdom to prove to sceptical friends that his native Ghana was a land of opportunity waiting for entrepreneurs with innovative business ideas.

With no start-up capital and little in the form of personal savings, no infrastructure and no equipment other than his old personal computer, Herman had to rely on the only resources available to him: his determination and creative talent for writing software programs. The company's first office was Herman's bedroom in his parent's home.

Globant is an Argentine software development and maintenance company formed in 2003 by four young entrepreneurs, Martín Migoya, Guibert Englebienne, Martín Umaran and Néstor Nocetti. Based in Buenos Aires the entrepreneurs saw the opportunities created in India by the IT and business process outsourcing sector and have exploited them. Globant has expanded revenue from $3 to $42 million and staff from 70 to 1500 and opened offices and in Chile, Colombia, the UK and the US.

Question

1 What global competitive capabilities are needed to create a born global IT business?

References: The other demographic dividend, *The Economist*, 7 Oct 2010.

specialized niche products and services. A group of young, well educated entrepreneurs are now having success in emerging markets, as Illustration 5.6 explains.

Increasing amounts of investment are now focused on the new emerging markets. The most adventurous SMEs recognize the need to be an early market entrant: thus, for some, the most promising markets for their specialized products and services are in Africa and South America but, at the same time, they are also the most risky.

Systems and support networks Typically SMEs tend not to have sophisticated systems and support networks for managing their international operations as is the case for large firms. Of course, advances in technology and the lower cost of IT systems, discussed in Chapter 12, are enabling SMEs to develop more advanced systems than they have had in the past. However, SMEs tend to rely on more informal, 'soft' systems and support networks that are based on personal contacts with family, friends, other business managers and officials for support, advice, information and knowledge.

Organization structure

As an SME increases its involvement in international markets, so it needs to set up an organization structure that will enable the leadership and management to support, direct and control its often widespread and growing organization effectively.

Sarathy, *et al.* (2006) have identified some of the variables which might influence the decision:

- size of the business;
- number of markets in which it operates;
- level and nature of involvement in the markets;
- company objectives;
- company international experience;
- nature of the products;
- width and diversity of the product range; and
- nature of the marketing task.

For a firm starting out in export markets, the decision is relatively simple. Either its international business is integrated within the domestic business or separated as a specialist activity. Setting up a separate export department allows greater independence to look specifically at international marketing opportunities.

However, this could indicate a less or more important activity and could, as a result, create conflicts between domestic and international market demands and ineffective use of company resources. As the company develops further, it is faced with deciding how its international operations should be organized, for example by area, by product and by function. Figure 5.6 and Figure 5.7 show typical organizational

FIGURE 5.6 Product structure

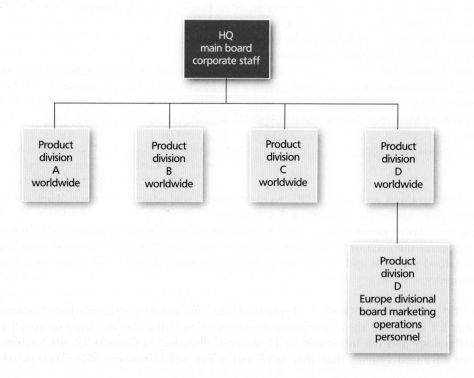

FIGURE 5.7 Geographic structure

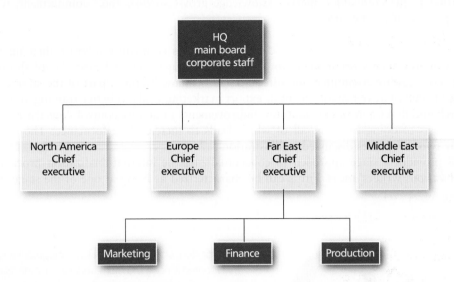

structures along geographic and product lines. Organization by function is only really appropriate for smaller companies with relatively simple product ranges.

As the firm grows it may decide to establish control in different ways – for example it may wish to control branding and corporate identity issues centrally through the use of international product managers – but at the same time it might wish to control the profitability of the business by having a senior executive in each individual country. In this way, the firm operates as a matrix structure within which individual managers might be responsible to different senior managers for different activities.

Skills, capability and the stages of internationalization Having discussed the alternative categories of international marketing and the strategies which SMEs adopt, we now turn to the process of SME internationalization and the factors which lead to success and failure. In looking at a cross-section of firms it is possible to find some firms with different mindsets regarding international trade including those that are taking the major step from being a solely domestic company to generating their first revenue from foreign country sales, others that are moving from the early stages of internationalization to a point where international marketing is totally integrated as part of the firm's activities, and a limited number of firms which are still small but have become confident world-class marketing companies.

The first step Firms typically approach involvement in international marketing rather cautiously, as the first step towards what may appear to them to be a rather unpredictable future. For small- and medium-sized firms in particular, exporting remains the more promising alternative to a full-blooded international marketing effort, since it appears to offer a degree of control over risk, cost and resource commitment.

The further internationalization of the firm is the process in which the enterprise gradually increases its international involvement. This evolves in an interplay between the development of knowledge about foreign markets and operations on one hand and an increasing commitment of resources to foreign markets on the other. Market knowledge and market commitment are assumed to affect decisions regarding the commitment of resources to foreign markets and the way current activities are performed. Market knowledge and market commitment are, in turn, affected by current activities and operational decisions.

Thus, firms start internationalization by going to those markets that they can most easily understand. There they will see opportunities, perceive low market uncertainty and gain experience – as they go through the internationalization process they will enter new more challenging markets where there is greater psychic distance. Psychic distance is defined in terms of factors such as differences in language, culture, political systems, etc., which disturb the flow of information between the firm and the market. This means that as the companies' market knowledge grows so does their commitment, which in turn affects the type of strategy they use.

More advanced stages of internationalization   As companies increase their international involvement so improvements occur in the organization, management and attitudes of those companies. Longer-term resources are committed and international business becomes part of the strategy rather than a tactical opportunity. Greater involvement in export marketing leads to better training and development, higher research and development expenditures, improvements in quality control, lower perceptions of risk and reduced costs of doing business, all of which leads to increased performance. The challenges have been faced by two companies discussed in Illustration 5.7.

Figure 5.8 provides a stage approach to conceptualizing the internationalization process based on a composite of various writers' ideas. Firms can be characterized as being at one of the stages shown.

© Norman Chan, iStockphoto.com

ILLUSTRATION 5.7

Tariff reduction prompts innovation

Suncoast Gold Macadamias (Aust) Limited

Australia's macadamia growers used to send their exports to the United States as raw nuts, but when the Australia–United States Free Trade Agreement (AUSFTA) came into force in January 2005, value-added tariffs on processed nuts began reducing. Suncoast Gold Macadamias (Aust) Limited is a cooperative of 150 macadamia nut growers in Gympie, Queensland. The cooperative's CEO, Jim Twentyman, said:

'The United States is the largest market for macadamias in the world. They consume half the world's production – so the drop in tariff through the AUSFTA made a very significant difference to our exports.'

With the reduction in costs Suncoast Gold has the opportunity to be more innovative in the ways nuts are packaged and processed. Suncoast Gold offers plain roasted, chilli, smoked, BBQ, honey roast and chocolate coated among the more traditional tastes. Suncoast developed macadamias flavoured with abalone and wasabi for Asian consumers but these have proved popular in Europe too, especially in Germany. Over 5 million macadamia trees are farmed Queensland and new South Wales, worth $75 million with 60 per cent exported thanks to the help received from Austrade, the government agency that supports exporters.

Saudi Fisheries Company

Saudi Fisheries Company has put Saudi Arabia on the map as a seafood producer. It bought the first of its 35 trawlers in 1981. It operates in the Gulf and Red Sea and has two processing plants for 90 tonnes a day and has its own shrimp fish farm. The farm is one of the most modern in the world and is managed to high ecological standards. The company distributes its products through owned and franchised retail shops, which offer special customer services, such as frying, grilling or roasting and retail counters in supermarkets in Saudi Arabia. It has built the largest franchised network in the Middle East. Maintaining quality throughout its operation is critical particularly as it wishes to increase exports to the EU, which has the toughest regulations.

Question

1 What are the key factors that help small businesses become more effective exporters?

References: www.austrade.gov.au and Ghani, (2010) Saudi fisheries: the Middle East's success story, *Asian Seafood Review*, issue 1, July–August.

For many firms the internationalization process of companies is not a gradual incremental process but a series of step changes. There may be a number of factors which might initiate a step change, for example, an unexpected product or market success, the recruitment of a new chief executive, serious failure leading to a reassessment of the business, loss of markets, the changing expectations of stakeholders, owners impatient for a more substantial return on their investment or business or family connections keen to share in the SME's success.

Grimes, Doole and Kitchen (2007) developed profiles of the internationalizing firms and it is possible to use this to characterize firms at each stage of internationalization.

The passive exporter
The passive exporter tends to lack any international focus, and perceives export markets as having a high hassle factor. Many passive exporters are relatively new to the export business, often reacting to unsolicited orders, and tend to see their market as essentially home based.

Such firms do not carry out research or invest in export promotion campaigns and have little direct contact with foreign companies. Firms at this stage perceive little real need to export and have no plans to do so in the future.

The reactive exporter
The reactive exporter sees export markets as secondary to the domestic markets but will put effort into dealing with key export accounts. Although they do not invest heavily in attracting export orders, once they have done business with a foreign customer they will follow up for repeat orders.

Such firms may have started to promote their export capacity and be starting to visit overseas clients. However, they have only a basic knowledge of their markets and are still undecided about their future role as an exporter.

The experimental exporter
The experimental exporter is beginning to develop a commitment to exporting and starting to structure the organization around international activities. They are in regular contact with key accounts and are beginning to develop alliances with export partners to build better products and services by using information from their successful markets.

Although they would prefer not to, such firms are prepared to make product adaptations to suit overseas customer needs and may have appointed dedicated export staff to look after this part of the business.

The proactive exporter
The proactive exporter is focused on key export markets, and devotes substantial amounts of time and resources to entering and developing new markets. Regular market assessment in the form of desk research and using partners' information is carried out, and promotional materials are produced in a number of foreign languages.

FIGURE 5.8 Levels of internationalization

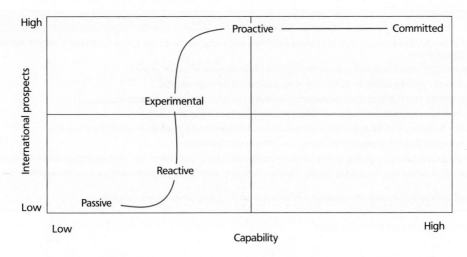

Senior management regularly visit key accounts to maintain healthy relationships with clients and exporting may account for up to 50 per cent of turnover. Exporting opportunities are welcomed and seen as crucial to the business.

The well-established exporter The committed exporter knows that exporting is integral to the business and sees the domestic market as just another market. The majority of the turnover is generated through international trade and significant amounts of time are spent on this activity, with senior and middle managers frequently visiting customers.

Investment in training is substantial as skills are needed in-house and thinking on export markets is both short-term tactical and longer-term strategic, with regular reviews of the overall mission and plan of action. Networks abroad provide excellent information and quality assured partners deliver on time, every time.

The firm's movement from one stage to the next, for example from reactive to experimental, experimental to proactive and proactive to world class, therefore, is not gradual. Each of these step changes requires a coordinated strategy to improve the performance of the firm. Doole, Grimes and Demack (2006) explored the management practices and processes most closely associated with high levels of export capability: from this ten benchmarks of international marketing practice are identified (Figure 5.9) which indicate the most critical areas of the firms' management skills. Closer examination of the nature of these benchmarks reinforces the idea that successful international marketing is a predictor of fast growth. Further analysis suggests three key areas that SME international marketers needed to focus on to ensure success:

1 developing the characteristics of a learning organization;

2 developing effective relationships; and

3 having a clear international competitive focus.

Learning organization A culture of innovation and learning throughout the firm is a common feature of successful firms that compete internationally. There is clear commitment from the top with senior management intent on building knowledge assets, and time and resources are invested in learning at all levels.

Investment in skills development enables the firms to be flexible in overcoming barriers and to be persistent in the face of difficulties. High levels of emotional energy are invested in the firm and staff are innovative and willing to learn. A shared vision and a sharing of experiences among internal partners are also key elements of the successful organizations' commitment to learning. Tight financial measurement and performance are seen as crucial.

FIGURE 5.9 Characteristics of successful international business-to-business marketers

Successful international business-to-business marketers:

1 Have a clear competitive focus in international marketplaces and a specific directional policy as to where the top management intend taking the firm.
2 Have high levels of repeat business and operate tight financial controls in export markets.
3 Have the tenacity and the resilience to face challenges and drive through change.
4 Have a perception that risk indicates a problem to be solved, not an insurmountable barrier.
5 View themselves as international niche marketers, not necessarily as good exporters.
6 Fully invest in ensuring they have thorough knowledge of the international markets in which they operate.
7 Are able to exploit distinctive product advantages in international markets.
8 Are strongly committed to supplying quality products and services to all their customers wherever they are in the world.
9 Build close relationships throughout the supply chain and invest in maintaining regular communications with their overseas partners.
10 Have a well-defined communications strategy and invest in good quality promotional materials.

Source: Adapted from Isobel Doole's PhD thesis (2000)

Effective relationships   Firms who compete successfully in international markets build close relationships, not only with customers but with others throughout the supply chain. Effective relationships are crucial and sometimes the focus of successful organizations. Competitive advantage may not be the product itself, but the added value given to the product and the ability to exploit opportunities by the close, meaningful and regular communication with customers, increasingly through e-commerce.

A commitment to quality procedures, a quality mission and the use of quality-assured intermediaries are seen as vital. Service reliability is key to the firm's relationships and underpins its contribution to the supply chain.

Clear competitive focus   Firms establish a clear and truly international focus, demonstrating a strong competitive position in a precisely identified market. Many successful firms adopt niche marketing strategies based on a clear mission statement and a planned development strategy.

Other features usually include clearly differentiated products, strong brand positioning and high levels of flexibility in adapting products to suit particular markets.

A thorough knowledge of markets is built up through innovative and informal means of collecting information and through focused research capability, concentrating resources where they are of most use. Most successful companies have primary markets which account for at least 30 per cent of their export turnover.

International entrepreneurship and fast growth

There are a small number of firms which achieve hypergrowth through commercially exploiting a revolutionary idea, innovative business method or adopting a marketing strategy which simply leaves all the competitors behind. While some of these firms succeed as a result of a new technical or scientific invention, more important is the entrepreneurial flair needed to exploit the idea commercially. Some of the greatest successes are, therefore, associated with individual entrepreneurs who have the vision, determination, ability and ambition to succeed.

The secret of high growth

For many firms high growth in revenue and profits is the ultimate goal, but this challenge is set against a global background of ever-greater competition and the increasing expectations of customers. During times of recession or more intense competition some firms still manage to grow at a spectacular rate. It is by studying these firms that the drivers of fast growth in SMEs can be identified.

Kim and Mauborgne (2005) explain that it is necessary to find market areas that are uncontested (the blue ocean). Slower growth firms typically focus upon the competition by benchmarking and seeking to meet the customers' (slightly) increased expectations. Their goal is to outperform their rivals, usually by offering a little more value for a little less cost. The competitive response from the rivals is to do the same and, inevitably, this leads to a cycle of small-scale leapfrogging. A lot of blood is spilled (red ocean) as rivals try to damage each other!

Becoming embroiled within this competitive scenario initiates a pattern of strategic behaviour which is, in fact, opposite of that which is associated with growth. Firms become reactive, drawing in resources to respond to the short-term competitive actions, and have no time or resources to think about the sorts of products and services that are needed for the future on a worldwide basis. Without this creativity the firms fall back on imitating competitors, believing the competitors' actions to be right for the market, rather than really exploiting the changes taking place in their customers' needs and wants.

By contrast, high growth firms leave the competitors to fight among themselves and, instead, seek to offer customers a quantum leap in value. The question that they need to pose is not what is needed to beat the competition but rather what is needed to win over the mass of customers. The implications of this are that it is necessary to challenge the conventional wisdom and assumptions of the industry about the basis on which firms compete and what customers value. An additional bonus from challenging the way the industry does things is that if the firm thinks on an international scale it can also lead to large cost savings as unnecessary operations are cut out. If the benefits really lead to a step change in value they will be perceived as such by customers all round the world.

© Ryerson Clark, iStockphoto.com

ILLUSTRATION 5.8

TerraCycle: Upcycling the world's plastic

Tom Szaky was 19 when he set up TerraCycle, a rubbish collecting and recycling business. The company has a $40 million turnover, has 70 employees and operates in 6, soon to be 17, countries. Szaky wants it to be the Google of garbage. The company makes 200 products from waste, for example, backpacks made from Kraft Capri Sun juice pouches and kites made from biscuit packets. Any person can sign up to join a brigade and collect the used packaging from featured brands. It is free to post and each item posted earns 2p to go to a charity or school of the sender's choice. The main motivation is reducing land-fill.

Companies, such as Kraft, Starbucks, Johnson and Johnson, Mars, Coca-Cola, Kellogg's and Nestlé

sponsor TerraCycle from their marketing budgets, to pay for the charity donations, shipping and website costs, as it is good PR for them. TerraCycle's original idea was upcycling – making a new product out of an item of rubbish, keeping its basic shape without adding heat or chemicals, but the cost of cleaning, sorting and manipulating the waste was too much and the company lost money. As a result the company began to focus on upcycling pre-consumer waste, which amounts to between 1 per cnet and 6 per cent of most company's production.

TerraCycle licenses companies to make bags, kites and pencil cases from this material around the world. TerraCycle has become the 'good housekeeping seal of approval' in the world of upcycling.

Now the company has expanded its activity to recycling – shredding, melting, adding chemicals – to re-use different grades of plastic to produce children's toys, furniture and household items. Szaky believes that the world would be better without plastic, because toxins are released during processing and usage that can seriously affect health. However, that is not likely to happen in the near future as the US alone has 30 million tonnes of plastic waste, so TerraCycle will continue to try to reduce the waste mountain.

Question

1 What advice would you give to Szaky to help his company become the 'Google of garbage'?

Cirque du Soleil was a small organization that challenged the ideas that circuses were for children and should have animals, which were expensive to keep. For many it was also unethical to keep animals. Instead they created a spectacular show for adults which focused on a combination of performance, art and music and quickly became a worldwide phenomenon with 4000 employees.

In starting to change the way the firm thinks about its competitive strategy, it should address the following questions:

- What factors that your industry takes for granted should be eliminated?
- What factors that your industry competes on should be reduced well below the standard?
- What factors that your industry competes on should be raised well above the standard?
- What factors should be created that your industry has never offered?

By finding answers to these questions the firm can create new markets and new expectations for customers in existing markets. The Apple iPod, low-cost airlines (South West Airlines, easyJet and Ryanair), online communities (YouTube and Twitter) and mobile phones (Nokia) show how providing a quantum leap in value to customers can reward the innovators. Typically it is smaller firms that are not weighed down by the industry traditions and standards that challenge conventional wisdom. If the ideas are sufficiently innovative and appealing they will create new international niche opportunities, as discussed in Illustration 5.8.

Shared values   The core advantages of SMEs and main factors for success are their innovative capability, responsiveness, adaptability and flexibility, which enable them to avoid direct competition from larger competitors. These values, which must come from senior management, must be shared and encouraged throughout the organization. They must also be underpinned by good strategic planning and management.

Because of the small scale of operations of SMEs, staff around the world often relate closely to and communicate regularly with the owner or senior manager of the SME, so it is often the personal values of the owner and their view of how the products and services should be marketed that become the shared values of the organization.

The reasons for failure   Many SMEs fail to reach their full potential because they do not manage effectively the international marketing and operational activities that are critical for international success. These factors include:

- failure to scan the international environment effectively;
- overdependence on one product;
- the ease with which larger, more powerful competitors or a number of smaller local competitors can copy the idea;
- failure to respond to worldwide changes in customer needs;
- failure to plan financial resources;
- failure to plan for fluctuation in currency values;
- failure to manage and resource both market and operations expansion;
- the prohibitive cost of enforcing patents and trademarks in foreign courts which may favour local firms.

One of the possible consequences of niche marketing is that success in one international market segment may lead to complacency and overdependence on that market, or the erroneous belief that the firm has built up barriers to entry which will prevent the entry of potential competitors. Against powerful global competitors the barriers are often an illusion. The product may be superseded by an even better idea from a competitor or, alternatively, larger competitors can often gain business with an inferior product simply because of their greater promotional power or their control over the distribution channels.

Because of the often ad hoc, unplanned way that SMEs develop internationally they underestimate the level of resourcing that is needed in both time and money, the difficulties and delays that may arise and consequently the length of time it takes to reach profitability in new foreign markets. The investment that is needed is often greater than the firms expect and they often fail to negotiate a suitable arrangement with their bank or other funders before difficulties emerge.

The main danger associated with international niche marketing is that the income stream is often dependent upon one single product or service idea or a very limited product portfolio. Given the capacity of competitors to copy product ideas, the firm must be absolutely sure that it has built in some unique competitive advantage such as a strong brand, unique technology or reliable business contacts to sustain it against the competition.

Creative SMEs find alternative ways to strengthen their international position, perhaps by finding a different way of expanding. This can be achieved by forming a joint venture or alliance with another firm, contracting out production to a firm with spare capacity, licensing the product or process or even agreeing to be taken over.

The future of SME internationalization

There are many pitfalls for an SME that is active in international markets. For some SMEs the greatest risk is internationalizing at all, particularly if they have no definable source of competitive advantage and little understanding of international marketing. However, with increasing globalization, firms such as these are no longer able to hide their inefficiency or lack of creativity in the domestic market as they will come under attack from international competitors. The global environment and the changing dynamics in markets can be equally challenging.

Almost as risky is operating as a traditional exporter – selling excess capacity into markets about which the SME has little or no information and with which its managers have little cultural empathy. Manufacturing SME exporters from developed countries struggle to compete with companies from emerging markets which have lower labour costs. However, small low-cost manufacturers in emerging markets are coming under pressure from manufacturers from less developed countries that can undercut their prices. For SMEs that are innovative and ambitious, are prepared to embrace new technology, use new routes to market and find new innovative ways of doing business, there are opportunities for success on a scale never before envisaged, provided they are willing to learn, have a clear competitive focus and a strong network of connections. For the most successful there is often an alternative opportunity to sell out, for example, Innocent smoothies by Coca-Cola, Pret A Manger by McDonald's, Ben and Jerry's by Unilever and Seeds of Change by Mars.

SUMMARY

- SMEs have always been involved in international marketing but now have greater opportunities to develop internationally and create wealth and employment for their domestic economy. New technology allows smaller firms to access information and communicate internationally in a way that was not possible before.

- Successful SME international marketers are those that build relationships with individuals and organizations that can help them understand the nature and value of the competitive advantage that they possess, and learn from their own experiences and those of others.

- The principles of international marketing can be applied to all categories of SME international activity, ranging from exporting manufactured goods, through e-commerce to marketing domestic attractions to tourists. However, SMEs use different ways of internationalizing and selecting countries for market entry from an incremental selection of countries, based on market potential or a network of contacts, through to high technology businesses that are 'born global'. This depends upon the context in which the firm is internationalizing.

- The chosen SME internationalization strategies are underpinned by generic marketing strategies but are often also affected by the management's perception of the barriers in the environment, the support that is provided in the domestic country and the specific market factors that affect their business sector.

- The stage of international development that the SME has reached reflects the company's capability, the confidence and attitude of the senior management to internationalization. It usually shows how the SMEs have utilized their inherent strengths of flexibility, adaptability, innovative capability and speed of response in developing their markets.

- There are a number of factors that lead to success and failure for SME international development, but the most significant factor is the ability of SMEs to offer customers a quantum leap in value by innovating throughout the marketing process.

KEYWORDS

Small- and medium-
    sized enterprises

*Domestically delivered or
    developed niche services*

Electronic commerce

Barrier to entry

International niche marketing

Reciprocal trading

Born global

Network

Market concentrators

Market expanders

Internationalization

Supply chain

Outsource

7S framework

Generic marketing strategies

Organization structure

Stages of internationalization

Courtesy of Q. Drum

CASE STUDY

Global marketing on a tight budget

At different points in this book we focus on the 'mindset' of the organizations that are developing their international marketing and it is interesting to compare, for example, the established global player with strong, well known brands, the company from an emerging market with the potential to become a global player, the entrepreneurial firm that successfully serves a global market niche or the global campaigning charity. Here, however, we focus on small firms that have very limited financial and human resources. They lack some of the international competitive capabilities, knowledge and skills that larger organizations have, so that often they do not have access to comprehensive market and cultural research, influential networks and allies, efficient supply chains and they cannot rely on a global brand to 'open the door' in foreign markets. They make up for this by being responsive to the specific needs of their customers, working hard to understand them and gain real insights into what they want. They are adaptable, changing quickly to the demands of customers and new market situations. They are flexible in the way they use their limited resources to provide new solutions. SMEs often too embrace different forms of social ownership and this can provide new levels of motivation and commitment from the staff.

Innovation is at the heart of small firm internationalization and at its most basic is about commercializing ideas, meeting unmet needs and solving problems in a way that larger firms are unwilling to do. African entrepreneurs provide us with excellent examples of innovation as a scenario for developing international marketing strategies for small firms.

Craft Silicon

Kamal Budhabhatti is the CEO of Craft Silicon, which is responsible for 90 per cent of Kenya's software exports, but with just 200 employees and a turnover of $15 million is still an SME. He is part of a growing number of entrepreneurs in the region that are helping Kenya to become East Africa's hi-tech hub. The country has a decent education system turning out skilled developers, the government sees the value of technology and is supporting it, tech firms, such as Google, IBM and Nokia, have set up there and are helping with skills development and profile raising and new undersea cabling has increased the perception of what might be possible. The opportunities for SMEs arise because western solutions may make sense to western markets, but not necessarily for African markets. There is a thirst for local content that meets the needs of the local market, so local versions of social media are growing.

Many services focus on the agricultural sector and mobile phones. A recent report suggests that 90 per cent of people in Kenya access the Internet through the mobile network, meaning slower speeds and smaller screens. Often it is the wealthy, older people that can afford to fully use the web. Many people do not have always-on connection, so mass-market, consumer services require other forms of interaction, such as SMS. Mobiles also provide the payment mechanism, such as M-Pesa. Agriculture offers interesting opportunities for entrepreneurs. Akira Chix is a collective of female programmers that are building a mobile platform for framers to crowdsource price information from markets.

The Q Drum

Technology, especially when connected with excellent design can also be important for entrepreneurs working to provide effective solutions for even the most basic needs, such as providing reliable solar powered lighting to replace hazardous kerosene powered lights as discussed and illustrated by National Geographic in *Big Ideas, Little Packages*, or the Ceramic Jiko portable charcoal stove that can reduce fuel consumption by 30–40 per cent, and thus is better for the environment and reduces toxic gas, resulting in better health for the user.

Clean water is essential to survival and a clean and accessible supply is a basic need of millions of people. The burden of fetching water over long distances falls to women and children who often suffer injuries as a result. Pieter Hendrikse was the inventor and is Managing Director of QDrum. The invention is a durable donut shaped plastic container that holds 50 litres of water and provides a hygienic solution to carrying water. A rope can be tied through the central hole in order to roll the drum across all terrain. With no handles or metal attachments the drum, made out of low density polyethylene is virtually indestructible. Even children can pull the Q Drum safely. The product has gained much publicity through articles and case studies of its use in international and national publications. Funding for new projects in different countries comes from sponsors and charities.

Questions

1 What are the main challenges faced by Craft Silicon and Q Drum as they spread into new international markets?

2 What advice would you give to the senior management of the two companies in terms of segmentation, growth strategies and brand development?

Reference: J. Fildes, 'Broadband world: Connecting Africa', BBC Online, 2 December 2010. 'Big Ideas: Little Packages', *National Geographic*, sourced at: http://ngm.nationalgeographic.com/big-idea/16/little-packages on 16 December 2010, www.qdrum.co.za and by D.M. Kammen, 'Cookstoves for the Developing World' at http://kammen.berkeley.edu//cookstoves.html.

DISCUSSION QUESTIONS

1 How can the smaller business compensate for its lack of resources and expertise in international marketing when trying to enter new markets?

2 Why is international niche marketing likely to be a superior approach to export selling?

3 As the leader of a rock group you have had moderate success in your home country but have noticed that you seem to be gaining fans in different countries. As you have not been signed up by a recognized music company, how might you exploit your popularity internationally?

4 How does the mindset of a proactive international marketer differ from a reactive marketer?

5 Small international marketing firms do not have the resources to carry out market research systematically. What advice would you give to a Danish renewable energy firm that wishes to enter the southern African market?

REFERENCES

1. Ansoff, I. (1957) 'Strategies for diversification', *Harvard Business Review*, 35 (5): 113–24.
2. Balabanis, G., Theodosiou, M. and Katsikea, E.S. (2004) 'Export marketing: developments and a research agenda', *International Marketing Review*, 21 (4/5): 353–77.
3. Balabanis, G. and Katsikea, E.S. (2003) 'The relationship between environment, export strategy development approaches and export performance', *Proceedings of the Annual Conference of the Academy of Marketing Science*, Washington DC, 26, 17–18.
4. Brown, L. and McDonald, M.H.B. (1994) *Competitive marketing strategy for Europe*, Macmillan.
5. Crick, D. (2009) 'The internationalisation of born global and international new venture SMEs', *International marketing Review*, 26 (4/5): 453–76.
6. Crick, D. and Spence, M. (2005) 'The internationalisation of "high performing" UK high tech SMEs: a study of planned and unplanned strategies', *IMR*, 14 (2): 167–85.

7. Doole, I., Grimes, A. and Demack, S. (2006) 'An exploration of the management practices and processes most closely associated with high levels of export capability in SMEs', *Marketing Intelligence and Planning*, 24 (6).

8. Global Entrepreneurship Monitor (2009) 'Adult Population Survey (APS) Global Entrepreneurship Monitor', accessed at: www.gemconsortium.org.

9. Grimes, A., Doole, I. and Kitchen, P.J. (2007) 'Profiling the capabilities of SMEs to compete internationally', *Journal of Small Business and Enterprise Development*, 14 (1): 64–80.

10. Hardman, D., Messinger, D. and Bergson, S. (2005) *Virtual scale: alliances for leverage, resilience report*, Booz, Allen, Hamilton, 14 July, accessed at www.strategy1business.com.

11. Harris, S. and Wheeler, C. (2005) '"Entrepreneurs" relationships for internationalisation: functions, origins and strategies', *International Business Review*, 14 (2): 187–207.

12. Katsikeas, C.S. and Leonidou, L.C. (1996) 'Export marketing expansion strategy: differences between market concentration and market spreading', *Journal of Marketing Management*, 12.

13. Kim, W.C. and Mauborgne, R. (2005) *Blue ocean strategy: how to create uncontested market space and make competition irrelevant*, Harvard Business Press.

14. Kulmeier, D.B. and Knight, G. (2010) 'The critical role of relationship quality in SME internationalisation', *Journal of Global Marketing*, 23 (1), Jan.

15. Leonidou, L.C., Katsikeas, C.S., Palihawadana, D. and Spyropoulou, S. (2007), 'An analytical review of the factors stimulating smaller firms to export: implications for policy makers', *International Marketing Review*, 24 (6), 735–70.

16. Mort, G.S. and Weerawardena, J. (2006) 'Networking capability and international entrepreneurship', *International Marketing Review*, 23 (5): 549–72.

17. Nicholls, A. and Opal, C. (2005) *Fairtrade: market-driven ethical consumption*, Sage.

18. Nueno, P. (2000) 'The dragon breathes enterprising fire', In S. Bailey and F. Muzyka, *Mastering entrepreneurship*, FT Prentice Hall.

19. OECD (2009) 'Top Barriers and Drivers to SME Internationalisation', Report by the OECD Working party on SMEs and Entrepreneurship, OECD.

20. Okpara, J.O. and Kabongo, J.D. (2010) *International Journal of Business and Globalisation*, 5 (2), 2 Aug 2010 169–87 (19).

21. Parrish, E., Cassill, N. and Oxenham, W. (2006) 'Niche marketing strategy for a mature market place', *Marketing Intelligence and Planning*, 24 (7): 694–707.

22. Porter, M.E. (1990) *Competitive advantage of nations*, Free Press.

23. Sarathy, R., Terpstra, V. and Russow, L. (2006) *International marketing*, 9th edn. Dryden Press.

24. Servais, P., Madsen, T.K. and Rasmussen, E.S. (2007) 'Small manufacturing firms involvement in international e-business activities', *Advances in International Marketing*, 17: 297–317.

CHAPTER 6

GLOBAL STRATEGIES

LEARNING OBJECTIVES

After reading this chapter you should be able to:

- Appreciate the various aspects of globalization and be able to compare and contrast the alternative global strategies

- Evaluate the factors that determine a firm's choice of global strategy

- Identify the challenges that firms particularly from emerging markets face in developing a global presence

- Appreciate the role of branding in globalization

- Understand the factors affecting global marketing management

INTRODUCTION

Having discussed the nature of international development in smaller firms we now consider the global marketing strategies of the largest firms that compete on a worldwide basis. The largest firms have the mindset of achieving **globalization** as the route to maximizing performance by introducing, where possible, standardized marketing programmes and processes to enhance efficiency and competitiveness, but at the same time, adapting certain operational activities to local needs in order to achieve effectiveness by maximizing short-term revenue generation. The problem that such firms face is exactly which aspects of their international activity to standardize and which to adapt because the decisions are often context specific and are affected by the particular factors which drive change within their particular industry. This leads to firms adopting a variety of global strategies, from those that are very similar from country to country to those that are substantially different in each country in which the firm operates and this substantially increases complexity. In the past global marketing has been dominated by firms from developed countries, such as Coca-Cola, McDonald's and Microsoft but an increasing number of firms, such as LG and Samsung, from recently emerging markets have become global players too. As the balance of economic power in global markets shifts further to the BRIC countries, many more firms from those markets are poised to continue the trend.

In this chapter we start by reviewing the dimensions of the concept and drivers of globalization before considering the alternative strategic approaches and the factors that drive strategic choice. This discussion is then followed by an examination of the strategy implementation issues that MNEs might face in managing their global business and building their global presence, with particular emphasis on global branding. We end the chapter with a discussion of the issues that must be addressed in order to manage global marketing effectively.

The alternative views of globalization

Over the past two decades the term globalization seems to have led to a polarization of views. For some, globalization is associated with opportunity, the removal of barriers to prosperity for all countries of the world and greater exposure to and understanding of different cultures. Others see globalization, capitalism and MNE activity as the same thing, believing global companies dominate international business, ruthlessly exploit the countries' resources and adversely influence the economy and culture of every country, moving their operations from country to country according to which offers the lowest wage rates, with no thought either for those who lose their jobs or the well-being of those who are paid extremely low wages. In the last few years the actions of global companies have been blamed for a number of world problems, such as the banks for the sub prime mortgages and the resulting recession of 2008 and BP for the Gulf of Mexico disaster.

In practice globalization is about progress towards an, as yet, undefined goal and few companies, even those with the most familiar brand names, are truly global. Table 6.1 lists the biggest firms in the world by revenues and it shows that many firms are strongly dependent on a large domestic market and a few additional key markets. This becomes clearer by contrasting this with Table 6.2, which shows the top 20 transnational companies (TNC) ranked by foreign assets. UNCTAD (2010) provides a measure of the real transnationality of multinationals by identifying an index of transnationality (TNI), which is an average of the measures of transnationality (foreign to total assets, sales and employment). This, perhaps, provides a more accurate picture of the most transnational companies ranked this time in order of TNI (Table 6.3). The reason that this list is different from Table 6.1 and 6.2 is that firms from the US have a huge domestic market in which to grow before embarking upon international, then global activity (note the positions of the US firms). By contrast, firms from smaller countries have always had to internationalize simply to grow.

The most dominant TNCs still come from developed economies and are typically from the motor, petroleum and telecommunications sectors. However, the TNCs from developing countries (top 20 in Table 6.4) are now gaining a significant presence. An increasing number of TNCs from emerging countries will appear in the top 100 in the world as emerging markets grow.

There is no doubt that the world's largest firms seek a worldwide presence. Driving this acceleration of global MNE activity appears to be increased competition which Sjobolom (1998) suggests is being

Table 6.1 The top companies in the world by revenues

	Corporation	Home economy	Industry[c]	Revenues
1	Wal-mart Stores	United States	Retail	408.2
2	Royal Dutch Shell	United Kingdom	Oil, gas	285.1
3	Exxon Mobil	United States	Oil, gas	284.6
4	BP	United Kingdom	Oil, gas	246.1
5	Toyota Motor	Japan	Motor vehicles	204.1
6	Japan Post Holdings	Japan	Banking, insurance, mail	202.2
7	Sinopec	China	Oil, gas	187.5
8	State Grid	China	Power distribution	184.5
9	AXA	France	Insurance	175.3
10	China National Petroleum	China	Oil, gas	165.5

Source: http://www.unctad.org © UNCTAD

Table 6.2 The top non-financial transnational companies: index of transnationality ranked by foreign assets

| Ranking by: | | | | Assets | |
Foreign assets	Corporation	Home economy	Industry[c]	Foreign	TNI[b] (Per cent)
1	General Electric	United States	Electrical and electronic equipment	401 290	52.2
2	Royal Dutch/Shell Group	United Kingdom	Petroleum expl./ref./distr.	222 324	73.0
3	Vodafone Group Plc	United Kingdom	Telecommunications	201 570	88.6
4	BP PLC	United Kingdom	Petroleum expl./ref./distr.	188 969	81.0
5	Toyota Motor Corporation	Japan	Motor vehicles	169 569	52.9
6	ExxonMobil Corporation	United States	Petroleum expl./ref./distr.	161 245	67.9
7	Total SA	France	Petroleum expl./ref./distr.	141 442	74.5
8	E.On	Germany	Utilities (Electricity, gas and water)	141 168	55.8
9	Electricite De France	France	Utilities (Electricity, gas and water)	133 698	42.2
10	ArcelorMittal	Luxembourg	Metal and metal products	127 127	87.2
11	Volkswagen Group	Germany	Motor vehicles	123 677	60.5
12	GDF Suez	France	Utilities (Electricity, gas and water)	119 374	56.4
13	Anheuser-Busch Inbev SA	Netherlands	Food, beverages and tobacco	106 247	87.9
14	Chevron Corporation	United States	Petroleum expl./ref./distr.	106 129	58.1
15	Siemens AG	Germany	Electrical and electronic equipment	104 488	73.0
16	Ford Motor Company	United States	Motor vehicles	102 588	54.3
17	Eni Group	Italy	Petroleum expl./ref./distr.	95 818	56.4
18	Telefonica SA	Spain	Telecommunications	95 446	70.3
19	Deutsche Telekom AG	Germany	Telecommunications	95 019	50.3
20	Honda Motor Co Ltd	Japan	Motor vehicles	89 204	72.2

Source: http://www.unctad.org © United Nations 2000–2011.

Table 6.3 The top non-financial transnational companies ranked by index of transnationality

TNI[b]	Corporation	Home economy	Industry[c]	TNI[b] (Per cent)
1	Xstrata PLC	United Kingdom	Mining and quarrying	93.2
2	ABB Ltd.	Switzerland	Engineering services	90.4
3	Nokia	Finland	Electrical and electronic equipment	90.3
4	Pernod Ricard SA	France	Food, beverages and tobacco	89.1
5	WPP Group Plc	United Kingdom	Business services	88.9
6	Vodafone Group Plc	United Kingdom	Telecommunications	88.6
7	Linde AG	Germany	Chemicals	88.3
8	Anheuser-Busch Inbev SA	Netherlands	Food, beverages and tobacco	87.9
9	Anglo American	United Kingdom	Mining and quarrying	87.5
10	ArcelorMittal	Luxembourg	Metal and metal products	87.2
11	Nestlé SA	Switzerland	Food, beverages and tobacco	87.1
12	Air Liquide	France	Chemical/Non-metallic mineral products	86.9
13	Liberty Global Inc	United States	Telecommunications	86.2
14	Astrazeneca Plc	United Kingdom	Pharmaceuticals	85.4
15	Teva Pharmaceutical Industries Limited	Israel	Pharmaceuticals	84.4
16	Lafarge SA	France	Non-metallic mineral products	84.2
17	Volvo AB	Sweden	Motor vehicles	82.3
18	Hutchison Whampoa Limited	Hong Kong, China	Diversified	82.0
19	Cemex S.A.	Mexico	Non-metalic mineral products	81.6
20	BP PLC	United Kingdom	Petroleum expl./ref./distr.	81.0

Source: http://www.unctad.org © United Nations 2000–2011.

brought about by four forces: changes in consumer expectations; technological change; deregulation; and regional forces. To become a truly global player requires huge resources and as Illustration 6.1 shows global ambitions sometimes have to be modified.

Table 6.4 Top 20 companies from developing countries: index of transnationailty ranked by foreign assets

Ranking by:				Assets	
Foreign assets	Corporation	Home economy	Industry[c]	Foreign assets US$ bn	TNI[b] (Per cent)
1	Hutchison Whampoa Limited	Hong Kong, China	Diversified	70 762	82.0
2	CITIC Group	China	Diversified	43 750	21.0
3	Cemex S.A.	Mexico	Non-metalic mineral products	40 258	81.6
4	Samsung Electronics Co., Ltd.	Republic of Korea	Electrical and electronic equipment	28 765	54.2
5	Petronas – Petroliam Nasional Bhd	Malaysia	Petroleum expl./ref./distr.	28 447	29.6
6	Hyundai Motor Company	Republic of Korea	Motor vehicles	28 359	36.5
7	China Ocean Shipping (Group) Company	China	Transport and storage	28 066	49.9
8	Lukoil	Russian Federation	Petroleum and natural gas	21 515	42.2
9	Vale S.A	Brazil	Mining and quarrying	19 635	38.3
10	Petróleos De Venezuela	Bolivarian Republic of Venezuela	Petroleum expl./ref./distr.	19 244	21.5
11	Zain	Kuwait	Telecommunications	18 746	61.2
12	Jardine Matheson Holdings Ltd	Hong Kong, China	Diversified	17 544	69.2
13	Singtel Ltd.	Singapore	Telecommunications	17 326	63.2
14	Formosa Plastics Group	Taiwan Province of China	Chemicals	16 937	40.9
15	Tata Steel Ltd.	India	Metal and metal products	16 826	69.8
16	Petroleo Brasileiro S.A. – Petrobras	Brazil	Petroleum expl./ref./distr.	15 075	16.2
17	Hon Hai Precision Industries	Taiwan Province of China	Electrical and electronic equipment	14 664	58.1
18	Metalurgica Gerdau S.A.	Brazil	Metal and metal products	13 658	48.6
19	Abu Dhabi National Energy Company	United Arab Emirates	Utilities (Electricity, gas and water)	13 519	69.5
20	Oil And Natural Gas Corporation	India	Petroleum expl./ref./distr.	13 477	23.8

Source: http://www.unctad.org © United Nations 2000–2011.

ILLUSTRATION 6.1

Vodafone: pragmatism over ambition?

For some years Vodafone has been one of the companies that topped the list of transnational firms, by foreign assets and by the transnationality index and at the start of the new millennium Vodafone seemed intent on becoming 'the Coca-Cola of mobile'. As part of its global development in 2000 it invested in China Mobile, which then had only 24 million customers. However, by 2010 China Mobile had 554 million customers, dwarfing Vodafone's 347 million, AND making it the largest operator in the world, even though it had no subscribers outside China. Now Vodafone, which has a market value of £81 billion, has given up its global ambition and changed its mindset to focus on a regional strategy and European, African and Indian markets. First it aims to dispose of its 20 per cent share of China Mobile for $4 billion, before deciding how to dispose of its 45 per cent stake in Verizon Wireless in the US and assets in France which together could be worth $40 billion. This will fund the developments in its target regions.

Many of the cross-cultural acquisitions it made resulted in controversy, for example, when taking over Mannesmann in Germany it encountered the problem of objection to national assets being taken over by a foreign company and it will need to be careful in selling off assets too. Vodafone can dispose of its China Mobile share to a strategic investor or sell the shares on the Hong Kong stock market, where China Mobile is listed, but it must be careful not to cause the share price to fall as it wishes to preserve close links with China Mobile as it collaborates on developing software 'apps' to challenge Apple.

Question

1 In what circumstances might aiming to be global not make the best business sense?

References: J Ashton, Vodafone in £4bn Chinese sell-off. *Sunday Times* 29 August 2010.

Globalization and standardization

In seeking to compete successfully in increasingly globalized markets multi-national enterprises realize that a precondition of long-term growth is a worldwide presence. In previous chapters we have discussed the nature of global markets and a fundamental question is whether global markets require standardized products. Two decades ago a number of writers such as Levitt and Kotler debated whether or not this would result in globally standardized products and services.

So far, there are few examples of product and service offers which have been completely standardized across the world and are probably limited to those sold over the Internet in the business-to-business sector. Some of the most widely available products which might be considered to be standardized in fact are substantially adapted. You can taste the Coca-Cola variants from around the world at the museum in Atlanta and try the different McDonald's menus as you travel. Computer companies use different language options in their service manuals. American baseball has the World Series competition in which only North Americans take part in contrast to the soccer world cup in which 204 teams applied to take part. The concept of globalization, therefore, is often characterized by contradictions, such as the need to standardize some elements of the marketing mix while, at the same time, accepting the need to respond to local needs and tastes by adapting the product or service. Some believe that the true nature of globalization is encapsulated in the phrase 'think global, act local', in which there is an acknowledgement of the need to balance standardization and adaptation according to the particular situation. Even this concept is challenged because it implies that the starting point for the strategy is based on a standardized marketing mix. For many MNEs the alternative – 'think local, act global' – may be more appropriate given that it implies focusing on local needs, but taking the opportunity, whenever feasible and appropriate, to standardize elements of the marketing mix and globalize support services. Against this background the word globalization is associated in a very imprecise way with many different aspects of the international marketing strategy process.

The drivers of globalization

Although globalization may be difficult to define satisfactorily, there are a number of drivers of globalization that can be used to explain its impact and discuss its implications:

- market access
- market opportunities
- industry standards
- sourcing
- products and services
- technology
- customer requirements
- competition
- cooperation
- distribution
- communication and information
- the company's strategy, business programmes and processes.

Globalization of market access has increased as the number of inaccessible markets has reduced following the political changes that have opened up markets, for example in Central and Eastern Europe and China, to much greater MNE involvement. While these 'new' markets have become more accessible, firms entering them usually face more difficult problems inviably establishing their global products there because of the differences in social and business culture and the lack of a reliable infrastructure, the unfamiliar and unpredictable legal framework and the varying standards and values of business practice, which often lead to corruption. While these markets offer attractive growth prospects, many Western global firms have shown themselves to be ill-equipped to exploit these opportunities. Initially they were unwilling or unable to 'go it alone' in these markets, which were unsophisticated by developed country standards, and found it necessary to form partnerships with local firms, with mixed results.

In the short period since these markets have opened up many local companies have experienced phenomenal domestic growth which has enabled them to build a platform from which they themselves can become global players.

Market access is also being improved by the increasing regionalization, resulting from the growth of trading blocs. Firms are reinforcing this effect by helping to reduce inter-country barriers and thus improve market access by operating more standardized pan-regional marketing programmes and processes such as product development and advertising. Indeed the market access challenges for global companies now relate not so much to externally imposed barriers but to internal management issues faced by competing in emerging markets against increasingly sophisticated competitors.

Globalization of market opportunities has increased with the continued deregulation of certain sectors, such as financial services where the traditional barriers between the various parts of an industry, such as banking, insurance, pensions, specialist savings, mortgage and loan suppliers, are being broken down. This has enabled supermarket groups to enter many market sectors, including financial services and pharmacy product retailing.

Removal of sector barriers has resulted in mergers or alliances of firms to form larger and more powerful groups which can offer a complete range of products or services to their customers in the sector. For such MNEs, the power base may be a large domestic or regional market, as has been the case with a number of mergers in financial services or in automobiles. As will be discussed later, Daimler (Germany) and Chrysler (USA), merged in 1998 to create a more comprehensive product range in their industry sector but as Illustration 7.8 shows this failed leading Daimler to sell Chrysler, but then embark on an alliance with Renault.

The privatization of government-owned utilities such as electricity, gas and telephone is leading to industry restructuring where previously there were monopolies with tight operating restrictions. This is allowing firms to compete in geographic areas and industry sectors from which they have previously been excluded.

The UK has allowed foreign ownership of many key state assets, for example six of its main airports are owned by a consortium led by Grupo Ferrovial, a Spanish firm, which includes South Korea's national pension service as a major investor. Owners of its utilities include EDF and GDF Suez (French) EON (Germany), RWE (Germany) Iberdrola (Spain), Macquarrie (Australia) and communications include Telefonica (Spain), Hutchinson Whampoa (Hong Kong), France Telecome and Deutsche Telecom (Germany), (Arnott, 2010).

Some governments, have raised money to fund social sector programmes and reduce budget deficits by selling off minority stakes in state owned assets. The Indian government has sold off 20 per cent of Power Grid Corporation, the biggest electricity transmission company and 10 per cent of Coal India, the biggest mining company in the world.

Globalization of industry standards is increasing as technical operating standards, professional rules and guidelines are being adopted more widely primarily due to the harmonization of regulations within trading blocs, but more generally around the world as a result of the increased mobility of experts and advisers, and the wider use of quality standards, such as ISO 9000. It is a precondition of supplying major customers that firms operate to certain product and service standards that can be recognized regionally and globally.

The largest MNEs are expected to work to ethical standards that cover such diverse areas as employment, environmental protection and unfair competition. As a result, MNEs demand that their staff work to exacting company standards. Professional staff are usually also regulated by national bodies and so greater regional harmonization is affecting standards of behaviour and performance. Despite this there is a long way to go. It has proved difficult for governments and regulators to agree and introduce standards for financial services to reduce a risk of the banking crisis in 2008.

Globalization of sourcing has increased as companies search the world for the best and cheapest materials, components and services rather than rely on local suppliers. Figure 6.1 identifies the benefits of global sourcing.

FIGURE 6.1 The benefits of global sourcing

- *Cheaper labour rates.* Fashion and clothing marketers obtain supplies from low labour rate countries such as China, Indonesia, Costa Rica, Vietnam and Latin America. There can, however, be problems of product quality and criticism of unethical behaviour as these firms resort to 'island hopping' to the new lower labour rate areas that result from changes in local country economic development, or their contractors may employ child labour.

- *Better or more uniform quality.* Certain countries and companies have competitive advantage over others as suppliers because of the local availability of materials and skills.

- *Access to the best technology, innovation and ideas.* Firms search the world to identify a particular research or design centre which might offer the specialist expertise they require. For example, Nissan set up design facilities in California and Microsoft has established research facilities close to Cambridge University in the UK.

- *Access to local markets.* Developing stronger links with a country through sourcing can help to generate new business in that country. For example, the aircraft maker Boeing has opened up the market in China following its decision to purchase components there.

- *Economies of scale advantages.* Where the location of a manufacturing or distribution operation is convenient to supply a whole region it can lead to significant cost advantages.

- *Lower taxes and duties.* Certain countries may offer tax advantages to manufacturers and low rates of duty when shipping goods to the customer. The relocation of some higher added value activities can help by spreading currency risk.

- *Potentially lower logistics costs.* Global transport and warehousing companies use IT more effectively to control product movement and inventory.

- *More consistent supply.* Some foods would be restricted because of seasonality if steps had not been taken to arrange supplies from countries with different growing seasons.

Stock.xchng

ILLUSTRATION 6.2

The changing geography of global outsourcing

The A.T. Kearney 2009 Global Services Locator Index (GSLI) suggests outsourcing is still expected to grow, as shortages are experienced in the talent pool in the home country and firms gain confidence in outsourcing higher added value functions. However, the geography of outsourcing is changing dramatically with some regions suffering falls, for example, in central European countries, such as Poland Czech Republic and Hungary, while countries in South East Asia and the Middle East are gaining. The reasons for this can be cost advantages but also improved labour quality in the outsourcing countries. Governments around the world are investing in the skills necessary to attract outsourcing business.

While India is the top destination, China has identified business process outsourcing and IT services as future key growth sectors. Different countries offer different advantages, for example, the prevalence of English or multilingual speakers, small time differences, for example South Africa has no more than two hours' difference with Europe, Egypt and Jordan have low cost, highly skilled workers that have worked as migrants in other Gulf states for years. Northern Ireland is close to the UK, but costs there are estimated by IBM to be 32 per cent cheaper than the rest of the UK.

Newer countries are emerging as outsourcing destinations including Vietnam and smaller islands, too, such as Jamaica and Mauritius.

Kearney observed that while offshoring slowed following the recession, the percentage of companies' staff offshore were likely to increase as companies sought to maintain service but reduce costs. Newer offshore facilities tended to be more efficient because onshore facilities tended to be older and more inefficient resulting from years of bad practices and legacy systems.

Question

1 What do you consider to be the key factors for successful outsourcing?

References: Twentyman, J. (2010) 'Where in the World', *Raconteur Media*, 10 August; and Kearney, A.T. (2009) *Global Services Locator Index* (GSLI).

Illustration 6.2 explains that new country destinations are being found for outsourcing.

The major risks in global sourcing are in dealing with countries where there might be political, economic and exchange rate risks. There are also specific risks associated with an individual supplier that might use the knowledge gained and power which results from a strong position in the supply chain to become a competitor. As increasing numbers of scientists and engineers are being trained in China, India and Central and Eastern Europe, so outsourcing of research and development now to these countries will lead to increased competition from there in the future. Quality and service provided by the supplier can be critical and if not managed can begin to affect the reputation of the customer. An example of this is shown in Management Challenge 6.1. What is crucial is that the MNE must retain its competitive advantage and not outsource its supplies to the point where it gives away all its technical and commercial secrets, power in the market or risks supply quality problems. This potential danger needs to be managed by purchasers improving their supplier–purchaser relationships or, perhaps, even forming longer-term strategic alliances. The additional benefit of better supplier–purchaser relationships can be improved communications and the avoidance of some unnecessary supply chain costs resulting from inadequate specifications, misunderstandings about quality and generally poor management. As we will see later the Internet has made the development of international supply chains easier but also changed their nature.

MANAGEMENT CHALLENGE 6.1

Toyota – growing too fast?

In the first few years of the new millennium the future prospects of the leading car makers changed. The US car makers lost out as high fuel costs hit demand hard for 4-wheel drive Sports Utility Vehicles and other large cars. The firms were crippled by very high healthcare costs and as the recession hit hard, they were all kept afloat by the US government. Chrysler only narrowly avoided bankruptcy.

By contrast Toyota had focused on being profitable and responding quickly to market changes and had developed a policy of manufacturing cars to suit the markets where they sell. However, even Toyota tried to become global too fast. Akio Toyoda, in written evidence to the US Congress, admitted that Toyota may have grown too quickly in its quest to become the world's number one car maker and put quantity before quality.

In the summer of 2006 Toyota's apparently perfect image was starting to become a little tarnished as the company recalled 2.2 million vehicles to correct faults, including potential power steering failure in its hybrid car, tyres bulging and possibly bursting in their small pick-up, and the possibility that air bags would not inflate in a crash. Worse was to follow when in 2010 it recalled around 10 million vehicles for various faults including faulty floor mats, sticking accelerator pedals, braking software problems and steering malfunctions.

Toyota's competitive advantage had always been built around quality and reliability, but of course as the development and manufacture of products was increasingly outsourced, it became more difficult to maintain high quality standards. Fast growth places considerable strain on effectively managing the supply chain especially where, as in Toyota's case, it constitutes such a high proportion of the car's value.

Question

1 How can Toyota maintain control of its reputation and brand image and build the capability and capacity to be leader in the sector?

References: Maynard, M. and Fackler, M. (2006) 'A Rise in Defects at Toyota Puts its Reputation at Stake', *New York Times*. 5 August. Clark, A. (2010) 'Toyota Boss Akio Toyota Apologises Ahead of US Grilling, www.guardian.co.uk, 23 February.

Globalization of core products and services. More and more products are reaching the mature phase of their product life cycle and this is leading to greater commoditization of products and services. Consumers see very little difference between the offerings of many competing suppliers as they become less loyal to a single brand. The increased speed at which new innovations can be copied by other competitors means that core benefits can no longer be a point of differentiation between competitors. MNEs are responding to this and gaining competitive advantage over local competition by differentiating their products through developing their marketing and customer service capability in the form of the brand image, higher levels of service or better technical support.

Globalization of technology. Technology is converging within and between industries, with similar processes and ideas being used, for example, in telecommunications, information technology hardware and software and entertainment and consumer electronics, so that new multifunctional products and services cross the traditional boundaries between the industry sectors. New technologies are adopted around the world at ever greater speeds. In many industries this is being driven by a small number of global players that have the market power to change the ways of working and generate sufficient demand from customers to make the wider application of the ideas more cost-effective. In this way the globalization of technology is contributing very significantly to the competitive advantage of the MNEs that are able to market products in a number of industry sectors because they have developed effective distribution channels and international promotion.

Globalization of customer requirements is resulting from the identification of worldwide customer segments, such as teenagers with similar worldwide tastes in music, fashion and fast food, and the very rich, who live the celebrity lifestyle and buy the most expensive fashion brands, fly first class or hire their own plane, stay at the same luxury hotels and own super performance cars. No matter where they originate they consume the same products and services. With industries becoming more globalized, the demands placed on the business support services, such as advertising agencies, accountants, law firms and consultants, are converging too. Customers in both the consumer and business-to-business markets are demanding and getting what they perceive to be added value global products and services which better meet their changing needs than those they have been used to receiving from national companies.

Globalization of competition between industry giants tends to result in the same fight being replicated in each corner of the world, with MNEs using largely similar competing product or service offers. Traditional national firms have been outmanoeuvred by aggressive fast-growing international competitors who are far better at exploiting technical changes and other globalization effects and winning customers with more sophisticated marketing. They are also able to cross-subsidize their activities between countries, so helping them to gain an unfair advantage over local competition.

Mature industries, as well as new technology sectors, are being affected by global competition. For example, while the majority of the top ten chemical companies are European, there is increasing competition particularly from Asian companies, which have different cost structures and systems of industry regulation. Success in these component and raw material industries has traditionally been dependent upon the product portfolio, the relationship with customers and the levels of technical service and support provided, but increasingly the fact that these are components in the supply chain of branded consumer products means that successful suppliers must carry out more effective marketing to members of the supply chain that are closer to the customer.

Globalization of cooperation. To compete in all the major world markets it is necessary to make available huge financial resources, often outside the scope of individual firms. This is leading to the formation of alliances between major MNEs, members of a supply chain or between firms with complementary activities. The Japanese *keiretsu* go further in that they are formal organizations between banks, manufacturers and trading companies with cross-share ownership, and have the huge resources necessary to build businesses in the major world markets. This has enabled them to make investments over a number of years to establish a dominant long-term market position in a particular industry.

Globalization of distribution is occurring, first, as the supply chain becomes increasingly concentrated on fewer, more powerful channel distributors, retailers and logistics companies; second, as e-business technology dominates the exchange and transfer of data and the whole process of product and service transactions, including methods of product and service selling, ordering, customizing, progress chasing, payment arrangement and delivery confirmation; and third, as logistics become a source of competitive advantage, for example in retailing, having contributed to the international success of Walmart, Ikea and Tesco. For many organizations it can be argued that a global approach to distribution means organizing according to factors such as proximity to the population and transport infrastructure, rather than country borders.

Globalization of distribution is particularly important for companies such as Amazon that use e-commerce as they must be able to make transaction and logistics arrangements to enable them to provide high levels of service and efficiency to customers, wherever they are located.

Globalization of communication and information. Major changes in telecommunications and information technology have had three effects. First, global communications such as satellite and cable TV, and the world wide web have made it essential that MNEs develop a consistent worldwide corporate identity and brand image. As consumers travel physically or virtually by way of the media or World Wide Web, they are exposed to communications and advertising originating from MNEs from many parts of the world. Consistency of the communication is vital for reinforcing brand familiarity, quality and values.

Second, digital technology is driving the localization and individuality of communications, for example through the proliferation of local TV channels, on-demand video and television and the development of the Internet, which allows greater exposure for individual communications. These developments go further than simply improving the accessibility of the traditional one-way communications with customers by adding a two-way, interactive dimension to the firms' relationships with their global customers.

Third, the explosion of social media through websites, such as Facebook and Twitter means that much more discussion of the MNE's activities takes place outside the influence and control of the company.

Courtesey of Tata Sons

ILLUSTRATION 6.3

Conglomerate breaks out from India

Unlike multinationals from developed countries that have focused on their core activities where there appeared to be the most attractive global market opportunities and sold off unwanted parts of the business firms from emerging markets have often adopted the conglomerate model, in which hundreds of often disparate businesses are held in an organization that perhaps resembles a private equity fund.

The activities that have bound these businesses together in the conglomerate model in the past have often been manufacturing or international trading.

Ratan Tata became chairman of Tata Sons, a disorganized family business in 1991. He is a shy and unassuming figure who shuns the trappings of wealth, despite being one of India's richest men. He took over at a time when the Indian government began removing the bureaucratic controls that had previously curtailed the development of Indian firms. He set about rationalizing the group's hundreds of businesses with the aim of making them more efficient. The organization is still

diverse, with interests in steel, cars, hotels, mobile telephony, chemicals and tea, and it is one of India's largest software firms. It is also in the top ten of global IT services firms.

A feature of most fast-growing companies from emerging markets is that they have lower costs than their competitors from developed countries. However, Tata's competitive advantage comes not just from the supply of low-cost, well-educated labour necessary for the technology-based activities. It has also built expertise in developing and operating automated, capital-intensive production, typical of steel making. Moreover during India's 1991 reforms Tata learned how to thrive in a highly competitive market place that still had a highly regulated environment and a poor infrastructure, and this serves them well as they pursue a strategy of mergers and acquisitions in different world markets.

Ratan Tata has single-handedly made the company into a respected MNE. In 2007 Tata completed a £6.7 billion takeover of Corus, the British–Dutch steel maker, in the process beating a Brazilian steel-making company CSN. This followed the acquisition of Singapore's Natsteel in 2004 and Thailand's Millennium Steel in 2005.

In 2000 Tata took over Tetley Tea, a British business with a global brand, with the intention of linking India tea production with the overseas tea markets. Tata decided that Tata Motors would make its own car, the Nano, turning away from the possibility of a joint venture with a more established manufacturer, however, Tata did acquire the Jaguar and Land Rover brands. Among many other acquisitions is Citigroup Global Services (US) as part of the group's development in business process outsourcing.

Investment does not only take the form of acquisitions. Tata made Bangladesh's single largest foreign investment of £1.1 billion when it agreed to build a power plant, steel unit and fertilizer factory after the government guaranteed a supply of gas for 20 years from its proven reserves.

Although he has made Tata's businesses more competitive and more global in outlook, the company has a tradition of being public spirited and Ratan Tata has said in interviews that he would prefer his legacy to be 'having caused no damage to others'. The company has a reputation for refusing to accept bribes and treating its workers well. Two-thirds of Tata Sons is owned by charitable trusts that do good works in India. Although the company is competitive, some foreign investors wonder if this approach is right for running the global business.

Question

1 What are the key issues that Tata faces as it progresses to becoming a global company?

References: 'Circle the wagons', *The Economist,* 12 October, 2006; 'Steely logic', *The Economist,* 28 October, 2006; 'The shy architect', *The Economist,* 11 January, 2007 and 'Bangladesh wins $2bn India deal', *BBC News online,* 19 August, 2004.

Thus while the globalization of communications leads to global access for customers, the need to integrate communications is becoming ever more difficult to manage.

Globalization of the company's strategy, business programmes and processes. The result of these globalization effects is to pose challenges to firms to achieve both improved global operational efficiency and greater global market effectiveness. The global firm's response to managing the complexity of international marketing must include developing an all-embracing global strategy supported by effective marketing programmes and processes that will integrate the various disparate activities of the firm's far-flung strategic business units.

In considering each of these areas of globalization in turn it is possible to identify business sector examples in which the globalization trend is relatively advanced and others in which it is in its early stages. For example, accountancy and associated consultancy is dominated by four major players, until the late 1990s retailing could be regarded as a largely national or, at most, subregional activity with few examples of retailers active in more than five or six countries. The challenge for global companies is to lead the development towards globalization in industry sectors where there is the greatest potential for growth. However, there is no guarantee that by simply being globally active in an industry sector a firm will benefit. Firms must be able to manage the environmental threats and exploit their market opportunities by building global competitive advantage. Illustration 6.3 shows how a firm from an emerging country has become a global player.

Alternative strategic responses

It is against the background of the trend towards globalization and the need to build a worldwide presence that firms must develop strategic responses which are appropriate to their situation and are feasible to implement. For MNEs, the question may be how to rationalize their activities to gain greater focus and effectiveness. For firms that have progressed through the early stages of expansion into new country markets, as we discussed in the previous chapter, the next stage is to decide whether or not to progress further and, if so, what strategy they might adopt to enable them to manage their involvement in many countries. Underpinning the growth strategy in either case must be some fundamental decisions about the product portfolio and expansion into new country markets.

The international competitive posture

The level of geographic development and product strength determine the strategic options available to a company. Gogel and Larreche (1989) identify four types of competitors along the two dimensions of product range and geographic coverage, as shown in Figure 6.2. The position of a company on the international competitive posture matrix will determine the strategic options.

Kings. Because these firms have a wide geographic coverage and strong product portfolio they are in a strong competitive position. They have been able to expand geographically and have not dispersed their resources into weak products. They are in the best position to have an effective global strategy and are the true global companies.

FIGURE 6.2 The international competitive posture matrix

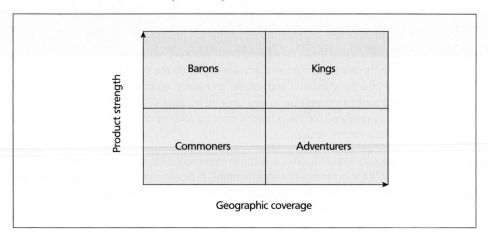

Source: Data adapted from Gogel & Larreche (1989)

Barons. These companies have strong products in a limited number of countries. This makes geographic expansion attractive to them unless their domestic and close-by markets are large and untapped in which case there is little need for international expansion. However, without domestic growth opportunities barons can be attractive to companies wishing to supplement their own product strength and therefore they may be takeover targets.

Adventurers. These have been driven to expand geographically, but they lack a strong portfolio. They are vulnerable to an increasing level of global competition. Their challenge is to consolidate their product position by focusing on internal product development, acquisition or by eliminating products to concentrate on a narrower portfolio in a classic global niche strategy.

Commoners. Commoners have a product portfolio with relatively weak international potential and narrow geographic coverage. They may have benefited from legal barriers protecting them from intense competition in their existing markets. They are likely acquisition targets, and before any geographical expansion they need to build their product portfolio. A likely international strategy could be one of supplying own-brand products to retailers.

Increasing geographic coverage and product strength means competition for resources and each quadrant of the matrix reflects the trade-offs that may become necessary. While the position of a firm on the matrix reflects how it has been able to balance its resources between consolidation and expansion of geographic coverage and product strength. Technology companies such as Microsoft were initially adventurers, marketing their operating system widely before building up their product range to become the 'kings' they are today. Companies from Asian markets frequently are 'barons', developing a strong product range and building their home or close regional markets before developing internationally.

Global strategy drivers

The fundamental driver of a global strategy is whether the market allows significant global standardization of the marketing activity or whether substantial adaptation is needed to address local differences and expectations. The challenge for global firm strategy development is to maximize the efficiency and effectiveness of their operations. While having a completely standardized marketing offer, products, services, communications, etc. would be very efficient, for most companies it would not maximize effectiveness in revenue generation, given the differing needs of customers from different countries and cultures. The second driver is what orientation the company adopts – in other words how it sees itself in the global market.

FIGURE 6.3 Company orientation in global strategy development

Global orientation	Focus
Ethnocentric	Because the domestic market is considered to be the most important, the company adopts home country standards and values, and assumes that the marketing offer in the home country will be acceptable in new country markets. Standardized products and services are typically designed for the domestic country and exported. The brand usually reflects the domestic country image.
Polycentric	Each country market is unique and the marketing offer is designed to meet the individual needs of the customers of each country. Typically a country manager would ensure that the products and services are adapted locally and the brand is developed to incorporate cultural differences. This would typically result in a multi-domestic strategy.
Regiocentric	Developing a regional strategy as the geographic market focus, for example, a company might develop a product and service portfolio for Europe, or for Southern Africa. The organization gives the regional managers considerable autonomy but the regional focus can leave missed opportunities to standardize.
Geocentric	This is the global or transnational company that sees the entire world as a potential market. The strategy adopted focuses on one global customer segment that requires a globally standardized product or service. Alternatively a geocentric company develops a transnational strategy that uses a strategy based on a standardized identity and well communicated values but then integrates standardized and adapted elements of the marketing offer to efficiently meet the diverse needs of customers.

Before looking at the market factors it is useful to consider the company orientation, shown in Figure 6.3.

The standardization and adaptation drivers lead to the worldwide strategy options illustrated in Figure 6.4 with, at one extreme, the concept of a multidomestic approach in which the firm has a completely different strategy for every single market and, at the other extreme, a global approach in which everything in the marketing activity is standardized in all countries. In addition, an ethnocentric firm that is very focused on the domestic market might seek to export its home market model with few modifications. In practice, firms adopt a combination of standardization and adaptation of the various elements of the marketing management programmes and processes by globalizing some elements and localizing others. In broad terms it is possible to categorize a firm's strategic development as multidomestic, global or regional, a third strategy in which separate, but largely standardized marketing strategies are implemented across a region of the world.

The largest, most complex companies in the world use a combination of all these strategies. A transnational approach is one in which the firm has a standardized identity and corporate values throughout the firm but delivers its strategic objectives through composite strategies which contain elements of multidomestic, regional and global strategies. The global marketing strategy is influenced significantly by the supply chain decisions relating to location of operations and outsourcing arrangements.

Zou and Cavusgil (2002) identify three perspectives of global marketing strategy: the standardization perspective, the configuration perspective and the integration perspective. The global firm locates its supply chain activities in those countries where they can be carried out most efficiently. Components are then transferred to another country for assembly, before the highly standardized finished goods are exported to the countries in which they will be sold, supported by largely standardized marketing. Global firms then integrate their activities and competitive moves to enable them to become major players in all major markets. Increased outsourcing makes these tasks more challenging as success depends on customer requirements being met on time.

FIGURE 6.4 Alternative worldwide strategies

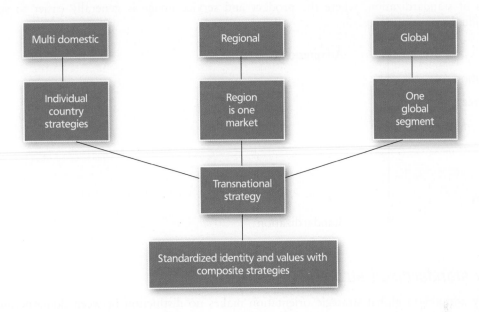

Standardizing the various elements of the marketing process has the aim of scale economies and experience curve effects in operations, research and development and marketing and concentrating value chain activity in a few country locations to exploit comparative advantage and so improve efficiency. The experience curve effect or learning curve relates to the relationship between experience and efficiency. In the 1960s research by Boston Consulting Group found that, provided that there was a desire to achieve results efficiency improved as the cumulative (lifetime) experience of carrying out the same tasks increased.

Standardization and adaptation

The challenge facing firms with aspirations to become truly effective global players appears to be turning widespread international presence into global competitive advantage. The critical success factor in achieving this is to offer added value for global customers by providing them with benefits that are significantly better than those provided by the competitors, particularly local competitors. The benefits can be tangible, for example a global product, such as Intel processors, that are broadly the same worldwide, or intangible, for example a brand such as Rolex that is recognized worldwide. At the same time they must aggressively seek cost efficiencies that will enable the firm to offer better value for money than their competitors.

In practice, firms manage these apparently incompatible requirements by using strategies that are appropriate to their own situation, and striking a balance between the different degrees of standardization or adaptation of the various elements of international marketing process.

In general:

- Marketing objectives and strategies are more readily standardized than operational marketing decisions.

- Within the marketing mix, products are most easily standardized, promotion less so and distribution and pricing only with difficulty.

- The more operational the decision the more likely it is to be differentiated.

Consequently the elements of marketing management should be seen as being at different points of a continuum of standardization, where the product and service image is generally easier to standardize than individual country pricing.

Pricing   ▲   Adaptation

Distribution

Sales force

Sales promotion

Product   │

Image

Objective

Strategy   ▼   Standardization

Globally standardized strategy

A company adopting a global strategic orientation makes no distinction between domestic and foreign market opportunities, seeking to serve an essentially identical customer segment appearing in many countries around the world and developing global strategies to compete with other global firms. Global marketing can be defined as the focusing of an organization's resources on the selection and exploitation of global market opportunities consistent with and supportive of its short-term strategic objectives and goals.

Global marketing is the realization that a firm's foreign marketing activities, in whatever form they take, need to be supportive of some higher objective than just the immediate exploitation of a foreign market opportunity. Global marketing can, therefore, involve the selection of a country for its potential contribution to globalization benefits, even entering an unattractive market which has global strategic significance – for example, the home market of a competitor. Thus an organization with such a global focus formulates a long-term strategy for the company as a whole and then coordinates the strategies of local subsidiaries to support this.

Many writers have offered views on this issue. For example Levitt (1983) suggested that in order to be competitive in the world market, firms should shift their emphasis from local customized products to globally standardized products that are advanced, functional, reliable and low priced. Buzzell (1968) argued that product standardization has the benefits of (a) economies of scale, (b) faster accumulation of learning through experience that can aid efficiency and effectiveness and (c) reduced costs of design modification.

In summarizing the forces at work in the standardization debate Meffet and Bolz (1993) describe the globalization push and pull factors, shown in Figure 6.5, which are driving marketing standardization. While many barriers to standardization have been removed or reduced, enabling cost savings to be made, some degree of adaptation is necessary in most cases and this usually involves additional cost. It is still possible to make cost savings even where the marketing programmes cannot be standardized by developing standardized processes even though the actual programme content may be different. For example, while it may not be possible to standardize the product range, advertising campaigns and prices it is possible to globally standardize the processes by which the product portfolio is managed, new products are launched, advertising is managed and advertising space is booked, and how the marketing information system and the marketing planning processes are integrated around the world. Therefore, some of the globalization drivers such as economies of scale and the experience effect (or learning curve) can be achieved through process standardization.

Other drivers illustrated in the model cover factors already discussed, such as globalization of customer demand, the globalization of competition and its effect on cross subsidization of markets.

FIGURE 6.5 Globalization push and pull factors

Source: Data adapted from Meffett and Bolz (1993) in Halliburton & Hunerberg (ed.) *European Marketing Readings and Cases*, Addison-Wesley.

Globalization of technology requires the high costs of innovation to be recovered more quickly, due to the shorter pay back cycles for new products, by quickly diffusing new products into all possible global markets.

However, market fragmentation has also increased and, in practice, global firms have to strike an appropriate balance between the relative advantages of standardization and adaptation to local tastes. There is little point in standardizing programmes for marketing products and services if consumers reject them and only buy the products and services that meet their specific needs.

McDonald's, for example, is not only adapting its traditional products to the tastes of different cultures but is also recognizing the need for greater variety on its menu. Coca-Cola uses different recipes around the world, varying sweetness according to local tastes.

Multidomestic strategies A company adopting a multidomestic orientation assumes that foreign market opportunities are as important as home market opportunities. However, the company takes the view that the differences between its international markets are so acute that widespread adaptation is necessary to meet market needs and to retain competitive leverage in local markets. Thus, the company essentially follows a differentiated marketing strategy with individual marketing mix strategies in many of their world markets.

For many major businesses there are few benefits to be obtained from widespread standardization of their activities. Consequently a well-organized and managed multidomestic strategy is an effective method for many companies for developing a global business.

An example of an organization which can be accurately characterized as having a multidomestic strategy is Asea Brown Boveri (ABB), discussed in Illustration 6.4.

A key factor in the strategy is encouraging senior managers to be entrepreneurial in responding to local customer needs, industry standards and different stages of economic development.

Thus, while there are many forces driving companies towards achieving a global strategy through standardizing as many marketing activities as possible, there are also very important prevailing arguments persuading companies that they can also achieve an effective worldwide strategy through a multidomestic approach. These forces are as follows.

ILLUSTRATION 6.4

© Tupungato, iStockphoto.com

ABB: a new model of global entrepreneurialism – good while it lasted?

ABB was formed by a merger of Sweden's ASEA and the Swiss company Brown Boveri. It had customers in the process industries, manufacturing and consumer industries and in utilities (oil, gas and petrochemicals). As chief executive Percy Barnevik was faced with merging two companies with different business cultures and operations, he decided to create a fundamentally different model of how a large MNE could be organized and managed. He created the new head office in Zurich to make the merger less like a takeover by the Swedes, and started dispersing the two head offices of 6000 staff among a number of front-line units.

He created a head office with 135 staff managing 1300 companies with 5000 profit centres. He cut 90 per cent of headquarters staff by moving 30 per cent into the small business units (SBUs), 30 per cent into free-standing service centres concerned with value-adding activities and eliminating 30 per cent of the jobs. Similar huge cuts in management were made in the headquarters of the subsidiaries.

The management within the SBUs, which usually had fewer than 200 employees, were given a substantially enhanced role in managing their business. ABB was one of the most admired firms of the 1990s. Bartlett and Ghoshall (2001) said that Barnevik's achievement was combining the contradictions of big and small, local and global, economies of scale and intimate market knowledge to create a truly global organization.

ABB employed 160 000 staff in 100 countries and a large part of their manufacturing was moved away from the developed countries to the developing countries, including Eastern Europe. By employing people in developing countries ABB was in a position to sell further expertise and services as they helped build the countries' infrastructure.

Barnevik was succeeded by Jorgen Centremann in October 2000, but he lasted less than two years as the company's share price halved. ABB missed its profit targets, it nearly ran out of cash as its debts mounted, and in 2002 it made its first loss of US $787 million. The problems were compounded by the threat that a US unit would go bankrupt because of the potential liabilities (capped at US$1.3 billion by a US court) resulting from a number of massive lawsuits involving asbestos.

Question

1 Could the model be blamed for ABB's problems?

Industry standards remain diverse For many traditional industries such as those based upon engineering and particularly those that involve large investment in plant and equipment, the cost of harmonization of standards is high and the progress to harmonization is slow. The markets for these industries often involve a country's infrastructure, transport and utilities and, consequently, depend on often protracted government spending decisions. Usually in making decisions such as these governments will give consideration not simply to market factors, but also to the impact on the economy, environment and the electorate's expectations.

Customers continue to demand locally differentiated products Cultural heritage and traditions still play a strong role in areas such as food, drink and shopping. While there are increasing moves to accept cross-border products, there is still resistance in many cultures.

Being an insider remains critically important The perceived country of origin effect of goods still has a bearing on take-up of products and local manufacturing of goods is frequently necessary to overcome this scepticism. In business-to-business marketing, there is a definite bias in favour of products sourced from particular areas, such as Silicon Valley in the US, and so IT/electronic firms often decide to set up local manufacture there.

A further factor is that companies that make a significant commitment to a country by establishing manufacturing, research and development capability are likely to be consulted by the government as they prepare new legislation. This should result in providing greater opportunities for influencing than would be possible for a company that shows little commitment to the country, perhaps, simply exporting to the country.

Global organizations are difficult to manage   In finding ways to coordinate far-flung operations, firms have to decentralize and replace home country loyalties with a system of corporate values and loyalties that is acceptable to the firm's staff around the world. For some companies this proves to be problematic and, in some cases, the head office values and culture can be significantly different from those of the workforce. Their desire to impose standardized products with little or no consultation on their country operations is very often seen as arrogant by local staff.

Management myopia   Many products and services that are suitable candidates for global marketing are ignored as managers fail to seize the opportunity to build their business in a wider range of markets. On the other hand products that work well in the managers' home markets are often believed to be acceptable to customers worldwide without being given full consideration. Self-reference criteria often makes it difficult for managers to take other than a narrow, national view of international marketing. Moreover, because there are no guarantees that a business can succeed, the firm must be willing to risk the heavy investment that the move from a multi-domestic to a global strategy requires. For some, the resources required and the risks involved are simply too great.

Regional strategy

One of the most significant developments in global marketing strategy is how firms respond to the rise of the regional trading blocs. Even in globalized industries, company strategies are becoming more of a composite of regionally focused strategies and programmes. For many companies, regionalization represents a more manageable compromise between the extremes of global standardization and multi-domestic strategies. For example, there are some obvious differences in the challenges of marketing to North America, Africa and South East Asia and different strategies are usually formulated for each region. One key question is when is the right time to enter emerging markets as Management Challenge 6.2 asks.

However, many firms create regional management for the convenience of creating manageable teams rather than to exploit regional similarities. For example, a number of MNEs create a regional division titled EMEA, which comprises Europe, Middle East and Africa – regions which might be characterized by their differences rather than their similarities.

Regional trading blocs tend to favour their own MNEs, and for those companies located outside the region there can be significant tariff and non-tariff barriers. Public–private sector committees decide on standards, such as car emissions, safety standards and security. By shifting operations and decision-making inside the region an MNE can gain advantage from being part of the consultation and decision-making process.

The key to developing effective regional strategies is deciding in what ways the marketing strategy for one region should be differentiated from the others, and being able to respond quickly to threats or opportunities that emerge in the region.

However, while regional strategies are built around the common elements within a region and the distinctiveness of the region, in practice the differences within the region are still huge. Cagni (2006) explains how with the enlargement of the EU there is an increasing management challenge, posed by conflict between the single market concentration and multimarket fragmentation, exacerbated by the mix of cultures, histories, economics and trends of the 'New Europe'. Big differences in the country environments and markets require more responsive approaches rather than centralized multinational

MANAGEMENT CHALLENGE 6.2

Banks timing their Africa entry

In many sectors the key to long term success in the emerging regions around the world is getting the timing right for early market entry. Africa is very attractive as a new market for banks. The collective annual GDP of the 53 countries is roughly equal to Brazil or Russia, Africa's trade with China is estimated to have increased from £3.5 billion in 1990 to more than $100 billion in 2008 and it is estimated that half the trade is with other 'emerging' markets. Management consultants McKinsey say there are more middle class people in Africa than India. The number of people wanting mobile phones, cars and televisions will increase rapidly over the next few years with improvements in education and further urbanization. Individually, economies are still small, for example, South Africa's GDP is the same size as that of Greece.

Barclays, Standard Chartered and JP Morgan have a significant presence resulting from the colonial legacy, but their position is being challenged by many competitors using a variety of market entry methods, such as China's ICBC that have taken a 20 per cent share of South Africa's Standard Bank and Bank of China that has a partnership with Ecobank, active in 29 African countries. Brazilian banks have entered Mozambique and Angola through joint ventures with Portuguese partners and Russia's Renaissance Capital investment bank has struck deals in West Africa.

Africa's working age population will increase from 500 million to 1.1 billion by 2040. As wage inflation occurs in Asia, companies will increasingly outsource their production to Africa, the last low wage region and banks see big opportunities for new business. The question, however, is whether the banks can cope with the risks of working in Africa. Nine bank bosses were sacked by a new financial regulator in Nigeria following the collapse of the system, which required a $4 billion bail out. Introducing banking to the rural areas is also problematic, and will require innovative solutions. For example, Barclays are using mobile phone technology to address this.

Question

1 What indicators signal the right time to enter a new market?

References: I Dey British banks join the rush for Africa, *Sunday Times*, 29 August 2010.

---

management. Companies are taking the opportunity from the formation of regional trading blocs to include regional objectives and plans as a significant part of their worldwide strategy and build on existing, or form new, cooperative trading relationships.

The prime motivation in the formation of the regional trading blocs is to enable indigenous companies to build the critical mass of activity within the home region necessary to enable them to compete effectively in global markets. The European Union, for example, has strived to create collaborative working between participants in a common supply chain, or those offering complementary or competitive products. Where the companies come from different countries political differences do still arise, particularly if national governments are concerned about the retention of jobs in sensitive industries, such as the defence and airline industries. Airbus is one such consortium in the manufacture of aeroplanes in Europe that has at different times benefited and suffered from political interference.

Transnational strategies If a firm has sufficient power and resources to exploit all the available opportunities on a worldwide basis, with little need to adapt strategies or involve partners to any great extent, then a simple strategy can be developed. However, many multi-nationals have a wide range of products and services, some of which might be suited to global and others to multidomestic development. The successful exploitation of these opportunities might require a much more flexible approach to strategic development, for example, it could involve a number of partners in licensing, joint ventures and strategic alliances as well as wholly owned operations.

Transnational companies integrate diverse assets, resources and people into operating units around the world. Through flexible management processes and networks, transnational companies aim to build three strategic capabilities:

■ Global scale efficiency and competitiveness.

■ National level responsiveness and flexibility.

■ Cross-market capacity to leverage learning on a worldwide basis.

Bartlett and Ghoshal (2001) argue that the aim of transnational companies is to further the firm's global scale efficiency and competitiveness in its totality. This task means the firm needs the ability to recognize market opportunities and risks across national borders. The overall goal is to achieve global competitiveness through a fully integrated strategy and operations. Thus, a transnational approach is not a particular strategy, but a strategic perspective that evolves as firms and the markets in which they operate increase in complexity. Hewlett Packard is a transnational organization because certain of its marketing operations and research and development are centralized and standardized, whereas other units operate with a substantial degree of independence. It has a strong corporate identity and some of its promotional themes, for example around e-business, are common throughout the firm. It has also formed strategic alliances with partners in order to carry out certain research and development activities where it is likely to benefit from the participation of partners. In such organizations the implications for strategic development are significant. A transnational strategy that is to achieve global competitive advantage needs to accommodate some, or all of the following:

■ Simple and complex individual product and market policies, which may be independent or interdependent.

■ Customer segments that are specific and unique to a cross-national niche market so the resultant segments are transnational and valid across borders.

■ Working closely with firms that are customers, suppliers, competitors and partners at the same time, but simultaneously ensuring that the values of the company are maintained and demonstrated to the external stakeholders through establishing clear and unambiguous positioning in all markets.

■ Maintaining and building meaningful and added value relationships in the supply chain.

International marketing management for global firms

So far in this chapter we have identified the changing trends in the business environment that are leading to increasing globalization and the factors that affect the firms' response to this, particularly in the way they standardize or adapt their marketing programmes and processes. We have shown distinct differences in the way global strategies can be developed to meet individual firms' situations. Implementing these global strategies, however, poses considerable problems and it is to these that we now turn.

As in the previous chapter, it is useful for the discussion to be based loosely upon the McKinsey 7S framework, which includes the hardware elements of strategy, structure and systems and the software elements of management style, staff, skills and shared values. Again we start with the hardware elements of strategy, systems and organization structure.

Global strategy implementation

Global firms have the objective of developing effective business operations in all the major markets in the world in order to maximize their performance. In the past they may well have prioritized the developed economies in North America, Europe and Asia, principally Japan. More recently these firms have developed a significant presence in many more markets. Now the focus for investment is China, India, Russia and Brazil, with their higher growth prospects in the future. Countries in the Middle East offer growth potential in many business sectors as they seek to diversify their business activity away from a dependence on oil and increasingly there is a view that companies will need to get a foothold in the other emerging markets of Asia, Africa and South America if they wish to benefit from the anticipated future development.

However, building a global presence is hugely expensive, and many firms see no value in expanding globally if their home country or region offers sufficient growth prospects without marketing their products and services in what they might perceive to be higher risk areas. US and Chinese companies have a large domestic market and, despite the rapid growth prospects of other regions of the world, their unfamiliarity often makes them unattractive. Despite this, with growth rates four times as high in Asia as in the rest of the world, almost all the Fortune 500 and leading European companies invested heavily in this area.

Opportunities in emerging markets for global firms

Most multinational enterprises, particularly from developed countries, focus on the customers that are wealthy enough now or will be in the future to purchase their premium goods and services and companies, such as McDonald's and Yum (see Integrative Learning Activity 3) are opening new outlets at unprecedented rates.

However, for many multinationals the very poorest parts of the world appear to be largely economically inactive and offer little opportunity for profitable growth. A small number of MNEs, such as Unilever discussed in the case study at the end of the chapter, have traded with these countries for many years, often buying and selling raw materials or selling processing machinery, and developing a presence by selling basic products to the consumer and B2B market. Prahalad and Hart (2002) have suggested that there is a pyramid of wealth, shown in Table 6.5, and emphasize that those with the lowest incomes still have the potential to create a significant demand for goods and services if they meet the specific needs of poor consumers and ensure that products and services are marketed to them in a sensitive way. While it might be expected that consumers from emerging markets simply want unsophisticated products, it may well prove a mistake to try to market to emerging markets those products that have reached the end of their life cycle and been replaced in developing countries. The particular situation in an emerging market may require a specific, innovative solution and this may miss out a particular technology development stage.

Hart and London (2005) have identified examples of innovative solutions that include not only products and services that satisfy customer demand but also create new routes to market that are more efficient in these emerging markets. This often requires the MNE to work with partners through less formal channels and networks than they are used to. The resulting solutions, such as lower cost manufacturing techniques, design and distribution can then be marketed to other parts of the world. For example, while a low cost car might be developed (Illustration 6.5) for emerging markets, it might also meet the needs of less affluent segments in developed countries.

The instability of emerging markets, crime and corruption are some of the main problems that MNEs have to deal with directly to ensure they protect their staff and reputation: however, their unfamiliarity with these markets makes this difficult, and here too local partners can prove invaluable.

Table 6.5 The global pyramid of wealth

	Global population (m)	Purchasing power (US$)
The wealthy	800	15 000
The emerging middle class	1500	1500–15 000
Low income markets	4000	<1500

Source: Adapted from Prahalad, C.K. and Hart, S.L. (2002) 'The fortune at the bottom of the pyramid', *Strategy and Business,* 26 (54): 67 Booz and Co.

Courtesey of LG

ILLUSTRATION 6.5

LG innovating to the top

LG started as an original equipment manufacturer for well know companies before it started marketing 'cheap and cheerful' products under its own brand. When Kim Sang-su took over as chairman in 2003 LG's white goods business was losing money, but he instituted a broad-based innovation programme to transform the business and help LG to attack the global high end market.

It became Korea's biggest and now the third-largest household appliance maker in the world after Whirlpool (US) and Electrolux (Sweden). It is the leader in home air conditioners, canister vacuum cleaners and microwave ovens and hopes to become number one in system air conditioners, front-loading washing machines and side by side refrigerators.

When CEO Yong Nam took over he realized that he needed to consolidate the improvements LG had made. LG jumped to number 7 in the most innovative companies list in 2010, but a key part of the success was the change he made to its procurement strategy, following the appointment of ex IBM purchasing manager Thomas Linton. Until then each procurement manager operated separately so the handset unit in Seoul did not know how much the flat screen TV unit in Mexico paid for the same chips from TSMC, the Taiwanese chip maker. Centralizing purchasing saved $2 billion off the company's $30 billion shopping bill. Better forward forecasting enabled it to save another $1 billion on purchasing wafers, the silicon disks used to make chips. The lower cost base that resulted enabled LG to get through the global downturn, increase its global competitiveness and offer attractively priced innovative products to the global market.

The procurement strategy helped it price the LG Cookie 30 per cent lower than competitor products. LG spent $1.2 billion to market its latest electronic devices including the LG Cookie helping it to become the world's third largest handset maker.

Question

1 What lessons can be drawn from LG's development from an OEM manufacturer to a global brand?

References: Ihlwan, M. 'Innovation Close-up: LG Electronics', *Business Week Magazine*, 15 April 2010.

The emergence of MNEs from emerging markets

So far we have focused on strategies of firms that already have a strong presence in developed countries and wish to extend that to emerging markets, but a current feature of global marketing is the emergence of future players. The high growth in the BRIC is providing the platform for the new generation of global players. Bracken (2007) suggests that it will be multinationals from emerging markets that could achieve the greatest growth in the future. Developing countries have traditionally depended upon foreign companies to supply job training and know-how and, in exchange, multinationals, usually from Western countries, could force concessions from national governments enabling them to build sales in new markets. Globalization and the requirements of a market economy, therefore, reduced the power of national governments. Now the governments of the strongest emerging countries are no longer willing to surrender their home market to foreign companies that exert undue influence in the industry sector and which might delay technology transfer into the developing country and so delay the economic development of the country. The size of the home markets in India and China provides domestic companies with a large base to build the potential multinational companies of the future. China, for example, has decided to develop its own car industry and India, following the removal of central planning and bureaucracy in the 1990s, has created some strong IT outsourcing businesses, such as Wipro, Tata and Infosys.

In emerging markets, volume and low cost have driven the hypergrowth and the ambitions of young managers. Entrepreneurs spot opportunities in other sectors than their own, so a property developer might move into computers (Economist, 2010 a).

Ghemawat and Hout (2008) suggest that in China at least established MNCs dominate the knowledge and brand intensive businesses, whereas Chinese businesses hold an advantage in industries, dominated by production and logistics. However, there is some evidence that this is changing partly through organic development and partly through acquisition. Tata is meeting the needs of local, first time, middle class consumers through its Nano car development, but has also taken over Citigroup's Global Services outsourcing division. China's BYD in batteries and Huawei, second largest supplier in the world to Ericsson in mobile telecom equipment, equally provide business customers with cost effective solutions. These companies are building their global presence also through acquisition, as discussed at various points (Economist 2010 b).

Multinationals from developed markets will now have to work harder to access these fast-growing emerging markets as it will prove to be much harder to go it alone and more difficult to exert control over local partners who now see the possibility of developing their own global businesses.

Multinationals from the last generation of emerging markets have already become global players with dominant market shares in Western markets. Toyota, from Japan, now close to becoming the leading US car maker, was virtually unknown in the west until 1965, and Samsung from South Korea was unknown ten years ago.

For firms wishing to build a truly global presence, there are a number of challenges, including:

■ Responding to the changing basis of competitive advantage.

■ Increasing global appeal by building the global brand.

■ Developing sustainable strategies.

■ Creating a global presence by achieving global reach.

■ Managing diverse and complex activities across a range of often similar but often disparate markets and cultures.

Global appeal and the changing basis of competitive advantage

All major firms today are capable of offering good-quality products and service that offer value for customers, so this is no longer a source of differentiation and competitive advantage as competitors quickly offer lower cost alternatives.

The rapid growth of the Japanese car industry was largely based on value for money criteria, with quality, reliability and performance at a reasonable cost being the basis of the appeal. However, as the Japanese manufacturers, such as Toyota, have continued to develop more sophisticated cars and establish local supply chains, their competitors from the emerging economies, such as Kia and Hyundai have replaced them in offering cheaper and even better value for money cars. At the same time a number of firms, such as Tata with its Nano, are competing for the very lowest price car segment. The car market is highly competitive and characterized by over-capacity, and it is becoming ever harder for major global players to be consistently profitable, and so the question is how and where they should compete particularly against the new players that are identifying new segments. A few of the car makers from the developed countries have substantially improved their quality and reliability and offer designs and brand imagery with better consumer appeal for the most affluent customers in developed and emerging markets.

It is possible to observe similar changes in the information technology industry as cost conscious consumers increasingly expect computer suppliers to offer improved performance, functionality, quality, security and greater reliability as well as becoming more 'user-friendly' – all at considerably reduced prices. To attract affluent consumers, firms must now offer more intangible benefits, including better styling, higher levels of service support and advice, more interesting and appealing software and online services and, a 'cool' brand. The spectacular performance of Apple was the appeal of the i-Mac, i-Pod, i-Phone and i-Pad to a design-conscious segment. Consumers are becoming more confident with technology, and are willing to experiment by downloading software and content from a variety of suppliers.

Consumers are also prepared to mix and match basic with expensive items. The cost of basic clothing sold through supermarkets and stores such as Zara and Primark has fallen dramatically in recent years, making it difficult for retailers to operate in the middle ground between high fashion and low cost. But high fashion – and cost – items, shoes and handbags are also matched with basic items.

In business-to-business situations, the basis of competitive advantage is also changing (*Strategy and Business*, 2010). For example, the chemical industry is moving to emerging markets because of commoditization of products that were once specialities and speciality niches becoming rarer reduce the possibility to add value and sustain the higher margins necessary for western companies. In engineered and technology products and service increasingly companies are competing on innovation as well as cost. In energy supply increasing legislation aimed at cutting carbon emissions, coupled with consumer behaviour towards reducing the use of energy and concerns about sustainability are leading to uncertainty and potential oversupply.

Increasing global appeal by building the global brand

Branding is usually considered within the marketing strategy as part of the product and service policy, and we have addressed the use of brands in international marketing there. Global brands, however, are inextricably tied up with achieving global appeal and building a global presence, so we have included a broader-based discussion of global branding at this point.

Global brand management

Holt, Quelch and Taylor (2004) noted that two decades ago Levitt was arguing that organizations should offer standardized products globally, but now consumers find it difficult to relate to generic standardized products, so firms have adopted 'glocal' strategies in which they have customized product features, selling and marketing to local tastes and instead build their efficiencies on a global scale around 'back office' activities of which customers are unaware.

Holt *et al.* found that most transnational firms are perceived differently from other firms because of their power, and have suffered from this because they have been major targets for anti-globalization protests. However, most people choose one global brand over another based on three dimensions: quality, indicated by the firms' global stature, the cultural myths and stories created by the firms, and the firms' efforts in corporate social responsibility. In the past for some brands the country of origin of the brand was important as it was often part of the cultural myth, but Holt *et al.* believe that this is no longer important. Indeed the trend for a number of global brands has been to dissociate themselves from their country of origin, for example, British Airways has renamed itself BA, British Petroleum has become BP and Kentucky Fried Chicken has become KFC.

For decades the power of the biggest global brands seemed to increase steadily but their dominant position now seems to be more dependent on success in newer markets and responding to changes in their existing markets.

Khashani (1995) draws attention to changes in a number of factors which affect the performance of the brands.

- Customers are better educated, better informed, more sceptical, more willing to experiment, less brand loyal, much more media aware and have higher expectations of the total package.
- Competition is more aggressive, with more rapid launches of higher quality 'me-too' products.
- Retailers have installed better electronic point of sale technology and, as a result, have greater awareness of brand performance. In response to better consumer information, they have introduced better quality private labels.

These changes in the brand market environment have been compounded by weaknesses in brand management, including:

- low investment;
- inadequate product development;
- poor consumer communication;
- an emphasis on quick paybacks rather than long-term brand building;
- too little innovation; and
- an emphasis upon small modifications.

For global brand success it is essential to listen to the market and get closer to global customers. It is necessary to be bold, think creatively, set new market and performance standards and take risks. The aim must be to think globally, launch products and services sequentially and rapidly across markets and build world brands. There are many 'almost great' brands but only a few are truly great.

While the progress of global brands seems to be unstoppable, they do not always succeed. Wal-Mart withdrew from South Korea and Germany in 2006 because financial losses could no longer be tolerated. Despite promising for years that performance could be improved, it never managed a turnaround. In both countries Wal-Mart failed to compete with dominant local companies that were better at catering for local tastes. Moreover, Barbaro (2006) notes that in Germany in the late 1990s Wal-Mart changed the name of its stores from a well known reliable local brand to Wal-Mart, a name that was unfamiliar to local shoppers.

The global development of brands can lead to some dilemmas. Both Google in China and Blackberry in the United Arab Emirates and Saudi Arabia have run into problems of government controls, explained in Illustration 12.7, which can result in the need to compromise on the brand values.

Business-to-business branding In business-to-business marketing, purchasers and users value the commitment of suppliers to the product and service and benefit from the added value from dealing with a firm. For example, buyers talk about suppliers such as Cisco or Vodafone as brands, which lends a sense of authority to the purchasing decision, or users might detail a specific product or service that must be purchased, e.g. i-Phone. In some situations there may be benefits which can be gained from co-branding with globally recognized branded components (e.g. Intel microprocessors in computers). This trend is becoming increasingly important as consumers become more influential in the choice of components and services in the supply chain and demand products that contain branded components.

In international business-to-business branding firms use different naming strategies, with some firms concentrating less on corporate brand endorsement and more on the individual brand in the same way as Procter and Gamble and Unilever do in consumer markets. For example, the pharmaceutical product brands Zantac and Tagamet are promoted by GlaxoSmithKline without any obvious association with the manufacturer in the brand name.

Ultimately, the rationale for the existence of brands in business-to-business marketing is the same as in consumer goods marketing – to avoid the commoditization of products, which leads to decisions being based only on price.

Brands are also important in the not-for-profit areas. For example, although the charity sector is fragmented into many thousands of organizations it is the global charities with well marketed brands, such as Red Crescent/Red Cross, Oxfam and Save the Children, that are the most successful in terms of scale of activities. When major disasters occur it is these organizations that have the resources to cope.

Creating a global presence by achieving global reach

The aim of many MNEs is to dominate their market sector by building a presence in every worthwhile market. However, few firms have the resources to build a strong presence in all the countries in the world and so rely on third parties to enable them to reach into similar markets. Many firms cannot afford to wait until they have built the products, services, image and resources through organic growth within the firm. Instead, they use a wide range of growth, market entry and marketing mix strategies to achieve global reach and these are discussed in later chapters. Acquisition and mergers are discussed here because they are used by MNEs to extend global reach much more quickly and achieve effective marketing worldwide, as the Chapter 6 case study shows.

Mergers and acquisitions The rationale for acquisitions and mergers has been that a well-managed company should take over a weaker rival marketer of competing or complementary products in order to achieve higher growth and savings in operating, management and marketing costs as discussed in Illustration 6.6.

As market entry methods, acquisition or mergers are used to facilitate access to particular markets. In some business sectors, however, there appears to be a view that it is only by operating on a very large scale

ILLUSTRATION 6.6

Stock.xchng

Airline mega-mergers

Regulators play a key role in deciding whether mergers can go ahead. For example, US competition regulators have traditionally opposed mergers between airlines that have a significant proportion of the domestic flights, and they have blocked tie ups in the past if they threatened to reduce the competition significantly and lead to higher prices and less choice for customers. However, when United and Continental airlines sought permission to merge their businesses in 2010, they gained approval, despite their domination of the New York routes.

The reason they gained approval was pragmatic. The recession, higher fuel prices and cutthroat competition had driven many airlines close to bankruptcy and the consequences of this could have been more disastrous for competition. This period led to consolidation of the sector in the US and Europe. The table of the largest players is the result of many mergers. Delta acquired Northwest, US Airways took over America West. In Europe, the largest airline was the result of a previous merger between Air France and KLM. BA and Iberian were joining forces and Lufthansa had bought up a number of airlines including Swissair

and BMI of the UK. The question was whether these mergers were simply delaying the inevitable failure of some airlines or whether the merged companies could reduce costs by getting rid of staff, to enable them to match the cost base of the low cost airlines such as Ryanair and easyJet. Most of the former national airlines had inefficient business models and high cost bases, which they always found difficult to correct.

World's top airlines by passenger numbers (million)

United	110
Delta	105
Southwest	101
American	85
Air France/KLM	74
China Southern	66
Ryanair	65
Lufthansa	53
US Airways	51
easyJet	45

Source: Iata

Question

1 In what circumstances are mega mergers likely to solve financial problems?

References: O'Connell, D., 'US airline mega merger cleared', *Sunday Times*, 29 August 2010.

on a worldwide basis that customers can receive the level and quality of service that they need. This seems logical in the case of aircraft manufacture where industry consolidation has left only two main players, Boeing and Airbus. Scale economies in accountancy may not be so obvious and, of course, there are still many small accountancy practices but the global sector is dominated by four companies, Deloitte, KPMG, Ernst and Young and PricewaterhouseCoopers, whereas there were eight major players in 1989.

Cross-border mergers and acquisitions are becoming increasingly common too, but often do not deliver the expected outcomes, for example, in telecommunications Vodafone (UK) with Mannesmann (Germany), and in automobiles Daimler-Benz (Germany) and Chrysler (US). One of the implications of mergers is the impact upon branding decisions and whether the merged firm will retain two separate brand identities or whether they will merge them. The decision often depends upon whether the senior management believes the brand is important for their particular company or industry sector. Smith (1998) reports research by McKinsey which suggests that there are three routes to brand consolidation:

- Phasing out brands over time, when the strategy is to retain loyal customers who will buy as long as the brand is available.
- Quickly changing some of the branding, which only works well if the firm has control over distribution, advertising and promotion.
- Co-branding to manage the transition, which is the most common approach, used, for example, when Whirlpool bought Philips domestic appliances.

The pitfalls of mergers and acquisitions   There are serious pitfalls associated with mergers and acquisitions, particularly where they involve cross-border ownership and cooperation. Finkelstein (1998) refers to a study of 89 US companies acquired by foreign buyers during the period 1977–90 and found the performance of most of them had not improved within one year.

As well as the obvious organizational challenges that follow from a merger, such as who will be in charge, whose products and services will be offered (or dropped) and where costs savings should be made, particularly if the merger or acquisition was not entirely harmonious, there are the cross-cultural challenges, such as the different ways of doing business in Europe, the US and Asia, different corporate governance, the status and power of different employee and management groups, job security guarantees, government regulations and customer expectations.

Finkelstein (1998) recommends that the integration process should focus on value creation by ensuring employees actually achieve the synergy that is promised before the deal is done, planning in detail how the various cross-border problems will be overcome and developing a clear communication plan to cope with the whole process.

Managing diverse and complex activities across a range of often similar but often disparate markets and cultures

The implications of pursuing a global strategy are that organizations must continually expand into what are likely to be less stable markets, perhaps tertiary opportunities from Figure 4.3 on page 104 or incipient markets in Figure 4.1 on page 101. Typically these will be in some way less attractive (at least at the present time) because of the associated political and economic risks of entering less developed markets, more difficult trading conditions and barriers to 'free' trade. By comparison with the firms' existing markets, these emerging markets may demand disproportionately high investment in management time and financial resources as well as involving the firm in considerable additional financial and reputation risk if things go wrong.

The risks associated with specific emerging country market involvement can be substantial, however, and include some or all of the following:

- financial loss associated with inappropriate investment, such as buying unusable assets, being unable to achieve acceptable levels of performance from the purchased assets, losing the assets by misappropriation to the host country government or to partners;

- damage to the firm's reputation through association with the country, its government and intermediaries, especially where they are seen to be corrupt, engage in unacceptable social or business practices, or have close relationships with other countries or organizations which are considered to be corrupt;

- litigation arising from offering an unacceptable product and/or service to the country, or becoming involved in questionable business practices;

- prompting an unexpected international competitor response by attacking a market which it considers to be its home territory;

- initially making arrangements with joint venture partners, distributors, agents or government agencies to secure entry but which become inappropriate in the medium to long term;

- damage to the firm's reputation through insensitivity in its operations in the country, when it might be accused of exploiting local labour, the country's resources or causing environmental damage to the country.

The problem for international strategic management in less developed countries is that the 'rule book' that managers rely on in developed countries does not always apply, because business infrastructure and processes are not well established.

Organization structure for transnational firms

While the simple organization structures discussed in the previous chapter are appropriate for managing the international strategies of SMEs, the largest transnational companies, by their very nature, have complex structures that are specific to the firms' context. As a result, organization structures differ from firm to firm.

Most firms operate using a form of matrix structure, but Majaro (1991) distinguished between a macropyramid structure in which companies such as McDonald's exert usually highly centralized control; the umbrella structure in which geographically based SBUs take responsibility for the global strategy of the MNE in specific activities; and the interglomerate, in which the SBUs of companies such as ABB, discussed in Illustration 6.4, and many Asian-owned comprises, such as Hutchinson Whampoa, Tata and Guandong Investments, operate as quite independent international businesses.

Systems, processes and control

Given the complexity of international strategic marketing in global firms it is essential that the organization operates effective processes for the management of its complex operations, processes and systems to enable managers to be able to share information effectively.

Control

Control is the cornerstone of management. Control provides the means to direct, regulate and manage business operations. A significant amount of interaction is required between the individual areas of marketing (such as market development, advertising and selling) and the other functional areas (such as human resources, finance, production, research and development).

However, for many firms, control means a separate activity through which senior managers are able to keep a check periodically (weekly, monthly or quarterly) on more junior levels of management, who often see this in terms of being called upon to justify their actions. Feedback and control systems should be regarded as an integrated part of the whole planning process, and they are essential in ensuring that the marketing plans are not only being implemented worldwide but are still appropriate for the changing environment in each country.

There are a number of benefits of an effective strategic control system. It encourages higher standards of performance, forces greater clarity and realism and permits corporate management to intervene when necessary. Moreover, it ensures that the financial objectives do not overwhelm the strategic objectives, encourages clearer definition of responsibilities making decentralization work more effectively and so provides more motivation for managers.

There are three essential elements of the control process:

1 *Setting standards*: The standards that are set need to be relevant to the corporate goals such as:

- growth and profits reported by financial measures, e.g. return on capital employed and on sales; and

- non-financial indicators, e.g. market share.

Intermediate goals and individual targets can be set by breaking the plan down into measurable parts which, when successfully completed, will lead to the overall objectives being achieved. The standards must be understandable, achievable and relevant to each local country situation.

2 *Measuring performance against standards*: To obtain measurements and ensure rapid feedback of information, firms use a variety of techniques, including reports, meetings and special measurements of specific parts of the marketing programme, such as:

- cost–benefit analysis of customers;

- product lines; and

- territories or marketing audits,

for a thorough examination of every aspect of marketing in a particular country. They also use benchmarking which allows comparisons of various aspects of the business, such as efficiency of distribution, customer response times, service levels and complaints, with other companies that are not necessarily from the same business sector.

3 *Correcting deviations from the plan*: Perhaps the most difficult decisions that must be made are to determine when performance has deviated sufficiently from the plan to require corrective action to be taken, either by changing the plan or the management team charged with the responsibility of carrying out the plan. Evaluation of the performance of a particular management team is particularly difficult in international marketing as the performance of a particular SBU can only be compared with its own plan, a plan determined by the headquarters or with the performance of a 'similar' SBU. There are obvious weaknesses in making any of these comparisons, resulting in considerable difference of opinion between the head office and subsidiary.

A key element in the control process is the input from people, both the directly employed staff of the company but also the staff of the other members of the supply chain. Various quality management models, e.g. Total Quality Management, Continuous Quality Improvement and Business Excellence, supported by international standards such as ISO 9000, are used by firms to underpin the control process. Consistency across the firm's global operations can be increased and general improvements made using a variety of techniques.

- Benchmarking against other SBUs within the firm, other firms within the business sector and the 'best in the class' in a particular activity, such as just in time operations control, service centre response rates or delivery performance.

- Identifying good practice wherever in the world it occurs and applying the lessons either in individual SBUs or across the firm.

- Encouraging performance improvement through self-assessment (individuals completing questionnaires and improvement plans alone), peer review(evaluation by staff at the same level) and appraisals completed by more senior managers.

Setting standards to achieve consistency and establishing continuous performance improvement projects throughout the global company can, however, be problematic because of cultural barriers, differences in language and ethical standards causing different levels of motivation, communications problems and misinterpretation of instructions and advice. In addition, different measuring techniques, standards and imprecise reporting procedures and processes can create difficulties in achieving a meaningful control process.

Return on marketing investment

One of the problems for marketing is the concern that marketing and promotion expenditure is simply seen as a cost to the business with no benefits linked to it. As a key control tool, therefore, measuring the return on marketing investment is essential for any business-to-business or consumer marketing manager looking to improve their ability to produce real results in revenue growth. In much of the traditional marketing activity it is difficult to define the specific benefits that can be attributed to one individual activity. With online marketing, as we shall see later, it is easier to link the marketing investment with its impact. In practice, firms need to measure the effect of an integrated marketing programme, in order to learn good and bad practice.

Planning systems and processes

The increasingly turbulent environment resulting from more rapid changes in technology, competition, consumer taste and fashion means that the traditional systems and processes for preparing the analysis, strategy development and action plans take too long. Balabanis *et al.* (2004) emphasized that global information systems are needed to enable HQ and subsidiary managers to keep track of environmental changes (opportunities and threats), facilitate the coordination and control of operations in different locations and assist in sharing of new ideas and knowledge.

Timescales must be reduced to make sure that the plan is still relevant when it is being implemented. Consequently, it is necessary to avoid planning that is too general and unfocused and to improve the quality of implementation and the relevance and responsiveness of the process.

As a result of this, increasing emphasis is being placed by MNEs on scenario and contingency planning to take account of things going wrong because of unexpected changes in the environment. Moreover, greater reliance is being placed on expert systems for understanding market changes, carrying out forecasting, resource planning and gap analysis. The plans prepared tend to be based on the understanding that they will be emergent, and will evolve during the timescale of the plan rather than be decided before the time period of the plan begins. The plans may be designed to be incremental, with the start of each new phase being prompted by a change in the environment or by the successful completion of a previous implementation phase.

Building skills in transnational organizations

While the structures outlined provide some general understanding of the alternative methods of organizing the management, they are for most companies an oversimplification. Cagni (2006) explains that old-fashioned, centralized, multinational management is no longer appropriate as it creates a single process overseen from head office. While this creates scale advantages, improved efficiency and the capability to share knowledge, local staff see a loss of autonomy, the creation of an ivory tower for the elite and the disempowerment of local managers, leaving them with less interesting jobs. The structure needs be developed in a way that avoids rigidity as flexibility is needed to respond to the changes in environment and market. However, Illustration 6.7 shows the benefit to LG of integrating activities as well as allowing business unit autonomy.

This has implications for the roles of the international marketing manager, as Bartlett and Ghoshal (2003) have concluded. The management of transnational businesses requires highly specialized, closely linked groups of global business managers, country or regional managers, and functional managers who work in networks. Global business or product division managers have the responsibility to further the company's global-scale efficiency and competitiveness. They must combine the strategist skills of recognizing opportunities and risks across national and functional boundaries, be the architect for worldwide resource and asset utilization, and the coordinator of activities and capabilities.

The country manager must play a pivotal role by sensing local customer needs, but also satisfying the host government's requirements and defending the company's market position. The country manager is likely to have objectives that conflict with the business manager and so must be prepared to negotiate to overcome the differences. The functional manager's role is the business environment scanner, cross-pollinator of ideas

© allOver photography / Alamy

ILLUSTRATION 6.7

Cars designed for emerging markets

Producing a car suitable for emerging markets has become a major objective of the global car firms. In the past the production lines of obsolete models were typically transferred to labour-intensive factories in developing countries. The problem was that car manufacturers in the past offered cars that they thought were wanted in developing countries without finding out exactly what was needed. However, over the last few years the move towards developing a

low-cost car has increased. As people in developing countries move up from bicycles, mopeds and rickshaws, more than 35 per cent of the market could be converted to low-cost cars.

Perhaps the first successful attempt to design a car specially was the Fiat Palio, which was launched in Brazil in 1996. More recently Renault took a radically different approach with the €5000 (£3125) Logan, a four-door saloon built in Romania. Tata of India, produced a step change when it launched a 600cc car in India for 100 000 rupees. Most of the other mass market manufacturers followed with their own low priced offers. Toyota, the world's leading car maker did not join the race to develop a car for emerging markets in Asia and South America until much later it announced plans to produce a small car, the Etios, in India. Although building locally was expected to reduce costs by 30–40 per cent, the car was expected to sell for below $10 000 but still well above the Nano price.

It is important that car makers do not confuse the different concepts – the low-cost car, the lightweight car, the economical car and the small car – because they are all different things and satisfy the needs of different segments. Moreover, the most innovative step would be to design and develop a car that leapfrogged fossil fuel technology and is based on new environmental technology and creates jobs, wealth and mobility for the world's poorest nations. But it probably also requires substantial investment in a new infrastructure in each country market to support the new technology.

Question

1 What do you consider to be the critical success factors for a car designed for emerging markets?

References: English, A. (2007) 'The Third World car war', *Daily Telegraph*, 31 March.

and champion of specific aspects of the business which are essential for success. The global manager may be required to play a number of roles and no one person can fulfil the required tasks alone. This manager must provide leadership, while acting as the talent scout and the developer of the other levels of management.

As a result, patterns of activity in a transnational company will vary considerably in each new situation. Innovations, for example, should be generated at several locations and in several ways throughout the world, so that the company is not restricted to making centralized decisions. For the past 10 to 20 years, firms such as Shell, Phillips and Unilever have used an integrated network approach, with resources and capabilities concentrated in various locations and accessed through the free flow of knowledge, technology, components, products, resources and people. By developing matrix structures, firms can achieve efficiency, responsiveness and the ability to develop and exploit their knowledge and capability for competitive advantage.

As the international operations of firms increase in diversity and tangible ties between the activities become strained, so the nature of the formal systems and organizational structures must change too. Training programmes, career path planning, job rotation, company-wide accounting, evaluation and data-processing systems become more important as part of the shared value system of the firm.

Staff and the problems of international management

Of the potential sources of problems of planning in international marketing, it is the relationship between headquarters and local subsidiary staff that is likely to be the largest single factor. Headquarters staff, as guardians of the overall company strategies, claim to have a far broader perspective of the company's activities and might expect that subsidiary staff should simply be concerned with implementation of the details of the plan. Subsidiary staff claim that, by being closer to the individual markets, they are in a better position to identify opportunities and should, therefore, play a large part in developing objectives and strategies. This situation must be resolved if the planning process is to be effective, so that all staff have a clear idea of their own role in setting, developing and implementing policy, and understanding how their individual contributions might be integrated into the corporate objectives and strategies.

Govindarajan and Gupta (2001) comment on the need to create teams comprised of many nationalities to benefit from the synergies and collective wisdom, superior to that of an individual. The failure rate of teams is high – in a survey one third of teams rated their performance as largely unsuccessful – and this is due to lack of trust, with hindrances, even when members speak in the same language, including semantics, accents, tone, pitch and dialects. Mortensen and Beyene (2009) explain that to build trust it is necessary to spend time onsite observing the people, places and norms of the distant locale as this not only leads to direct knowledge of the other but also leads to knowledge of self as seen by the other (reflected knowledge), thus affecting trust through identification, adaptation and reduced misunderstanding.

Sebenius (2002) note that decision-making and governance processes vary widely not only in terms of legal technicalities but also the behaviour and core beliefs that drive them. The solution is to map out the decision-making process and anticipate problems before they arise.

The difficulties of planning in international markets are further developed by Brandt *et al.* (1980), in a framework of international planning problems, and Weichmann and Pringle (1979), who identified the key problems experienced by large US and European multi-nationals.

Many companies recognize that for strategies to be successful they must be owned and so staff at all levels must be involved in the marketing planning process. This is becoming more difficult as MNEs have ever greater numbers of their workers employed outside the head office country. As the company grows, therefore, a company-wide planning culture should be developed, with the following objectives:

- planning becomes part of the continuous process of management rather than an annual 'event';
- strategic thinking becomes the responsibility of every manager rather than being restricted to a separate strategic planning department;
- the planning process becomes standardized, with a format that allows contributions from all parts of the company;
- the plan becomes the working document, updated periodically for all aspects of the company, so allowing performance evaluation to be carried out regularly; and
- the planning process is itself regularly reviewed and refined through the use of new tools and techniques in order to improve its relevance and effectiveness.

Brett, Behfar and Kern (2006) identify the advantages of multicultural teams in international firms, including deep knowledge of different product markets and culturally sensitive customer service, but also note the problems caused when cultural differences affect team effectiveness, direct versus indirect communication, trouble with accents and fluency, differing attitudes to hierarchy and authority and conflicting norms for decision-making. The authors emphasize the need to pinpoint the root cause of the problems, intervene early and see the challenges as stemming from culture rather than personalities.

What makes a good international manager

For many of the most powerful businesses increasing globalization is the future scenario, and the most successful will be managed by people who can best embrace and thrive on the ambiguity and complexity of transnational operations. Using Illustration 6.8 it is interesting to consider the changes in organization culture that take place as a result of globalization.

A number of researchers have emphasized the need for managers to be able to handle national differences in business, including cultural divergence on hierarchy, humour, assertiveness and working hours. In France, Germany, Italy and a large part of Asia, for example, performance-related pay is seen negatively as revealing the shortcomings of some members of the work group. Feedback sessions are seen positively in the US but German managers see them as 'enforced admissions of failure'.

The international manager, therefore, must be more culturally aware and show greater sensitivity, but it can be difficult to adapt to the culture and values of a foreign country while upholding the

© Catherine Yeulet, iStockphoto.com

ILLUSTRATION 6.8

Leadership for a new world order

It is hard to imagine the changes that new executives in Middle East companies have faced. Suliaman Al-Muhaidib is chairman of the family owned Al-Muhaidib Group, a conglomerate based in Saudi Arabia that has investments in financial services, real estate, consumer goods, energy and utilities. When he first joined the firm his father told him to learn from the other traders in the same street the business skills he would need in order to manage the firm in the future. His decision-making skills were built around the local culture but Suliaman's son has developed his judgement very differently. He is general manager of a subsidiary, has a staff of 500 and deals with suppliers from around the world.

As the oil rich Middle East nations of Bahrain, Kuwait, Oman, Qatar and Saudi Arabia have invested heavily it has become more open to worldwide business. The managers of the companies created have become leaders of multinationals – a far cry from their humble backgrounds and nomadic family life of 50 years ago when even running water was not widely available. They must bridge the divide between the traditions of the past as well as enthusiastically exploring the global future. The region has new opportunities and can exert new types of influence but they have to manage risk too, typified by the economic crisis in Dubai. In the past the companies relied on expatriates but now many of the new leaders are nationals under 25. Women are also beginning to play a greater role, but not on the scale of their counterparts in other regions of the world. Saddi *et al.* comment that there is a shortage of leaders to manage the rapid growth and highlight three qualities which future leaders need;

■ Farsighted vision to build sustainable institutions.

■ Pragmatic openness and seek ideas from around the world and customize them for the region.

■ Conscious presence in recognizing the need to build not only their own organization but also work together to establish the region as a global player.

Question

1 What are the main differences in leading a national business compared to a global company?

References: Saddi, J., Sabbagh, K. and Shediac, R. (2010) 'Measures of Leadership', *Strategy and Business*, Summer: 59, May 25.

culture and values of a parent company. The only way is to give managers experience overseas, but the cost of sending people abroad is typically two-and-a-half times that for a local manager, so firms look for alternatives, such as short-term secondments, exchanges and participation in multicultural project teams.

Wills and Barham (1994) believe that international managers require four sets of attributes. They must:

1 Be able to cope with cognitive complexity and be able to understand issues from a variety of complicated perspectives.

2 Have cultural empathy, a sense of humility and the power of active listening. Because of their unfamiliarity with different cultural settings international managers cannot be as competent or confident in a foreign environment.

3 Have emotional energy and be capable of adding depth and quality to interactions through their emotional self-awareness, emotional resilience, ability to accept risk. They must be able to rely on the support of the family.

4 Demonstrate psychological maturity by having the curiosity to learn, an awareness of time constraints and a fundamental personal morality that will enable them to cope with the diversity of demands made on them.

Management culture

There has been considerable discussion about the difference between the Asian and Western models of management and the reasons for the differences, such as the elements of a deeply embedded culture and more recent history, for example, the effects on management of working within a centrally planned economy. Deshpandé *et al.* (2004), however, also note the differences between Asian management cultures and suggest that Chinese and Vietnamese firms, emerging from centrally planned economies to some form of market socialism, tend to be bureaucratic. Indian firms tend to be entrepreneurial. Japanese culture is the most consensual and the least entrepreneurial. Hong Kong tends to be about average in that it reflects the mixed Chinese and Western influences on its management culture.

They conclude that there are in fact four organizational culture types:

1 Competitive or market culture which is characterized by an emphasis on competitive advantage and market superiority.

2 Entrepreneurial or adhocracy culture which emphasizes innovation and risk-taking.

3 Bureaucratic or hierarchy culture in which regulations and formal structures are important.

4 Consensual or clan culture which emphasizes loyalty, tradition and internal maintenance.

They found that in each country more competitive and entrepreneurial firms perform better and consensual and bureaucratic firms perform worse than their national peers. They also noted that market orientation has a greater effect on performance in Asia and innovativeness has a greater effect in the more industrialized nations.

Research by PricewaterhouseCoopers and Cranfield School of Management (2007) suggests that firms should plan the return of expatriate executives that have carried out assignments abroad. They show that 40 per cent of executives that return home from overseas postings resign after being frustrated at being sidelined after successfully completing their assignment. Firms often offer generous financial packages to help the overseas transition but fail to meet the expatriate's expectations of an increase in salary and status on their return. The cost of an overseas posting averages US$311 000 for a typical 29-month assignment. The executives are usually given high levels of support from personnel managers and only 4 per cent return prematurely. However, when they returned their measured performance did not match that when abroad and only 24 per cent managed to move up the promotion ladder in the first year back, despite the fact that these executives were typically among the best in the company.

Management style and shared values

The different contexts and stages of global development of firms mean that there is no proven right and wrong management style and shared values for the firm. Indeed the shared values, as we have seen earlier, may be the only common aspect of the company that binds the various parts together and may be based upon a long tradition in the firm, built up over many years. This is particularly the case in companies dominated by extended family ownership, such as in many Asian businesses, or where the principles of the founding family of a business are maintained.

What is important to recognize is that although global businesses are complex and diverse, the chief executive can have a major effect on the business. The personality of entrepreneurs such as Ratan Tata, Steve Jobs, Michael Dell and Richard Branson shapes the management style and shared values of the businesses they create from their early days.

SUMMARY

- The increase in global business activity has resulted from a number of drivers in the environment, particularly through technological developments. Clearly it is communications and information technology that have had the greatest effect on creating a global marketplace. Firms have also accelerated the move towards greater globalization by developing a worldwide presence and strategy, and offering similar products and services.

- To exploit global markets firms have developed appropriate strategies for their particular situation. These range from multidomestic strategies, in which each market is seen as separate and individual, through to globally standardized strategies in which the firm has identified one global segment with similar needs. In practice, the largest firms are too complex for one simple strategy to be appropriate and so they use a combination of different strategies to build global efficiency, local effectiveness and knowledge assets.

- In the past global trade has been dominated by MNEs from developed countries, but now companies from emerging markets that have built their capability and resources in the domestic market, are becoming global players investing in developed countries too. The competitive advantage that they have built in their home market must then be tested in the global marketplace.

- To succeed globally firms must build global appeal through globally recognized brands, but also innovate, as the basis of competitive advantage in many industries changes continually.

- An increasingly common feature of transnational strategies is the greater level of cooperation between firms that would otherwise be competitors, customers or suppliers.

- To enable managers to set and control the operations of the business an appropriate organization structure is needed. International managers must also be able to recruit and develop the right staff that will have the skills necessary to deal with the complexity, diversity and conflicting challenges of global business development.

KEYWORDS

Globalization	Standardization	Global brand
Transnationality	Adaptation	Global reach
Market access	Global presence	Business-to-business marketing
Global sourcing	Competitive Advantage	Control
World Wide Web	Global appeal	International manager

CASE STUDY

Unilever: redefining product policy for a global future

Unilever illustrates many of the challenges faced in developing and managing a global strategy.

Brand culling and underperformance

When Patrick Cescau took over as CEO of Unilever in 2005 the company was still suffering from the shock of its first ever profits warning. The previous CEO, Niall Fitzgerald, had developed a five-year 'Path to Growth' plan which involved reducing the company's portfolio of brands from 1600 to 400 in the belief that focusing resources and effort would deliver the target 5–6 per cent growth per annum. However, the sales of a number of high-profile brands, such as Surf and Slim-fast, significantly underperformed expectations.

By 2007 the performance of Unilever was back on course with sales growth of 3.8 per cent and profits up 7 per cent. The turnaround was achieved by focusing resources on those specific products with the most potential for growth, for example its care brands such as Dove and Lifebuoy, its 'vitality' brands that encourage healthy living, such as Knorr Vie, Flora and Blue Band Idea.

Restructuring the organization

Cescau also changed Unilever's organization. He slimmed down the executive board and removed one of the two joint executive chairmen. Previously one represented the British side of the business and one the Dutch, a tradition started in 1930 when Lever Brothers, a British soap maker, merged with Marga-rine Unie of the Netherlands. Unilever's global business started in the nineteenth century when the two companies sent out young men on ships from Rotter-dam and Liverpool to various parts of the world to build businesses, set up plantations, build factories, establish distribution and supply systems. Because of the long communication lines these companies de-veloped a high level of independence which then be-came difficult to manage due to the complexity, and they changed to achieve a more efficient and effective global business. But this early colonization meant that Unilever has a more established position in many emerging markets than its rivals and so the opportu-nities are greater. However, this meant that until Ces-cau's reorganization Unilever operated as a federation of national businesses. The chairmen of country op-erations were responsible for managing everything from the local supply chain to advertising and human resources and they wanted to be self-sufficient. This led to complexity and fragmentation. The executive in charge of marketing deodorants across Europe recalls that the firm's Swiss marketing director argued that a different size of roller ball was needed on the deodor-ant dispenser because Swiss armpits were of a differ-ent size! It took some persuasion before the standard sized product was accepted.

While the old structure encouraged entrepreneur-ship in the national businesses it inhibited exploitation of innovation – any local innovation would have only a 50 per cent chance of being adopted in one more country and innovations in food often stayed local. For example, despite the success in Europe of *Pro Activ*, the range of cholesterol-lowering margarines, yoghurt and drinks, it had not been adopted in the US despite the obesity and coronary disease pro-blems there. Cescau believed the reason was the 'not invented here' syndrome – but the brand was eventually launched in the US in 2007.

The role of the country operations became one of 'getting things done' and managing relationships with the big customers – the retailers, instead of consu-mers. Indeed Cescau took on personal responsibility for the biggest retailers – Wal-Mart and Tesco. Sup-port services such as HR, IT management and busi-ness processing were outsourced. The company continued with considerable rationalization. For exam-ple, there were 64 variants of tomato soup in Europe. The 64 pieces of advertising for the Pond's range of beauty products in Asia was reduced to four. Two or three adverts were created for Axe (Lynx in the UK) where previously there were 30 or 40. However, cul-tural difference still needed to be respected, particu-larly in advertising. For example, in the Dove ads women in Brazil hug one another, but that is not ac-ceptable in the US where they stand slightly apart.

At an operating level there was additional complexity, for example the company had three operating companies in China, each of which had its own chairman, who reported to two regional presidents, who answered to two members of the executive committee. The rationalization Unilever undertook resulted in a loss of over 50 000 jobs worldwide, the closure of 50 of its 300 factories and 75 of its 100 regional centres. Its top management tiers in Europe alone were cut from 1200 to 700 people.

Focusing on growth

For the next CEO, Paul Polman, the recession of 2008 changed the shape of world markets. He could not see prospects for economic or business growth in the developed markets for at least five years, but Unilever's emerging markets in Asia, Africa and Latin America had become 'decoupled' from the developed economies and were showing sales volume increases of 10 per cent per annum. As 50 per cent of Unilever's revenue came from these markets the company could be optimistic.

Polman was the first 'outsider' to become CEO of Unilever and even more surprisingly had previous spells working for rivals, P&G and Nestlé. Following the earlier underperformance of Unilever some analysts were still critical of the growth prospects for the company but Polman saw no reason why the company could not double in size from its current £33 billion. The aim was to make the company leaner, faster and more focused on consumers and customers through quicker innovation, more centralization and pay incentives. Polman had a marketing focus and believed that as the aim was growth more money should be spent on marketing whereas the restructuring required a financial focus and executive. Unilever is probably unique among its major rivals in that its products range from food, to household goods to personal care products. Although this might appear to be a disparate range of products Polman believed that the connection between the businesses was that the customer buys the complete range and so there was no reason for Unilever to divest itself of some of its businesses.

Company integrity

Polman had a strong belief too in company integrity, believing that the communities that the companies work in should also be successful. His view was that it is necessary to work together to solve global warming, poverty, water shortage, population growth and obesity. Unilever aims to balance its desire for growth with addressing these aims, for example, by producing detergents that use less hot water, making healthier ice cream and reducing the environmental impact of its packaging. Producing concentrated versions of its laundry products reduced packaging usage by 10–20 per cent saving 1300 tonnes of plastic and 1700 tonnes of cartons in 2008. It also took 2350 lorries off the road and saved 26 football fields worth of shelf space. Using concentrated packs could save 4.3 million tonnes of CO_2 a year, the equivalent of taking a million cars off the road.

Another environmental concern is the production of palm oil, a raw material that is widely used in half its best selling foods, such as Kit Kat and Flora margarine and in its toiletries, such as Dove soap. Unilever has strongly opposed palm oil deforestation and when two of its palm oil producers in Indonesia were alleged to be destroying rainforests by Greenpeace and the BBC, Unilever cancelled the contracts. Clearing jungles results in loss of habitat for endangered species, such as orang-utan and snow leopard and release of huge amounts of greenhouse gasses.

Developed markets

The era of 'continual consumption', which generated growth in the US and Europe, ended with the recession as consumers are increasingly sought to pay as little as possible for what they need, for example, by substituting the branded products for own label alternatives. For a long period the customer promotions and discounts (two for ones and 20 per cent free) were used to maintain loyalty, but to win more market share, or grow the market again innovation was needed. The key to innovation for companies like Unilever, P&G and Reckitt is to know what customers want before they know it themselves. Unilever is innovating new shampoos, deodorants and washing powder. Innovation should be about not reducing prices. Consumers want something better and Unilever have introduced Dove conditioner, which repairs damaged hair, and deodorants, which are effective longer.

However, the big brands must be cost competitive to prevent loss of business to supermarket own label products. This has meant that supermarket own label products, which make up 20 per cent of the Unilever's European markets, have not gained significant additional market share and in the US, where own label is only 12 per cent of the markets, only a small proportion of branded market share has been lost.

Unilever's emerging markets

The growing affluence and population in emerging markets and its strong market position over a long period is the reason for the Polman's optimism. Unilever is the largest manufacturers of deodorants in the world with brands, such as Rexona, Shields, Lynx, Axe and Sure and has, for example, a 70 per cent market share in Argentina. But only 7 out of 100 Asians use deodorants and many Russians only use them for special occasions, such as weddings, so there is huge potential.

From its colonial heritage Unilever has a strong position in many markets but the jewel in the crown is Hindustan Unilever, – listed on the Mumbai stock exchange – which is India's biggest consumer goods company and biggest advertizer. It caters for all segments by adapting products and prices, for example, offering Surf Excel for the affluent, Rin for the 'aspiring class' and Wheel for poorer people, who generally live in the countryside. One-use sachets amount to 70 per cent of shampoo sales as India's poor cannot afford to buy a bottle.

Social and political issues and the Corporate Social Responsibility agenda have an increasing focus. Unilever has operated in South Africa for 100 years and recently worked with INSEAD, a French business school, to evaluate its impact on the country, looking at training, medical care, pensions, skills transfer, black empowerment initiatives and environmental standards. For example, in addition to its 4000 employees, through its 3000 direct suppliers and extended supply chain, 100 000 jobs depend on the company, 0.8 per cent of the country's employment and 0.9 per cent of GDP.

Proctor and Gamble

One of Unilever's main global rivals is Procter and Gamble (P&G) makers of Pampers, Gillette razors, Duracell and Oral-B toothpaste who also see increasing growth opportunities in their emerging markets but although P&G's global analysis is similar, the company has lagged behind Unilever in emerging market development. Although P&G is the larger company only 32 per cent of sales came from emerging markets in 2009. In Africa, for example, it has a weak web presence but things are changing fast as the company made progress in its ambition to add 1 billion new consumers, largely in emerging markets, by 2015. It added 200 million people to its reach in 2010 and expected almost all its new production plants to be sited in emerging markets, such as the $176 million diaper factory in Cairo.

P&G's entry strategy for Africa is based around its Egypt arm, which exports to North, East and West Africa. It strongest markets have included Lebanon and Jordan but demand is also picking up in Kenya and Ethiopia where demand is being driven by big populations and increasing wealth and also in Iraq, where the challenge is to ensure the safety of staff, particularly when they were doing 'on the ground' marketing in stores.

At the moment P&G is avoiding direct competition with Unilever, for example, deciding not to enter South Africa with laundry detergents where Unilever's Omo and Surf brands are very strong, but instead promoting products where it has a better chance of becoming number one. P&G is adapting its products and pricing to reflect local needs. For example, the company has adapted its product and priced Tide Naturals in India at 30 per cent below the regular product, has a mid-price version of its Mach 3 razor for Asian and Latin American men and developed a new men's skin care product in China.

A key challenge for P&G in its most attractive markets is to get all its product categories out into all its markets. For example, P&G has 36 product categories on sale in the US and only 16 in China.

Questions

1 Carry out a full analysis of the environment in which Unilever is operating and identify ten key challenges it faces.

2 What do you consider to be the main competitive advantages that Unilever have in developing a global strategy for developed and emerging markets?

3 What competitive capabilities do Unilever need to develop to enable them to continue to grow successfully?

References: D. Reece, 'Vitality treatment from man of action', *Daily Telegraph*, 9 February, 2007; and B. Lawrence 'Unilever gets its global act together', *Sunday Times*, 18 March, 2007. A. Wilson 'Western shoppers stay on the shelf', *Daily Telegraph*, 6 August 2010. A. Davidson, 'Would-be priest's gospel of change for Unilever', *Sunday Times*, 8 August 2010, 'The legacy that got left on the shelf', *The Economist,* 31 Jan 2008. J. Bleby, 'Procter and Gamble targets "low hanging fruit"', www.allafrica.com, 26 July 2010. M. Hickman, 'Unilever drops palm-oil producer', BBConline, accessed 22 February 2010. S. Goldstein, 'Unilever tackles environmental impact of laundry products', *Packaging News*, 24 July 2009; and J. Birchall, 'Emerging markets spur P&G global aims', *Financial Times*, 3 August 2010.

DISCUSSION QUESTIONS

1   What do you consider to be the differences between a global, regional and an international mindset? What are the arguments for and against setting a firm's aim to be a global player rather than a regional or international player?

2   Identify the reasons why international strategies sometimes fail in their objective to build competitive advantage. What capabilities do firms need to compete internationally?

3   What is the rationale behind mega mergers and major acquisitions? Using examples, explain the advantages and disadvantages of this approach to achieve global reach?

4   What are the critical success factors in developing a global brand? What must an international firm do for its brand to achieve 'global' status? Give examples to support your opinion.

5   What are the main challenges that are faced by international managers in contributing to the management and control of a global marketing strategy? What advice would you give to a manager with this responsibility?

REFERENCES

1. Arnott, S. (2010) 'Who owns Britain: Watchdog launches first UK stock take', *The Independent*, 15 May.
2. Balabanis, G., Theodosiou, M. and Katsikea, E.S. (2004) 'Export marketing: developments and a research agenda', *International Marketing Review*, 21 (4/5): 353–77.
3. Barbaro, M. (2006) 'Wal-Mart profits falls 26%, its first drop in 10 years', *New York Times*, 16 August.
4. Bartlett, C.A. and Ghoshal, S. (2001) *Managing across borders: the transnational solution*, HBS Press.
5. Bartlett, C.A. and Ghoshal, S. (2003) 'What is a global manager?', *Harvard Business Review*, 81 (8): 101–8.
6. Boston Consulting Group (2009) 'The 2009 BCG New Global challengers'.
7. Bracken, P. (2007) 'Revenge of the domestic tigers', accessed at www.strategy-business.com on 10 April.
8. Brandt, W., Hulbert, J. and Richers, R. (1980) 'Pitfalls in planning for multinational operations', *Long Range Planning*, December.
9. Brett, J., Behfar, K. and Kern, M.C. (2006) 'Managing multicultural teams', *Harvard Business Review*, 84 (11): 84–91.
10. Buzzell, R.D. (1968) 'Can you standardise multinational marketing?', *Harvard Business Review*, 46 (6): 101–14.
11. Cagni, P. (2006) 'Think global, act European', available at www.strategy-business.com.
12. Cranfield School of Management (2007) 'International Assignments', accessed at www.som.cranfield.ac.uk/som/news.
13. Deshpandé, R., Farley, J.U. and Bowman D. (2004) 'Tigers, dragons and others: profiling high performance in Asian firms', *Journal of International Marketing*, 12 (3): 5–29.
14. Economist (2010 a) 'The world turned upside down', *The Economist,* 15 April.
15. Economist (2010 b) 'Grow, grow, grow. What makes emerging-markets companies run', *The Economist*, 15 April.
16. Finkelstein, S. (1998) 'Safe ways to cross the merger minefield, Mastering Global Business Part 4', *Financial Times*, 20 February.
17. Ghemawat, P. and Hout, T. (2008) 'Tomorrow's Global Giants', *Harvard Business Review*, 86 (11): 80–88.
18. Gogel, R. and Larreche, J.C. (1989) 'The battlefield for 1992: product strength and geographical coverage', *European Journal of Management*, 17: 289.
19. Govindarajan, V. and Gupta, A.K. (2001) 'Building an effective global business team', *MIT Sloan Management Review*, 42 (4): 63–71.
20. Hart, S.L. and London, T. (2005) 'Developing native capability: why multinational corporations can learn from the base of the pyramid', *Stanford Social Innovation Review*, Summer, accessed at www.ssireview.org/.
21. Holt, D.B., Quelch, J.A. and Taylor, E.L. (2004) 'How global brands compete', *Harvard Business Review*. 82 (9): 68–75.
22. Khashani, K. (1995) 'A new future for brands', *Financial Times*, 10 November.
23. Levitt, T. (1983) 'The globalisation of markets', *Harvard Business Review*, May/June.
24. Majaro, S. (1991) *International Marketing*, Routledge.
25. Meffet, H. and Bolz, J. (1993) 'Standardization of marketing in Europe needs effort', in C. Haliburton and R. Hunerberg (eds) *European Marketing Readings*, Addison-Wesley.
26. Mortensen, M. and Beyene, T. (2009) 'Firsthand experience and the subsequent role of reflected knowledge in cultivating trust in global collaboration', Working papers Harvard Business School Division of Research, 1–65.
27. Prahalad, C.K. and Hart, S.L. (2002) 'The fortune at the bottom of the pyramid', *Strategy and Business*, 26 (54): 67.
28. Sebenius, J.K. (2002) 'The hidden challenge of cross-border negotiations', *Harvard Business Review*, 80 (3): 76–85.

29. Sjobolom, L. (1998) 'Success lies one step ahead of the consumer, Mastering Global Management', *Financial Times*, 6 February.

30. Smith, A. (1998) 'The conundrum of maintaining image', *Financial Times*, 8 May.

31. Strategy and Business (2010) 'Six industries in search of survival', *Strategy and Business,* 8 March.

32. UNCTAD (2010) *World investment report 2009*, UN conference on Trade and Development, available at http://www.unctad.org.

33. Weichmann, U.E. and Pringle, L.G. (1979) 'Problems that plague multinational marketers', *Harvard Business Review*, July/August.

34. Wills, S. and Barham, K. (1994) 'Being an international manager', *European Management Journal*, 12 (1).

35. Zou, S. and Cavusgil, S.T. (2002) 'The GMS: a broad conceptualisation of global marketing strategy and its effect on firm performance', *Journal of Marketing*, 66: 40–56.

CHAPTER 7

© R_R, Shutterstock

MARKET ENTRY STRATEGIES

LEARNING OBJECTIVES
After reading this chapter you should be able to:

- Identify the alternative market entry options available to firms seeking to develop new country markets

- Compare the different levels of involvement, risk and marketing control of these market entry methods

- Understand the criteria for selecting between the market entry options

- Appreciate the advantages and disadvantages of the different market entry methods

- Understand the motivations and challenges of market entry partnership strategies, such as alliances and joint ventures

INTRODUCTION

For the majority of companies, the most significant international marketing decision they are likely to take is how they should enter new markets, and how they will maintain and build their involvement in existing markets to increase their international competitiveness. Having identified potential country, regional and world markets in previous chapters and discussed the development of international marketing strategies in both smaller and global firms, in this chapter we examine the different market entry options open to firms to enable them to select the most appropriate method for their given situation. For most small- and medium-sized businesses this represents a critical first step, but for established companies, the problem is how to exploit opportunities more effectively within the context of their existing network of international operations and, particularly, how to enter new emerging markets.

There are advantages and disadvantages with each market entry method: critical in the decision-making process are the firm's ambition and capability, assessment of the cost and risk associated with each method and the level of involvement the company is allowed by the government. These factors determine the degree of control it can exert over the total product and service offer and the method of distribution.

There is, however, no ideal market entry strategy and different market entry methods might be adopted by different firms entering the same market and/or by the same firm in different markets. We particularly focus on the collaborative strategies adopted by the very largest firms.

The alternative market entry methods

The various alternative market entry methods are shown in Figure 7.1. They cover a span of international involvement from almost zero in domestic purchasing, when the firm merely makes the products available for others to export but effectively does nothing itself to market its products internationally, to total involvement where the firm might operate wholly-owned subsidiaries in all its key markets. These are approximate relative positions and vary according to the specific situation. E-commerce might be placed in a range of positions depending upon the particular business model adopted. For Facebook and Google it is the complete offer, whereas for the manufacturer of capital equipment it might be simply an information source.

The market entry decision is taken within the firm and is determined to a large extent by the firm's objectives and attitudes to international marketing and the confidence in the capability of its managers to operate in foreign countries. In order to select an appropriate and potentially successful market entry method, it is necessary to consider a number of criteria including:

- the company objectives and expectations relating to the size and value of anticipated business;
- the size and financial resources of the company;
- its existing foreign market involvement;
- the skill, abilities and attitudes of the company management towards international marketing;
- the nature and power of the competition within the market;
- the nature of existing and anticipated tariff and non-tariff barriers, and other country specific constraints, such as legal and infrastructure limitations;
- the nature of the product itself, particularly any areas of competitive advantage, such as trademark or patent protection; and
- the timing of the move in relation to the market and competitive situation.

This list is not exhaustive, as the entry method might be influenced by other factors which are specific to the firm's particular situation. For example, the laws of a host country might prevent a firm from owning 100 per cent of an operation in that country. Trade embargos put in place by the United Nations may prevent a firm entering the country, during times of war or terrorism the country of origin of the product or service may make market entry inadvisable.

Timing is another particularly important factor in considering entry. For example, emerging markets typically have bursts of optimism and growth often followed by setbacks caused by political or economic factors, or changing customer expectations. The Asian approach of allocating time and resources in the expectation of improved trading conditions in the future has paid off in many emerging markets.

FIGURE 7.1 Market entry methods and the levels of involvement in international markets

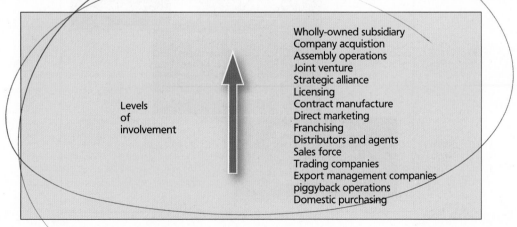

Levels
of
involvement

Wholly-owned subsidiary
Company acquistion
Assembly operations
Joint venture
Strategic alliance
Licensing
Contract manufacture
Direct marketing
Franchising
Distributors and agents
Sales force
Trading companies
Export management companies
piggyback operations
Domestic purchasing

Chinese companies are investing heavily in the infrastructure in Africa in exchange for valuable resources and assets and in the expectation that the economies of African countries will improve in the near future. This approach contrasts with that of many Western companies who seem to invest only when a particular country is about to 'take off', but it may be too late if their Asian rivals are already well entrenched.

Risk and control in market entry

We referred earlier to the fact that one of the most important characteristics of the different market entry methods is the level of involvement of the firm in international operations. This has significant implications in terms of levels of risk and control and is shown in Figure 7.2. Figure 7.2 also shows the four categories of market entry methods: indirect and direct market entry, cooperation and direct investment.

The cost of resourcing the alternative methods usually equates closely to levels of involvement and risk. The diagram does suggest, however, that higher levels of involvement bring greater potential for control over its foreign country marketing activities and also higher potential risk, usually due to the high cost of investment. In practice this is an oversimplification, because firms whose products are marketed internationally through domestic purchasing are at risk of losing all their income from international markets without knowing why, because of their total reliance on their customer's strategy for success.

Partnerships, in the form of joint ventures and strategic alliances, have become increasingly common over the past few years because they are thought to offer the advantage of achieving higher levels of control in market entry at lower levels of risk and cost, provided that there is a high degree of cooperation between companies and that the individual objectives of the partner companies are not incompatible.

In making a decision on market entry, therefore, the most fundamental questions that the firm must answer are:

- What level of control over our international business activities do we require?
- What level of risk are we willing to take?
- What cost can we afford to bear?

In answering these questions it is important to consider not just the level of control, risk and cost, but also the relative importance that the firm might place upon the different elements of its marketing activity. For example, lack of control over certain aspects of the marketing process, such as after-sales

FIGURE 7.2 Risk and control in market entry

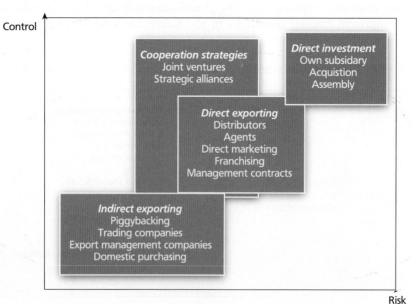

servicing which is often undertaken by third party contractors, may affect the reputation and image of a company or brand because consumers frequently blame the manufacturer rather than a distributor or retailer for the poor quality of after-sales service that they have received.

Indirect exporting

For firms that have little inclination or few resources for international marketing, the simplest and lowest cost method of market entry is for them to have their products sold overseas by others. The objective of firms which use this method of entry may be to benefit from opportunities that arise without incurring any expense or simply to sell off excess capacity into foreign markets with the least possible inconvenience. Firms such as these often withdraw from this activity as soon as their sales into the home market improve. While indirect exporting has the advantage of the least cost and risk of any entry method, it allows the firm little control over how, when, where and by whom the products are sold. In some cases the domestic company may even be unaware that its products are being exported.

There are four main methods of indirect exporting and these are by using:

1 domestic purchasing;
2 an export management company (EMC) or export house (EH);
3 piggyback operations; and
4 trading companies.

Domestic purchasing

Some firms or individuals do not realize that their products or services have potential export value until they are approached by the buyer from a foreign organization, who might make the initial contact, purchase the product at the factory gate and take on the task of exporting, marketing and distributing the product in one or more overseas market. Examples of this include purchasing beads from the Maasai and cocoa beans from farmers in Africa, discussed in Chapter 5. Body Shop sourced naturally occurring ingredients for its ranges of toiletries and cosmetics and made domestic purchasing from deprived regions of the world a feature of its marketing activity. Taking a moral stance and demonstrating environmental concern, however, can make the firm a target for detractors. Ben and Jerry's took this route, in sourcing ingredients for their ice cream from community-based suppliers, but when fashions changed and certain ingredients were no longer popular, they were criticized for stopping supply arrangements with community based social enterprises.

Local subcontractors to original equipment manufacturers (OEMs) fall into this category, as their international market potential is derived entirely from being a member of the OEM's supply chain. While for the manufacturer or supplier domestic purchasing could hardly be called an entry strategy, it does provide the firm with access to and limited knowledge of international markets. However, the supplying organization is able to exert little control over the choice of markets and the strategies adopted in marketing its products. Small firms find that this is the easiest method of obtaining foreign sales but, being totally dependent on the purchaser, they are unlikely to be aware of a change in consumer behaviour and competitor activity or of the purchasing firm's intention to terminate the arrangement. Illustration 7.1 shows how Chinese manufacturers are gaining sales in developed countries, but have little control over marketing so their opportunity to add value and increase profitability is very limited. Moreover, raw material, energy and wage inflation places ever greater pressure on costs.

If a company is intent upon seeking longer-term viability for its export business it must adapt a more proactive approach, which will inevitably involve obtaining a greater understanding of the markets in which their products are sold.

© Alex Segre/Alamy

ILLUSTRATION 7.1

In search of the 99p bargain

One of the fastest-growing markets is the world is the single price item. The concept has its origins in the US with Dollar Tree and Dollar General, which started in the 1950s. Supermarkets around the world want to sell items for 99p, 99 cents, 100 yen or one euro and some shops are set up just to sell these items. Consumers want to buy cheap 'things' – things that when you get them home you realize you should not have bought – but console yourself that they were cheap. Low income groups see the items as essentials at knock down prices. But Poundland the fast growing UK version finds that AB social classes are up to 22 per cent of shoppers.

The source of the 'things' is China and the hundreds of thousands of factories that are listed on Alibaba.com and MadeInChina.com that make toys, trivia and accessories, usually from plastic. Buyers from importers, distributors and agencies scour the factories or go to the 'biggest wholesale market in the world' at Yiwu, where 100 000 businesses are represented, doing deals at high speed and expecting the vast orders to be shipped within 30 days. The calculation works in sterling as follows. Of the 99p, 17.3p will go in VAT and the supermarket will keep 81.7 pence. To make their profit margin the supermarket will want to buy the product at 45p from the importer, who will want to buy the products landed in the UK at 31.5p. When shipping, customs duties, insurance and unloading are taken off, the products must be bought 'free on board' for 22p from the supplier. Typically raw materials would cost around 15.5p leaving the factors 6.5p to cover wages, overheads and wafer-thin profits, meaning of course that very low wages are paid and even big percentage increases in wages will not make very much difference to the costs.

There are many stories of buyers making huge sums of money through 'kickbacks' (bribes from the supplier), frauds when a supplier has taken money for orders and disappeared and goods that are short, defective, broken or dangerous.

Question

1 What advice would you give to the factories to enable them to improve their performance and growth prospects?

References: M. Sheridan, 'The crown jewels of the China trader', *Sunday Times*, 18 February, 2007. J. Finch, 'Posh shoppers buy into bargain paradise', *The Observer*, 9 May 2010. J. W. Miller, 'Africa's new car dealer: China', *Wall Street Journal*, 28 August 2007.

Export management companies or export houses

Export houses or export marketing companies (EMCs) are specialist companies set up to act as the export department for a range of companies. They can help small- and medium-sized companies to initiate, develop and maintain their international sales. As well as taking orders from foreign buyers, they provide indirect access to international market information and contacts. By offering ranges of products from various companies they provide a more attractive overall sales package to foreign buyers, and by carrying a large range they can spread selling and administration costs over more products and companies, and reduce transport costs because of the economies of making larger shipments of goods from a number of companies.

EMCs deal with the necessary documentation and their knowledge of local purchasing practices and government regulations is particularly useful in markets that might prove difficult to penetrate. The use of EMCs, therefore, allows individual companies to gain far wider exposure of their products in foreign markets at much lower overall costs than they could achieve on their own, but there are a number of disadvantages too. The export house may specialize by geographical area, product or customer type (retail, industrial or institutional) and this may not coincide with the suppliers' objectives. As a result of this, the selection of markets may be made on the basis of what is best for the EMC rather than the manufacturer. As EMCs are paid by commission, they might be tempted to concentrate upon products with immediate sales potential rather than those that might require greater customer education and sustained marketing effort to achieve success in the longer term. EMCs may also be tempted to carry too many product ranges and as a result the manufacturer's products may not be given the necessary attention from sales people. The EMC may also carry competitive products which they promote preferentially, again to the disadvantage of a particular firm.

Care is needed in selecting a suitable EMC and resources should be allocated to managing the relationship, monitoring performance and learning more about the markets in which products are being sold in order to seize new opportunities. As sales increase, the firm may wish to manage its own exporting but the transition may not be very easy. First, the firm is likely to have become very dependent on the export house and unless steps have been taken to build contacts with foreign customers and increase market knowledge, moving from using EMCs could prove difficult. Second, the firm could find it difficult to withdraw from its contractual commitments to the export house. Many agreements are based only on the current and short-term situation. Third, the EMC may be able to substitute products from an alternative manufacturer and so use their customer contacts as a basis for introducing new competition against the original exporter.

E-business was expected to have a very significant adverse effect on EMCs and even threaten their survival. However, in assessing the impact of e-business Varinder (2005) found that by linking e-business with their market-based assets, EMCs could still play an efficient and effective role.

Piggybacking

In piggybacking, an established international distribution network of one manufacturer might be used to carry the products of a second manufacturer. The second manufacturer is able to ride on the back of the existing reputation, contacts and administration of the carrier with little direct investment themselves.

The carrier is either paid by commission and so acts as an agent, or alternatively, buys the product outright and so acts as an independent distributor. There are also advantages in piggybacking for the carrier as they are able first, to carry a wider product range and so present a more attractive sales package to potential buyers and second, to benefit from economies of scale by increasing their revenue without incurring additional costs of marketing, selling administration and distribution.

There can, however, be problems as the terms and conditions of the marketing arrangements are often poorly thought out because piggybacking often starts on a 'try it and see' basis. Either company might become locked into an arrangement that proves unsatisfactory for them, particularly as a firm's strategic objectives change over a period of time. Decisions about such marketing mix issues as branding might not suit both companies, and arrangements for providing technical support and service for products often prove to be a source of disagreement and difficulty.

For smaller firms, piggybacking can work when two products are interdependent, or if the second product provides a service for the first. Larger companies, too, have found it successful, particularly when the rider has experienced some kind of barrier to entering particular markets, or the use of an existing distribution network can provide faster market development.

A form of piggybacking occurs when an MNE moves into an emerging market. This provides the opportunity for their key suppliers, such as advertising, market research and consultancy companies, to set up local offices there.

Trading companies

Trading companies are part of the historical legacy from the colonial days and although different in nature now, they are still important trading forces in Africa and Asia. The United Africa Company, part of Unilever, for example, was once claimed to be the largest trader in Africa and the *Sogo shosha* have traditionally played an important role in Japanese international business although, as Illustration 7.2 shows, different patterns of business activity could result in them becoming less significant in some sectors.

One of the major benefits of using trading houses is that their extensive operations and contacts allow them to operate in more difficult trading areas. One important aspect of their operations is to manage countertrade activities, in which sales into one market are paid for by taking other products from that market in exchange. The essential role of the trading company is to quickly find a buyer for the products that have been taken in exchange.

Indirect exporting is often a small company's first experience of international marketing: it has the advantages of being a simple and low-cost method of gaining exposure of products in foreign markets without the company first having to gain the necessary expertise in the various aspects of international trading. However, the company has little control over its international marketing activities and is restricted to simply reacting to new situations and opportunities as they arise. It is extremely difficult to build up international marketing knowledge and expertise by marketing at arm's-length, or to develop any significant long-term product and promotional strategies. Moreover, because of the lack of direct contact between the firm and the market, indirect entry approaches are usually perceived as lacking long-term commitment. As a result, customers and other members of the distribution channels are likely to withhold their full commitment to the firm and its products until the firm becomes more involved in the market, by adopting a more direct approach.

Direct exporting

If a company wishes to secure a more permanent long-term place in international markets, it must become more proactive through direct involvement in the process of exporting. Indeed exporting is the most popular approach for firms as it requires less resources, has little effect on existing operation and involves low investment and financial risks (Leonidou, Katsikeas and Samiee (2002)). However, this requires definite commitment from the company and takes the form of investment in the international operation through allocating time and resources to a number of supporting activities. The key components of the export marketing mix are summarized in Figure 7.3.

The benefits of direct over indirect exporting are that the proactive approach makes it easier to exert more influence over international activities, resulting in a number of specific advantages for the exporter such as greater control over the selection of markets, greater control over the elements of the marketing mix, improved feedback about the performance of individual products, changing situations in individual markets and competitor activity and the opportunity to build up expertise in international marketing.

The disadvantages of direct exporting are that the direct investment necessary is considerable because the whole of the marketing, distribution and administration costs will now be borne by the company. In taking this decision, the company must be quite sure that the costs can be justified in the light of the market opportunities identified.

Illustration 7.3 shows how an exporter from an emerging market has eliminated competition in a global market.

For those firms wishing to change from indirect to direct exporting or to significantly increase their marketing efforts the timing can be critical, as the extra costs involved can often place a huge financial burden on the company. The solution to this is, wherever possible, to make the transition gradually and in a well-planned way, starting with a beachhead or initial landing in one nearby foreign market.

ILLUSTRATION 7.2

© Jiang Dao Hua, shutterstock.com

The future of *Sogo shosha*

In Japan after the Second World War, the dominant industrial powers that emerged tended to be the *keiretsu* (industrial groups), which grew out of the pre-war conglomerates, and the *zaibatsu* (financial cliques) such as Mitsui, Mitsubishi, Sumimoto and Yasuda. These had evolved from family business empires and government favour and were a key part of the government's expansion abroad. Each *zaibatsu/keiretsu* has its own *Sogo shosha* (trading company), which in the seventeenth century were simple import–export businesses. Their influence was enormous because their employees, 'shosha-men', spent years overseas developing their expertise. For example, it was suggested that during the Gulf War the Japanese foreign ministry relied on these contacts rather than its own diplomatic sources. The *Sogo shosha* played a major role, for example, in facilitating the relocation of Japanese production facilities by developing industrial parks in Thailand, Indonesia, Philippines, Myanmar and Vietnam with distribution centres for suppliers and finished goods.

At the height of their power the *Sogo shosha* wielded great power: for example, in 1991 they accounted for 43 per cent of Japan's exports and 79 per cent of imports. Now things are changing. The top five, Mitsubishi, Mitsui, Sumimoto, Itochu and Marabeni, are still major players, but are having to restructure and embark on joint ventures to maintain their position. Under great pressure from the government and banks they are having to get rid of non-performing assets, to partner with other firms and to cut costs. Because they are trading companies their gross turnover is huge but their profits are very thin. Some estimates suggest that up to 30 per cent of a *Sogo shosha's* subsidiaries and ventures could be loss-making at any one time. They suffered in the 1990s due to the long recession in the Japanese economy, where they conduct 50 per cent of their transactions. The need for Japanese companies to adopt global standards in management and more transparent accounting procedures led to harder decisions being taken on loss-making subsidiaries. The problem was that Japanese employers were reluctant to sack workers in large numbers, especially when this might lead to sacking staff in other firms with which they were closely tied.

The pressure was greater for the smaller *Sogo shosha*. The sixth and eighth largest, Nissho Iwai and Nichimen, merged with the loss of 4000 jobs. This was a big shock for the *shosha*-men: until a few years ago, like lawyers and doctors, being a *shosha*-man was a very honourable lifetime career for a university graduate.

The *Sogo shosha* have a history of reinventing themselves when it has become necessary. However, the main problem they are facing is caused by the change in business practice. For example, Nippon Steel bought from all the *Sogo shosha* to maintain good relations, but have now cut suppliers and buy in greater volumes at lower prices. Moreover, e-commerce has the potential to cut out the intermediary's role altogether.

Question

1 What must they do to survive?

References: S. Kawakami 'Goodbye to the glory days', February, 2003, www.japaninc.net.

ILLUSTRATION 7.3

High-flying Brazilian exporter

Asked to name the product made by Brazil's top value private sector exporter, some readers might suggest soccer players and others brazil nuts! (In fact your Brazil nuts are more likely to originate from Bolivia.) The answer could be aircraft from Embraer. This is surprising, especially as North American and European manufacturers, such as Boeing and Airbus, dominate the global market for aircraft. Embraer has demolished its opposition to become the fourth-largest commercial airline manufacturer.

The origins of the Brazilian aircraft industry, however, go back a long way. While the Wright brothers' flight in 1903 was not witnessed and recorded by the authorities, the powered flight three years later by the Brazilian Alberto Santos Dumont in the Bois de Boulogne near Paris was. (Consequently many Brazilians believe that they really invented powered flight.)

Inspired by Santos Dumont, the country has become a leader in small, 30 to 50 seat regional jets that are necessary in a country larger in size than the US. The firm was set up in 1969 as a state industry with a mix of domestic and foreign investment. Despite the scepticism – even from Brazilians – the firm has thrived. There used to be nine manufacturers in the market but now only Bombardier Aerospace of Canada is a competitor. A number of well-known producers of small planes have gone out of production including Fairchild Dornier (US–Germany), British Aerospace (UK), Fokker (Netherlands), Saab (Sweden) and Shorts (UK). At the same time Embraer has developed exports worldwide and even sold products to its Canadian rival.

How did Embraer succeed? The company had vision and a degree of luck and ignored turbo-propeller planes, which effectively died in the 1990s. Instead it went straight to producing jets, which were ideal for the growing air travel market in the US, especially since it was deregulated. It employs 19 000 people and its production facilities are midway between Rio and São Paulo and probably just as sophisticated as Boeing and Airbus. As part of its growth plans Embraer has launched a 70-seater plane which can compete with the smaller aircraft in the Airbus range.

Question

1 What makes an exporter from an emerging market successful against worldwide competition?

References: J. Walters, 'Brazil's winged victory', *The Observer*, 8 December, 2002, 'The jet set, Embraer bucks the trend', *The Economist*, 9 September, 2010.

Factors for success in exporting

A considerable amount of research has been carried out into the barriers and motivations for new exporters and the stages of internationalization, and this was discussed this in Chapter 5.

Katsikeas, Leonidou and Morgan (2000) concluded that the way exporting performance is assessed is important. The simplest measure is whether firms do or do not export. Measurement of the financial performance of the firm in terms of export sales volume, growth and profitability, and the ratio of export to total sales is useful to measure longitudinal firm performance, but is less useful for comparing firm performance between industry sectors because the industry sectors may be structured quite differently. Subjective measurements of the performance of the management of the firm are often helpful but pose a problem, too, in their comparability between firms and sectors.

FIGURE 7.3 The components of the export marketing mix

Product:	selection, development and sourcing
Pricing:	policy, strategies, discount structures and trading terms
Promotion:	corporate promotions and local selling, trade shows and literature
Distribution:	sales force management, agents, distributors and logistics
Services:	market research, training and sales servicing
Finance and administration:	budgets, order processing, insurance and credit control
Technical:	specifications, testing and product quality

Katsikeas *et al.* did, however, conclude that a number of factors were important in contributing to successful exporting:

- commitment of the firms' management;
- an exporting approach in the firm which emphasized the importance of augmenting and maintaining skills;
- a good marketing information and communication system;
- sufficient production capacity and capability, product superiority and competitive pricing;
- effective market research to reduce the psychic distance between the home country and target country market given that it is knowledge that generates business opportunities and drives the international process;
- an effective national export policy which provides support at an individual firm level, and emphasizes the need for knowledge-based programmes which prioritize market information about foreign market opportunities.

They found that the cost of export planning incurred by the firm did not correlate with export performance, and suggested that this might be explained by the fact that a major source of strength in exporting is flexibility and adaptability to export opportunities and the ability to make an immediate strategic response. Moreover, firm size and the managers' experience were not critical factors in export success, but they did recognize that these factors may be the source of the export stimuli in the first place, and could be major determinants of the firm's commitment to exporting and its ability to solve problems.

It is generally accepted, therefore, that in small business, attitudes and commitment to international expansion are crucial for success, whereas in larger companies other factors can have a bearing on performance. The size of a company can either hinder or encourage international development because of the variations in the capability of the staff for planning, the lack of consistency of information and the degree to which adaptation of the mix is necessary. A number of other factors, such as the types of strategies that are pursued, segmentation, product and pricing can also affect export success.

International marketing of services is more fully explored in Chapter 8, but early stage exporting of services is different from exporting of products. Styles, Patterson and La (2005) found there is limited research into the unique success factors in the sector but report some key success factors, emphasizing appropriate use of the tangible and intangible assets and personnel-related factors where there is high face-to-face contact.

Selection of exporting method

The choice of the specific individual markets for exporting was discussed in the first section of this book, but it is important to re-emphasize that the more subjective factors, such as a senior executive's existing formal or informal links, particular knowledge of culture or language and perceived attractiveness of markets, may well influence an individual firm's decision.

Once individual markets have been selected and the responsibilities for exporting have been allocated, the decision needs to be taken about precisely how the firm should be represented in the new market. Clearly the nature, size and structure of the market will be significant in determining the method adopted. In a large market, particularly if a high level of market knowledge and customer contact is needed, it may be necessary to have a member of the firm's staff resident in or close to the market. This cannot be justified if the market is small or levels of customer contact need not be so high. Alternatively a home-based sales force may be used to make periodic sales trips in conjunction with follow-up communications by telephone, fax and email.

Many other factors will affect the cost–benefit analysis of maintaining the company's own staff in foreign markets, such as whether the market is likely to be attractive in the long term as well as the short term and whether the high cost of installing a member of the firm's own staff will be offset by the improvements in the quality of contacts, market expertise and communications. The alternative, and usually the first stage in exporting, is to appoint an agent or distributor.

Agents

Agents provide the most common form of low-cost direct involvement in foreign markets and are independent individuals or firms who are contracted to act on behalf of exporters to obtain orders on a commission basis. They typically represent a number of manufacturers and will handle non-competitive ranges. As part of their contract they would be expected to agree sales targets and contribute substantially to the preparation of forecasts, development of strategies and tactics using their knowledge of the local market. Agents do not take ownership of the goods but work instead on commission, sometimes as low as 2–3 per cent on large value orders.

The selection of suitable agents or distributors can be a problematic process. The selection criteria might include:

- The financial strength of the agents.
- Their contacts with potential customers.
- The nature and extent of their responsibilities to other organizations.
- Their premises, equipment and resources, including sales representatives.

Clearly, the nature of the agreement between the firm and its agent is crucial in ensuring the success of the arrangement, particularly in terms of clarifying what is expected of each party, setting out the basis for the relationships that will be built up and ensuring that adequate feedback on the market and product development is provided.

There are various sources for finding a suitable agent at low cost to the exporter:

- Asking potential customers to suggest a suitable agent.
- Obtaining recommendations from institutions such as trade associations, chambers of commerce and government trade departments.
- Using commercial agencies.
- Using agents for non-competing products.
- Poaching a competitor's agent.
- Advertising in suitable trade papers.

Achieving a satisfactory manufacturer–agent relationship

To achieve success the exporter–agent relationship needs to be managed by:

- Allocating time and resources to finding a suitably qualified agent.
- Ensuring that both the manufacturer and agent understand what each expects of the other.
- Ensuring that the agent is motivated to improve performance.

- Providing adequate support on a continuing basis including training, joint promotion and developing contacts.
- Ensuring that there is sufficient advice and information transfer in both directions.

Distributors

Distributors buy and stock the product from the manufacturer, organize selling and distribution and so take the market risk on unsold products as well as the profit. For this reason, they usually expect to take a higher percentage to cover their costs and risk.

Distributors usually seek exclusive rights for a specific sales territory and generally represent the manufacturer in all aspects of sales and servicing in that area. The exclusivity, therefore, is in return for the substantial capital investment that may be required in handling and selling the products. The capital investment can be particularly high if the product requires special handling equipment or transport and storage equipment in the case of perishable goods, chemicals, materials or components.

The issue of agreeing territories is becoming increasingly important as in many markets, distributors are becoming fewer in number, larger in size and sometimes more specialized in their activity. The trend to regionalization is leading distributors increasingly to extend their territories through organic growth, mergers and acquisitions. Also, within regional trading blocs competition laws are used to avoid exclusive distribution being set up for individual territories. However, the car industry in the EU was allowed to retain exclusive distribution until block exemption was removed. In anticipation of this Mercedes decided to take over its dealerships in order to retain control.

Other direct exporting methods

There are three other modes of exporting which are considered to be direct: management contracts, franchising and direct marketing, typically online buying.

Management contracts Management contracts emphasize the growing importance of services, business skills and management expertise as saleable commodities in international trade. Normally the contracts undertaken are concerned with installing management operating and control systems, and training local staff to take over when the contract is completed. Many construction projects, such as the rebuilding of Afghanistan and Iraq, were undertaken in this way.

Other examples of management contracts may be as part of a deal to sell a processing plant as a turnkey operation, in which the capital plant and a management team are provided by the firm to set up and run the plant for the first few months of operation, and then train the local team to take over. With increased privatization and outsourcing of facilities management by public and private sector organizations there is a substantial growth in management contracts and in firms providing these services. Business process outsourcing has become a rapidly increasing international growth opportunity for companies such as Wipro and IBM, who provide a wide range of IT, human resource and operations processing services.

Franchising Franchising is a means of marketing goods and services in which the franchiser grants the legal right to use branding, trademarks and products, and the method of operation is transferred to a third party – the franchisee – in return for a franchise fee. The franchiser provides assistance, training and help with sourcing components, and exercises significant control over the franchisee's method of operation. It is considered to be a relatively less risky business start-up for the franchisee but still harnesses the motivation, time and energy of the people who are investing their own capital in the business. For the franchiser it has a number of advantages, including the opportunity to build greater market coverage and obtain a steady, predictable stream of income without requiring excessive investment.

Chan (1994) identifies two types of franchise. With product/trade franchises, for example car dealerships, petrol service stations and soft drinks bottlers, the franchisees are granted the right to distribute a manufacturer's product in a specified territory. Business format franchise is the growing sector and includes many types of businesses, including restaurants, convenience stores and hotels. This type of franchise includes the licensing of a trademark, the system for operating the business and the appearance of the location.

Franchising can take the form of single-unit franchising in which the arrangement is made with a single franchisee, or multi-unit in which the franchisee, operates more than one unit. The multi-unit franchisee may be given the responsibility for developing a territory and opening a specified number of units alone or, as is common in international markets, operating a master franchise, in which the master franchisee can sub-franchise to others. In this case the master franchisee is responsible for collecting the fees, enforcing the agreement and providing the necessary services, such as training and advice.

Duckett (2008) found that franchising is becoming increasingly popular as a method for achieving international growth. Trading companies have frequently been appointed as master franchisees and, while this has helped to accelerate the growth of franchising, it has also influenced the franchiser's internationalization process. Because of the global power of these trading companies they are able to challenge the franchiser's decisions in the franchise process and have a considerable say in the strategic development of the business. There is an imbalance in power in franchising and Weaver, Frazer and Giddings (2010) noted that four government enquiries took place in Australia between 2006–08 to try to resolve problems and they conclude that a lack of due diligence and unrealistic expectations increase the likelihood of relational conflict.

There are also differences in the way local culture affects franchise operations, and one of the main problems for franchisers is deciding to what extent the franchise format should be modified to take account of local demands and expectations; for example, McDonald's have added spaghetti to the menu to compete more effectively with Jollibee in the Philippines, Pizza Hut find that corn and not pepperoni sells well in Japan and KFC find that gravy, peas and pumpkin are popular in Australia.

Most US hotels are part of branded groups but considerable scope exists in China and India, where hotels remain independent. The group sells off hotels to investment companies but offers franchises and management contracts to ensure a steady flow of bookings.

Direct marketing and online purchasing Direct marketing is concerned with marketing and selling activities which do not depend for success on direct face-to-face contact. This includes mail order, telephone marketing, television marketing, media marketing, direct mail and electronic commerce using the Internet. We discuss e-commerce developments more fully in Chapter 12. There is considerable growth in all these areas, largely encouraged by increased availability of information and the development of information and communication technology to analyze it and client management systems to manage customer contacts. The changing lifestyles and purchasing behaviour of consumers, and the increasing cost of more traditional methods of entering new markets are further drivers of this trend. The critical success factors for direct marketing are in the standardization of the product coupled with the personalization of the communication. While technical data about the product might be available in one language, often English, the recipients of the direct marketing in international markets expect to receive accurate communications in their domestic language. International direct marketing, therefore, poses considerable challenges, such as the need to build and maintain up-to-date databases, use sophisticated multilingual data processing and personalization software programs, develop reliable credit control and secure payment systems.

However, it can offer an advantage in entering new markets. Whereas American firms had trouble breaking into the Japanese market, catalogue firms were successful because they were positioned as good value for money for well-known clothing brands, compared to Japanese catalogues which were priced higher for similar quality items.

Direct marketing techniques can also be used to support traditional methods of marketing by providing sales leads, maintaining contact or simply providing improved customer service through international call centres. Where multiple direct channels are used for market entry, it is the integration of channels through effective customer relationship management systems that is essential to ensure customer satisfaction.

Foreign manufacturing strategies without direct investment

Having so far considered market entry strategies that have been based upon the development, manufacture and supply of products and services from the firms' domestic operations, we now turn our attention to strategies which involve production and service supply from overseas plants. Before discussing the alternatives available for ownership and control of overseas operations, it is necessary to consider the factors which may lead a firm to start having its products and services produced in one or more of its international markets.

Reasons for setting up overseas manufacture and service operations

The benefits of overseas manufacturing and service operations are:

Product. Avoiding problems due to the nature of the product, such as perishability.

Services that are dependent for success on local intellectual property, knowledge and sensitivity to the local market.

Transporting and warehousing. The cost of transporting heavy, bulky components and finished products over long distances is reduced.

Tariff barriers/quotas. Barriers to trade, which make the market inaccessible, are reduced.

Government regulations. Entry to some markets, such as central and Eastern Europe, are difficult unless accompanied by investment in local operations.

Market. Local manufacture and service operations may be viewed more favourably by customers.

Government contacts. Firms are likely to be viewed more favourably if they contribute more to the local economy.

Information. A strong local presence improves the quality of market feedback.

International culture. Local presence encourages a more international outlook and ensures greater commitment by the firm to international markets.

Delivery. Local manufacture and service operations can facilitate faster response and just-in-time delivery.

Labour costs. Production, distribution and service centres can be moved to lower labour cost markets provided there are appropriate skills and adequate information technology infrastructure to maintain satisfactory quality.

For most companies, the cost of setting up an overseas operation is initially much higher than expanding the domestic facility by an equivalent amount, as we indicated earlier in this chapter. While the equipment costs are likely to be similar, and other costs such as labour, land purchase and building may even be cheaper, it is the cost involved in transferring technology, skills and knowledge that normally proves to be expensive and often underestimated.

Transferring operations from a domestic to an overseas plant reduces the demand on the home plant, which might have traditionally supplied all the firm's overseas markets and the firm must plan either to quickly reduce the cost of running the domestic plant or find new business to replace the production that has been transferred abroad, otherwise the viability of the domestic plant might be put at risk. Setting up new plants overseas involves large cash outflows and can put a significant strain on the firms' finances. Poor planning, underestimation of costs or unforeseen problems associated with setting up a plant overseas have frequently caused businesses to fail or be vulnerable to takeover.

The reason for locating the manufacturing plant close to the market may be due to the nature of the product but increasingly it is the costs of manufacture (including labour, raw materials and government support) as well as the costs of transport. For many firms, setting up foreign country operations for market entry reasons has prompted them to review their business and frequently resulted in them closing down their domestic operation and transferring labour-intensive activity to lower labour-cost countries.

Regionalization is also having a significant effect on plant location; for example, in the car industry location decisions are being based on a variety of factors, such as the participation of the country in monetary

MANAGEMENT CHALLENGE 7.1

Dangote showing that Africa is a good place for capitalism

The most enduring image of Africa over the last few years has been associated with poverty, thanks to the Charity brands 'Live Aid' to provide Food for Ethiopia in 1985 and 'Live 8, Make Poverty History' in 2005. But many of the countries of Africa are working hard to change this image. Botswana, for example, was one of the fastest growing world economies in the last decade.

Of great significance, therefore, was when Aliko Dangote, the Group President and CEO of the Dangote Group was named as the 51st richest person in the world by Forbes 2011 Billionaires with $13.8 billion demonstrating that entrepreneurs can make money in Africa. Dangote has built a diversified conglomerate largely through investment in a range of industries in Nigeria, including cement, sugar, flour, salt, pasta, beverages and real estate. The company has embarked on new projects in the oil and Natural gas, telecommunications, fertilizer and steel industries. The Group focuses on providing local, value-added products and services that meet the needs of the African population and this has led to the company's international development in other African countries including Benin, Cameroon, Ghana, Nigeria, South Africa and Zambia, through direct investment. One example is a US$400 million investment in a 1.5 metric tonnes capacity cement plant in Zambia.

Question

1 What are the benefits and risks of developing a diversified portfolio of products focused on a small number of country markets?

union, the different levels of productivity and the need to be closer to the most attractive potential markets. Mexico has expanded its car manufacturing business within NAFTA. Hutton (2006) observed that Eastern Europe has become the new Detroit: General Motors, Volkswagen, Audi, Renault Daewoo, Suzuki, Toyota, Peugeot, Hyundai, Skoda and Kia all have factories there. Interestingly South Korean firms are looking to 'make where they sell' to avoid paying tariffs and high transport costs, but Kia noted that wage rates in Slovenia were one-fifth of those in South Korea. Reversing this trend, however, Hyundai invested $1 billion in an assembly plant in Alamaba to produce Sports Utility Vehicles and the Sonata.

Having emphasized that a move into overseas manufacturing and service operations involves high cost and risk, firms can choose between different levels of financial commitment. They can, for example, embark upon foreign manufacturing strategies which do not involve direct investment, such as contract manufacture and licensing agreements, or strategies which do involve direct investment albeit at different levels of cost and risk, for example, assembly operations, wholly-owned subsidiary, company acquisition, joint venture and strategic alliances. Management Challenge 7.1 not only show how the success individual entrepreneurs can help create a new brand for African countries but also shows that building a strong base in value added manufactured products in an emerging market can provide a springboard for international expansion.

Contract manufacture

A firm which markets and sells products into international markets might arrange for a local manufacturer to produce the product for them under contract. Examples include Nike and Gap, both of whom use contract clothing and shoe manufacturers in lower labour-cost countries. The advantage of arranging contract manufacture is that it allows the firm to concentrate upon its sales and marketing activities and, because investment is kept to a minimum, it makes withdrawal relatively easy and less costly if the product proves to be unsuccessful.

Contract manufacture might be necessary in order to overcome trade barriers and sometimes it is the only way to gain entry to a country in which the government attempts to secure local employment by insisting on local production. If political instability makes foreign investment unwise, this may be the best way of achieving a marketing presence without having the risk of a large investment in manufacturing. The disadvantage of contract manufacture as an entry method is that it does not allow the buyer control over the manufacturer's activities.

Outsourcing from contract manufacturers allows firms such as Sara Lee to be very flexible by supplying differentiated food products for different regional markets and adjusting costs more quickly when necessary. It also has the financial benefit of lower capital employed, but the risks are that the local contractor may not achieve the desired quality levels or may not gain the necessary knowledge to market the product themselves and compete directly with the international marketer. The marketing firm has less control over the conditions in the factory (intentionally or unintentionally). Some years ago Nike and Gap had bad publicity with the sweatshop conditions in plants it has used in Asia. As a result they had to sever contracts with plants which refused to comply with company standards for wage levels, working conditions and the use of child labour.

Two Scottish companies, Young's and Dawnfresh, provide further examples of contract manufacture. They are processors and marketers of shellfish caught in Scottish waters. However, both companies announced that they were closing their processing plants in Scotland with the resulting loss of 190 jobs. Young's decided to ship 120 000 tonnes of scampi 12 000 miles to Thailand for peeling before they make the return journey. Dawnfresh shipped its scampi to China for peeling.

Licensing

Licensing also requires relatively low levels of investment. Organizations involved in the film, television and sports industries, as diverse as Disney, the Olympic Games Committee and Manchester United Football Club, have been particularly successful in licensing the use of brands, characters and themes, generating huge sales of licensed products (an example appears in Illustration 7.4). It is estimated that the global merchandizing industry is worth $191 billion and instantly recognizable logos or characters are key, with cartoon characters making the most successful brands. The Simpsons is the most successful licensed TV show in history, with sales of more than $8 billion. It is a form of management contract in which the licenser confers to the licensee the right to use one or more of the following: patent rights, trademark rights, copyrights and/or product or process know-how. In some situations, the licensor may continue to sell essential components or services to the licensee as part of the agreement.

There are a number of reasons why licensing is a useful entry method. Financial and management commitments can be kept low, the high cost of setting up a manufacturing, retailing or marketing subsidiary can be reduced and tariff and non-tariff barriers can be avoided. Licensing is particularly useful, therefore, to deal with difficult markets where direct involvement would not be possible, and where the market segments to be targeted may not be sufficiently large for full involvement.

Licensing usually has a number of benefits for the licenser. The licensee pays for the licence normally as a percentage of sales and thus, as the sales grow, so does the revenue to the licenser. Considerable control exists as the licensee uses the rights or know-how in an agreed way for an agreed quantity of product, and the licensee markets and purchases products for an agreed fee.

For the licensee, there are a number of advantages. For a relatively low outlay, it is possible to capitalize on established know-how with little risk and avoid the high research and development cost associated with launching a new product in many markets. This is particularly important in the industrial market, for example, where licensing of proven technology enables companies to enter markets with products which would be prohibitively expensive to develop.

Problems can occur in licensing if the licenser does not respond to changes in the market or technology, or does not help to develop the market for the licensee. A very capable licensee may have learned so much about the market and product that the contribution from the licenser is no longer required. The licensee too may either be unwilling or unable to develop the market in the way that the licenser would wish. These sources of conflict often arise as a result of the environment, competitors and market demand changing over the licensing period.

Sarathy et al. (2006) identify a number of techniques that can be adopted in order to minimize the potential problems of licensing:

- develop a clear policy and plan;
- allocate licensing responsibility to a senior manager;

ILLUSTRATION 7.4

Copyright © Astley Baker Davies/Entertainment One

Peppa Pig: from muddy puddle to global superstar

Helped by brother George and Mummy and Daddy pig, Peppa with her characteristic laugh and love of muddy puddles is the most popular British pre-school cartoon and her adventures are shown in 180 countries. Peppa Pig's owner, Entertainment One and Nickelodeon, the most watched children's channel in the US agreed a partnership to screen Peppa, surprisingly for American TV keeping the British accents. Entertainment One will be looking to recreate the success of the UK licensing model in the US and hope to attract a number of licensees over the coming year.

In the UK the brand is worth £150 million and in the US could be worth ten times that. British television exports run at just below £1.5 billion. Nickelodeon is also showing The Tales of Peter Rabbit in the US, Canada and Latin America and sharing with owners' Chlorion the licensing and merchandizing of dolls, drinks, bags and other items. Other deals will follow for the rest of the world. Peppa and Peter Rabbit could be the next billion dollar brands, following in the footsteps of Winnie the Pooh and Thomas the Tank Engine.

Question

1 What do you consider to be the key elements of a global TV brand?

References: A. Mostrous, 'From muddy puddles to global superstar, Peppa is laughing all the way to the bank', *The Times*, 11 October 2010. Please note that Peppa Pig facts are correct as of March 2011.

- select licensees carefully;
- draft the agreement carefully to include duration, royalties, trade secrets, quality control and performance measures;
- supply the critical ingredients;
- obtain equity in the licensee;
- limit the product and territorial coverage;
- retain patents, trademarks, copyrights;
- be an important part of the licensee's business.

Foreign manufacturing strategies with direct investment

At some point in its international development, a stage is reached when the pressure increases upon a firm to make a much more substantial commitment to an individual market or region. The reasons for investment in local operations are:

- *To gain new business.* Local production demonstrates strong commitment and is the best way to persuade customers to change suppliers, particularly in industrial markets where service and reliability are often the main factors when making purchasing decisions.

- *To defend existing business*. Car imports to a number of countries are subject to restrictions and as their sales increase, so they become more vulnerable to locally produced competitive products.

- *To move with an established customer*. Component suppliers or service providers often set up their own local subsidiaries in order to retain their existing business, compete with local component makers and benefit from increased sales.

- *To save costs*. By locating production facilities overseas, costs can be saved in a variety of areas such as labour, raw materials and transport.

- *To avoid government restrictions* which might be in force to restrict imports of certain goods.

For most multi-nationals there is a strong requirement to demonstrate that they have a permanent presence in all their major markets. The actual form of their operations in each market is likely to vary considerably from country to country but they must also reduce their own manufacturing and operations costs through making the supply chain more cost-effective. Some firms, for example, in the shoe and footwear industries obtain component or finished product supplies from the lowest labour cost areas; Ford locates its component suppliers on a manufacturing campus close to its assembly plants.

Assembly

A foreign owned operation might be set up simply to assemble components which have been manufactured in the domestic market. It has the advantage of reducing the effect of tariff barriers, which are normally lower on components than on finished goods. It is also advantageous if the product is large and transport costs are high, for example in the case of cars. There are other benefits for the firm too, as retaining component manufacture in the domestic plant allows development and production skills and investment to be concentrated, thus maintaining the benefit from economies of scale. By contrast, the assembly plant can be made a relatively simple activity requiring low levels of local management, engineering skills and development support.

There is an argument that assembly plants do not contribute significantly to the local economy in the long term. In initially attracting Nissan, Honda and Toyota assembly plants, the UK government claimed that many jobs would be created at relatively low cost but critics claimed that the number of jobs created in the assembly plants was not very significant and, unless the components were made locally, little transfer of technology would be achieved and the assembly plants could relatively easily be moved to a new location. In practice as other car manufacturers withdrew from the UK market these Japanese manufacturers became the only major established firms. Both to counter threats such as this and also to generate further employment, countries can take steps to develop the component supply business either by interrupting the component supply chain through imposition of import or foreign exchange rate restrictions or, as in the case of CzechInvest, the inward investment arm of the Czech Republic, by supporting local component manufacturers who can supply 'just in time'. Coca-cola uses 50 per cent owned bottling and distribution companies in local countries, supplying them with concentrate to maintain control over the recipes.

Wholly-owned subsidiary

As we indicated in Figure 7.2 at the start of the chapter, for any firm the most expensive method of market entry is likely to be the development of its own foreign subsidiary, as this requires the greatest commitment in terms of management time and resources. It can only be undertaken when demand for the market appears to be assured. Illustration 7.5, however, illustrates the pitfalls of inadvisable acquisition.

This market entry method indicates that the firm is taking a long-term view, especially if full manufacturing facilities are developed rather than simply setting up an assembly plant. Even greater commitment is shown when the R & D facilities are established in local countries too. If the company believes its products have long-term market potential in a relatively politically stable country then only full ownership will provide the level of control necessary to fully meet the firm's strategic marketing objectives. There are considerable risks too, as subsequent withdrawal from the market can be extremely

ILLUSTRATION 7.5

HSBC buying problems in the US

If expansion is too rapid it can cause problems. In February 2007 HSBC announced its first profits warning for 142 years. The unexpected profit underperformance was attributed to Household (renamed HFC and later HSBC Finance Corporation) its US subsidiary which was bought for $15 billion in 2003. HSBC had to increase its bad debt provision by £900 million

when US borrowers failed to make their mortgage repayments. Perhaps most surprisingly, given that HFC was the leading profit generator in the six months to June 2006, there was no American representative on HSBC's main board. However far worse to was to come.

HFC was a major sub prime mortgage lender and the bad debts by the company destroyed the value of the company. Moreover, HFC's credit card loans, with many again in the sub prime market, stood at $49.6 billion, around two thirds of all HSBC credit card loans, and the credit card operation was forced to write off $5.4 billion in bad or doubtful loans. 800 HFC branches were closed in an effort to shrink its exposure to the sub prime market amid calls for HSBC to walk away from HFC.

Question

1 How can an organization reduce the risk of new market entry?

References: P. Aldrick 'HSBC "to axe loan arm chiefs"', *Daily Telegraph*, 9 February, 2007. R. Wachman, 'HSBC faces crisis over us credit cards', *The Observer*, 12 April 2009.

costly, not simply in terms of financial outlay, but also in terms of the firm's reputation in the international and domestic market, particularly with shareholders, customers and staff.

Company acquisitions and mergers

In the previous chapters we discussed the role of acquisitions and mergers in achieving globalization. Illustration 7.6 illustrates the justification for using acquisition as a means of strategic development to strengthen a long term position but also shows that governments can play an important role in the process, and can foil takeover attempts.

The considerable pressure to produce short-term profits means that speed of market entry is essential and this can be achieved by acquiring an existing company in the market. Among other advantages, acquisition gives immediate access to a trained labour force, existing customer and supplier contacts, recognized brands, an established distribution network and an immediate source of revenue. Companies from emerging markets have used acquisition as a fast route to acquiring a globally recognized brand, for example, Lenovo's acquisition of IBM's PC division, Aspen Pharamacare's takeover of Australia's Sigma Pharmaceuticals to acquire market share or India's Bharti Airtel's acquisition of the African assets of Kuwait's Zain to build its African telecoms business.

In certain situations acquisition is the only route into a market. This is the case with previously state owned utilities. Many utilities and infrastructure companies in the UK are foreign owned, for example water companies are owned by Australian investment fund Macquarie, Suez, Vivendi and Bouygues (France), Union Fenosa (Spain) and YTL (Malaysia), the British Airports Authority by Ferrovial of Spain and electricity companies by EDF of France.

Courtesy of Absolut

ILLUSTRATION 7.6

Absolut privatization in Sweden

A change of government in Sweden, when the Alliance for Sweden party replaced the Social Democrats led to a huge privatization of previously state-owned assets. It was expected that the sale of around 50 nationally owned organizations would raise almost SEK 150 billion. Goldman Sachs, Deutsche Bank and Morgan Stanley all opened up new offices in Stockholm in anticipation of new fees for banking, legal services and consultancy. Nordea Bank, telecom group TeliaSonera, mortgage lender SBAB, the stock market operator OMX and property company Vasakronan were the first candidates. Other organizations to be privatized included SAS airlines, Svenska Spel (the gambling network), Vin and Sprit and the pharmacy monopoly Apotoket. The privatization coincided with a rapid downturn in the Swedish economy and the sales of V & S, Telia Sonera and OMX generated SEK 100 billion which was used to help reduce debt.

One of the most interesting privatizations was Vin and Sprit, owners of Absolut Vodka, a world-beating brand and world number three in spirits sales which generated SEK 55 billion. The company was nationalized in 1917 to stop rampant drunkenness and under a string of politician bosses with MPs on the board it performed extremely well, showing real international marketing flair. Absolut's brand was created around an old medical flask spotted in the window of a Stockholm antique shop, and US artist Andy Warhol was persuaded to paint a picture of the bottle with the caption 'Absolut Warhol'.

Of course, privatization is not welcomed by all Swedes, and some think it a disgrace to let Russian, Chinese or French companies get control of the country's infrastructure and prize assets.

Question

1 How might the type of ownership of a MNE affect its international marketing performance?

Expropriation is the opposite of privatization and occurs when a government, usually a non-democratic regime, takes strategic assets from a company, such as an oil well or mine. Even the most powerful companies are unable to stop this and often receive little compensation.

Sometimes the reasons for international business acquisition are, perhaps, not driven by business logic as it seems questionable whether any of the takeovers of British premiership football clubs will make money, starting with Roman Abramovitch's purchase of Chelsea and the Glazer family ownership of Manchester United, even though the marketing opportunities are huge.

An acquisition strategy is based upon the assumption that companies for potential acquisition will be available, but if the choice of companies is limited, the decision may be taken on the basis of expediency rather than suitability. The belief that acquisitions will be a time-saving alternative to waiting for organic growth to take effect may not prove to be true in practice. It can take a considerable amount of time to search and evaluate possible acquisition targets, engage in protracted negotiations and then integrate the acquired company into the existing organization structure.

Another disadvantage of acquisition is that the acquiring company might take over a demotivated labour force, a poor image and reputation and out of date products and processes. All of these problems can prove costly and time-consuming to overcome.

While takeover of its companies is often accepted by governments as a way of increasing investment, takeover of companies which are regarded as part of a country's heritage or key to security can raise considerable national resentment if it seems that they are being taken over by foreign firms. This is often a problem at the time of privatization, as Illustration 7.7 shows. A country looking to develop its own

© Jeffrey Heyden-Kaye, iStockphoto.com

ILLUSTRATION 7.7

BHP Billiton: Trying to acquire growth

In 2010 BHP Billiton made a $39 billion hostile bid for Canada's Potash Corporation and the justification was based on the expectation that rising food demand would cause a significant growth in demand for potash, a key component of fertilizers used to maximize the supply of healthy crops. The company also produces nitrogen and phosphate based fertilizer products.

The world population is predicted by the UN to rise from 6.8 billion to 9 billion by 2050. Demand for grain is rising, particularly as more people are eating meat, as they become wealthier and switch from starch to protein based diets. For example, each pound of beef requires seven pounds of grain to produce. While China has 20 per cent of the world's population it now only has 6 per cent of the arable land, due to previously fertile land being polluted by industrialization. Extreme weather, such as flooding in Pakistan and failure of the wheat harvest in Russia in 2010, exacerbated the shortages. A Royal Society paper estimated that global food supplies need to increase by 70 per cent in the next 40 years. Potash could play a key part in increasing yields as, for example, China and India use only half as much fertilizer as the US.

Acquisition of existing mines is seen as the best approach because digging new mines can be more expensive and can take seven or eight years to build and become productive. There are risks, however, as in 2009 the potash market fell sharply with sales down 30 million tonnes as farmers delayed projects. The price per tonne fell from $1000 in 2008 to $374 in 2010. New technology and genetically modified crops might also reduce the demand for fertilizers, but this is likely to take some time to take effect.

However, the Canadian government made overly stringent demands on BHP Billiton including what the company considered an unprecedented monitoring and compliance regime. BHP Billiton claimed it had committed $820 million investment into the region, promised increased employment and community projects and even offered a position on the board to a Canadian official. Market analysts began to fear protectionism by Canada as the company withdrew its bid. Just preparing the bid had cost $350 million, which had to be written off.

Question

1 How might the stakeholder interests conflict in this situation?

References: R. Wachman, 'Resource wars: the global crisis behind BHP's bid for Potash', *The Guardian*, 22 August 2010: 41. H. Ebrahimi, 'BHP lashes out at Canada as it pulls $38bn bid', *Daily Telegraph*, 15 November 2010.

technology and manufacturing is likely to believe that acquisition of a domestic company by a MNE is not as desirable as the MNE setting up a local subsidiary.

Moreover, acquisition by a large international firm is often associated with job losses and transfer of production facilities overseas. In the past few years there has been considerable debate about acquisition and mergers as a method of achieving rapid expansion. The rationale that is used for acquisition is that an ineffective company can be purchased by a more effective company which will be able, first, to reduce costs, second, improve performance through applying better management skills and techniques and third, build upon the synergy between the two companies and so achieve better results. Many takeovers in the UK and US were financed by huge bank loans justified on the basis that an improvement in future profits would be used to pay the high interest charges. In practice few companies are able to realize the true benefits of synergy. If the other parts of the acquirer's business underperform, for example during a recession, then the acquired company is used to service an increasing debt and is starved of investment.

Some firms use acquisition to focus on their core business and sell off peripheral activities to raise the necessary investment funds for new projects or to plug holes in their finances. As part of its commitment to raise $30 billion by the end of 2011 to meet the obligations of the Gulf of Mexico oil spill BP sold assets in many countries around the world.

Cooperative strategies

There are a number of situations in which two or more firms might work together to exploit a new opportunity. The methods that are adopted are joint ventures, strategic alliances and reciprocal ownership, in which two firms hold a stake in each other's business.

Joint ventures

Joint ventures occur when a company decides that shared ownership of a specially set up new company for marketing and/or manufacturing is the most appropriate method of exploiting a business opportunity. It is usually based on the premise that two or more companies can contribute complementary expertise or resources to the joint company, which, as a result, will have a unique competitive advantage to exploit. Table 7.1 shows the contributions of partners from developed and developing countries.

While two companies contributing complementary expertise might be a significant feature of other entry methods, such as licensing, the difference with joint ventures is that each company takes an equity stake in the newly formed firm. The stake taken by one company might be as low as 10 per cent, but this still gives them a voice in the management of the joint venture.

There are a number of advantages of setting up joint ventures. These include:

- Countries, such as the Philippines, try to restrict foreign ownership.
- Many firms find that partners in the host country can increase the speed of market entry when good business and government contacts are essential for success.
- Complementary technology or management skills provided by the partners can lead to new opportunities in existing sectors, for example, in mobile communications.
- Global operations in R & D and production are prohibitively expensive, but necessary to achieve competitive advantage.
- The two companies can share investment costs and risk.
- The firms can learn from each other, particularly how to participate in local markets.

There are, however, some significant disadvantages of joint ventures as a market entry method. As joint venture companies involve joint ownership, there are often differences in the aims and objectives of the participating companies which can cause disagreements over the strategies adopted by the particular companies. If ownership is evenly divided between the participant firms, these disagreements can often lead to delays and failure to develop clear policies. In some joint ventures the greater motivation of one partner rather than another, particularly if they have a greater equity stake, can lead to them becoming dominant and the other partner becoming resentful. Some firms more effectively learn their partners' skills, so in a General Motors – Toyota joint venture, Toyota learned about supply logistics and managing US staff, whereas GM failed to learn Toyota's manufacturing methods.

Table 7.1 Who provides what in partnerships between firms from developed and developing countries

Developed	Developing
Marketing systems	Customer insights
Brands and communication	Land
Financial management	Buildings and equipment
Forecasting	Distribution networks
Planning	Skills
Technology	Low costs
Information systems	Beneficial wage rates
Capital	
Supply chain management	Tax relief
Know-how	Political connections
Human resources	Neighbouring markets
Financial incentives	

Source: Data adapted from Schiffman, L.G. and Kanuk, L.L. (2000) *Consumer Behaviour*, Prentice Hall.

The other disadvantages of this form of market entry compared to, for example, licensing or the use of agents, is that a substantial commitment of investment of capital and management resources must be made in order to ensure success. Start up costs for management and control and developing cultural understanding can be high. Many companies would argue that the demands on management time might be even greater for a joint venture than for a directly owned subsidiary because of the need to educate, negotiate and agree with the partner many of the operational details of the joint venture.

Some experts recommend that a joint venture should be used by companies to extend their capabilities rather than merely exploit existing advantages, and is not recommended if there are potential conflicts of interest between partners. The role of the government in joint ventures can be particularly influential, as it may control access to the domestic market. Moreover, a government may be persuaded to adapt its policy if a firm is bringing in advanced technology or is willing to make a major investment. Most of the major multi-nationals have increased their involvement in joint ventures, but the implications of this are that it leads to increasingly decentralized management and operations, more closely aligned to transnational operation than to global standardization, in which more centralized control is necessary.

Where joint ventures are used for emerging market entry there is also the possibility of a conflict of objectives which can occur between the international company, which wishes to develop a new market, and the local company which wishes to develop its own foreign markets or withdraw profits from the joint venture to finance other projects.

In analyzing the results of joint ventures in China, Vankonacker (1997) observes that joint ventures are hard to sustain in unstable environments and concludes that more direct investment in China will be wholly-owned, offering Johnson and Johnson's oral care, baby and feminine hygiene products business as a success story. Moreover, as Management Challenge 7.2 shows, there can be a danger of creating a new competitor.

MANAGEMENT CHALLENGE 7.2

Creating competitors for airspace

High technology companies face a dilemma, because the fast growing China market offers the prospect of immediate sales but to gain access it is necessary to co-operate with Chinese companies that in the future will become rivals. Passenger traffic in China is increasing at 20 per cent a year and 10 airports opened in 2010, with an increase expected from the current 176 airports to 250 by 2020.

In 2010 Boeing delivered its 800th plane to China but had a backlog of $30 billion worth of sales. So far Boeing's main global competitor has been Airbus, which established its first assembly line outside Europe in China in a 51 per cent owned joint venture with a Chinese Consortium, delivering its first A320 jet to Sichuan Airlines in 2009. The major threat to the duopoly of Boeing and Airbus is the state owned Commercial Aircraft Corporation of China (Comac) with its C 919, 190 passenger, single-aisle aircraft. Comac expected to sell 2509 C919s over 20 years with the first due to enter service in 2016. Several US companies that are suppliers to Boeing have contracts for the C919. They include General Electric (GE), Honeywell, Rockwell Collins, Eaton, Goodrich and Parker Hannifin.

The question is whether they will transfer the latest technology to the C919, whether they will get Intellectual Property guarantees if the factories are government-run and whether they will embark on local joint ventures. Already the C919 will get a world class fuel efficient engine from CFM International, a GE–Safran (France) joint venture. GE also formed a joint venture with Aviation Industry Corp of China to build the C919 housing and gear, and an electronics system. Eaton formed a joint venture with Shanghai Aircraft Manufacturing Co, a subsidiary of Comac to develop fuel and hydraulic systems for the plane.

Comac provides the entry ticket to a lucrative Chinese market for aeroplane manufacturers and their supply chain partners and it can trade this for access to the latest technology from the US and Europe. However, in the future Comac could develop indigenous suppliers to replace the foreign suppliers it is currently using and it could soon develop bigger two aisle jets and thus become a much stronger competitor – much of Boeing's backlog is for the 787 Dreamliner. The aircraft and aircraft parts businesses are US export strengths and there is a real danger that in the rush to tie up supply deals the companies might be creating competitors for the future.

Question

1 How should Boeing and Airbus manage their interests in China?

References: R. Krause, 'China's jet ambition a boon to suppliers – or their bane', *Investor's Business Daily*, 19 August 2010.

Strategic alliances

While all market entry methods essentially involve alliances of some kind, during the 1980s the term strategic alliance started to be used, without being precisely defined, to cover a variety of contractual arrangements that are intended to be strategically beneficial to both parties but cannot be defined as clearly as licensing or joint ventures. The Star alliance of airlines that includes Lufthansa, BMI, Scandinavian Airlines, Singapore Airlines and South African Airways and many more is one example. Bronder and Pritzl (1992) have defined strategic alliances in terms of at least two companies combining value chain activities for the purpose of competitive advantage.

Some examples of the bases of alliances are:

- technology swaps
- R & D exchanges
- distribution relationships
- marketing relationships
- manufacturer–supplier relationships
- cross-licensing.

Perhaps one of the most significant aspects of strategic alliances has been that many involve cooperation between partners that might also be competitors. This can pose problems for the participants, who must be careful about sharing information with their alliance partner but avoid information leakage where the organization may be competing.

There are a number of driving forces for the formation and operation of strategic alliances.

Insufficient resources: the central argument is that no organization alone has sufficient resources to realize the full global potential of its existing and particularly its new products. Equally, if it fails to satisfy all the markets which demand these products, competitors will exploit the opportunities which arise and become stronger. In order to remain competitive, powerful and independent companies need to cooperate.

Pace of innovation and market diffusion: the rate of change of technology and consequent shorter product life cycles mean that new products must be exploited quickly by effective diffusion out into the market. This requires not only effective promotion and efficient physical distribution but also needs good channel management, especially when other members of the channel are powerful, and so, for example, the strength of alliances within the recorded music industry including artists, recording labels and retailers, has a powerful effect on the success of individual hardware products such as the MP3 players.

High research and development costs: as technology becomes more complex and genuinely new products become rarer, so the costs of R & D become higher.

Concentration of firms in mature industries: many industries have used alliances to manage the problem of excess production capacity in mature markets. Sometimes this leads to takeovers as has occurred in the One World between BA and Iberia.

Government cooperation: as the trend towards regionalization continues, so governments are more prepared to cooperate on high-cost projects rather than try to go it alone. There have been a number of alliances in Europe – for example, the European airbus has been developed to challenge Boeing, and the Eurofighter aircraft project has been developed by Britain, Germany, Italy and Spain.

Self-protection: a number of alliances have been formed in the belief that they might afford protection against competition in the form of individual companies or newly formed alliances. This is particularly the case in the emerging global high technology sectors such as information technology, telecommunications, media and entertainment.

Market access: strategic alliances have been used by companies to gain access to difficult markets; for instance, Caterpillar used an alliance with Mitsubishi to enter the Japanese market.

As with all entry strategies, success with strategic alliances depends on effective management, good planning, adequate research, accountability and monitoring. It is also important to recognize the limitations of this as an entry method. Companies need to be aware of the dangers of becoming drawn into activities for which they are not designed.

Voss *et al.* (2006) emphasize the importance of cultural sensitivity in cross-border alliances and the implications for trust and quality information exchange.

Minority stake share holdings

In this chapter we have considered many different methods of cooperation between partners. Over the years many firms have taken an equity stake in another firm for a variety of reasons. Russia, for example, restricts foreign ownership to 49 per cent. The main reason is that it is regarded as less risky to build an ownership stake over time to reduce uncertainty in the workforce. Volkswagen took a 31 per cent stake in Skoda and gradually increased this to 70 per cent, the remainder is owned by the Czech government. It might provide the opportunity to influence the strategy of that firm, create a basis upon which to share expertise between the firms or establish a platform that might lead to a more formal business relationship, such as a merger, as well as generating an immediate return on the investment. Renault took a stake in Nissan to save the company from bankruptcy and succeeded in turning the company around by helping it to launch a more attractive and competitive range of cars. Renault then became the recipients of Nissan's expertise in improving quality and production efficiency. A further interesting alliance is discussed in Illustration 7.8 between Renault, Nissan and Daimler, which follows a previous alliance failure.

Courtesy of Daimler AG

ILLUSTRATION 7.8

Daimler collaborating again

In 2010 Daimler AG tried again to succeed in a collaborative venture, this time in a three way equity sharing alliance with Renault and Nissan. Daimler's last major collaboration had been a disastrous merger in 1998 with Chrysler that was finally ended in 2008 after nine years of losses, when Chrysler was sold off by Daimler AG to Cerberus Capital Management. This was timely as the US government saved Daimler AG from bankruptcy in 2009.

Daimler AG, Renault and Nissan emphasized that there was no intention of merging their interests this time. Carlos Ghosn Chairman and CEO of both Renault and Nissan said that the small cross shareholding in each company (around 3 per cent) was intended to be 'a signal inside the companies to co-operate'.

The impetus for this new collaboration was that from 2012 companies will face a penalty in the European Union if the total average emissions of their cars exceed 120g of CO_2 a kilometre. In 2010 the average was 158g, so the companies need a product portfolio that includes small fuel efficient cars to balance the higher powered cars in the range. Nissan and Renault were already partners on their own but this deal enabled them to gain access to Daimler's technology on high performance cars while Daimler AG would get its hands on Renault and Nissan's small car technology to develop its Smart range and compact Mercedes Benz ranges. Together the partners intended to work on a new generation of the Renault Twingo and Daimler's Smart Fortwo, including electric versions.

Question

1 What will be the critical factors in making this alliance a success?

Reference: Daimler AG, 'Nissan and Renault announce three-way tie-up', BBCOnline, 7 April 2010.

What is quite clear is that global firms are adopting a range of market entry partnership arrangements to maximize their global performance and presence. The businesses are becoming increasingly complex as they embark on joint ventures, with the associated formal responsibilities, strategic alliances, short-term contractual obligations and shareholdings which might be the basis for closer future cooperation.

Inevitably the challenge for management is to manage the various stakeholder expectations and maximize the opportunities that come from synergy and the complementary activity of the partners. To do this it is necessary to select partners that are willing and able to contribute at least some of:

■ complementary products and services;
■ knowledge and expertise in building customer relationships;
■ capability in technology and research;
■ capacity in manufacturing and logistics;
■ power in distribution channels; and
■ money and management time.

The management must also deal with the added complexity and potential for conflicts between two quite different partners that arise because of differences in:

■ objectives and strategies;
■ approach to repatriation of profits and investment in the business;
■ social, business and organization cultures; and
■ commitment to partnership and understanding of management responsibilities.

While cooperative strategies promise synergy, the potential for cost saving and faster market entry, it requires considerable management effort to overcome the inherent difficulties and dedication to see the partnerships through to success.

SUMMARY

- For a firm at the start of internationalization, market entry can be regarded as a critical first step which is vital not only for financial reasons, but also because it will set a pattern of future international involvement. It determines not just the opportunities for sales but also a valuable source of market information.

- Market entry methods can be seen as a series of alternatives available to international firms, and a global strategy might utilize a number of different approaches. A firm can make individual decisions based on the factors affecting one specific country or the whole region and choose the most appropriate method for the particular set of circumstances.

- The choice of market entry method should be based on an assessment of the firm's desired involvement in the market and the level of control of its marketing mix in the country, set against the financial and marketing risks.

- For large established companies that already have extensive involvement in international markets, the market entry decision is taken against the background of the competitive nature of the market, the environment, its global strategy and an existing and substantial network of operations.

- The company's competitive strategy is likely to require simultaneous decisions affecting its arrangements in a number of markets in order to improve its competitive position by entering untapped or emerging markets, or expanding its activities in existing markets.

- In order to achieve these objectives within a very short timescale, rather than relying on organic growth the companies have used a variety of market entry strategies, including joint ventures and alliances, often with competitors. This is leading to increasingly complex operations being created in which companies strive to balance the opposing forces of competitiveness and cooperation, and quite frequently such arrangements fail to deliver the expected benefits.

KEYWORDS

Market entry	Trading companies	Wholly-owned subsidiary
Market involvement	*Sogo shosha*	Contract manufacture
Risk and control	Exporting	Licensing
Indirect exporting	Distributors	Acquisitions
Domestic purchasing	Management contracts	Joint ventures
Export houses	Franchising	Strategic alliance
Piggybacking	Direct marketing	

CASE STUDY

When joint ventures go wrong

A few years ago the arguments for strategic alliances and joint ventures as international market entry strategies for companies from developed countries entering a developing country seemed clear and compelling. They seemed particularly appropriate for China and in some cases appeared the only way. The theory was that the Chinese company provided access to cheap labour, local regulatory knowledge, knowledge of consumer behaviour and access to what appeared to be a relatively small, high-risk domestic market. The foreign partner provided capital knowledge, access to international markets and the promise of jobs in China. The attraction was that the market was promising, although at the same time it was geographically vast with very complex, contradictory and often invisible rules. Many of the largest companies in the world pursued collaborations of this type with what were then local Chinese companies in the belief that the arrangement would reduce risk but still allow high levels of control over the marketing strategy in China.

In practice many joint ventures and alliances have failed to deliver the original promise, involving companies from just about every industry sector, including Peugeot (cars), Remy Martin (spirits), Foster's (beer), News Corporation (media) and many telecoms firms. Chinese companies originally were keen to receive money, technology and business 'know-how', but they now have global ambitions of their own and do not want to be constrained by a global multinational partner who may want to curtail these ambitions. The joint venture partners frequently argued about the allocations of profits and decisions on investments.

China itself has also changed, having become a member of the World Trade Organization it agreed to be more open in legal matters. As the domestic economy grew more rapidly than anyone expected domestic capital was freely available, with the result that there was little need for money from foreign investors. As the Chinese market became one of the most attractive in the world and sentiment in China became more nationalistic and self-reliant the balance of power shifted between the Chinese and foreign partners, and providing access to China for foreign partners was of much less interest to indigenous companies.

Danone, a French Food multinational, acquired a 51 per cent stake in the Chinese firm Hangzhou Wahaha Beverage and believed they had struck an excellent deal. Wahaha originally knew little about the new business and welcomed a partner. The company was managed by Zong Qinhou, the entrepreneurial founder of Wahaha. He had developed the company from a milk selling stall to China's largest beverage company in 20 years.

Danone had very little success in the Chinese market prior to this joint venture and provided little input to the management of the new company believing they knew best. Without challenge from Danone, Zong was the main decision-maker, and the Confusion culture with its business model of the family reinforced his authority as an autocratic leaders. He was headstrong, did not want to share control, viewed the western model of corporate governance as inefficient and saw Danone as the provider of passive capital. Zong travelled 200 days per year around China testing consumer preferences. Danone could not appoint executives and Zong ended the contracts of high ranking R&D and marketing staff that Danone employed.

The lack of control by Danone allowed Zong to set up parallel companies so displacing profits from the joint venture. He was able use the trademark outside the joint venture because Danone had not challenged a court ruling in the early days of the joint venture. Zong was able to gain sympathy for his dealings outside the joint venture because foreign ownership had become politically sensitive in China.

Zong was able to use the fact that Danone has set up other joint ventures in China with other local companies such as Robust, Aquarius, Mengniu Dairy and Bright Dairy Food and allowed directors to sit on other boards in breach of Chinese law. The companies became involved in an acrimonious public dispute with 30 lawsuits on 3 continents. Chinese society is relationship rather than law driven. The Chinese step outside the law when they feel justified, but Danone came to realize that this becomes a disadvantage when a dispute arises. Danone resolved the problem only by pulling out of its joint venture resulting in a loss of £3 billion of income, around 10 per cent of its worldwide sales. Its other Chinese joint ventures also failed suggesting that Danone simply had not got to grips with the culture.

The moral of this experience confirms conventional wisdom about forming joint ventures – to undertake the most careful planning and stay closely involved in the operations of the new organization. Alliances may be formed for local business reasons but they need to be part of a coherent alliance portfolio. It is necessary too to maintain trust with existing partners when embarking upon new alliances and the alliance can cause problems as a result of using a partner's technology, products and services resulting quite often in the creation of a new competitive threat.

Questions

1 What are the factors that a multinational firm should consider when deciding to use a joint venture as a market entry strategy for a developing country? What are the potential benefits and risks in taking this course of action?

2 Develop an outline international marketing strategy for a joint venture between Danone, a French multinational food company, and a food producer from a developing country. Explain which companies you feel should be responsible for providing the leadership and decision-making for the various activities detailed.

References: U. Wassmer, P. Dussauge and M. Planellas (2010) 'How to Manage Alliances Better Than One at a Time', *MIT Sloan Management Review*, 1 April. J. Yao, (2008) 'Why Danone's ventures failed', *International Financial Law Review*, March, 27 (3): 46–48.

DISCUSSION QUESTIONS

1   What market entry options does a small firm that has developed specialist security equipment for use at airports have when seeking to develop internationally? Specify what you consider to be the important criteria in deciding the appropriate entry method.

2   As a consultant you have been asked to advise a leisure and hotel complex in southern Africa on how they should increase the number of international visitors. Explain their options and potential risks, and how they might control the way their offer is marketed, particularly if you have recommended the use of third parties.

3   International marketing of intellectual property, such as technological inventions, creative works, the performing arts and consultancy provide opportunities and pose particular challenges for market entry. Using examples to illustrate your answer, explain what the opportunities are and identify the specific cross cultural challenges of marketing this intellectual property internationally.

4   Why is acquisition often the preferred way for companies from emerging markets to establish wholly-owned operations abroad, and what are the limitations of acquisition as an entry method?

5   Explain the alternative approaches to collaboration that firms might adopt in their quest to become global players. What are the advantages of collaboration, and what are the potential pitfalls?

REFERENCES

1.   Bronder, C. and Pritzl, R. (1992) 'Developing strategic alliances: a conceptual framework for successful co-operation', *European Management Journal*, 10 (4).

2.   Chan, P.S. (1994) 'Franchising: key to global expansion', *Journal of International Marketing*, 2 (3).

3.   Duckett, B., (2008) 'Business format franchising: a strategic option for business growth – at home and abroad', *Strategic Direction*, 24 (2): 3–4.

4.   Hutton, R. (2006) 'Eastern Europe the new Detroit', *Sunday Times*, 15 October.

5. Katsikeas, C.S., Leonidou, L.C. and Morgan, N.A. (2000) 'Firm-level performance assessment: review, evaluation and development', *Journal of Academy of Marketing Science*, 28 (4): 493–511.

6. Leonidou, L.C., Katsikeas, C.S. and Samiee, S. (2002) 'Marketing strategy determination of export performance: a meta analysis', *Journal of Business Research*, 55: 51–67.

7. Sarathy, R., Terpstra, V. and Russow, L. (2006) *International marketing*, 9th edn. Dryden Press.

8. Styles, C., Patterson, P.G. and La, V.Q. (2005) 'Executive insights: exporting services to South East Asia: lessons from Australian knowledge-based service exporters', *Journal of International Marketing*, 13 (4): 104–28.

9. Vankonacker, W. (1997) 'Entering China: an unconventional approach', *Harvard Business Review*, March–April.

10. Varinder, S. (2005) 'Export management companies and e-business: impact on export services, product portfolio and global market coverage', *Journal of Marketing Theory and Practice*, 13 (4): 61–71.

11. Voss, K.E., Johnson, J.L., Cullen, J.B., Sakano, T. and Takenouchi, H. (2006) 'Relational exchange in US–Japanese marketing strategic alliances', *International Marketing Review*, 23 (6): 610–35.

12. Weaver, S., Frazer, L., and Giddings, J., (2010) 'New perspectives on the causes of franchising conflict in Australia', *Asia Pacific Journal of Marketing and Logistics*, 22 (2): 135–155.

CHAPTER 8

INTERNATIONAL PRODUCT AND SERVICE MANAGEMENT

LEARNING OBJECTIVES

After reading this chapter you should be able to:

- Understand the nature of international product and service marketing and appreciate the elements that make up the product and service offer

- Evaluate the factors affecting international product and service strategy development both external and internal to the firm

- Explain the issues that affect international product and service management across borders

- Identify the implications of the image, branding and positioning of products and services in international markets

- Understand how innovation contributes to the international product and service strategy

INTRODUCTION

Success in international marketing depends to a large extent upon the value proposition, satisfying the demands of the market and ultimately, on whether the product or service offered is suitable and acceptable for its purpose. More markets are reaching maturity and fewer products can be differentiated by their core benefits and so are becoming commodities. In defining the term 'product', therefore, we include additional elements such as packaging, warranties, after-sales service and branding that make up the total product and a complete package of tangible and intangible benefits for the customer. Services are taking an increasing share of international trade, but managing services internationally poses particular challenges. This is because the delivery of services is so dependent on the context, which is usually influenced by the varying cultural perceptions of what is acceptable service. In both product and service markets increasing customer expectations and competition mean that it is essential for firms to continually add better value through innovation and new product development. Much of this innovation is related to technological developments.

In this chapter we focus upon some of the key aspects and recent trends of international product policy by considering the changes in the nature of the products and services offered individually and within the portfolio, their relationship with the market and how innovation can create new products and services. Particularly important is the need to provide customers around the world with a satisfactory experience when using the product or service. To achieve this requires a clear understanding of when to meet the similar needs and wants of transnational customer segments and when to adapt to local tastes and requirements.

The nature of products and services

The reason that the majority of companies initially develop international markets is to generate new market opportunities, increase sales of an existing product or service or to offload excess capacity. However, the product must be seen as a bundle of satisfactions, providing people not just with products but with satisfying experiences in terms of the benefits they provide rather than the functions the products perform. These concepts are particularly important in international marketing, because, for example, the growth of such global consumer products as McDonald's and Coca-Cola cannot be attributable solely to a distinctive taste. Much of their success might be attributed to the aspirations of their international customers to be part of the 'Coca-Cola Culture', by deriving satisfaction from a close association with the product and the brand and also being reminded of the experiences associated with the product such as enjoying music, being with friends or watching sport.

In understanding how products can provide satisfying experiences and benefits for people, it is necessary to clearly identify and understand the motivations of the target consumer and not make assumptions about them. A typical response to Nike sports shoes, reported in *Sky* magazine was: 'It's kind of like, Nike don't give a * * * * what you do, they don't care where you come from and they don't want to hear you talk about it. They just want to see what you can do'.

International product and service marketing

The term 'product' is used in marketing to refer both to physical goods, such as a can of baked beans or a refrigerator, and services such as insurance or a holiday. In fact few products can be described as pure product with no service element – salt is often suggested as approaching a pure product. Education is probably the closest to a pure service. All offers are a combination of product and service components, as shown in Figure 8.1. Before considering the total product 'offer' in more detail, it is important to consider the specific characteristics of services and the challenges they pose in international marketing.

Services are characterized by their:

- Intangibility: air transportation, insurance and education cannot be touched, smelled or seen. Tangible elements of the service, such as food, drink and personal video on airline flights; a written policy and a free gift in insurance and a certificate and a photograph of graduation for success in

FIGURE 8.1 The product-service continuum

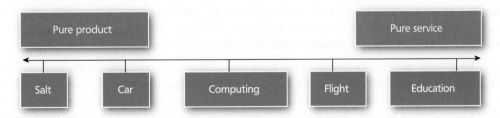

education, are used as reminders and reinforcements of the service in order to confirm the benefit provided and enhance its perceived value. However, the physical evidence of the service that is offered may be valued very differently from country to country.

■ Perishability: services cannot be stored – for example, the revenues from unfilled airline seats are lost once the aircraft takes off. This characteristic causes considerable problems in planning and promotion in order to match supply and demand at busy and quiet times of the day. Predicting unfamiliar patterns of demand and managing capacity in distant and varied locations is particularly difficult.

■ Heterogeneity: services are rarely the same, because they often involve interactions between people. For fast food companies this can cause problems in maintaining consistent quality, particularly in international markets where there are quite different attitudes towards and expectations of customer service.

■ Inseparability: the service is created at the point of sale. This means that economies of scale and the experience curve benefits can be difficult to achieve and supplying the service in scattered markets can be expensive. Where the service involves some special expertise, such as pop music, the number of consumers is limited by the size and number of venues that can be visited by the performer. If the fans are in a market which is remote, they are unlikely to see the artist and need other forms of communication, such as videos, website and books, in order not to feel too separated from the performer. Twitter has been used by celebrities to maintain continual contact with their devoted followers.

The three additional marketing mix elements
These differences between product and service offers have certain implications for the international marketing mix and, in addition to the usual four Ps for products – product, price, place and promotion – another three Ps for services are added. Because of the importance and nature of service delivery, special emphasis must be placed upon:

■ *People*. Consumers must be educated in order for their expectations of the service to be managed, and employees must be motivated and well trained in order to ensure that high standards of service are maintained. However, because of cultural differences the staff and customers in various countries often respond differently not only to training and education but also in their attitudes to the speed of service, punctuality, willingness to queue and so on. However, firms such as consultancies, advertising agencies or IT management supplying services around the world to an MNE customer, will be expected to maintain the same standards at every country location, but local staff and customers may have different attitudes to service in each.

■ *Process*. As the success of the service is dependent on the total customer experience, a well-designed delivery process is essential. Customer expectations of process standards vary with different cultures and standardization is difficult in many varied contexts. Frequently the service process is affected by elements for which the service deliverer may be blamed by frustrated customers but over which they have little control. Sports fans might travel to an event at great expense only to experience delays at an airport, excessive policing or bad weather. Although their team may perform well the fans may be reluctant to travel to future matches because of their unsatisfactory overall experience. At its most basic the process of customer management should make it easy for the customer to deal with the firm no matter where they are in the world.

■ *Physical aspects*. Many physical reminders, including the appearance of the delivery location and the elements provided to make the service more tangible, can enhance the overall customer experience. Apart from using appropriate artefacts to generate the right atmosphere, constant reminders of the firm's corporate identity help to build customer awareness and loyalty. For example, the familiar logos of Vodafone, Google, CNN and Cathay Pacific airline may give the reassurance necessary for a consumer to use a service in a foreign market.

Low-cost airlines, such as Ryanair and easyJet, have put pressure on the national flag carriers by changing each element of the marketing mix, using their website for managing most transactions, yield management software to maximize revenue generation rather than price maintenance and charging for every 'extra' after the customer has purchased a seat. There are some specific problems in marketing services internationally. There are particular difficulties in achieving uniformity of standards of the three additional Ps in remote locations where exerting control can be particularly difficult. Pricing, too, can be extremely problematic, because fixed costs can be a very significant part of the total service costs but may vary between locations, for example, in the case of mobile telephony. As a result the consumer's ability to buy and their perceptions of the promised and received service may vary considerably between markets, resulting in significantly different prices being set. Increasingly important in service marketing is the need to provide largely standardized services customized to individual requirements. This clearly poses considerable challenges to international service providers. For example, a MNE might employ an international law firm to protect its interests but the scope for offering a standardized service is limited by the fact that every country has its own different legal system.

There are a number of generalizations that can be made about international marketing of services. Foreign markets present greater opportunities for gaining market share and long-term profits for MNEs if local firms are less experienced in customer management and communication and quality of service delivery. If cultural sensitivity and local knowledge is key then local service companies are likely to succeed. Companies such as Google, eBay and Facebook have lost out to local imitators in China and India. Information technology and the development of expert knowledge networks are the sources of competitive advantage for international service marketers. Due to the high initial cost of financing overseas operations, joint ventures and franchising are rapidly growing entry methods, and frequently the market entry strategy is based on forming alliances or piggybacking as existing clients move into new markets. Government regulations and attitudes to the protection of local suppliers vary considerably from country to country, but more new markets are opening up.

While it might seem appropriate to categorize physical goods as tangible and services as intangible, marketing increasingly appears to be concerned with blurring this distinction. For example, a product such as perfume is not promoted as a complex chemical solution, but instead, as one perfume house executive put it, 'dreams in a bottle'. Many services appear to compete over tangible 'add-ons' as we discussed earlier in this chapter.

The international marketing of service

One of the achievements of the Uruguay Round of negotiations on the General Agreement on Trade in Services (GATS) was to identify four modes of delivery or ways in which services may be exported. This is useful in detailing the nature of international services:

1 *Cross-border trade*, where the trade takes place from one country to another, without the movement of persons. Only the service itself, for example, market research or training, crosses the border electronically (email), by telecommunications (telephone, radio) or by infrastructure (air, rail).

2 *Consumption abroad*, where the customer travels to the country where the service is supplied (tourism, education or training, legal services).

3 *Commercial presence*, where the supplier establishes a commercial presence abroad (banks, construction project offices or warehousing and logistics).

4 *Movement of natural persons*, where the provider of the services crosses the border (arts and culture, recreation and sports).

Any of the four modes constitute trade so long as the local firm is being paid by the foreign firm, no matter where the service is provided.

Illustration 8.1 shows how ISS has created a new approach in the facilities service sector and used acquisition to develop its international markets.

'Invisible' services contribute to all aspects of economic activity. For example, infrastructure services (transport, communications and financial services) provide support to any type of business. Education, health and recreational services influence the quality of labour available, and professional services provide the specialized expertise to increase firms' competitiveness. Services make up an increasing proportion of GDP and are also used to add value to the product offer as outlined in the following section.

ILLUSTRATION 8.1

© Pedro Castellano, iStockphoto.com

ISS: Cleaning up in the world

ISS is one of the world's largest Facility Services providers with a market presence in 50 countries across Europe, Asia, South America and Australia. Most people think that contract cleaning is done by small local operators, using unskilled, part time, casual, low paid and largely unmotivated staff. Danish company, ISS is proof that it can be done another way as they now employ over 500 000 people.

ISS has grown rapidly on the back of the move by both private and public sector organizations to focus on their core activities and outsource support services and facilities management. ISS offers facilities management services including cleaning, catering, security, office support and property services.

ISS spotted the opportunity to rejuvenate and restructure the cleaning business, which traditionally was characterized by having a negative external image, many small-scale, local and rather unprofessional operations and poor management.

The success of ISS is due to its expertise in contract tendering, project management, its investment in the training of all staff and not just managers to ensure quality and avoid accidents, the use of the appropriate technology, such as the use of the correct cleaning agents and the effective use of time and supplies.

It believes in peer pressure and so even for contracts with SMEs, where normally one person would do the work, ISS provides a two or three person 'hit squad'. This ensures that even a huge multinational has a local 'face'.

ISS's international growth comes partly from winning new contracts and partly from taking over existing cleaning companies that already have a customer base, staff, contacts and a recognized presence in the market.

Every interaction between the cleaner and the customer is vital to the success of the contract and the successful delivery of the services is more important than offering low prices for a service that the customer may not be able to rely on. Relationship management is key, therefore, especially as customers are often reluctant to change a service provider without good reason. Often contracts will be renewed for years. But if there are complaints the contract will be terminated very quickly and the news very rapidly goes through the industry, damaging the firm's reputation.

Good techniques, management systems and human resource processes are essential for dealing with people. Of course, service expectations and service delivery are affected very much by cultural considerations, so this is often a key consideration in maintaining service delivery consistency.

Question

1 Referring to the characteristics of services, how does culture affect delivery of cleaning services?

The components of the international product offer

In creating a suitable and acceptable product offer for international markets, it is necessary to examine first, what contributes to the 'total' product, and second, decide what might make the product acceptable to the international market. Kotler (2002) suggests three essential aspects of the international product offer, which should be considered by marketers in order to meet consumer needs and wants:

1 *Product benefits*: the elements that consumers perceive as meeting their needs and providing satisfaction through performance and image.

2 *Product attributes*: the elements most closely associated with the core product, such as features, specifications, styling, branding and packaging.

3 *The marketing support services*: the additional elements to the core product which contribute to providing satisfaction, and include delivery, after-sales service and guarantees.

These elements form the augmented product, an extended version of which is shown in Figure 8.2. Moving down and to the right of the diagram shows the elements that are relatively more difficult to standardize in different country markets.

Having introduced the concept of the total product offer, it is essential to evaluate each aspect of the product in terms of what benefits the consumer might expect to gain and how the offer will be perceived by consumers. This can be done by answering the following six questions for each market:

1 For what purpose has the product been developed and how would the product be used in that country?

2 What distinctive properties does the product have?

3 What benefits is the consumer expected to gain?

4 How is the product positioned and what image do consumers perceive it to have?

5 Which consumer segments of the total market are expected to buy it, on what occasions and for what purposes?

6 How does the product fit into the total market?

FIGURE 8.2 The three elements of the product or service

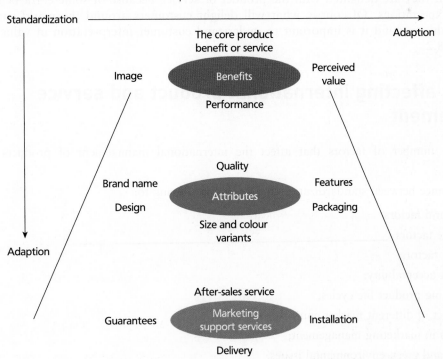

The main issue for a company about to commence marketing internationally is to assess the suitability of the existing products for international markets. As a minimum, a purchaser in an overseas market expects to have a clear explanation of how a product should be used, so the instructions on the domestic packaging usually have to be translated for international markets. Interestingly, one cosmetics marketer found that in some countries customers objected if their language was not printed first on multilingual packs.

The question is, however, to what extent the components of the total product offer can and should be adapted for international markets. In the case of a product where only the packaging needs to be changed, the effect on the overall cost is likely to be minimal, but if more fundamental changes to the product itself are required, because of differences in use or safety regulations, the higher cost might prove prohibitive for a small company. Such problems can be circumvented by taking an alternative market entry approach such as licensing or franchising.

Products, services and value propositions

The distinction between products and services is becoming increasingly blurred. In practice there are few 'pure' products and services and most offerings from firms are a combination of the two but to succeed it is essential they focus on value based marketing, which requires:

- a deep understanding of customer needs and decision-making processes;
- the formulation of value propositions that meet the needs of customers and create a differential advantage;
- the building of long term relationships with customers, so that loyalty and trust is built on the satisfaction and confidence in the supplier; and
- the necessary superior knowledge, skills, systems and marketing assets (including brand) to deliver superior value.

At this point it is worth noting that customer expectations are increasing. A value proposition that simply claims to offer a good quality product or reliable service no longer satisfies customers. Customers will be dissatisfied if they do not receive good quality products and service, but they will only be satisfied if they are delighted with the product or service because of some extra benefits that exceed their expectations. Of course, what will delight customers around the world varies considerably. With this in mind it is important to understand customer interpretation of value as shown in Illustration 8.2.

Factors affecting international product and service management

There are a number of factors that affect the international management of products and services including:

- the balance between standardization and adaptation owing to:
  - cultural factors
  - usage factors
  - legal factors;
- product acceptability;
- shortening product life cycles;
- the effect of different market entry methods;
- changes in marketing management;
- ethical and green environmental issues.

© Charles Polidano/Touch The Skies/Alamy

ILLUSTRATION 8.2

Flying low cost with frills or no frills

Over the last decade there has been a huge growth in low cost airlines around the world. The Irish airline Ryanair has been particularly successful. The no frills airlines followed a model pioneered in the US by South West Airlines. To do this the company cuts the 'included' service to the bone. Food on board has to be paid for, there is no seat allocation and seat bookings and check-in are made on the Internet and charged. Payment by most types of credit and debit cards incur extra costs. Destination airports are often not the closest airport to the flier's destination and appear to be chosen because landing charges are less. The compensation for 'no frills' is low prices.

The pricing model is based on yield management software that is designed to maximize the revenue achieved on each flight, by rewarding early customers with low prices and charging high prices to latecomers. This model contrasts with the full service airlines which have traditionally tried to maintain high ticket prices, even when running the plane half-full, and have focused on alliances with other airlines to ensure that long-haul passengers have a seamless service.

The chief executive of Ryanair, Michael O'Leary, is outspoken and combative and has attacked any moves by stakeholders to add costs to the business model, restrict the airline's activities or criticize its activities – governments putting green taxes on flights, airport authorities increasing landing charges and pressure groups criticizing the contribution to carbon emissions. Although the basic price of a flight might be very low, the cost to the customer can be much higher when taxes are taken into account. Moreover Ryanair adds other charges, for example, for payment by credit card and for carrying luggage over a certain weight.

Many competitors have followed the example and the no frills airlines have transformed regional air travel where distances are short.

Question

1 What are the challenges of running low-cost airlines and what will the critical success factors be in the future?

Towards standardization

The discussion in Chapter 6 on globalization leads to the conclusion that for the largest companies in the world the benefits of marketing standardized products are very significant indeed, but while firms may be prepared to invest heavily to achieve standardization, in practice, virtually all products must be adapted to some degree. The issue then becomes to what degree their industrial or consumer product or service should be standardized or adapted to the needs of the local market. Even the most obviously global companies achieve only partial standardization of products. For example, while Coca-Cola adopt a global standardized branding strategy, they modify the product for particular customer segments by offering Diet and Caffeine-Free Coca-Cola and altering the sweetness for different national tastes. McDonald's, too, alters its menu in different countries to cater for local tastes.

All firms must identify the benefit or satisfaction that the consumer recognizes and will purchase. This benefit must provide the basis upon which the company differentiates its products from those of its competitors. For a product such as the mobile phone, when it was first introduced, the competitive advantage was a technical breakthrough, the first portable long distance mobile voice communication, and so standardization of the core benefit was possible. As products were copied and developed so new sources of competitive advantage were sought for the mobile phone and this led to standardization of non-core elements of the augmented product, for example, additional functions such as texting, camera facilities, music and video downloading and so on. Fragmentation then occurs as manufacturers choose to

BAKER & McKENZIE

ILLUSTRATION 8.3

Courtesy of Baker & McKenzie

Working within the law in South America

Despite the drug cartels and natural disasters, there is optimism in Latin America. The banks are coping with the financial crisis and the middle class population is growing. Given the opportunities for development, especially in the oil and gas industry, international law firms are starting to seek opportunities, but their first steps are rather cautious. Bar rules are very protectionist and in most countries the law does not allow foreign firms to practise local law. Davies, Arnold and Cooper, the US–UK firm has just one office – in Caracas – staff spend much of their time on planes and in hotels trying to cover the region.

Baker & McKenzie is the exception. It moved into Latin America in the 1950s from its Chicago base and now has 500 lawyers practising across Latin America and has always emphasized its local operation. It is able to use this alongside its global network, especially its Asian practice, for example, acting on both political and legal issues on an oil and gas joint venture for a Chinese client in Argentina.

How do you get a foothold in the market? For international firms with no strong local base the answer is to use local partners to do the local work and deal with the bureaucracy and complex tax regimes across the region, while the international firm does the US, European and international law. Then they can gradually build up the local presence. Often it is specialist expertise, for example, Clyde and Co in investment and aviation, that provides the catalyst, or Davis, Arnold and Cooper's use of the relationships of its office in Spain and strength in insurance to give it a bridgehead in Mexico.

Question

1 What are the benefits and risks for a law firm entering the Latin American market?

References: E. Fennell (2010) 'Latin Americas market warms up', *The Times,* 2 September.

---

differentiate their product in different ways, such as design, greater functionality, a more robust product for rough use or producing a very basic phone that will appeal to specific segments. Also different business models such as 'Pay and Go' accelerated usage. Sometimes, however, the differentiation does not appeal. Vodafone withdrew a very basic phone soon after its introduction because of lack of demand.

The decision for most companies to standardize or adapt is based on a cost–benefit analysis of what they believe the implications of adaptation and standardization might be for revenue, profitability and market share. In normal circumstances, the cost of adaptation would be expected to be greater than the cost of successful standardization. Only if the needs and tastes identified in the target market segment are significantly different and substantial additional business will be generated, can the extra cost involved in making and delivering adapted products be justified. Illustration 8.3 shows how law firms need to adapt to the different practice requirements to gain a foothold in new markets.

While some companies are tempted to adopt a policy of adaptation in order to satisfy immediate demand, others believe that continual exposure to the standardized products will redefine customer needs and ultimately change their tastes, leading to greater market share in the longer term. Summarizing the advantages of product standardization, the company benefits from more rapid recovery of investment, easier organization and control of product management, the possibility to reduce costs through economies of scale and the experience effect throughout most of the firm's operations, such as production, advertising and distribution.

Product standardization is both encouraging and being encouraged by the globalization trends in markets, including:

1 markets are becoming more homogeneous;

2 there are more identifiable transnational consumer segments; and

3 there is an increase in the number of firms moving towards globalization, so forcing greater standardization throughout industry sectors.

There are some disadvantages of product standardization too; for example, market opportunities might be lost when it is impossible to match very specific local requirements. Some managers of local subsidiaries who are only expected to implement global or regional product policies can become demotivated and miss market opportunities if they are not given the opportunity to be entrepreneurial.

Greater standardization of products makes it easier for competitors to copy at ever-lower prices, but this leads inevitably to standardization within a product category so that consumers are unable to differentiate between competing products, with the result that a 'commodity market' is created. To counter this, competition is focusing increasingly upon the augmented product elements. In the family car market, for example, there is very little to choose between the performance, reliability and economy of the main competitors, including Ford, General Motors, Renault, Toyota, Peugeot and Nissan. Against this background, the promotion of individual cars focuses upon design, image, warranties and financing arrangements and rather less on individual performance comparisons. The industry is also continually developing products for subsegments, examples being the Smart car, Toyota Prius hybrid energy source car and sports utility vehicles.

Reasons for adaptation of the product

In some instances, product standardization may not be possible due to environmental constraints either through mandatory legislation, because of such reasons as differences in electrical systems, legal standards, safety requirements or product liability, or because the firm believes that the product appeal can be increased in a particular market by addressing cultural and usage factors.

Cultural factors   Certain products and services, such as computers and airline flights, are not culturally sensitive as the benefits they offer are valued internationally. Here the adaptation is peripheral to the main benefit, for example, translation of instructions into different languages. Other products and services are more culturally sensitive and might need to be adapted more substantially. Food is a particularly difficult area for standardization, as the preparation and eating of food are often embedded in the history, religion and/or culture of the country. This presents specific problems for fast food firms, for example, where the main ingredients of McDonald's and Burger King, beef and pork, prove unacceptable to many potential customers, and the necessary ingredients for fast food, such as the specific type of wheat for pizza bases, suitable chicken and mozzarella cheese are unavailable or are of variable quality in certain countries.

One example of service development is Islamic banking, which for many years was regarded as a small niche activity. However, the growing sense of religious identity in the Muslim world together with the significant increase in construction in the Middle East has led to rapid growth in the sector, which by 2006 was estimated to be worth US$1000 billion and forecast to treble in the following five years (Ringshaw 2006).

Changes are taking place in product acceptance however. For example, fashion is becoming increasingly globalized and the traditional domination of the fashion industry by Western designers is gradually being broken down. Denim jeans infiltrated countries like India which had hitherto only accepted traditional dress. Some people believe that the erosion of the country's traditional heritage and culture, particularly by the media and MNE advertising, is unethical and should be resisted. Others suggest that larger countries such as India and China simply take those international products which serve a particular need and ignore other global products.

Usage factors   The same product might be used in quite different ways in different markets, partly due to the culture of the country, but also due to the geographical factors of climate and terrain. Unilever and Procter & Gamble have a large variety of products adapted and branded for different markets because of the different ways products are used. For example, French people wash clothes in scalding hot water, while the Australians tend to use cold water. Most Europeans use front-loading washing machines, whereas the French use top-loaders. Equipment supplied to armies fighting in unfamiliar and inhospitable climates has often proved ineffective.

Honda found that when they first introduced motorcycles into the US they were unreliable and frequently broke down. Whereas Japanese riders were only able to travel short distances, American riders were used to riding the bikes over longer distances and much rougher terrain. Honda quickly realized, however, that Americans were fascinated by their 50cc bikes and promoted them instead. Honda quickly became established and were able to introduce better performing larger bikes too.

Legal standards The standardization of products and services can be significantly affected by legislation. Legal standards are often very country-specific, sometimes because obscure laws have been left unchanged for decades. There have been considerable problems for the European Union in attempting to harmonize standards during the creation of the single market and it took a number of years to achieve agreement on relatively simple products, such as confectionery, jam and sausage.

Lack of precise, reliable, understandable and universally accepted scientific information, for example in food safety (beef, lamb and chicken), serves only to make it more difficult to achieve a satisfactory industry standard. Pharmaceutical companies experience problems in introducing products into different markets, because individual governments have differing standards of public health and approaches to healthcare. Many countries insist that they carry out their own supervised clinical testing on all drugs prior to the products being available on the market and, for example, the instructions and contraindications might need to be changed and agreed with health authorities locally.

Product liability In the US, over the past few years there has been a considerable increase in litigation, with lawyers seeking clients on a no win–no fee basis. For marketers, particularly those selling potentially life-threatening products such as pharmaceuticals and cars, this demands much greater caution when introducing standard products based on the home country specification into these markets. In extreme circumstances litigation can lead to huge financial settlements, for example in cases related to the oil, tobacco and asbestos industries.

Product acceptability

Consumers generally are becoming much more discerning and have greater expectations of all the elements of the augmented product. The manufacturer must take responsibility for controlling the pre- and post-purchase servicing and warranties provided by independent distributors and retailers. The packaging, branding and trademark decisions are becoming increasingly important because the global social media no longer allows mistakes and failures to go unpublicized.

Consumers, too, have different perceptions of the value and satisfaction of products and their view of what is acceptable will vary considerably from country to country. The product usage, production process or service offered may not fit with the culture and environment of the country and the product or service may not be acceptable for its intended use. Certain healthcare services, such as abortion, gambling, banking products and alcohol are unacceptable to some cultures.

Shortening product life cycles

The merging of markets through increasing globalization is leading to greater concentration of powerful suppliers who have the resources to rapidly copy a competitor's product or develop their own products to exploit a new market opportunity. The increasing pace of technology means that a technical lead in a product is not likely to be held for very long, as competitors catch up quickly. This means that product life cycles are becoming shorter and improvements are introduced more frequently. To this must be added the much higher cost of research, development and commercialization of new products, which places much greater pressures on the firm to distribute the new product throughout world markets as quickly and widely as possible in order to achieve a high return on research and development investment before new products are introduced.

Franchising, joint ventures and alliances

The pressure to exploit new technology and products as quickly and widely as possible has encouraged the rapid expansion of more creative and cost-effective ways of achieving cooperation in research, development and distribution, such as franchising, joint ventures and strategic alliances. As discussed in the previous chapter, while these market entry methods allow less control than total ownership, they do enable firms to develop a wider sphere of activity than they could do alone. Of course, the challenge is to find partners with truly complementary expertise, knowledge and capability.

Marketing management

These trends have led to significant changes in the way that marketing management operates, allowing a more creative approach to be adopted in developing product policy. First, there are a wider range of options available in international marketing management, particularly through innovation and integration of the marketing mix elements which will be discussed later in this book. Second, there have been significant improvements in the tools available for performance measurement, real time data analysis and planning. Third, there are more insightful and widely available sources of information through online marketing research, involving customers, suppliers and the web community in product and service evaluation and innovations, which allow greater power for global brand management. It must be pointed out that success in using these tools requires managers to be more flexible in redefining niche segments and creative in innovating in all areas of the marketing mix. Fourth, with improved internal and external networking, new product development can become much more integrated within the firm's strategies and be capable of more satisfactorily meeting customer needs through the management of supply chain relationships.

Green environmental issues

By way of contrast, unscrupulous companies have exploited the different legal controls and lower risks of litigation by sending for disposal hazardous products, such as chemical waste, to less developed countries with lower standards. However, this practice is being increasingly challenged by international pressure groups and is backed up in the US courts, which have the power to control the actions of US subsidiaries abroad.

Concern for environmental issues is becoming greater in many countries and has considerable implications for product policies, but the nature, patterns and strength of interest vary considerably from country to country.

Howard (1998) highlights a number of things that are making it necessary for firms to pay more attention to global green environmental concerns. These are:

- greater public awareness following the publicity given to environmental disasters, such as floods and fires in Indonesia and Thailand, oil spill in the Gulf of Mexico, deforestation of the rain forest, water pollution and reduction in biodiversity;
- greater national and local regulation of actions which are likely to affect the environment;
- greater stakeholder awareness of MNE activity through better global communications;
- greater expectations that MNEs will be more responsive because of their need to preserve a good image of corporate citizenship;
- increasing cross-border concerns being shown, with the effect that more powerful countries can exert pressure and influence on MNE activities wherever they are.

Against this background MNEs must respond in an appropriate way to the global and local concerns by taking a more comprehensive approach to dealing with environmental issues by anticipating and, where appropriate, initiating changes. They must also evaluate and manage proactively all the effects on the environment of their operations.

Malagasy is a gourmet food company that sells high-quality products to supermarkets. It has partners in Madagascar that produce and package the chocolate, nuts, spices and honey it uses. It is a social enterprise that balances its commercial aims with social and economic objectives. The company realized that with many firms 95 per cent of the final value of a chocolate bar is created outside the country from which the chocolate ingredients originate. However, more value can be retained in the country where the ingredients originated if the finished product is made and packaged in that country – and that is what Malagasy do (Stone 2006).

A number of companies have set corporate strategies which address these issues. Sony for example incorporate environmental considerations into the planning of every product, and Ford has adopted the environmental standard, ISO4001 worldwide.

MANAGEMENT CHALLENGE 8.1

Apple superfactories not so super

Many of the technological devices used around the world are made in huge quantities in super-factories mainly in China, but also in Taiwan, Singapore, the Philippines, Malaysia, Thailand, the Czech Republic and the US. The factories are capable of assembling a wide variety of devices and work on contracts for companies such as Apple. The Taiwanese company, Foxconn, is one of Apple's biggest suppliers. The superfactories employ as many as 300 000 workers, who live in self contained cities. The workers, who are paid as low as $130 per month, sleep in corporate dormitories. Management is strict, given the need to maintain low production costs to avoid the loss of new contracts. As well as the work being repetitive and boring the conditions are so poor and there is repeated criticism that Apple uses factories that abuse workers. The problem for Apple is that they have become so dependent on these factories for supplies that they have limited power to intervene if they are to avoid letting down their customers.

- In 2008 25 children were discovered working at factories that supply Apple.
- A Foxconn employee committed suicide after being accused of stealing an Apple prototype and being beaten by security staff.
- An Apple report admitted that at least 55 out of 102 factories that produce its goods ignored Apple's rule that staff could not work more than 60 hours per week.
- Only 65 per cent of factories were paying their staff correct wages and benefits and 24 factories did not even pay China's minimum wage (800 yuan per month).

Question

1 How can a high profile marketing company manage insatiable customer demand as well as ethical concerns?

References: M. Moore (2010) 'Apple admits using child labour', *Daily Telegraph*, 27 February. (2010) 'How much do you really want an iPad', *The Observer*, 30 May.

The goal is to achieve environmental excellence with firms such as The Body Shop, 3M, British Telecom, Johnson Matthey, Merck, Norsk Hydro and Rank Xerox taking a strategic approach rather than making *ad hoc* decisions. There are many problems in building environmental considerations into corporate strategy, including the uncertainties of the science, for example different views on global warming, and the difficulty of deciding on appropriate action because replacement processes or chemicals often give rise to new problems. Management Challenge 8.1 shows how working conditions in superfactories for producing the latest gadgets can be highly questionable, at best.

Product policy

Having considered the factors which underpin the development of an international product portfolio, the next steps are to look first at the suitability of the existing products before embarking on the development of new or modified products. The decision about which products should be included in the range to be marketed internationally is determined by several factors:

- the company's overall objectives in terms of growth and profits;
- the experience, philosophies and attitude of the company to international development, and which of the company's financial and managerial resources will be allocated to international marketing;
- the characteristics of the markets, such as the economic development and the barriers to trade of the firm's domestic and host countries;

ILLUSTRATION 8.4

© Thomas Polen, iStockphoto.com

Fly tipping a jet

Recycling is a global business but is not always high tech. In 2004 Ryanair sold an old Boeing 737-200 to Autodirect Aviation in the US, which sold it to Diversified Aero Services in Miami, which contracted two UK firms to dismantle it. Many years later a Scottish local authority environmental officer spotted a pile of broken seats, broken fuselage, oxygen masks and in-flight magazines fly tipped alongside the docks, simply abandoned.

The problem is that aircraft manufacturers use ever more complex composite materials to increase strength and reduce weight to improve fuel efficiency. These materials contain carbon fibres and nasty chemicals to bond them together and these do not break down in the environment and are almost impossible to re-use. The manufacturing processes also cause considerable waste. As a result it all usually goes to landfill. There are few regulations for the disposal of jets and they are often parked in the US desert for years, after being stripped of the most valuable parts, such as the engine components, electronics and aluminium hull. In the next 20 years 6500 planes will be scrapped and there will be increasing pressure on Boeing and Airbus and their suppliers to work out how to recycle the materials from worn out planes and make better use of the waste created during manufacture.

Question

1 Who should be responsible for disposing of or recycling difficult-to-reuse materials?

References: M. Harris, (2010) 'Grounded: The jet fly tippers', *Sunday Times*, 29 August.

- the requirements, expectations and attitudes of the consumers in the market;
- the products and services themselves, their attributes, appeal and perceived values (their positioning), the stage that they are at in the life cycle and economies of scale;
- the ease of distributing and selling them;
- the support the products require from other elements of the marketing mix and after-sales services;
- environmental constraints (such as legal or political factors) which must be overcome;
- the level of risk that the company is prepared to take.

Illustration 8.4 shows how even at the end of the life of a product its disposal should be a matter of concern.

Product strategies

Against the background of so many variables, it is inevitable that companies adopt a very wide range of product strategies in international markets. In formulating product policies, Mesdag (1985) postulated that a company has three basic choices:

SWYG   Sell What You have Got.

SWAB   Sell What people Actually Buy.

GLOB   Sell the same thing GLOBally disregarding national frontiers.

All three strategies have been used for a long time. Heinz, Mars, Heineken and Johnnie Walker have been international brands for decades using global product and brand strategies to enable them to clearly position their products as global brands. The Danes have long dominated the UK bacon market by following a SWAB strategy as have the French in their marketing of Cheddar cheese in the UK. The disadvantage of the SWAB strategy is that it is only possible to penetrate one market at a time. It may be also difficult to compete with local firms on their own terms. Furthermore, it is sometimes difficult for a foreign company to establish credibility as a supplier of products which have a strong domestic demand; for example, Suntory of Japan made good whisky but could not market it in the UK so it acquired Morrison Boxmore Distillers, which produces distinctively Scottish single malt whisky brands.

The SWAB approach is the classic differentiated approach, but while it is responsive to market needs it does make considerable demands on the firm's development, manufacturing, logistics and financial resources and is often impractical for these reasons.

SWYG are the most common form of export strategies, but they are also the most common reason for failure. The key objective for most firms following such strategies is to fill production lines at home rather than meet a market need, but by concentrating only on a few markets, many companies do successfully implement this kind of strategy. Mesdag argues also that some of the most successful global products started off as domestic products with a SWYG strategy, for example pizza, hamburgers and yoghurt. Success has been the result of the company's ability to meet new international emerging demand for the convenience of fast foods. The products may not necessarily be formulated identically across markets but they appeal to a pan-regional or global need and can therefore be positioned as cross-frontier brands. The success of the strategy has been based on identifying and meeting the needs of transnational customer segments. Heineken, the Dutch brewing firm, took over Egypt's only brewery, Al Harham Beverages, in 2002 and in so doing acquired Fayrouz, a fruit flavoured non-alcoholic malt drink popular in Egypt and certified Halal by Al Azhar, a leading Sunni Islam religious institution. Heineken then had the opportunity to market Fayrouz in the Indian subcontinent and to Muslims in the UK, Germany, Netherlands and France.

Keegan and Green (2011) has highlighted the key aspects of international marketing strategy as a combination of standardization or adaptation of product and promotion elements of the mix, and offers five alternative and more specific approaches to product policy.

One product, one message worldwide These are the truly global brands. Since the 1920s, Coca-Cola have adopted a global approach, which has allowed them to make enormous cost savings and benefit from continual reinforcement of the same message. While a number of writers have argued that this will be the strategy adopted for many products in the future, in practice only a handful of products might claim to have achieved this already. A number of firms have tried this and failed.

Product extension, promotion adaptation While the product stays the same, this strategy allows for the adaptation of the promotional effort to target either new customer segments or appeal to the particular tastes of individual countries; for example, Yoplait yoghurt attempts to capture the mood of the country in its various television adverts.

Product adaptation, promotion extension This strategy is used if a promotional campaign has achieved international appeal, but the product needs to be adapted because of the local needs. Many suppliers of capital goods, IT management and consultancy, promote the idea of providing technical solutions rather than selling industrial plants or computer hardware; and IBM have used 'Solutions for a small planet'.

Dual adaptation By adapting both products and promotion for each market, the firm is adopting a totally differentiated approach. This strategy is often adopted by firms when one of the previous three strategies has failed, but particularly if the firm is not in a leadership position and, instead, must react to the market or follow the competitors. This is closest to a multidomestic strategy.

Product invention Product invention is adopted by firms, usually from advanced nations, who are supplying products to less well-developed countries. Products are specifically developed to meet the needs of the individual markets. After watching a programme on TV about AIDS in Africa, Trevor Bayliss invented the clockwork radio to help the news to be spread to areas which did not have electricity and could not afford batteries. The radios were made by disabled staff by BayGen in South Africa.

Managing products across borders

The product life cycle

In the domestic market models such as the product life cycle and Boston Consulting Group's portfolio matrix are used to manage a portfolio of products. The concepts can be applied in international markets to the management of a product, brand or product range across a portfolio of countries.

The life cycle concept is used as a model for considering the implications for marketing management of a product passing through the stages of introduction, growth, maturity and decline, and can be applied to international marketing.

The international product life cycle suggests that products in international markets can have consecutive 'lives' in different countries. Soon after the product was launched in its domestic market it was introduced into another developed country, A. Later it was introduced to other developed and newly industrialized countries, B and C, and only recently to a less developed country, D. In the domestic market and country A, a replacement product is required, while considerable growth is still possible in the other countries. This illustrates the dilemma that firms often face: they must decide how to allocate scarce resources between product and market development (Figure 8.3).

In some high technology markets it is now possible to accurately predict when new technology will force a new product's introduction. As a result it is now necessary for the product to be project managed

FIGURE 8.3 The international product cycle

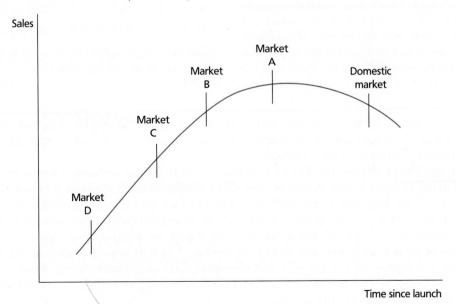

Courtesey of Gillette

ILLUSTRATION 8.5

Gillette planning a close shave

In the late 1970s and 1980s the change to disposable razors by many consumers in the US and Europe meant that shaving products appeared to be turning into a commodity market. For Gillette, which had a 65 per cent share of this market, this was extremely serious. Gillette in the US cut advertising by a quarter and appeared to have almost given up on razors.

In Europe, however, Gillette started to spend on a pan-European campaign featuring the slogan 'Gillette – the best a man can get' to promote the top-of-the-range Contour Plus brand, and this led to a gain in market share and an increase in margins.

Gillette's mission statement over the past 25 years has been 'There is a better way to shave and we will find it', and Sensor, launched in 1989, spearheaded Gillette's fight back. Sensor was shown to be significantly better than anything else on the market and user tests showed that 80 per cent of men who tried it kept on using it. Gillette decided to centralize its marketing by combining the European and US sections into one group, headed by the previous European head, to ensure an effective launch of Sensor. Previously, marketing had been carried out by brand managers in each local country.

Sensor helped Gillette to a 70 per cent share of the world razor market, but by 1997 the sales growth was flattening, signifying the need for a new product. The successor, Mach 3, cost well over US$1 billion to develop but sold at a premium of 25–35 per cent over the price of Sensor, which Gillette retained as it does not withdraw older products.

The competition started to fight back: Schick, recently taken over by Energiser, using the Wilkinson Sword brand in some markets with its four-blade Quattro, followed by Schick Hydro, and a South Korean company, Dorco, which developed a Mach 3 competitor with prices 30 per cent cheaper than Gillette. Men and women do not shave more often, so the only way to increase sales and profits is to increase prices in developed countries, persuade customers to buy more products and win new customers in emerging markets. The Fusion range was the last new product to be introduced before Procter and Gamble bought Gillette in 2005. Five years passed before the Fusion ProGlide Series became the first introduction under P&G. With its five blade razor and range of skincare products, Gillette's aim was to 'address every aspect of interaction with hair and skin' claiming in tests involving 30 000 men there was a 2:1 preference for ProGlide over Fusion. Gillette sells in over 75 countries.

Questions

1 How should Gillette keep its technological lead?

2 Will technology be the only factor in its future success in the global shaving market?

for a limited and specific lifetime to ensure that by the end of its life the product has been profitable, recouped the initial investment and a replacement new innovation is ready for launch. Illustration 8.5 shows how Gillette is addressing this situation.

The most significant change for life cycle models is that global communications lead to global companies having to launch new products into many markets simultaneously to meet customer expectations, and so the sequential approach to marketing and manufacturing that is encapsulated in the original model applies less frequently. However, as we established earlier, not all companies operating internationally are global corporations, nor based on leading edge technology and it is therefore important not to ignore the model altogether. The concept of phases in the life cycle is still useful for a company that is not in a fast-changing market, perhaps simply exporting specialist engineering components and tools from an advanced economy or rolling out a service into new country markets as the opportunity arises.

On balance, therefore, although the validity of the product life cycle has at various times been attacked by a variety of writers, it does have a role to play for certain types of company insofar as it is a model that provides a framework for thinking in detail about product policy, new product development, product introduction and product elimination.

Product portfolio analysis

The use of portfolio approaches in international product management centres around the Boston Consulting Group's (BCG) Growth–Share Matrix, the General Electric/McKinsey Screen and the Arthur D. Little Business Profile Matrix. They are designed primarily to clarify the current strategic position of a company, its products and those of its competitors, and to help identify any future strategic options.

The complexity of the analysis increases as the competitive positions occupied by a product and the intensity of competition differ significantly from one market to another. Comparing the strength of a portfolio across a variety of markets becomes difficult as the analytical base constantly changes. For these reasons, the BCG matrix, for example, might be based on one product range or on one brand with the circles in the matrices representing country sales instead of different product sales, as shown in Figure 8.4. This then provides a basis for analyzing the current international product portfolio, assessing competitors' product/market strengths and forecasting the likely development of future portfolios both for itself and its competitors. The key decisions will be whether to use cash generated in 'cash cow' countries to maintain the position by introducing new products or to build positions in emerging markets (stars and question marks) where growth will be higher.

FIGURE 8.4 The portfolio approach to strategic analysis (BCG matrix)

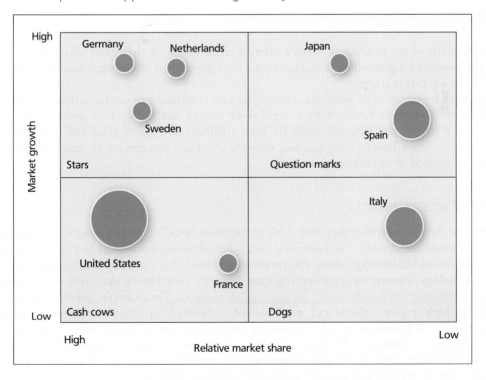

Introduction and elimination activities

While the major focus of product policy is upon new product and service development, the increased pace of the activity has a number of consequences for product management at both ends of the product life cycle. The factors that need to be taken into account in managing the product portfolio are:

- the firm's objectives;
- the profitability of the company's existing range of products and services;
- the stage in the life cycle that the products and services have reached;
- the manufacturing and service delivery capacity available;
- the likely receptiveness of the market to the new product or service; and
- the competitive structure of the market.

These factors have a number of implications for the product policy. Too many product and service introductions can risk overburdening the firm's marketing system. There is a constant need for a regular review of the range and for elimination decisions to be made where a product or service is either in its decline stage or simply failing to generate sufficient profit. The international perspective, however, means that decision-making is more difficult, since a product may be manufactured principally in a plant in one country but exported to many countries, be a 'cash cow' in one market and a 'dog' in another. Careful analysis is therefore needed before the product elimination decision is taken. The identification of overlaps in the product range or poor performance of specific products may necessitate elimination of products if they are in the declining stage of the product life cycle, have been duplicated or have been replaced by a newer product.

The complexity of managing a wide portfolio of products is shown in the Unilever case study at the end of Chapter 6 and it raises some fundamental issues about the product strategy alternatives.

Image, branding and positioning

Of all the elements of the product or service offer, it is the image of the brand which is the most visible and it is the perceived value which consumers attach to this that is the central factor in positioning the products in the various markets.

The image and reputation of products, companies and countries can confer different values to consumers in different countries. Research by a number of writers has shown that products from particular countries have a stereotyped national image for such attributes as quality, price and reliability. Individual corporate brands either benefit from positive country of origin perceptions or must overcome negative perceptions to succeed in international markets.

Country of origin effects

Buyers evaluate the products that they may wish to purchase based on their assessment of intrinsic – taste, design, performance and quality – and extrinsic cues – brand names, packaging and country of origin.

Where the buyers' knowledge about the product is limited, for example because they do not understand the technology, country of origin perceptions influence their buying decisions. The consumers' perceptions of companies are usually based on national stereotypes. For example, Japanese products tend to be regarded as high quality, reliable and 'miniaturized', whereas US products are seen as big and 'brash'. German products are perceived as well engineered and of high specification, whereas products from developing countries are often seen by Western consumers as low quality, unreliable, inexpensive and usually copies of products from developed countries. This was the perception of Japanese products some decades ago, and shows that it is possible to change consumer attitudes.

There are significant differences between countries in the willingness of consumers to buy locally produced products. Usually this appears to be related to the feeling of nationalism that exists in the country at the particular time the assessment is made. As countries develop there is often a greater satisfaction with home produced products and services,

The country of origin effect does extend further. For example, the stereotyping relates just as much to developed countries. For example, there are strong associations between countries and the products that they are known for: Italy and pizza and Germany and machine tools. Overcoming these stereotypes is often the first challenge for international marketers who must prove that their product does not reinforce negative stereotypes. This is particularly important as customers become more knowledgeable. For example, many new car buyers know where their car has been designed and manufactured as well as the country of origin of the brand. Increasingly, of course, the MNE's headquarters, the brand's perceived 'home', the location of product design and places of manufacture may all be in different countries. Many MNEs such as Nike are marketing, not manufacturing companies and source products from many countries. Their brand becomes the 'badge of quality' that overlays the country of origin effect.

Product image: As we have already emphasized, product image is one of the most powerful points of differentiation for consumers. The aspirational and achiever groups of purchasers wish to belong to particular worldwide customer segments and are keen to purchase products associated with that group. This is a major buying factor that has driven the sales of Apple's iPhones, iPods and iPads. An interesting example of this is that the sales of luxury goods remained buoyant during recent recessions due to increased sales to emerging countries as the 'new' rich sought to buy similar products and services to the 'old' rich.

Company image is becoming increasingly important in creating a central theme running through diverse product ranges. It reinforces the vision and the values of the company, which can be recognized by employees and customers alike. For this reason many companies have spent considerable effort and resources on controlling and enhancing the corporate identity through consistent style and communications, discussed in more detail in Chapter 9.

Image can be equally important at the other end of the product spectrum to luxury goods. Aldi (Germany), Netto (Denmark) and Lidl (Sweden) use a no-frills approach to retailing by reinforcing their message of low prices with simple decor, warehouse-type displays and single colour understated packaging.

The image of a company also plays a vital role in business-to-business marketing, for example, when quoting for international capital projects. Decisions are likely to be made on the grounds of the perceived reputation of the company as, without a strong international presence, it can be quite difficult to break into a small elite circle of international companies, even if very low prices are quoted.

Connections too can be important. Reconstruction projects following wars are extremely lucrative and are usually awarded to global companies, such as the Halliburton group which has strong political connections in the US – it was once led by Vice President Dick Cheney.

International branding

The image and reputation of an organization and its products and services are increasingly important differentiators from competitors' offers in international markets and the management of international branding is vital in adding value. The role of branding, important as it is in domestic markets, takes on an additional dimension in international markets as it is the most visible of the firm's activities particularly for global companies, as we discussed in Chapter 6. Brands allow customers to identify products or services which will 'guarantee' satisfaction by providing specific benefits, such as performance, price, quality or status. Brands have the potential to add value to the organization by providing the following benefits:

Price premium: They should allow higher prices to be charged than for products that have an equivalent specification but no brand.

Higher volumes: Alternatively branded products can generate higher volumes than non-branded products if they are priced at market rates, rather than at a premium.

Lower costs: Higher volumes should lead to cost reduction from the economies of scale and the experience effect, so improving competitiveness.

Better utilization of assets: The predictably high level of sales should lead brand managers to make effective use of assets such as equipment, the supply chain and distribution channels.

The constituents of the brand can include both tangible benefits, such as quality and reliability, and intangible benefits which may bring out a whole range of feelings, such as status, being fashionable or possessing good judgement by purchasing a particular brand. Very young children are now fully aware of which fashion label is 'cool' at the moment and advertisers are well aware of the effects of 'pester power' on all the family purchasing decisions.

Brand categories

Three brands categories are identified (Doyle 2000):

1 *Attribute brands* are created around the functional product or service attributes, such as quality, specification and performance, to build confidence among customers in situations where it is difficult for them to evaluate the difference between competitive products. The brand provides a 'guarantee'. Examples include Volvo for safety, Wal-Mart for everyday low prices and Intel for computer processing.

2 *Aspirational brands* create images in the minds of customers about the type of people who purchase the brand and convey the standards and values that the brand is associated with. Such brands do not simply deliver the customer's functional requirements of the products and services, such as high specification and quality, but also recognize the customer's status, recognition and esteem that can be associated with the brand. Examples include Ferrari, Rolex and high fashion.

3 *Experience brands* focus on a shared philosophy between the customer and brand and on shared associations and emotions, but not necessarily on claims of superiority. Examples include Nike, Virgin and Skoda.

The appeal of these different types of brand varies according to the context of the purchasing decision. In luxury product markets aspirational brands are likely to be most successful, whereas in consumer markets, where there is little to distinguish between the attributes and performance of products, experience branding is more appropriate. Attribute branding would be more appropriate in business-to-business markets where the purchasing process should be more rational, objective and based on specifications.

In global markets, too, because of different culture, customer expectations and market sophistication, the appeal of a particular branding approach might be more relevant for a similar product. For example, in some cultures, such as in Germany, the attributes, functionality and specification may be more important, whereas in others, such as emerging markets, aspirational branding might be more appealing.

The brand value equation (Figure 8.5) draws attention to the offer to consumers of the intangible benefits that the brand adds over and above the tangible, functional benefits of a commoditized product or service. The challenge for international branding, of course, is to what extent the intangible benefits from branded products and services vary between countries, cultures and individuals.

Apple products are the 'must haves' for the teenage and young adult generation not just because of their functionality and design but also because of peer pressure.

FIGURE 8.5 The brand value equation

Tangible and intangible benefits

$$\text{Brand value} = \frac{\text{Benefits received by customers}}{\text{Costs to customer of brand purchases}}$$

Total cost of ownership

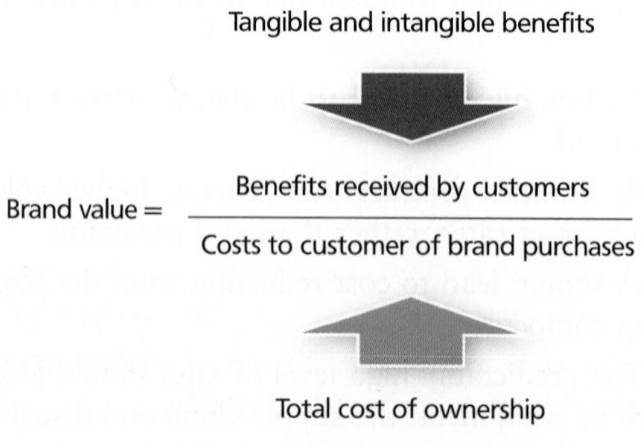

Rappa and Hirsh (2007) found that superb service was the indispensable ingredient of successful high-end brands and identified four principles to deliver customer satisfaction:

- Create a customer-centred culture.
- Use a rigorous staff selection process.
- Constantly retrain employees.
- Systematically measure and reward customer-centric behaviour.

Tangible and intangible benefits must also be valued against the background of the total cost of ownership of the branded product by the customer. The total cost of ownership and the tangible and intangible benefits are accrued over the lifetime of the product. For example, car ownership offers different benefits and costs in different markets, especially when considering the longer-term implications of, for example, warranty and servicing costs, car resale value and changing car fashions. Brand strength for cars is, to some extent, determined by the second-hand car values, with car marques such as BMW and Mercedes holding their value exceptionally well and some cars, such as Ferrari, even increasing in value.

Brand value

It has been suggested that the strongest brands convey a core value to all their customers by the associations that are made with their name. By adding '-ness' to the brand names consumers instantly associate values which are globally recognized – 'Pradaness', from 'Gucciness', and 'Appleness' from 'Sonyness'. Traditionally the great brands (Table 8.1) have achieved their global status through high levels of investment and consistent management across their country markets of the dimensions used to value the brand over a long period of time. Usually the investment includes a large commitment to advertising but other factors, such as understanding their customers' needs and wants, totally consistent quality, reliability and continuous innovation are just as important to achieve widespread customer loyalty and recommendations. To illustrate this point the value of the Google (+36%) and Apple (+37%) brands showed the highest increase, whereas the Toyota brand decreased by 16 per cent due to the recalls and the Nokia brand decreased by 15 per cent due to increased competition.

Brand valuation is inevitably subjective to some degree, but the dimensions indicated in Figure 8.6 suggest that building the brand requires dedicated management of the complete marketing mix across the various markets, and there is evidence of this in all the successful brands. Brands can, of course, also decline in value from time to time due, for example, to failure to understand changing customer expectations (some fast food brands), to inappropriate brand stretching (a number of the top fashion brands), to failure to respond to market problems (banks and financial institutions) or product and service problems (Toyota) or failure to respond to new competition (formerly state-owned airlines and telecoms businesses and many of the developed world car manufacturers at some point in their recent history).

Branding strategies

Branding strategies and the brand portfolio The first decision is to choose between the alternative branding strategies that can be applied to the brand portfolio. The alternatives are:

- *Umbrella brands*: occurs when one brand supports several products, as is the case with Philips electrical products.
- *Product brands*: occur when, for example, Unilever, Procter & Gamble and pharmaceutical firms give each product a unique and distinctive brand.
- *Line brands*: occur where a company has a number of complementary products sharing the same brand concept. L'Oréal sells haircare products under the Studio Line of products.
- *Range brands*: are similar to Line brands but include a broader range of products. Heinz uses Weight watchers and Nestlé uses Findus for frozen foods.

Table 8.1 The best global brands 2010

Rank	Previous Rank	Brand	Country of Origin	Brand Value ($bn)
1	1	Coca-cola	United States	70.5
2	2	IBM	United States	64.7
3	3	Microsoft	United States	60.9
4	7	Google	United States	43.6
5	4	General Electric	United States	42.8
6	6	McDonald's	United States	33.6
7	9	Intel	United States	32.0
8	5	Nokia	Finland	29.5
9	10	Disney	United States	28.7
10	11	Hewlett-Packard	United States	26.9
11	8	Toyota	Japan	26.2
12	12	Mercedes Benz	Germany	25.2
13	13	Gillette	United States	23.3
14	14	Cisco	United States	23.2
15	15	BMW	Germany	22.3
16	16	Louis Vuitton	France	21.9
17	20	Apple	United States	21.1
18	17	Marlbro	United States	20.0
19	19	Samsung	South Korea	19.5
20	18	Honda	Japan	18.5
21	21	H&M	Sweden	16.1
22	24	Oracle	United States	14.9
23	23	Pepsi	United States	14.1
24	22	American Express	United States	13.9
25	26	Nike	United States	13.7
26	27	SAP	Germany	12.8
27	25	Nestlé	Switzerland	12.7
28	28	Ikea	Sweden	12.5
29	37	J.P. Morgan	United States	12.3
30	30	Budweiser	United States	12.2

Source: Adapted from Best Global Brands 2010, accessed at: www.interbrand.com on 2 December 2010.

- *Endorsing brands*: is a weaker association of a corporate name with a product brand name and is often used after acquisition. Over time, Nestlé has gradually increased the size of 'Nestlé' on the packaging of its acquired brands, such as Kit-Kat. This may be one step towards umbrella branding.

- *Source brands*: occur where products are double branded with a corporate or range name and a product name, for example, Ford Mondeo.

Essentially the decision about which strategy to use is determined by whether the benefits of a shared identity outweigh the importance of differentiation between the individual product brands.

A further branding strategy, private branding, is the practice of supplying products to a third party for sale under their brand name. The two South Korean companies, Samsung and LG, achieved success initially largely by being original equipment manufacturers (OEM), but have rapidly developed internationally to the point where they now have high shares of certain product categories by building their own brands. Management Challenge 8.2 shows that Taiwanese manufacturer HTC has embarked on a similar strategy.

Private branding is used widely in retailing and as the major retailers become more powerful, so the private brand share of the market has increased significantly, especially during times of recession. This is because the consumers perceive private brands as providing value for money, and this has been supported as retailers have promoted their own label products and continually improved the quality too.

Brand piracy

One of the most difficult challenges for brand management is dealing with brand piracy. Research suggests that the problem of forgery of famous brand names is increasing, and many but by no means all fake products have been found to originate in developing countries and in Asia. It is important to recognize the differences between the ways in which forgery takes place. Kaitiki (1981) identifies:

- *Outright piracy*: in which a product is in the same form and uses the same trademark as the original but is false.

- *Reverse engineering*: in which the original product is stripped down, copied and then undersold to the original manufacturer, particularly in the electronics industry.

- *Counterfeiting*: in which the product quality has been altered but the same trademark appears on the label. Benetton, Levi Strauss and LaCoste have all been victims.

- *Passing off*: involves modifying the product but retaining a trademark which is similar in appearance, phonetic quality or meaning – for example Coalgate for Colgate and Del Mundo for Del Monte.

- *Wholesale infringement*: is the questionable registration of the names of famous brands overseas rather than the introduction of fake products. This might be considered brand piracy but it is entirely within the law. This has been very prevalent in e-business with the registration of dotcom sites by individuals hoping to sell the site later, at substantial profit, to the famous name.

There is a vast trade in pirated brands and copied products. It has been estimated that 90 per cent of the software used in India and China is counterfeit. However, some cultures do not accept that individuals should gain from ideas which should benefit everyone, so there are substantial differences in the

FIGURE 8.6 Brand Valuation

The most basic criteria for brand evaluation include:

- title to the brand has to be clear and separately disposable from the rest of the business.

- the value has to be substantial and long term, based on separately identifiable earnings that have to be in excess of those achieved by unbranded products.

MANAGEMENT CHALLENGE 8.2

HTC – the next global mobile brand?

HTC was founded in 1997 as a contract manufacturer of mobile handsets, including personal digital assistants (PDAs) for Compac. It followed a Taiwanese model of manufacturing products for other companies and HTC was largely unknown outside the industry. However, in 2002 Microsoft awarded HTC a contract to supply smartphones and quickly it became the top producer of Windows phones, setting up its US headquarters close to Microsoft's head office.

Without a brand a contract manufacturer remains a low-margin manufacturer of mass volume products. Provided the company keeps a tight control of costs and secures high volume contracts the model is profitable, but similar companies in South Korea, LG and Samsung, have successfully made the transition to become successful as companies with a global brand.

When Apple introduced the iPhone in 2007 the market was ignited and Chairman Peter Chou decided to create a HTC brand. The firm allocated $400 million a year on advertising and quickly became the fourth largest smartphone brand after Nokia, RIM (Blackberry) and Apple. According to Chou, the move to branding has had a good effect, as other firms in the supply chain are now more keen to develop partnerships. Even the partnership with Microsoft has changed as HTC is no longer the junior partner.

Innovation is the key to HTC's ambition and this is backed up by around a quarter of the company's 8000 staff holding engineering related jobs. The company looks at what is possible, puts in the necessary resources and is quite prepared to take risks. It became the top maker of handsets using Microsoft's Windows Mobile operating system, producing unbranded devices for Verizon, T-mobile, Spirit Nextel and NTT DoCoMo of Japan. As it developed its expertise it built the first phone powered by Google's Android operating system for T-mobile and the Nexus One for Google and quickly became market leader in the one segment growing faster than Apple's iPhone.

The HTC Android devices are making rapid progress and Chou is keen to expand sales in China and the US and develop a global brand and supports this with an international top team and the use of English for all business documents. By 2010 HTC was listed in the top 50 innovative companies by Bloomberg Business Week.

Question

1 What lessons can be learned from LG, Samsung and HTC that can help a firm move from being an own label supplier to a global brand?

References: M. Amdt and B. Einhom (2010) 'The 50 most innovative companies', *Bloomberg Business Week*, 15 April. B. Einhom (2010) 'A former no-name from Taiwan builds a global brand', *Bloomberg Business Week*, 28 October.

perception of the importance of counterfeiting. Others believe that the development of many underdeveloped economies would have been set back considerably if they had paid market rates for software, which raises the ethical question of whether oligopolistic companies such as Microsoft should be allowed to make fortunes for certain individuals by charging very high prices, while effectively excluding customers in underdeveloped countries who cannot afford to pay.

The issue of brand piracy clearly is costing MNEs vast revenues, and the US has led the way in insisting that governments crack down on the companies undertaking the counterfeiting. However, such firms have sophisticated networking operations, with much of their revenue coming from sales to consumers in developed countries. Trying to reduce or eliminate their activities is costly and time-consuming and unlikely to be a priority for governments in less developed countries. Moreover, pursuing legal action in foreign markets can be expensive, particularly for small companies, and can result in adverse publicity for larger firms.

The music industry has particularly suffered from illegal practices. The myth of music piracy was of a victimless crime, but the International Federation of the Phonographic Industry (IFPI) claims that billions of dollars goes to support criminal gangs as well as sucking out money from the legitimate music industry.

Positioning

Closely related to brand strategy and at the heart of its implementation is positioning. Positioning is largely concerned with how a product or service might be differentiated from the competition. However, it is important to stress that it is the customers' perceptions of the product or service offer that will indirectly confirm the positioning and so determine its success. Firms can only seek to establish and confirm the positioning in the consumers' minds through their management of the marketing mix. In countries at different stages of economic development the customer segments that are likely to be able to purchase the product and the occasions on which it is bought may be significantly different. For example, while KFC and McDonald's restaurants aim at everyday eating for the mass market in the developed countries, in less developed countries they are perceived as places for special occasion eating, and out of reach of the poorest segments of the population. A Mercedes car may be perceived as a luxury car in many countries but as an everyday taxi in Germany.

Unilever has a different approach. It introduced a new logo for its ice cream so that while the familiar names stay the same, for example Wall's in the UK and Ola in the Netherlands, the background design and font are being standardized around the world.

There appears to be an increasing demand for standardized products among market segments that are mobile and susceptible to influence by the media and through travel, and there is a strongly emerging demand for the same products among consumers in the less developed countries, too. Achieving unique positioning for a product or service must come from the creative dimensions of positioning rather than resorting to simple price positioning.

In confirming the positioning of a product or service in a specific market or region, it is necessary, therefore, to establish in the consumers' perception exactly what is the value proposition and how it differs from existing and potential competition.

Innovation and new product development

A recurring theme of discussions of international marketing issues is the increasing need for companies to have a dynamic and proactive policy of innovation for developing new products and services in order to satisfy the apparently insatiable demand of consumers for new experiences and to reinforce and, where necessary, renew, their source of competitive advantage. Some companies have new product development as a corporate objective. Johnson and Johnson generates 35 per cent of its sales from products that are less than five years old compared to 30 per cent in 1980. Lim, Sharkey and Heinrichs (2006) argue that faster new product development capability is essential for firms striving for a higher degree of export involvement. At the outset, however, it is important to stress that the most competitive firms encourage innovation in every aspect of their marketing activity. The space in which innovation takes place includes new products and services; new processes; position innovation which includes creativity in brand identity and communication; and paradigm innovation, which changes the underlying mental models that frame what the organization does. For example, IBM has reinvented itself from being a hardware company (International Business Machines), to a software and solutions provider, to a business process outsourcing company. Nestlé's new medical nutrition division aims to create a new industry between food and pharmaceuticals, in which foods are developed for people suffering, for example, from metabolic disorders. An increasing trend among online businesses is architectural innovation, Tuschman and Anderson (2004), and the adoption of innovative business models. For example, Google does not charge for search but generates income from advertisers. Mobile phone companies give away expensive phones for free and generate income from monthly rental contracts and connection.

While product or technological innovation is quite obvious, Jana (2007) maintains that service innovation is hidden, giving the example that the average person knows that Edison invented the light bulb, but getting the bulbs into houses and schools, and setting electricity is service innovation. IBM, Oracle and other tech companies have formed a non-profit consortium www.thesri.org to advance the concept using an open web social networking community and public archive. It maintains that innovation is about culture and values rather than processes and notes that the best ideas are, at first, laughable. If an innovation is truly and substantially new, it must by definition carry with it uncertainty and ambiguity.

The most innovative companies

Deciding which are the world's most innovative companies rather depends on which measure you use. Jaruzelski and Dehoff (2010), for example, in Booz and Company's annual study of the world's biggest R&D spenders note that automobiles, computing and electronics, and healthcare were the biggest industries for R&D spending and the top five companies were Roche, Microsoft, Nokia, Toyota and Pfizer. By contrast a survey of innovation executives to explore the relationship between innovation capabilities, corporate strategy and financial performance resulted in overwhelming votes for Apple, Google and 3M as the world's most innovative companies.

Patent filing is used by some as another measure of the innovativeness of firms. Huawei Technologies, China's largest telecoms equipment maker, was the world's top international patent seeker followed by Panasonic and Philips Electronics which had dominated for a decade. They were followed by Japan's Toyota and Fujitsu, Germany's Robert Bosch and Siemens, Finland's Nokia, South Korea's LG Electronics and Sweden's Ericsson. China was the sixth-largest patent filer by country, behind the United States, Japan, Germany, South Korea and France.

The nature of new product development

Few new products and services are actually revolutionary and Figure 8.7 shows the various categories of new products in terms of their newness to the market and company. Innovative firms encourage their staff to undertake incremental innovation in every aspect of business activity as a continual improvement process intended to refresh and reinforce the product range by complementing the existing company and brand image, rather than causing a change of direction.

Periodically step change innovation occurs as a result of a technological break through, such as the mobile phone, or groundbreaking, creative ideas often related to marketing that achieve a change of industry direction. Renewable energy innovations require technological and business innovations, step change and incremental. However, as Illustration 8.6 shows, there may be constraints to gaining access to the essential components for leading edge innovations.

Usually, developing new technologies is hugely expensive. For example, it is estimated that the cost of developing a new drug is estimated to be between US$800 million – $2 billion and takes over 15 years. In order to recover the research and development costs it is necessary to market new ideas simultaneously in all developed countries, as the time taken by competitors to copy or improve products and circumvent patents is shortening. Moreover, when pharmaceutical products come out of the patent period, they can

FIGURE 8.7 New product categories

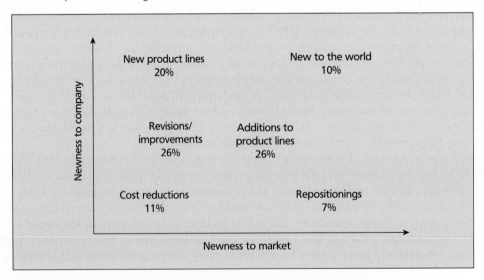

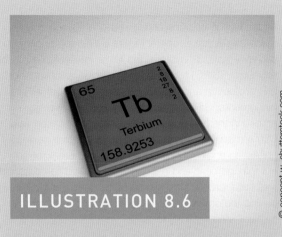

© concept w, shutterstock.com

ILLUSTRATION 8.6

China controlling rare metals, controlling innovation

China accounts for 97 per cent of the world output of rare earth metals, such as terbium, thulium, cerium and lanthanum. These metals are essential for many high tech products, such as iPads, plasma TVs and lasers. Each Toyota Prius uses a number of these metals and so the company has purchased the rare metals dealer Wako Bussan. Cerium is used for catalytic converters for diesel engines and Terbium is essential for low energy light bulbs. Much of the high tech defence equipment uses these rare earths too.

In 2010 China announced that it was cutting export quotas by 72 per cent on the basis that its own industry was forecast to need most of the output for the next three or four years. The US had been self sufficient in these metals until the 1990s when China flooded the market with exports and the US production closed down, as their German and Japanese owners switched operations to China. If countries cannot get access to these rare earth metals they will not play a significant part in the high tech future. Japan has been stockpiling them for five years, whereas the West and particularly the US has been caught off guard. Rare earth metals are not in fact rare but rarely occur in viable concentrations for mining and the processing is very complex. While a number of countries are now considering opening new or reopening mines, the only other option for manufacturers is to move their operations to China. To some observers, placing export limits to compel firms to locate plants in China looked like a breach of the WTO rules.

Question

1 What action can a high tech company take to ensure supplies of essential components?

References: A. Evans-Pritchard, *Daily Telegraph*, 2 August 2010. 'Rare earth blockade shows how China plays the globalisation game', *The Times*, 27 August 2010.

---

legitimately be copied as generic drugs – companies such as Ranbaxy in India and Aspen in South Africa have grown fast and built a strong global business doing this.

Even the largest companies do not have sufficient resources on their own to achieve rapid diffusion of a new product or service into all world markets, so this is at least as important a part of the process as the initial idea. This leads to the use of different market entry methods, such as licensing, franchising and strategic alliances, to secure cost-effective diffusion.

The new product development process

In its simplest form, developing products follows a similar process for international markets to that in domestic situations:

- idea generation
- initial screening
- business analysis
- development
- market testing
- commercialization and launch.

©Junial Enterprises, shutterstock.com

ILLUSTRATION 8.7

China supporting IP rights

In response to major criticism in recent years that there was widespread patent infringement in China and following its acceptance in the WTO, the country made Intellectual Property Rights (IPR) a top priority. It set up a national system, the State Intellectual property Office (SIPO) for accepting patent applications for IPR protection and handling complaints about IPR infringements. SIPO noted that 1076 cases were prosecuted in the first half of 2006. Isle of Man-based Strix Ltd, a manufacturer of electric kettle controls took legal action against two Chinese manufacturers for patent infringement and a Beijing court ruled the patent was valid, ordered the two manufacturers to stop producing the controls. Protection from Chinese courts is a major step forward for small firms, but against this small firms face the problem that getting a patent issued now takes an average of three years in the US and four years in Europe, so delaying innovation in fast moving markets for an unacceptably long period.

Question

1 What are the advantages and disadvantages for multinational firms such as Strix Ltd in legally protecting their intellectual property rights in this way?

References: P. Prowse, 'Patent attorneys welcome latest sign that Chinese courts respect UK companies' IP rights', www.cipa.org.uk, 19 February 2010.

Particular emphasis must be placed upon the quality of the information system, as it is essential that the product or service meets the needs of the customers and is positioned accurately in each market from the outset. With this in mind, the international development process should incorporate the following elements.

Idea generation must ensure that ideas worldwide are accessed so that duplication is avoided and synergy is optimized by effectively using all available internal and external resources to generate new ideas, including employees, R & D departments, competitors, sales people, customers, distributors and external experts.

Initial screening involves establishing rigorous international criteria, including both production and marketing factors, to test the ideas for suitability in all world regions so that opportunities and limitations are not overlooked. Ideas that may, for example, be inappropriate for Western Europe might be appropriate for South America. In doing this an assessment should be made of the degree of adaptation that will be necessary for individual markets.

Business analysis must involve establishing criteria for potential success or failure of the product and linking the criteria with regions and/or markets. It must make provision for contingencies such as environmental and competitive situations and unexpected events which might adversely affect the business case.

Product development must include ensuring that all relevant functions such as production, design and packaging become involved in the process. The most appropriate R & D centres for the development process should be selected, with particular attention being paid to such factors as access to technological expertise and location near prime target and lead markets.

Market testing must involve ensuring the test area is representative of the prime target markets, an adequate infrastructure in terms of the necessary services such as advertising and market research agencies, and an appropriate distribution network. It should also take account of potential competitor response both in the test market and globally.

The launch must be planned either to be sequential, with an initial concentration upon prime markets or lead markets, or to be a simultaneous launch. Allowance must be made for aggressive competitive responses, as few competitors will give up market share without a fight.

To protect the firm's competitive advantage the company needs to pay particular attention to defending its intellectual property, as Illustration 8.7 shows, and anticipate the ability of competitors to copy a new product and launch it in a separate market. There are a number of actions that companies might take to protect their intellectual property, such as taking strong patent protection, or entering into licensing arrangements to ensure fast, widespread penetration of the world or regional markets.

Timing is perhaps the most critical element of the process, not only in terms of exploiting an opportunity or competitive weakness at the right moment but also minimizing the time to market – how long it takes from when the idea was first generated to making it available commercially and the time it takes to achieve the desired level of diffusion.

Approaches to technology transfer and the benefits for marketing

This traditional, sequential and largely internal approach to new product development has considerable disadvantages because of a number of factors, including:

- the shortening of product life cycles;
- the cost and risk of funding development internally;
- the time needed to get the new product to market;
- 'non-core' activities such as product and packaging design and process development, as part of the in-house development process.

In an attempt to resolve these problems, many firms are adopting a more interactive approach in which new product and service developments are carried out jointly between the manufacturer, component maker, designer and technology supplier. Chesbrough (2003) explained that open innovation is an approach in which a variety of specialist organizations including design companies, R & D companies and universities might be used by a lead firm to increase the speed, effectiveness and quality of innovation. The main benefits of an interactive approach to new product development for the company are the concentration of skills and expertise on core activities, the ability to condense timescales and access to the best knowledge available on a particular topic. Increasingly web based firms are involving their customers in innovation in their business, as we discuss in Chapter 12.

It can be difficult to obtain contributions to the innovation process from staff around the world. Eppinger and Chitkara (2006) note that companies in many industries have engineering teams located in different parts of the world, but that without frameworks to support collaboration, managers find it difficult to achieve the necessary cohesion in the operation to drive efficient growth and innovation. The authors highlight Hyundai, Hewlett Packard and Alcatel as firms that have achieved this.

To further speed up the NPD process the stages can be regarded as simultaneous rather than linear. For example, testing the concept on customers around the world, carrying out the detailed analysis for the business case and designing the product packaging, could go ahead at the same time.

Research and development strategies

No matter which approach is adopted, major international companies must still decide upon the aims of their own R & D, the exact nature of the activities undertaken and where they should be located. They must take decisions on:

- the location of their own internal R & D facilities;
- the extent to which they embrace open innovation and contract out certain parts of their research and development programme, as large pharmaceutical companies do;
- whether they might acquire a company which can provide either the required new technology or a new product;
- licensing the technology and process from another company; or
- funding joint ventures or strategic alliances with companies that have complementary technology.

In general, the R & D activities of international companies tend to follow an evolutionary path, but for many the major question is whether or not they should move away from the dominance of their domestic country R & D location and if so, where should their R & D facilities be located.

Many companies still concentrate a large proportion of R & D activity in their country of origin, but as they move increasingly towards transnational operations so the concept of the home country becomes increasingly meaningless. It is, however, useful to consider the arguments for and against the centralization of R & D activities, and these are shown in Figure 8.8.

Success and failure in new product development

One of the most difficult aspects of NPD is to reduce the high levels of risk (and therefore the cost) of new product failure. The classic studies of success and failure of new products in developed countries, particularly the US and UK, emphasize that for success it is necessary to place greater emphasis upon marketing rather than technical factors. The key to success is an effective NPD strategy which includes the development of the central and supporting processes, in order to generate a flow of new products that might vary in market impact, but will include some high revenue or high-margin generators. In emerging markets the key is to develop products and services that meet the needs of customers for more basic items and the concept of 'frugal engineering', has been introduced as Illustration 8.8 shows. The aim of the innovation is to completely re-engineer products and services rather than simply try to reduce the costs of the established processes. These new products created are not inferior quality and will find new markets in developed countries too.

FIGURE 8.8 The arguments for and against centralization of R&D

Arguments for centralization	Arguments against centralization
- economies of scale	- pressure from subsidiaries
- easier and faster communication	- pressure from governments
- better coordination	- benifits of public relations
- greater control over outflow of information with implications for secrecy	- use of wider range of skills and abilities
- greater synergy	- benifits from comparative advantage
- avoiding duplication	- greater sensitivity to local tastes
- overcoming problems of ownership	- better monitoring of local competitive activity
	- closeness to possible acquisitions
	- access new technology wherever it is located

Stock.xchng

ILLUSTRATION 8.8

Meeting emerging market needs with frugal engineering

Over many years innovation has (and still is) mainly concerned with improvements that embrace new technology and typically add value for those customers that can afford to pay for increasingly sophisticated products and services. In Chapter 6 we introduced the concept of customers at the bottom of the pyramid highlighting the huge number of people particularly in markets such as China, India and Brazil that are moving out of poverty, enjoying prosperity for the first time and shopping for basics, rather than 'nice to have' features.

The term 'frugal engineering' has been coined not to describe stripped down engineering – removing features to enable products to be sold at lower prices – but to take a 'clean sheet' approach, where cost discipline is an intrinsic part of the process and avoids needless costs in the first place. In developed nations expansion of features has contributed most to the profitability of firms so, for example, many car manufacturers make profit on the top of the range models and little or no profit on the low specification models. But this means that production lines are not geared to producing basic items, for example, manual car windows are virtually extinct in the US. Firms in emerging markets, such as Tata with its Nano, are showing how 'frugal engineering', a term coined by Renault CEO Carlos Ghosn, can create products with costs that are unimaginable in the developed nations.

It is not just cars that are fit for purpose in emerging markets but also 'Little Cool' refrigerators with a fan rather than a compressor, basic function lap top computers, unsophisticated X ray machines and mobile phones that just make calls. Western firms are beginning to wake up to the opportunities, so after watching customers using mobile phones in India Nokia developed it best selling phone costing between $15–$20. It sends and receives calls and texts, has a monochrome display, lacks complex software so extending battery life, and is designed to cope with high humidity and dust. Its one added feature is an energy efficient flashlight, popular where blackouts are common.

Some customers in developed countries also see the value in frugally engineered products. Deere from the US started selling small, lower powered tractors in India but did not sell them into the US until an Indian company, Mahindra and Mahindra beat them to it. Now Mahindra and Mahindra are competing for Deere's large tractor market. By contrast GE is selling in the US its low cost electrocardiogram machine, developed for India.

Question

1 How can firms such as Tata, Nokia and GE manage their portfolio to include 'frugal engineering' but also include top of the range models for more demanding customers?

References: V. Sehgal, K. Dehoff and G. Panneer (2010) 'The importance of frugal engineering', *Strategy and Business*, Summer: 59. Accessed at: www.strategy-business.com, 25 May 2010.

Griffin (2003) suggests three fundamental requirements of the innovation process:

- Uncover unmet needs and problems.
- Develop a product with competitive advantage.
- Shepherd the products through the firm.

Tzokas, Hart and Saren (2003) suggest that market information is central to achieving success in NPD, and summarize the research studies that have highlighted its role within the strategic success factors:

- Ensuring product performance improvements over what is already available.
- Achieving synergy with existing firm technologies and manufacturing capability and learning new capabilities quickly.

- Achieving marketing synergies, such as channels and promotion, often because of the need to target a new segment.
- Integrating the contributions of marketing and R & D.
- Identifying attractive markets with growth potential.
- Effectively carrying out the NPD process, including pre-development activities, such as idea generation, screening, concept and business case investigation.
- Obtaining support from top management.
- Speed in development.

Key to success in technology sectors is generating a continual flow of new product introductions, but success is by no means guaranteed. Even for technologically leading edge companies not every idea will make it to the market and be a commercial success, so risk-taking and tolerating failure must be accepted by the firm's management. The main focus, however, should be to add value to meet the needs of customers wherever they are in the world.

SUMMARY

- In many business sectors product and service strategies are being affected by the increased globalization of consumer tastes, communications, technological advances and the concentration of business activity. At the same time, however, given the level of competition and choice available, there is an increasing expectation among customers that their individual needs will be met.
- Product managers are balancing the efficiency benefits of standardization in terms of economies of scale and the experience effect with the need and cost of adapting products and services to meet the needs of local customers, regulations and usage conditions.
- The growth of international services is a feature of international marketing and it is being driven by low labour costs and increasing demand in developing countries and the increased possibilities for transferring information through information technology and communications.
- As more products are reaching the mature phase of the life cycle they are becoming commodities, and there is a need to use additional services to differentiate them from competitor offerings. However, services are often difficult to standardize globally because they are affected significantly by the different expectations of service delivery that exist in different cultures.
- The product or service strategy is usually at the centre of international marketing operations. Branding is a key part of product and service management, particularly in international markets, but it is difficult to establish truly global brands that are truly distinctive and have images that appeal to cross-cultural customer segments.
- New product and service development and innovation throughout the marketing process are essential for growth and the renewal of the international portfolio and, particularly for culturally sensitive products and services, it is vital to obtain input from the different stakeholders around the world in order to ensure that they will be successful.

KEYWORDS

Intangibility	Adaptation	International branding
Perishability	International product portfolio	Branding strategies
Heterogeneity	Product strategies	Brand piracy
Inseparability	International product life cycle	New product development
International product offer	Country of origin effect	
Standardization	Services	

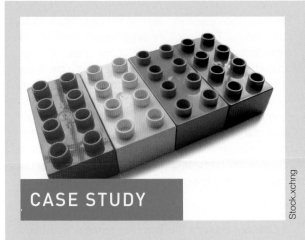

CASE STUDY

Stock.xchng

Lego playing with its strengths

Lego is one of the world's best known toy brands, yet for many years things have not gone well, but now the company has turned around. For 70 years Lego, the leading European toymaker, prospered, promoting learning and development through play by explaining that play is 'nutrition for the soul'. Lego sells its colourful bricks in 130 countries, claiming that on average everyone on earth has 52 bricks.

However, in 1998 it made its first loss and in 2004, following six years of declining sales and profits it made a huge loss of US$240 million, and rumours circulated that it would be taken over by Mattel, America's biggest toy maker. Lego was still owned by the family of Ole Kirk Christiansen, the Danish carpenter who founded the company in 1932. The family decided to stand by the company, injected their own money and appointed Jorgen Vig Knudstorp, a former management consultant for McKinsey, as the new CEO.

Lego had years of unbroken sales growth and for 50 years the plastic bricks faced little competition. Today children are growing up more quickly. Although Lego recognized this, some commentators felt they had lost their way in trying to address the problem. After the company posted its first losses in 1998 it negotiated lucrative tie-ins with Disney, the Harry Potter and Star Wars movies. More than one million Hogwarts Castle Lego sets were sold when the first two Harry Potter films came out, helping the firm back into profits in 2001 and 2002, but the company became too dependent on these licensing agreements and sales slumped again when no blockbuster Harry Potter films were released.

Other brand extension strategies failed to deliver the desired growth, when products such as Galidor, a cartoon-related series of Lego figures, was criticized because it lacked the open-ended imaginative play that the Lego brand was known for. Lego branched out and co-produced a kids TV show called *Galidor: Defenders of the Outer Dimension*, which was meant to encourage further sales, but it was dismissed as a predictable 30 minute TV advert. Lego music builder, aimed at pre-school children, under performed. Lego phased out the Duplo brand, established in 1969, and replaced it with Lego Explore but parents thought Lego no longer made larger sized bricks for children aged 18 months to 5 years and Lego's revenues in the pre-school market halved. Poor forecasting in the US of what its best sellers in its popular Bionicle range would be resulted in being overstocked in some products and out of stock in some successful products, and there were worldwide complaints that colours did not match.

With the aim of becoming a lifestyle brand, Lego had diversified into clothes, watches and video games. Lego had also tried to attract more girls. However, it had neglected its core customer segment of boys aged 5–9. Knudstorp believed that Lego had become arrogant and had stopped listening, so he went around to talk to the retailers. They told him that Lego should not change the core brand and the company should stick to what it had always been good at.

The traditional toy market was slimming down due to low-cost copies, hi-tech competitors and falling birth rates in developed countries. The turnaround plan, begun in March 2004, was painful as 3500 of the firm's 8000 workers lost their jobs. Half the 2400 jobs in Billund, the home of Lego, were due to be phased out. Factories in Switzerland and the US were closed and production moved to Eastern Europe and Mexico. Major stakes in the four Legoland theme parks and other assets in America, South Korea and Australia were sold off.

The management structure was simplified and a more commercial culture was fostered through a performance-based pay scheme and frank discussions about the financial position of the company took place between the management and employees, who had never before been used to talking about money. By 2006, having placed greater emphasis on the core business, the company had returned to profit and was increasing sales.

Although much of its diversification was stopped some parts were paying off well. Its Bionicle range, based on Polynesian mythology, was expanded and further new toys based on tie-ins with films such as Star Wars and Harry Potter were developed under licence. The Lego Star Wars video game in which Lego figures enact Star Wars was a best seller.

Reflecting on the problems years Lego's executive vice president for markets and products, Mads Nipper, believed that the problem was that the designers had too much freedom, but it was management to blame. Lego believed that giving the designers whatever pieces they asked for would unleash their creativity. But the designers had come with ever more complex models, which required the company to make new components. In seven years the number of components had increased from 7000 to 12 400 hugely increasing supply costs. Pieces for the previously successful Lego City line became stylized and no longer resonated with kids, who found them difficult to play with resulting in the line reducing from 13 per cent to 3 per cent of the sales in 2004. Lego's solution was to restrict the designers, made them work with non-creative staff, such as product and marketing managers, who had researched what kids wanted. The designers returned the Lego range to its core ranges. The Lego City range had an overhaul and now accounts for 20 per cent of the sales. They reduced the number of components (it is now back around 7000). Lego has competitors, such as MEGA brands of Canada, and they consistently undercut Lego on price but parents buy Lego because they believe the quality is better and because it offers the most creative collection of models to build, not just a collection of bricks and not just a stylized collection of models to simply look at.

Questions

1 Critically evaluate the branding strategy that Lego pursued in its effort to re-establish itself in the global market since 1998, identifying its future options.

2 Develop an outline international marketing strategy for Lego based on your preferred strategic option.

References: *The Economist*, 28 October 2006. J. Greene, 'How Lego revived its brand', *Bloomberg Businessweek*, 23 July 2010, and other public sources.

DISCUSSION QUESTIONS

1   Identify the major macro environmental trends in world trade. Using examples from one product and one service sector explain how these trends have affected product and service portfolio management across international markets.

2   In an ideal world companies would like to manufacture a standardized product. What are the factors that support the case for a standardized product and what are the circumstances that are likely to prevent its implementation?

3   Examine the ways in which a major company operating in many countries around the world can use new product development and commercialization to enhance its ambitions to become a global company.

4   What challenges would you expect to face in marketing products and/or services from:

(a)   A developing country to a developed country?

(b)   A developed to a less developed country?

5   How might these challenges be overcome? Illustrate your answer by focusing on a product or service of your choice.

6   International services marketing is a major growth area. Using one service sector as an example, explain what the main barriers to success are and what strategies might be used to overcome them.

REFERENCES

1. Chesbrough, H., (2003) 'The new imperative for creating and profiting from technology', Harvard Business School.

2. Doyle, P. (2000) *Value based marketing strategies for corporate growth and shareholder value*, Wiley.

3. Eppinger, S.D. and Chitkara, A.R. (2006) 'The new practice of global product development', *MIT Sloan Management Review*, 47 (4): 22–30.

4. Griffin, A. (2003) 'Marketing's role in new product development and product decisions', in *Marketing best practice*, Thomson South-Western.

5. Ho, S. (1997) 'The emergence of consumer power in China', *Business Horizons*, September–October.

6. Howard, E. (1998) 'Keeping ahead of the green regulators', *Mastering Global Management*, Part 10, *Financial Times*.

7. IFPI (2003) *Commercial piracy report*, July, London, available at: www.ifpi.org.

8. Jana, R., (2007) 'Service innovation: the next big thing', *Bloomberg Businessweek*, 29 March.

9. Jaruzelski, B. and Dehoff, K. (2010) 'The Global Innovation 1000: How the Top Innovators Keep Winning', *Strategy and Business*, Winter 2010: 61 sourced at: www.strategy-business.com.

10. Kaitiki, S. (1981) 'How multinationals cope with the international trade mark forgery', *Journal of International Marketing*, 1 (2): 69–80.

11. Keegan, W.J. (1989) *Multinational marketing management*, Prentice Hall.

12. Keegan, W.J. and Green, M.C. (2011) *Global Marketing*, 6th edn, Pearson.

13. Kotler, P. (2002) *Marketing management: analysis, planning, implementation and control*, Prentice Hall.

14. Lim. J., Sharkey, T.W. and Heinrichs, J.H. (2006) 'Strategic impact of new product development on export involvement', *European Journal of Marketing*, 40, 44–60.

15. Mesdag, M. van (1985) 'The frontiers of choice', *Marketing*, 10 October.

16. Rappa, R. and Hirsh, E. (2007) 'The luxury touch', accessed at: www-strategy-business.com, 3 April.

17. Ringshaw, G. (2006) 'Bankers face Mecca', *Sunday Times*, 15 October.

18. Stone, A. (2006) 'Profits save the world', *Sunday Times*, 10 December.

19. Tuschman, M.L. and Anderson, P. (2004) *Managing Strategic Innovation and Change*, 2nd edn, New York: Free Press.

20. Tzokas, N., Hart, S. and Saren, M. (2003) 'New product development, a marketing agenda for change' in S. Hart, *Marketing changes*, Thomson.

INTERNATIONAL MARKETING PLANNING: STRATEGY DEVELOPMENT

Introduction

In the Integrated Learning Activity 1, against the background of information on the market structure and customer needs, a segmentation approach was developed. In this activity we focus on possible strategic alternatives and the development of a global marketing strategy by companies from emerging markets who are becoming global players in the industries within which they operate.

Arguably the most significant change in international marketing over recent years has been the changing competitive landscape globally, as major players who were previously national champions in their own countries in emerging economies, ranging from China and Taiwan to Korea and Brazil, have developed as potential global players.

These companies have not really developed their global strategies through the traditional multi-national route, but they are becoming global by developing global brands, either organically or by buying Western companies to aid their global growth. However, as they develop, considering the possible alternative approaches to transnational development is valuable, given the very different contexts in which they operate. In this activity we consider a number of companies from emerging markets who are highly competitive and who are aiming to become truly global. You are able to choose one to investigate, but essentially the activity is about analyzing the basis of the competitive capability of the firms involved and thinking through how this has to develop and shift if they are to build and sustain a global competitive advantage. This gives you the opportunity to consider how a changing global competitive landscape modifies the competitive behaviour of companies in their struggle for a global competitive advantage. It is these issues and how the company you choose should resolve them that are explored in this activity.

Learning Objectives

On completing this activity should be able to:

- Critically appraise the global marketing strategy that a company is following and evaluate the potential for their success or failure

- Understand the role and value of global marketing planning and its implications for the organization structure

- Understand the concept of globalization and how it affects the strategies of organizations

The scenario: The future global players from emerging markets

Boston Consulting Group (BCG) have identified 100 newcomers (called the RDE 100) from developing economies, such as China, India, Brazil, Mexico and Russia – firms who are cash rich and hungry for global growth. BCG have also identified 40 fast growing and globalizing companies from Africa

Previously newcomers from emerging markets have focused on building their competitive advantage through marketing low-value manufacturing and service activities. These firms, however, are building the capability to compete with the established firms by the use of much more sophisticated marketing approaches: for example, by using their success in meeting customer needs in their huge and rapidly growing domestic markets as a platform for global expansion. The question for all of these companies is whether they can compete on a more sustainable basis in the global marketing environment.

Not too many years ago companies such as Toyota, LG and Samsung would have been regarded as 'newcomers' from emerging markets and, more recently, companies that have been discussed in earlier editions of this book have rapidly become quite established global operators in their particular sectors in a period of 20 years. These companies include Mittal, an unknown steel producer in Indonesia, now as ArcelorMittal it is the world's largest steel producer. Lenovo, which bought IBM's personal computer division is the fourth largest PC maker, and South African Breweries, a local brewer in South Africa is now one of the three largest companies. Which companies will be the stars of tomorrow?

The following ten firms are typical of the firms identified by BCG

1 Shoprite: www.shoprite.co.za

The Shoprite Group of Companies is based in South Africa and is Africa's largest food retailer, operating in more than 1068 corporate and 275 franchise outlets in 17 countries across Africa, the Indian Ocean Islands and southern Asia. It employs more than 75 000 people. Its outlets include supermarkets, non-foods, furniture and fast food.

2 Marcopolo: www.marcopolo.com

Founded in 1949 in Brazil, Marcopolo is one of the biggest manufacturers of bus bodies in the world and recently initiated activities in the LCV sector, parts and components and also in the plastic products sector. It has factories in Brazil, Colombia, Argentina, Mexico, India, Egypt and South Africa.

3 Etisalat: www.etisalat.ae

Etisalat is one of the largest telecommunications companies in the world and the leading service provider in the Middle East. The company operates in 18 countries across Asia, the Middle East and Africa and has 100 million customers.

4 Suntech: www.suntech-power.com

Suntech develops, manufactures and delivers solar energy solutions. Founded in 2001 by a solar scientist Dr Zhengrong Shi, Suntech systems has offices in 13 countries, including regional headquarters in California, Switzerland and China and is listed on the New York stock exchange. Its solar modules are installed in over 80 countries.

5 Aspen Pharmacare: www.aspenpharma.com

Aspen Pharmacare of South Africa is Africa's largest pharmaceutical manufacturer and a major supplier of branded pharmaceutical, health care and nutritional products to southern African and other international

markets. Its revenues have grown by 37 per cent annually for the past decade and the international share of its business in 44 per cent. The company has manufacturing plants in East Africa, India, Latin America, Germany and South Africa, and has the right to distribute GlaxoSmithKline's drugs in South Africa, in return for Glaxo taking a 19 per cent stake in Aspen.

6 Embraer: www.embraer.com

A Brazilian Company listed is Embraer (the Empresa Brasileira de Aeronáutica S.A.), a Brazilian aircraft manufacturer. They produce commercial, military and corporate aircraft and are one of the three top exporters in Brazil. It has a workforce of 17 000, and a firm order book totalling US $15 billion. This means that globally Embraer has the third-largest yearly delivery of commercial aircraft (behind Boeing and Airbus) and the fourth-largest workforce (behind Boeing, Airbus and Bombardier).

7 Huawei: www.huawei.com

Huawei is a telecom solutions provider using fixed line, wireless and IP technologies, Huawei's products and solutions have been supplied in over 100 countries and its customers include 45 of the world's top 50 telecom operators, as well as one third of the world's population.

8 Infosys: www.ifosys.com

Infosys Technologies was started in 1981 by seven people with $250. Today, the company is a global leader in 'next generation' IT and consulting with revenues of US$5.4 billion in 2010.

Infosys defines, designs and delivers technology-enabled business solutions for major companies offering business and technology consulting, application services, systems integration, product engineering, software development, IT infrastructure services and business process outsourcing.

9 Grupo Bimbo: www.grupobimbo.com

Grupo Bimbo was established in Mexico in 1945 and is a major baking company with production in 17 countries in the United States, Latin America and Asia encompassing over 7000 products and more than 150 brands.

10 United Spirits: www.unitedspirits.in

United Spirits Limited (USL) is the largest spirits company in India and among the top three spirits companies in the world with 17 millionaire brands (selling more than a million cases a year) in its portfolio. It has a 59 per cent market share for its first line brands in India, including brands such as Whyte & Mackay and Bouvet Ladubay. It exports to over 59 countries.

Developing a strategy for a global challenger from an emerging market

You are required to select one of the companies listed, all of whom come from emerging markets and are embarking on global expansion. Your brief is to develop an outline global marketing strategy to enable it to challenge the existing competitors in the market.

You should prepare a report of approximately 3500 words.

The task

1 Critically and briefly evaluate the trends in the international market sector in which the company operates.

2 Against the background of your answer to Question 1, comment on how well your chosen firm is placed to develop globally.

3 Advise the company on how to develop a sustainable long-term global marketing strategy.

The report should include the following sections:

Section 1

- Trends in the environment and market for the sector.
- The market structure for the sector, including the geographic spread of products, customer segmentation, competitive positioning of key global players.

Section 2

- Summary of product and market focus, including reasons for the company's domestic, regional and international success to date.
- Basis of current competitive advantage.
- The strategic marketing challenges it is likely to face as it aims to improve its international competitive position.

Section 3

- Recommendations on how to build sustainable competitive advantage in the future.
- Implementation actions that will be critical in building competitive advantage.

Useful websites

Shoprite www.shoprite.co.za

Marcopolo www.marcopolo.com

Etisalat www.etisalat.ae

Suntech www.suntech-power.com

Aspen Pharmacare www.aspenpharma.com

Embraer www.embraer.com

Huawei www.huawei.com

Infosys www.ifosys.com

Grupo Bimbo www.grupobimbo.com

United Spirits www.unitedspirits.in

www.businessweek.com

www.telegraph.co.uk

www.oecd.org/statistics

www.ft.com/markets/emerging

www.businessmonitor.com/risk

Getting started

In this section the case study focuses on the companies from emerging markets that are developing global competitive positions. You should use the information outlined above to obtain an understanding of who the companies are, where they come from and why they may be interesting to examine, as well as for general background information. It is important of course to use the information to decide which company you are going to use as a basis for this learning activity. To complete the learning activity, however, you will need to access a range of research material from libraries and web-based sources as well as perhaps external sources of information.

In Task 1 we build on the skills developed in ILA 1. However, in this task it is important to pay particular attention to the key trends affecting the development of the company you have chosen, their competitive positioning and how the trends in the market are impacting on the way the global market is structured.

In considering Task 2 you will need to carry out some research to understand the company background, its activities and progress to date and you will also need to gain an understanding of the competition and the market environment.

Given that your company may be relatively unknown, you should not expect to obtain very detailed information on the company and you should not try to carry out a critical evaluation of its strategy.

You are, however, required to demonstrate your understanding of the global challenges (threats and opportunities) that a firm from an emerging market faces and you are encouraged to be creative in your response to the questions asked.

The starting point for Task 3 is articulating an overall vision and setting appropriate corporate objectives for the firm in terms of developing globally. The global marketing strategy that is developed should be based on a relevant response to the analysis you have developed in answering questions 1 and 2. Against the background of the firm's capabilities, existing and potential future competition, the firm should consider the strategic options it has and develop a positioning statement that will ensure the firm can build a global competitive position in which its products and services are clearly differentiated from the competition.

Key decisions in the strategy development will relate to the degree to which the firm wishes, and is able, to standardize its product and service offerings or needs to adapt them to the requirements of the local markets. Market entry methods need to be selected if it is to enter new markets and the products and services that will be the portfolio need to be chosen. You also need to consider how the recommendations made contribute to the development of a long-term global competitive advantage across the region and the implications your recommendations have for resource allocation and portfolio management for the specified company. In summary, in completing the task you need to ensure you consider the key factors listed in the key pointers below.

Key pointers for the integrated learning activity 2

Task 1

- the key international trends impacting on the development of the market.
- an evaluation of how the global market is structured/segmented.
- the competitive positioning of the key global players.
- the ability to analyze and synthesize material from a variety of sources.
- relevance and coherence of analysis.

Task 2

- assessment of current competitiveness of the specified company.
- identification of the key strategic marketing issues the company need to address to compete effectively in the global market.

Task 3

- clearly stated recommendations
- ability to contextualize
- clear and logical link between analysis and response
- innovation and creativity in your response
- coherence and justification of your recommendations
- appreciation of the contribution to a long-term global competitive advantage.

The way forward

The task in this activity shows how the diversity encountered in developing a global marketing strategy is a difficult activity to carry out satisfactorily. After studying Part 3 of the text you may wish to revisit the solutions you have recommended in this activity, and consider how your recommendations could be successfully implemented.

In doing so you may wish to consider such aspects as:

- What is an appropriate organization management structure for delivering your strategy?
- How can you ensure a systematic planning system throughout the globe that will enable the company to satisfactorily implement the strategy, organize the diverse operations and ensure the managers around the globe respond to the challenges you have identified?

All of this is hard to achieve in a global marketing strategy. For senior managers, the problem is how to maintain cohesion between all staff in order to ensure uniform standards, a coherent worldwide strategy, retain a unique vision and purpose and yet at the same time create an operation which has empathy with consumers in each host country.

For most firms the international planning process is concerned with managing a number of tensions and ambiguities. It is how you would resolve such tensions that you may wish to consider on completion of Part 3. There is a need to adopt a regular, thorough and systematic sequence, but at the same time provide the flexibility which allows more junior managers to realize opportunities and address problems when and where they occur. While detailed analysis is necessary to fully appreciate the complexities of a situation at the host country level, there is also a need for a clear uncluttered vision, shared by all staff, of where the company intends to go.

References

The 2009 BCG 100 new global challengers http://www.bcg.com/documents/file20519.pdf, and the African challengers: global competitors emerge from the overlooked continent, accessed at: www.bcg.com 2 June 2010.

PART III: IMPLEMENTATION

AIMS AND OBJECTIVES

Having defined the international marketing strategy and determined the market entry method and product policy in Part 2, we now turn to implementation. The aim of this, Part 3 of *International Marketing Strategy*, is to examine the implementation issues and determine the activities that will ensure that the strategies are competitive and sustainable, the products and services are effective in meeting the needs of the customers. While we address the elements of the marketing mix in turn, throughout the section we emphasize the need to integrate the various elements of marketing activity, as they are mutually reinforcing. Where possible, many firms seek to standardize their marketing activities but recognize too that they need to be adapted to the needs of the specific markets in which they are operating. In this respect market entry and product and service management are also considerations in both strategic development and implementation.

The first chapter in Part 3, Chapter 9, is a broad examination of the importance of integrating communications. International communications is not only concerned with the promotion of products and services and differentiating them from those of competitors: it is also about achieving effective communications internally, establishing a corporate identity that is understood worldwide and building long-term relationships with customers.

In Chapter 10, we turn to the more operational aspects of the marketing mix, involving the distribution of goods and services that make up a significant proportion of costs and contribute to customer satisfaction. This includes the different retailing infrastructures around the globe and the challenges of physically distributing products.

For most firms pricing is a complex area, especially so when pricing across international markets. Firms face currency risks, transaction risks and the risks of not being paid at all. In Chapter 11 we examine the problems companies face when pricing across foreign markets and look at some of the tools and techniques used by companies to combat these problems.

Finally, in Chapter 12 we explore the increasing role technology plays in providing a source of growth and enabling managers to implement their international marketing strategy efficiently and effectively. Technology is expected to provide the solution for many global sustainability problems and we discuss corporate social responsibility in this chapter too.

9 International communications

10 The management of international distribution and logistics

11 Pricing for international markets

12 Technology enabled sustainable international marketing

Part 3 Integrative Learning Activity

INTERNATIONAL COMMUNICATIONS

LEARNING OBJECTIVES

After reading this chapter you should be able to:

- Appreciate the nature and role of communications in implementing international marketing strategies

- Understand the challenges faced in the successful management and effective integration of international marketing communications

- Be able to explain the use of the elements of an international communications strategy, including corporate identity, products and services promotion and the development of relationships with customers

- Identify the use and the limitations of the communications tools in international marketing

- Recognize the value of integrating the communications to meet the requirements of different audiences offline and online

INTRODUCTION

The geographical and cultural separation of the company from its marketplaces causes great difficulty in communicating effectively with its stakeholders. In this chapter we take a broad view of communications and include not just the traditional promotional mix of personal selling, advertising, sponsorship, sales and public relations but also other methods of communications which have the objective of developing better and more personalized relationships with global customers, often using online media. In our discussions we acknowledge the fact that the target audience extends beyond existing and potential customers and includes other stakeholder groups that have a potential impact on the global development of firms and their international reputation.

In doing this, the development of internal relationships between staff from different strategic business units within the global organization and with close business partners is vital in influencing overall performance. Some remote strategic business units often appear to have a closer relationship with their customers and competition than they have with the parent organization, and ensuring good communications seems to be particularly important as firms embark on joint ventures and strategic alliances.

Building a convincing value proposition for stakeholders and achieving cost-effectiveness requires the integration of marketing communications and the distribution channel. Success in this depends upon building good relationships with all of these interested parties.

The role of marketing communications

Marketing communications are concerned with presenting and exchanging information with various stakeholders, both individuals and organizations to achieve specific results. This means not only that the information must be understood accurately but that, often, elements of persuasion are also required. In a domestic environment this process is difficult enough, but the management of both offline and online international marketing communications is made particularly challenging by a number of factors including the complexity of different market conditions, differences in media availability, languages, cultural sensitivities, regulations controlling advertising and sales promotions and the challenge of providing adequate resourcing levels.

A variety of approaches have been taken to define and describe the marketing mix area, which is concerned with persuasive communications. Some writers refer to the 'communications mix', others to the 'promotional mix' and others, for example Kotler (2002), use the two terms interchangeably to mean the same thing. Communications, embracing as it does the ideas of conveying information, is the most helpful term and implies the need for a two-way process in international marketing and is at the core of the digital media. It also includes internal communications between the organization's staff, especially as organizations become larger, more diverse and complex. In addition 'internal staff' might include collaborative partners that add value to the organization's offer and are part of the supply chain. Some online organizations encourage greater involvement of customers in the business and these situations redraw the boundaries between internal and external staff.

Figure 9.1 shows the external and internal marketing communication flows and emphasizes the need to consider three dimensions: external, internal and interactive or relationship marketing.

Internal marketing

For a large diverse multi-national firm it is a key task to ensure that all staff employed in its business units around the world are aware of the strategies, tactics, priorities and procedures to achieve the firm's mission and objectives. Increasingly organizations form closer collaborations with supply chain and distribution channel members, work with joint venture and strategic alliance partners and participate in

FIGURE 9.1 External, internal and interactive marketing

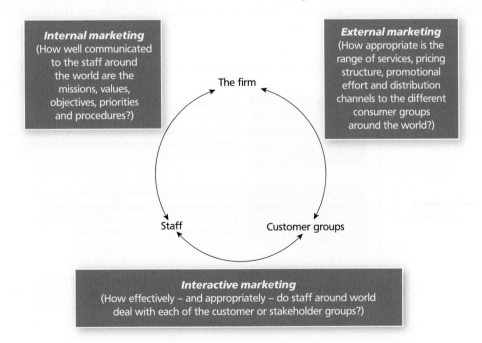

marketing networks. Organizations are dependent on staff in the extended organization working to a common set of objectives and they need to be informed about the appropriate marketing strategies.

Staff in remote locations are often overlooked in communications or receive messages that become unclear as they cross cultural and language boundaries, in the same way that external audiences may misunderstand the firm's external communications. As a result staff in remote locations can become closer to the staff of local customers and even competitors, making it vital that they regularly receive helpful information about the strategy as well as being reminded of the organization's standards and values.

Interactive marketing

Because many customers of MNEs are MNEs themselves it is essential for staff around the world to deliver consistent service. This includes service delivery staff, call centre operators, service engineers and salespeople in each location. Staff are trained how to communicate with stakeholders in a consistent way, take appropriate decisions that fit with the strategy and deliver a standardized service, so that the reputation of the organization is enhanced.

Consistent and effective two way interactive communication is at the heart of online marketing businesses, where the Internet provides the underpinning link between the staff undertaking the various business functions and their customers. As we discuss later it is this process that creates the nature of the relationship that online businesses strive to build and maintain.

External marketing

The traditional role of international marketing communications is largely concerned with providing a mechanism by which the features and benefits of the product or service can be promoted as cost effectively as possible to existing and potential customers in different countries, using the promotion mix, which includes online and offline communications, personal selling, advertising, sales promotion and public relations with the ultimate purpose of persuading customers to buy specific products and services. International marketing communications, however, have now become much more important within the marketing mix and the purposes for which marketing communications might be used externally in international markets are now more diverse. They include the need to communicate with a more diverse range of stakeholders, including supply chain partners, industry regulators, pressure groups and the community in general, and build higher levels of customer service through interactive or relationship marketing. International marketing communications could now be considered to include the three distinct strategic elements shown in Figure 9.2.

FIGURE 9.2 The dimensions of external marketing communications

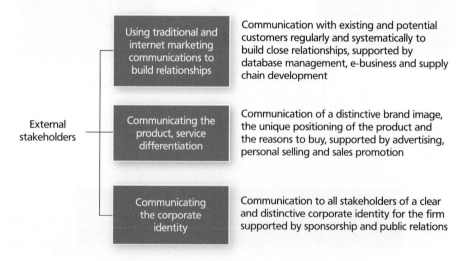

External stakeholders

Using traditional and internet marketing communications to build relationships — Communication with existing and potential customers regularly and systematically to build close relationships, supported by database management, e-business and supply chain development

Communicating the product, service differentiation — Communication of a distinctive brand image, the unique positioning of the product and the reasons to buy, supported by advertising, personal selling and sales promotion

Communicating the corporate identity — Communication to all stakeholders of a clear and distinctive corporate identity for the firm supported by sponsorship and public relations

Communicating product and service differentiation

As we have discussed in Chapters 6 and 8, increased competition and the maturation of markets have led to many firms offering largely similar core product and service specifications, with the result that in addition to its traditional role of promoting products and services, international marketing communications is increasingly used to provide the firm with an important source of differentiation. For example, by providing customers with an easily recognizable and distinctive brand image, or by explaining the unique positioning of the product.

Online and mobile communications have contributed to the vast increase in the range and volume of communications to which consumers are exposed as they go about their normal work and leisure, and making one product or service distinctive becomes an increasing challenge. There are a wide variety of promotional tools that might be used to persuade customers to buy the firm's products and services, and the newer information and communications technologies are increasing this choice all the time. The challenge for the firm is to use these tools as cost-effectively as possible to reach out to consumers – wherever they are in the world.

Communicating the corporate identity to international stakeholders

As stakeholders in general have become more aware of how they are affected by international organizations – both good and bad – companies have found it necessary to justify their international activities by constantly and more widely communicating their core values and standards to their internal and external audience. This is essential in order to demonstrate their responsibility to shareholders, trustworthiness to

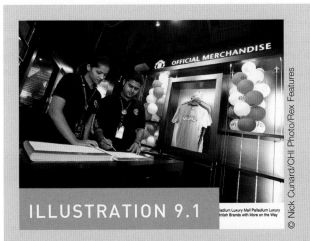

ILLUSTRATION 9.1

© Nick Cunard/CHI Photo/Rex Features

Manchester United Scoring in India

Manchester United, the UK premier league soccer team, is one of the most valuable clubs in the world and has successfully developed a worldwide following due to the popularity of premier league matches being screened on TV in Asia and this had led to huge sales of merchandize carrying the club's logo and colours. Occasional visits to the countries by the team enabled the supporters to see the club's stars

in action and fuelled the brand growth. India is a nation of sport enthusiasts but until recently they preferred cricket. After securing a five-year sponsorship deal with Bharti Airtel worth £12 million, Manchester United sought to build on their popularity in India. They carried out research which showed they had 20 million supporters in the country, resulting from their games being broadcast to 1.15 billion homes. 287 million watched their May 2008 Champions league final game with Chelsea. United held an event for the +91 Europe network of Indian CEOs to explain the value of partnerships and of sport sponsorship. Only 10 per cent of all sponsorship in India goes to sport, whereas in Europe the figure is 86 per cent. Rakesh Rawal founder of the network commented that ten years ago everybody returning to India from the UK would be asked to bring back a bottle of Johnnie Walker whisky, but now it would be the red Manchester United shirt.

Question

1 How might Manchester United build its brand in India?

References: Ogden, M. 'United target expansion on new frontier in India', *Daily Telegraph*, 18 March 2010.

customers and care and concern for the local community, environment and local employees. The corporate image or logo is the most visible part of the identity and, in some firms, is the only standardized element of the marketing mix, because it constantly reminds stakeholders of the organization's reputation. The corporate identity of the firm should be deeper and more pervasive and reflected in a clear and distinctive message supported by appropriate and proactive public relations activity. Illustration 9.1 shows the value of a strong corporate identity with iconic images for a football club when it communicates with new international markets.

Using communications to build relationships

More intense global competition has provided consumers with greater choice of products and services which they perceive to be capable of satisfying their needs and providing new experiences. Customers also feel that there is less risk of dissatisfaction in switching to alternative products and services, and so are becoming less likely to stay loyal to one supplier or brand.

With the increasing cost of marketing communications and the need to reach an ever wider international audience, organizations are becoming much more aware of the high costs of winning new customers and the relatively lower costs of retaining existing customers. Attention has been drawn to how much a single customer of one product might purchase over his or her lifetime. Readers might like to calculate how much they buy from a food retailer, car manufacturer or a travel company if they stay loyal to that supplier for 5, 10 or 20 years. Food retailers offer incentives for customer loyalty, such as bonus cards and money-off vouchers for other products and services they offer, such as petrol and insurance services. They routinely communicate with consumers using direct mail to inform them of new product offers.

The concept of relationship marketing has taken on greater significance with e-commerce where communications, promotion and delivery of services have been integrated with customer relationship management (CRM) systems to enable firms to communicate in a much more intelligent, efficient and effective way by basing their messages on a better knowledge of the characteristics and responses of their existing and potential customers and a better understanding of what they might wish to hear. In this way firms are able to be sensitive to different cultures and environmental contexts and develop better relationships with their customers and other influential stakeholders, irrespective of their location in the world. It is useful to reflect on the key characteristics of the Internet in Table 9.1 to appreciate the integration of interactive marketing that is possible.

Table 9.1 The characteristics of the Internet – the Six 'I's

	Characteristics
Interactivity	Customer initiates contact Marketer has 100 per cent customer attention and can store responses
Intelligence	Ability to collect and analyze information continuously and make individually focused offers.
Individualization	Tailored communication using stored data to achieve mass customization.
Integration	Achieve integration of communication and manage customer switching channels during purchasing.
Industry restructuring	Disintermediation involved removal of traditional intermediaries. Reintermediation to gain presence on websites.
Independence of location	Reach extended to countries where a physical support presence would not be viable.

Source: Referenced from Deighton, J. (1996) 'The future of interactive marketing', *Harvard Business Review*, November–December 151–42.

The fundamental challenges for international marketing communications

All forms of international marketing communication have a fundamental purpose, which is to ensure that the intended messages (those which are part of the firm's international marketing strategy) are conveyed accurately between the sender and the receiver, and that the impact of unintentional messages (those which are likely to have an adverse effect on the firm's market performance and reputation) are kept to a minimum. The communications process should be two-way and the sender should always make provision for feedback to ensure that the receiver has understood the message as it was intended and has responded positively to it as Figure 9.3 shows.

In practice this apparently simple process poses considerable challenges for firms trying to manage their international marketing communications. This is often discussed in the business press, which contains many serious but frequently amusing anecdotes about the failed attempts of major firms to communicate in international markets. Mistakes in the use of language, particularly using messages which do not translate or are mistranslated are a particular problem: more serious is a lack of sensitivity to different cultures among international communicators. Management Challenge 9.1 also shows how product advertising can meets customer needs but still prove controversial.

Many of the failures of communications are unintentional, of course. Following negotiations with the Council on America–Islamic Relations, Nike had to scrap almost 40 000 pairs of sports shoes because the flame design which was used bore a resemblance to the Arabic for Allah. Two years earlier Nike was forced to withdraw a billboard showing a basketball player above the caption 'They Called him Allah' when it caused an outcry among Muslims.

Besides the often highly visible failures which make firms appear to be incompetent and insensitive there are many examples of wasted effort and resources which are not so widely publicized. There are a number of reasons for international marketing communications' failure, including:

- Inconsistency in the messages conveyed to customers by staff at different levels and from different countries and cultures.
- Different styles of presentation of corporate identity, brand and product image from different departments and country business units which can leave customers confused.
- A lack of coordination of messages, such as press releases, advertising campaigns and changes in product specification or pricing across the various country markets.

FIGURE 9.3 Model of communication

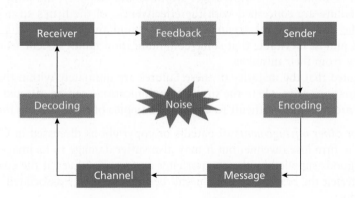

MANAGEMENT CHALLENGE 9.1

Advertising whitening – an ethical dilemma?

In what is being called the 'Snow White syndrome' in India, sales of whitening creams are outstripping sales of Coca-Cola and tea. The market is worth $432 million and is rising about 18 per cent per year. The implication of the business is that the whiter the skin, the more attractive you are. Once it was women that wanted to be fair, but now men are also buying products that range from 50 cents to $150 per jar. The reason for the increased demand is that there is a tendency to discriminate against a person's skin colour, particularly in rural areas. The TV message is not so subtle either. In one commercial two men, one with dark skin the other with light skin, are standing on a balcony looking over the neighbourhood. The dark skin guy says in Hindi 'I am unlucky because of my face'. His light skin friend replies 'Not because of your face, because the colour of your face'. The light skin guy throws his friend a whitening cream. In many similar ads it is the light skin guy that gets the girl and the dream job and they imply 'at least you will get noticed'.

Hindustan Unilever's Fair and Lovely is the leader in women's lightening cream products and Calcutta's Emami Group's Fair and Handsome is the male equivalent best seller, with 70 per cent market share and good export sales too to Gulf countries and the Middle East. Olay, Neutrogena and L'Oreal all sell products through promotion featuring Bollywood stars. Some people are critical with dermatologists pointing out that the products contain steroids and warning of potential side effects, while others believe that skin whitening commercials could be considered to be racist.

Question

1 Do you consider skin whitening commercials to be racist?

References: Guha Ray, S. (2010) 'India's unbearable lightness of being', BBC Online, accessed 5 November. Sidner, S. (2010) 'Skin whitener advertisements labelled racist', CNN, accessed 5 November.

■ Failure to appreciate the differences in the fields of perception (the way the message is understood) of the sender and receiver. The field of perception tends to be affected significantly by the self-reference criteria of both parties. This is, perhaps, where the greatest problems arise because, as we have already discussed, avoiding this requires knowledge of different market environments, cultural empathy and the willingness to adapt the communications programmes and processes to local requirements.

Illustration 9.2 shows the importance of appreciating the subtlety of language and tone in communications.

While this last area is influenced by knowledge, attitudes and empathy, the other three areas of potential communications failure are concerned with the effectiveness of the firm's strategy and planning and the degree to which the staff within the organization understand and are involved in the communications planning process. It is almost inevitable that some communication failures occur from time to time and it is vital that firms learn from their mistakes.

While it can be argued that the majority of these failures are ultimately within the control of the company, a number of situations arise where the firm's communications can be affected by factors which are outside its control or are extremely difficult to control. Examples of these are situations where:

■ *Counterfeiting or other infringements* of patents or copyright as discussed in Chapter 8 take place. Not only does the firm lose revenue, but it may also suffer damage to its image if consumers believe the low-quality goods supplied by the counterfeiter are genuine. Even if the customer knows the product is counterfeit the brand name might still be subconsciously associated with a poorly performing product.

■ *Parallel importing*, which is discussed in greater detail in Chapter 11, communicates contradictory messages that do not reflect the image of the brand and thus confuse consumers. This can be

ILLUSTRATION 9.2

Negativity in advertising

Global firms see the cost benefits and brand-building benefits of standardization of creative work. However, to understand the reason why advertisements might or might not cross borders requires more subtlety, particularly in Asian markets.

There are many reasons. One is the issue of negativity. If a person in some western countries is asked, 'How are you?', the answer might be 'Good' or 'Fine'. It also might be 'Not bad', which really also means good. For many on the Indian subcontinent, 'Not bad' is more precise and often means neutrality – neither this nor that. They place great significance on negative expressions, such as non-violence, non-greed and non-hatred, which are embedded in the culture and convey important personal values. In Western advertising, the appeal might be based on an unacceptable or annoying situation that can occur if a particular product is not bought. A Western advertisement for a TV set might emphasize the picture is 'free from distortion', whereas in Asian markets a TV that has a clear picture might communicate a more precise message.

In Western advertising there is little distinction between praise and flattery, whereas in Sinhala and Tamil languages, spoken in Sri Lanka, flattery is regarded as deceitful and false. In this case, care needs to be taken with over positive expressions in advertising.

In the West, emphasis is placed on logic and rationality in advertising, whereas the Asian view is that the truth will emerge.

Question

1 How can managers responsible for cross-border campaigns ensure that they will convey the message effectively?

References: *Marketing Business*, 2000.

---

particularly problematic if the parallel importer seriously undercuts the prices charged by the official channel, leading customers to feel they have been 'ripped off'.

- *Competitors, governments or pressure groups* attack the standards and values of the MNE by alleging, fairly or unfairly, bad business practice. Despite their huge resources, some of the largest firms are not very effective in responding to allegations from relatively less powerful stakeholders. Companies such as Shell, Exxon and McDonald's have suffered following criticism of their lack of concern for the environment. The lack of standards and controls on the Internet has made the problem worse, for example, anti Coca-Cola websites post negative communications without the need to substantiate the messages.

Customers increasingly believe reviews posted on websites rather than more rigorous and independent assessments, perhaps not realizing how much these informal reviews can be manipulated. The most significant challenge is that anyone can now comment on a firm's product and service through social media and this is increasingly at the expense of formal communications. The firm has less control or even influence over the identity, image and reputation created in the media.

International marketing communications, standardization and adaptation

The most obvious tactic for reducing instances of international communications failure might appear to be to adopt a strict policy of standardization in the implementation of communications plans. Firms adopt this principle, for example, in their use of corporate identity and global advertising campaigns. However, given the need to also demonstrate cultural sensitivity and empathy with a wide range of international customers *and* to avoid the type of mistakes referred to earlier, it is necessary to adapt the international communications to local market needs with sensitivity.

Towards standardization

The drivers for standardization of international marketing communications come first, from the organization's desire to improve efficiency. Cost-saving activity in marketing communications includes benefits from economies of scale, for example, in advertising creative work, media buying, making better use of staff time and from the experience effect, by achieving efficiencies through replicating successful marketing communications programmes and processes in different countries.

Customers believe that they gain additional benefit and value from a consistent and widely recognized brand image that reflects their own self-image; for example, teenagers (as well as rather more elderly sports enthusiasts too) gain peer recognition, credibility and prestige from wearing branded sports wear which has strong associations with international sports stars. A company may use a top international business consultancy or advertising agency with a prestigious image just as much because the association is perceived positively by the company's suppliers and customers rather than for the cost-effectiveness of the work that is carried out.

Consistency in the corporate identity and branding, reinforces awareness in stakeholders' minds and provides the familiarity with the company which leads to a feeling of confidence, trust and loyalty. For example, it may be reassuring for a visitor to see the familiar logo and appearance of a fast food outlet, hotel chain or bank in a foreign country that they are visiting.

Over the years changes have led to greater prosperity and thus greater buying power – at least for some people – has resulted in greater acceptance of imported products. Consumers and business-to-business customers often prefer internationally available products with which they have become familiar through increased travel, Internet, radio and television communications and the written media. Satellite and cable television have created worldwide customer segments for many more globally standardized products and services.

The Internet allows customers to access products from organizations from very distant locations. It allows specialist suppliers to make their standard products and services globally available to customers, and enables smaller companies to compete essentially on equal terms with their much larger competitors, so 'punching above their weight'. Of course, companies that only communicate using the Internet are limiting their customer base to those customer segments that can access the Internet or buy online.

At an operational level, advertising standardization is possible when:

- visual messages form the main content of the advertisement;
- well-known international film stars, popular celebrities and sports personalities are featured;
- music is an important part of the communication;
- well-known symbols and trademarks are featured. For example, the Grand Canyon in the US can be used to symbolize certain types of outdoor American values.

Advertisements do not travel well to other countries:

- when the use of spoken and written language forms an important part of the communication;
- if humour is used – humour is often *very* specific to certain cultures;
- if personalities are used who are well-known in one country but are not known internationally;
- if campaigns are used that rely on specific knowledge of previous advertising.

Towards adaptation The principal drivers of international marketing communications adaptation are the cultural differences that must be managed when communicating with customers in different countries. As we have already seen in this book, there are some fundamental differences in the ways that consumers from different cultures respond to different communication approaches. More specifically, however, in a comparison between the US and Chinese responses to advertising Zhang and Neelankavil (1997) observe that, overall, US subjects preferred the individualistic appeal (self-orientation, self-sufficiency and control, the pursuit of individual gains) whereas Chinese subjects favoured the collective appeal (subordination of personal interests to the goals of the group, with emphasis on sharing, cooperation and harmony, and a concern for the group's welfare). It is these differences which must be recognized, but there is also likely to be continuing convergence across cultures and moves toward standardization.

Advertisers believe that advertising is most effective when it is relevant to the target audience – one area where there are significant differences is in the portrayal of women in advertising.

Siu and Au (1997) report that research studies of advertising suggest that:

- over 80 per cent of voiceovers are male;
- women are depicted as housewives, mothers and/or sex objects;
- females are shown as product users whereas males are shown in the roles of authority.

However, the role of women is changing rapidly as many more women are entering the workforce. In research carried out by Siu and Au in China and Singapore, they found that sex-role stereotyping was more apparent in China – women were depicted as product users and men as having product authority – whereas in Singapore women generally appeared as the spokesperson for the product, to have product authority and be the providers of help and advice.

There are many local reasons why firms may need to adapt their communications strategy. Many companies have to change their brand names because of different meanings they have when they move to new markets. The New Zealand Dairy Board, a large exporter of dairy foods, uses the brand name Fern for its butter in Malaysia, although Anchor is the flagship brand well known in Western Europe. In Malaysia Anchor is a widely advertised local beer, and Malaysian housewives are unlikely to buy dairy products for their children which they would subconsciously associate with alcohol.

When Johnson and Johnson entered the Hong Kong market they used the name *zhuang-cheng* which means 'an official or lord during feudal times'. This upper-class association was seen as inappropriate for China, and the more upbeat modern tone of '*qiang-sheng*', meaning 'active life', was used instead, to better reflect the drive for modernization.

The differences in appeal between Western and Asian communications are more fundamental than simply changing brand names. Chan and Huang (1997) suggest that brands can be enhanced if names and/or symbols of favourite animals and flowers and lucky numbers are used. In Asia written figures may be perceived as potent symbols; thus, as Schmitt and Pan (1994) point out, in Asian countries the emphasis may be heavier on the distinctive writing and logo of the brand than on the jingles that Western marketing communications favour.

Firms use a variety of ways of becoming more sensitive to cultural differences. Unilever has set up innovation centres in Asia in order to bring together research, production and marketing staff to speed up development of international brands which have a local appeal. In Bangkok there are innovation centres responsible for ice cream, laundry detergents and hair care. Asian Delight is a regional brand of ice cream – between the Magnum brand and local brands – and uses English and Thai on its packaging in Thailand, but English only in Malaysia, Singapore and Indonesia. It is sold from Wall's mobile units and cabinets in convenience stores and supermarkets. The flavours have a local appeal and include coconut-milk based ice cream mixed with fruits and vegetables traditionally used in desserts or chewy strings of green flour, black beans and sago.

International marketing communications strategy

So far in this chapter we have highlighted the need to consider the nature and role of international marketing communications more broadly than was the case in the past, by focusing upon both internal and external communications and a wider range of communications tools. In thinking about developing strategy there are two significant issues to address. First, there is a need to state clear and precise objectives for the international marketing communications strategy and, second, how the various communications activities might be coordinated to maximize their cost effectiveness.

The promotional objectives can be categorized as sales-related and brand/product communications-related, which might be stated in terms of increasing sales by:

- increasing market share at the expense of local and/or international competitors;
- identifying new potential customers;

- obtaining a specific number of responses to a promotional campaign;
- reducing the impact of competitors in the market,

and brand/product communications-related by:

- increasing the value of the corporate brand and product image;
- helping to establish the position or to reposition the product or brand;
- increasing awareness levels especially in new country markets;
- changing consumers' perceptions of products, brands or the firm.

These objectives must be set for each country or region in order to fit with the firm's international development ambition.

The options that are available for a generic marketing communications strategy centre on the extent to which a **push or pull strategy** could and should be adopted (Figure 9.4). A push strategy means promoting the product or service to retailers and wholesalers in order to force the product or service down the distribution channel by using promotional methods, such as personal selling, discounts and special deals. A pull strategy means communicating with the final consumer to attract them to the retailer or distributor to purchase the product. In this case mass advertising, sales promotions and point of sales promotions are the most obvious promotional methods. In domestic markets firms realize the need to have a combination of push and pull strategies, including both encouraging the intermediaries and retailers to stock the products and attracting end users to buy.

In international markets the nature of the market structure that already exists may well affect the degree to which push and pull strategies are used; for example, how well the distribution channel is established, how powerful the retailers or distributors are, how well established the competitors are and whether the firm marketing its products or services wishes to, or has the power to, challenge the existing 'route to market' by setting up a new channel.

Frequently, the international marketing communications strategy of a firm has to be adapted because of the variation in the market structures and distribution channels from country to country (for example, some are highly fragmented, while others are very concentrated). More often than not, however, it is the

FIGURE 9.4 Push and pull strategies

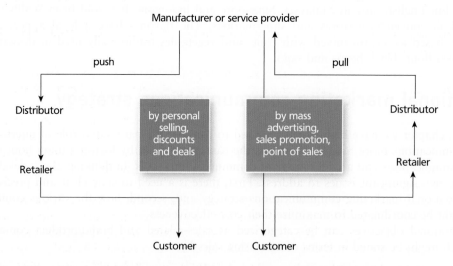

lack of resources, expertise and local knowledge of the firm in the target country markets that limits its communications strategy options. It may well not be able to transfer its successful domestic strategy to the new market. The firm may be forced into making use of and relying heavily upon established intermediaries to do the promotion for them through existing channels. For this reason it is possible to find organizations that have a pull strategy in their domestic or other established markets and a push strategy in their newer markets.

Having determined the objectives and decided upon the degree to which a push and pull strategy might be used, the dimensions of the international marketing communications implementation strategy can be defined. These are:

- the message to be communicated;
- the target audience to which the message will be directed;
- the media that will be used to carry the message;
- the ways in which the impact of the communications will be measured.

As we said at the start of this chapter, continually evaluating the impact of the communications is vital, not only in improving the effectiveness of the communication but also in assessing the degree to which each of these dimensions can be standardized across international markets.

Communicating with existing and potential customers

Given that the primary objective of international marketing communications is to persuade customers to buy products and services which will meet their requirements, it is appropriate to consider how international marketing communications are used strategically to influence each of the stages of the buying process and to help customers to complete their purchase.

A number of writers have developed models of buying behaviour which tend to vary according to the context of the study, but all acknowledge that there are a number of stages in the buying process. A simplified version of these stages (AIDA) includes:

- Awareness of the firm, its products and services and their reputation. Illustration 9.3 provides an example of raising awareness for a specific segment.
- Interest in the products and services, because they may be suited to the consumers' needs and worthy of consideration for potential purchase.
- Desire to buy the product or service, in preference to that of the competitor, after consumers have become better informed about its performance.
- Action by the customer in overcoming any remaining reservations or barriers and purchasing the product or service.

Different messages must be prepared and the most appropriate promotional tool selected for each part of the buying process in order to persuade customers to move to the next stage. There are significant differences between consumer markets, business-to-business and institutional market purchasing. For example, in fast-moving consumer goods marketing, advertising can be used to raise awareness, create interest and encourage consumers to purchase, but only if the messages are sensitive and appealing and the customers have access to the media used for advertising. Other tools such as point of sale promotion can be used to support the strategy, provided it is possible for the firm to maintain some level of control over the displays used by local retailers.

Capital equipment usually depends more on personal selling and providing technical service to a buying committee. This would typically be supported by awareness-raising in the trade press, using PR and corporate advertising. Here the need for monitoring the consistency of approach and ensuring good communications with the manufacturing operation must be balanced against the need for sensitivity to the way that business is done in that particular country. Institutional purchasing is often undertaken through competitive tenders which often, directly or indirectly, favour local suppliers.

© Steve Stock/Alamy

ILLUSTRATION 9.3

Building cool brand

When China first opened up to Western brands initially it was their 'foreignness' that made them attractive to consumers, but now the brands have to work harder and be more creative. A number of Western brands are using the emerging youth culture as a way of connecting with new consumers. In a country where ancient traditions have emphasized conformity and respect for elders and education has centred on rote learning, the youth culture is emerging as 'the right to be unique'. Brands, such as Wrangler, Motorola, Levis, Pepsi, Ben Sherman, Nokia, Budweiser, Umbro and Converse, sponsor rock festivals or use retail spaces or galleries as impromptu concert venues in an attempt to be the new 'cool'. The approaches of the brands reflect their view of their target customer segment, so Pepsi looking for a mainstream segment staged an American Idol style battle of the bands, where 6000 bands from 121 cities auditioned for a 10-part, 10-band competition with cash and a production deal for the winner. By contrast Converse shoes, going to the cultural fringe, used a brand promotion to provide tickets for the hard rock P.K.14's Love Noise tour of underground rock venues.

Question

1 Is cross cultural sponsorship likely to be effective in building a brand in new markets for the sponsor?

References: Foster, P. (2009) 'Kingdom of the sing dynasty', *Daily Telegraph*, 21 November.

The integration of communications

Stakeholders receive messages, both intended and unintended, from every part of the organization's activities. Davidson (2002) explains that an organization communicates in eight ways:

1 Actions – what it does.
2 Behaviour, how things are done, for example, how the telephone is answered.
3 Face-to-face by management: through talks, visits and meetings it shows what the management thinks is important.
4 Signals, from the organizations' actions, facilities and objects, including executive bonuses, dress, buildings.
5 Product and services, and particularly their quality.
6 Intended communications, such as advertising, which is not always received as the organization expects.
7 Word of mouth and word of Web (including email).
8 Comment by other organizations, such as pressure groups, competitors and the media.

As the number of communications have increased dramatically and customers have become more critical and sceptical, the importance of integrated marketing communications has been emphasized in order to avoid conflicting messages and instead communicate consistent and mutually supporting messages. Fill (2006) points out that traditional mass-communication strategies have given way to more personalized, customer-oriented and technology-driven approaches. To be successful the firm requires a completely different approach, focusing on the individual customer and Kotler (2003) says that 'companies need to orchestrate a consistent set of impressions from its personnel, facilities and actions that deliver the company's brand meaning and promise to its various audiences'.

Shimp (2006) provides a definition of integrated marketing communications which puts the customer at the centre:

1 Start with the customer or prospect.

2 Use any form of relevant contact.

3 Achieve synergy through consistency across the communication elements.

4 Build relationships.

5 Affect behaviour.

The emphasis of Shimp's approach is on marketing promotion whereas, digital media encourages a two-way communications process and interactivity between the organization and its customer is a key component of integration. For example, seeing the comments of customers in social media can help a firm reduce the gap between its intended image and that perceived by customers.

The benefits of integration Given the fact that individual messages on their own have little overall impact on customers it follows that the effect of communications will be significantly greater if the many messages are consistent, uniform and mutually supporting in the way that builds the image of the brand, product and service and reinforce the reputation, standards and values of the organization around the world.

It is easier to justify the cost and control communications activities if they are integrated so that the cumulative effect, rather than individual effect, is assessed. Measurement of individual actions is difficult, given the 'noise' in the environment, and so it is more sensible to measure the effects of the combined actions.

Integration with the global strategy Although usually considered to be a part of the marketing mix, in many organizations communications takes on a much more important role. It is essential in explaining the organization's corporate, business unit and marketing mix strategies to stakeholders, including shareholders. Global integration is needed so that the consistency of internal and external communications across borders is maintained.

Business unit integration At business unit level, managers in charge of communications must work closely with colleagues responsible for development, operations, key account management, sales and customer service centre management to develop a highly integrated global approach that offers a seamless service to customers.

Marketing mix integration Customers continually receive communications from the organization that are the result of marketing mix actions. Every element of the marketing mix communicates with customers.

It is important to remember that non-verbal communication in many markets has a greater impact than verbal communications or written words, especially given the amount of time (milliseconds!) that a customer concentrates on one communication. For example, the colours and styles used in creative packaging or signage work communicate non-verbally with the customers, reinforcing the images and customer perceptions, but this differs between cultures. Customers can pick up small errors in colour matching and design, so discipline in the use of the corporate identity is essential. In different cultures the significance of colours, symbols and numbers is so great that they alone could deter customers from buying a product.

Coordination and planning of the international marketing communications strategy

To achieve its objectives, the communications strategy will almost certainly include a variety of promotional tools. The key to success is integrating the various promotion elements in a cost-efficient way and adding value through choosing the communications methods that will have the most impact on the customers. The actual mix chosen will depend upon a number of issues surrounding the context of the purchasing situation, including:

- the market area and industry sector;
- whether it is consumer, institutional or business-to-business marketing;
- the customer segment to be targeted;

FIGURE 9.5 Internal and external international communications programmes

Marketing programmes influencing communications	International communication aims
Internally focused programmes	
Corporate identity	Consistency in all aspects of company logo, signs and image
Internal marketing communications	Reinforce motivation through telling staff what is happening
Sales force, dealer and distributor training and development	Training through conferences, manuals and brochures
Retailing merchandising	Point of sale persuasion through displays and shelf facings
First contact customer service	Welcoming first contact through telephonist and receptionist training
After-sales service	Customer retention and satisfaction through staff training and brochures
Quality management	Assuring a continuous quality approach in all programmes
Brand management	Achieving common brand standards and values
Externally focused programmes (marketing mix)	
Product attributes	Offering innovative, high-quality products
Distribution channel	Ensuring easy access to products and frequent customer encounters with the products
Price	Messages about quality and status
Product/service promotion	Managing customer expectations through the integration of the marketing mix communications
People	Using staff–customer interactions to reinforce the aims, standards and values of the firm
Customer service process	Providing a satisfactory total experience through the service offer
Physical evidence for the service delivery	All contacts with the facilities reinforce the firm's messages

MANAGEMENT CHALLENGE 9.2

Self-reference criteria in advertising decisions

Advertising managers who are involved in cross-border campaigns face the problem of self-reference criteria. A European brand manager for Heinz, based in the UK, was responsible for approving advertising campaigns that had been developed by local agencies for the local country subsidiary as part of a pan-European campaign. In Germany the local agency produced a television advertising campaign. The European brand manager, his boss and his boss's boss, all English, turned down the agency's creative work.

The advertisement was meant to be humorous but they did not find it at all funny, and they were concerned that it would devalue the brand and the campaign. The agency insisted that they had tested the ad on consumers and the humour would work in Germany. After various delays the manager had to make the decision whether or not the ad should go ahead on the following Monday. However, it was the weekend and he could not reach his bosses for help

with the decision. The campaign would cost £1 million which would be lost if it did not go ahead. If the campaign adversely affected the product it would be a greater disaster – his job could be on the line! Against his better judgement, and overcoming his self-reference criteria, he decided the advert should be broadcast. The campaign was a great success!

Western firms also realize that it is important to appreciate the levels of intelligence and sophistication of emerging markets. When Heinz first launched tomato ketchup in Russia they used an existing TV ad from the UK with minor modifications. Now it would be unacceptable as the Russian audience is more sophisticated. Russian actors would be needed on the advertisement. Heinz is particularly sensitive to the need to adapt to local markets and this is part of their strategy.

Consumers are very knowledgeable and well aware when some big brands are behaving in an arrogant manner and telling them what to buy. They can become annoyed when firms insult their intelligence. A number of firms have seen their reputation and share price suffer because of insensitive promotion and PR.

Question

1 Should a firm insist on standardization and consistency of its communications approach, and when should they trust partners with local knowledge?

- the participants in the purchasing process, their requirements and expectations and the best methods to reach and influence them;
- the country or region, the culture, the communications infrastructure and the preferred methods of communicating;
- the resources made available by the organization and the implications for the level of involvement and control it wishes to exert over the communications process.

The value of different promotional methods varies according to the context in which the marketing communications are being used and the degree to which they are integrated within a marketing communications strategy, as shown in Figure 9.5.

The critical issue is the extent to which they must be adapted so that they can be effective in international markets. Management Challenge 9.2 shows how difficult it is for managers to make decisions that require them to go against their instincts and self-reference criteria.

The marketing communications tools

There are a number of offline and online marketing communications tools for the external market and it is to these that we now turn. For convenience we have grouped these tools within broad categories. In practice there is some flexibility in the way the tools are used within a coordinated strategy but the tools are listed as follows:

Communicating product and service differentiation. This group includes personal selling and word of mouth communications, exhibitions and trade fairs, trade missions, advertising and the use of agencies, sales promotion and direct marketing.

Communicating with a wider range of stakeholders. This includes corporate identity, sponsorship and public relations.

Online communications are used in all areas of communications, both complementing and replacing offline communications.

Personal selling and word of mouth

For many companies the first proactive communication tool to promote exports is personal selling. Selling is often used to gain the first few orders in a new market and as the main component of a push strategy to persuade distribution channel members, such as agents, distributors or retailers to stock the product. It is expensive, however.

The use of personal selling tends to be limited to situations in which benefits can be derived from two-way information flows, negotiation is required and when the revenue from the sale is sufficiently high to justify the costs. This is typically the case with business-to-business marketing and in consumer markets where the purchase price and complexity of negotiations justifies the high cost of personal selling, for example for cars, holidays, homes and consumer durable products. Even here the need for personal selling is being challenged as direct marketing, particularly using the Internet, is now being used routinely to purchase these products.

In countries where labour costs are very low, personal selling is used to a greater extent than in high cost countries. This ranges from street and market trading to quite sophisticated multilevel distribution chains for business-to-business products. In high labour-cost countries personal selling of low unit cost products is used rarely, except for illegal trading, for example of drugs.

Effective selling in international business-to-business and consumer markets involves a wide range of tasks and skills, including product and market knowledge, listening and questioning skills. However, it is in the core selling activities of negotiation and persuasion discussed in Chapter 3 that higher-order expertise is required. It is likely that local people will be more effective than home-based representatives in understanding the subtleties of the negotiation process as they apply within the local business culture. They will have fluent language skills and an intimate knowledge of the culture of the country.

However, negotiation of high-value contracts may well require specialist technical knowledge, an understanding of the processes and systems and strict adherence to the firm's standards and values. For these reasons the company may well prefer to use staff from its head office to ensure that the sales people are well informed about the firm's capabilities and that their activities can be controlled.

This is particularly the case if the opportunities to make a sale are very infrequent (e.g. with capital goods) when high levels of technical skill and an understanding of the company's systems are needed but not easily learnt by new people. For example, Rolls-Royce use a complete team of UK-based engineers, accountants and sales people to sell aero engines to customers in foreign markets. Some of the team will make frequent visits, others will be based in close online and offline contact with the customer for a period of many months. The sheer complexity of the contracts means that only Rolls-Royce employees could understand the detail sufficiently to handle the negotiations. The high contract price provides sufficient revenue to pay for the costs of the UK-based sales team.

An alternative to employing local or head office sales staff (both have their advantages and disadvantages) is to employ expatriates, staff from the domestic country to work for extended periods in the host country in order to bridge the culture and company standards gap.

In practice the expatriate is likely to experience a culture shock caused by living in a foreign culture where the familiar symbols, cues and everyday reassurances are missing, often causing feelings of frustration, stress and anxiety. The expatriate can respond to the situation in one of three ways. At one extreme, adjustment is made to the expatriate culture only. In effect the expatriate adjusts to the way of life of a ready-made cultural island within the host country and makes little attempt to adjust to the host culture.

At the other extreme the expatriate completely embraces the host culture and minimizes contact with the expatriate community – and the firm too. Ideally the expatriate adjusts to both the local culture and the expatriate culture. In this way the expatriate retains the home country's and firm's system of values and beliefs, but is considerate and respectful towards the people of his or her host country and to their culture. It is this last option that is usually most beneficial for the firm's sales effort.

Whichever approach to selling is adopted, it is through relevant training that firms aim to manage their sales staff's involvement with the firm and the market, and maintain their enthusiasm for selling. Honeycutt (2005) explains that global firms have a training culture, employ a more formal training curriculum and focus on 'soft' competencies, whereas local Singaporean firms used more on the job training and did not appear to understand how sales training could be used for competitive advantage. As the cost of personal selling is increasing, so firms are seeking ways of improving their cost-effectiveness by using more systematic ways of analyzing customer requirements and carrying out the sales role, rather than relying on a good firm handshake for closing the deal.

Exhibitions, trade fairs and experiential marketing

Exhibitions and trade fairs are an effective way of meeting many existing and potential customers from different countries. The cost of exhibiting at international trade fairs is very high when the cost of the stand, space rental, sales staff time and travelling expenses are taken into account. It is for this reason that the selection of the most appropriate fairs for the industry is critical. Also important are the creative work for the stand, preparation of sales literature and selection of suitable personnel for the stand, bearing in mind the need for cultural and language empathy.

To obtain the maximum benefit from an exhibition it is essential to publicize the firm's attendance at the event to encourage potential customers to visit and also to ensure that all leads are followed up. Shimp (2006) explains that the real cost of exhibitions can be two or three times higher than the cost of the event itself.

An additional benefit of exhibitions is that they can provide experiential marketing, a rapidly growing communications approach also called customer experience marketing, in which customers obtain an engaging, entertaining and interactive brand experience. There are of course other ways of providing experiential marketing. For example, Apple operates stores in which customers can try out their products and Harley Davidson provides opportunities for visitors to ride its bikes.

Given the importance of context in many markets, such as Asia, experiential marketing, involving life experiences at events for external communications to customers and internal communications, were shown to be valuable (Whiteling 2007).

Trade missions

Trade missions are organized visits to a country or region by a group of senior business managers from a number of firms, perhaps from the same geographic region or the same industry. They are often subsidized by national or local government. Discussions with potential customers are arranged in advance in the host country.

Trade missions are usually associated with exporting, and may be used to carry out introductory talks with prospective clients or to negotiate a contract. As with trade fairs, good preparation work before the visit is essential to ensure that meetings are arranged with appropriate customers where there is a genuine possibility of business being generated. Usually the home country's local embassy staff will provide support for trade missions and often, too, depending on the importance of the mission, there will be discussions with the host government, civil servants and politicians about how trade between the two countries can be developed.

Advertising

Online and offline advertising are usually the most visible forms of communication and are often considered the most important part of the whole strategy for consumer products in countries with a well-developed media industry. Traditionally offline advertising has disadvantages because it is essentially a one-way method of communication and in international marketing, for example, it can be difficult to control the reach of TV (the geographic area in which consumers are exposed to the messages and specific customer segments). The objective is to obtain the maximum exposure of the product or brand to the largest possible target audience.

In most business-to-business markets advertising tends to be used as a supporting activity, for example, to increase awareness or interest in the company as a whole or in a new concept. In business-to-business markets the number of important customers is often comparatively small and it is essential that advertising is precisely targeted, using appropriate specialist trade media.

Together with the increased harmonization of consumer demands for some products and the benefits of standardized products and services to firms, there is a strong move to pan-regional advertising campaigns. Consumers increasingly share common values and characteristics but there are differences: for example, consumers in developing markets are still developing their habits as consumers.

There are considerable differences in the availability and usefulness of other advertising media such as radio, cinema and posters. These differences make it essential to obtain data about media effectiveness in order to make informed decisions about international media schedules. For instance, in remote regions exposure to certain media is prevented because of the poor transmission output quality from radio stations, lack of electricity to power TVs or computers, the target audience having insufficient disposable income to afford television or radio and low adult literacy levels preventing significant numbers of adults from reading printed advertising.

Mass communications are becoming less effective for reaching target segments, particularly in developed countries because of the increasingly fragmented nature of the national press and television. Many households have access to multiple TV channels, films and TV on-demand, and alternative leisure activities such as gaming and social media. The traditional channels have lost audiences, particularly in the 16–24 age group. Vollmer, Frelinghuysen and Rothenberg (2007) explain the changes taking place in the balance between offline and online advertising.

In these situations it may be necessary to develop a campaign based upon a multitude of individual media activities, but this does mean that the measurement of the cost-effectiveness of the campaign is extremely difficult, given that individual components of the campaign may produce different effects.

Mass marketing is still valuable in emerging markets and to help organizations create a global brand. Increased spending has led to Coca-Cola becoming the best-selling soft drink in China and overtaking Pepsi in a number of central and Eastern European republics. Pepsi response to this has been to embark on diversification by buying a stake in Russia's largest food group, Wimm-Bill-Dann. Conglomerates from emerging countries such as Hyundai, HTC and Huawei, recognize the value of moving from product orientation to marketing orientation and have built substantial brands through global advertising.

Table 9.2 shows the top ten advertising spenders worldwide and in the US, Asia and Europe. It also compares their spending in the three major trading regions.

Television advertising

The main influence on television advertising expenditure is the size of the economy in gross domestic product per capita, but the regulatory environment also affects spending, particularly television which tends to be more closely regulated than other media.

Cable and satellite television have contributed to a proliferation of television channels so that viewers can receive a rapidly increasing number of programmes. This means that there is a greater capacity for television advertising but, of course, there is greater competition for prime television advertising spots (and much higher costs) if there is likely to be a large audience. Both satellite and cable television have the potential to cross country borders and attract large audiences for programmes of common international interest, for example major sporting events.

It is not only overt television advertising in large amounts that sells. The prominent placing of products on television shows or sponsorship of programmes that are likely to be transmitted in other countries can also become an important part of the advertising campaign, particularly as placements and sponsorship cannot be removed by viewers 'zapping' between channels. An interesting development is

Table 9.2 Top 10 global advertisers

Rank	Advertiser	Spending Worldwide US$billion
1	Proctor & Gamble	9.73
2	Unilever	5.72
3	L'Oreal	4.04
4	General Motors	3.67
5	Toyota	3.20
6	Coca-Cola	2.67
7	Johnson and Johnson	2.60
8	Ford	2.45
9	Reckitt Benckiser	2.37
10	Nestlé	2.31

Source: Reprinted with permission from Advertising Age (2006). Copyright Crain Communications Inc.

shown in Illustration 9.4 which shows how offline and online communications can be integrated. With a more sceptical and knowledgeable audience, advertisers are adopting different, more inclusive approaches to win over customers.

Press advertising

Media availability and effectiveness are particularly important in deciding the nature of campaigns, because they can vary from country to country. The lack of mass-circulation national titles might cause distribution difficulties too, as it is easier to distribute quickly in small compact countries than in much larger ones such as France or Spain. Vast countries like the USA have a regional press. Newer publishing and printing technology has allowed many more local and free newspapers and specialist magazines to be introduced to both consumer and business-to-business markets. By their very nature they tend to be highly targeted at specific market segments and can be useful to niche marketers. Sales of mass audience newspapers in many countries are declining as readers turn to the Internet for general and specialist news coverage. For mass marketers the resulting fragmentation of readership means that national campaigns are more difficult to coordinate.

The use of agencies and consultancies

Most companies in which marketing communications are an important part of the marketing mix use agencies and consultancies. The reasons why this is so can be explained by financial considerations, specialist knowledge, creative input and external perspective.

Financial. Advertising agents that are recognized by the media are eligible for a commission based on booked advertising space. The agency can, therefore, perform the advertising services of creation, media planning and booking more economically than the client.

Agencies and consultancies can use specialist people and resources, such as a database for media planning, with a number of clients. This helps spread costs for both the agency and client.

Specialist knowledge. By concentrating on one particular area, agencies and consultancies can become experts in specialized techniques, for example international database marketing or training sales people.

wrinkled?

wonderful?

Will society ever accept 'old' can be beautiful?

campaignforrealbeauty.co.uk Dove

Courtesy of The Advertising Archives

ILLUSTRATION 9.4

Dove uses consumer-created ads

The academy awards ceremony is the second most watched TV programme in the US after the Super-bowl. In 2007 Unilever took a very expensive 30 second spot for its new product, Dove Cream Oil Body Wash. The featured advertisement was the winning entry in a contest in which consumers created their own advertisement. It was a reflection of the combination of new and old media, and a move to engaging consumers through user-generated content, rather than simply pushing the product. It followed on Dove's award-winning global campaign that featured ordinary-looking women and departed from conventional ideas of beauty. The Evolution ad won a Grand Prix best commercial ad at Cannes in 2007.

The creators of the Dove campaign were Ogilvy and Mather, and CEO, Shelly Lazarus explains that whereas in the past advertising a brand simply meant coming up with a good idea for a few television and print ads and intruding into the lives of its viewers, campaigns must now be an invitation to them, using the most appropriate media and communication tools available.

The Dove campaign was an illustration of this new approach and was designed to banish stereotypes and prompt a debate about beauty by involving consumers in 'Real Beauty' online workshops through the combination of traditional make up, digital enhancement and altering of the resulting images to prompt a debate over the Internet.

Dove's 'Campaign for Real Beauty' was launched in 2004 and as part of it, and reflecting the research that found only 2 per cent of women in the world think they are beautiful, Unilever were persuaded by Ogilvy to launch a worldwide 'self-esteem fund' to persuade girls and young women to embrace more positive images of themselves.

To manage Dove's worldwide integrated campaign it was necessary for Ogilvy to change its way of working. It brought together previously separate creative departments so Internet 'types' would sit together with television, print, outdoor advertising, direct marketing and public relations specialists to develop an integrated 'idea' that would appeal to the boss of the client company, who are much more aware of the importance of reputation, image and being a good corporate citizen.

Question

1 What factors will have most impact on traditional advertising?

References: 'Queen of Madison Avenue',*The Economist*, 22 February 2007. G. Haycock, 'Unilever's Dove ad flies home with top prize', *Reuters*, 23 June 2007: accessed at http://uk.news.yahoo.com and from http://www.unilever.com/ourbrands/personalcare/dove.asp.

Client companies might have an infrequent need for these services and so find it more cost-effective to subcontract the work.

Creative input. Creativity is very important in marketing communications. The organization culture of client companies is unlikely to encourage true creativity in external communications. The challenge of new and different projects for different clients contributes to the creativity of agencies.

External perspective. The external view of agencies reduces some of the myopia of the client company. This might be particularly valuable at times of major transition, for example in moving from international marketing towards global marketing.

The selection of agencies and consultants is an important business decision. If the agency is going to be involved over a long period and be trusted with large expenditures of time and money the decision process will be significant. A dilemma for global marketers is whether they should select one central agency or many local agencies in their target countries, both of which approaches have advantages and disadvantages.

Sales promotions

Sales promotions are used as an extra incentive for the purchaser at the point of sale. In some markets there may be no meaningful differences between a number of companies or brands, except for the degree of attractiveness of the sales promotion offer. The customers' perception of the relative value of the alternative promotions depends to a great extent on their cultural values and differences, which lead to certain types of sales promotion being very successful in one country but failing in another.

Legal restrictions also affect the opportunity for firms to standardize sales promotion across country borders. There are limitations on the amount of cash discounts and special sales promotions in some countries in Europe. Different legal definitions of the rules for lotteries, too, prevent some competition-based promotions being operated across borders.

Direct marketing

In the past, direct marketing has usually taken the form of direct mail or telephone selling, but in markets with high computer ownership the Internet has taken the lead. The key elements of direct marketing are an accurate up-to-date database, the ability to purge the database of incorrect data and to merge the database with a firm's promotional message. Usually firms subcontract direct marketing to specialist agencies which provide the various services, such as list brokering, purging and merging.

Communicating with the wider range of stakeholders

At the outset we said that the principal objective of the international marketing communications strategy was to sell products and services. However, customers in a host country are unlikely to even contemplate buying from a foreign firm that is unknown, or worse still, perceived to be exploiting its local workers, bribing government officials, showing little regard to environmental protection issues, offering poor or variable product quality or is likely to pull out from the country at any moment and thus be unable to fulfil its guarantees and obligations. A foreign firm can build increased loyalty among its customers at the expense of local firms if it is perceived to offer better quality and value for money, to be a more reliable supplier, more caring about the local community and, in some cases, through association, to be respected by world personalities.

Firms need to build their reputation with all their influential stakeholders, pressure groups and the community in general as well as customers. They do this in a number of ways:

- Corporate identity.
- Sponsorship.
- Public relations and lobbying.

Corporate identity

Corporate identity is concerned with consistently communicating not just what business the firm is in and what image it wishes to project in the market, but also how it does its business. It must reflect the standards and values it aims to uphold in its dealings with all its stakeholders. Corporate philanthropy is a key factor as Illustration 9.5 shows, but the aims of the organization and recipients of corporate giving may not always coincide. For this reason there are two distinct elements. For many MNEs the focus is upon the image it wishes to create, which is reinforced by consistency in the way the company name and logo is presented and applied to the vast range of physical outputs and assets of the company including signs, staff uniforms, letterheads, visiting cards, gifts, annual reports, packaging specification and promotional literature.

In principle, while these can all be controlled by the firm, there are many challenges in applying them consistently in all the countries where the firm operates, especially where it develops alliances with partners who might also wish to maintain their corporate identity in joint communications.

Arguably of more importance is the underlying identity of the firm and its beliefs, standards and values, which will show through in everything it does. These may pose more difficulties in the firm's attempts to achieve consistency and a favourable impact throughout the world because of the different cultural values of its staff and stakeholders in different countries.

© Geoffrey Kidd/Alamy

ILLUSTRATION 9.5

Corporate giving – not meeting real needs?

Corporate giving is an effective way of using PR to enhance the organization's corporate social responsibility reputation internationally, and the pride, loyalty and commitment of staff. BSkyB responded to the Haiti earthquake not only by adding 50 per cent extra to all the money raised by its staff but also by launching the Red Button Appeal, which meant that Sky customers could press the red button on their television to make a donation. This also had the additional effect of demonstrating the possibilities that interactive television offers to potential advertisers.

Glaxo SmithKline works with charity partners as a member of the Partnership for Quality Medical Donations alliance of donating pharmaceutical companies and humanitarian agencies, and provides specialist advice and donates medicines for community healthcare and disaster relief. The company believes donations should only be made on the advice of people with local expertise, including the area director. A key part too is keeping its own staff informed using a website to reassure them of the efforts being made.

One problem in corporate giving is that levels of donations have been hit by many businesses replacing charitable donations with employee volunteering. The advantage for employees is that they see the direct benefit of their work but the volunteering may not always address the priority needs of the charity and could in some circumstances reduce the opportunity for the charity to employ local people in need of work too.

Question

1 How can the PR benefits of enhanced reputation be maximized through corporate giving?

Sponsorship and celebrity endorsement

Sponsorship involves a firm (the sponsor) providing finance, resources or other support for an event, activity, firm, person, product or service. In return the sponsor would expect to gain some advantage, such as the exposure of its brand, logo or advertising message. Sponsorship of music, performing arts and sporting events provides opportunities for:

- brand exposure and publicity;
- opportunities to entertain and reward customers and employees;
- association between brands and events, with the events often reinforcing the brand positioning;
- improving community relations by supporting community-based projects;
- creating the opportunity to promote the brands at the event, either through providing free products or gifts such as T-shirts carrying the brand logo.

Expenditure on global sponsorship has expanded rapidly over the past two decades, and it is being used much more for the following reasons:

- restrictive government policies on tobacco and alcohol advertising make sponsorship the most effective way of communicating the brand imagery to a mass market, for example in Formula 1 car racing;
- the escalating costs of media advertising;
- increased leisure activities and sporting events;
- the cost effectiveness of sponsorship of successful events;
- endorsement of the product or service through association with the event;
- greater (free) media coverage of sponsored events;
- the reduced efficiencies of traditional media advertising because of clutter and zapping between television programmes, especially during advertising breaks.

Masterson (2005) explains the need to achieve a fit between the sponsor and the activity being sponsored, introduces the concept of integrated product relevance and explains the ways in which this can be used to affect the consumers' responses to the sponsor's products, by focusing on function and image similarity.

There has been an increase in the amount of broadcast sponsorship in film, television and radio programmes. This can result in the benefit of the event sponsorship being reduced. For example, Heinz sponsored a Rugby World Cup only to find that Sony sponsored the national commercial television coverage in the UK, resulting in most viewers thinking that Sony had sponsored the whole event.

Product placement and celebrity endorsement

Because many television viewers record programmes and are able to fast-forward through advertising, product placement within the programmes is becoming more attractive. Those films that will gain a global TV audience, such as James Bond, offer the most potential from product placement for global firms.

Sponsorship of individuals such as sports stars and the use of celebrities to endorse brands are very beneficial because of the perceived shared values and image association between the celebrity and the brand. The problem is that individuals can be unpredictable and this can lead to unfortunate and undesirable associations. Celebrities are increasingly advertising their own merchandize on TV shopping channels and Illustration 9.6 shows how they are being paid for web endorsements.

Global brands ambassadors need to be leaders in their field and recognizable by global consumers. As David Beckham came towards the end of his footballing career, he was replaced as the face of Gillette by Tiger Woods, Thierry Henry and Roger Federer. Woods attracted unfavourable media comment because of his behaviour in his private life, which adversely affected his sporting performance too.

© thesuperph, iStockphoto.com

ILLUSTRATION 9.6

Celebs Paid to Tweet Endorsements

Many social media sites have started up with the focus being social communication or business networking but without an overtly commercial focus. Their value for business takes time to recognize. In the B2C market celebrities, from Snoop Dogg to Kirstie Alley from US sitcom Cheers, are paid up to £32 000 per month to plug products ranging from clothes to cars on the Twitter social networking site. While the US regulations force celebrities to declare that the celebrities have benefited from their 140 character endorsements, in the UK there is no obligation for them to do so and fans cannot distinguish between an honest comment and a paid recommendation. For celebrities the attraction of Twitter is that they can maintain contact with their fans around the world (and make money from it too), but of course they risk their reputation if they inadvertently write something that is inappropriate.

Twitter itself has been slow to identify ways of making a profit from its micro blogging platform but it is now partnering with Disney Pixar, to promote 'trends', its first being Toy Story 3.

Businesses initially find Twitter difficult to use, not because it is complicated because it is not, but it is difficult to work out how it can be used for marketing purposes. One-way targeted messages replicating traditional advertising are unlikely to generate any value but listening to others can be the starting point because it can provide help with marketing, sales, recruitment, feedback, support or staying close to geographically spread networks. It is a fast, cheap way of hearing about dissatisfaction and provides an opportunity to respond. It can be a cost effective marketing tool when resources don't stretch to more expensive methods, such as conventional advertising, PR and conferences. It can help with formulating marketing messages as the discussion can identify value adding elements of the offer. By working with other social media platforms, it can be used to provide integrated, interactive, communications.

Question

1 What online information sources influence your purchasing decisions?

References: J. Harlow and J. McGinnes, 'Tweet-talking stars cash in', *Sunday Times*, 24 October 2010. S. Israel, 'In business, early birds twitter most effectively' B*loomberg Business week*, 8 October 2009. M. Warman, '"Promoted tweets" finally bring advertising to Twitter', *Daily Telegraph*, 17 June 2010.

Public relations

Public relations is concerned with communicating news stories about the firm, its people, standards and values – particularly its attitude to social responsibility – products and services through the media and without charge to develop relationships, goodwill and mutual understanding between the firm and its stakeholders. The press is always hungry for stories in order to fill their ever-expanding programmes and newspapers, and are grateful for interesting and newsworthy stories that are inexpensive to obtain.

The purposes of PR are as follows:

- helping to foster the prestige and reputation of the firm through its public image;
- raising awareness and creating interest in the firm's products;
- dealing with social and environmental issues and opportunities;
- improving goodwill with customers through presenting useful information and dealing effectively with complaints;
- promoting the sense of identification of employees with the firm through newsletters, social activities and recognition;
- discovering and eliminating rumours and other sources of misunderstanding and misconceptions;
- building a reputation as a good customer and reliable supplier;
- influencing the opinions of public officials and politicians, especially in explaining the responsible operation of the business and the importance of its activities to the community;
- dealing promptly, accurately and effectively with unfavourable negative publicity, especially where it is perceived to be a crisis which might damage the firm's reputation;
- attracting and keeping good employees.

An important aspect of PR is explaining the corporate social responsibility policy of organizations and dealing with the cynicism of pressure groups and individuals communicating online and using traditional media.

Public relations is concerned with a wide variety of activities in order to deliver these objectives, including:

- dealing with press relations;
- arranging facility visits;
- publishing house journals and newsletters;
- preparing videos, audiovisual presentations, printed reports and publications describing the firm's activities;
- training courses;
- arranging community projects;
- lobbying governments.

From a communications perspective the effect of public relations-generated stories in the media is different from advertising. The viewer, listener or reader will perceive the information differently. Editorial material in the media is perceived by consumers to be factual and comparatively neutral whereas advertising material is expected to be persuasive and present a positive statement for the advertisers' products. Whereas the firm controls every aspect of advertising, a press release covering a firm's news story will be interpreted by the journalist who writes the story for the press or edits the videotape for television.

Crisis management

In international marketing one of the most important responsibilities of public relations is to manage unexpected crises which occur from time to time. Over the past few years there have been a number of examples of good and bad practice in managing information when dealing with a crisis such as environmental pollution, unethical promotion, exploitation of labour and health scares caused by food contamination. The golden rule is that the firm should be seen to act, before the media or government forces it to do so, in order to show that it is sorry that an incident has occurred. However, it should neither accept responsibility nor apportion blame until the evidence is investigated and the real cause of the problem identified.

Illustration 9.7 shows how BP's PR in the aftermath of the disastrous Gulf of Mexico oil spill was woeful and contributed to the company's predicament.

ILLUSTRATION 9.7

© Donald Johansson, iStockphoto.com

BP's PR disaster

In 2010 11 people died and 17 were injured when a torrent of oil and gas shot up 3.5 miles of drilling pipe, broke through the floor of the Horizon rig and ignited. The rig sank two days later and for 87 days crude oil, estimated to be of the order of 200 million tonnes leaked into the Gulf of Mexico. BP set up a pot of $20 billion for the clean up and to cover claims for compensation from individuals and organizations that had lost out. It was the PR failures that made things worse however. Carl-Henric Svanberg, BP's chair-man, was forced to apologize for his apology when he patronizingly expressed his concern for the 'small people of the US', effectively reinforcing people's perceptions of the arrogance of global MNEs. Chief Executive, Tony Hayward, an otherwise well respected executive, gave a lamentably poor and evasive performance in front of US congressmen, presumably after having been given legal advice, when he appeared to abdicate all personal responsibility for the disaster and refused to answer any question about what might have caused it.

Throughout the crisis BP played down the scale of the disaster, underestimated the public mood and was slow to respond to each event that occurred. In this way it unnecessarily created international political and media hysteria and at one point this threatened the company's existence.

Question

1 How should a company such as BP respond to a crisis?

References: J. Warner, 'The Gulf of Mexico oil spill is bad but BP's PR is even worse', *Daily Telegraph*, 18 June 2010.

Many MNEs consider government lobbying an essential part of international communications, with the aim of influencing foreign governments both directly and indirectly through asking the home country government to help. Recent examples of lobbying have been US firms seeking to reduce Chinese piracy of products and services and allowing greater access to Japanese markets.

As government lobbying becomes increasingly important it raises issues for the company about how high profile it should be in pressing its case, particularly where it is seen to be exerting undue pressure on politicians or civil servants to behave unethically or reverse policy.

Some firms go one stage further by making donations to political parties. This, of course, can have the effect of alienating other stakeholders. There is little doubt that firms are increasingly making lobbying a major responsibility of senior management, given the pivotal role of governments in making decisions which might affect MNE.

Online communications

In Chapter 12 we discuss the use of technology in shaping the international marketing strategy of firms at greater length and, clearly, facilitating communications is at the heart. Here, however, we discuss the tactical use of online integrated marketing communications.

The nature of online communications

A number of online tools are used by marketers to create brand awareness, product and service associations and drive users to their websites, where customers might obtain further information, purchase an item from an online store or direct the customer to a traditional store. One significant advantage of online communications is that it is easier to measure the actions of customers and their response and so marketing metrics are more accurate.

Advertising is placed on partner sites that charge a 'click-through' fee in return for providing the sales lead and link. Search engines and comparative pricing sites provide sales leads by listing websites based on brand searches or brand associations with key words. Being listed on the first page of a key word search is essential and firms pay heavily and also manage their web content carefully to ensure that this happens in all their international markets.

Websites Some websites are clearly defined as marketplaces either owned by one specific organization or where links to commercial sites should be expected, for example, financial services supermarkets, online travel agents or insurance brokers.

Email Organizations use email to convey their marketing messages directly to their customers. However, many customers have been irritated by the large volume of spam they receive. Godin (2002) found that customers were bombarded by up to 500 marketing messages per day from traditional communication sources but today customers can expect to see up to 3000 messages, because of the rise in online communications. This means that the effect of individual messages is diluted among this volume of what he refers to as interruption marketing (spam). He has introduced the term 'permission marketing' to suggest that the communications will be more effective if customers agree to receive more communications from the firm. This opt-in approach is preferable to an opt-out, in which the customer would have to take the initiative in asking a firm not to send messages.

Viral marketing has extended the effectiveness of online communications by encouraging recipients of email messages to pass them onto the others to create a 'buzz' in the marketplace. As discussed in Illustration 9.8, social networking sites provide a platform for sharing informal views about products and services that can have considerable effect on the success of marketing campaigns, but they are outside the control of the marketer, and thus it is difficult to obtain advertising benefit.

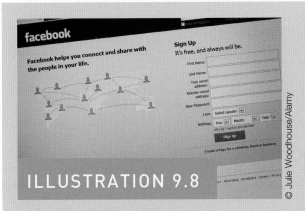

© Julie Woodhouse/Alamy

ILLUSTRATION 9.8

Social networking: searching for a new advertising model

Social networking became the global phenomenon that changed the advertising industry for ever, as two thirds of the Internet population visited a social network or blogging site. It overtook email to become the fourth most popular sector after search, portals and PC software applications, accounting for 10 per cent of all Internet time spent. It is interesting to see the different patterns of development.

For example, Germany and Switzerland were quite late to embrace the phenomenon, perhaps due to natural German reserve in disclosing personal data. Facebook, the market leaders, did not immediately launch a German language interface and by the time they did, five local start-up competitors were already more popular.

Facebook started out as a service for university students and the early dramatic growth was driven by younger people, but its appeal to a wider age group brought about a demographic change such that its 35–49 year old audience outstripped its 18–34 audience. US market leader, MySpace, focused more on music and video entertainment, and self expression, (with customizable profile pages), so appealing more to teenagers and young adults, but in other countries it is regarded as a niche player. Local players became leaders in many markets, for example, Google-owned Orkut in Brazil, Wer-kennt-wen in Germany and Mixi in Japan. The particular mix of factors in each country provides a challenge for the international players. Because the global growth of social networking was so rapid in many countries these local players established themselves, forming partnerships with the portals, before the international players had time to enter the market. For example in China the different language and regulatory issues of doing business, and the mindset needed for running a Chinese social network that understands the cultural nuances and network behaviour, made the strong local players such as the leading social network 51.com more likely winners. In Japan Mixi is an invite only system that appeals more to the 'humble' Japanese mindset. Facebook, which launched without effective local leadership and sensitivity to the local culture failed to make an impact.

The social networking players whether local or global constantly face new challenges as new network models, such as Twitter, discussed in Illustration 9.6, become the next global phenomenon or fad, and consumers are increasing their demands and expectations for easier mobile social networking.

The challenge for advertisers

For advertisers social networking provides the potential opportunity for targeting all demographic groups in a focused way and achieving high levels of engagement with the audience, but so far advertising on social networking sites has not been successful. Unlike traditional media where they simply consume content, members of social networks both consume and supply content. The sense of ownership they feel over the content means that advertising is intrusive and less acceptable. A well used analogy is that it is like gate crashing a party.

The personal data of consumers available on networks is attractive to advertisers as it allows highly targeted ads, but consumers see this as invading their privacy. Research by Nielsen suggests that consumers are becoming less tolerant of online advertising and the term they most closely associate with advertising is 'false'.

Bearing in mind these factors advertising on social networks must be through conversation, rather than by using a 'push model'. Authentic, candid and humble messages similar to 'word of mouth' approaches are needed to overcome the lack of trust. Nielsen suggest that standard 'ad' formats are not acceptable, different approaches, trial and error and a closer relationship between the advertisers and the social networks than is common in traditional media advertising will be essential.

Social networks are a communication channel like traditional media, and advertisers have to understand the nature of engagement and new approaches to connect with consumers. Consumers are keen to offer opinion and co-create content, as discussed in Illustration 12.1, so advertisers can no longer simply push content to the audience and sit back and wait for a reaction. They must genuinely interact and crucially they must think of their consumers as people with whom they want a dialogue.

Question

1 Will advertising in social media become acceptable?

References: 'Global faces and networked places', Nielsen, March 2009 accessed at: www.nielsen.com.

Mobile communications For some time it has been predicted that mobile communications would be valuable and, as we saw in earlier chapters, multifunctional mobile devices, such as the iPhone, iPad provide now provide more comprehensive services and interactive communications. In Africa, mobile internet access is more prevalent.

Privacy There is a conflict between the interests of the firm and customer in developing databases. In order to offer more individually targeted, personalized and relevant communications, the firm requires ever more detailed and potentially sensitive information from the customer. However, the customer is reluctant to give firms personal information. They appreciate that certain firms such as insurance companies might need the information in order to process a transaction, can be trusted and will respect local country privacy laws, such as the 1998 Data Protection Act in the UK. They have more concern over the possibility of the firms passing on the sensitive information – deliberately or accidentally – to other firms that will not be so scrupulous in its use. It is very easy to pass information electronically to other companies or countries.

Developing profitable, long-term marketing relationships

So far in this chapter we have focused upon the communications strategies that might be used to ensure that the firm's broad base of stakeholders around the world are aware of the company's standards and values, the distinctiveness and quality of its brands, products and services and that customers are exposed to the messages that will encourage them to buy the firm's products and services rather than the competitor's. Once customers have been won over, usually at a considerable cost, firms increasingly realize that it is less costly if they can persuade them to stay loyal to the firm rather than lose them to a competitor and so face the cost of winning them over again.

Customer retention is particularly important for B2B marketing, where the number of opportunities to win over new customers may be very limited and the loss of a major customer could have a disastrous effect on the firm. The lifetime value of the customer is considerable, but the cost to the customer of changing to a new supplier can be considerable too. Both supplier and customer have something to gain from the relationship marketing (RM) concept, which is concerned with developing and maintaining mutually advantageous relationships between two or more firms in a supply chain and using their combined capability and resources to deliver the maximum added value for the ultimate customer. It involves a more holistic approach to understanding the market dynamics and developing implementation strategies to respond to the changes in the market needs that have been identified.

The concept of relationship marketing

There are significant differences between adopting a traditional marketing approach based on individual transactions, in which the emphasis is placed on the 4Ps of the product marketing mix (particularly the product P) and an approach based upon building relationships by emphasizing the three extra Ps of the service mix (particularly the people P). At the core of relationship marketing is the idea that rather than simply trying to add customer service onto a predetermined product offer, based on a rigid marketing mix, the firm should provide customer satisfaction by using the marketing mix flexibly to meet the customer's evolving needs.

Horovitz (2000) suggests that in relationship marketing the 4Ps of the traditional marketing mix are changed altogether and replaced by the 4Cs of relationship marketing: customer needs and wants; costs; convenience and communication. Clearly given the need to meet diverse cultural requirements, relationship marketing makes sense for high-involvement B2B purchases where value can be added and sales generated by RM but less so for low-involvement purchases of consumer packaged goods. It is important to recognize that consumers do not want a relationship as such but do want interactivity, 1:1 marketing and more personalized communications and this can be done by replacing conventional offline with online communications.

Throughout the firm the objectives of relationship marketing are to:

- Maintain and build existing customers by offering more tailored and cost-effective business solutions.
- Use existing relationships to obtain referral to business units and other supply chain members that are perhaps in different parts of the world and not currently customers.
- Increase the revenue from customers by offering solutions that are a combination of products and services.
- Reduce the operational and communications cost of servicing the customers, including the work prior to a trading relationship.

Relationships must be built with those that might influence the final purchase decision, and includes internal staff as individuals and groups, experts, celebrities and other influential individuals that have the power to connect the organization with the market.

The power and influence of the organization's stakeholders in these markets will vary considerably around the world and their relative importance depends upon the specific context of the firm's activity. In the technology sector, for example, key influencers and high profile, lead customers may be located in a particular country market but their decisions might influence purchasing decisions across the world.

Database development

Managing and influencing potentially millions of interactions between staff, customers and partners requires a systematic approach. Chaffey *et al.* (2003) explain that the key objectives are: customer retention, customer extension (increasing the depth and range of customers) and customer selection (segmenting and targeting).

The starting point is to build an information technology system that will integrate the RM activity. Central to the system is a database that will identify those customers with which it is worthwhile developing a relationship. The database can best be built from the company records of its interactions with customers and then supplemented with purchased lists of possible customers. Chaffey *et al.* (2003) explain that the details about the customer should include:

- Personal and profile data, including contact details.
- Transaction data including purchase quantities, channels, timing and locations.
- Communications data, including response to campaigns.

Wasserman, Khermouch and Green (2000) explained that data mining is used to 'discover hidden facts contained in databases'. Identifying trends in behaviour and attitudes from data provides a basis for targeting prospective customers cost-effectively, developing cooperative relationships with other companies and better understanding the patterns of customer purchasing behaviour.

Customer relationship management

International consumer markets are characterized by their sheer size and the relative anonymity of their customers. Even small retailers cannot possibly know their customers' individual behaviour, attitudes, intention to purchase and experiences (good or bad) in dealing with the firm, whereas an industrial marketer with only a few customers possibly can. As we have discussed in the section on databases, technology has been developed to try to integrate RM activity and manage the vast amounts of supporting information. Customer relationship management (CRM) is effectively computer software coupled with defined management processes and procedures to enable staff throughout organizations to capture and use information about their customers to maintain and build relationships. Companies such as Siebel (US) have built their business around such concepts.

Although CRM should play a decisive role in integrating communications and developing relationships with the customer as the focus, Kotler (2003) points out that in practice, many firms have embraced the concept and spent between $5 million and $10 million on CRM systems, but been less than satisfied with the results. He quotes the CRM Forum research that suggests less than 30 per cent of companies are satisfied with their systems. The problems that companies identify in establishing the systems tend not to be associated with software failure (2 per cent) but rather organizational change (29 per cent), company politics/inertia (22 per cent), lack of CRM understanding (20 per cent), poor planning (12 per cent), lack of CRM skills (6 per cent), budget problems (4 per cent), bad advice (1 per cent) and other (4 per cent).

The problems arise when firms see CRM systems as a quick fix to try to manage vast amounts of data. They make broad generalizations about customer segments and are often too insensitive to different consumer cultures and concerns. Too often CRM is not adopted on an organization-wide basis and instead is adopted by individual departments for very specific reasons. It also gets modified because of the need to interface it with existing legacy systems and so becomes fragmented and, rather than reducing cost, actually increases it. The introduction of CRM leads to raised expectations of service levels among customers and staff and if this is not delivered CRM can have a detrimental effect on the business.

The opportunities for relationship marketing to offer benefits are increasing because of improvements in communications, IT and increased cross-border purchasing. However, it is important to understand that the consumer is not necessarily a willing participant in the relationship mission and, unless this is recognized, relationship marketing will prove to be of limited value. Indeed the question must be asked whether the majority of consumers will derive any benefit from a relationship with a MNE – the benefits will be mainly with the firm.

For relatively low purchase price items there is a danger that the costs to the firm of building customer loyalty might outweigh the costs of a more traditional approach to marketing products and services. It is difficult to measure the relative merits of short-term costs against longer-term revenues and few companies are willing to take a long-term view based upon their assumptions of what might happen in the future.

In practice the methods of relationship marketing in the consumer markets are diverging from relationship marketing in the business sector. In consumer markets relationship marketing will become more concerned with making one-to-one connections with customers through interactivity and promoting and placing products and services in the appropriate media at just the right moment.

SUMMARY

- To be effective in global markets external international marketing communications are driven by the need to have a uniform corporate identity, clearly differentiated product and service offers supported by consistent promotion and strategies in place to build long-term customer relationships.

- Firms also need to focus on internal and interactive communications and ensure that their staff and partners' staff in remote locations deliver consistent and integrated international marketing communications.

- There are benefits to the firm of standardizing the promotion processes and programmes to benefit from economies of scale and the learning effect, wherever possible, but communications are extremely sensitive to local culture and conditions and, without attention to detail, they can be the source of problems worldwide for firms.

- The communication tools must be used appropriately to suit the context of the markets being served, different customer needs and the firm's objectives. Media availability, cultural and legislation differences and the nature of the products and services being marketed will influence the communications strategy decisions and choice of tools.

- Customer perceptions can be damaged by poor communications management within the firm and by external factors over which the organization may have no control. The international firm must concentrate on communicating consistency in its image, standards and values to a diverse range of stakeholders as well as making its direct appeal to existing and potential customers. It must also integrate the traditional communications with online communications to further develop interactive, one-to-one customer relationships.

- Because of the high cost of winning and losing customers, firms, particularly in the business-to-business market, must build relationships to retain their most valuable customers in the long term. They must also measure the impact of their marketing communication investment as far as possible to ensure value for money.

KEYWORDS

Communications mix	Failures of communications	Push or pull strategy
Promotional mix	Standardization of international marketing communications	Communications tools
Corporate identity		Product and service differentiation
Relationship marketing	Communications adaptation	Transactions
Customer relationship management		

GREENPEACE
CASE STUDY

Greenpeace – global campaigner

Competition in global markets continues to intensify and the charity sector is no different. Over the last few years the competition for donations between different charities has increased substantially. For a campaigning charity such as Greenpeace it is essential also to recruit new members committed and prepared to give their time to its various causes.

Greenpeace campaigns to change attitudes and behaviour, in order to protect and conserve the environment and to promote peace in a number of areas, such as: Energy conservation, reducing waste of resources and use of hazardous chemicals, promoting sustainable agriculture, protecting the world's great forests, the animals and plants and people that live in them, and its oceans, working for disarmament, elimination of nuclear weapons and tackling the causes of conflict.

The global credit crunch means that not only have donors got less money to donate to the charity but, when hard pressed financially, many people are more concerned about their own personal problems and, perhaps, cannot afford to worry so much about the future of the world.

Among its various stakeholders it is governments and large commercial organizations that are its primary targets as it is the politicians and policy makers that Greenpeace must influence if it is to achieve its objectives. Given their primary targets Greenpeace only raise funds from individual donors and do not accept donations from any commercial or politically based organizations. Clearly given the high levels of donations needed to fund its worldwide campaigns this poses Greenpeace with a particular challenge. Greenpeace adopts professional marketing strategies and management but most of its activities are controversial. Greenpeace's main marketing weapons are high profile actions that make dramatic news items in the worldwide media, drawing attention to a particular campaign, such as its anti-whale hunting campaign. To support these public relations campaigns Greenpeace uses a wide range of marketing communications to get its message across.

Although it is a global operation, Greenpeace's international strategy is based on a franchise system in which each country-based Greenpeace operation is responsible for local management, campaigns and raising funds, but contributes 17.5 per cent of its income to Greenpeace International to fund global campaigns. This reflects the fact that different cultures and geographically based audiences may place a different emphasis on the relative importance of Greenpeace's campaigns.

Of course more professional management and marketing can create tensions. Many donors want every penny to be spent on campaigns, but in practice when some of the donations are spent in developing effective marketing communications and charity management, higher levels of donations are usually received and the charity can achieve more. There is a further dilemma. While it is often easier to increase donations by using shock tactics that might involve breaking the law this can alienate some donors and members too.

For charities such as Greenpeace there is increasing pressure to maintain and grow their level of funding over the longer term from donors. A starting point to achieving this is Greenpeace's recognition that different segmentation strategies are required for each market and that individuals cannot just be divided into 'donors' and 'members'. As people go through life, their charity giving, their contributions to the causes and their political and economic influence also go through different stages, so Greenpeace are now trying to segment the market in a way that reflects these different stages.

Direct mail has long been an important tool in the communications armoury of Greenpeace, however, they are now increasingly using e-marketing, social media and CRM strategies to develop viral marketing campaigns and build longer-term relationships with potential donors and in their quest to turn non-committed donors into committed long-term givers. The challenge they now face is how to make better use of the database information they can build through e-marketing to make strategic marketing decisions by which they can maximize the life time value of individual donor population.

Questions

1 Advise Greenpeace on the strategic marketing decisions they need to consider if they are to maintain and grow their level of donations and increase their membership over the longer term.

2 In light of your answer to question 1, recommend to Greenpeace how they can develop an integrated communications strategy which would help them to achieve their long term objectives.

References: The above data has been based on a real-life situation, but details have been changed for assessment purposes and may not be an accurate reflection of reported news.

DISCUSSION QUESTIONS

1 Communications are becoming increasingly fragmented. Why is this so and what are the critical success factors in planning, executing and controlling an integrated international communications strategy?

2 Critically examine the case for and against using one advertising agency to create and implement an international advertising campaign.

3 How might a small firm with few resources use online communications to build its international business? Using examples show how this might be done (1) in the business to consumer market and (2) in the business-to-business market.

4 Select an economic region. Identify the advantages and disadvantages of pan-regional advertising. How would you manage a pan-regional campaign for a product or service of your choice?

5 A key element of communications for a global company of your choice is maintaining relationships with all its international stakeholders. Identify the various stakeholders and prepare an outline international communications plan to promote the company's values reputation, and increase its profile.

REFERENCES

1. Chan, A.K. and Huang, Y. (1997) 'Brand naming in China: a linguistic approach', *Marketing Intelligence and Planning*, 5 (15): 227–34.
2. Chaffey, D., Meyer, R., Johnston, K. and Ellis-Chadwick, F. (2003) *Internet marketing: strategy, implementation and practice*, FT Prentice Hall.
3. Davidson, H. (2002) *Committed enterprise: how to make values and visions work*, Butterworth-Heinemann.
4. *Economist, The* (2006) 'The blog in the corporate machine', *The Economist*, 2 November 2006.
5. Fill, C. (2006) *Marketing communications: engagement, strategies and practice*, FT Prentice Hall.
6. Godin, S. (2002) *Permission marketing: turning strangers into friends and friends into customers*, Free Press.
7. Honeycutt, E.D. (2005) 'Sales training in a dynamic market: the Singapore service industry', *Services Marketing Quarterly*, 26 (3): 55–70.
8. Horovitz, J. (2000) 'Using information to bond customers', in D. Marchand (ed.) *Competing with information*, Wiley.
9. Kotler, P. (2002) *Marketing management*, Prentice Hall.
10. Kotler, P. (2003) *Marketing insights from A to Z: 80 concepts every manager needs to know*, John Wiley.
11. Masterson, R. (2005) 'The importance of creative match in television sponsorship', *International Journal of Advertising*, 25 (4): 471–88.
12. Neelankavil, J.P., Mummalaneni, V. and Sessions, D. (1996) 'Use of foreign language and models in print advertisements in East Asian countries: a logit modelling approach', *European Journal of Management*, 29 (4): 24–38.
13. Schmitt, B.H. and Pan, Y. (1994) 'Managing corporate and brand identities in the Asia Pacific Region', *Californian Business Review*, Summer.
14. Shimp, T.A. (2006) *Advertising, promotion, and other aspects of integrated marketing communications*, Thomson South-Western. Shimp, T.A.(2009) *Integrated Marketing Communications in Advertising and Promotion, International Edition*, (Paperback) – 26 April.
15. Siu, W. and Au, A.K. (1997) 'Women in advertising: a comparison of television advertisements in China and Singapore', *Marketing Intelligence and Planning*, 15 (5).
16. Vollmer, C., Frelinghuysen, J. and Rothenberg, R. (2007) 'The future of advertising is now', accessed at: www.strategy-business.com on 17 January 2007.
17. Wasserman, T., Khermouch, G. and Green, J. (2000) 'Mining everyones' business', *Brandweek*, February.
18. Wentz, H. (1997) 'A single Europe: reality or mirage', *Advertising Age International*, May.
19. Whiteling, I. (2007) 'Emerging markets: the China experience', http://eventsreview.com/ accessed 8 February 2007.
20. Zhang, Y. and Neelankavil, J.P. (1997) 'The influence of culture on advertising effectiveness in China and the USA: a crosscultural study', *European Journal of Management*, 31 (2): 134–49.

CHAPTER 10

THE MANAGEMENT OF INTERNATIONAL DISTRIBUTION AND LOGISTICS

LEARNING OBJECTIVES

After reading this chapter you should be able to:

- Strategically evaluate potential foreign distribution options for a given situation

- Discuss the complexities of efficiently managing intermediaries in an international marketing context

- Appreciate the difference in retailing infrastructures across the globe

- Advise and recommend potential solutions to developing a logistics strategy in foreign markets

- Understand the export documentation process

INTRODUCTION

In Chapter 7, we examined strategies for international expansion and the options available for firms entering foreign markets. In this chapter we will build on the issues discussed in Chapter 7, but focus on managing the distribution and logistics within foreign markets.

The management of foreign channels of distribution is a key area in a firm's efforts to gain competitive advantage. As products become more standardized across the world, the ability to compete on customer service becomes more vital. In order to be effective in this area, a firm must have a well-managed **integrated supply chain** within foreign markets and across international boundaries.

International marketing involves companies operating in countries other than their own. The trend to a more globalized world implies an interconnected and inter-dependent world where capital, goods and services are freely transferred across national frontiers. As companies continue to pursue global strategies and operate in more and more countries, customers in every corner of the world expect to be served better, faster and by whatever channel suits them. To meet those expectations, organizations need to give a global, holistic view of their customers and really understand how to develop a globally integrated distribution system.

The ultimate goal may be to have a single system that offers all global customers a streamlined efficient service. For many companies in many markets in order to achieve that they first have to develop a real understanding of the mechanics of the operations of the distribution systems of the countries in which they operate.

In this chapter, we will examine the strategic issues in managing distribution channels and discuss the issues of selecting intermediaries and how to build long-term effective relationships in international markets. We will also examine the developments in retailing and the differences in retailing across markets at different levels of economic development.

Finally, we will examine the logistics of physically moving goods across national boundaries and the importance of efficient distribution management to minimize costs in international markets.

The challenges in managing an international distribution strategy

Distribution channels are the means by which goods are distributed from the manufacturer to the end user. Some companies own their own means of distribution, some only deal directly with the most important customers but many companies rely on other companies to perform distribution services for them. These services include:

- the purchase of goods;
- the assembly of an attractive assortment of goods;
- holding stocks or inventory;
- promoting the sale of goods to the end customer;
- the physical movement of goods.

In international marketing, companies usually take advantage of a wide number of different organizations to facilitate the distribution of their products. The large number is explained by considerable differences between countries both in their distribution systems and in the expected level of product sales. The physical movement of goods usually includes several modes of transport – for example, by road to a port, by boat to the country of destination and by road to the customer's premises. The selection of the appropriate distribution strategy is a significant decision. While the marketing mix decisions of product and marketing communications are often more glamorous, they are usually dependent upon the chosen distribution channel. The actual distribution channel decision is fundamental as it affects all aspects of the international marketing strategy.

The key objective in building an effective distribution strategy is to build a supply chain to your markets that is, as Kotler *et al.* (2009) said, 'a planned and professionally managed vertically integrated marketing system that incorporates both the needs of the manufacturer and the distributors'.

To achieve this across international markets is a daunting task and will mean the international marketing manager has to meet a number of important challenges in order to ensure they develop a distribution strategy which delivers the effective distribution of products and services. The major areas they will need to consider are as follows:

- *Selection of foreign country intermediaries.* Should the firm use indirect or direct channels? What type of intermediaries will best serve their needs in the marketplace?
- *How to build a relationship with intermediaries.* The management and motivation of intermediaries in foreign country markets is especially important to firms trying to build a long-term presence, competing on offering quality services.

- *How to deal with the varying types of retailing infrastructure across international markets.* Achieving a coordinated strategy across markets where retailing is at varying stages of development and the impact of the growth of retailers themselves globalizing are important considerations in the distribution strategies of firms competing in consumer goods markets.

- *How to maximize new and innovative forms of distribution.* Can be achieved particularly through opportunities arising through the Internet and electronic forms of distribution.

- *How to manage the logistics of physically distributing products across foreign markets.* Firms need to evaluate the options available and develop a well-managed logistics system.

In the following sections of the chapter, we will examine the issues in each of these areas of international distribution and logistics.

Selecting foreign country market intermediaries

A distribution decision is a long-term decision, as once established it can be difficult to extract a company from existing agreements. This means that channels chosen have to be appropriate for today and flexible enough to adapt to long-term market developments.

In some instances, difficulties may arise because of legal contracts, as in the case of the termination of an agency; in other situations they result from relationships that need to be initiated and then nurtured. For example, the development of sales through wholesalers and distributors might be substantially influenced by the past trading pattern and the expectation of future profitable sales. Therefore, a long-term relationship needs to be developed before a firm is willing to invest significantly in an intermediary.

The long-term nature of distribution decisions forces a careful analysis of future developments. If new forms of distribution are emerging, for example, TV and mobile phone shopping, interactive media and e-retailing, this has to be considered early in the planning stage of the distribution channels for your market.

Another important challenge is the comparative inexperience of managers in the channel selection process in international markets. In domestic marketing, most marketing managers develop marketing plans which will usually be implemented within the existing arrangement of the company's distribution channels. This is quite a different proposition to the pioneering process of establishing a distribution channel in the first place and then achieving a well-supported availability through channel members in different country markets.

Furthermore, if foreign market channels are being managed from the home market, there may be preconceived notions and preferences that home market systems can operate elsewhere. Because they are unfamiliar with the market, managers may underestimate the barriers to entry erected by local competitors and even government regulations. For instance, in both France and Japan there are restrictive laws which inhibit the growth of large retailers. In Japan no one can open a store larger than 5382 square feet without permission from the community store owners: thus it can take eight to ten years for a store to win approval.

Indirect and direct channels

One of the first decisions to make in selecting intermediaries for international markets is: should the product be distributed indirectly? In other words, using outside sales agents and distributors in the country; or should the product be distributed directly, using the company's sales force, company-owned distribution channel or other intermediaries in a foreign country? The former option is an independent channel which is non-integrated and provides very little or no control over its international distribution and affords virtually no links with the end users. On the other hand, direct distribution, which is an integrated channel, generally affords the supplier more control and, at the same time, brings responsibility, commitment and attendant risks. As we have discussed, distribution decisions are difficult to change and so it is important for firms to consider the alternatives available and the differing degrees of commitment and risk, evaluate the alternatives and select the most appropriate type of distribution.

Integrated (direct) channels of distribution are seen to be beneficial when a firm's marketing strategy requires a high level of service before or after the sale. Integrated channels will be more helpful than independent channels in ensuring that high levels of customer service will be achieved.

Indirect channels on the other hand require less investment in terms of both money and management time. Indirect channels also are seen to be beneficial in overcoming freight rate, negotiating disadvantages, lowering the cost of exporting and allowing higher margins and profits for the manufacturer. An independent channel, therefore, allows the international firm to tap the benefits of a distribution specialist within a foreign market, such as economies of scale and pooling the demand for the distribution services of several manufacturers.

The advantages and disadvantages of indirect exporting were discussed in Chapter 7. In this section we will focus on issues facing firms who have made the decision to involve themselves with intermediaries in foreign country markets, either through the use of agents or distributors or using their own company-owned sales force. These intermediaries offer a wide range of services.

■ *Export distributors* – usually perform a variety of functions including: stock inventories, handling promotion, extending customer credit, processing orders, arranging shipping, product maintenance and repair.

■ *Export agents* – responsibilities often include: buyer/seller introductions, host market information, trade fair exhibitions, general promotional activities.

■ *Cooperative organizations* – carry on exporting activities on behalf of several producers and are partly under their administrative control (often used by producers of primary products – e.g. bananas, coffee, sugar).

A company-owned sales force may be one of three types:

1 *Travelling export sales representatives*. The company can begin by sending home-based sales people abroad to gather important information, to make the necessary customer contacts and to conduct the negotiating and selling process.

2 *Domestic-based export department or division*. An export sales manager carries on the actual selling and draws on market assistance as needed. It might evolve into a self-contained export department performing all the activities in export and operating as a profit centre.

3 *Foreign-based sales branch or subsidiary*. A foreign-based sales branch allows the company to achieve greater presence and programme control in the foreign market. The sales branch handles sales and distribution and may also handle warehousing and promotion. It often serves as a display centre and customer service centre as well.

The choices available to a firm may well be determined by whether they are operating in the business-to-business (B2B) or business-to-consumer (B2C) sector. Figure 10.1 illustrates the choices for a supplier in the business-to-business market internationally.

The main channels in the B2B market, therefore, tend to be agents, distributors and companies' wholly-owned sales force. The main distribution channels in the B2C market are shown in Figure 10.2.

Over the past few years there have been considerable developments in retailing across national boundaries. In a later section in this chapter, we will examine these trends and other new forms of retailing. First, however, we will look at the factors to consider in selecting channels of distribution and then building effective relationships with intermediaries.

FIGURE 10.1 Distribution channels for business goods

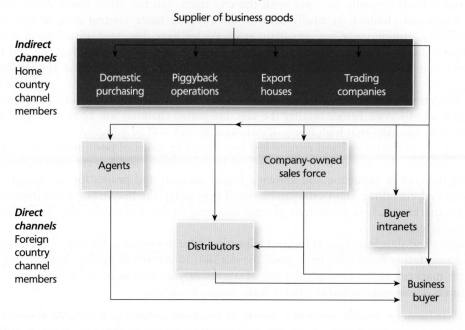

FIGURE 10.2 Distribution channels for consumer goods

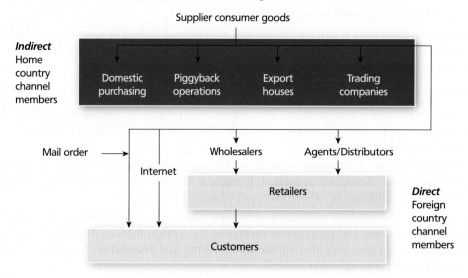

Channel selection

In selecting appropriate channel intermediaries, a firm has to consider many factors. Czinkota and Ronkainen (2009) suggested the 11C model to explain the factors a firm should consider in their selection process. The 11 elements to consider are:

1 Customer characteristics
2 Culture
3 Competition
4 Company objectives
5 Character of the market
6 Cost

7 Capital required

8 Coverage needed

9 Control issues

10 Continuity provided

11 Communication effectiveness.

Customer characteristics and culture

Channels of distribution have usually developed through the cultural traditions of the country and so there are great disparities across nations, making the development of any standardized approach difficult.

The distribution system of a country can vary enormously. In Finland, The main sectors of the Finnish economy are dominated by oligopolies. Consumables for everyday use are marketed by an integrated system of distribution dominated by three big groups: Kesko, the S Group (SOK) and Tradeka which control more than 90 per cent of the markets in the country. In Japan, the entire distribution system is based on networks with lots of wholesalers selling to other wholesalers. There are over 300 000 wholesalers and over 1.2 million retailers. Because the price of land is so high in Japan, many wholesalers cannot carry stock in the traditional sense, so may order on a daily basis. This means that there are many layers between the foreign company entering the market and the final consumer.

The Japanese system centres on distributor linkages to *dainyo* manufacturers, where the distributor accepts a subservient social status in return for economic security. From this interaction emerges vertical distribution networks called *Ryūtsū keiretsu*, in which units are arrayed in hierarchical layers and power resides at the 'commanding heights' of large *keiretsu*.

Keiretsu refers to a uniquely Japanese form of corporate organization. A *keiretsu* is a grouping or family of affiliated companies that form a tight-knit alliance to work toward each other's mutual success. It can best be understood as the intricate web of relationships that links banks, manufacturers, suppliers and distributors with the Japanese government.

Distributors at 'lower' layers in the structure are tied to the *Ryūtsū keiretsu, (Distribution Keiretsu)* system by bonds of loyalty, mutual obligation, trust and power that extend throughout existing distribution structures. While this arrangement guarantees members some degree of security, it also deprives them of economic freedom. Distributors that choose to deal with firms outside of the established group risk severing their ties with the group.

While distributors lack the freedom to transact with whomever they wish, they are also relieved of many costs associated with being independent – for example, smaller distributors in the system need not shoulder the risk of carrying inventories of products that will not sell and can depend on reliable delivery and financial help where necessary.

In the past decade the power of the *keiretsu* has started to diminish. Many faced debts through bad loan portfolios and were forced to merge or go out of business. Furthermore, companies from outside the *keiretsu* system, such as Sony and new international retailers entering Japan such as Toys'R'Us and McDonald's, have managed to grow by circumventing the system and outperforming their counterparts within the *keiretsu* networks, this has led to an overall loosening of keiretsu alliances. E-retailing has also had a major impact on the power of the *keiretsu* as can be seen in Illustration 10.1.

Sometimes non-Japanese businesses are described as *keiretsu*. The Virgin Group (UK) and Tata Group (India) and airline alliances such as Oneworld and the Star Alliance (USA) are seen to have similar characteristics to those of the Japanese *keiretsu*.

Thus, the characteristics of the customer and the cultural traditions of the country have a major impact on the choices available to a firm. A Belgian shopper may buy groceries from huge hypermarkets, concentrating on purchases which have long shelf lives and are easy to store in their spacious apartments and houses. The Japanese customers on the other hand can be characterized by their logistical imperatives, as confined living space makes storage of goods very difficult. Therefore, customers make frequent visits to shops and rely on stores to keep their inventories. Moreover, Japan's narrow roads and lack of parking space (except for suburbs) predispose most of its population to do its shopping on foot.

ILLUSTRATION 10.1

© Payless Images, shutterstock.com

Internet retailing helps Western countries penetrate Japan

Non-store retailing is gaining popularity in Japan, mainly driven by the expansion of Internet retailing and home shopping. The impact of Internet retailing is proving to be powerful in the more restricted economies like Japan. This is because by increasing price transparency and competition the Internet is having its greatest impact on those economies that have built-in structural inefficiencies.

Japan, with high distribution margins, is starting to see considerable price erosion and big gains in efficiency. By exposing firms to more intense global competition in order to compete effectively, businesses are having to rethink old inefficient habits and seek new ways to eliminate market rigidities that have previously protected them from international predators.

In Japan the Internet strikes at the heart of the archaic and expensive *keiretsu* distribution system that holds prices artificially high. Suppliers and retailers tend to be tied to manufacturers. This allows manufacturers to control prices by restricting distribution to their own retailers. The Internet, by giving more power to the consumer through price transparency, is allowing Western companies to bypass the many layers of middlemen that have in the past proved to be such a formidable barrier to them. Foreign companies that have failed to penetrate the market previously are finally being able to reach potential consumers in the Japanese market.

Question

1 What are the other benefits of using Internet marketing in countries with high operational barriers?

Company objectives and competitive activity

The channel choice will also be determined by the company's objectives and what the firm's competitors are doing in a particular market. The distribution policy is part of a firm's international direction. Therefore, the distribution system developed will depend on the company's objective, i.e. whether their strategic objective is long-term or short-term and how quickly they need to realize their investment.

Most firms operating in international markets will endeavour to maintain a cost-effective balance between direct and indirect channels of distribution. Firms will use direct channels, perhaps their own sales force, in foreign country markets where their company's objective is to deliver high-value solutions to buying problems in order to maximize customer satisfaction. Thus, the firm is practising 'interaction' marketing as opposed to 'transaction' marketing. A firm whose objective is to build long-term, stable relationships with its foreign customers will have quite different objectives in the building of relationships throughout the supply chain than a firm with relatively short-term objectives in foreign country markets who purely wishes to complete the transaction before moving on to the next customer.

Character of the market

The characteristics of the market will also determine the choice available. Products often are introduced later into international markets than to the home domestic market; the company's image and awareness is normally lower, in many cases much lower, than in the domestic market and the market share attainable in the market is lower, at least initially. This makes it a much less profitable business proposition for distribution channel intermediaries. Furthermore, distribution channels are already being used by other companies who will have built up relationships with the intermediaries. This provides less space and opportunity for firms newly entering the market.

Developing countries are characterized by distribution systems consisting of a myriad of intermediaries and retail outlets. Such fragmentation results in cost inefficiencies as large volumes of product cannot be centralized and moved quickly from manufacturers to wholesalers to retailers.

Fragmented and circuitous channels also diminish possible competitive advantage by reducing the abilities of firms to get their products and services quickly and efficiently to masses of buyers. This is particularly the case for time-sensitive products. For example, overnight package couriers in some markets have failed in some cases to live up to delivery promises due to flight cancellations, poor road conditions and insufficient phone lines.

Often in emerging markets, the problems of fragmented distribution are compounded by legal restrictions as to which channels of distribution can be used by foreign importers.

The World Trade Organization is working towards the opening up of participation in distribution systems by foreign firms in a number of countries. India and Indonesia have eased restrictions, making it much easier for international companies to develop their own distribution systems. Previously foreign companies had not been allowed to set up their own distribution networks. Thailand has welcomed foreign investment, but then Tesco (UK) faced severe restrictions in Thailand when Thailand's ruling military council restricted their expansion plans in the country. However, many regions are actively encouraging the development of a global retailing industry. Illustration 10.2 gives an example in the Middle East.

ILLUSTRATION 10.2

Courtesey of Waitrose

Global retailers are drawn to the Middle East

The retail sector in the Middle East region is growing rapidly. The increasing household consumption, affluent population and booming services industry (tourism, banking and trading sectors) are propelling growth in the region's retail industry. Also, the modern shopping malls anchoring state-of-the-art hypermarkets and various shopping events like Dubai Shopping Festival, makes the region a highly profitable destination for global retail players. The Middle East region has a growing population, growing economy and a large availability of retail space which makes the region all the more attractive for incoming retailers. This is especially so as there is marked trend of consumers preferring to shop at modern retail formats and a preference for international brands.

Galeries Lafayette, the prestigious French retailer, Bloomingdale's, America's leading department store, Hamley's, London's famous toy store have all now established a presence there. Now even Waitrose, the UK food retailer has opened its first ever store outside the UK in Dubai. It is not just western retailers that are building a presence in the region, Kinokuniya, a bookstore chain originating in Japan, also building a strong presence in the region.

Question

1 What do you see are the challenges and opportunities of developing a retailing operation in the Middle East?

References: RNCOS, 'Middle East Retail Sector Analysis (2007–2010)', and Emaar (2008), 'Over 165 retailers open their first Dubai outlets at The Dubai Mall,' *Property Wire*.

Capital required and costings

In assessing the financial implications of channel selection, a firm needs to assess the relative cost of each channel, the consequences on cash flow and the capital required.

The relative costs of each channel   It is generally considered that it may be cheaper to use agents than set up a firm's own sales force in international markets. However, the firm has little control and may have little commitment from the agent. Also, if the company has long-term objectives in the market, then as sales develop the use of agents may be more expensive than employing the company's own sales force. A break-even analysis is necessary to evaluate the relative cost of each channel alternative over time.

Consequences on cash flow   If a firm uses wholesalers or distributors then traditionally they take ownership of the goods and the risks. This has a positive impact on cash flow. If the firm wishes to circumvent such channels and deal direct with the retailer or even the consumer, it means they have to be prepared to take on some of the traditional wholesaler services, e.g. offering of credit, breaking bulk, small orders. This means the firm will have capital and resources tied up in managing the distribution chain rather than developing the market.

Capital required   Direct distribution systems need capital injected to establish them. Non-recurring capital costs, as well as the recurring running costs when evaluating expected return in the long-term, have to be taken into account.

A company also needs to evaluate whether it can raise the finance locally or whether borrowing restrictions are placed on foreign companies, what grants are available and what the regulations on earnings capital repatriation will be.

The coverage needed

Required coverage will also be a determining factor. In some markets, to get 100 per cent coverage of a market, the costs of using the company's own sales force may be too high making indirect channels more appropriate, especially in countries which are characterized by large rural populations. However, firms who rely on sparse retail outlets can maximize the opportunities that fragmented distribution channels afford. Avon has recruited and groomed armies of sales representatives to sell its cosmetics directly to millions in all reaches of Brazil, Mexico, Poland, China and Argentina. Altogether Avon is successfully operating in 26 emerging economies and targeting more (e.g. India, South Africa, Russia and Vietnam). They now have over 5 million Avon representatives worldwide achieving sales of over US$10 billion.

Control, continuity and communication

If a firm is building an international competitive advantage in providing a quality service throughout the world then channels that enable the firm to achieve rapid response in foreign markets will be important, as will the development of a distribution system which gives them total control in the marketplace and effective direct communication to their customer.

It is the drive to achieve high levels of quality of service that, to some extent, has led to the breakdown of conventional barriers between manufacturers, agents, distributors and retailers, as firms strive to develop effective vertical marketing systems. Such firms will be selecting intermediaries which will enable them to be solution-oriented service providers operating on high margins across a multitude of international markets.

To achieve this, some manufacturers have bought themselves into retailing and other parts of the supply chain, while others, such as Benetton, have pursued similar results by franchising. From small beginnings Benetton now operates in 120 countries and has over 6000 franchised stores in the Benetton network.

The selection and contracting process

Having evaluated the criteria discussed above, a firm must select intermediaries capable of helping the firm achieve its goals and objectives. The intermediaries chosen must provide the geographic coverage needed and the services required in the particular international market(s). It is often desirable to select intermediaries that are native to the country where they will be doing business as this will enhance their ability to build and maintain customer relationships.

The selection process for channel members will be based upon an assessment of their sales volume potential, geographic and customer coverage, financial strength (which will be checked through credit rating services and references), managerial capabilities, the size and quality of the sales force, any marketing communications services and the nature and reputation of the business. In some countries, religious or ethnic differences might make an agent suitable for one part of the market coverage but unsuitable in another. This can result in more channel members being required to give adequate market coverage.

Before final contractual arrangements are made, it is thought wise to make personal visits to the prospective channel member. The long-term commitment involved in distribution channels can become particularly difficult if the contract between the company and the channel member is not carefully drafted. It is normal to prescribe a time limit and a minimum sales level to be achieved in addition to the particular responsibilities for each party. If this is not carried out satisfactorily, the company may be stuck with a weak performer that either cannot be removed or is very costly to buy out from their contract. The difficulties that can arise when contracts in international markets are interpreted differently by the parties concerned are illustrated in the Merry Management case study at the end of the chapter.

Building relationships in foreign market channels

Management of sales activities and business relationships across international boundaries is a particularly complex and often overwhelming task. The combination of diverse languages, dissimilar cultural heritages and remote geographic locations can create strong barriers to building and maintaining effective buyer–seller relationships. Further, in international settings, communications are often complicated by a lack of trust – a critical dimension in any business relationship. Non-verbal cues, product origin biases, sales force nationality issues and differences in intercultural negotiation styles add even more complexity to the international business environment. Added to the traditional responsibilities of a sales manager, these factors make managing international relationships in distribution channels a unique and challenging task. Thus, it is crucial for firms and their sales managers both to understand and be able to work within various international markets throughout the world.

Motivating international marketing intermediaries

International marketing intermediaries can pick and choose the products they will promote to their customers. Therefore, they need to be motivated to emphasize the firm's products. As difficult as it is for manufacturers to motivate their domestic distributors or dealers, it is even more difficult in the international arena. The environment, culture and customs affecting seller–intermediary relationships can be complicating factors for the uninitiated.

Motivation, whether in the context of domestic or international channels, is the process through which the manufacturer seeks to gain the support of the marketing intermediary in carrying out the manufacturer's marketing objectives. Three basic elements are involved in this process (Rosenbloom 2009):

1 finding out the needs and problems of marketing intermediaries;

2 offering support that is consistent with their needs and problems;

3 building continuing relationships.

First, the needs and problems of international marketing intermediaries can be dramatically different from those at home. One of the most common differences is in the size of the intermediary. In emerging economies in Asia, Africa and Latin America dealers may be family businesses with little desire to grow larger. This may also be true for more developed economies in Eastern Europe, Japan and Italy. Thus, they may not aggressively promote a foreign manufacturer's product.

Second, the specific support programme provided by the manufacturer to its international intermediaries should be based on a careful analysis of their needs and problems. Factors to be included are:

- the adequacy of the profit margins available;
- the guarantee of exclusive territories;
- the adequacy and availability of advertising assistance;
- the offer of needed financial assistance.

In light of the cost structures faced by many foreign market distributors and dealers, the need to provide them with good margin potentials on the imported products they handle is even more important. Doing so, however, may force manufacturers to change their ideas of what constitutes a 'fair' or 'reasonable' margin for foreign market distributors.

Territorial protection or even the guarantee of exclusive territories sought by many distributors in the domestic market can be even more desirable in foreign markets. On some international markets distributors, many of whom may have quite limited financial resources, will not want to assume the risk of handling and promoting a foreign manufacturer's product line if other distributors will be competing in the same territory for the same customers.

Advertising assistance for distributors and dealers is another vital form of support. A foreign manufacturer, especially a large one, can have an advantage over indigenous firms in providing advertising support because of its often greater financial resources and experience in the use of advertising. For example, firms such as Johnson Wax (with extensive distribution in Europe) and 3M (in Asia) have used their considerable resources and advertising expertise to support distributors to very good advantage in those markets.

Financial assistance in countries where intermediaries are small and fragmented is essential. Levi-Strauss found in Russia that they needed to give a six month credit period to persuade intermediaries to stock their products. Their usual credit period was 30 to 60 days. Such constraints do not mean that manufacturers selling through foreign market intermediaries cannot build strong relationships with them; it is certainly possible to do so. However, the approach used may have to be quite different from that taken with intermediaries in their home market. Companies from the USA predominantly motivate distributors through financial incentives. However, in many other cultures motivating factors such as status, personal recognition and if some cases management support are much more important.

It is important to keep in regular contact with intermediaries. A consistent flow of all relevant types of communications will stimulate interest and sales performance. The cultural interface between the company and the channel member is the essence of corporate rapport. Business people from low context cultures may be thought to be insensitive and disrespectful by agents in high context culture countries. The problem can be compounded if sales performance is discussed too personally. According to Usunier and Lee (2005), precise measurement of sales people's performance, for example of the agent or the distributors, may be considered as almost evil in some countries. In South East Asia the ethic of non-confrontation clearly clashes with an objective to review performance. Various types of motivation need to be considered. In some cultures, intrinsic and group-related rewards work best. In the US, a country in which individualism and rationalism are the foundations of its society, individual and extrinsic rewards work best.

Controlling intermediaries in international markets

The process of control is difficult. Control problems are substantially reduced if channel members are selected carefully, have appropriately drafted contracts which have been mutually understood and agreed and are motivated in a culturally empathetic way.

Control attempts are often exercised through other companies and sometimes through several layers of distribution intermediaries. Control should be sought through the development of written plans with clearly expressed performance objectives. These performance objectives would include some of the following: sales turnover per year, number of accounts, market share, growth rate, introduction of new products, price charged and marketing communications support. Control should be exercised through a regular report programme and periodic personal meetings.

Evaluation of performance and control against agreed plans has to be interpreted against the changing environment. In some situations, economic recession or fierce competition activity prevent the possibility of objectives being met. However, if poor performance is established, the contract between the company and the channel member will have to be reconsidered and, perhaps, terminated. In an age in which relationship marketing is becoming more important in the Western world, the long-term building of suitable distribution relationships provides something of the Eastern flavour of obligation and working together.

Channel updating

In managing distribution channels, firms need to ensure that as they increase their involvement in global markets they are able to adapt and update their channel strategy accordingly. Thus, the management monitoring and control mechanisms a firm puts in place should give them the ability to develop their presence in the marketplace. In China, Kodak ensured this capability was in place in their early negotiations when setting up their local manufacturing and distribution operations by taking over three loss-making Chinese companies. They also offered a package to all their distributors offering help including marketing assistance to corner shops in exchange for becoming a Kodak Express and evicting competing film brands from the stores. Dell built a global brand by focusing on a direct sales model. However, they too have adapted their strategy in response to customer needs and have introduced a retail presence.

Developing a company-owned international sales force

Firms with expansion plans and an interest in becoming more involved in global markets will eventually take control of implementing their own marketing strategies and establish and manage their own international sales force. Generally, the firms begin to gradually move from indirect exporting to direct exporting via marketing intermediaries to a company-owned sales force (Kotler *et al.* 2009). The company can do this in several ways, including travelling export sales reps, a domestic-based export department or division and a foreign-based sales branch or subsidiary.

The advantages of using a company-owned sales force include:

- it provides far greater control over the sales and marketing effort because the sales force is now directly employed by the company;
- it facilitates formation of closer manufacturer–customer relationships;
- once established, the company-owned sales force can be helpful in identifying and exploiting new international marketing opportunities.

The disadvantages of developing a company-owned sales force include:

- a relatively larger resource commitment;
- somewhat higher exit costs should the firm decide to no longer serve a particular market;
- increased exposure to unexpected changes in the political/social environment of the host country.

One common strategy is to begin export operations by establishing a domestic-based export department and/or using home-based travelling salespeople. Then, as sales reach a certain volume in the new market, the decision is made to set up a foreign-based sales branch or subsidiary in the country.

The new unit may be strictly a marketing/sales arm or may also involve a production or warehouse facility. In either event, the firm must make a commitment of resources to develop its own direct sales force to sell the firm's offerings and build relationships with the firm's customers in that market.

It may well be that a firm uses its own sales force for key accounts and agents and distributors for small accounts. Equally, its own sales force may work in conjunction with international intermediaries, building links directly with customers but always with and through the intermediaries. This has the advantage of enabling the firm to build relationships with the customer and the intermediaries while not having to make the capital investment required to run a wholly-owned subsidiary.

However, for many multi-nationals, managing international operations is an issue of 'does the company control operations centrally or allow sales subsidiaries around the world a high degree of autonomy?' In some countries they may have little choice, due to the strength of local competition and the loyalty of local distributors to locally made brands.

Trends in retailing in international markets

Retailing structures differ across countries, reflecting their different histories, geography and politics. Retailing varies across the different levels of economic development and is influenced by cultural variations. The cultural importance attached to food in France provides the opportunity for small specialist food retailers to survive and prosper. In other developed countries, for example the US, the trend is towards very large superstores which incorporate a wide range of speciality foods. The French approach relies on small-scale production by the retail proprietor. The US approach encourages mass production, branding and sophisticated distribution systems to handle inventory and freshness issues.

In this section, our discussion will be concerned with three important issues for international marketers. First, the differences in the patterns of retailing around the world with particular reference to emerging markets and developing countries. Second, the internationalization of retailers and its impact on distribution channel structures and, third, the emergence of new forms of retailing which are particularly relevant to firms competing on international markets.

The differing patterns of retailing around the world

The concentration of the retailing industry varies significantly between markets. Low concentration ratios of retailer ownership give more power to the manufacturer. A 'no' decision from any one retailer does not make a big impact on total sales. While the low concentration ratios to be found in Japan and Italy and in many lesser developed countries increase the relative power of the manufacturer, there are problems. First, low concentration ratios in retailers might be counterbalanced by powerful wholesalers. Second, the costs of the sales force in calling on a multiplicity of very small retailers and the logistics of delivering products to them can reduce the manufacturer's profitability. If economies are sought by using wholesalers, the power balance might tilt away from the manufacturer to the wholesaler.

The main differences between traditional retailing structures found in lesser developed countries and the advanced retailing structures in more developed economies are illustrated in Table 10.1.

Table 10.1 Retailers – typical differences between developing and developed countries

Retailing issues	Traditional retailers in developing countries	Advanced retailing structures in mature economies
Concentration of retail power	Low	Often high
Site selection and retail location	Limited to the immediate locality	Very important, often sophisticated techniques to pinpoint the most valuable sites
Size of outlet	Limited	Large and tending to get larger
Retailer initiation of product assortment	Limited to the buy/no buy decision	Wide range of stock possible. Use of own-label and store-specific sales promotions
Retail concepts, images and corporate identity	Rarely used	Very important
Retailer-initiated sales promotion	Rarely used. Reliance on manufacturer and wholesaler-developed sales promotion and point of sale material	Very important
Use of retail technology	Limited	Vital e.g. EDI, EPOS
Service	Mainly counter-service	Mass customization, sophisticated CRM systems

© Mark Pearson/Alamy

ILLUSTRATION 10.3

Nakumatt drive through East Africa

Nakumatt Holdings is the parent company of Kenya's leading chain of retail stores which has over 32 stores dealing in general retail merchandize and employs more than 3000 Kenyans, making it one of Kenya's leading employers. It is currently expanding to the wider East African region including countries such as Rwanda, Uganda and Tanzania. Planet Retail has highlighted the company as the retailer to watch in Africa.

Nakumatt's goal is to create a chain of superstores in strategic locations delivering quality, value, service, variety and lifestyle, with convenient opening hours giving everyone the opportunity to shop at any of its stores countrywide. In this way the retail chain hopes to stay ahead of competition.

Nakumatt's store formats range from supermarkets to hypermarkets that display distinctive, world-class shopping floor layouts and amenities. All Nakumatt branches offer a range of over 75 000 quality products. Nakumatt stores look and feel just like Wal-Mart, Tesco and other giant retail stores around the world. However, it is not just a look-a-like, as it is also incorporating leading retailing technology into its business operations.

The retail chain is proud of its cutting-edge Oracle retail IT system that took an investment of more than KSh 32 million (2 million US dollars) to roll out. Nakumatt's environment and quality policy ensures that customers are afforded products and goods that meet world environmental and quality standards. Nakumatt have now launched a range of gold and silver Nakumatt Visa credit cards, heralding their entry in the financial services sector.

Nakumatt prides itself in conforming to local and international laws, policies and regulations. Nakumatt Holdings has, in keeping with global standards, managed to bag a string of internationally recognized awards and certifications. All the awards and certifications confirm Nakumatt's world-class superiority. They include:

- PriceWaterhouseCoopers East Africa most respected service sector award.
- East Africa Bureau of Standards ISO 9001:2008 Quality Management system.
- Planet Retail Global Ranking.
- East Africa Superbrand 2007/2008 and 2009/2010.
- GCR Credit rating.
- CEO – top 50 emerging market business leaders.
- Environment Audit due diligence.

Question

1 What do think are the main challenges to building a retailing business in East Africa?

References: http://www.superbrandseastafrica.com/assets/Featured-Brands/PDFs/129-nakumatt.pdf and http://allafrica.com/stories/201002080080.html

Retailing in developing countries is characterized by low levels of capital investment. The large size, purpose-built retail outlet, full of specialist display shelving and electronic point of sale equipment, is rarely found in less developed countries (LDCs). The more likely picture is of a very small space with goods sold by the counter service method and technology limited to a cash register or a pocket calculator. That does not mean to say that there are not innovations or exciting things happening in these markets. As you can see in Illustration 10.3 Nakumatt, an East African retailer are changing the way retailing business is done in that region.

Retail stores are often managed by the owner/proprietor and staffed by the extended family. The lack of capital input is partially offset by large quantities of low-cost labour and the management style is usually based on limiting risks. The retailer will seek to stock goods with a proven demand pattern. In addition, the retailer will try to obtain interest-free credit from the interface channel partners: the wholesaler and the manufacturer.

Straddling the pyramid

Dealing with distribution problems can lead to some surprising innovations and even generate entirely new businesses. The Future Group, India's largest retailer, has introduced 'organized chaos' into its shops to make consumers feel at home, breaking up long aisles with untidy-looking displays. New technology can also work wonders for distribution. The India Tobacco Company, one of the country's biggest conglomerates, has created a network of more than 5000 Internet kiosks known as *e-choupals* to help farmers communicate with both the supply and the distribution chains. Farmers can bring their goods for sale and ITC will display their products.

However the big challenge in emerging markets is how do competing companies '**straddle the pyramid**', in other words how do they serve both the people at the bottom of the pyramid and those at the top? Proctor and Gamble and Unilever have used many innovative methods ranging from different packaging and being responsive to local cultural behaviours, e.g. washing clothes with a soap bar. Nokia have also been working hard to produce phones for every market, from rural models designed to cope with monsoons to fashion accessories that will look cool in a Shanghai nightclub. The cheap phones are sold through a vast network of local outlets, such as mom-and-pop stores and rural markets, and the upmarket models through shops in fashionable city centres.

However, straddling the pyramid in emerging markets remains for many companies a critical challenge in how they set up and manage their distribution in these markets.

Questions

1 For an emerging market of your choice discuss how a company can respond to the challenges of establishing a distribution strategy which straddles the pyramid.

2 What recommendations would you make to them?

References: http://www.economist.com/node/15879299, http://findarticles.com/p/articles; accessed 20 March 2011.

Distribution channels in developing countries depend on manufacturers and wholesalers for their sales promotion ideas and materials. In developed countries retailers often take the initiative regarding sales promotions and will develop their own schemes. The opportunities for the manufacturer to influence the retailer in advanced countries are becoming fewer and fewer.

Small-scale retailing limits the opportunities to follow own-label strategies. The minimum economies of scale cannot be reached by the small urban and rural retailer in developing countries. The balance of power lies with the manufacturer to innovate and adapt products.

The proliferation of very many small-scale retailers means that the retail market is widely dispersed. The levels of concentration of ownership are much lower than are found in mature economies with relatively structured levels of retailing.

These differences give rise to principally four stages of retailing around the world: traditional, intermediary, structured and advanced.

Traditional retailing

'Traditional retailers' are typically found in Africa, Asia, Latin America and Japan. The concentration of operators is weak, segmentation is non-existent and the level of integration of new technology is very low. These are often small-scale family retailing businesses employing few people and with a low turnover. Traditionally the retail market in India fell into this group and was largely unorganized; however with changing consumer preferences, organized retail is gradually becoming popular. Unorganized retailing in India consists of small and medium grocery store, medicine stores, subzi mandi, kirana stores, paan shops, etc. More than 90 per cent of retailing in India fall into the unorganized sector, the organized sector is largely concentrated in big cities. India's organized retail trade has generated a lot of interest among domestic and global retailing operators as it is viewed as being on the brink of change and poised for substantial growth. Organized retail in India is expected to grow 25–30 per cent yearly and is currently worth in the region US$24 billion. This divergence in the sector brings particular challenges to global operators (see Illustration 10.4).

Intermediary retailing

Retailing in Italy, Spain and Eastern Europe is in the process of transformation, being both modern and traditional and so examples of intermediary retailing. Most businesses are independent with a turnover lower than the European average. However, there is a marked tendency towards concentration, particularly in the food sector, where the number of food retailing outlets per 1000 people is dropping. The importance of wholesalers and voluntary chains is still very strong, particularly in Italy, where there are 192 000 wholesale businesses.

© Pierdelune, shutterstock.com

ILLUSTRATION 10.4

Comparative retailing traditions

In the UK consumers are used to shops being open 7 days a week and in the US 24–7. In Germany,

however, it is only recently that shops have been allowed to open on Saturday afternoons: a new federal law allows city centre shops to open until 8 p.m. However, outside the city most still close at 4 p.m. for the weekend and Sunday opening is still highly restricted. This is much the same as New Zealand where stores close at 5.30 p.m. except for one night each week when they are open until 9.00 p.m. Stores are also closed on Sundays and many are closed on Saturday afternoons.

In India opening hours are unrestricted but most retail stores are family owned and are much smaller in size. With the exception of a few (small) super bazaars, consumers are not allowed to walk freely inside the stores, examine and compare labels of different brands before making the selection. Instead, consumers approach shops with a predetermined list of items to purchase, which are then pulled out of the bins by the salesperson.

Retailing in Greece, on the other hand has until recently been small-scale and highly traditional. The majority of stores are family owned and small in size and shopping for pleasure is less popular. However, the entry into the country of some of the big global retailers is starting to change the face of retailing there.

Question

1 How can a company achieve a global distribution strategy when retailing infrastructures vary so much?

In the major cities of China there have been huge developments in the retail structure of the country, taking retailing in the major cities to a very advanced status. China is encouraging mergers and partnerships between indigenous retailers to reduce costs and improve competitiveness and ensure they have the capacity to compete against such global operators as Wal-Mart and Carrefour, who are fighting for a share of the US$1.8 trillion retail market. Shanghai Bailian Group Co. Ltd, China's largest retailer is a vertical-integrated organization that manages the entire operation process from product design, to production, to sales. At present, products under the brand name of 'Bailian' are sold in more than 300 direct outlets throughout China. However, like India, outside the major cities of Shanghai and Bejing, China's retail sector is still dominated by small neighbourhood stores and local markets.

Countries with intermediary retailing structures are obviously attractive locations for retailers expanding internationally as they are seen as latent markets ripe for expansion. The level of economic development and the intermediary structure of retailing has historically meant that these countries are not host to large domestic retailers, making entry into the market relatively easy.

Over the course of the past decade, the entry of foreign operators into regions such as Latin America have altered the retailing landscape. There are now hypermarkets, variety stores and non-food specialists which have stimulated competition and greatly modernized retailing across the continent.

Structured retailing

Retailing in the north of Europe tends to be fairly structured, reflecting the level of economic development. Denmark, Luxembourg, the Netherlands and France have enterprises larger in size, have a higher level of concentration and a greater level of productivity per employee than Southern European retailers.

In these markets, retail competition is fairly well developed and there is a mature relationship between suppliers and retailers.

Retailers also have introduced fairly sophisticated technologies facilitating more elaborate competitive strategies. They are also, themselves, finding growth through opportunities overseas and new retailing formats.

Advanced retailing

The US, Germany and the UK are all examples of countries in which retailing is the most advanced in terms of concentration, segmentation, capitalization and integration. In Germany and the UK there are about 60 retailing businesses per 10 000 inhabitants, 98 being the European average. Retailer strategies are advanced and are very market focused, and generally incorporate five important dimensions.

Interactive customer marketing. Targeting of customers as individuals, developing strategies to improve retention and increase sales per shop visit.

Mass customization. Retailers are looking for improved margins through higher volumes, reduced costs and achieving low levels of returns.

Data mining. Retailers are using technology and electronic point of sale (EPOS) information to improve knowledge of customers, ensure the ability to make targeted offers which are timely and clearly differentiated. Data mining is beginning to be used by retailers in emerging and developing markets where previously there has been little reliable data on which to base decisions as can be seen above in Illustration 10.3 in the case of Nakumett.

Category management. Retailers are aiming to achieve improved levels of customer satisfaction through reducing costs, reducing mark downs and optimizing product assortment.

Effective consumer response. Retailers are establishing permanent links with manufacturers, establishing electronic data interchange (EDI) systems for efficient inventory replenishment and ensuring a continuous just in time delivery of supplies.

In these markets the balance of power in the supply chain, for the present at least, seems to lie firmly with these large retailers, who are increasingly dictating the trends in their home markets and as these reach maturity are seeking growth opportunities by expanding internationally.

The globalization of retailing

One of the key trends in international distribution over the past few years has been the aggressive strategies pursued by many major retailers as they have pursued global marketing objectives. Tesco, the French hypermarket groups Auchan, Carrefour and Promodes, and the German discount food retailers Aldi, Lidl and Swartz have all expanded globally. The food retailing sector especially is now dominated by huge global retailers and Table 10.2 gives the top ten in the world. However, it is not just in food that retailers are going global; the US retailer Wal-Mart and specialists Toys'R'Us, Home Depot, Staples, Benetton, Body Shop and Hertz are all now global retailers. Hong Kong retailers A S Watson and Dairy Farm entered neighbouring countries with supermarkets and pharmaceutical chains and Japanese department stores Takashimaya and Isetan have established outlets across Asia. More recently this trend has accelerated, with German retailers Metro, Rewe and Tengelmann expanding into the Czech Republic, Hungary and Poland, often using joint ventures with former socialist cooperatives. Three Western European retailers, Tengelmann (Germany), Ahold (Netherlands) and Delhaizae Le Lion (Belgium), now generate more sales and profit from their foreign activities, which include the US, Central Europe and Asia, than they do in their home markets. Tesco, already strong in Ireland, Central Europe and Asia are now expanding into the USA, opening a number of Tesco Express stores on the West Coast. The smaller high-growth economies such as Ireland (see Illustration 10.5 below on freight forwarders) have also been generating the particular interest of the expanding globals.

The expansion of international activity of retailers around the world has given rise to four different types of international retailers: the hypermarket, the power retailers, the niche retailer and the designer flagship stores who target particular global cities for their stores. Examples of these cover a range of product categories including fashion, jewellery, food and beverage, home furnishings and specialty stores. Alberta Ferretti, Joseph, Alexander McQueen, Manolo Blahnik, Agent Provocateur, Galliano, Tom Ford and Lanvin are leading names in the global high fashion niche retailing.

Besides the growing sophistication of the industry and the opening up of new markets around the world, the globalization of retailers can be attributed to a number of 'pull' and 'push' factors.

The 'push' factors are:

- saturation of the home market or over-competition;
- economic recession or limited growth in spending;

Table 10.2 Top ten global food retailers

	Sales (US$bn)	No of stores
Wal-Mart (US)	405	8 416
Carrefour (France)	120	14 215
Metro (Germany)	91	2 127
Tesco (UK)	89	4 835
Schwartz (Germany)	81	9 902
Kroger (US)	77	3 619
Rewe (Germany)	71	13 148
Costco (US)	70	560
ALDI (GERMANY)	70	69
TARGET (USA)	64	1 740

Source: www.supermarketnews.com, accessed August 2010.

ILLUSTRATION 10.5

Freight forwarders

A freight forwarder is a company that dispatches shipments via carriers and books or otherwise arranges space for shipments. Carriers could include vessels, airplanes, trucks or railroads.

Freight forwarders arrange cargo to an international destination and have the expertise that allows them to prepare *and* process the documentation and perform activities that are needed for international shipments. Some of the information reviewed by a freight forwarder is the commercial invoice, shipper's export declaration and other documents required by the carrier or country of export, import or transhipment. Common services of freight forwarders are: Air freight, Sea freight, Shipping, Logistics management, Trucking, Rail freight, Specialized transportation. They will also give advice on every aspect of freight forwarding – the best freight transport route, the documentation needed, as well as the timings and the costs a company should expect.

Question

1 Assess the role of a freight forwarder in helping a company develop a global logistics operation.

- a declining or ageing population;
- strict planning policies on store development;
- high operating costs – labour, rents, taxation;
- shareholder pressure to maintain profit growth;
- the 'me too' syndrome in retailing.

The 'pull' factors are:

- the underdevelopment of some markets or weak competition;
- strong economic growth or rising standards of living;
- high population growth or a high concentration of young adults;
- a relaxed regulatory framework;
- favourable operating costs – labour, rents, taxation;
- the geographical spread of trading risks;
- the opportunity to innovate under new market conditions.

Marketing implications for development of international distribution strategies

The internationalization of retailing has meant a new era of distribution is developing. This new competitive landscape in distribution has a number of implications for the development of the distribution strategies of international firms. The most important of these are:

- power shifts in supply chains towards retailers;
- intense concentrated competition with significant buyer power across country markets;

- rapidly advancing technology facilitating global sourcing and global electronic transactions;
- unrelenting performance measures being demanded of suppliers by international retailers;
- smart, demanding consumers expecting high levels of customer service.

Thus, power in many international markets is moving from the supplier down the supply chain to the consumer. This means effective management is critical to suppliers competing in international markets. It again highlights the importance of ensuring the distribution strategy across international markets is driven by an understanding of the target market segments, both within each foreign country market and across national market boundaries.

This intensive growth in the size and power of retailers in countries with advanced retailing structures and retailers internationalizing means there is now tremendous pressure on suppliers to improve the quality of service to them. Retailers are demanding:

- streamlined and flexible supply chains;
- suppliers who can guarantee quality and reliability across global markets;
- the ability to supply high volumes and close relationships with intermediaries in the supply chain;
- suppliers who can meet the global sourcing requirements of large-scale retailers who wish to buy centrally across the globe.

It could mean, therefore, that the firms who are successful are the firms who develop the capability to compete effectively in the supply chain activities compared to their international competitors. It is for this reason that the distribution strategy of the international company has taken on such an important dimension in recent times.

Internet retailing

Multimedia technology has provided a number of opportunities for interactive shopping which offer particular opportunities in international markets. Tele-shopping and the Internet offer suppliers the retailing opportunities for direct contact with consumers throughout the globe. What is more, they can achieve this without the problems and expense of having to establish infrastructures in foreign country markets. For example, Amazon.com, the bookshop which sells purely over the Internet, carries no books as they are directly shipped from the publishers' or distributors' warehouses. This means Amazon have few inventory or real estate costs. They offer 2.5 million titles including every English language book in print whereas even the largest bookstore would only stock 170 000. EToys, the Internet competitor to Toys'R'Us, has no retail outlets but a higher market capitalization than Toys'R'Us. EToys and Amazon proactively trap individual information on consumer purchases and then flash messages back telling consumers of other products bought by consumers making similar purchases, as do Amazon. The diffusion of the Internet is increasingly challenging the traditional channels of distribution. It has the capacity to bring together buyers and sellers around the world through the creation of an online marketplace. However, despite exponential growth in access to the Internet, consumers are still limiting their purchases to relatively few product lines. It is estimated that nearly 40 per cent of all Internet purchases are for travel, another 26 per cent for the purchase of tickets for events and concerts and 25 per cent is spent on books and CDs.

In international marketing the major impact, as we will discuss in Chapter 12, has been the ability of the Internet to enable small- and medium-sized companies to access niche markets around the globe that were previously too logistically difficult for them to access. By simply setting up their own sites, a company in effect becomes global and can sell goods and services throughout the world. However, there has also been the development of market sites which have impacted on the way business transactions take place internationally, such as:

- *Auctions.* Online marketplaces where negotiations of price between independent buyers and sellers are implemented through a standard auction open to all participants (e.g. eBay, Dabsexchange, On Sale).

- *Single buyer markets.* Where a large buyer establishes an online intranet market for its own suppliers (e.g. GE Trade Web), usually for them to gain access to the site the suppliers will have achieved the status of approved supplier.
- *Pure exchanges.* Where individual buyers and sellers are matched according to product offers and needs.

The most promising products are often those where existing intermediaries do not perform many of the traditional 'wholesaler' functions for a broad market owing to the high cost of servicing small diverse and geographically or functionally dispersed players. There are several market characteristics in international markets which favour the development of Internet-based distribution:

- *Inefficiencies in traditional distribution channels,* as in Japan where it is difficult for international operators to penetrate the market so sellers cannot gain access to customers.
- *Market fragmentation.* Niche market players where customers are geographically dispersed across the globe and are not concentrated in any one country.
- *Minimum scale barriers.* Smaller exporters have traditionally been restricted from operating globally because of the costs and difficulties of exporting, and therefore lose out to larger players who reap economies of scale and exploit distribution relationships.
- *Commodity-type products.* Products with well-known technical specifications, or manufacturer brands that can easily be price-compared across countries and do not require substantial after-sales service.
- *Short life-cycle products.* Product-markets with short life-cycles create large quantities of obsolete and discontinued items. Customers may experience difficulty finding spare parts or compatible accessories for earlier generations of product.

The management of the physical distribution of goods

Physical distribution management (PDM) is concerned with the planning, implementing and control of physical flows of materials and final goods from points of origin to points of use to meet customer needs at a profit (Kotler *et al.* 2009).

In international physical distribution of goods the total distribution costs will be higher than domestic distribution. The extra activities, increased time taken and the need to adapt to special country requirements will all increase costs. The extra costs centre around three areas:

1 *Increased distance*; this means, in terms of costs, increased transport time, inventory, cash flow and insurance.
2 *New variables to consider*; new modes of transport (air, sea, rail, road), new types of documentation, packaging for long transit times.
3 *Greater market complexity*; language differences requires the translation of documents, the extra costs of bureaucracy and longer lines of communication.

It is important for the firm to take full account of all these extra costs when evaluating alternative distribution strategies. In taking the total distribution cost approach, firms will include the costs of transport, warehousing, inventory, order processing, documentation, packaging and the total cost of lost sales if delays occur. Companies find that changes to one element of distribution influence the performance and the costs of other elements, as Cisco found to its advantage in Management Challenge 10.2.

The logistics approach to physical distribution

Many writers on physical distribution use logistics and physical distribution as terms meaning the same thing. Kotler *et al.* (2009) makes the distinction between physical distribution as a more

MANAGEMENT CHALLENGE 10.2

Cisco Systems

Cisco Systems enforces very high-quality, control standards on all its suppliers. This has always involved the company in lengthy and cumbersome processes of certification which proved very costly. Furthermore, whenever the company put anything out to tender evaluation of those tenders was very time-consuming. In order to maintain their competitive advantage internationally the company prioritized this area as one where significant cost savings could be made.

The dilemma is, how can this be achieved without compromising standards?

traditional activity and logistics as being more market-oriented. In this way, physical distribution thinking starts with the finished product at the end of the production line and then attempts to find low-cost solutions to get the product to the customer. Logistics thinking, on the other hand, considers the customer and then works back to the factory. In this section we will use the market-oriented view. We will use the term logistics to mean an integrated view of physical distribution management in which customer demand influences are at least as important as cost-cutting forces. More and more companies are integrating their physical distribution strategies and linking their operations in different countries with more common processes, thus rationalizing their manufacturing and distribution infrastructure to make more effective use of business resources and so taking a logistical view of their distribution operations.

In Europe 75 per cent of businesses operating across European markets have a pan-European logistics or distribution strategy in place. McKinsey Consultants estimate the European logistics market to be worth about US$400 billion. The logistics function is having an increasing influence in many parts of the business, especially in inventory planning, information technology, purchasing and manufacturing.

There are a number of factors influencing this change:

■ Customers demanding improved levels of customer service.

■ Electronic Data Interchange (EDI) becoming the all-pervading technology for firms to build links with customers, suppliers and distribution providers.

■ Companies restructuring their physical distribution operations in response to the formation of regional trading blocs.

In the following sections, we will briefly examine the developments in each of the above areas.

Customer service

The main elements of customer service will revolve around:

■ order to delivery time;
■ consistency and reliability of delivery;
■ inventory availability;
■ order size constraints;
■ ordering convenience;
■ delivery time and flexibility;
■ invoicing procedures, documentation and accuracy;
■ claims procedure;
■ condition of goods;

- salesperson's visits;
- order status information;
- after-sales support.

In developing customer service levels it is essential to use the elements of service that the customer regards as important. Delivery reliability might be more important than a quick order to delivery time that is unreliable in meeting delivery schedules. Understanding the way in which the international customer perceives service is important. There will be considerable differences. Customers who are distant might be more concerned about the guarantees of reliable rapid availability than customers much closer to the production source. The corporate capability to meet widely differing customer requirements in different countries needs to be managed.

In all countries, customers are becoming increasingly demanding. Partnership arrangements are becoming significant in many sectors as supply chains become more integrated. These developments are usually driven by customer-led demands for improved service. Consumers are demanding ever-quicker delivery and ever more added value from their products that increasingly require just in time distribution. Companies increasingly allow customers to track the progress of products through the distribution system via the Internet. The websites which allow customers to track the progress of their packages are attracting 1 000 000 hits a day. The other major area of IT involvement is in stock control and buying. Despite having 600 stores in 14 countries and using 12 different own labels, C&A is still able to deliver nine times a day to its stores due to its efficient centralized buying operation for men's and children's wear in Brussels and women's wear in Düsseldorf.

The restructuring of physical distribution operations

In mature trading regions such as the US and Europe, a large number of firms have restructured their distribution networks in response to changes in the trading structures in the region. Cross-border deliveries have increased and the number of factories and warehouses has decreased. The number of distribution centres serving more than one country has increased whereas there has been a decrease in the number of warehouses dedicated to within-country movements.

Lucent Technology dispatches all its products from its factory in Spain to a test and assembly centre in Singapore before final delivery. It might go back to a customer sitting 10 kilometres away from the factory in Spain, but it will still go to Singapore. The company gives a 48-hour delivery guarantee to customers anywhere in the world, posing demanding logistical challenges.

The physical movement of goods is a high-cost activity. Companies often incur 10 to 35 per cent of their expenditure on physical distribution. Because distribution is so expensive, it is now receiving close attention from general management and from marketing management.

The logistics approach is to analyze customer requirements and to review what competitors are providing. Customers are interested in a number of things: deliveries to meet agreed time schedules, zero defect delivery, supplier willingness to meet emergency needs, supplier willingness to replace damaged goods quickly and supplier willingness to engage in just in time (JIT) delivery and inventory holding.

If a company is to achieve a logistically effective system of distribution it will become involved in a highly complex and sophisticated system and will, therefore, need to:

- clearly define areas of responsibility across foreign country markets;
- have a highly developed planning system;
- have an up to date and comprehensive information support system;
- develop expertise in distribution management;
- have a centralized planning body to coordinate activities and exercise overall control.

Thus, a logistical system helps the company to pay attention to inventory levels and think through market relationships, to minimize costs of stock out and maximize distribution efficiency across a large number of markets.

In developing an efficient logistical system of physical distribution across international markets there are a number of important considerations:

- how intermediaries such as freight forwarders can enhance our service;
- what modes of transportation should be used;
- how the firm can make effective use of export processing zones;
- what documentation is required;
- what are the packaging requirements for transit and the market;
- how should the export sales contract be organized.

In the following sections, we will briefly discuss some of the important issues in each of these areas.

The use of intermediaries

Traditionally, intermediaries such as forwarders and freight companies simply offered transportation by land, sea and air. There are now many types of intermediaries which offer global logistical services. FedEx, UPS and DPWN (Deutsche Post World Net, which absorbed DHL) have global networks to offer express-delivery services which they also use to offer customized logistics solutions. Broking houses such as Kuehne & Nagel offer their skills in tying together different modes of transport. Other companies offer specialized services, for instance transport and warehouse-management firms which organize the physical movement and storage of goods. Still others are dedicated contract carriers and freight forwarders, who buy capacity on ships and cargo planes, and put together loads from different companies to fill them. Most freight forwarders will offer services such as preparation and processing of international transport documents, coordination of transport services and the provision of warehousing. (See Illustration 10.5).

However, as we have seen in the above section, recent trends such as just in time delivery, outsourcing of non-core activities, cutting inventories and the trend to build to order (BTO) have meant international firms have had to build a comprehensive but flexible logistical operation to ensure goods reach their customers around the world in the right place at the right time. This is such a challenging task that companies are no longer able to do it all themselves, so more of them are using intermediaries and outsourcing the logistical functions. This has meant the global freight-transport industry itself has had to reshape, as manufacturers seek service suppliers with global reach. Manufacturers want custom-designed delivery systems, using all types of transport – land, sea and air. Many of the larger firms now offer a whole range of options beyond their original specific function. This has meant that distinctions between the various intermediaries, such as freight forwarders, transport companies, express couriers and logistics services, are blurring.

All intermediaries deal with three parallel flows: physical goods, information and finance (leasing, lending and brokerage). What is happening now is that while previously intermediaries specialized in one of the flows they are now offering the full range of services. Even global manufacturers are entering the logistics business. Caterpillar, which makes construction equipment, uses the global distribution network it has already developed as a channel for the products of other manufacturers.

There have been two driving forces for this. First, global competition has meant a downward pressure on costs. This has spawned the phenomenon that began in the logistics sector with outsourcing but has extended to the whole range of other services now regarded as legitimate logistics tasks. Indeed, many of the multi-national logistics companies such as DPWN, FedEx, UPS and TNT, the so-called integrators, themselves outsource the functions they take on to small specialist suppliers.

Second, the technological advances discussed earlier mean that logistics specialists are able to offer increasingly sophisticated services to exporters that firms cannot provide in-house. For example, a firm's products might once have passed from factory to national warehouse and then on to a foreign regional warehouse, then to a local depot, before delivery to the end consumer: a wasteful process in terms of time and cost. Today, using state-of-the-art systems, a logistics specialist taking responsibility for the warehouse function will deliver to the customer direct from the main warehouse, cutting out three of four links in the chain.

At the more advanced end of the logistics services spectrum, companies are handing control of more and more roles to their logistics partners. This is partly driven by the sheer geographical complexity of many exporters' operations where, for example, head office, factory and customer may be separated by thousands of miles.

As more companies attempt to develop the newly opened emerging markets where they have little knowledge or understanding of the distribution system, the use of third party intermediaries to organize logistics is becoming an essential part of a global marketing strategy.

Transportation

The physical handling and movement of goods over long distances will practically always have to be performed by third parties.

Transportation is the most visible part of the physical distribution strategy. The main options are:

- *Ocean transport*: capacity for large loads of differentiated products, raw materials, semi-finished goods, finished goods. Handling of goods in bulk, in packaged or unitized form, pallets, containers.
- *Inland waterway transport*: heavy and bulk products. Growing container transport. Restrictions because of need for suitable loading/unloading terminals.
- *Air transport*: urgent shipments, perishables, low-density light/high value, relatively small shipments.
- *Road transport*: most flexible door-to-door transport for all kinds of products but mostly finished goods. Container transport.
- *Rail transport*: long distance heavy and bulk products. Container transport.

Ocean and inland waterways Sea and inland waterways provide a very low-cost way to transport bulky, low value or non-perishable products such as coal and oil. Water transport is slow and is subject to difficulties caused by the weather; for example, some ports are iced over for part of the winter. Water transport usually needs to be used with other modes of transport to achieve door-to-door delivery.

One of the policies used to encourage growth in South Korea, a newly industrialized country, has been the stimulation of its shipping and shipbuilding industry.

Ocean shipping can be open market, i.e. free ocean where there are very few restrictions, or it can be organized in conferences which are essentially cartels that regulate rates and capacities available on routes.

As in other areas of distribution, the containerization of ports and the impact of information technology have meant sea transport has become a capital-intensive industry where there is high pressure to achieve full capacity utilization.

The costs of ocean freight, as a result, have declined over the past decade and so it is still the most cost-effective method of transporting goods to distant markets.

The average cost for a six-metre dry cargo container to be shipped from the UK to Shanghai in China will be £1000–£1550 and the approximate transit time would be 20–25 days.

However, a number of hidden costs can arise in overseas shipping:

- overseas warehousing costs due to having to send large inventories in container loads;
- inventory losses from handling spoilage, theft, obsolescence and exchange rate charges in manual time;
- cost of time in transit;
- lost sales from late arrival.

Inland waterways are very important in countries with poor infrastructures. In Vietnam the most popular mode of transportation is by water. A dense network of waterways exists, although even this system will suffer the vagaries of both flood and drought conditions.

Air Air freight is considerably more expensive per tonne/kilometre than the other modes of transport. Air freight is particularly appropriate for the movement of high-value low-bulk and perishable items. For example, diamonds, computer software, specialist component parts and cut flowers use air freight. Air freight is extending its market through promoting its advantages. The higher freight charges can often be offset. Packing costs and insurance rates are significantly less by air. Storage en route, overseas warehousing and inventory losses may all be less by air as will the actual cost of the time in transit. In addition, the development of larger and more flexible aeroplanes for air freight has helped reduce costs.

Road Very flexible in route and time. Schedules can deliver direct to customers' premises. Very efficient for short hauls of high-value goods. Restrictions at border controls can be time-consuming, however, and long distances and the need for sea crossings reduce the attractiveness of freight transport by road. In some parts of the world, particularly in LDCs, road surfaces are poor and the distribution infrastructure poor. In Vietnam, an attractive emerging market for many international firms, the majority of the road network is beaten track which, during the wet season (six months of the year), makes transporting anything by road very difficult. The problems of transporting goods across African countries due to poor road infrastructure can be seen in Illustration 10.6.

Rail Rail services provide a very good method of transporting bulky goods over long land distances. The increasing use of containers provides a flexible means to use rail and road modes with minimal load transfer times and costs.

In Europe, we are seeing the development of the use of 'Bloc Trains' as a highly efficient means of rail transport. In the US they use 'Double Bloc' trains to transport goods across the vast plains. In a number of markets, rail transport is fraught with difficulties. In China, a shipment from Shanghai to Guangzhou, a distance of approximately 2000 kilometres, can take 25 days. Across the interior it is even slower. Shanghai to Xian, 1500 kilometres, can take 45 days. Much of the rail capacity is antiquated and many of the rail lines are old, leading to frequent derailments.

The final decision on transport The decision concerning which transport mode to use is discussed by Branch (2005). He identifies four factors as decisive in choosing transport: the terms of the export contract, the commodity specification, freight and overall transit time.

In the terms of the export contract, the customer can specify the mode(s) of transport and can insist on the country's national shipping line or airline being used. In considering different modes of transport, the specification of the commodity will have a strong influence on modal choice. For example, transport of fresh food will have requirements to prevent spoilage and contamination. The cost of transport is of major importance: it creates extra costs above the normal domestic cost. It is important, therefore, that transport options are researched thoroughly so that the best value arrangements can be made for both the buyer and the supplier.

Export processing zones

The principle of the export processing zone (EPZ) started with the opening of the world's first EPZ at Shannon in the Republic of Ireland. Since then there has been a proliferation in the establishment of EPZs worldwide, with notable examples being Jebel Ali at Dubai in the UAE and Subic Bay in the Philippines. The principle of the EPZ has been embraced as a worldwide instrument for national economic development by the United Nations.

The concept of the EPZ concerns the duty-free and tax-free manufacture or processing of products for export purposes within a customs-controlled ('offshore') environment. Components may be imported into the zone duty free and tax free to be processed or manufactured into the finished product, or stored for onward distribution and then re-exported without any liability of import duties or other taxes. The purpose of the EPZ is to ensure that at least 70 per cent of the zone-produced articles are re-exported. The remaining percentage of items produced within the zone may be imported into domestic territory upon payment of the appropriate import duty and tax for the finished article.

Companies trading from within the export processing zone can be wholly-owned by foreign-based enterprises and, in most cases, all profits may be repatriated to the home country. Foreign direct investment by overseas-based companies is encouraged in zone operations, since normal national rules regarding profits or ownership do not apply. It is also possible for locally based companies to engage in zone operations as long as they are involved in import and export operations.

ILLUSTRATION 10.6

© Peter Treanor/Alamy

Nightmare logistics in Cameroon

Douala, Cameroon's major port is one of Africa's busiest ports, handling 95 per cent of Cameroon's international trade. It also serves Cameroon's neighbours, Chad and the Central African Republic.

Douala was once considered one of the worst ports in the world; however, since borrowing money from the World Bank and investment by the government in the port infrastructure things have improved somewhat. The main problem now is once the goods have landed in the port to transport them safely to their destination. The only viable route is by road and that can be very problematic. Douala suffers from horrendous traffic problems and once outside the city, roads have been built on soft soil with little foundations. Roads are poorly maintained and subject to bad weather, since fewer than 7 per cent of the roadways are tarred. The heat and the rain soon cause wide potholes and huge cracks. Besides the potholes, motorists must dodge the wrecks of cars that have smashed. Under Cameroon law, these cannot be moved until the police have given permission. The many frequent roadblocks often serve little other purpose than to allow police and gendarmes to collect bribes.

Companies like Coca-Cola and Guinness transporting drinks face nightmare problems. On a journey through Cameroon they may lose up to a third of a truckload. The cost of distribution alone can be as much as 15 per cent higher than in a country with decent roads. This is besides the traumas of police controls, local government bureaucracy and the longer length of time it takes for a truck to make a simple journey.

Global operators use specialist logistics companies to deal with such logistical problems. In order to transfer a production unit of the Cameroon Brewery Company from Cameroon to Benin, TBC Logistics organized a special convoy made up of trucks and oversized machines and tanks. They managed to pass through Nigeria and cover a distance of about 5000km. To do this the convoy had to pass through thickly populated towns as well as small isolated villages with tracks rather than roads.

Question

1 What are the ways in which companies can minimize logistical problems in countries like Cameroon?

References: www.economist.com, www.tbclogistics.com and wikipedia.org/wiki/Cameroon.

It is also likely that the workforce used will cost the zone company less than for home-based operations, since the majority of the EPZs are located in developing countries, especially East and South East Asia and Central America.

The advantages for companies in taking advantage of EPZs are:

- All goods entering the EPZ are exempted from customs duties and import permits.
- Firms can use foreign currency to settle transactions.
- EPZs can be used for assembly of products and so help reduce transportation costs.
- EPZs give a company much more flexibility and help avoid the unwanted bureaucracy of customs and excise.

China has developed 124 export processing zones in the coastal regions and special economic zones (SEZs) in the interior of China to help develop export sea trade. Examples of EPZs in China are Hong Kong, Shenzen, Shanghai and Tianjin.

Administrative problems resulting from the cross-border transfer of goods

For many companies, particularly those that are infrequent exporters or that have insufficient resources for effective export administration, the process of ensuring that goods reach their ultimate destination is beset with difficulties: goods held in customs warehouses without apparent reason, confusing paperwork, high and apparently arbitrary duties, levies and surcharges and the need to make exorbitant payments to expedite the release of goods. The UN Conference on Trade and Development (UNCTAD) believe these additional costs to world trade could be as much as 10 per cent of the US$12.5 trillion total world trade. UNCTAD also believes that those costs could be cut by US$250 billion by improved efficiency. It is unlikely, however, that such changes as these will happen quickly, and so companies face a series of decisions about how to manage their own risks and costs, while still providing an effective service to their customers.

Documentation

A number of different documents are required in cross-border marketing. These include invoices, consignment notes and customs documents. SITRO, the Simpler Trade Procedures Board, has been involved in developing simpler documentation and export procedures with the aim of encouraging international trade. EDI is expanding and now providing a fast integrated system which is reducing documentation preparation time and errors.

The process of documentation has more importance than its rather mechanistic and bureaucratic nature would suggest. Errors made in documents can result in laws being broken, customs regulations being violated or, in financial institutions, refusing to honour demands for payment. Country variations are considerable with regard to export documentation procedures. Different documents are required in different formats. Figure 10.3 shows a typical export order process.

Documentation problems have five main causes: complexity, culture, change, cost and error. Complexity arises from the number of different parties requiring precise documents delivered at the correct time. In addition to the customer, banks, chambers of commerce, consulates, international carriers, domestic carriers, customs, port/terminal/customs clearance areas, insurance companies and the exporting company or freight forwarding company are being used by the exporter.

Different countries require different numbers of copies of documents, sometimes in their own language and sometimes open to official scrutiny that is strongly influenced by the culture of that country. Document clearance can, therefore, be slow and subject to bureaucratic delays.

FIGURE 10.3 The export order and physical process

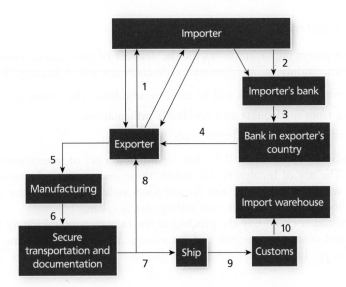

Errors in documentation can have serious consequences. The definition of an 'error' is open to interpretation. Errors can result in goods being held in customs or in a port. Clearance delays cause failure to meet customer service objectives. In extreme cases, errors result in goods being confiscated or not being paid for.

The development of regional trading blocs is reducing some of the complexity of documentation. Previous to the single European market, a firm transporting goods from Manchester (UK) to Milan (Italy) would require 38 different documents. Now, theoretically, none are required! Some companies seek to minimize their exposure to documentation problems by using freight forwarders to handle freight and documentation. Other companies develop their own expertise and handle documentation in-house.

Packaging

Packaging for international markets needs to reflect climatic, geographical, economic, cultural and distribution channel considerations. In this section we will concentrate on the specific requirements that particularly relate to transport and warehousing.

The main packaging issues of interest for the exporter are: loss, damage and the provision of handling points to cope with the range of transport modes and the levels of handling sophistication and types of equipment used throughout the entire transit.

- *Loss.* The main concerns of loss of goods relate to misdirection and to theft (pilferage). The use of containers has reduced some of the opportunities for theft. Misdirection can be minimized by the appropriate use of shipping marks and labelling. High-value consignments need to be marked in such a way as to avoid drawing them to the attention of potential thieves. Marking needs to be simple, security-conscious and readily understandable by different people in different countries.

- *Damage.* The length of transit and variations in climate and physical movement give rise to many opportunities for damage to occur. Goods stowed in large ships might be contaminated by chemical odours or corroding machinery. Goods might be left out in the open air in equatorial or severe winter conditions. Wal-Mart found that local Brazilian suppliers could not meet their standards for packaging and quality control.

A good balance needs to be achieved between the high costs of the substantial export packing required to eliminate all or almost all damage and the price and profit implications that this has for the customer and the exporter.

Over the years, export packaging has been modified from wooden crates and straw, etc., towards fibreboard and cardboard cartons. Different countries have different regulations about what materials are acceptable. In addition, export packaging influences customer satisfaction through its appearance and in its appropriateness to minimize handling costs for the customer.

The export sales contract

The export sales contract covers important terms for the delivery of products in international trade. There are three main areas of uncertainty in international trade contracts which Branch (2005) identifies as:

- uncertainty about which legal system will be used to adjudicate the contract;
- difficulties resulting from inadequate and unreliable information;
- differences in the interpretation of different trade terms.

The International Chamber of Commerce (ICC) has formulated a set of internationally recognized trade terms called Incoterms. The use of Incoterms will reduce these uncertainties. However, because there are many different ways in which the customer and the supplier could contract for the international delivery of products, the possibility of ambiguity can exist unless care is taken.

At one extreme the customer could buy the product at the factory gate, taking all the responsibility for permits, arrangements and costs of transport and insurance. At the other extreme the supplier can arrange and pay for all costs to the point where the product is delivered to the customer's premises.

There are a variety of different steps between manufacture and delivery to the customer. Keegan and Green (2010) identify nine steps:

- obtaining an export permit, if required. For example, for the sale of armaments;
- obtaining a currency permit, if required;
- packing the goods for export;
- transporting the goods to the place of departure. This is usually road transport to a seaport or to an airport. For some countries, for example within continental Europe, transport could be entirely by road;
- preparing a bill of lading;
- completing necessary customs export papers;
- preparing customs or consular invoices as required in the country of destination;
- arranging for ocean freight and preparation;
- obtaining marine insurance and certificate of the policy.

There are many Incoterms specifying many variations of responsibility for the required steps in the delivery process. The main terms are defined below:

- *Ex-works* (EXW). In this contract the exporter makes goods available at a specified time at the exporter's factory or warehouse. The advantage to the buyer in this arrangement is that of obtaining the goods at the lowest possible price.
- *Free on board (FOB)*. In this contract the exporter is responsible for the costs and risks of moving the goods up to the point of passing them over the ship's rail. The FOB contract will specify the name of the ship and the name of the port. The benefit to the buyer in this arrangement is that the goods can be transported in the national shipping line of the buyer and can be insured using a national insurance company. In this way the amount of foreign currency needed to finance the contract is reduced.
- *Cost, insurance, freight (CIF)*. This contract specifies that the exporter is responsible for all costs and risks to a specified destination port indicated by the buyer. The buyer benefits from receiving the goods in the home country and is, therefore, spared the costs, risks and management of the goods in transit. The exporter can benefit from a higher price for the contract. Whether the contract is more profitable will depend on the extra total distribution costs associated with the CIF contract. From a national point of view, the use of CIF contracts by a country's exporters is preferred as invisible earnings through extra freight and insurance services are increased when CIF contracts are used rather than FOB contracts.

Governments of all types of political and economic persuasion sometimes develop policies to favour their own national companies, and they can try to influence the availability of transport modes. In addition, the extra incentive to increase foreign currency earnings can change the export sales contract and with it the specification of the Incoterms.

SUMMARY

- The management of international distribution channels and logistics is challenging because it is frequently determined more by the available infrastructure and host country channel structure than by what the firm would like to do.
- The lack of experience in distribution decision-making is exposed further by explicit and implicit cultural differences. It is important to understand and manage cultural differences among different members of the variety of distribution channel arrangements in different country markets.

- Cultural differences add to control difficulties. Typically, companies have less control over international channels than they have in their domestic market. The usual pattern is to have a smaller market share and to use longer distribution channels, that is, using more layers of distribution intermediaries. Both of these factors reduce the power of the manufacturer. Less channel power usually results in less control over other channel members.

- The changing nature of retailing patterns influences distribution planning. The long-term commitments that form the basis of successful distribution need to be nurtured. However, change also implies some adapting of distribution channel arrangements. It is a considerable challenge to add new types of distribution intermediaries while holding on to long-established accounts.

- Successful management of international distribution channels and logistics represents a significant challenge to the international marketer. The proximity of the company, the distribution intermediaries and the customer make cultural interactions an important influence on success.

- Success in international distribution channel and logistics management has to be based on high-quality strategic decisions and consistent and efficient tactical implementation.

KEYWORDS

Integrated supply chain	Interactive customer marketing	Logistics or distribution strategy
Foreign market channels	Mass customization	Electronic Data Interchange
Indirect channels	Data mining	Build to order
Direct channels	Category management	Open market
Buyer–seller relationships	Effective consumer response	Export processing zone
Distribution channel structures	Interactive shopping	Export administration
Straddle the pyramid	Total distribution cost	

© Art Directors & TRIP/Alamy

CASE STUDY

Merry Management Training

Merry was a training consultancy producing a range of management training courses. Their own staff delivered the courses. They also marketed a range of distance learning management courses which they marketed internationally through agents.

A client that successfully completed a training course would receive a Merry certificate.

Recently John Razor of Merry investigated the possibility of entering the Middle East. Research had shown that there were potential opportunities for distance learning management programmes, particularly in the Gulf States. By chance he met Yabmob Nig, the managing director of a small management consultancy firm based in Dubai called Ala-Meer Ltd. Ala-Meer was owned by two partners, Yabmob Nig and a silent partner who took no part in the management of the business. The silent partner, a local Dubai businessman, was necessary because Yabmob Nig was an expatriate from India and so could not be sole director of the business.

Yabmob and John had a series of meetings and developed a good rapport. It was not thought necessary to draw up a detailed contract at this stage and so a brief memorandum of understanding (MOU) was signed. The main terms of the MOU were as follows:

1 Ala-Meer had exclusive rights to market and recruit clients throughout the Middle East.

2 Ala-Meer would receive 20 per cent of the fee income.

3 Ala-Meer would charge for other services as agreed.

4 All fees would be made payable to Merry but collected by Ala-Meer.

Ala-Meer were very effective marketers. They very easily got potential clients to sign up for a course but were finding it hard to get clients to make the payments direct to Merry.

Yabmob Nig persuaded John Razor to change the method of payment. The new method of payment allowed clients to pay Ala-Meer in the local currency who would then pass on the payments to Merry. Ala-Meer were then able to market the courses much more easily and were soon recruiting clients from most of the countries in the Middle East. They did this by newspaper advertising, mail shots, Web advertising and subscribing to a number of search engines on the Internet.

Client numbers grew rapidly and everyone was pleased with the market development. Merry was dispatching a large volume of material to the Middle East and Merry staff were conducting seminars in the region on a regular basis. This was the honeymoon period for the business relationship, as both parties had a common objective – to grow sales. A high degree of trust existed between the parties at this stage.

At the end of the first two years of operations Merry undertook a financial audit of the partnership. However, this was quite difficult to do, as there were no proper audited accounts. Under Dubai law, firms do not have to publish audited accounts. Even so, the auditors found evidence to indicate that the business could be a profitable partnership. However, the cash flow was poor. They found that few clients were making payments

directly to Merry; most were making payments to Ala-Meer. The audit also showed there was a substantial sum of money that should have been paid to Merry by Ala-Meer which had not been paid.

Yabmob Nig was holding back payment as he and John Razor disagreed on the amount of fees that were outstanding. Ala-Meer were claiming a large amount of expenses that Merry argued had not been agreed in the contract. Ala-Meer saw the 20 per cent margin as pure profit whereas Merry had assumed costs would be defrayed from this percentage. Ala-Meer were also aggrieved that Merry had started marketing their courses in Turkey; they thought they had exclusive rights to the whole of the Middle East, and, to them, that included Turkey.

After long negotiations Merry found it almost impossible to agree the sum that Ala-Meer should pay as a result of the fees they had collected. Ala-Meer were constantly claiming 'additional costs' and reporting lower recruitment figures than Merry had delivered material for. In the end Merry had to send out its own accounting staff to audit Ala-Meer records and agree how much Ala-Meer had to pay to Merry. The relationship between the two parties deteriorated rapidly from this point on and Merry terminated the relationship.

Questions

1 Why did this promising business relationship go so badly wrong?

2 How could Merry have protected their business in the Middle East more effectively?

3 What lessons can be drawn from this case regarding cross-cultural negotiations?

Source: Nick Payne, Sheffield Hallam University.

DISCUSSION QUESTIONS

1 How might companies use the Internet to increase the competitiveness of their international distribution strategy?

2 How might the analysis of the retailer infrastructure and retailer marketing practices in advanced economies influence the development of marketing plans for retailers based in less-developed countries?

3 Discuss what factors contribute to the increasing complexity of global logistics operations. Explain why cooperative relationships are so important in this aspect of international marketing operations.

4 The arrival of the global village has had a major impact on companies' distribution methods. Identify four factors involved and explain how each has influenced distribution.

5 Fully evaluate the statement: 'Distribution and logistics are increasingly becoming the battleground in international markets as companies seek to gain global competitive advantage.'

REFERENCES

1. Alexander, N. and Doherty, A.M. (2008) *International Retailing*, Oxford University Press.

2. Branch, A.E. (2005) *Export practice and management*, 5th edn. Thomson Learning.

3. Cateora, P.R. and Ghauri, P. (2006) *International marketing*, 2nd edn. McGraw Hill.

4. Coughlan, A.T., Anderson, E., Stern, L. and El-Ansary, A.I. (2006) *Marketing channels*, 7th edn. Prentice-Hall.

5. Czinkota, M.E. and Ronkainen, I.A. (2009) *Principles of International marketing*, 9th edn. S.W. College.

6. Keegan, W.J. and Green, M.J. (2010) *Global Marketing Management*. 6th edn. Pearson.

7. Kotler, P., Keller, K.L., Brady, M., Goodman, M. and Hansen, T. (2009) *Marketing Management*, Pearson.

8. Rosenbloom, B. (2009) *Marketing Channels, a Management View*, 8th edn. FT Prentice Hall.

9. Albaum, G. and Duerr, E. (2008) *International Marketing and Export Management*, 6th edn. Addison-Wesley.

10. Usunier, J.C. and Lee, J.A. (2005) *Marketing Across Cultures*, 5th edn. Prentice Hall.

11. Waters, D. (2010) *Global Logistics: New Directions in Supply Chain Management*, Chartered Institute of Logistics & Transport (UK).

CHAPTER 11

PRICING FOR INTERNATIONAL MARKETS

LEARNING OBJECTIVES

After reading this chapter you should be able to:

- Discuss the issues that affect international pricing decisions

- Evaluate different strategic options for pricing across international markets

- Differentiate between the problems facing companies engaged in foreign market pricing and those faced by companies trying to coordinate strategies across a range of global markets

- Find solutions to the problems of pricing in high-risk markets

INTRODUCTION

Many organizations believe that pricing is the most flexible, independent and controllable element of the marketing mix and that it plays a major role in international marketing management. This is largely based on the fact that pricing changes appear to prompt an immediate response in the market. However, despite the apparent simplicity of using pricing as a major marketing tool, many managers find pricing decisions difficult to make. This is in part due to the fact that while most firms recognize the importance of pricing at a tactical level in stimulating short-term demand, far fewer recognize the importance of the strategic role of pricing in international marketing.

In this chapter, we focus upon both the internal and external factors that affect international pricing decisions, the role that pricing plays in developing strategies to meet corporate objectives, and the relationship between pricing and other aspects of the firm's activities. In addition to considering the stages involved in developing a comprehensive international pricing policy, we discuss the specific problems associated with pricing in international marketing which do not affect the domestic business. We then go on to explore the financial issues in managing risk in pricing and of non-payment of debts.

Domestic vs international pricing

For many companies operating in domestic markets, pricing decisions are based on the relatively straightforward process of allocating the total estimated cost of producing, managing and marketing a product or service between the forecast total volume of sales, and adding an appropriate profit margin. Problems for these firms arise when costs increase, sales do not materialize or competitors undercut the prices. In international markets, however, pricing decisions are much more complex, because they are affected by a number of additional external factors, such as fluctuations in exchange rates, accelerating inflation in certain countries and the use of alternative payment methods such as leasing, barter and countertrade. Since the global financial crisis of 2008 the complexities of pricing in a global market where there is economic and political uncertainty has made this decision area even more difficult for many companies who are often now trading in countries with high levels of debt, high unemployment and political tensions.

In recent years, too, it has become more apparent that customer tastes have become much more sophisticated, and that purchase decisions are made less frequently on the basis of price consideration, but are increasingly influenced by wider expectations of product performance and perceptions of value. This has particular implications for international products, which are often perceived to be of significantly different value – higher or lower – than locally produced products. Pricing strategies are also strongly influenced by the nature and intensity of the competition which exists in the various local markets.

For these reasons, it is important to recognize at the outset that the development and implementation of pricing strategies in international markets should go through the following stages:

1 Analyzing the factors which influence international pricing, such as the cost structures, the value of the product, the market structure, competitor pricing levels and a variety of environmental constraints.

2 Confirming what impact the corporate strategies should have on pricing policy.

3 Evaluating the various strategic pricing options and selecting the most appropriate approach.

4 Implementing the strategy through the use of a variety of tactics and procedures to set prices at SBU level.

5 Managing prices and financing international transactions.

The factors affecting international pricing decisions

A firm exporting speculatively for the first time, with little knowledge of the market environment that it is entering, is likely to set a price based largely on company and product factors. Because of its restricted resources, the firm places particular emphasis on ensuring that sales revenue generated at least covers the costs incurred. However, while it is important that firms recognize that the cost structures for production, marketing and distribution of products and services are of vital importance, they should not be regarded as the sole determinants when setting prices. Sarathy, Terpstra and Russow (2006) identify many other factors that firms should take into consideration – environment, market, company and specific product factors – these are summarized below. It is by giving full recognition to the effect of these factors on pricing decisions that the company can develop a strategic rather than a purely tactical approach to pricing.

Factors influencing the pricing strategy
Company and product factors

- corporate and marketing objectives;
- firm and product positioning;

- product range, life cycle, substitutes, product differentiation and unique selling propositions;
- cost structures, manufacturing, experience effect and economies of scale;
- marketing, product development;
- available resources;
- inventory;
- shipping costs.

Market factors

- consumers' perceptions, expectations and ability to pay;
- need for product and promotional adaptation, market servicing, extra packaging requirements;
- market structure, distribution channels, discounting pressures;
- market growth, demand elasticities;
- need for credit;
- competition objectives, strategies and strength.

Environmental factors

- government influences and constraints;
- currency fluctuations;
- business cycle stage, level of inflation;
- use of non-money payment and leasing.

Companies operating internationally must consider all the above factors detailed for each specific country market. However, as with all the other marketing mix factors, the individual country pricing policies need to be integrated and coordinated within a wider regional or global strategy in order to enable corporate objectives to be met.

While it is important that companies consider all the factors listed, some of them, such as corporate objectives, market and product factors, consumer perceptions, competitor responses and cost structures are of particular significance.

Company and product factors

Corporate objectives The short-term tactical use of pricing such as discounts, product offers and seasonal reductions is often emphasized by managers, at the expense of its strategic role. Sometimes firms will use export markets if they have excess production capacity to dump excess products. This means they use marginal pricing strategies, pricing at really low prices so they cover only the variable costs. Yet pricing over the past few years has played a very significant part in the restructuring of many industries, resulting in the growth of some businesses and the decline of others. New global brands from emerging markets such LG and Haeir have approached a new international market for a specific product with the intention of building market share over a period of years, through maintaining or even reducing pricing levels, establishing the product, the brand name and setting up effective distribution and servicing networks. As a result of this strategy they are now beginning to dominate a whole range of market sectors especially in markets such as consumer electronics. This has usually been accomplished at the expense of short-term profits, as the company will have a long-term perspective on profits.

By contrast, US firms have relied in the past more on international corporate strategies with greater emphasis on factors such as advertising and selling, believing that these reduce the need to compete on price. The reason for this is that the cost base of US manufacturing is usually much higher than that of its foreign competitors. However, the rapid growth of brands from China, Korea and the Asian economies has led to a change in the priorities of US firms. In a recent survey US firms ranked pricing as more important than any other element of the marketing mix, whereas Asian firms, which have been aggressively reducing their cost base for years, now place greater emphasis upon other factors as they seek to build global brands. The move of many Asian manufacturers from being contract manufacturers to marketing their own brands globally has seen them placing much more emphasis on innovation and marketing as they upgrade and develop their products and differentiate themselves by building their own distinctive brands.

The international nature of competition leads to the question of whether firms should aim for a broadly standardized price structure, or whether prices should be adapted in each country.

Product and service factors

While in theory standardization in pricing might appear easier to manage and therefore be preferable, in practice the different local economic, legal and competitive factors in each market make it rarely achievable. The occasions when price standardization is achievable are more usually related to the nature of the product and its stage in the life cycle – for example, standardized pricing can be adopted for certain hi-tech products where limited competition exists. Myers, Cavusgil and Diamontopolous (2002), in their examination of export pricing, note that when the technology becomes more freely available, the marketers adopt more market-led pricing. Aircraft makers, for example, because of the relative uniqueness and complexity of the technology, tend to charge the same price regardless of where the customer is based. However, in contrast, shipbuilders, with products in the mature phase of the product life cycle, adapt prices to meet each particular purchase situation.

In developing pricing strategies, a company needs to be aware of the price dynamics of specific products in the various markets. Five characteristics of the product are important in pricing:

- *Frequency of purchase*. Frequently purchased products, for example baby food, petrol, tea and bread, tend to be very price-sensitive in all international markets, whereas occasional purchases are not.
- *Degree of necessity*. If a product is essential for its users, price changes are unlikely to affect the market size, except in countries where extreme poverty exists and people cannot afford even the most basic necessities.
- *Unit price*. High-priced products such as holidays and cars are evaluated in greater detail in terms of the consumer's perceptions of value for money, and so, for example, reliability, style and features of cars are extremely important to consumers besides price.
- *Degree of comparability*. Consumers are less price-conscious about insurance policies than grocery products, because the alternatives are more difficult to compare. Price-setting is particularly difficult in certain services, such as advertising, consultancy and accountancy, which have a different perceived value from country to country.
- *Degree of fashion or status*. The high prices of luxury goods are seen as establishing their quality and it is usually the goods that have a prestige image, often created in other countries, which are not price-sensitive. However, even non price sensitive luxury products suffer from cross border cut prices as can be seen in Management Challenge 11.1.

Developing pricing strategies for services across international markets is difficult for several reasons. Services are highly perishable, and human resource constraints often restrict the capacity to grow a service business in foreign country markets, and so companies are restricted by the high costs of expansion and managing short-term capacity issues. Likewise the intangibility of services compared with goods may lead to higher marketing costs because the company has to build the market reputation on the actual service experience of consumers rather than building a brand image in anticipation of the consumer experience. This means positioning optimum prices in foreign country markets can be difficult to judge. In business-to-business marketing, where the growth of international services predominates, managers are often tasked with developing effective global pricing strategies for B2B customers that are characterized by different cultures and differing perceptions as to the value of the different service attributes they are buying. The intensive customer contact, extensive customization requirements, and the costs of building

MANAGEMENT CHALLENGE 11.1

Luxury goods gain EU protection

The European Commission has issued revised rules to allow luxury goods manufacturers who own less than 30 per cent market share in any particular market to restrict the distribution of their goods through online resellers. The means that the manufacturers are able to protect an exclusive off-line distributor from active sales by other distributors in other territories who operate across country boundaries on-line. This ruling they hope will encourage the distributor exclusively allocated territory or customer group to invest in the territory.

This new rule is of particular importance to online retailers such as EBay and Amazon. Under the new rules manufacturers could impose 'hardcore' restrictions on on-line resellers forcing them to refuse sales in particular markets or to reroute customers to particular resellers. The commission has indicated that it will monitor the application of the law for any abuses.

Question

1 In an age of global communications and borderless territories how can such rules impact on a manufacturer's pricing strategy?

---

a service quality reputation in the market make the challenge of formulating international pricing strategies for services across international markets particularly problematic.

Price positioning and value for money

The characteristics of the product or service, particularly the high unit price items, lead international marketers to adopt local pricing strategies which are broadly similar for individual markets, so that the positioning of specific products remains consistent from country to country. Marks and Spencer sell basic foods at higher prices than other food retailers in the UK, by guaranteeing extremely high consistency of quality. This difference is not perceived to be so great in other countries, however, where consumers feel that the general quality is not significantly different to justify a substantially higher price.

Price plays an important role in product differentiation by enhancing the perceived value of the product and helping consumers to distinguish between offers from different competitors in order that their needs can be met. Watch prices, for example, range from very little for a child's watch, to a high premium price for a Rolex. Within this range, individual manufacturers normally confine specific brands within particular pricing bands which are linked to the positioning of the brand and the profile of the watches within the range, and to the characteristics of the target segment.

The key role of price in differentiating products within a category and within a particular market can be used as an offensive strategy. This is demonstrated by the South Korean car manufacturer, Kia, which entered the US car market knowing that its brand name had little credibility there and that the market was already saturated with broadly equivalent products. It targeted its Japanese equivalents, the Honda Civic and Toyota Corolla, by offering a similar car at a 25 per cent lower price.

The influence of cost structures on pricing

There is a close relationship between prices, costs and sales volume of a product, because the price charged affects sales volume by increasing or decreasing the overall demand. As a result of producing or marketing larger volumes the unit cost of an individual product reduces, and so, of all the factors, this often becomes the initial stimulus for firms taking the decision to export.

The relationship between demand and sales volume

The way price affects demand is influenced by many factors. Some products are characterized by having elastic demand and being extremely price-sensitive, so that sales volumes increase significantly as prices are reduced. In underdeveloped markets, where there is low penetration but considerable desire for Western products such as soft drinks or fast food, sales will increase rapidly if the price is reduced relative to consumers' ability to pay.

By contrast, other products are characterized by inelastic demand. For example, suppliers of power generation equipment cannot significantly stimulate demand in individual markets by reducing the price. For such firms, an increase in business revenue is largely determined by changes in external factors, such as an improvement in the economy. The potential market for the European power generation equipment suppliers National Power and ABB was increased by the political decision in Malaysia to partially privatize state utilities.

The relationship between cost and sales volume

A second situation of inelastic demand occurs if a firm finds that it has reached saturation in its home market so that even if prices were reduced, there would not be significant extra sales to offset the loss of profit. The firm might conclude that exporting would provide an alternative method of increasing sales and thereby generate additional profit.

This is especially so when firms can increase sales by entering an export market, make use of existing spare production capacity and so price purely to cover their variable costs. Consider the situation shown in Table 11.1 where all the fixed costs are absorbed by the sales in the domestic market, but in addition, 10 per cent extra sales are obtained in export markets at the same prices. Provided there are no increases in fixed costs, there would be recovery of the fixed costs because of the additional 10 per cent export business. This recovery of fixed costs by the export business would be shown as an additional contribution to the general overheads of the business. The contribution from the export business would all be additional profit.

The fixed production cost of the product includes depreciation of equipment, building rental and business rates. General overheads include advertising, selling, distribution and administration.

The example shows that in practice the additional £100 000 sales have generated an additional £40 000 profit (6.3 per cent on total sales) – far greater than the $30 000 profit generated on the £1 million domestic sales (3 per cent profit on total sales). The firm could, therefore, afford to reduce its

Table 11.1 The effect of additional export sales on contribution

	Domestic sales (100 000 units) £000	+ 10 % Export sales	Domestic + 10 % export sales (110 000 units) £000
Sales	1000	100	1100
Fixed production costs	300		300
Variable production costs	500	50	550
Total costs	800	50	850
Contribution to general overheads	200	50	250
General overheads	170	10	180*
Profit	30	40	70

Note: *General overheads are higher due to additional exporting costs

export price considerably and still make a profit, provided that no extra general overhead costs were incurred, as long as there was spare production capacity and no extra investment had to be made.

In export markets, the firm might choose one of the following four alternatives, setting the selling price at:

- Production cost plus general overhead plus added profit (this would normally be the list price).
- Production cost, but without general overhead or profit added.
- Below production cost.
- Production cost with specific export costs added.

The choice of alternatives will depend on the firm's objectives in entering international markets. The first leads to the safest, albeit least competitive, price and is frequently the approach adopted by new exporters who are unwilling to take any significant risk. The firm might even take the list price, including the domestic gross margin, and add to it all the costs of exporting such as marketing, distribution and administration, resulting in the export price being far greater than the domestic price. In most international markets, however, a list price calculated in this way is unlikely to gain significant market share, and so a lower selling price is required.

The arguments for using the second option, to set a lower export selling price, are based on the belief that export costs should not include domestic sales costs such as advertising, marketing research, domestic and administration costs. While this option has some merit, it might well fail to take account of high specific export costs.

The third option is clearly quite risky as it is designed to substantially increase volume. The danger, of course, is that if the increased volume generated does not absorb the fixed and general overhead costs, the product will be unprofitable and losses will result. This approach is often used in overseas markets and is based on marginal costing, whereby unused production capacity or extended production runs can provide extra goods for sale with little or no change in fixed costs, so that the extra production can effectively be produced at a lower cost than the original production schedule. Another risk with this strategy is that the firm could be accused of dumping excess capacity in foreign markets. This sometimes is exacerbated as a result of government policy, particularly in declining industries, for example, if governments continue to subsidize their own inefficient industries by providing various incentives such as subsidies.

The fourth option begs the question of whether or not export pricing should reflect the entire costs specific to export sales, and if so, which costs can be directly attributable to exports. It can be argued that, particularly if a firm intends ultimately to commence manufacture in foreign markets, it is vital to know exactly what the realistic costs for foreign markets are. Allocating costs such as research and development accurately and appropriately, however, can be difficult.

Specific export costs

While export volumes are small in comparison to the domestic market, some experimentation in export pricing is possible, but as exporting becomes a more significant part of the activities of the company, perhaps requiring the allocation of dedicated equipment or staff, it is necessary to reflect all costs that are specific to export sales. These costs include tariffs, special packaging, insurance, tax liabilities, extra transport, warehousing costs and export selling as well as money transmission, hedging and foreign exchange costs. This can be quite a minefield as Apple discovered when they launched the iPad as shown in Illustration 11.1.

However, often when operating across international markets cost elements can frequently be overlooked or under-estimated by companies, these include:

- Additional freight and handling costs due to a misunderstanding of trading terms.
- Last-minute product modifications to meet an export standard.
- Packaging and labelling requirements (language, ingredients, use-by dates).

© Oleksiy Maksymenko Photography/Alamy

ILLUSTRATION 11.1

Apple iPad gets it wrong

Many global customers were dismayed at the global launch of the Apple iPad when they realized that in most countries it was a higher price than in the USA. One of the reasons was that published prices in the USA do not include sales tax.

But there are other reasons for the difference. Apple say there are increased overheads for distribution and so the 'cost of business' in countries outside the USA is usually higher. Foreign exchange rates and government legislation can also make a difference.

But, even a company as big as Apple can get its facts wrong. In Germany a special copyright tax is imposed by the government *for* computers. A number of countries have laws to protect authors and musicians by taxing sales of digital recorders and DVD players, products regularly used to illegally copy their works. Germany extended this protection into the 'digital age' by taxing sales of modern devices that make for easy copying and transferring of copyright-protected material. France followed suit, with its tax targeting sales of CD-Rs (recordable CDs) and DVDs.

Apple announced at its launch that German iPad prices would be a bit higher than in other countries. The reason for that, as explained by Steve Jobs himself, was the newly introduced €15 copyright tax that Apple added to every model to meet German legislative requirements. This meant that iPad prices in Germany were about 15 euros higher than those in France and Italy, with the extra copyright tax being applied due to the iPad's classification as a 'PC without burner'.

Unfortunately for Apple their information wasn't quite correct. The copyright tax in Germany doesn't affect computers with less than 40GB of memory (or indeed mobile devices). When Apple realized its mistake it had to close its online store, only to reopen it later with the correct lower pricing for the 16GB and 32GB German iPads.

Question

1 What are the other hidden costs in exporting that could impact on the price of a product in different international markets?

- Documentation requirements such as certificates of origin and invoices.
- Insurance (including credit insurance), finance and banking charges.
- Delays in customs clearance if documentation, packaging and labelling is not in order.
- Vaguely worded contracts or agreements.

The most immediate and obvious result of all these costs being passed on is that the price to the consumer in an export market is likely to be much greater than the price to a domestic consumer. An example of this is shown in Table 11.2.

This raises the question of whether foreign consumers will be prepared to pay a higher price for imported rather than locally produced goods. Justifying the cost of the product on the basis of its added value might be possible in the short term, but is unlikely to provide the international marketer with a basis for long-term viability in each local market. A strategy must be developed to deal with

Table 11.2 Escalation of costs through exporting using the 'Cost Plus' Export Pricing Model

FOB	Free on Board	
	EXW Price Plus	100
+	Transport to carrier (eg wharf, airport)	17
+	Customs clearance	8
+	Additional packaging/labour for transport	5
+	Agent's commission	13
	FOB	143
CFR	**Cost and Freight**	
	or	
CPT	**Carriage Paid To**	
	FOB Price Plus	143
+	Sea/air freight charges to wharf/airport	32
+	Sea/air document fees (e.g. Airway Bill, B/L)	11
+	BAF (Bunker Adjustment Factor)	2
+	Transport contingency	2
	CFR or CPT	190
CIF	**Cost, Insurance, Freight**	
	CFR or CPT Price Plus	190
+	Marine Insurance Premium	2
	CIF	192
DDP	**Delivery Duty Paid**	
	CIF Price Plus	192
+	Import duty/tax (calculated as 20% of CIF price)	39
+	Customs clearance fees	8
+	Delivery charge from airport to customer	10
	DDP	249

Source: www.austrade.gov.au, *Austrade Guide to Export pricing*.

this situation in which the cost to the ultimate consumer is reduced. The main options available to the exporter include:

- aggressively reducing production costs, modifying the product if necessary and sourcing overseas;
- shortening the distribution channel, for example, by selling direct to retailers;
- selecting a different market entry strategy, such as foreign manufacture, assembly or licensing to avoid the additional costs of exporting.

The implications of changing the market entry and distribution strategy have been dealt with in earlier chapters of this book; here we discuss strategies for reducing cost.

Cost reduction

The rationale behind any firm's decision to enter international markets is usually to increase profitability, and this is based upon a recognition of the fact that the size of the firm's actual market share is a primary determinant of profitability. Thus the argument goes that firms with a larger market share normally have lower unit costs, and they are perceived by customers to market higher-quality products, leading to relatively higher market prices. Both of these factors result in higher profits for the firm.

Most companies in international markets have the potential to benefit from driving down costs through achieving economies of scale, exploiting the benefits of the learning curve and making strategic decisions on the location or relocation of manufacturing plants within the context of worldwide operations.

Economies of scale

Economies of scale are obtained as a result of manufacturing additional products with the same or only slightly higher fixed costs, so that, in practice, for every additional product produced, the unit cost reduces. This is a slight over-simplification of the situation as, for example, installation of new plant might in the short term increase unit costs during the period when the plant is running at below its economic capacity. While in domestic markets the benefits from economies of scale follow directly, in international markets these economies must more than offset savings achieved by having local plants, which result in reduced transport costs and the avoidance of import tariffs.

Learning curve

Some authors have suggested that, although it is less well-known than economies of scale, the learning curve has potentially greater benefit for cost reduction. Its origins lie in the production of aircraft in the Second World War. The observation that the time needed to perform a specific task reduced as the operatives become more familiar with it was made. Since then a series of studies by the Boston Consulting Group have found evidence that the effect was much more widespread than this, and covered all aspects of business, including high and low technology, products and services and consumer and industrial products. They point out that there is a direct relationship between the cumulative volume of production and the costs incurred in producing the same product benefits. The major sources of savings from the experience gained through the learning curve are:

- greater labour efficiency;
- task specialization and method improvement;
- new production processes;
- better performance of existing equipment;
- changes to the mix of resources;
- greater product standardization;
- improved product designs.

Thus the learning curve provides an opportunity for cost reductions, although if managers do not make a concerted effort, costs will rise.

The combined effects of economies of scale and the learning curve were seen in the electronics market, where aggressive firms slashed prices to gain market share, knowing that cost reductions would follow. For example, Sony set the price of its DVD players in the US market at a third of the actual manufacturing cost, on the basis that the volume generated by increased demand would force component and assembly costs down, through a combination of these two effects. A key issue in international marketing is how best these effects can be exploited, particularly as the skills and experience are spread throughout the world. The efficient transfer of these skills and knowledge between different strategic business units then becomes paramount.

Location of production facility

Driven by the continual need to reduce costs, companies have increasingly considered selective location or relocation of production facilities. As firms increasingly market their products globally, so their choice of manufacturing locations is determined by many other considerations, than simply being close to particular markets. They might choose to locate a factory in a less developed country in order to take advantage of lower labour costs, but also they may well develop specific skills and areas of specialization in those locations. For example, a large proportion of televisions, radios, calculators and jeans are manufactured in China and South East Asia.

India, with over 1 billion inhabitants, 125 million of whom are considered to represent a financially aware middle class, presents the attractive opportunity of an emerging market as well as a huge skilled but cheap workforce for multi-nationals seeking low-cost manufacturing bases. Thomson-CSF (France), Coca-Cola, Motorola, IBM and Hewlett Packard and many others have invested heavily in the region.

Problems associated with manufacturing in Western countries have helped to accelerate this transfer of manufacturing. Lagging productivity, reluctance to source materials and parts globally, strong unions and high standards of living were the causes of the decline in the US manufacturing base. Many regions and countries are responding to this opportunity for inward investment by marketing a variety of incentives and attractions to companies wishing to relocate.

It is not only in manufacturing that relocation of activities can benefit from lower labour costs. For instance, the introduction of fibre optic cables allows considerably more information to be transferred quickly and accurately by telecommunications, and so can lead to high labour-content jobs such as data input, order processing and invoicing being carried out in other countries. It is on this foundation that India has built a global advantage in offering high tech services such as data processing, call centres and software application.

Market factors

Consumers' response   Perhaps the most critical factor to be considered when developing a pricing strategy in international markets, however, is how the customers and competitors will respond.

There are nine factors which influence the sensitivity of customers to prices and all have implications for the international marketer. Price sensitivity reduces:

- the more distinctive the product is;
- the greater the perceived quality;
- the less aware consumers are of substitutes in the market;
- if it is difficult to make comparisons, for example in the quality of services such as consultancy or accountancy;
- if the price of a product represents a small proportion of total expenditure of the customer;
- as the perceived benefit increases;
- if the product is used in association with a product bought previously so that, for example, components and replacements are usually extremely highly priced;
- if costs are shared with other parties;
- if the product or service cannot be stored.

The issue with all these factors is that it is customer perceptions and purchasing behaviour which are most important in setting prices. In France, EuroDisney suffered considerably from weaknesses in its financial structure. The fundamental problems were that customer perceptions and demand for EuroDisney were out of step with forecasts. The explanation for the weaknesses in their offer was found to be in the factors affecting price sensitivity. High interest rates and high labour costs were underestimated and the availability of disposable income of potential consumers overestimated. After a five-year major effort EuroDisney became profitable. Customers' perception of credit can also influence purchasing behaviour. In Central Europe and Asia, consumers have been reluctant to borrow money to buy goods.

Competitors' response   As competition increases in virtually every product and market, the likely response of the competitors to a firm's pricing strategy becomes increasingly important. An attempt should be made to forecast how competitors might react to a change in pricing strategy by analyzing the market and product factors which affect them, consumer perceptions of their product offers and their internal cost structures. Competitors' pricing strategies will be affected by such issues as their commitment to particular products and markets, and the stance that they might have adopted in the past during periods of fierce competition.

Before implementing pricing strategies and tactics, therefore, it is essential to estimate the likely consumer and competitor response by evaluating similar situations which have arisen in other international markets or countries. The responses of competitors who adopt a global strategic approach are likely to be more easily predicted than a competitor adopting a multidomestic strategy.

It is useful to consider how these factors have affected the competitive responses of a number of companies such as Gillette, Kodak and Philip Morris.

Developing pricing strategies

Having discussed the factors which firms should consider in the pricing process, we now turn to the development of international pricing strategies. The first question to be addressed is to what extent prices should be standardized across the markets. There are three approaches to international pricing strategies.

Standardization, or ethnocentric pricing, based on setting a price for the product as it leaves the factory, irrespective of its final destination. While each customer pays the same price for the product at the factory gate, they are expected to pay transport and import duties themselves, either directly or indirectly, and this leads to considerable differences in the price to the final consumer.

For the firm, this is a low-risk strategy as a fixed return is guaranteed and the international buyer takes all the exchange rate risk. However, no attempt is made to respond to local conditions in each national market and so no effort is made to maximize either profits or sales volume. This type of pricing strategy is often used when selling highly specialized manufacturing plant.

Adaptation, or polycentric pricing, allows each local subsidiary or partner to set a price which is considered to be the most appropriate for local conditions, and no attempt is made to coordinate prices from country to country. The only constraints that are applied when using this strategy relate to transfer pricing within the corporate structure.

The weakness with this policy is the lack of control that the headquarters have over the prices set by the subsidiary operations. Significantly different prices must be set in adjacent markets, and this can reflect badly on the image of multi-national firms. It also encourages the creation of grey markets (which are dealt with in greater detail later in this chapter), whereby products can be purchased in one market and sold in another, undercutting the established market prices in the process. Firms marketing on the Internet find it very difficult to pursue such strategies, because of the free flow of information across markets. Gap customers soon discovered they could save up to 40 per cent of the price of a garment by buying online rather than in their local store, leading to a speedy change in their pricing strategy.

Invention, or geocentric pricing, involves neither fixing a single price, nor allowing local subsidiaries total freedom for setting prices either, but attempts to take the best of both approaches. While the need to take account of local factors is recognized, particularly in the short term, the firm still expects local pricing strategies to be integrated into a company-wide long-term strategy. The benefits of this approach are shown in the following example. A firm which intends to establish a manufacturing base within a particular region may need to rapidly increase market share in order to generate the additional sales necessary for a viable production plant. In the short-term, the local subsidiary may be required to sell at what for them is an uneconomic price, so that by the time the new plant comes on stream, sufficient sales have built up to make the plant and the individual subsidiaries profitable.

The objectives of pricing

The objectives of the firm's pricing strategy are directly related to the various factors which have been discussed, but it should be emphasized that they will be affected as much by the prevailing company culture and attitudes to international marketing as by market and environmental conditions. The most common pricing objectives for companies are listed below, but it must be recognized that firms also adapt or add other specific objectives according to their own specific and changing circumstances. The alternative approaches are:

- *Rate of return.* Cost-oriented companies set prices to achieve a specific level of return on investment, and may quote the same ex-works price for both domestic and international markets.

- *Market stabilization.* A firm may choose not to provoke retaliation from the leader, so that market shares are not significantly changed.

- *Demand-led pricing.* Prices are adjusted according to an assessment of demand, so that high prices are charged when demand is buoyant and low prices are charged when demand is weak.

- *Competition-led pricing.* In commodity markets such as coffee and wheat, world market prices are established through continual interaction between buyers and sellers. Selling outside the narrow band of prices that have been mutually agreed will either reduce sales or unnecessarily reduce profits.

- *Pricing to reflect product differentiation.* Individual products are used to emphasize differences between products targeted at various market segments. Carmakers, for example, charge prices for the top of the range models which are far higher than is justified by the cost of the additional features which distinguish them from the basic models, but problems arise in different international markets, as consumers' perceptions vary as to what is considered to be a basic model.

- *Market skimming.* The objective of market skimming is for the firm to enter the market at a high price and lower the price only gradually, or even abandon the market as competition increases. It is often used by companies in recovering high research and development costs.

- *Market penetration.* Low prices can be used by a firm to rapidly increase sales by stimulating growth and increasing market share, but at the same time discouraging competition. Japanese companies have used this strategy extensively to gain leadership in a number of markets, such as cars, home entertainment products and electronic components.

- *Early cash recovery.* Faced with liquidity problems, products in the mature or declining phase of the product life cycle, or products with an uncertain future in the market because of changes in government policy, a firm may aim for early cash recovery, to increase sales and generate cash rapidly. A variety of mechanisms are used, including special offers, discounts for prompt payment and rigorous credit control; all this type of pricing is a form of marginal cost pricing.

- *Prevent new entry.* Competitors can be discouraged from entering a market by establishing low prices which will indicate to potential competitors the prospect of low returns and price wars. Domestic firms have used this strategy to attempt to prevent entry by international competitors; however, the danger is that the other firm might successfully enter the market with a quite different positioning, such as higher specification or quality, or with improved service levels. The defending firm, due to its low-price strategy, may not have the income to make the necessary investment to compete with the new entrant.

Setting a price

Having determined suitable strategies for pricing in international markets, a company must then consider the options available in setting individual prices. Companies can decide on the basis of their knowledge, objectives and situation to take either a cost, market or competition-oriented approach.

Cost-oriented approaches are intended to either:

- achieve a specific return on investment; or
- ensure an early recovery of either cash, or investments made to enter the market.

Market-oriented pricing approaches give the company the opportunity to:

- stabilize competitive positions within the market;
- skim the most profitable business; or
- penetrate the market by adopting an aggressive strategy to increase market share.

Competition-oriented approaches are designed to:

- maintain and improve market position;
- meet and follow competition;
- reflect differences in the perceived value and performance of competitive products; or
- prevent or discourage new entrants in the market.

No matter which of these broad strategies are adopted, the process for determining export pricing is essentially the same:

- determine export market potential;
- estimate the price range and target price;
- calculate sales potential at the target price;
- evaluate tariff and non-tariff barriers;
- select suitable pricing strategy in line with company objectives;
- consider likely competitor response;
- select pricing tactics, set distributor and end-user prices;
- monitor performance and take necessary corrective action.

Problems of pricing and financing international transactions

There are a number of specific problems which arise in setting and managing prices in international markets. Problems arise in four main areas:

1 *Problems in multi-national pricing.* Companies find difficulty in coordinating and controlling prices across their activities sufficiently to enable them to achieve effective financial performance and their desired price positioning:

- How can prices be coordinated by the company across the various markets?
- How can a company retain uniform price positioning in different market situations?
- At what price should a company transfer products or services from a subsidiary in one country to a subsidiary in another?
- How can a firm deal with importation and sale of its products by an unauthorized dealer?

2 *Problems in managing foreign currency and fluctuating exchange rates.* Considerable problems arise in foreign transactions because of the need to buy and sell products in different currencies:

- In what currency should a company price its products in international markets?
- How should the company deal with fluctuating exchange rates?
- How can a company minimize exchange rate risk over the longer-term transactions?

3 *Problems of obtaining suitable payment in high-risk markets.* Obtaining payment promptly and in a suitable currency from the less developed countries can cause expense and additional difficulties:

- How might/should a company deal with selling to countries where there is a risk of non-payment?
- How should a company approach selling to countries which have a shortage of hard currency or high inflation?
- How can a company obtain payment upfront on long-term transactions?

4 *Administrative problems of cross-border transfer of goods.* Problems of bureaucracy and delays arise as a result of simply moving goods physically across borders:

- At what point should an exporter release control and responsibility for goods?
- What steps can be taken in the export order process to minimize delays?

These four major problem areas will now be dealt with in the following four sections.

Problems in multi-national pricing

Coordination of prices across markets

The pressure on companies to market truly global products backed by globally standardized advertising campaigns is caused by three major trends: the homogenization of customer demand, the lowering of trade barriers and the emergence of international competitors. At the same time these largely undifferentiated global products can be sold at very different prices in different countries, based on factors such as purchasing power, exchange rate changes and competition and consumer preferences.

Until recently this has been a perfectly acceptable practice. However, in the past decade it has become increasingly difficult for companies to maintain a differentiated pricing strategy across international markets when they are marketing similar if not standardized products. Readily available information on worldwide prices through modern data transfer and the Internet have greatly increased price transparency. Advances in telecommunications systems have also greatly reduced international transaction costs. Global companies who obviously follow differentiated pricing policies are often threatened, first by an erosion of consumer confidence as customers learn of the more attractive pricing policies in other markets and second by grey marketing which can result in the cannibalization of sales in countries with relatively high prices and damaging relationships with authorized distributors.

European Monetary Union The issue of achieving price coordination across markets has become particularly pertinent in the European Union (EU) since the establishment of the European Monetary Union (EMU). The EMU, sometimes called the Euro zone or Euro area, is the name given to the union of countries using the Euro as a domestic currency.

National price levels across the EU are far from uniform. Among the Euro zone countries, Austria and Finland are viewed as high-priced markets, France, Belgium and Germany are seen as average, Portugal and Spain as having much lower prices. Price levels in Scandinavia can be 40 per cent higher than in southern parts of the Euro zone. This has caused some difficulties for companies who have tried to differentiate prices as in the case of GSK in Spain in Illustration 11.2.

Differences in taxation and excise duties as well as disparities in production costs and wage levels lead to price differentials and difficulties in managing problems in the economy Firms in product markets have

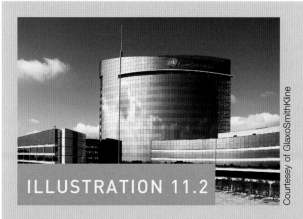

Courtesy of GlaxoSmithKline

ILLUSTRATION 11.2

GSK v The EU

The pharmaceuticals manufacturer GlaxoSmithKline Unlimited ('GSK') entered into an agreement with 75 Spanish wholesalers establishing a two tier price structure for medicinal products sold in Spain and those exported from Spain to other parts of the EU. The purpose of this differentiated pricing structure was to discourage parallel market sales of pharmaceuticals. However this was considered to in breach of European competition laws.

GSK argued the agreement should be exempt from the rules as:

■ competition in the pharma sector was already restricted because national governments set the price of most drugs;

■ restrictions on parallel trade generated positive benefits as they enabled pharmaceutical companies to make higher profits that could be used for R&D;

■ by contrast parallel trade in pharmaceuticals gave rise to no benefit to consumers (i.e. national health services or patients) since parallel traders generally did not compete on price in the country of import but kept the difference between the price in the lower-priced country and that in the higher-priced country.

However, after much legal wrangling and several appeals the European Court of Justice, made a final judgment. This was that the GSK agreement violated European rules against competitive restrictions. The Court also found that in order to be subject to an exemption, an agreement must contribute to improving the production or distribution of goods or to promoting technical or economic progress. Their view that the agreement GSK had entered failed to do this.

Question

1 Discuss the arguments for and against the GSK case.

tended to adapt their prices to the buying power, income levels and consumer preferences of national markets. However, in the service sector and particularly the tourism industry it is not very easy to differentiate prices to reflect the differences in buying power and consumer preferences of the variety of national and international consumers that a company may be targeting.

Prior to the formation of the EMU these differences were largely concealed from the European consumer, despite the formation of the Single European Market. The formation of the EMU and the introduction of the euro has changed all that. Now prices are no longer distorted by fluctuating exchange rates. This means companies competing on the European market need to consider the implications of the price transparency in the Euro zone. The onset of price transparency impacts on firms in different ways. Highly specialized products with few direct rivals are largely immune to the risk of price transparency generating more intense competition. However, companies marketing goods that are supplied direct to the consumer have come under increasing pressure from retailers to reduce margins if retailers themselves have had to cut prices to meet new price points set in euros. Furthermore, more retailers and businesses have moved to a policy of European-wide sourcing and using the Internet to search for the lowest prices for products. It has, therefore, become virtually impossible for companies to operate on the European market without a sophisticated strategy to effectively coordinate prices across the EU. It is this that has led to so many companies revamping their approach to managing their European marketing strategies.

Firms who have failed to meet this challenge have left themselves open to the threat of grey market goods cannibalizing their sales in high-priced national markets.

ILLUSTRATION 11.3

Stock.xchng

Dealing with non-SEPA payments

The Single Euro Payments Area (SEPA) was formed in 2008 between the countries of the Euro zone. The aim was that banks dealing with transfers in Euros between members of the Euro zone (SEPA Credit Transfers) would charge no more for such cross border transfers than they charged for domestic transfers. In practice, this means no charge at all in several countries where domestic transfers are free of commission. Banks outside the Euro zone still charge substantial commissions for cross border transfers of funds. Typical remitting costs from the UK are £9 per transaction for small personal payments, and £20 and upwards pro rata for commercial payments. This means that non-Euro payments made to SEPA destinations attract charges at the remitting end, and then are often charged commission of €30 or more by the receiving bank within the SEPA for converting the received funds into Euros. This meant that pricing decisions made by non Euro zone businesses trading in Europe would have to factor these costs into their prices, possibly affecting their competitiveness in their European markets.

Since 2008, non Euro zone businesses wishing to transfer funds to SEPA beneficiaries can save by ensuring that the funds are converted into Euros by the remitting bank, as SEPA rules now forbid the receiving bank from levying commission on incoming Euro transfers as long as IBANs (International Bank Account Numbers) and BICs (Bank Identifier Codes) of the beneficiary are correctly quoted on the transfer.

Additionally, the SEPA Direct Debit Scheme was introduced in November 2009 to enable Euro payments to be collected by creditors more quickly and cost efficiently than was previously possible. Clients using this scheme will need to operate a Euro account with a bank in a SEPA country.

Question

1 What can businesses in the UK who trade with Euro area businesses do to save on bank transfer commissions?

Source: Peter C. Mcgregor, Sheffield Hallam University.

Single European Payments Area

Economic and Monetary Union and the Euro were introduced to help achieve the goal of a single European market. One particular objective was to create a single market where currency could move as freely and cheaply in the Euro zone as it could within national markets. However, to achieve a truly single market, integration of payment facilities across borders was needed to create a single financial services market across the Euro zone. This is known as the Single European Payments Area (SEPA).

The key problem SEPA resolves for companies marketing across the Euro zone is the differences they face between the way domestic and cross-border payments operate and are priced. With the SEPA in place, companies can execute any payment within the Euro area as easily and at the same cost as they could in their existing domestic markets.

The objective of SEPA introduced in 2008 was to create a single payment area where consumers and businesses can make cross-border payments as easily, safely and efficiently as they can within their own countries and perhaps most importantly, as cheaply. Cross-border Euro payments are treated exactly like domestic payments whatever their amount. It could still take three business days from order to receipt for cross-border payments, as opposed to a single day within a country, and it still means companies face cross-border pricing difficulties with customers outside the SEPA (see Illustration 11.3). In the SEPA there has been a consolidation of the cross-border payment infrastructure which means there are now common rules for clearing and settlement, which means costs are minimized and processes quicker. The harmonized European payments infrastructure also makes it possible to implement efficient e-solutions. According to GTnews.com, e-payments will soon account for 95–99 per cent of the total volume of payments.

What is grey marketing?

As said above, grey marketing has become a particular problem for companies operating across Europe where there are huge price differentials and trade barriers so goods are able to flow freely across borders. Grey marketing is a business phenomenon that has seen unprecedented growth in the past few years as information on prices has flowed across countries and consumers have discovered how varying prices can be when companies try to pursue highly differentiated pricing strategies across markets that can no longer be kept separate.

Grey marketing occurs when trademarked goods are sold through channels of distribution that have not been given authority to sell the goods by the trademark holder. This could occur within a country but more and more it is becoming common across countries. This becomes problematic, especially for global marketers trying to manage a coordinated marketing strategy across different markets. Coca-Cola had to bring forward the European launch of Vanilla Coke after it found the product was already being sold in the UK by a distributor who had imported it directly from Canada, where it had been launched several months previously. Typically, however, grey market goods are international brands with high price differentials and low costs of arbitrage. The costs connected with the arbitrage are transportation, tariffs, taxes and the costs of modifying the product, i.e. changing the language of instructions.

It is perhaps important to point out that there is nothing illegal about grey market goods; it is purely the practice of buying a product in one market and selling it in other markets in order to benefit from the prevailing price differential. Grey markets tend to develop in markets where information on prices for basically the same product in different countries is cheap and easy to obtain (e.g. cars, designer goods, consumer durables). KPMG estimates the revenue generated by international grey marketing activities to be about US$25 billion a year. While grey marketing is seen by its critics as a free-riding strategy, it is being increasingly seen as a viable international strategy by smaller firms who, with limited resources, can use it to compete against larger firms in international markets.

There are three types of grey markets (see Figure 11.1):

1 *Parallel importing.* When the product is priced lower in the home market where it is produced than the export market. The grey marketer in the export market will parallel import directly from the home market rather than source from within their own country; for example, there is a strong parallel import trade in Levi jeans between the USA and Europe. Levi Strauss took out a lawsuit against the retail chain Tesco for selling Levi jeans they sourced directly from outside the EU. Levi insisting that jeans in Europe should only be sourced from authorized dealers within the EU.

FIGURE 11.1 Three types of grey market

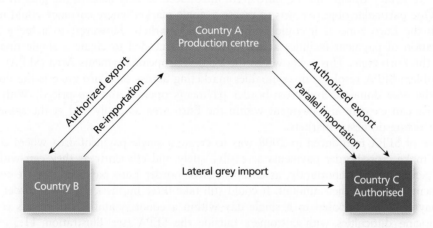

Note: Price in Country B < price in Country C

Source: Adapted from: Assnus, G. and Wiesse, C. (1995) 'How to address the gray market threat using price coordination', in I. Doole and R. Lowe, *International Marketing Strategy: Contemporary readings*, International Thomson Business Press.

ILLUSTRATION 11.4

Clamp-down on grey marketing

IBM has unveiled a series of measures designed to help stamp out grey market activity in its channel.

It has harmonized hardware pricing, boosted transparency in its supply chain and is 'systematically extending' compliance programmes. They hope this will reduce the scope for arbitrage business in the grey market by minimizing regional price differences.

The firm has also harmonized pricing on accessories, which will now carry bar codes and serial numbers so it can more effectively monitor the supply chain to detect breaches of distribution agreement. They have warned their partners they intend to take a hard line and that rule-breakers could see their agreements terminated or face legal action.

IBM along with Cisco and HP is a member of the Alliance for Grey Market and Counterfeit Abatement (AGMA), a vendor-led industry body whose objective is to clamp down on the IT market's unauthorized sector.

Question

1 Do you think large international companies should manage grey marketing in the distribution channels through legal means or let the market itself act as a regulator?

Sources: http://www.microscope.co.uk/news/reseller-news/ibm-clamps-down-on-grey-marketing/&: and http://www.gammaglobal.com/aboutus_articles. Accessed August 2010.

The judgment by the court, which shocked consumer rights groups everywhere, was that Tesco should not be allowed to import jeans made by Levi Strauss from outside the EU and sell them at reduced prices without first getting permission from the jeans maker. The high tech market in particular suffers from grey marketing which is why global companies like IBM have taken steps to clamp down on it (see Illustration 11.4).

2 *Re-importing.* When the product is priced cheaper in an export market than in the home market where it was produced; re-importation in this case can be profitable to the grey marketer.

3 *Lateral importing.* When there is a price difference between export markets, products are sold from one country to another through unauthorized channels.

A disturbing example of this can be found in the pharmaceutical industry, where it is estimated that US$18 million of reduced-price HIV drugs intended for African markets were diverted back to Europe to be sold at much higher prices on the grey market.

Price coordination strategies

Typically firms try to defend themselves against grey market activities by calling for government intervention or legal protection. As seen in the previous section, companies may resort to imposing restrictions or even threats to retailers. In the US, Wal-Mart sourced products through grey markets and suffered the resultant threats from firms such as Adidas and Levi jeans. Other reactive measures have included the refusal to issue warranties in certain markets, or even buying out the grey marketer.

Companies competing in international markets who wish to develop more effective strategies to deal with the problem of price coordination across increasingly interdependent markets and the threat of grey market goods have four options open to them.

1 *Economic measures.* The company can influence the country manager's pricing decision by controlling the input into those decisions. A multi-national can do this through transfer pricing (see the later section in this chapter). By raising the price by which it transfers products to the low-priced country the headquarters essentially imposes a tax on that market. Closely related to transfer

pricing is rationing the product quantities allocated to each country or region and so limiting the number of units sold in the diverting country.

2 *Centralization.* The company can move towards more centralization in the setting of prices. Traditionally many multi-national companies have given country managers a high degree of decision-making autonomy. Usually they are in the best position to assess consumer response to any given pricing decisions and they are able to react swiftly to competitor activity. A centralized approach, however, could overcome difficulties with grey market goods although it does usually result in dissatisfaction among country managers. A compromise approach is to shift the decision-making authority in pricing from a country to a regional level; however, increasingly grey market goods are becoming a global issue.

3 *Formalization.* The company can standardize the process of planning and implementing pricing decisions. Thus the company influences prices at the local level by prescribing a process that is followed by country managers when establishing pricing policy.

4 *Informal coordination.* A number of companies have moved towards a more informal system of coordination without either a high degree of centralization or formalization. This thinking is usual in the transnational company where international subsidiaries make differentiated and innovative contributions to an integrated worldwide operation. While this approach may incorporate a variety of techniques, the essential asset is that there are common shared business values across the subsidiaries that are backed by compatible incentive systems.

In a proactive approach to coordinating its pricing decision across international markets, a company has to select the appropriate strategy which will in effect be determined, first, by the level of local resources available, and then by the level of environmental complexity, as illustrated in Figure 11.2.

Transfer pricing in international markets

Transfer pricing is an area that has created complications for many international marketing firms. It is concerned with the pricing of goods sold within a corporate family, when the transactions involved are from division to division, to a foreign subsidiary or to a partner in a joint venture agreement. While these transfer prices are internal to the company, they are important externally because goods being transferred from country to country must have a value for cross-border taxation purposes.

The objective of the corporation in this situation is to ensure that the transfer price paid optimizes corporate rather than divisional objectives. This can prove difficult when a company internationally is organized into profit centres. For profit centres to work effectively, a price must be set for everything that is transferred, be it working materials, components, finished goods or services. A high transfer price, for example from the domestic division to a foreign subsidiary, is reflected in an apparently poor performance by the foreign subsidiary, whereas a low price would not be acceptable to the domestic division providing the goods. This issue alone can be the cause of much mistrust between subsidiaries – at best leading to fierce arguments, and at worst leading to loss of business through overpricing.

There tend to be three bases for transfer pricing:

1 *Transfer at cost.* In which the transfer price is set at the level of the production cost, and the international division is credited with the entire profit that the firm makes. This means that the production centre is evaluated on efficiency parameters rather than profitability.

2 *Transfer at arm's-length.* When the international division is charged the same as any buyer outside the firm. Problems occur if the overseas division is allowed to buy elsewhere when the price is uncompetitive or the product quality is inferior, and further difficulties arise if there are no external buyers, making it difficult to establish a relevant price. This is the strategy most preferred by national governments and the agreed a general principle of the OECD. The OECD say this principle should govern transfer pricing transactions and has published detailed guidelines to guide companies.

3 *Transfer at cost plus.* Is a compromise, where profits are split between the production and international divisions. The actual formula used for assessing the transfer price can vary, but usually

FIGURE 11.2 A framework for selecting a coordination method

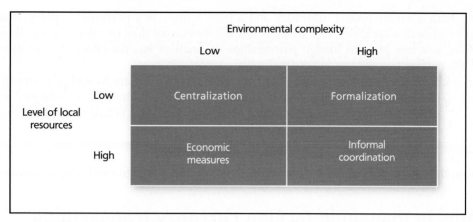

Source: Assnus, G. and Wiesse, C. (1995) 'How to address the gray market threat using price coordination', in I. Doole and R. Lowe, *International Marketing Strategy: Contemporary readings*, International Thomson Business Press.

it is this method which has the greatest chance of minimizing executive time spent on transfer price disagreements, optimizing corporate profits and motivating the home and international divisions. Often a senior executive is appointed to rule on disputes.

However, the real interest of transfer pricing is how it is used strategically by companies either to act as a barrier to entry, or to marshal resources around the world.

To create barriers to entry

Most oil companies are vertically integrated, from oil exploration right through to selling petrol at the pumps, and use transfer pricing as part of their strategy to maintain barriers to entry. The major cost for oil companies is at the exploration and refining stage and so, by charging high transfer prices for crude oil, profits are generated at the refining stage of the process, rather than in distribution, where it is relatively easy to enter the market. Oil companies, therefore, attempt, by the use of transfer pricing, to make petrol distribution unattractive to potential competitors. Supermarkets and hypermarkets, with their huge purchasing power, have managed to challenge the dominance of the oil companies by using low-priced petrol as a loss-leader to entice customers to stores.

To avoid domestic tax liabilities

When countries have different levels of taxation on corporate profits, firms try to ensure that profits are accumulated at the most advantageous point. Companies operating in countries with high corporation tax may be tempted to sell at low transfer prices to their subsidiaries in countries with lower corporate taxation.

To avoid foreign tax

Foreign tax authorities wish to maximize the taxable income within their jurisdiction, and there are a number of strategies a company might use to avoid tax – for example, by charging lower transfer prices if there is high customs duty on goods. The impact of such avoidance strategies is diminishing, as customs authorities become more aware of this practice. Recently the US government demanded huge taxes from Sony when it discovered that it generated 60 per cent of its global sales in the USA but very little profit due to Sony's management of transfer pricing. Japan then retaliated by doing the same to Coca-Cola. However, it can be argued that as the general level of import duties is reducing as international trade agreements come into effect, so the need to take avoiding action is declining.

To manage the level of involvement in markets

If a firm has both a wholly owned subsidiary and a joint venture in a particular country, it will wish to sell at a higher price to a company with which it has a joint venture than one that is a wholly-owned subsidiary. Selling at a low price to foreign partnerships or licensees has the effect of sharing more of the profit with the partner.

Transfer pricing is an area where profit objectives, managerial motivations and government regulation interact and so the expertise of many people – accountants, legal counsel, tax advisors and division managers – is needed to achieve an agreement. The international marketing manager's contribution is primarily concerned with two aspects of the problem:

- achieving an effective distribution of goods to world markets;
- ensuring that the impact of the transfer price does not affect foreign market opportunities.

Problems in managing foreign currency transactions

Perhaps the most critical issue for managers is how to deal with the various problems involved in managing transactions which involve currency exchange; a second difficulty is what action to take when selling to countries where there is high inflation.

What currency should the price be quoted in?

In any international marketing transaction, the exporter has the option of quoting in either the domestic or the local currency. If the exporter quotes in their own domestic currency, then not only is it administratively much easier, but also the risks associated with changes in the exchange rate are borne by the customer, whereas by quoting prices in the foreign currency the exporter bears the exchange rate risk. However, there are benefits to the exporter in quoting in foreign currency:

- it could provide access to finance abroad at lower interest rates;
- good currency management may be a means of gaining additional profits;
- quoting in foreign currency could be a condition of the contract;
- customers normally prefer to be quoted in their own currency in order to be able to make competitive comparisons and to know exactly what the eventual price will be.

Furthermore, customers in export markets often prefer quotations in their own currency to enable them to more easily compare the tenders of competitors from a range of countries.

Often the choice of currency for the price quotation depends partly on the trade practices in the export market and the industry concerned. Suppliers competing for business in the oil industry, wherever in the world they may be supplying, may well find they are asked to quote in US dollars. In the airline industry things are more complicated. EADS, the European group manufacturing the Airbus plane, has all its costs in Euros, but on the global market, planes are priced in US dollars. This gives the US company Boeing an advantage competing on international markets, because they do not have the same exchange risk as EADS and can forecast their costs and prices with much more certainty than their arch rival Airbus.

When exporters experience a period of strong home currency it reduces their competitiveness on international markets and makes them vulnerable to price-cutting pressures from international customers, as happened to MDL (see Management Challenge 11.2).

Thus, as well as the decision as to what currency to quote in, the main worry for both suppliers and customers on international markets is fluctuating exchange rates and how to deal with them.

The introduction of the Euro has effectively eliminated exchange rate risk in the Euro zone countries. Even countries like the UK, who have decided not to enter the EMU for the present time, increasingly find that companies selling goods into Europe are pressurized to quote prices in the Euro.

MANAGEMENT CHALLENGE 11.2

Can we avoid the currency risk without losing our customers?

Management Development Ltd (MDL) is a small firm specializing in management training and development. The firm delivers training programmes using a combination of self-study material and study weekends and operates in the UK, Middle East and the Far East.

Ten years ago the firm took a strategic decision to enter the Malaysian market. They appointed an agent in Malaysia to market the courses and recruit students. To encourage students to join training courses payment could be made in stages.

The majority of the firm's costs, developing study material, tutoring, etc. were incurred in sterling.

The income from selling in Malaysia would normally be in ringgits. Income in ringgits and costs in sterling meant MDL faced a currency risk. Traditional methods for avoiding currency exposure (hedging) were not considered appropriate due to the small scale of the operation.

Over the last ten years the financial results from the contract had been poor. Prices had been going up by 5 to 10 per cent per year and recruitment had been good but still the firm was failing to make a reasonable return. MDL's accountant said you only need to look at the HM Revenue and Customs exchange rate data base to find the reason (http://www.hmrc.gov.uk/exrate/malaysia.htm).

Question

1 How should MDL resolve their dilemma?

Source: Fiona Elspeth.

Should prices be raised/lowered as exchange rates fluctuate?

One of the most difficult problems that exporters face is caused by fluctuating exchange rates.

Sarathy, Terpstra and Russow (2006) identified three types of risk affecting firms, arising from exchange rate fluctuations:

1 *Transaction risk*. This occurs when the exporter quotes in a foreign currency, which then appreciates, diminishing the financial return to the firm. US hoteliers in Hawaii experienced a noticeable decline in Japanese tourism when the dollar rose in value from ¥90 to ¥120 in just over a year.

2 *Competitive risk*. Arises because the geographic pattern of a firm's manufacturing and sales puts them at a disadvantage compared to their competition. If, for instance, the firm is manufacturing in a country with an appreciating currency but trying to compete in a marketplace where currencies are depreciating, it could lose out to a local manufacturer. Firms may then try to maximize their expenditure in the market place. This is why Mercedes and BMW are now manufacturing in the USA.

3 *Market portfolio risk*. Ths risk occurs because a company with a narrow market portfolio will be influenced to a much greater extent by changes in exchange rates than a diversified firm that is better able to balance changes in exchange rates through operating in many countries.

Various tactics can be adopted to deal with currency fluctuations. When the domestic currency is weak, the firm should:

■ compete on price;

■ introduce new products with additional features;

■ source and manufacture in the domestic country;

■ fully exploit export opportunities;

- obtain payment in cash;
- use a full-cost approach for existing markets, but use marginal costs for new more competitive markets;
- repatriate foreign-earned income quickly;
- reduce expenditure and buy services (advertising, transport, etc.) locally;
- minimize overseas borrowing;
- invoice in domestic currency.

When the domestic currency is strong, the firm should:

- compete on non-price factors (quality, delivery, service);
- improve productivity and reduce costs;
- prioritize strong currency countries for exports;
- use countertrade for weak currency countries;
- reduce profit margins and use marginal costs for pricing;
- keep the foreign-earned income in the local country;
- maximize expenditures in local country currency;
- buy services abroad in local currencies;
- borrow money for expansion in local markets;
- invoice foreign customers in their own currency.

Problems in minimizing the risk of non-payment in high-risk countries

The international marketing manager increasingly needs to be knowledgeable about the various complexities of financing international marketing transactions and sources of finance to support international marketing strategies, especially when trading with markets is seen to be high risk due to adverse economic and political conditions, high inflation or perhaps lack of hard currency. For a company exporting goods to such markets there is a considerable risk of non-payment for a variety of reasons, such as:

- the buyer failing or refusing to pay for the goods;
- insolvency of the buyer;
- a general moratorium on external debt by the host;
- government political and legal decisions;
- war;
- failure to fulfil the conditions of the contract;
- lack of hard currency;
- high inflation.

Traditionally managers will seek financial support to help reduce the risk of non-payment due to these factors through home governments, commercial banks or some kind of cooperation agreement.

Government-sponsored finance   Governments are often willing to financially support companies in financing international trade transactions in the hope that increased exports will generate economic growth at home and boost employment. National governments approach such support in a variety of ways but in most countries there is an export–import bank or perhaps export bank or, as in the UK, a government department (Trade Partners UK) who fund a variety of support packages to help companies finance export strategies. Governments will also provide low-cost export guarantee insurance to protect their exporters against non-payment by foreign buyers. However, such protection may not be available in particularly high-risk markets.

Commercial banks   Commercial banks compete intensively to offer international trade services to companies operating in international markets. However, they tend only to be willing to support low-risk activities, which sometimes makes it difficult for companies expanding into emerging markets. Commercial banks may also be more interested in short-term financing, and so potentially not such a good source for companies making a long-term investment decision in incipient markets where it may be several years before a full return on investment can be achieved. Many banks who made long-term loans to developing markets have suffered losses when countries not experiencing the growth rates expected have been unable to meet debt repayments. This has led to a number of banks being less willing to expose themselves in long-term high-risk markets.

One of the ways banks can help against the risk of non-payment is by forfaiting.

Forfaiting   This is a way of financing without recourse. It means that companies selling products essentially transfer the transaction risk to a forfaiting house. A bill of exchange, usually requiring a bank guarantee or, as in the US, a back up letter of credit, is drawn up to the value of the contract and the seller transfers the claim resulting from the transaction to the forfaiting house. The seller immediately receives the full amount of the contract minus the discount agreed for the period of the contract. This discount will vary depending on the length of the contract, the level of country risk and whether the invoice is guaranteed by a commercial bank. For the company it provides a source of finance to support medium-term contracts in a market and a means of reducing the risk of non-payment.

Cooperation agreements   These agreements are special kinds of countertrade deals (see below) that extend over long periods of time and may have government involvement. They may be called product purchase transactions, buyback deals or pay as you earn deals. For instance, a company may obtain finance to help set up a factory in a particular country if they then agree to buy back the output of the plant.

Countertrade and leasing

So far in this chapter we have focused upon largely conventional approaches to international pricing; however, over the past two decades there has been a dramatic increase in the use of leasing and countertrade deals, which are used as a response to the lack of hard currency, particularly among less developed countries.

Counter trade deals are more prevalent when companies are trying to enter emerging or less developed markets. The reason for this is threefold:

■ It is sometimes difficult to obtain finance commercially to enter such markets.

■ The markets themselves may have limited access to hard currency which means the finance of joint ventures or strategic alliances has to be sought through less traditional means.

■ Emerging markets may see such deals as a way of encouraging job creation in their own countries and so actively encourage such financing deals.

What is countertrade?   Countertrade covers various forms of trading arrangements where part or all of the payment for goods is in the form of other goods or services, and price-setting and financing are dealt with together in one transaction. The original and simple barter system has been developed in order to accommodate modern trading situations. Estimates of countertrade activity range from 20 to 30 per cent of world trade, and it is predicted to grow further due to its ability, first, to overcome market imperfections and, second, to provide opportunities for extraordinary profits to be made.

ILLUSTRATION 11.5

Countertrade deals for GEC

GEC – the Marconi electronics subsidiary – became involved in three offset countertrade deals to help them develop their markets in the Middle East. A contribution to the local economy, in the form of investment in a furniture factory in Abu Dhabi, was made in return for an arms contract. In the deal, local craftsmen assemble furniture and fittings for palaces, hotels, etc. in UAE. GEC is in partnership with local sheikhs and a Birmingham company for the venture, who agreed to export at least 50 per cent of the output to Europe and the Far East.

Other offset countertrade projects include the formation of a local company to charter ships for an Emirate group and a joint venture to provide geological and topographical information to help evaluate water, oil and gas and other natural resources.

Question

1 What are the advantages and disadvantages of such deals?

There are many variants of countertrade, resulting from the need to adapt arrangements to meet the needs of individual transactions. The following are the basic forms:

Barter. This is a single exchange of goods with no direct use of money, and does not require intermediaries. It is the simplest form, but has become unpopular because, first, if the goods are not exchanged simultaneously then one participant is effectively financing the other, and second, one of the parties may well receive unwanted goods as part of the deal. Coca Cola has entered several barter deals in Eastern Europe, Russia paid Coca-Cola in vodka. Poland did the same with Coca-Cola but paid in beer.

Compensation trading. This involves an agreement in which payment for goods is accepted in a combination of goods and cash.

Counter-purchase. This involves the negotiation of two contracts. In the first, the international marketer agrees to sell the product at an established price in local currency. In the second, simultaneous, contract the international firm buys goods or services for an equivalent or proportionate cash payment from another local supplier.

Offset. This is similar to counter-purchase, but in this case national governments cooperate to support the deal. Sometimes called a product purchase transaction, it is a way in which the international firm is able to obtain more saleable goods from the country in exchange. For example, Boeing sold AWACS aircraft to the British Ministry of Defence on the basis that the purchase price would be spent on British goods (see Illustration 11.5).

Switch deals involve a third party (usually a merchant house), which specializes in barter trading, disposing of the goods. For example, if an Eastern European company importing Western products can only provide in return heavily discounted relatively low-quality products, which may not be saleable in the West, a third country will need to be found in order that a switch deal can be set up in which these lower-quality goods can be exchanged for other products that are more suitable for the original Western markets.

Cooperation agreements. These can cover buyback deals (see Illustration 11.6), pay as you earn deals or a range of other beneficial arrangements made between two parties. It is an arrangement whereby part or all of the cost of purchase of capital equipment might be paid for in the form of production from the equipment supplied, either over time or in the form of some other benefit.

In Japan and South East Asia compensation and offset are the most frequently used forms of countertrade. Barter and counter-purchase tend to be more common in lesser developed countries.

So far, the examples of countertrade have involved deals of products, but many other less tangible elements such as know-how, software and information can be included in agreements. Many of the deals set up are complicated and in some cases have stretched over many years.

Advantages and limitations of countertrade

The advantages of countertrade are as follows:

- New markets can be developed for a country's products, as marketing and quality control skills are often 'imported' with the deal, and it can lead to gaining experience in Western markets.
- Surplus and poorer quality products can be sold through countertrade whereas they could not be sold for cash. Moreover, dumping and heavy discounting can be disguised.
- Countertrade through bilateral and multilateral trade agreement can strengthen political ties.
- Countertrade and contract manufacture can be used to enter high-risk areas.
- Countertrade can provide extraordinary profits as it allows companies to circumvent government restrictions.

However, there are disadvantages and limitations in using countertrade:

- There is a lack of flexibility, as the transactions are often dependent on product availability, and countertraded products are often of poor quality, overpriced or are available due to a surplus.
- Products taken in exchange may not fit with the firm's trading objectives, or may be difficult to sell.
- Dealing with companies and government organizations may be difficult, particularly in locating and organizing countertrade products.
- Negotiations may be difficult, as there are no guide market prices.
- Countertrade deals are difficult to evaluate in terms of profitability and companies can, through countertrade, create new competition.

It is likely that in the future, countertrading will develop further in the form of longer-term rather than shorter-term partnerships as multi-nationals seek permanent foreign sources for incorporation in their global sourcing strategy. LDCs offer the benefits of low-cost labour and materials, as well as relatively untapped markets for goods. This has resulted in multi-nationals reversing the traditional countertrade process by first seeking opportunities, and then identifying potential countertrade partners with which to exploit the opportunities.

Leasing

Leasing is used as an alternative to outright purchase in countries where there is a shortage of capital available to purchase high-priced capital and industrial goods. Usually the rental fee will cover servicing and the costs of spares too, and so the problem of poor levels of maintenance, which is often associated with high technology and capital equipment in LDCs, can be overcome. Leasing arrangements can be attractive, too, in countries where investment grants and tax incentives are offered for new plant and machinery, in which case the leaser can take advantage of the tax provisions in a way that the lessee cannot, and share some of the savings. It is estimated that leased aircraft account for about 20 per cent of the world's aircraft fleet.

Deciding at what stage of the export sales process the price should be quoted

Export price quotations are important, because they spell out the legal and cost responsibilities of the buyer and seller. Sellers, as previously mentioned, favour a quote that gives them the least liability and responsibility, such as FOB (free on board), or ex-works, which means the exporter's liability finishes when the goods are loaded on to the buyer's carrier. Buyers, on the other hand, would prefer either franco domicile,

© RIA Novosti/Alamy

ILLUSTRATION 11.6

IKEA's buy back strategy?

IKEA is a Swedish home products retailer that sells ready-to-assemble furniture, accessories, and bathroom and kitchen items in their retail stores around the world. The company, which pioneered flat-pack design furniture at affordable prices, is now the world's largest furniture retailer.

The chain has 313 stores in 37 countries, most of them in Europe, North America, Asia and Australia. The IKEA Group itself owns 276 stores in 25 countries and the other 37 stores are owned and run by franchisees.

Central to its marketing strategy is the standardization of its core concept of Swedish democratic designs. However, its competitive prices are the mainstay of its competitive edge, and IKEA manages its supply route specifically to ensure it can keep prices down. It has suppliers in 50 countries, roughly two thirds of its products are sourced from Europe with about one third from Asia. A small amount of products are produced in North America. In Eastern Europe an essential part of their procurement strategy is the buyback contract, a form of countertrade in which machinery and equipment for increasing and

upgrading production is leased to Eastern European companies in exchange for an export contract. In this way the suppliers are able to meet IKEA's high-quality standards and specifications. The repayment period is between three and five years, and in return, IKEA usually buys three to four times the value of the equipment supplied.

IKEA has now expanded into the Russian market with similar deals and they successfully developed IKEA MOS, a shopping centre located on a site adjacent to one of IKEA's two existing stores in the Moscow region of Russia. The objective for IKEA was to introduce into Russia a totally new concept of retail and provide local customers with an innovative, customer-oriented retail environment. However IKEA's developments of the Russian market have been beset with difficulties. They have been campaigning vigorously against corruption and indeed last year froze their investments in the country in protest at the bureaucratic hurdles it faced. They also had huge difficulties with the unspoken rule that you needed to pay bribes to get things agreed with local government officials. However, in spite of its high-profile anticorruption stand, IKEA has had to sack two senior executives in Russia for allegedly turning a blind eye to bribes paid by a sub-contractor to secure electricity supplies for its St Petersburg outlets.

Questions

1 Evaluate the pros and cons of countertrade strategies in helping IKEA to sustain its competitive advantage across international markets over the longer term.

2 How would you respond to the demand for payment from officials in return for agreements needed to run your business in a country?

where responsibility is borne by the supplier all the way to the customer's warehouse, or CIF port of discharge, which means the buyer's responsibility begins only when the goods are in their own country.

Generally, the more market-oriented pricing policies are based on CIF, which indicates a strong commitment to the market. By pricing ex-works, an exporter is not taking any steps to build relations with the market and so may be indicating only short-term commitment. The major stages at which export prices might be quoted are articulated through internationally agreed terms called incoterms. The main ones are as follows:

- Ex ws: ex-works or ex point of origin.
- FAS: free alongside ship.
- FOB: free on board.

Table 11.3 Incoterms stages and services at each stage of the export sales process

Services	EXW	FAS	FOB	C&F	CIF	DAF	DEQ	DDP
	Ex Works	Free Alongside Ship	Free Onboard Vessel	Cost and Freight	Cost Insurance and Freight	Delivered At Frontier	Delivered Ex Quay Duty Unpaid	Delivered Duty Paid
Warehouse Storage	Seller	Seller	Seller	Seller	Seller	Seller	Seller	Seller
Warehouse Labour	Seller	Seller	Seller	Seller	Seller	Seller	Seller	Seller
Export Packing	Seller	Seller	Seller	Seller	Seller	Seller	Seller	Seller
Loading Charges	Buyer	Seller	Seller	Seller	Seller	Seller	Seller	Seller
Inland Freight	Buyer	Seller	Seller	Seller	Seller	Seller	Seller	Seller
Terminal Charges	Buyer	Seller	Seller	Seller	Seller	Seller	Seller	Seller
Forwarder's Fees	Buyer	Buyer	Seller	Seller	Seller	Seller	Seller	Seller
Loading On Vessel	Buyer	Buyer	Seller	Seller	Seller	Seller	Seller	Seller
Ocean/Air Freight	Buyer	Buyer	Buyer	Seller	Seller	Seller	Seller	Seller
Charges On Arrival At Destination	Buyer	Buyer	Buyer	Buyer	Buyer	Buyer	Seller	Seller
Duty Taxes & Customs Clearance	Buyer	Buyer	Buyer	Buyer	Buyer	Buyer	Buyer	Seller
Delivery To Destination	Buyer	Buyer	Buyer	Buyer	Buyer	Buyer	Buyer	Seller

Source: Adapted from: www.austrade.gov.au, *Austrade Guide to Export pricing*.

- C. and F.: cost and freight.
- CIF: cost, insurance freight.
- DAF: Delivered at Frontier
- DDP: Delivered duty paid to destination point.

In deciding at what stage of the export sales process to price in a company has to be clear about the responsibilities and the costs it is including in its price and what responsibility they wish to pass onto the buyer. Table 11.3 illustrates these costs for each of the main stages in the export sales process.

The export order process

To further emphasize the complexity of managing international pricing, a major task of the marketer is to choose payment terms that will satisfy importers and at the same time safeguard the interests of the exporter. The transactions process for handling export is illustrated in Figure 11.3.

In the process, the customer agrees to payment. The customer begins the process (1) by sending an enquiry for the goods. The price and terms are confirmed by a pro-forma invoice (2) by the supplier, so that the customer knows for what amount (3) to instruct its bank on the method of payment (4). The method of payment is confirmed and arranged. If this is by letter of credit this will be opened by the issuing bank (5) in the supplier's country.

When the goods are shipped (6) the shipping documents are returned to the supplier (7), so that shipment is confirmed by their presentation (8) together with all stipulated documents and certificates for payment (9). The monies are automatically transmitted from the customer's account via the issuing bank. The customer may only collect the goods (10) when all the documents have been returned to them.

While letters of credit and drafts are the most common payment method, there are also several other methods of payment:

- A *draft* is drawn by the exporter on the importer, who makes it into a trade acceptance by writing on it the word 'accepted'. A *sight draft* is an unconditional order to pay a sum of money on demand or to the order of a specified person. Drafts which are payable at a future date are called *term drafts*.

FIGURE 11.3 The export order process

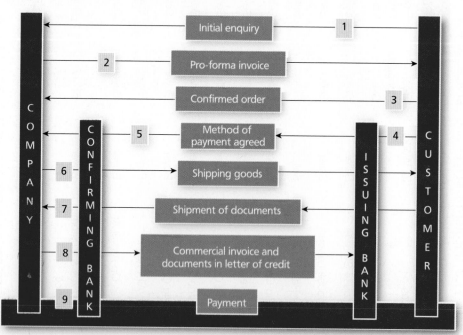

- *A letter of credit* is similar to a draft, except it is drawn on the bank and becomes a bank acceptance rather than a trade acceptance. There is greater assurance of payment, as an unconditional undertaking is given by the bank that the debts of the buyer will be paid to the seller.

- *A bill of exchange* is an unconditional order in writing which is signed by one person and requires the person to whom it is addressed to pay a certain sum of money on instruction at a specified time.

- *A documentary collection* is when a bill of exchange is presented to the importer via the banking system or alternatively the exporter can present the bill direct. If the importer pays the bill of exchange on presentation, usually by authorizing the bank to transfer funds to the exporter's bank account, then no further action is required.

- *Open account* is when the sales terms are agreed between buyer and seller, but without documents specifying clearly the importer's payment obligations. There is less paperwork but greater risk of non-payment, so it is only used when a trusting relationship has been developed between the trading parties. In countries where foreign exchange is difficult to obtain, drafts and letters of credit will be given priority in any currency allocation.

- *A consignment note* is when the exporter retains title of the goods until the importer sells them. Exporters own the goods longer in this method than any other, and so the financial burden and risks are at their greatest. In addition, the recovery of either goods or debt could be very difficult, and it is for this reason that consignments tend to be limited to companies trading with their subsidiaries.

The credit terms given are also important in determining the final price to the buyer. When products from international competitors are perceived to be similar, the purchaser may choose the supplier that offers the best credit terms, in order to effect a greater discount. In effect the supplier is offering a source of finance to the buyer, and in some countries – for example Brazil – government support is given to firms to help them gain a competitive advantage through this method. There has been a variety of international agreements to try and stop such practices, but it is still quite prevalent in some countries.

SUMMARY

- In international markets pricing decisions are much more complex, because they are affected by a number of additional external factors, such as fluctuations in exchange rates, accelerating inflation in certain countries and the use of alternative payment methods such as leasing, barter and countertrade.

- Many factors and problems contribute to making effective pricing management one of the most difficult aspects of international marketing to achieve. As well as the market factors associated with pricing decisions in each country it is necessary to deal with the complexities of financing deals based in different currencies and trying to maintain cross-border consistency of pricing.

- While there are cost benefits in standardizing products, services and processes, local factors affect the cost base in individual countries and make it difficult to maintain similar prices in different markets.

- In addition to this strategic role, there are a number of issues relating to the detailed operational management of international transactions. These particularly relate to the reduction of risk in carrying out international trade transactions, especially when trading in high-risk countries.

- There are also areas of specific management expertise in pricing that exist in international marketing. These include, for example, the management of transfer pricing between business units within an MNE, grey marketing and countertrade and the administration of cross-border transfers of goods.

- What becomes quite clear in developing international pricing is that there is a need not only to use pricing in a key role in achieving a company's financial objectives, but also as part of an integrated strategy, for example along with other marketing mix elements, to respond positively to the opportunities and threats of the various markets in which it operates.

KEYWORDS

Price standardization	Internal cost structures	Production costs
Elastic demand	Ethnocentric	Price transparency
Inelastic demand	Polycentric	Transfer pricing
Fixed production cost	Geocentric	Foreign currency
Marginal costing	Marginal cost pricing	Exchange rate risk
Dumping	Exchange rate	Euro zone
Economies of scale	Grey marketing	Countertrade
Learning curve	Price coordination	Market-oriented pricing

Courtesey of WABCO

CASE STUDY

WABCO

Introduction

WABCO Holdings Inc. develops, manufactures and sells braking, stability, suspension and transmission control systems primarily for commercial vehicles. It produces pneumatic anti-lock braking systems, electronic braking systems, automated manual transmission systems, air disk brakes and an array of conventional mechanical products, such as actuators, air compressors and air control valves. The company also supplies electronic suspension controls and vacuum pumps to the car and sport utility vehicle (SUV) markets. In addition, it provides replacement parts, diagnostic tools, training and other services to commercial vehicle distributors, repair shops and fleet operators. Its customers also include a commercial vehicle distributor network that provides replacement parts to commercial vehicle operators, trailer manufacturers and car and SUV manufacturers.

The company markets its products primarily in Europe, the Americas and Asia through a global sales force. WABCO Holdings markets its products primarily in Europe, the Americas, and Asia. The company was founded in 1869 and is headquartered in Piscataway, New Jersey. It has 9,900 employees in 31 countries around the globe and generates sales of around $2.2 billion (2010). See www.wabco.com for more details.

The global challenges facing WABCO

In maintaining its global market presence WABCO and the whole automotive supply industry generally, face a number of challenges.

A major challenge generally is that while there is a highly educated and skilled workforce which is valued for its expertise, it has a development team that has a strong technological focus to "pioneer breakthrough technologies". To market pioneered breakthrough technology is always a challenge at the beginning of a product lifecyle, referring to the P for Product in the Marketing Mix. With its focus on bespoke design new products are generally developed in response to the performance specification of the customer when they place an order. This is generally for the development of a new system or component for a new vehicle platform. Although WABCO drives a best cost country strategy (see company presentation), the ability to exploit economies of scale and design efficiencies of the learning curve always has scope for further improvements.

This area for improvement could be exacerbated by the desire and drive of some engineers to provide impressive technical solutions to sophisticated technical problems. At the same time, efficient and effective solutions in a given time period for a given cost base are needed to keep the company at the same high level and road of success. This means that the bespoke solutions provided must be efficient in terms of time and resources expended. Otherwise, in more stringent financial times, the sustainability of providing such a high level of solution service would no longer be financially viable for the company as it would become difficult to compete in a market where customers are now looking for cost effective solutions.

Consequently, the second challenge to companies is calculating a sales price across the global markets, because automobile customers are very price-sensitive - referring to the P for price in the Marketing Mix. Traditionally, companies used a full absorption costing approach to their pricing. The fixed costs, material costs, labour and process and full export costs and a defined margin would be included in a bottom up approach to building the price for all quotation requests across the global markets. But this would give the global sales force little flexibility when negotiating in different country markets. Those companies would be unable to respond to local market conditions, nor are they able to take into account the strategic significance of the customers in helping build those markets. Furthermore this approach does not allow them to respond to local competitive conditions. This means that those companies would find it particularly problematic in pitching themselves against competitors who have bases in countries with a much lower cost base.

WABCO acts differently. As a flexible, modern company carefully watching the economic environment, WABCO has responded to this challenge by the initiation of a value based pricing approach to its global markets to continue their success story. The aim of the programme is to help focus the engineering resources to those developments which clearly build value to the customers and for which the customer is therefore willing to pay. This will enable the company to achieve higher value margins in targeted areas and focus resources on those areas which will deliver a high margin. Using this approach, the basis on which they price a product or solution is by evaluating the

value of the technical solution sought to the voice of the customers and then orientating the pricing package to this. The aim of the company is to avoid setting prices that are either uncompetitively high for customers to pay or lower than they would be willing to pay. This creates a win-win situation for the supplier and the customer.

This whole strategy is part of the general marketing strategy, promoted and visible to the public at the 2010 IAA truck show in Hannover, Germany. An example of the WABCO value based approach to pricing is the method used to price the NG Next Generation disc brake. This brake consists of a turning disc which is mounted to the axle and on top a brake calliper, carrying the brake pads and the adjuster unit. The brake calliper traditionally consists of two separate halves which need to be assembled together. WABCO's highly skilled development engineers developed a mono bloc brake calliper, which could be reduced in weight. The better distribution of the forces within the single bloc use less material than in the previous version of two halves screwed together. In terms of the value based approach to pricing the evaluation of WABCO showed (fictitious numbers, dependent on several variables but fulfilling the explanatory purpose):

- Mono bloc brake callipers are more expensive in production, assumed around €20..
- Mono bloc brake callipers provide a weight reduction of 10kg per wheel end.
- A heavy commercial truck has in average three axles and runs in average 120 000 km per year in a three-year period.
- The fuel saving for 1000 kg for 100km is assumed to be 0.6l with a fuel price of €1.20 per litre in Europe.
- The emission reduction for 1 litre less fuel is assumed to be 2.7kg CO_2.

By using the value based pricing approach with the figures above, it could be possible to justify a €5 higher price or added value for the monobloc solution than with the cost-plus approach. By communicating and explaining those commercial advantages to a major European truck manufacturer, the customer was willing to pay for the clear added value and the delivery contract was extended over a five-year period. This generated additional sales with a higher margin and improved customer satisfaction. At the same time it was also possible to support the green brand image of the customer by reducing CO_2 emission without any further investment.

Questions

1 Recalculate the value for the customer for fuel saving and CO_2 emission.

2 Critically evaluate the global pricing strategies pursued by WABCO and the industry.

3 Discuss how far the value based approach to pricing meets the global challenges outlined in the case study.

4 What are the key learning points of the case for B2B companies setting a global pricing strategy?

Source: Authored by (Wolfram Klussmann (by courtesy of Vincent Pickering, CLO WABCO – solely using publicy available sources).

DISCUSSION QUESTIONS

1   What are the arguments for and against using price and non-price factors when competing in international markets?

2   What pricing problems might a multi-national company face in marketing to less developed countries, and how might they be overcome?

3   Increasingly competing on global markets requires substantial investment, often undertaken by two or more firms in a joint venture or strategic alliance. Consider the implications of such ventures in developing a strategic approach to coordinating pricing strategies across international markets.

4   Why should a domestic supplier invoice export goods in a foreign currency? What are the advantages and disadvantages of foreign currency invoicing?

5   The Internet is increasing price transparency across international markets. Fully evaluate the problems and opportunities this brings to the company trying to build a global competitive advantage.

REFERENCES

1.   Albaum, G. and Duerr, E. (2009) 'International Marketing and Export Management', *Financial Times*, Prentice Hall.
2.   Myers, M.B.S., Cavusgil, S.T. and Diamontopolus, A. (2002) 'Antecedents and actions of export pricing strategy: a conceptual framework and research propositions', *Journal of European Marketing*, 36 (1/2).
3.   Sandslatt, P. (2009) 'Transfer Pricing: The global divergences regarding the documentation requirements', *VDM publication*.
4.   Sarathy, R., Terpstra, V. and Russow, L. (2006) *International marketing*, 9th edn. Dryden Press.
5.   Sugden, D. (2009) *Gray Markets: Prevention, Detection & Litigation*, Oxford Press.

CHAPTER 12

TECHNOLOGY ENABLED SUSTAINABLE INTERNATIONAL MARKETING

LEARNING OBJECTIVES

After reading this chapter you should be able to:

- Understand how technology presents opportunities and poses challenges for international marketing strategy development

- Appreciate the role of the enabling technologies in the international marketing strategy process

- Identify the approaches to achieving sustainability and corporate social responsibility

- Understand the integration of solutions to international marketing strategy problems through the use of enabling technologies

- Identify the opportunities and challenges posed by the use of enabling technologies now and in the future

INTRODUCTION

Technology is at the forefront of economic development as it drives business growth in most business sectors and connects the increasingly global marketplace. Many of the changes taking place in global marketing, such as global sourcing, social networking and mobile access to the media, have been accelerated because of advances in technology. New technology has also generated new products, services and processes that have contributed in no small part to the unsustainability of the world today. Technology is expected by many to solve the global problems, such as the generation of renewable energy and making better use of resources. International marketing is at the heart of many of these new initiatives.

As we saw in the first section of the book, technology is a major driver of both the pace and magnitude of change in international marketing. It provides more immediate methods of gathering marketing information from around the world, quicker and more effective methods of analysis and prediction of future customer needs and wants. It is revolutionizing individual and organizational communications and so provides the enabling mechanism by which effective and integrated responses can be made to changing marketplaces. It is, therefore, an essential element in the development of the international marketing strategy. Technology underpins the choice of implementation strategies of the marketing mix, facilitates the process of learning and sharing best practice, and enables more effective control of a firm's diverse international activities.

In this chapter, therefore, we focus upon the ways in which technological, business and marketing innovation facilitate further development of international marketing, in providing solutions to international marketing problems and the mechanisms to exploit opportunities. The technology tools that are available to develop appropriate strategic responses are identified. As we shall see, this involves integrating separate elements of international marketing into a cohesive approach. We then discuss how firms can pull together the various aspects of corporate social responsibility discussed throughout this book into a cohesive sustainable strategy. Finally, we focus on the challenges and opportunities faced in international markets in the future and consider the role enabling technologies will play in them.

The enabling technologies

Down the centuries, advances in technology, business and marketing innovations have provided solutions for business problems, such as in design, manufacturing, operations, internal and external communications, inventory control, managing finances and so on. Technological advances have enabled innovative firms to make product and service developments that provide distinctive benefits to customers. The technology is either industry sector specific or generic in nature. Of course, a specific industry technology may sometimes start off being used in one sector and over time be transferred to others. For example, the Internet was initially developed for use in the defence industry and Facebook was initially built for college students.

Marketing and business innovations have often built on and enhanced technological inventions, for example, in the mobile phone sector, marketing pay-as-you-go and monthly contracts, which included 'free' sophisticated phones, provided the impetus for global growth. Technological platforms provide opportunities for many and varied new developments, for example, the Internet has generated many social media developments and Apple iPhones and iPads provide a platform for hundreds of thousands of apps.

The Internet has had the effect of 'shrinking the world' and has facilitated the worldwide integration of the different technologies, systems and processes in supply chains that are used locally by different parts of the organization and its partners. It enables experts around the world to be accessed virtually and instantly. When some advanced GE medical equipment being used to treat a child broke down in the middle of the night in the US the customer was not able to get hold of a local engineer. However, it was normal working hours for the call-centre in France. The problem could be diagnosed online and expert help provided from France to solve the problem.

We refer here to enabling technologies, because there is no single technology that supports international marketing. The major steps forward in recent years have been associated with the integration of many technologies, such as those that support e-commerce, information management and search, mobile communications and social media, customer relations management, computer-aided design, process, inventory and logistics management. So, enabling technologies in international marketing provide the solutions to old problems, such as:

- How can customers in remote locations around the world contribute to the design of a new global product as much as the customer next door?

- How can an organization use the advocates for its products to share their good experiences with potential customers around the world? and

- How can a ten-person business market its products or services to its potential customers in 40 or 50 countries when managing market entry in so many countries through agents and distributors would probably be beyond the resources of most small businesses?

ILLUSTRATION 12.1

Stock.xchng

EMERGING MARKETS IMPROVING ENERGY EFFICIENCY

The emerging markets are expected to make an increasingly significant contribution to energy efficiency. There are extremes with highly publicized,

old, very energy inefficient factories but also, due to their fast growth, many new facilities that tend to be built with energy efficiency in mind. By contrast firms in the developed countries largely put efficient technology in old infrastructure. The economies, climate and topographies also affect the focus of work, so China's contribution is improving the energy efficiency of factories, whereas in Latin America it is reducing emissions from deforestation and land degradation. Brazil is forging ahead with sugar cane based ethanol production. Most of its new cars can switch between ethanol and petrol and it launched its first electricity generating plant from ethanol. Suzlon Energy, a former textile business in India is the third largest wind turbine supplier. South Africa plans to build the world's largest solar energy park in the Northern Cape. Abu Dhabi is using oil wealth to invest in sustainable energy development and aims to create Masdar in the desert as a zero-carbon city. Small scale initiatives are important too. In Ghana and Kenya the World Bank is funding a programme to replace polluting kerosene lamps with LED lanterns.

Question

1 How can firms make sense of the many technology-based initiatives that might affect their international markets and their potential impact on the firm?

References: S. Murray, 'Emerging markets: Developing nations count up the opportunities', *Financial Times*, 3 June 2010.

Technology does not remove the elements, challenges and dilemmas associated with the international marketing process, such as the need for cultural sensitivity, the need to make products and services available to customers worldwide with minimum investment, or the need to be both efficient and effective by achieving an appropriate balance between the standardization and adaptation of the international marketing process and programmes. It does have a major impact on the nature of the international marketing strategy that is used and enables creative solutions to be found which will increase the organizations' competitive capability.

Technological innovation

In considering the application of technology it is useful to focus specifically upon how technological advancement both creates new marketing opportunities and poses new challenges for firms, for example, in energy generation and conservation, discussed in Illustration 12.1, and waste recycling discussed in previous chapters. For international marketers, timing of the introduction of innovations is critical. Boston Consulting Group (2010a) explain how the future is closer for alternative energy than people think as the prospects for advanced biofuels, Concentrated Solar Power, Solar Voltaic and electric vehicles are

FIGURE 12.1 The vicious circle of technology and competitive advantage

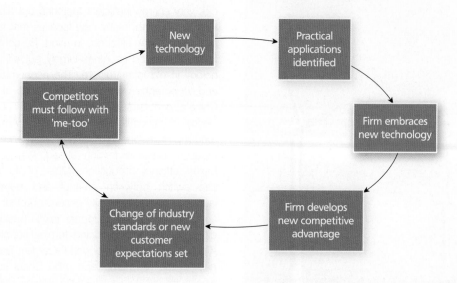

starting to look attractive as technological problems are overcome and costs are reduced, so that the technologies are likely to be competitive in a few years. Decision-making by governments around building the necessary support infrastructure will still be critical to the timing of major international marketing promotion.

As illustrated in Figure 12.1, it is important to emphasize that technology is of no value until it has a practical application. Those firms that are first to embrace a new technology and find a practical application, for example in creating a new product or service, a new route to market or a lower energy consuming process, will gain a new source of competitive advantage. This sets new standards for the industry sector that means competitors also have to achieve those standards if they wish to compete in the future. Global communications make customers worldwide aware of the latest products and create new stakeholder expectations so all competitors in the sector, wherever they are in the world, have to catch up by embracing the new product and service offers and industry standards if they wish to survive.

Disruptive technologies

From time to time technological advances make existing products and services redundant, as discussed in Illustration 12.2 and sometimes challenge the very existence of businesses if they fail to react quickly enough. For example, the conventional worldwide photography sector was virtually destroyed by digital camera technology, severely damaging companies such as Kodak. Traditional fixed line telephony was the cornerstone of the former state-owned telecommunications firms for over a century, but the introduction of mobile and Internet systems, such as Skype, has completely changed the economics of the sector. Often it is entrepreneurial born global firms that exploit the disruptive technology if a new competence is required that the organization that previously led the sector does not have.

A more recent trend, frugal engineering, discussed earlier has challenged the assumption that innovation should focus on adding additional features for wealthy customers. Technological innovation is being applied to address the needs of cost conscious customers in emerging markets. Potentially this could be disruptive for many established companies. Significant innovation is occurring in the Middle East and Africa, with the World Economic Forum (2009) identifying Tunisia (30th), South Africa (36th) and Kenya (50th) in the top 50 innovative countries in the world, on a par with Brazil and India.

ILLUSTRATION 12.2

© HSNPhotography, iStockphoto.com

When technologies die

Product life cycles often show a gradual decline in demand over a period of years as laggards in the diffusion curve still cling to dying products, but new technologies seem to have a much more limited life, then die quickly and are replaced usually by something better. This process of creative destruction is critical for global businesses because if they do not invest quickly enough in the next technology, even a powerful global business can be put at risk, even face bankruptcy, as a new competitor company exploits the new technology faster and more effectively. Of course, some technologies evolve, are reinvigorated by newer complementary technologies and become useful for other purposes, for example, landline telephones, whereas other technologies like fax machines simply die. Predictions have been made of the demise of Adobe's flash software (Steve Jobs of Apple), email (Sheryl Sandberg of Facebook) and single lens reflex cameras (Anssi Varjoki). For international marketers the question is one of timing when customers will prefer a new technology and, of course, new technologies are 'hyped' by the media often

before they are ready. Some dying technologies might include:

- The combustion engine
- Consumer video cameras
- Credit cards
- Desktop PCs
- DVDs and Blu-ray
- Digital music players
- E-readers
- Fax machines
- Games consoles
- Pagers
- Dashboard mounted GPS systems
- Keys
- Landline telephones
- 3D TVs with glasses
- Point and shoot cameras
- Personal Digital Assistants (PDAs)
- Power cables
- Remote controls
- USB memory sticks

A key change is technology convergence, so that iPhone apps and tablet computers might couple with cloud computing and replace many individual product technologies, so changing the way that consumer and business customers select and buy products and services.

Question

1 What are the critical success factors for global technology companies?

References: J. Stonington, 'Old tech never fades away; it just dies', *Bloomberg Businessweek*, 21 October 2010.

Convergent technology

An important trend is the integration of technologies and technology gadgets for business and consumer markets so, for example, the mobile phone has became a mobile communications and computing device that embraces not just voice, text and games but also downloaded music, video, television and Internet access, particularly to the social media. As the functionality increases so mobile computing is replacing 'fixed position' computing. In the same way traditional home television and recording devices are being wirelessly connected with personal computers and global communications. Integration goes further because revenues can be generated by products (such as the hardware, including mobile devices, Blu-ray or

MANAGEMENT CHALLENGE 12.1

Technology convergence: one brand or pick and mix?

The integration of technologies, supported by communications technologies, leads to fully mobile computing that allows 'computing' to control multiple functions, for example, it can control many activities within the home – not just leisure, but also security and energy efficiency. There are a handful of extremely powerful global players that are driving consumer integration innovation, such as Sony, Apple and Microsoft, but their strategies are based upon persuading consumers to purchase their own complete solution of hardware and software products. In the recent past companies have moved away from competitive strategies of this nature and, perhaps mainly driven by the open access nature of the Internet, towards a 'pick and mix' strategy, which allowed consumers to freely choose products, services and content from different providers because they were usually compatible.

There would not be room for more than a small number of very dominant global brands, supported by their supply chain partners to offer complete integrated solutions. Independent firms that supply associated products (and customers) have to decide whether or not they wish to align themselves with one major supplier. If a rival solution proves to be most popular and successful, it could be an expensive mistake for the 'losing' global brand, their supply chain and customers.

Question

1 What are the arguments for and against aligning a firm's marketing strategy alongside one powerful brand in the consumer electronics market?

DVD player), services (e.g. broadband Internet access) and content (e.g. music, podcasts, videos, games, and social media).

Major players such as Apple, Microsoft and Google are trying to establish themselves as dominant, branded players at the centre of this convergence, while other less powerful firms, are seeking to connect a more open and inclusive network as Management Challenge 12.1 shows.

The Internet and international business communications

The Internet is the central pillar of the economies of developed countries, and the growth of emerging economies is increasingly dependent on the Internet too. A report by Boston Consulting Group (2010b) ranked Denmark highest on its 'e-intensity index', a measure of the reach and depth of the Internet, followed by Japan, South Korea and Holland. The report noted that Britain was a net exporter of e-commerce goods and services, exporting £2.80 for every £1 imported, whereas in the 'off-line economy, only 90p was exported for every £1 imported.

In the business-to-business market the development of the Internet external networks and extranet internal organizational networks has revolutionized demand and customer information management, supply and value chain management, distribution channel management and control. It has speeded up the process so that real time decisions can be made in virtual, global market places or 'hubs' that manage supply and demand. To support high speed decision-making mobile technology is essential.

In consumer markets communications technology is regarded as a utility, similar to power and water. It has helped people around the world to become more aware of changes in the market environment and exciting new products and services that are introduced anywhere in the world. Customers have changing lifestyles, are more easily bored with their existing products and services and are always looking for innovative new products and services that will regain their interest. They are less brand-loyal, so if one firm does not meet the needs of international customers then a competitor will. Customers find out online about new products and services, have new ways of assessing their suitability and likely performance, believing online peer reviews more than company advertising, becoming deeply sceptical of the communications of multinational organizations and suspicious of the motives of the most powerful. Information must be available in two or three clicks of the mouse and the products must be accessible to purchase quickly and more cost-effectively and delivery should only take a day. Customers want it and they want it now!

The key function of the Internet is provided by search engines (such as Google and Yahoo!) enabling users to find the information and services they need. This is critical for international marketers who want potential customers to be able to find them. Customers are impatient so it is vital for organizations that they appear high in the list of results of search. Many would argue that the current search functions can be highly frustrating and little progress has been made over the last ten years by the dominant providers to satisfy the needs of average users. However, there is evidence to suggest that the search providers are at last aiming to improve. Google suggests that there are three layers of search: content, social and local and the firm is aiming to capture the market for location based search with its Place Search function

© Cliff Parnell, iStockphoto.com

ILLUSTRATION 12.3

The B2B mobile future in South Africa

Research by World Wide Worx found that by 2010 three quarters of South African companies were deploying smartphones, compared to almost none, two years previously. Managers regarded 'enterprise mobility solutions' as essential for businesses that wished to be competitive, responsive and efficient, not just to improve internal efficiencies and communications but to interact more effectively with increasingly mobile global customers.

The research also found that within the next two years 84 per cent of firms intended to have a 'Software as a Service' strategy in place and 60 per cent of firms intended to have a 'Cloud' computing strategy in place to make more efficient use of new technology, including outsourced storage and archiving systems, software deployment, hardware upgrades, network capacity and bandwidth increases to improve their cost effectiveness, flexibility and mobility.

While the company of the future's buildings and infrastructure may still be confined to a specific site its people, activities, information, documentation and data have been freed from location. A number of firms are developing solutions to support these initiatives. For example, IBM in partnership with open source software firm, Canonical, has introduced Smart Work, a flexible software package for low-cost netbooks that leapfrogs traditional PCs and proprietary software, such as that of Microsoft, and provides IBM's 'industrial strength' software using the 'cloud' service approach. To build a new mass B2B audience in Africa, IBM must reduce the cost of traditional business computing.

Question

1 What advice regarding investment in information and communications technology would you give to an African company seeking to develop its international business?

References: Adapted from Smartphone 'revolution' at SA firms, http://www.southafrica.info/business/trends/new business/smart-250210.htm, 26 February 2010.

the hope of significantly reducing the number of searches needed to get a satisfactory answer. It should also provide new sources of revenue by attracting local advertisers. Given the number of mobile phones (well in excess of six billion) the market for efficient search continues to grow. Microsoft's Bing also aims to achieve a step change in performance. It also provides huge potential for advertising if a suitable format can be developed. Google has so far dominated online advertising but Apple could significant increase its own revenues by perfecting mobile advertising.

All businesses must respond to these opportunities and threats, so they must embrace new methods of communicating in order to gain more customer insights, retain and connect better with their customers. Many people in emerging economies do not even have access to old technologies, such as reliable electricity, fixed line telecommunications, radio and television, let alone the latest information and telecommunications technology, but increasingly these markets are being recognized for their potential. It is possible to leapfrog existing technology with innovations that are appropriate to the specific situation, such as the developments for remote areas of Africa of the wind-up radio, solar energy systems to power communications equipment and recharge mobile phone batteries and mobile phones as a tool for making online payments. The cost of a fixed line telecommunications structure would be prohibitively expensive in most of the largely rural countries of Africa. But with in excess of 500 million mobile subscriptions there is a high level of demand. With 14 per cent of the world's population, Africa accounts for only 2 per cent of Internet use. Of the 20 countries with the most expensive broadband subscription fees (over $1000 per month in some countries) 14 are in sub Saharan Africa. The technological leap will be interesting. Cable systems are being laid around coasts, so bandwidth increase will become huge and costs will fall sharply. The challenge will be to connect the rural broadband users with wireless technologies through 3G networks to the communications provider. For international marketers to and from Africa this will bring about another industrial revolution and this is discussed in Illustration 12.3.

Email is increasingly frustrating for users. Other communications mechanisms, such as Twitter which limits message size to 140 characters, work differently but are preferred by many users for social and increasingly business networking. Technology platforms enable customers around the world to continually develop more efficient and effective integrated communication of word, stationary and video imagery, sound and complex data.

Online strategies

The advances in communications technology enable internationally trading firms to develop new international marketing strategies. No longer is international marketing limited by the physical boundaries of the media footprint or the salesperson's or distribution company's territory. At a local level new developments in hand-held devices, allow connection between users that is almost unlimited, offering opportunities for promotions close to location and point of sale (for example, of restaurants, entertainment and shops) but few of these opportunities have yet been exploited.

The Internet provides a global marketplace that is open to everyone. It is also:

- a method of collecting, searching for and exchanging marketing and business information;
- an alternative route to market to traditional distribution channels;
- a means of building customer relationships;
- a device for the digital delivery of certain information services;
- a networked system for managing the supply chain; and
- a virtual marketplace, trading floor and auction house.

The Internet also provides a mechanism for social networking through dedicated websites. The relevance of social networking for international marketing, which will be discussed in more detail later, is that it provides the opportunity for individuals and groups to discuss new products and services, problems encountered in dealing with organizations and dissatisfaction with the behaviour of organizations.

The purpose of websites

Websites are created by individuals and organizations as a shop window or for facilitating activities. While they are used for many purposes, their relevance for international marketing falls into the following main categories:

- Organization sites;
- Service online;
- Information online;
- Business transactions online (E-commerce websites).

Organization sites

Many organizations use their website to provide information to their stakeholders about the organization, ranging from its origins, business mission and areas of activity, standards and values, brands, financial performance, job opportunities and contact points through to quite specific information about products and their applications. Firms appealing to global customers must consider the degree to which their website should build much closer relationships with customers by providing a site in the local language. Wenyu, Boonghee and Ma (2003) explain the increasing use in global communications of ethnic portals for those whose first language is not English.

There are, of course, dangers too in just translating web content without addressing the need for it to be sensitive to cultural needs.

As well as providing information about products, some sites take customers through the purchasing process. For example, BMW help customers to design their new car from a range of options, such as whether to have cruise control, petrol or diesel, metallic paint and alloy wheels, but when the customer has designed the car they are then referred to their local dealer to complete the purchase.

Service online

Online banking puts customers more in control of their accounts, enabling them to obtain information from anywhere in the world and make transactions any time of the day or night. The saving to the bank is automation and being able to reduce the resourcing of bank branches and service centres and cut the cost of individual banking transactions.

Firms delivering packages, such as Federal Express, have been able to make huge savings on staff employed to answer queries from customers about where their package is, by providing an online tracking service around the world. The system involves applying a barcode to the package, which is then scanned each time it progresses past a key point on its journey. This information can then be transferred to the website and accessed by customers worldwide. Another example is real-time in-flight information that can be accessed online by those that are going to meet a flight, letting them know if the plane is going to be late.

Information online

Organizations in the business of providing information, such as Wikipedia or the *Financial Times*, provide websites that enable customers to access current and archived past files of news, data and images. Often, such sites provide one level of access free, but may charge a subscription for heavier users or may require payment for more valuable information. As this information is in digital form it can be accessed and delivered online anywhere in the world.

Sites of media organizations, such as the BBC or CNN are used to maintain and build the relationship with their consumers considerably beyond the scheduled content.

Business transactions online

These websites typically include elements of the previous categories but in addition enable customers to complete a transaction and purchase products or services online. The websites comprise two parts, the first providing the shop window, which must be eye catching for the potential customer and an easy-to-use check out process, that also assures the buyer of its security, particularly important where the purchase is cross-border.

Social networking

The disadvantage of websites is that consumers have to go to them to receive the information they want, whereas it is suggested that platforms and networks will become more important for sharing information. One example is Digg which aggregates social media news and provides links to interesting stories that are voted on by users.

Social networking has always been a feature of the Internet and, for example, people recorded web logs before the term 'blogs' was coined. As early as 1995 Amazon allowed users to write reviews and consumer guides. The phrase Web 2.0 was coined to indicate a second generation of Web services including social networking websites and online communications tools and emphasizes collaboration using the web as a platform, users owning and exercising control over the data rather than hierarchical control being exercised.

Weblogs, chat rooms and community websites, such as Taobao, MySpace and Ibibo provide a platform for millions of consumers to air their views. Blogs are updated thousands of times an hour. Many of the comments relate to product, services and opinions about companies and it is essential for organizations to know what is being said about them. This requires intelligent search engines, such as Attentio, that can dig deeper than general searches and aggregate the data to provide a fuller picture of the trends and conversations that are taking place.

Businesses increasingly see the benefit of some involvement in other types of websites, even if the purpose is only to hear what is being said about the company, its competitors and their products. Blog and Forum websites, such as Google's Blogger enable people to meet others with common views and thus enable firms to quickly hear about dissatisfaction. They can also be used by companies to inform and keep their staff around the world up to date. Social websites, such as Facebook, are effectively member groups or communities with common interests. File sharing websites, such as Flickr and YouTube, have on numerous occasions been used to share both photo and video files that have either enhanced the reputation of a company and its staff or proved embarrassing. Perhaps the most significant developments are likely to come from mobile device websites that support smartphones.

International e-markets and e-marketing

There are a number of e-marketing business models and e-marketplaces that originally started as digital extensions of physical marketing models. These business models focus on business to business marketing discussed next and business to consumer marketing, and other models are discussed later.

Business to business (B2B)

The interactions involved in B2B marketing are much more complex because they involve the exchange of significant amounts of information between the seller and customer before, during and after any transaction. The information includes such things as specifications, designs and drawings, purchase contracts, supply chain management, manufacturing and delivery schedules, inventory control, negotiation of price, distribution channel management and delivery. The information comes from different departments within the firms and is exchanged between the firms involved in the value chain.

For many years firms have been using information technology to improve the efficiency and effectiveness of the internal firm processes, for example demand forecasting, inventory control, computer-aided design and manufacturing: the Internet enables this to be linked with external organizations and customers. The Internet has enabled a far wider range of data to be exchanged without restriction on the number of participant organizations. The mechanisms by which the exchanges take place and business can be transacted are Web portals. These are 'hubs' where all the interested participants congregate. Typically there are two types of hubs:

- industry-specific hubs, such as automobile or aerospace manufacturing; and
- function-specific hubs, such as advertising or human resource management.

Using e-hubs, firms improve the efficiency of the processes of transactions and thereby lower costs. The hubs can reduce the transaction cost by bringing together all the purchasing requirements of many hundreds of customers worldwide (Kaplan and Sawhney 2000). E-hubs attract many buyers who are able to negotiate bulk discounts on behalf of a range of smaller, individual buyers.

If the products are commodities with no need to negotiate specifications then dynamic pricing enables buyers and sellers to negotiate prices and volumes in real time. In sectors such as energy purchasing the peaks and troughs of supply and demand can be smoothed.

The US originally dominated B2B and much of the innovation in B2B came from the US, but firms around the world recognize that the potential savings can be quite significant with the increasing internationalization of sourcing and supply chain management. A culture change in the attitude of firms is needed as companies that may normally be competing can cooperate for the mutual benefit of reducing costs. Illustration 12.4 shows how Jack Ma has helped millions of Chinese entrepreneurs to access global business markets.

© Lou Linwei/Alamy

ILLUSTRATION 12.4

Jack Ma creating Chinese entrepreneurs

To thousands of Chinese, Jack Ma has achieved rock star status to the point where he needs bodyguards to hold back the adoring fans. He is listed in *Time* magazine's top 100 most influential people in the world and has achieved this status by enabling many Chinese to become their own boss – a dream ingrained in the Chinese culture. Ma set up Alibaba which is now the world's largest B2B market place and, through the acquisition of Yahoo! China, enables the company to challenge US global online giants, Google, eBay, Yahoo! and Amazon. Alibaba has become a leader in its own right though its own innovations that deliver value to users.

Alibaba has two B2B websites at its heart, alibaba.com, a marketplace for firms across the world to trade in English, and china.alibaba.com, a domestic Chinese service. While the aim of rival western sites, such as Ariba and Commerce One, was to cut the procurement costs for multinationals, Alibaba's was to build markets for many Chinese SMEs, which make a vast array of manufactured goods available to western traders, who might resell on eBay.

Ma has led the Chinese development of online communities and social networking with a consumer auction site, Taobao, that has an innovation that reflects a cultural difference. Whereas eBay transactions are between largely anonymous buyers and sellers, Taobao facilitates instant messaging, voicemail and allows personal photographs and details to be posted, creating a community of 'friends' in a country where there is still a lack of trust. By 2010 Taobao claimed it had 190 million customers in China and transactions worth £19 billion. Ma has also addressed the problem of settlement risks in online payments in China, where there are no credit cards, by introducing AliPay, which holds cash in an escrow account until the goods are delivered. AliPay is effectively an online bank that is able to maintain many thousands of supplier and customer credit histories.

Alibaba International claims to be the world's largest B2B marketplace for global trade with 500 000 people visiting the site every day and Alibaba China is the largest site for domestic China trade with 16 million registered users. Taoboa has 30 million registered users and is the largest e-commerce website in Asia.

The interesting aspect of Ma is that he is a business entrepreneur rather than a computer geek like the founders of Yahoo! and Google. He believes that 'someone as dumb as me should be able to use technology'. He will not accept a new feature unless he can understand it and use it.

Question

1 What are the critical success factors in creating a successful B2B and C2C electronic market place?

References: 'Jack Ma is attracting a following among entrepreneurs in China and Internet companies worldwide' *The Economist*, 21 September, 2006. 'Taobao's Alipay Will Charge Fees', 16 March, 2007, http://www.chinatechnews. com: and 'Alibaba IPO would touch US$1 billion', 1 June 2007, accessed at: http://www.chinaeconomicreview.com/ it/category/services/.

The benefits of e-procurement, such as convenience and cost saving through group purchasing, appeal to governments for public sector and private–public sector purchasing. However, often progress is much slower than in private business.

Disintermediation and re-intermediation

The Internet offers the possibility for an organization to efficiently handle many more transactions than was possible previously. With the benefit of the enabling Internet technology many organizations have re-assessed the value contribution of the intermediaries (distributors and agents) with the intention of managing the distribution themselves and cutting out the intermediary. The benefits to the organization are the removal of channel infrastructure costs and intermediary margins and the opportunity to develop a direct relationship with the final customer. 'Cutting out the middleman' is described as disintermediation. Chaffey *et al.* (2006) observes that at the start of the e-business boom it was expected that there would be widespread disintermediation. While it has happened in some sectors, in others there has been little change and the results of disintermediation is some sectors have been disappointing with the marketing organization incurring substantial additional IT, order management and logistics costs, offsetting the forecast savings.

The counter to disintermediation is re-intermediation and the creation of new firms that add value in the purchasing situation, such as travel and household goods. While many financial services products and offers from utilities lend themselves to online selling, it is a laborious task to compare the many offerings from competing companies. Consequently many brokers have set up websites such as Uswitch and moneyextra to allow customers to compare many different financial product offerings. Of course this means that the Internet marketer must ensure that they are represented on key sites where there are high volumes of potential customers and ensure that they are offering competitive prices.

The alternatively strategy is for the marketer to set up his own intermediary to compete with the existing intermediaries: this is referred to as counter-mediation. A group of airlines set up www.Opodo.com as an alternative to www.expedia.com to offer airline tickets.

Business to consumer

In the B2C sector, well designed websites, whether from small or large companies, provide a satisfying experience for the online shopper and this means customers are able to browse through the information that is available about the products and services they are seeking to buy and, do so at their leisure. The best websites offer potential customers the choice of which language they wish to communicate in and are sensitive to the local culture and legal frameworks. Having selected the product they enable customers to easily purchase and pay for the product online, using credit cards to make payment. In practice, many more customers are prepared to use the Internet to carry out their information search on companies, products and services, but are still unwilling to pay online because of fears about the security of online payment and the potential for fraud, or, in emerging markets, unable because of the lack of a suitable payment method such as a credit card. Firms that have both virtual and physical stores allow customers to find out information and then choose whether to buy online or go to the store.

Some services can be supplied as digital services online over the Internet. For example, information, software, financial advice, ticketless travel and music can be downloaded direct to the customer's computer. For physical products, however, the supplier still needs a suitable distribution method to deliver the goods to the consumer. Fulfilment of the order depends on more traditional distribution, with its associated limitations of the country's existing infrastructure and the availability of appropriate logistics in each customer's country. Small items such as DVDs and books can be posted but delivering valuable bulky goods such as furniture or goods that require special storage conditions, such as food, directly to the door also requires arrangements to be made for the customer to receive them.

Using the Internet simply to transact business underutilizes its potential, however, and does little to build competitive advantage, or improve the overall effectiveness of the operation in winning global customers and developing their loyalty. Moreover, without building competitive advantage and unique selling propositions, firms using the Internet to sell their products are vulnerable to lower priced offers from other global competitors, because sophisticated search engines identify the cheapest offers of comparable products or services. Many companies believe they can survive and grow by offering the lowest priced products direct to customers, but inevitably new entrants will always offer lower prices, even if they are not sustainable in the longer term.

E-business operations are expensive to establish and maintain, given the large outlay for information technology, systems, management and website development. Moreover, e-commerce firms require sophisticated systems to fulfil orders promptly and accurately and need to innovate constantly to retain customer interest and loyalty. The challenge for a business is therefore to maximize income. Chaffy *et al.* (2006) identify a number of opportunities for generating income from a website, for example, by charging for sponsorship, advertising and 'click-through' fees, for sales generated by a second firm that has a direct link to its own site.

Consumer to consumer (C2C)

Timmers (1999) has identified other Internet business models involving exchange between supplier and customer. These include C2C in which consumers sell to each other through an online auction. The most successful site for trading between individuals by online bidding is eBay. This type of buying and selling tends to become almost a hobby in itself for customers. They take a fee to insert the advertizement and a fee based on the final value. It has been successful internationally but has had problems competing in certain markets. It pulled out of Japan and failed to compete with Alibaba, partly because it did not really understand the Chinese culture.

New models of international business are being developed that incorporate a number of aspects of business, consumer and social networking websites and an example of this is discussed in Illustration 12.5, which uses viral marketing as a key step.

International marketing solution integration

The most significant international marketing strategy development that is facilitated by technology is business solution integration. As competition increases, so firms must seek to find new sources of competitive advantage, secure ever-lower costs, increase their speed of action and responsiveness, demonstrate their adaptability to new situations and flexibility in offering new innovative products and services

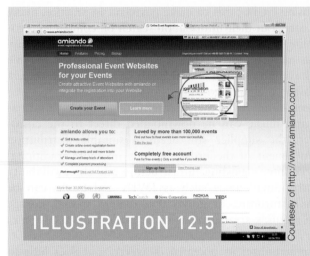

Courtesey of http://www.amiando.com/

ILLUSTRATION 12.5

Viral ticketing

Five friends from Munich organized a party in their back garden for several hundred people to watch Germany's opening match of the 2006 World Cup on the understanding that everyone would contribute 20–23 euros for food and drink. After the event it occurred to them that they had a business opportunity and formed Amiando, now Europe's leading online service for on-demand event organization and ticketing. The initial idea was to create a platform for selling tickets to an event, initially e-invites for private parties but this was soon followed by a payment and ticketing system, promotion, demand management attendee registration. The company generates income through a percentage of the ticket price. The key to the business was harnessing social media, such as Facebook and Twitter as a mechanism to release viral tickets. If you buy a ticket through Amiando, you can share the event with friends either by email or through sites such as Facebook, Twitter and LinkedIn. When the friend or colleague buys a ticket, they get a discount and you get a refund on the original ticket price. For the event organizer the benefits include reduced cost and a lower investment in traditional marketing and advertising.

Viral marketing is not new but the benefit of this model is that it provides incentives and benefits for participants. Other companies have developed similar models. For example, on one site artists and event organizers can create an event and then recruit 'reps', usually in the 16–24 age group to push it through their extended network. Traditional middlemen that have charged high booking fees and manipulated the market for the highest profile events will come under pressure as these companies grow. Amiando claims more than 100 000 events per year, supports 15 currencies with offices around the world, and has high profile clients such as BMW, News Corporation and Nokia.

Question

1 How might viral marketing be used by international firms to create a new business model or to promote their business?

References: F. Graham, 'Viral ticketing: Catching a bigger audience on Facebook', *BBC News Online*, 29 October 2010.

perceived by customers to be valuable. They must also develop better relationships with their customers and business partners in order to retain their business. The strategy to achieve these outcomes is based on the effective integration of the elements of the marketing and business processes.

Knowledge management

The move to an increasingly global market served by e-business has prompted firms to redefine their sources of competitive advantage. In a global market the traditional sources of competitive advantage can be easily challenged. A company that operates in a small number of countries or within a restricted business sector may believe that its competitive advantage comes from low-cost manufacturing, design capability, sales expertise and distribution efficiency. However, when exposed to global competition it may find that its own competitive advantage cannot be transported to new countries and discover, instead, that regional or global competitors have even greater competitive advantage in their own domestic market as well as in the target country market.

By contrast, knowledge, expertise and experience have the potential to be transferable if they can be effectively collected, stored, accessed and communicated around the world (hence the term knowledge management). Below we discuss the processes for managing knowledge to support the customer–client interface, but knowledge management is essential to maximize added value throughout the supply chain. There is a danger in building competitive advantage through knowledge management, of course, because the knowledge assets of a firm are locked into their staff and their records, typically contained in their computers. Staff are becoming increasingly mobile, computer systems are still notoriously insecure and the potential loss of knowledge to a competitor is an ever greater problem for firms. Business espionage is growing in many countries.

Supply chain management

Technology-enabled supply chain management has helped firms to grow through exploiting market development opportunities, reducing investment by buying rather than manufacturing components and enabling small firms to have similar costs to large firms through e-procurement. It is vital that each part of the supply chain of the product maximizes the added value and this is made possible by integrating the activities. A supply chain for a complex product might typically involve such distinctly different activities as design, manufacture of raw materials, component assembly, advertising, logistics and local servicing. It is highly unlikely that one company could be the leader in each of these areas of activity, particularly when the most efficient members of the supply chain will increasingly be located around the world.

The implications, of course, are that through using e-commerce for procurement, partnerships can be set up and dissolved instantly. Of course, suppliers need to have huge flexibility and excellent systems to manage the rapid changes that are necessary to survive in this type of market. Suppliers are in completely open competition with other firms around the world.

Cost savings can be made in all areas of the supply chain, such as inventory reduction and just in time sourcing. Amazon is able to offer millions of books and music titles and other items by quickly obtaining stocks held anywhere in the world, whereas an average traditional bookstore might physically hold only 170 000 titles. Savings can be made in evaluating suppliers, specifications and delivery times and arranging scheduling. Marketing costs can be reduced because it is easier, quicker and cheaper to make alterations to Web content than incur the design and printing costs of a new brochure.

Advantest America Inc. supplies measuring instruments, semiconductor test systems and related equipment. It outsourced its delivery of its replacement parts, e-commerce and supply chain management services to FedEx Corporation, which provides transport. Using FedEx's sophisticated, integrated systems it was able to reduce its delivery times by more than 50 per cent, to 48 hours in Asia and 24 hours for customers in America and Europe. Previously, starting from the time the order was taken, it could take between 25 and 42 hours even to get through customs and onto a commercial aeroplane. Extending the system to the firm's customized printed circuit boards would avoid the need for the customer to hold stock on site, thus considerably reducing their inventory.

Every element in the logistics process must be tackled in order to improve performance. In service call centres the cost of employing a person capable of dealing with service calls in India is about one-tenth of the cost of employing a person in the UK for an equivalent level of performance. Very often service centre calls are routine and technology can be used to make further savings by replacing people-based transactions with 'intelligent' computer-based responses.

Value chain integration

The key question is how effectively the individual supply chain members around the world work in partnership to maximize the effectiveness of their contributions towards improving efficiency and adding value across the entire value chain, so-called value chain integration. Success is then likely to be dependent on the effectiveness of the working relationship between the members of the supply chain, the speed and openness of information sharing and the degree of collaboration between each company, its suppliers and customers, with the objective of adding value and removing transaction costs.

So, for example, a supermarket chain will allow its hundreds of suppliers to have access to its data warehouse, so they will know how their particular product is selling in each individual store, and to the inventory system to ensure that the supermarket never runs out of stock. This system makes it easier for additional suppliers to be included and managed at low additional cost, allowing consumers more choice and more competitive prices. Hagiu and Yoffie (2009), however, explain that although multisided platforms (MSPs), such as Microsoft, Google and Apple, can lower costs, there are dangers with online collaboration as firms cede too much power to the MSPs. Toys'R'Us signed a ten-year 'exclusive' agreement with Amazon with the intention of creating an online retail business to dominate its category and paid them $50 million annually, plus a percentage of sales, but Amazon recruited small third party merchants to sell toys and games directly through its website. Toys'R'Us lost money and successfully sued Amazon for $200 million in damages.

Virtual enterprise networks

The possibility for Internet technology-supported collaboration between supply chain members is being extended and applied to SMEs and individuals with complementary expertise that form themselves into a virtual enterprise network to bid for and carry out projects and routine business. Snyder (2005) explains that the Internet has reduced transaction costs and outsourcing risks, enabling the individuals and organizations to form a more efficient form of organization, based on virtually integrated collaborative networks rather than hierarchical bureaucracies. Virtual enterprise networks are expected to become more common, international in nature and focused on international marketing opportunities.

Customer relationship management

Customer relationship management (CRM) is the process of identifying, attracting, differentiating and retaining customers (Hoffman 2003). It allows a firm to focus its efforts on its most lucrative customers, no matter where they are from, and is based on the 'rule' that 80 per cent of a firm's profits come from 20 per cent of its customers. It is also designed to achieve efficient and effective customer management. As pressures on costs and prices increase firms must manage customers as inexpensively as they can without losing customer loyalty. To answer a customer query with an automatic Web-based service can be less than a tenth of the cost of a person handling it by telephone through a service call centre, but the question is whether it can be as responsive to customer queries.

CRM allows customers to be categorized on the basis of their past profitability. The most profitable customers will be recognized and will be routed to the area that will handle calls fastest. For example, this can be done automatically by transferring telephone calls with a particular number. The profitable customers can then be targeted with attractive deals. The information is shared throughout the company to ensure integration of the firm's activities so that profitable customers get priority service throughout the firm and also from partner firms.

To deliver a CRM strategy the key component is the database of customer information. Techniques and systems are used to manage and extract data (data mining) to identify trends and analyze customer characteristics that enable the targeting to be carried out. Javalgi, Radulovich, Pendelton and Scherer (2005) have developed a framework for providing managerial insights into building and sustaining a competitive advantage using a consumer-centric approach, coupled with CRM technology on a global scale.

The system involves the retention of large amounts of detailed information about individual customers in a firm database. Customers often resent firms holding information about them and in some countries it would infringe privacy laws. Companies analyze the data that they have but only past behaviour has been recorded and so this data may not be an accurate predictor of future behaviour. Finally, there is an assumption that customers want a 'relationship' with suppliers and that in some way they will benefit from it. If the benefit is not clear, then customers will not remain loyal.

Customization

As we have suggested on a number of occasions, customers increasingly want to be treated as individuals and not simply be the unwilling targets of mass market advertising. The Internet allows companies to mass customize their offering and a variety of firms are exploiting the flexibility of online mobile communication. A number of firms are providing software applications that are designed to personalize or more individually target the firm's interactions. For example, Lindgren (2003) explains how Poindexter (US) uses statistical analysis to identify the shared characteristics of online advertising viewers, and be able to cluster those customers who respond to websites and online advertizements in a similar way. The clusters can then be offered a customized marketing mix and customized promotions and product offers. For example, an online shopper who puts products in an online basket but does not go through with the purchase immediately might be offered a discount by the online retailer, as an incentive to go through with the purchase. As more viewers are analyzed the system learns the best response and so delivers better performance.

Customers can be targeted and made aware of special deals being offered in their own neighbourhood, perhaps on travel, at a restaurant or at the wine shop. Global positioning systems coupled with mobile telephony enable firms to text consumers about deals available in the shop that they are just passing.

The impact on international marketing strategy

Having discussed the central role of the Internet as a technology enabler of international marketing and highlighted the various elements of the electronic marketplace, we now turn to how these can both influence and support the much more dynamic approach to international marketing strategy development that we mentioned at the start of this chapter.

The impact of technology on analysis

Demand patterns are now changing more quickly because of changes in the environment, customer needs and wants and competition, and so it is increasingly vital for firms to be able to track changes through an effective marketing information system. Much of the data that must be gathered from around the world can be more effectively collected, managed and communicated through integrated Web-based systems. Firms can track political, economic and legal changes and new product launches by competitors as they are announced by using search engines and sites that provide up to date expert analysis. Point of sale information can be collected and analyzed by retailers on a daily basis to provide information about what products are selling and not selling so that appropriate action can be taken to avoid unnecessary inventory, and build a supply chain that is flexible and responsive. For example, for clothing products sourced from Asia to sell in the US, the fabric production, garment making and logistics must be fast, flexible and quickly adaptable to changing fashion needs to avoid stock write-offs or write-downs.

In the past fashion magazines and newspaper articles provided information about the latest trend and images of celebrities wearing the next 'cool' brand or 'must have' product. Now social networking websites provide the response from customers that are likely to affect their purchasing habits. Because of the informal, non-regulated nature of the websites firms can influence their perceptions of the products, as we discuss later in this section.

The Internet provides not only general information about the firm's products but also makes it easier and faster to apply questionnaires to existing and potential customers around the world by using the Internet. Customer behaviour can be monitored on websites by tracking navigation through the site to provide new insights, thought processes and predict likely purchasing intentions. Egol, Clyde and Rangan (2010) explain how online shopping behaviour can lead to six consumer segments:

- *Shoppers 2.0*, the most technologically advanced group, price sensitive with little brand loyalty.
- *Deal Hunters*, are price sensitive but although they gather information online they get the best deal in store.
- *On-line window shoppers*, again gather information online and in-store, but are less price sensitive and less likely to switch brands.
- *Channel surfers*, hunt out the brands they love and try to source the brands at reasonable prices.

- *Loyalists*, are least likely to switch brands or retail formats.
- *Laggards*, are least likely to change behaviour and carry out little online research.

The Internet provides some negative information as well, from blogs and social networking sites. Firms can suffer considerable damage at the hands of such sites.

As we discussed in Part 1, organizations are collecting this type of information in a much more systematic way. For example, Procter & Gamble and Unilever have a database of observed behaviour accessible to staff worldwide through an intranet.

A huge amount of data can be generated and analyzed but Ofek and Wathieu (2010) observe that while managers recognize major social, economic and technological trends, their focus is often on short term goals and they often fail to realize the significance of these trends in reshaping the business.

The impact of technology on international strategy development

For some firms their international marketing strategy is inextricably linked to technology either because of the nature of the business, in the case of firms such as IBM, Microsoft and Acer, or because it is the route to market in the case of Expedia, Dell and Bloomberg.

For firms in most industry sectors technology, business and marketing innovations are a major source of international competitive advantage. As we discussed earlier, organizations in developed countries cannot compete against the low labour and other associated costs, operational scale benefits and lower research and development costs of firms from developing countries, such as India and China.

Their source of competitive advantage in the future, therefore, is likely to come from technological, business process and marketing innovation, from knowledge management of the organization's intellectual property and assets, its ability to manage effectively and the contributions of the supply chain to maximize the customer value. For these reasons technological competence and capability, understanding the competitive market position and gaining in-depth customer insights will become key success criteria in the future.

Internet-based market entry

The Internet provides a market entry method that is particularly suitable for smaller, widespread niche markets. While the website might be accessible worldwide, however, the firm may need to select markets to focus on, possibly excluding those where there may be particular barriers, such as language, legal, payment and over-fulfilment problems. The cost of organizing to serve certain markets might outweigh the possible benefits. For firms that already have a strong presence in many markets the Internet supports all aspects of their activity.

Web-based services will be successful if firms develop a global strategy based upon the integrated value chain. As this is a pervasive method of entry, based on global communications, it can facilitate lower-risk access to difficult markets. By building online delivery capability it is possible to serve markets profitably where there might be limited demand. Of course, an e-commerce strategy is limited in scope simply because it appeals to a very specific transnational segment – those that are able to gain access to the firm's website – but as Internet access, particularly high speed access, continues to grow this is a diminishing problem.

The impact of technology on strategy implementation and control

Product and service management   Technology supports the delivery and control of all the elements of the augmented product and service offer (Figure 8.2) and integrates the worldwide members of the supply chain, as discussed earlier in this chapter. It is also used to speed up innovation and facilitate worldwide contributions to new product and service development activity.

In doing this, technology is increasingly supporting, on the one hand, the standardization of the components of the product, and creating worldwide product 'platforms'. For example, car firms such as VW,

ILLUSTRATION 12.6

Crowd-sourcing at Mountain Dew

There is an increasing trend for major brands, such as Amazon, Chevrolet, Doritos, HP and Peperami to use 'Crowd-sourcing' involving consumers in the production of creative marketing campaigns, so by-passing ad agencies or relegating them to a role in implementing the plan. Mountain Dew at www.mountaindew.com used a contest in which any agency, independent film company or individual person could submit 12 second clips outlining their ideas for line extension products. The line extensions, Distortion, Whiteout and Typhoon were created by consumer product development too.

Mountain Dew is a Pepsi acquisition and it launched in 2007 with an online game. The company is now using Facebook, Twitter and its private online Dew Labs to determine the flavour, colour, packaging and names of new products.

Question

1 What are the advantages and disadvantages of crowd-sourcing for international product development and marketing?

References: N. Zmuda, 'New Pepsi "Dewmocracy" push threatens to crowd out shops', www.adage.com, 11 February 2009.

and household appliance manufacturers such as Whirlpool, use a common platform and make minor adaptations for different models and markets. On the other hand, however, it is enabling firms to offer increased customization of products and services and one-to-one marketing. Illustration 12.6 shows how customers can be encouraged to provide innovative ideas for new products and communications, using so-called crowd sourcing.

Pricing As we discussed earlier in the chapter, technology is driving down costs and prices through supply chain efficiencies, economies of scale, the experience curve effect and greater price transparency. Price transparency for customers and other stakeholders is created because of the ease with which it is now possible to compare prices offered by competing potential suppliers across borders by searching through the information on their websites. Some sites such as Expedia in travel and Kelkoo on a range of products in B2C markets and the sector and function e-hubs in B2B provide the opportunity for customers to compare prices on one site. The sophistication and usefulness of Web search activity is improving as competition between firms such as Google and Microsoft increases.

The Internet makes grey marketing easier and also makes it much more difficult for firms to operate specific geographic territories and price differentials across country borders, so grey marketing may become less of an issue in international markets as firms give up hope of trying to control it. Price transparency has the effect of driving mature products towards commoditization in which products become less differentiated and competition is based largely on price. When there are many competitors, price transparency forces down prices as suppliers have to respond by cutting the costs of their products and services. This usually forces them to find ever-lower cost sources. The alternative is to innovate and develop new products and services or add additional services, many of which, such as loyalty reward schemes, are operated online. However, these strategies will only work if customers around the world perceive the additional services to be valuable and of additional benefit over the commodity product alternative.

Customization is clearly the opposite of commoditization and, therefore, can be used partially to counter price transparency. Because international pricing embraces both pricing and financing the transaction, technology allows pricing to be customized. It can enable complex calculations to be made to facilitate the negotiation of mutually beneficial deals between supplier and customer with flexible pricing and financing and also control non-standard repayment schedules that ensure that the transaction is ultimately profitable. An example of this from personal finance is that it is possible to offset longer-term loans, such as a mortgage to buy a house, against savings in a current account and pay interest daily on the balance outstanding.

Channel management Electronic marketing has encouraged disintermediation, or the removal of intermediaries from the supply chain, as suppliers market directly to customers. Technology now enables firms to efficiently manage thousands of small transactions that previously would have been left for a local intermediary to undertake. This is possible because e-marketing has typically lower transaction costs and is capable of managing large inventories, logistics, ordering and payments but also allows the virtual bundling of products that might be sourced from different partner suppliers. Disintermediation provides the manufacturer with stronger control of its activities in the market and avoids being so reliant on third parties. It also enables the distribution channels to be customized to the specific needs of the customers.

For those firms that are maintaining intermediaries within their distribution channel, technology allows much closer cooperation through sharing of market information but also greater control of intermediaries by making it easier to check on a daily basis that they are fulfilling their commitments to the supplier.

Communications The main advantage of e-marketing communications is that they are targeted and are often based on one-to-one communications. The most important aspect is that they are interactive. Customers are required to do something rather than being passive recipients of untargeted advertising or other promotion. As customers become more involved, so they are more likely to buy.

Marketing through websites, even interactive ones, is reactive, because potential customers must take the initiative and locate the site first typically by using search, which is critically important. It is essential that the firm features high on the list of search results. Word of mouth referral or viral marketing is important in building traffic to the website, but to gain a large market in unexciting business sectors it is not enough just to have a website. It is also necessary to proactively market and promote the brand and the site in the traditional media. The fundamental questions of marketing need to be asked, such as who are we targeting, where will we find the target customers on the Internet and how will we get them directed to our site? How best can we then communicate our message to them globally and at low cost? The key is to deliver the right message to the right people at the right time in the right place using the right e-based communication channels.

Control, evaluation and learning Technology enables firms to collect, transfer and analyze vast amounts of data from anywhere in the world. Using Enterprise Resource Planning (ERP) software they are able to control the use of resources and improve the efficiency of their operations. Financial management and control can be more immediate and more detailed. Firms use other processes and systems to control the supporting operations to ensure quality and efficiency of the manufacturing, distribution operations, and measure the effectiveness of the marketing processes and programmes.

These techniques can be applied in worldwide operations because they can be supported by information technology and systems. Underpinning all these techniques is the need to develop a learning organization that follows good practice, shares new ideas and creates greater confidence in the abilities of its staff so that they can be empowered to take decisions in their own area of expertise and knowledge.

Some limitations of e-commerce for international marketing strategy

There are some disadvantages in operating e-business globally, including the high cost of providing a global website with 24-hour service for customers who expect interactive capability, wherever possible, in their own language and culture and adapted to their own environment. There are also some significant perceived and real dangers associated with e-commerce. Customers are concerned with data security and the risks, for example, of credit card fraud. Customers are also concerned with identity theft, data protection and the use, storage and passing on to third parties of personal information to firms anywhere in the world. Of course technology is being continually developed and improved to try to overcome these difficulties.

Firms basing their business on e-commerce must recognize that there are typically low entry barriers and competitors have greater and easier access to information that can be used to challenge the existing supplier. For example, Yell the business directory company blamed a decline in profits on a rival business set up by ex sales staff made redundant in the US by the company. Computer systems are still prone to system failure and corruption and it is still alarmingly easy for computer hackers and computer viruses to cause severe damage to multi-national enterprises. Often MNEs, particularly banks, do not publicize such difficulties as it may well deter customers. There is also a proliferation of anti-MNE websites and through social networking that can publicize damaging stories – true or not – virtually without challenge. This is possible, of course, simply because of the relatively uncontrolled nature of the Internet.

International e-business marketing businesses face some challenges:

1 The decisions of customers in e-commerce are strongly affected by cultural issues. Customers from some countries, typically low-context countries, embrace the Internet in different ways to those in high-context cultures, because of the lower emphasis placed on implicit interactions when building relationships and purchasing products.

2 Brand values often depend on the different communication methods that people use, both explicit and implicit, such as image, reputation, word of mouth and continual exposure online and offline. This emphasizes the need for an integrated communications approach involving virtual and physical media.

3 By being global, e-commerce still favours global players. Consumers expect high quality of performance and image but these can be severely tarnished by a low-cost, poorly performing website and slow or inaccurate order fulfilment.

4 The effectiveness of websites is influenced by such factors as the ease of navigation, company and products information, shipping details and sensitivity to language and culture.

5 The barriers to entry must be significant if the defenders of domestic or limited country niches wish to retain their market share. It must be recognized by marketers that the marketing skills to ensure success in e-business are different from traditional skills, in that success depends on attracting consumers to sites and this is typically more difficult because of the increased media 'noise'.

6 The development of intelligent agents that search for specific pieces of information on markets and potential suppliers means that marketers cannot base their appeal to customers on traditional marketing-mix factors but must find a new sustainable competitive advantage.

Legislation

The aspect of the Internet that seems to raise most concern is the fact that there is very little control exerted and consequently the Internet is used for unethical and illegal purposes and to circumvent the law. The Internet has grown extremely rapidly and the application of existing law and introduction of legislation to control activities has lagged behind. Governments do not want to stifle development and so legislation is being developed not in anticipation but only as problems arise.

Problems of application of existing law to the Internet

The Internet removes traditional geographic boundaries, so that virtually anyone anywhere in the world can access a website. Zugelder, Flaherty and Johnson (2000) explain that a particular difficulty, of course, is the fact that websites are subject to the laws of individual countries, both home and host country, where customers are based. Websites are also subject to regional trade agreements (e.g. EU and NAFTA) and regulations of organizations such as the WTO, the World International Property

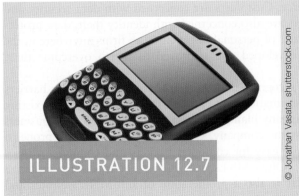

© Jonathan Vasata, shutterstock.com

ILLUSTRATION 12.7

Collecting too much information?

Five hundred thousand users of the Blackberry were affected by a ban imposed by two Gulf states, Saudi Arabia and the United Arab Emirates The Government of the UAE wanted to stop users accessing email, web browsing and instant messaging because of national security concerns and claimed that Blackberry applications allowed people to 'misuse' the service. The UAE regulator complained that users' data was being automatically sent to overseas servers and managed by foreign, commercial organizations, allowing users to behave without any legal accountability, causing judicial, social and national security concerns. It claimed the suspension was due to the lack of compliance with UAE telecoms regulations. Saudi Arabia decided to ban instant messaging saying the ban was intended to encourage the owners of Blackberry, Research in Motion, to release data from users 'when needed'. Activists said that the Blackberry system made it more difficult for conservative countries, which actively censor websites to monitor what users were saying. Google has faced a challenge from the Chinese government for allowing customers to access information on sensitive issues such as Tibet and took the decision to withdraw its China site.

Google also violated the Canadian privacy laws when it inadvertently collected personal information with its Street View by accidentally intercepting and storing data including emails and, separately, names of people suffering from certain medical conditions.

Question

1 How much attention should global firms pay to local laws and should there be limits to the collection, storage and sharing of data?

References: E. Rowley, 'Blackberry faces ban in Gulf States over security concerns', *Daily Telegraph*, 2 August 2010. J. Halliday, 'Google Street View broke Canada's privacy law with Wi-Fi capture', at: www.guardian.co.uk, accessed 20 October 2010.

Organization (WIPO) and the Berne Convention on copyright law. Many countries either do not conform or interpret many conventions differently. Illustration 12.7 shows how country laws, lack sensitivity to users' needs and the freedom of the Internet.

The result is a chaotic situation in which multiple and contradictory laws apply to the same transaction, leaving a marketer open to the possibility of unintentionally violating the laws of a foreign country. A whole series of issues arise in e-marketing, including what constitutes a contract in cyberspace, how international tax can be harmonized and how tax should be collected for online transactions.

There are many issues of intellectual property protection, including copyright infringement, inappropriate linking to information from another website and trademark infringement, such as the registering of existing trademarks as domain names for the website. Because of the demand for domain names, second-level (for example .co, .org and .com) and third-level country names (.uk and .de) have been added. Countries, including the UK, Mexico and Russia, have taken a 'first come, first served' approach to this, and companies such as Nike, Chrysler and Sony initially failed to register as widely as they should have and have suffered as a consequence.

Consumer protection for international consumer clients must be provided to avoid unfair and deceptive trading practices, such as unsubstantiated advertising claims and false endorsements. Relationship marketing is based, especially for small firms, on building substantial data on customers in order to retain their loyalty, but in a number of countries gathering such information is illegal as laws exist to protect consumer privacy. Marketers must also know the difference between what is considered free speech and what is defamation and disparagement.

Other Internet problems

The problems discussed so far have related to the application of largely existing legislation to the new medium and the fact that the Internet crosses country borders indiscriminately. Other issues are the ease of access and lack of control of illegal activity. It has been estimated that a large percentage of international consumer e-commerce is devoted to pornography and a worrying part of this traffic is illegal and supporting paedophilia. It requires close cooperation between country law enforcement agencies to catch the culprits.

The ease of communicating with many recipients makes it easy to send out 'junk mail' (spam). Millions of messages can be sent out worldwide in the hope of getting just a few responses. Many firms sell to potential customers through emails and text messages. However, if this is overused it degenerates into spam. Spam is the intrusive, offensive and often pornographic junk email that fills up the inboxes of email systems. It threatens to create gridlock on the Internet if it is not controlled. The US has proposed opt-out legislation so that spam would be legal unless the receiver has opted out of receiving it. The EU legislation is opt-in – spam could not be sent unless the receiver had given consent to receive it – and would be more effective in controlling spam.

Moving to a customer-led strategy

The Internet and developments in the media have revolutionized business communications and transactions and changed marketing for ever by allowing anyone anywhere in the world to buy online from anyone else. The range of communication methods has increased significantly as a result of technological advances and entrepreneurialism. The growth in social networking has transformed communications. Sometimes blogging is well informed and sometimes it is completely incorrect and often malicious, but it strongly influences consumer purchasing and usage decisions. The technology advances were expected to level the playing field between small and large firms so that the most innovative firms, small or large, would become the winners. It was thought that the technologists rather than the marketers would be in control. In reality consumers have become more sophisticated in their use of technology and media, and used it to their advantage. As a result consumers are increasingly in control of events and so even greater customer insights are needed and marketing expertise has never been more vital. Management Challenge 12.2 provides one example of how the current generation of teenagers might be consuming media.

At the start of the chapter we proposed the idea that technology is an enabler, and Hamill and Stevenson (2003) suggest that technology facilitates cost-effective relationship building, but does not automatically achieve a customer-focused approach. Ritter and Walter (2006) examine the impact of information technology on customer relationships in the B2B context. They conclude that while IT competence can replace parts of relationship management, it cannot do so totally.

Technology has shifted the balance of power from suppliers to customers. Consequently, customer dominance must be accepted and those arrogant firms that take customers for granted will suffer. Organizations must adopt a customer-led approach in order to achieve sustainability. This means that they must develop innovative approaches to sales, marketing and overall corporate strategy that are driven by what customers need and want.

The objective of being customer-led is to identify, acquire, retain and grow 'quality' customers. Nykamp (2001) suggests that organizations must achieve competitive differentiation by building impermeable customer relationships and the challenge is to use the interactive power of the Internet to facilitate this by helping the organization to build close one-to-one relationships with their most valuable and growable customers.

Many firms have recognized the need to be customer-led and have responded by implementing sophisticated and expensive customer relationship management systems. Hamill and Stevenson suggest that many of these systems have failed to produce the expected return because they have been technology driven rather than customer-led. The term CRM has been hijacked by software vendors promising 'out-of-the-box' solutions to complex strategic, organizational and human resources problems. They claim that technology has a part to play but customer-led is not about software, database marketing, loyalty programmes, customer bribes or hard selling. It is about building strong one-to-one relationships with

MANAGEMENT CHALLENGE 12.2

How teenagers consume media

When Morgan Stanley in the UK asked Matthew Robson, a 15 year old schoolboy to write a report on how he and his friends consume media they were surprised to see the results. We have included some of the points made here to illustrate some differences between the generations and prompt a discussion about how teenagers consume media in different countries. The changing preferences for media consumption have major implications for marketers to this segment now and in the future, and to those that wish to communicate with them, one example discussed is the end of chapter case study.

Teenagers do not regularly listen to music on the radio and instead rely on online sites streaming music for free. They prefer sites that allow users to listen to their choice rather than that of the radio presenter. They watch TV selectively, boys generally watch more during the football season and choose regular programmes, such as soap operas, but they have less time available to watch TV. Services that allow you to watch what you want are more popular and teenagers switch to other channels or do something else while the adverts are running. Teenagers cannot be bothered to read newspapers, except free sheets while travelling and they only like compact size papers, which are easier to read.

The Wii has increased the interest in gaming of girls and younger players, and teenagers tend to game in longer sessions over one hour, rather than in short bursts. Connection to the Internet allows voice chat between users for free over the console, which teenagers prefer, whereas they would be unwilling to pay to use the phone.

Teenagers are heavily active on social networking sites, with the most common being Facebook, which allows wide scale interactions. Teenagers do not use Twitter although most sign up to the service. They would prefer to text friends rather than tweet, which they see as pointless as no-one views their profiles. They use YouTube to watch videos and use it as a background music player. Google is the favoured search tool.

While teenagers enjoy and support viral marketing because of the often humorous and interesting content, they see website ads (pop ups and banners) as irritating, annoying and pointless.

Teenagers listen to a lot of music while doing something else but are reluctant to pay for it and instead download illegally. They prefer to have a 'hard copy' of the music they like in order to share it as they wish. iTunes is unpopular with many because of the cost. Going to the cinema is common among younger teens 13–14, not because of the film, but because of the opportunity to get together with friends, but when they can no longer go to the cinema at children's prices it becomes less popular.

Almost all – 99 per cent – teenagers have a mobile phone on pay-as-you go and usually only use the phone for texting and calling. Other features are considered too expensive, such as Internet features and mobile email – as they can use the PC when they get home. They use mobile phones to send songs and videos even when it is illegal. Every teenager has access to a basic computer with Internet and has Microsoft Office installed to help them do their homework, but most do not have sophisticated computers.

They like anything with a touch screen, phones with large capacities for music, portable devices and really big TVs. They don't like anything with wires, clunky phones and devices with a short battery life.

Question

1 What patterns of media consumption by teenagers do you detect and how do these differ between cultures and countries?

References: M. Robson, 'Teenager causes City sensation with research on media', *Daily Telegraph*, 13 July 2009.

quality customers, achieving customer loyalty, maximizing customer lifetime earnings and re-engineering the firm towards satisfying the needs of 'quality' customers on a customized and personalized basis. The most convincing reason for a customer to buy from any company in the world is that they are totally satisfied, have no reason to complain about the service they receive and are surprised and delighted by some of the firm's innovative actions. Illustration 12.8 discusses the future of gaming and recognizes the value of technological advances, but then asks whether culture still affects success in global markets.

To deliver this requires a more fundamental reinvention of the firm if it wishes to really succeed in the future. A new mindset is needed together with an innovative approach to the strategy. In practice firms will need to:

- Focus not on markets but on quality customers from anywhere in the world. By quality customers it is the strategically significant, most valuable and 'growable' customers that should be given the highest priority. The suggestion is that, over time, firms have moved from supplying markets to serving market segments, and are now focusing on serving individual customers one at a time.

- Focus on one-to-one relationships. To do this firms must learn about customers and deliver personalized and customized products, services and support in order to maximize the up- and cross-selling opportunities. The implications of this are that at one level firms must be sensitive to the customer's business and social culture and the customer's business dynamics. At another level the firm must be able to form supply and value chain alliances that enable the up- and cross-selling to be developed for the customer's benefit.

- Increasing both lifetime and short-term revenue from customers. Firms must focus on the delivery of exceptional value by developing an effective worldwide supply chain, building ever-closer relationships both with customers and partners and finding ways to erect barriers to entry by competitor firms.

- Win-win. The long-term business relationships must be valuable for both supplier and provider and so long-term value for the customer and firm must be maximized. This could require some compromises by both parties to achieve this.

- Integrated and coordinated approach. The success of a customer-led relationship building approach is that it requires commitment at all levels, creating, communicating and delivering value. For all businesses, but particularly global businesses, this is clearly a major challenge.

Most firms would claim to be customer led, but the real test for them is whether they would be willing to change their strategy radically because of the trends that are being perceived in the marketplace. Lindstrom and Seybold (2003) reports on research that suggests that marketing strategies in the future may need to be changed radically in order to be customer led. Very young, computer literate child consumers have a large influence on family purchasing decisions. They are extremely well-informed through online networking sites that influence their behaviour. It is necessary to ask just how far firms should change their international marketing strategy to respond to these changes.

Sustainability and corporate social responsibility

Sustainability is the topic of ever more intense public attention and debate, and we have discussed various aspects of sustainability and corporate social responsibility in this book. Much of the public debate has centred on the green environment, reduction in the consumption of the world's non-renewable energy and other resources, the dumping of waste and pollution of the landscape and sea, and so on. It is becoming increasingly important for global firms to address these issues responsibly as they will affect the reputation of the company and its brand value. However, for some firms the failure to secure viable energy and resources, minimize waste and develop a sustainable, competitive cost base they will put at risk the future of the business. Technological solutions from renewable sources of energy, recycling and using recycled components, and improved processes are essential.

Corporate Social Responsibility covers many more areas from treating staff well and paying them a living wage, not using child labour, paying suppliers a fair price, treating customers fairly to adopting fair competition practices, not resorting to bribery, fraud or other illegal practices. Berns *et al.* (2009)

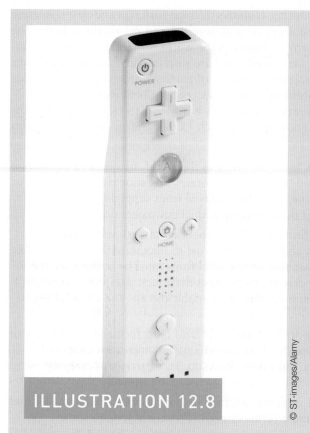

ILLUSTRATION 12.8

© ST-images/Alamy

The future of gaming

For years gaming was simply a digital extension of traditional arcade shooting and driving games, a solitary, immature pursuit in which the player huddled over a control pad furiously pressing buttons. In 2006 the Nintendo Wii changed all that, transforming gaming into a fun form of entertainment for family and friends. Using motion sensor controllers to control the on screen action Wii introduced a wide range of consumer segments, female as well as male, old as well as young to 'casual' video games.

By using a high tech camera Microsoft's Kinect moved gaming to a higher technology level, more accurate and responsive than Wii, allowing players to use their whole body to play the game, recognizing players in multi-play games and using gestures and voice to control menus.

By removing the physical 'barriers' of keyboards, controllers and even touch screen the technology enables real connection between players and on-screen images, for example, allowing in 'Kinectimals' a child to bond with an animal by stoking it. The so called 'gesture interfaces' that allow people to operate their phones or computers with intuitive physical commands also demonstrate the future for controlling TV or browsing media.

The success of each generation of gaming devices depends not just on the hardware but the range and interest of the games available to consumers from different cultures too. The success of the Wii was attributed to the large range of games that were available to keep people hooked.

The challenges of international marketing in gaming are interesting because it might be assumed that, while the technology might be considered 'culturally neutral', cultural differences will create preferences in the nature of the games. Poplak (2010) explains Hezbollah developed a video game called 'Special Force' as an alternative to western games in which Arabs and Muslims are frequently portrayed as terrorists. The games were meant to show the problems of American games and to be a recruitment tool. From his experiences and research in 30 cities in the Muslim world Poplak concludes that most kids don't care whether they are the American or Bangladeshi hero, so long as they get to blow the heads off the bad guys, whatever religion, creed or species they are.

In India consumers are embracing gaming through social networking too. Ibibo, one of the challengers to Facebook in India believes that social gaming is the way to build relationships between friends and this requires an understanding of the local culture. One of the games is 'The great Indian Parking Wars' where users collect points by parking legally or illegally and removing idle cows. Ibibo users can make micro payments for the virtual currency by texting from their mobile phones to buy virtual tractors, fertilisers and even mini skirts that are important for success in gaming.

Question

1 How important is cultural adaptation and technological advances in winning over consumers of gaming?

References: *Economist* (2010) 'Five Things: The Sheik's Batmobile', 2 September. Poplak, R. (2010) *The Sheik's Batmobile: In Pursuit of American Pop Culture in the Muslim World*, Soft Skull Press. Chibber, K. (2010) 'The Great Indian Parking Wars', BBC News Online, 14 October.

found from a survey of 50 global thought leaders that the barriers that impede decisive corporate action include:

- a lack of understanding of what sustainability is and means to the enterprise;
- difficulty modelling the business case; and
- flaws in execution after a plan has been developed.

The growing awareness of consumers of the issues and their ability to access information about company practices worldwide means that more firms will come under pressure to provide answers. The Gulf of Mexico oil spill nearly caused the collapse of one of the largest companies in the world, BP, so all companies will have to address these issues. Along with technological advances, marketing will need to provide the answers.

SUMMARY

- Technology is creating new market opportunities and continually changing the way business is done in international markets. New technology provides solutions to solve old problems but also sets new challenges for international marketing management. Firms will under perform or even fail if they are not able to exploit the global opportunities offered by the new technology or if they take the wrong decisions about how new technology might affect their industry sector.

- Consumer e-marketing, and especially innovative business models attract the interest of global consumers and facilitate new routes to market. Consumers are enthusiastically embracing new ways of communicating, through mobile devices and social media, collecting information about products and services, sharing opinions and making purchase and usage decisions.

- Although the Internet and advances in telecommunications have had the most dramatic effect on international marketing, other technologies and software to support integrated marketing solutions, particularly in B2B marketing, have been part of this change. For example, e-procurement through e-hubs enables purchasing to be more efficiently managed worldwide.

- Greater cooperation because of improvements in communication and the ease of information sharing make supply chains more effective. However, excess capacity and increased competition mean that the power in the supply chain is increasingly favouring the customer.

- Technology will provide some of the solutions to achieve sustainability of resources and strategies, and companies will have to take a more responsible attitude to the green environment but so too, they will have to adopt greater corporate social responsibility as communications increasingly enable the community to scrutinize their actions.

- Because of this, firms will need to work ever harder to find new customers, gain deeper insights about the behaviour and opinions of different global segments and retain the loyalty of existing customers. Their international marketing strategies will have to be customer led to develop compelling added value offers.

KEYWORDS

Internet	Information technology	Knowledge management
Enabling technologies	Industry-specific hubs	Customer relationship management
E-commerce	Function-specific hubs	Mass customize
Websites	Supply chain management	Legislation
Business to business marketing	E-procurement	Customer-led
Business to consumer marketing	Online auction	

© Anthony Brown, iStockphoto.com

CASE STUDY

Which way forward for global broadcasting

During the cold war the state broadcasters had big budgets to fight propaganda wars about the virtues and vices of capitalism and communism. Powerful short wave transmission was expensive and big and rich countries fought over frequencies. The landscape has now changed drastically, however, as new technology has cut costs and there are few barriers to market entry. Customers increasingly have access to the Internet, satellite and fibre optic cable broadcasting, so hugely expanding their choice of programmes. Of the six taxpayer-financed US broadcasters that measure their reach, five see a decline. The BBC World Service has lost eight million viewers and listeners. Inevitably tax payer funding will be less freely available to the state owned broadcasters if they are less effective than the private sector firms, and so the decline might well accelerate.

In the past a favourite Soviet tactic was to jam the broadcasts and now a similar tactic, carried out in some countries, is preventing websites from including material that might not be acceptable. Google, for example, has had to rethink its strategy in China. However, the old international broadcasters have plenty of solutions to deal with censorship, or banning reporters. For example, the BBC used clandestine and surrogate news gathering in Zimbabwe from where they were banned. More subtle pressure is also now applied because of the change to rebroadcasting on local FM networks. Voice of America's Russian service is carried by only one of the 85 domestic stations that carried it seven years ago and the BBC Arabic service to northern Sudan was shut down.

The bigger problem is competition. In the last four years China, France, Iran, Japan and Qatar have launched English-language TV news channels. China's commitment of over $7 billion to international news is more than 15 times the annual budget of the BBC, and it broadcasts in more languages than any other state backed organization. China radio has doubled its short wave output, while the BBC has abandoned short wave broadcasts in Latin America, North America and most of Europe. Voice of America has cut its short wave broadcast frequencies by 24 per cent.

Short wave listeners tend to be older, poorer and more rural listeners, but the main battle is for the opinion formers, who mainly consume media from satellite and the Internet. Here Al Jazeera, supported by the Emir of Qatar, has been the winner, dominating the Middle East. Recent research in six countries found that 39 per cent watched it more than any other channel, while the figure was 1 per cent for Alhurra, the well funded, US channel. Al Jazeera now has 80 offices, often small, but adequate for news gathering, that use small, lightweight, modern digital cameras. It is established in Asia and has poured resources into tough countries, such as Zimbabwe. Perhaps surprisingly it is the preferred channel of US military in Afghanistan. There is also huge growth in small local channels in poor countries, especially in Africa. In 20 years TV channels in Kenya have grown from one state-owned service to 20 broadcasters and 80 licensed radio stations.

The nature of broadcasting and media consumption is changing even further, however. While Voice of America has been virtually driven out of Russia, 2.3 million of its videos were watched in one month on YouTube. Fewer customers are prepared to accept formal broadcasting formats and prefer to select what they want to watch themselves. Internet audiences are busier and hurried, and access is still patchy. In Kenya Internet access is only 10 per cent. German broadcaster, Deutsche Welle is responding to this by trying to provide a dependable rather than a loud, mass market voice, concentrating on the urban elite segment of the audience.

There are some major decisions to be made by the big state owned broadcasters, particularly as, under continual criticism from the private sector, their generous state funding may seem unfair. For example, the three biggest radio stations in Afghanistan are run by the BBC. The local competitors complain these outsiders compete unfairly, lure away staff with promises of higher salaries and visas to the west. The big broadcasters have for a long time promoted the idea of freedom on their channels but the consequences may not always be palatable for them.

Questions

1 Identify the technology changes, cross cultural consumer preferences and the key trends affecting the broadcasting market.

2 Selecting a broadcaster of your choice, prepare an outline strategy that will provide the international customer segments with the services that they require using their preferred technologies.

References: 'Waves in the web', *The Economist*, 12 August 2010.

DISCUSSION QUESTIONS

1 The fundamental concerns of international marketing strategy analysis, development and implementation are to add stakeholder value and remove unnecessary costs. How can innovation in information and communications technology assist in this process of global consumer marketing?

2 For a company providing international consultancy to major multinationals in the use of renewable energy identify the key areas for decision-making in the marketing process.

3 How might mobile computing change international marketing?

4 Write a report to the chief executive of a small company supplying gaming software to be used by the global gaming hardware brands, analyzing the use of social and business networking sites in marketing the business.

5 As the marketing manager of a global, fast moving consumer goods company of your choice identify the key decisions that will be needed to ensure the company has a sustainable future.

REFERENCES

1. Berns, M., Townend, A., Khayat, Z., Balagopal, B., Reeves, M., Hopkins, M.S. and Krushwitz, N. (2009) 'The business of sustainability, what it means to managers now', *MIT Sloan Management Review*, Fall, 51 (1): 20–26.

2. Boston Consulting Group (2010a) 'What's next for alternative energy', available at: www.bcg.com.

3. Boston Consulting Group (2010b) 'The Connected Kingdom: How the Internet Is Transforming the UK Economy', accessed at: www.bcg.com, 28 October.

4. Chaffey, D., Mayer, R., Johnston, K. and Ellis-Chadwick, F. (2006) *Internet marketing*, FT Prentice Hall.

5. Egol, M., Clyde, A., and Rangan, K. (2010) 'The new consumer frugality', www.strategy+business.com, 15 March.

6. Hagiu, A. and Yoffie, D.B. (2009) 'What's your Google strategy', *Harvard Business Review*, April, 87 (4): 74–81.

7. Hamill, J. and Stevenson, A. (2003) 'Customer-led strategic Internet marketing', in S. Hart (ed.), *Marketing changes*, Thomson Learning.

8. Hoffman, K.D. (2003) 'Services marketing', in *Marketing Best Practice*, Thomson Learning.

9. Javalgi, R., Radulovich, L.P., Pendelton, G. and Scherer, R.F. (2005) 'Sustainable competitive advantage of internet firms: a strategic framework and implications for global marketers', *International Marketing Review*, 22 (6): 658–72.

10. Kaplan, S. and Sawhney, M. (2000) 'E-hubs: the new B2B marketplaces', *Harvard Business Review*, 78 (3): 97–103.

11. Lindgren, J.H.E. (2003) 'Marketing', in *Marketing best practice*, Thomson Learning.

12. Lindstrom, M. and Seybold, P. (2003) *BRAND child*, Kogan Page.

13. Nykamp, M. (2001) *The customer differential*, AMACOM.

14. Ofek, E. and Wathieu, L. (2010) 'Are you ignoring trends that could shake up your business?' *Harvard Business Review*, July/August 2010, 88 (7/8): 124–131.

15. Poplak, R. (2010) '*The Sheikh's Batmobile: In Pursuit of American Pop Culture in the Muslim World*', Soft Skull Press.

16. Ritter, T. and Walter, A. (2006) 'Matching high-tech and high-touch in supplier-customer relationships', *European Journal of Marketing*, 40 (3/4): 292–310.

17. Snyder, D.P. (2005) 'Extra-Preneurship', *Futurist*, 39 (4): 47–53.

18. Timmers, P. (1999) *Electronic commerce strategies and models for business to business trading*, Wiley.

19. Wenyu, D., Boonghee, Y. and Ma, L. (2003) 'consumer patronage of ethnic portals', *International marketing Review*, 20 (6): 661–77.

20. World Economic Forum (2009) 'The Africa Competitiveness Report 2009', available at: www.weforum.org.

21. Zugelder, M.T., Flaherty, T.B. and Johnson, J.P. (2000) 'Legal issues associated with international Internet marketing', *International Marketing Review*, 17 (3).

INTERNATIONAL MARKETING PLANNING: IMPLEMENTATION, CONTROL AND EVALUATION

Introduction

In the previous two special focus sections on planning we explored the dimensions of analysis and strategy development. We now turn to the implementation of the plan through the application of the marketing mix that has been covered in the chapters in Part 3. In practice, of course, some of the content of the previous chapters needs to be revisited because there is no clear distinction between what might be considered strategy development and implementation. This is especially true of product and service strategy, where many decisions can be regarded as operational, and market entry, where many decisions are closely associated with distribution.

The starting point for implementation is planning the international marketing mix. This includes completing the product and service plan and preparing communications, distribution and pricing plans. The plan should explain how relationships with key partners can be built and managed within the supply chain, how customer relationships can be developed and how technology can be used to facilitate the firm's international marketing plan implementation.

The success of the implementation plan is dependent on the planning ability, management capability and motivation and effectiveness of the firm's staff. The global market environment is constantly changing and competition from existing and new companies is intensifying. As we saw in ILA 2, while organizations may perceive themselves to have competitive advantage, such as a new product idea, low cost manufacturing or a strong brand, this can be quickly eroded by a new competitor, so the key to successful implementation is having competitive capability – the ability to continuously compete internationally – no matter what challenges are faced. In the implementation stage this means being able to quickly assess situations, develop innovative solutions, make strategic decisions when necessary and implement new plans.

Management need to anticipate and plan for potential problems that might arise in managing the implementation stage. Of course, these problems may well originate in topics that were considered in the first two parts of the book. We also consider how to establish appropriate performance standards and measurement techniques that can be used to maintain control over the plan and the evaluation that will enable corrective action to be taken whenever the firm's performance deviates from the plan (as it surely will).

In this activity the focus is on developing the skills of decision-making in a local business unit at an operational level, while still keeping in mind the implication of the firm's global strategy on these local decisions.

Learning Objectives

On completing this activity you should be able to:

- Appreciate the opportunities for growth in an international business sector and how they are influenced by the strategy implementation
- Use appropriate concepts and an analysis of market factors to develop marketing mix implementation strategies
- Appreciate the benefit of developing better customer relationship management
- Identify the methods that should be used for the management and control of the business

The scenario: Multinational organizations

This integrative learning activity can be applied to any multinational organization, but we have chosen to provide a short case study of Yum Brands, which is the largest restaurant business in the world, slightly ahead of McDonalds. The company has reached an interesting point in its history as its growth opportunities now exist in emerging rather than traditional markets. In developed countries the debate about healthy eating has intensified and in emerging markets, as the demand grows for branded fast food, so local competitors have begun to emerge too. A lot of information and comment is available online and in the media to support the activity and so the information presented is there merely to present the scenario to start your study.

Yum brands – eating into new markets

Yum brands is the world's largest restaurant group with 37 000 restaurants in 110 countries with revenues of over $11billion, followed by McDonald's and Subway each with 32 000, Starbucks with 17 000 and Burger King with 12 000.

In October 1997, Yum! Brands was spun off as Tricon Global Restaurants, Inc from PepsiCo, which owned and franchised the KFC, Pizza Hut and Taco Bell brands worldwide. The aim was to build brands through running restaurants in three divisions, the US, China and Yum Restaurants International (YRI) which develops business in over 110 countries. Yum Brands spends over $500 million globally on marketing.

Yum US

Until recently the US division provided all the profits for the company from the 17 500 restaurants carrying the KFC, Pizza Hut, Taco Bell, A&W and Long John Silver's brands, but now there is a decline in sales. Yum's competitors are seeing similar patterns. McDonalds gets 75 per cent of revenues from the US and Europe but is seeing a decline in same store sales in these regions. Starbucks has 75 per cent of its stores in the US and has seen same store sales decline of 5 per cent.

Yum China

KFC was the first quick service restaurant chain to enter China in 1987. It is still the market leader with 3000 units in 650 cities, and the fastest growing, opening 500 new KFC restaurants in 2010. The development of the Chinese market has been much faster than the company anticipated, and is due to the establishment of an effective and efficient supply chain and distribution

infrastructure, building a strong network of partners in the process. The Chinese restaurants are 95 per cent owned by the company and each requires on average a cash investment of over $500 000 which can be repaid out of profits in two to three years.

The market is expected to expand fast as the middle class is forecast to grow from 300 million to 800 million in 25 years. As incomes grow Yum China will further exploit its other brands and meal formats, such as Pizza Hut, the leading casual dining and pizza delivery brand.

Yum Restaurant International (YRI)

Yum Restaurant International has 14 000 units in 110 countries, having opened 898 new restaurants in 2009 across six continents, making it the ninth year of opening over 700 restaurants. YRI is mainly a franchise driven model with 1000 franchisees opening 90 per cent of new restaurants. Sales are split: Europe 30 per cent, Asia 27 per cent, Americas, 19 per cent, Middle East/South Africa 13 per cent and Australia/New Zealand 11 per cent.

YRI divides its markets into three regions: Developing; developed – underpenetrated (mainly France and Germany); and developed – established. Future growth in both outlets and profitability will come from the developing and the underpenetrated developed markets.

In the developing world the aim of YRI will be to increase its lead in existing markets, enter new markets and increase its business particularly in India and Russia, where both countries will see a growing middle class. India and Russia offer massive market potential as both countries are attracted to western brands. Both have well established local infrastructure and generate high returns on investment. India is a huge consuming economy on the scale of China, with a $1 trillion GDP and eating out market of $64 billion.

In the developed world (underpenetrated) the aim must be to narrow the gap against the competition, particularly in France and Germany where the company has huge potential, given that at the end 2009 KFC had 160 units whereas McDonald's had in excess of 2500 units.

In the developed world (established) the aim will be to capture the remaining development potential, and improve margins. Yum's developing markets are significantly underpenetrated both in terms of current spending power and the potential growth of competition.

Given that Yum brands needs to build the loyalty of the next generation of consumers it must make decisions on the best ways to communicate with them. The traditional model of promotion using TV advertising at the heart of the strategy will not be enough to win over these consumers.

In the media there has been considerable discussion about the fast food operators' approach to sustainability and corporate social responsibility, including topics ranging from encouraging child obesity, ill treatment of staff, overuse of packaging, questionable sourcing of food products and cultural insensitivity. Yum will have to work hard to maintain its corporate reputation.

Americana – partner or competitor?

As indicated previously, Yum uses franchisees to build its international business and we have provided some details about one such franchise operator. Americana Group began in Kuwait in 1964 with the establishment of a small trading company, which then opened its first restaurant (Wimpy) in 1970. Its main lines of business are operating food and beverage outlets, as well as manufacturing food products which find their way into millions of Middle East and North African households every day. It now operates international franchises like Hardee's, TGIF's, Krispy Kreme, KFC Costa Coffee and Pizza Hut.

It has grown into one of the largest and most successful corporations in the Middle East and North Africa region (MENA) with over 1200 outlets spanning 14 countries with over 45 000 employees and 17 factories producing its food products. Americana Group has learned through its international franchising and gained a thorough understanding of Middle Eastern tastes.

This has led it to create six of its own home-grown brands, including Chicken Tikka, Fish Market, Samadi, Maestro, Grand Café and Fusion and the company claims these to be as successful with consumers as their global counterparts.

Yum brands realizes that it has to adapt the KFC and Pizza Hut menus to local taste and is going a stage further in China by trialling a new Chinese food chain, East Dawning, to further utilize its effective distribution operation. Internationalization of its brands has not been entirely successful. Its Mexican food brand, Taco Bell, has continually tried to develop business outside the US for 30 years but the brand still only generates 3 per cent of its revenue from the international markets.

Yum must maintain its business and profitability in its traditional markets, too, and this means continuing to respond to healthier eating. To maintain the company's financial health it is looking to switch the US business from being company owned to franchise owned.

Useful websites

www.americana-group.net

www.yum.com

www.starbucks.com and

www.mcdonalds.com

References

N. Ziegelasch, J. Jackson and M. Gilligan, Yum! Brands, www.killik.co.uk, 27 September 2010.

S. Foley, The Pepsi spin-off – owner of KFC, Pizza Hut and Taco Bell – has grown so fast that it's now bigger than McDonald's. *Independent*, 14 July 2010 and other public sources.

The task

1 Critically evaluate the global marketing implementation strategy of Yum Brands, paying particular attention to whether the company is responding to the changing nature of expectations of customers and consumer purchasing behaviour in markets around the world, not forgetting that in a franchising model the company has multiple levels of customers and some powerful global and well entrenched local competitors.

2 Having identified the challenges Yum Brands faces, develop an international marketing implementation strategy in outline both for the consumer and franchisee market that both leverages and builds competitive advantage. Focus on the marketing mix implementation issues, including an assessment of the key brand, product, service and communications issues. Identify, too, the factors that will influence the pricing strategy.

3 Prepare a plan for the control, management and continuous improvement of the operations, including appropriate measurement, and outline the processes that are required to achieve sustained success. Explain particularly the key dimensions of the marketing culture that is needed and how consistent that is across the global markets.

Getting started

This section focuses on the global consumer markets but you also need to consider the importance of managing relationships with the franchisees and supply chain. You should use this case study not only to focus on the implementation issues of the strategy process but also to study in greater depth the particular issues involved in managing this service sector model.

Clearly the effective marketing of services requires an understanding of customer requirements and service expectation as well as staff motivation and management, customer relationship building and the cultural issues that underpin much of this.

Task 1 requires an analysis of the factors that have led to the growth in fast food in international markets, particularly in emerging markets over recent years and of the factors that will determine the nature of consumer purchasing in the future – and consequently how important relationship-building with global customers will be in the future. By now you should have a very good understanding of how you can access and analyze research material from libraries and online sources to complete this task. There is a huge amount of information and comment about the fast food market and the competition in the literature and business press to help you complete Tasks 2 and 3, but you must also include your own creative approaches. You require an understanding of the sector and how it differs in the markets around the world.

Customer satisfaction is very dependent on the customers' perception of the brand but also the suitability of the product in appealing to local taste and service expectations. Consequently, setting realistic customer expectations, motivating and training staff, managing the supply chain effectively and managing a cost-effective fast food service are all critical for success. Task 3 requires you to think about how you would organize and manage this on a global basis.

In completing the tasks you need to consider the issues highlighted in the following framework shown in Table III.

The way forward

Strategy development and planning is a continuous process. Having completed the tasks in this section, you will have gained a better understanding of the fast food market and the perceived value that consumer and franchisee customers are able to obtain, You should now be well informed to revisit the strategy development process.

You should return to the Part 1 planning framework earlier to review the current market environment for Yum Brands as the basis for their ongoing strategy. The most important issue is to decide where and how the firm can further build its strong global position, using an assessment of the market environment, customer demands and competitor activity. Given the fast growth of the sector you should review the firm's ambitions particularly in developing markets, and focus on the market factors in these countries and use the market information and research framework to identify further growth opportunities. You should also consider the more traditional markets that are still significant to assess the opportunities to increase market share. Finally, you might reassess the company capability and expertise that will be expected to underpin its continued expansion.

You should then return to the topics of Part 2 and again using the framework on page 25, review the firm's vision and objectives as stated on the website and decide if they are still appropriate. You should re-evaluate and restate the firm's competitive advantage and assess how this informs the international positioning of the various Yum Brands. Using the recent data available online you should assess the market entry methods used and the effectiveness of these methods in delivering the strategy.

Checklist for success

Having completed the integrative learning activities you should think about how comprehensive your work is and whether you really have addressed the fundamental issues that could well make the difference between a failing and a successful strategy. To help you do this we have identified some of the issues you should consider. Clearly you may not be able to answer these in detail because you will not have sufficient detail about the firm's operations, but you should have thought about how you would address the issues given access to the information.

Does the plan contain:

- Assumptions about the world economy and the environmental trends in the principal markets?

- Details of historical performance (sales, costs, profitability)?

- Forecasts of future performance based on (a) an extrapolation of the past, (b) alternative scenarios?

- Identified opportunities and threats?

- Analysis of the company strengths, weaknesses and future capabilities in comparison with local and international competition?

- Long-term aims and objectives and the strategies to achieve them?

- One-year marketing objectives and individual strategies (for example, budgets, brand objectives and development of personnel)?
- Country-by-country forecasts and targets?
- Country-by-country plans for all marketing activities and coordination with other functions (for example, supply chain management)?
- An explanation of how country plans will be integrated regionally or globally if appropriate? It might be useful to comment on the current structure of the company.

- A summary of the critical factors for success?
- An assessment of the likely competitor response? If your objective is to increase market share in some markets, your competitors will not simply lie down and let you take their business without fighting back!
- A contingency component for when the unexpected happens and things do not go to plan?
- A control process for feedback, evaluation and taking corrective action?

Table III Key factors to consider in evaluating the implementation of the strategy

The element of the plan	Some concepts, models and issues to be addressed
Environmental analysis	• Identify the global trends that have provided the opportunity for growth in the sector • Analyze the nature of customer needs and the nature of competition in the sector • Evaluate the firm's strategy and its regional focus
Marketing mix	• Building the corporate identity and managing the brand • Product differentiation and the three service Ps • Communication to customers and other stakeholders • Managing the delivery to achive customer satisfaction • Managing cost and the pricing strategy • The use of technology
Relationship marketing	• The methods of identifying current and potentional high value customers • Knowledge and database management • Customer relationship management
Control and management	• The organization and management structure using the **7S** framework • Internal communications with its own staff • Financial and marketing measures and controls • Performance management and improvement processes, incuding benchmarking, balanced scorecard and self-assessment and improvement • Technology-enabled systems

GLOSSARY

7S framework Framework devised by consultants McKinsey & Co for analyzing how well the organization is positioned to deliver its objectives

Acquisition A market entry strategy in which the firm invests in assets outside the home country

Adaptation Flexible approach to marketing that aims to vary the marketing mix programmes to meet the local conditions in each country market

Asian Free Trade Area (AFTA) The name of the free trade area the members ASEAN plan to complete by 2015

Association of South East Asian Nations (ASEAN) A free trade area of 580 million across Thailand, Indonesia, Singapore, Brunei, Malaysia and the Philippines, Vietnam, Myanmar, Cambodia and Laos

Attitude a complex mental state involving beliefs and feelings and values and dispositions to act in certain ways

Balance of payments a system of recording all of a country's economic transactions with the rest of the world over a period of one year

Barrier to entry Real or perceived reason why a firm might be prevented from marketing its products and services in a new market

Beliefs The psychological state in which an individual holds a proposition or premise to be true

Born global Firm that internationalizes at birth, entering a number of country markets to secure sales of (usually) high technology products and services

Brand piracy Naming a product in such a way that it confuses customers, or enables the pirate firm to sell forgeries and fake products

Branding strategies The alternative approaches to applying names (or brands) to a product and groups of products to achieved the desired positioning

Build to order When a product is scheduled and built in response to a specification and confirmed order received from a final customer

Business to business marketing Marketing products and services to other organizations

Business to consumer marketing Marketing products and services to people who will consume them

Buyer–seller relationships Collective term for the categories of relationship between a buyer and seller. These can be categorized into transactional relationships, collaborative relationships, alliances and reciprocal relationships

Category management Category Management is a retailing concept in which the total range of products sold by a retailer is broken down into discrete groups of similar or related products; these groups are known as product categories

Communications adaptation Marketing communication strategies that are flexible, allowing variation in the use of the mix between countries to meet local conditions

Communications mix Often used interchangeably with promotions mix, the Communications mix implies a broader range of uses of offline and online, interactive tools

Communications tools The range of tools a marketer can use, including personal selling, advertising, sales promotion, public relations, sponsorship and online media

Comparative advantage The advantage a nation has by being able to produce products or services more efficiently and at lower cost than a competitor nation

Comparative research Comparative research is a research methodology in the social sciences that aims to make comparisons across different countries or cultures

Consumer behaviour the behaviour of individuals when buying goods and services for their own use or for private consumption

Contract manufacture Arrangement in which a subcontractor undertakes manufacturing (or service provision) under license

Control The management responsibility for measuring performance and taking corrective action when deviation from the standards set occurs, so that the goals of the organization are achieved

Corporate identity The corporate personality demonstrated in branding and other communications to reflect the values and culture of the organization

Countertrade exchanging goods or services which are paid for, in whole or part, with other goods or services, rather than with money

Country of origin effect The perceptions and attitudes that exist towards the products or brands on the basis of their country or origin, design or manufacture

Cross-cultural dealing with or comparing two or more cultures

Cross-cultural research the conducting of a research project across a number of nations or culture groupings

Cultural identity Cultural identity is the identity of a group or culture, or of an individual as far as one is influenced by one's belonging to a group or culture

Cultural paradoxes a terms used to describe the cultural sensitivities in a market where there evidence both of the westernization of tastes and the assertion of ethnic, religious and cultural differences

Cultural sensitivity cultural sensitivity is the quality of being aware and accepting of other cultures. This is important because what seems acceptable in some countries can be rude or derogatory in others

Customer relationship management The process of storing and analyzing data relating to customers, to enable the organization to serve their needs efficiently and effectively

Customer-led Adopting marketing approaches that primarily focus on the needs and expectations of customers

Customs The overt forms of behaviour and significant events which symbolize the particularistic characteristics of a particular culture

Data mining A technique for searching large-scale databases for patterns; used mainly to find previously unknown correlations between variables that may be commercially useful

Differentiated marketing Strategy whereby a company attempts to appeal to two or more clearly defined market segments with a specific product and unique marketing strategy tailored to each separate segment

Direct channels Distribution channel in which a producer supplies or serves directly an ultimate user

Direct marketing Online or offline communication with potential consumers or business customers designed to generate a response, such as an order or request for more information

Distribution channel structures Path or 'pipeline' through which goods and services flow from vendor to the consumer. A distribution channel may include several interconnected intermediaries such as wholesalers, distributors, agents, retailers

Distributors Firms that buy and stock products from a manufacturer before adding a margin and selling them to the final customers

Doha Round Commenced 2001, the name given to the current negotiations being undertaken by members of the WTO are attempting to liberalize trading rules in a number of areas, including agricultural subsidies, textiles and clothing, services, technical barriers to trade, trade-related investments and rules of origin

Domestic purchasing International trade in which a foreign firm approaches a non-exporter, buys the product 'at the factory gate' and takes the responsibility for all aspects of exporting, without involvement from the seller

Domestically delivered or developed niche services Services that are marketed to international customers but delivered in the home country

Dumping When a manufacturer in one country exports a product to another country at a price which is either below the price it charges in its home market or is below its costs of production

E-commerce The exchange of goods, services and cash using the Internet

Economic and Monetary Union The creation of a single currency bloc within the European Union which began on 1st January 1999

Economies of scale Unit cost reductions which result from increasing total output

Effective consumer response Supply chain partnerships which work together towards making the retail sector more responsive to consumer demand and promote the removal of unnecessary costs from the supply chain

Elastic demand Demand for a product that changes substantially in response to small changes in price; when demand is elastic, a small decrease in price may substantially increase total revenues

Electronic commerce Exchange of goods and services using the Internet or other online network

Electronic data interchange Electronic Data Interchange (EDI) refers to the structured transmission of data between organizations by electronic means It is used to transfer electronic documents from one computer system to another, i.e. from one trading partner to another trading partner

Emerging economies Emerging markets are nations with social or business activity in the process of rapid growth and industrialization

Enabling technologies The use of a variety of largely integrated technologies that facilitate fast and effective international marketing processes

Enculturation Enculturation is the process by which a person learns the requirements of the culture by which he or she is surrounded

E-procurement The use of the Internet or other online services to manage the purchasing and delivery of services and products

Ethical challenges challenge of setting the ethical values in international marketing strategies and then driving those through long distribution channels across geographical markets with different ethical values

Ethnocentric centred on a specific ethnic group, usually one's own

Euro zone The eurozone, officially the euro area, is an economic and monetary union (EMU) of 16 European Union (EU) member states which have adopted the euro currency as their sole legal tender

European Union an international organization of European countries formed after World War II to reduce trade barriers and increase cooperation among its members

Exchange rate rate of exchange: the charge for exchanging currency of one country for currency of another

Exchange Rate Mechanism The European Exchange Rate Mechanism, ERM, was a system introduced by the European Community in March 1979, as part of the European Monetary System (EMS), to reduce exchange rate variability and achieve monetary stability in Europe, in preparation for Economic and Monetary Union

Exchange rate risk the potential to lose money because of a change in the exchange rate

Existing markets product/service markets where customers demands are served from a number of suppliers and the infrastructure to support the market is established

Export administration the management of the processes that allow an export transaction to take place

Export houses (also Export management Companies) Specialist firms that act as the export department for a range of companies and take on the role and responsibilities that would normally be done by those companies

Export marketing marketing of goods and/or services across national/political boundaries

Export processing zone Designated area or region where firms can import duty-free as long as the imports are used as inputs into the production of exports

Exporting Selling abroad products produced in the home country, typically without significant adaptation to foreign market needs

Failures of communications When the recipient does not receive the marketing messages as intended

Fixed production cost Costs of production that are fixed and unrelated to the volume of production

Foreign currency any currency that is in use in a foreign country, but not in one's own

Foreign market channels channels of distribution within countries outside a firms domestic operations

Franchising A contractual arrangement whereby a parent company (the franchisor) allows another firm (the franchisee) to operate a business that it has developed in return for a fee, provided that it adheres to the stated policies and practices

Free Trade Area of the Americas Scheme to unite all free economies (excluding Cuba) of the Western Hemisphere, by eliminating tariffs and employing common investment and trade rules among the 34 member countries by 2005

Function-specific hubs Electronic market places where buyers and sellers meet using the Internet to trade in business services, such as HR services or business process management

Generic marketing strategies Marketing strategies that can be applied to all market contexts, based on segmentation, targeting and positioning and underpinned by Porter's generic growth strategies (cost leadership, focus and differentiation)

Geocentric Having the earth as the centre

Global appeal The attraction of certain products and services to a global customer segment

Global brand A brand that has a similar name, similar distinctive image and positioning around the world

Global marketing The process of conceptualizing and then conveying a final product or service worldwide with the hopes of reaching the international marketing community

Global presence Ensuring that the company has assets and operations located in all (major) country markets

Global reach The ability of the marketing efforts of the firm to connect with customers around the world, where appropriate using third parties

Global sourcing The process of arranging goods and services to be supplied irrespective of geographic location

Globalization The process of progressing towards trading in all major regions and most country markets

Grey marketing the trade of a commodity through distribution channels which, while legal, are unofficial, unauthorized or unintended by the original manufacturer

Gross national income National income plus capital consumption allowance

Hard currency A currency that is not likely to depreciate suddenly in value

Heterogeneity Because services are delivered and received by individual people the concept suggests that each interaction will be unique

High-context cultures Cultures in which the context is at least as important as what is actually said

Incipient markets markets where economic conditions suggest a market may develop but the market as yet does not exist

Indirect channels the selling and distribution of products to customers through intermediaries such as wholesalers, distributors, agents, dealers or retailers

Indirect exporting Market entry methods in which firms commit few resources to international marketing and largely rely on third parties to build their international business

Individualism Individualism is the moral stance, political philosophy, ideology or social outlook that stresses the moral worth of the individual

Industry-specific hubs Electronic market places where buyers and sellers meet using the Internet to trade components and services required in particular industries, such as aerospace manufacture

Inelastic demand The demand that exists when price changes do not result in significant changes in the quantity of a product demanded

Information technology The organization's management process for creating, storing, exchanging and using information

Inseparability In the marketing of services, the service is created, delivered and consumed at the same point whereas in product there is usually separation between manufacture and consumption

Intangibility Whereas products are physical entities, services are characterized by being intangible – they cannot be touched, smelled or seen

Integrated supply chain The optimization and control of the supply chain network of suppliers, factories, warehouses, distribution centres and retailers through which materials are acquired, transformed and delivered to the customer

Interactive customer marketing Ability to address an individual and the ability to gather and remember the response of that individual leading to the ability to address the individual once more in a way that takes into account his or her unique response

Interactive shopping Allow the consumer to play an active role in the selection and customization of his/her order

Internal cost structures Cost elements that correspond to a specific internal operations of a company

International branding A brand that is known in a region of the world or in a cluster of countries

International Development Association An agency of the United Nations affiliated with the World Bank

International manager A member of staff with the responsibility of managing across country borders

International marketing The process of planning and conducting transactions across national borders to create exchanges that satisfy the objectives of individuals and organizations

International Monetary Fund A United Nations agency to promote trade by increasing the exchange stability of the major currencies

International niche marketing Marketing a differentiated product or service to different countries, usually to a single customer segment (a group of customers with a distinctive, common characteristic)

International product life cycle A concept that enables the firm to describe the stages (introduction, growth, maturity, decline) that its product portfolio has attained in different country markets

International product offer The bundle of benefits for international customers that are presented in the total product 'package'

International product portfolio The firm's chosen range of products and services that provide a complete and satisfactory offer to customers

International trade International trade is exchange of capital, goods and services across international borders or territories. It refers to exports of goods and services by a firm to a foreign-based buyer (importer). In most countries, it represents a significant share of gross domestic product

Internationalization Pursuit of market opportunities outside the home country

Internet The network of computers that enable digital files, such as emails to be sent

Joint ventures A market entry approach whereby two or more companies share ownership of a newly created firm

Knowledge management Strategies and practices used by organizations to identify, share and enable adoption of the insights and experiences, that constitute knowledge

Latent markets A group of people who have been identified as potential consumers of a product that does not yet exist

Learning curve A learning curve is a line graph displaying opportunities across the x-axis, and a measure of performance along the y-axis

Legislation The legal framework enacted by governing bodies that determines how business can be carried out. The Internet is subject to the laws of many governing bodies

Less developed economies The name given to a country which, according to the United Nations, exhibits the lowest indicators of socioeconomic development, with the lowest Human Development Index ratings of all countries in the world

Licensing A market entry strategy in which a firm makes assets, such as an image or know how, available to another firm in exchange for royalties

Logistics The management of the flow of goods, information and other resources, including energy and people, between the point of origin and the point of consumption in order to meet the requirements of consumers

Logistics or distribution strategy Management's plan for moving products to intermediaries and final customers

Low-context cultures Are those where people are more psychologically distant so that information needs to be explicit if members are to understand it

Management contracts Service projects undertaken by partner firms in conjunction with a supplier, typically of major infrastructure installations

Marginal cost pricing The outcome of perfectly competitive markets in which the price of each good is equal to its marginal cost

Marginal costing An accounting technique whereby the effect on costs of a small increment or decrease in output may be estimated. Assuming that the change in output does not affect the elements comprising fixed costs, the marginal cost will be the variable cost per unit of output

Market access The opportunity for firms to enter sectors, from which they were previously barred

Market concentrators Typically smaller firms that focus their internationalization on a small number of geographic markets

Market entry The approach that a firm uses to pursue market opportunities outside its home market

Market expanders Typically larger firms that focus their internationalization on a large number of geographic markets

Market involvement The degree to which a firm commits resources to a specific market, enabling it to directly control its marketing activities, rather than rely on third parties

Market-oriented pricing Determining the initial price of a product by comparison with competitors' prices

Market profile analysis An analysis that draws a marketing profile of a country

Market segmentation A market segment is a sub-set of a market made up of people or organizations sharing one or more characteristics that cause them to demand similar product and/or services based on qualities of those products such as price or function

Marketing information A system in which marketing information is formally gathered, stored, analyzed and distributed to managers in accord with their informational needs on a regular basis

Marketing research Research that gathers and analyzes information about the moving of good or services from producer to consumer

Mass customization The use of flexible computer-aided manufacturing systems to produce custom output

Mass customize The use of flexible computer-aided manufacturing and service systems to produce output that is designed to meet the individual requirements of the customer

Mercosur Regional common southern market integrated by Argentina, Brazil, Paraguay and Uruguay

Mergers of equals Firms with similar market power merge their operations in the belief that to succeed globally, scale advantages are required

Multi-country study A market research study that is carried out across a number of countries

Multinational enterprise An international or transnational enterprise which has productive capacity in several countries

Multimedia technology The knowledge and use of tools, techniques, systems or methods of organization of media and/or content that uses a combination of different content forms

Network A collection of individuals that are willing to share information

New product development The process of ensuring that new products and services are created to meet changing customer needs, and replace those that are no longer satisfactory

Next eleven The Next Eleven (or N 11) are eleven countries identified as having the potential to become among the world's largest economies in the 21st century

Non-tariff barriers Trade barriers that restrict imports but are not in the usual form of a tariff

Non-verbal communication Gestures, body language, facial expression, sign language are all ways of communicating without the spoken word

North American Free Trade Area North American Free Trade Area, formed between Canada, Mexico and the United States of America

Omnibus surveys A survey covering a number of topics, usually for different clients. The samples tend to be nationally representative and composed of types of people for which there is a general demand

Online auction Participants are able to bid to purchase products and services using the Internet

Online databases An electronic collection of information

Open market A competitive market where buyers and sellers can operate without restrictions

Organization structure Explanation of how tasks are allocated, activities co-ordinated and staff supervized in the delivery of the organization's strategy

Outsource Obtaining supplies or services from another firm (typically in a lower cost country), rather than carrying out the work within the firm

Pareto Law Also known as the 80–20 rule, states that for many events, 80 per cent of the effects come from 20 per cent of the causes. In marketing, 80 per cent of the sales often come from 20 per cent of the customers

Perception of risk The subjective judgment that people make about the characteristics and severity of a risk

Perishability Services cannot be stored and, hence, if an opportunity for a sale is missed, then it is lost for ever

Piggybacking A market entry approach based on riding on the back of an already successful international marketer by persuading the firm to carry non-competing products

Piracy A contemporary security concern for shipping; annual cargo crime losses are estimated at $30–50 billion internationally

Polycentric Having many centres, especially centres of authority or control

Price coordination The attempt to co-ordinate prices across dispersed geographical markets with the objective of achieving a consistent pricing policy across those markets

Price standardization Setting a standard, identical price in all markets, regardless of whether they are foreign or domestic

Price transparency The accessibility of information on the order flow for a particular stock, allowing knowledge of the quantities of stock being offered and the bids at the various price levels

Primary data Data observed or collected directly from first-hand experience

Product and service differentiation The process of distinguishing a product or service offering from competitive offerings to make it more attractive to a particular target market

Product strategies The approach adopted to selection and positioning of products and services, and the marketing support provided to satisfy customer needs

Production costs The cost-of-production theory of value is the theory that the price of an object or condition is determined by the sum of the cost of the resources that went into making it. The cost can compose any of the factors of production (including labour, capital or land) and taxation

Promotional mix The mix of communications tools used to persuade customers to buy and use products or services

Pull strategy Pull strategies involve promoting the product or service to the intended consumer, who will demand supplies from the intermediaries

Purchasing power parity The situation where the exchange rate between two currencies represents the difference between the price levels in the two countries

Push strategy Push strategies involve promoting the product or service to intermediaries, who will then promote them to the final consumers

Qualitative research A set of research techniques in which data is obtained from a relatively small group of respondents and not analyzed with statistical techniques

Reciprocal trading Trading in which the supplier also purchases products or services from the customer

Relationship marketing The creation of mutually beneficial long term value through building customer relationships rather than relying on converting customers through advertising and sales promotions

Research process The ordered set of activities focused on the systematic collection of information using accepted methods of analysis as a basis for drawing conclusions and making recommendations

Risk and control The necessary balance to be struck in entering new markets, which involves accepting risk of failure, set against committing sufficient resource in an attempt to exert control in the market and 'guarantee' success

Secondary data Data collected and recorded by another

Self-reference criterion The assumption that a product can successfully be sold abroad on the basis of its success in the home market

Services Intangible, largely experience based economic activity

Silent language Non verbal signals in a communication

Single European Market The complete integration of the economies of member states of the European Union

Small- and medium-sized enterprises Small (typically up to 50 employees) and Medium (from 50–250 employees) firms that have a different approach and mindset to large multinational organizations

Social and cultural factors The macros factors in environmental analysis relating to social and cultural factors

Sogo shosha Historically highly successful Japanese trading companies typically part of a major conglomerate

Spoken language Spoken language is a form of communication in which words derived from a large vocabulary

Stages of internationalization An international marketing concept in which firms progress through a series of steps as they develop from a domestic to a global company. Each step has distinctive characteristics

Standardization Approach to marketing that aims to reduce marketing mix variation between countries and regions of the world

Standardization of international marketing communications Where possible, reducing variation in the use of the communications mix between different countries and regions

Straddling the pyramid A strategy for serving both the people at the bottom of the income pyramid and those at the top. Particularly prevalent in emerging markets where the income distribution is highly polarized

Strategic alliance A contractual arrangement whereby two or more firms form a partnership to exploit a market opportunity together, so that they reduce risk

Supply chain A group of firms that undertake support activities in the manufacture and supply of materials and components, conversion into finished goods and making them available to buyers

Supply chain management The management of a group of firms that contribute to the development, manufacture and delivery of a final product to maximize efficiency and effectiveness

Tariff Duty: A government tax on imports or exports

Total distribution cost The total cost incurred by an exporter in the distribution of merchandize internationally including transport, warehousing, inventory holding, order processing, documentation, taxes, packaging, etc.

Trade deficit A negative balance of trade

Trading blocs A trade bloc is a type of intergovernmental agreement, often part of a regional intergovernmental organization, where regional barriers to trade (tariffs and non-tariff barriers) are reduced or eliminated among the participating states

Trading companies Organizations involved in the exchange of products, services and cash that were particularly important in opening up new markets in underdeveloped countries

Transactions The exchange of items of value, including information, goods, services and money

Transfer pricing The price that is assumed to have been charged by one part of a company for products and services it provides to another part of the same company, in order to calculate each division's profit and loss separately

Transnational segmentation Entering foreign markets with a solid marketing plan that helps a company create a positive brand presence and resonates with residents of the foreign country

Transnationality The pursuit of opportunities in all parts of the world by integrating and coordinating sourcing of products and services from all parts of the world and serving multiple country markets across all world regions

Values Monetary or material worth, as in commerce or trade

Websites Collections of related web pages containing images, videos or other digital material

Wholly-owned subsidiary Independent business unit in a foreign location owned by a parent firm with headquarters in the home country

World Bank An international banking organization established to control the distribution of economic aid between member nations, and to make loans to them in times of financial crisis

World trade The value of the trading of goods and services across the globe

World Trade Organization The World Trade Organization (WTO) deals with the rules of trade between nations at a global or near-global level

World Wide Web Global network of computers connecting the sites that supply a variety of data, audio and visual resources

Index